I0874995

THE CONTINENTAL LEGAL HISTORY SERIES

Published under the auspices of the

ASSOCIATION OF AMERICAN LAW SCHOOLS

A HISTORY
OF
GERMANIC PRIVATE LAW

BY

RUDOLF HUEBNER

PROFESSOR OF LEGAL HISTORY IN THE UNIVERSITY OF GIESSEN

TRANSLATED BY

FRANCIS S. PHILBRICK

PROFESSOR OF LAW IN THE UNIVERSITY OF CALIFORNIA

WITH AN EDITORIAL PREFACE BY

ERNEST G. LORENZEN

PROFESSOR OF LAW IN YALE UNIVERSITY

AND INTRODUCTIONS BY

PAUL VINOGRADOFF

CORPUS PROFESSOR OF JURISPRUDENCE IN OXFORD UNIVERSITY

AND BY

WILLIAM E. WALZ

DEAN OF THE FACULTY OF LAW IN THE UNIVERSITY OF MAINE

THE LAWBOOK EXCHANGE, LTD.
Clark, New Jersey

ISBN 978-1-58477-065-7

Lawbook Exchange edition 2000, 2025

The quality of this reprint is equivalent to the quality of the original work.

THE LAWBOOK EXCHANGE, LTD.
33 Terminal Avenue
Clark, New Jersey 07066-1321

Please see our website for a selection of our other publications and fine facsimile reprints of classic works of legal history:
www.lawbookexchange.com

Library of Congress Cataloging-in-Publication Data

Hübner, Rudolf, 1864-1945.
[Grundzüge des deutschen Privatrechts. English]
A history of Germanic private law / by Rudolf Huebner ; translated by Francis S. Philbrick ; with editorial preface by Ernest G. Lorenzen and introductions by Paul Vinogradoff and by William E. Walz.
p. cm.
Originally published: Boston : Little, Brown, 1918. (The continental legal history series ; v.4)
Includes bibliographical references and index.
ISBN 1-58477-065-1 (cloth : alk. paper)
1. Civil law—Germany—History. I. Title. II. Continental legal history series; v. 4.

KK993.6 H83 2000
346.43—dc21 99-055138

Printed in the United States of America on acid-free paper

THE CONTINENTAL LEGAL HISTORY SERIES

Published under the auspices of the

ASSOCIATION OF AMERICAN LAW SCHOOLS

A HISTORY

OF

GERMANIC PRIVATE LAW

BY

RUDOLF HUEBNER

PROFESSOR OF LEGAL HISTORY IN THE UNIVERSITY OF GIESSEN

TRANSLATED BY

FRANCIS S. PHILBRICK

PROFESSOR OF LAW IN THE UNIVERSITY OF CALIFORNIA

WITH AN EDITORIAL PREFACE BY

ERNEST G. LORENZEN

PROFESSOR OF LAW IN YALE UNIVERSITY

AND INTRODUCTIONS BY

PAUL VINOGRADOFF

CORPUS PROFESSOR OF JURISPRUDENCE IN OXFORD UNIVERSITY

AND BY

WILLIAM E. WALZ

DEAN OF THE FACULTY OF LAW IN THE UNIVERSITY OF MAINE

BOSTON

LITTLE, BROWN, AND COMPANY

1918

Norwood Press
Set up and electrotyped by J. S. Cushing Co., Norwood, Mass., U.S.A.
Presswork by S. J. Parkhill & Co., Boston, Mass., U.S.A.

THE CONTINENTAL
LEGAL HISTORY SERIES

Volume Four

A HISTORY OF GERMANIC
PRIVATE LAW

The Continental Legal History Series

Published under the auspices of the

Association of American Law Schools

I. A GENERAL SURVEY OF EVENTS, SOURCES, PERSONS, AND MOVEMENTS IN CONTINENTAL LEGAL HISTORY. By VARIOUS AUTHORS. Translated by RAPELJE HOWELL, F. S. PHILBRICK, JOHN WALGREN, and JOHN H. WIGMORE. $6.00 *net.*

II. GREAT JURISTS OF THE WORLD, FROM PAPINIAN TO VON IHERING. By VARIOUS AUTHORS. Illustrated. (Extra volume. By arrangement with John Murray, London.) $5.00 *net.*

III. HISTORY OF FRENCH PRIVATE LAW. By J. BRISSAUD, late of the University of Toulouse. Translated by RAPELJE HOWELL, of the New York Bar. $5.00 *net.*

IV. HISTORY OF GERMANIC PRIVATE LAW. By RUDOLPH HUEBNER, of the University of Giessen. Translated by FRANCIS S. PHILBRICK, of the University of California. $4.50 *net.*

V. HISTORY OF CONTINENTAL CRIMINAL PROCEDURE. By A. ESMEIN, late of the University of Paris, with chapters by FRANÇOIS GARRAUD, of the University of Lyon, and C. J. A. MITTERMAIER, late of the University of Heidelberg. Translated by JOHN SIMPSON, of the New York Bar. $4.50 *net.*

VI. HISTORY OF CONTINENTAL CRIMINAL LAW. By LUDWIG VON BAR, late of the University of Göttingen. Translated by THOMAS S. BELL, of the Los Angeles Bar. $4.00 *net.*

VII. HISTORY OF CONTINENTAL CIVIL PROCEDURE. By ARTHUR ENGELMANN, Chief Justice of the Court of Appeals at Breslau, with a chapter by E. GLASSON, late of the University of Paris. Translated by ROBERT W. MILLAR, of Northwestern University. $4.00 net.

VIII. HISTORY OF ITALIAN LAW. By CARLO CALISSE, of the Italian Council of State. Translated by JOHN LISLE, late of the Philadelphia Bar. $5.00 *net.*

IX. HISTORY OF FRENCH PUBLIC LAW. By J. BRISSAUD, late of the University of Toulouse. Translated by JAMES W. GARNER, of the University of Illinois. $4.50 *net.*

X. HISTORY OF CONTINENTAL COMMERCIAL LAW. By PAUL HUVELIN, of the University of Lyon. Translated by ERNEST G. LORENZEN, of Yale University. $5.50 *net.*

XI. THE PROGRESS OF CONTINENTAL LAW IN THE 19TH CENTURY. By A. ALVAREZ, L. DUGUIT, J. CHARMONT, E. RIPERT, and others. Translated by L. B. REGISTER, of the University of Pennsylvania. $5.00 *net.*

EDITORIAL COMMITTEE

OF THE

ASSOCIATION OF AMERICAN LAW SCHOOLS

LIST OF TRANSLATORS

THOMAS S. BELL, of the Los Angeles Bar.

JAMES W. GARNER, Professor of Political Science in the University of Illinois.

RAPELJE HOWELL, of the New York Bar.

JOHN LISLE, late of the Philadelphia Bar.

ERNEST G. LORENZEN, of the Editorial Committee.

ROBERT W. MILLAR, Professor of Law in Northwestern University.

FRANCIS S. PHILBRICK, Professor of Law in the University of California.

LAYTON B. REGISTER, Lecturer on Law in the University of Pennsylvania.

JOHN SIMPSON, of New York.

JOHN WALGREN, of the Chicago Bar.

JOHN H. WIGMORE, of the Editorial Committee.

I might instance in other professions the obligation men lie under of applying themselves to certain parts of History; and I can hardly forbear doing it in that of the Law, — in its nature the noblest and most beneficial to mankind, in its abuse and debasement the most sordid and the most pernicious. A lawyer now is nothing more (I speak of ninety-nine in a hundred at least), to use some of Tully's words, "nisi leguleius quidem cautus, et acutus praeco actionum, cantor formularum, auceps syllabarum." But there have been lawyers that were orators, philosophers, historians: there have been Bacons and Clarendons. There will be none such any more, till in some better age true ambition, or the love of fame, prevails over avarice; and till men find leisure and encouragement to prepare themselves for the exercise of this profession, by climbing up to the vantage ground (so my Lord Bacon calls it) of Science, instead of grovelling all their lives below, in a mean but gainful application of all the little arts of chicane. Till this happen, the profession of the law will scarce deserve to be ranked among the learned professions. And whenever it happens, one of the vantage grounds to which men must climb, is Metaphysical, and the other, Historical Knowledge. HENRY ST. JOHN, Viscount BOLINGBROKE, *Letters on the Study of History* (1739).

Whoever brings a fruitful idea to any branch of knowledge, or rends the veil that seems to sever one portion from another, his name is written in the Book among the builders of the Temple. For an English lawyer it is hardly too much to say that the methods which Oxford invited Sir Henry Maine to demonstrate, in this chair of Historical and Comparative Jurisprudence, have revolutionised our legal history and largely transformed our current text-books. — Sir FREDERICK POLLOCK, Bart., *The History of Comparative Jurisprudence* (Farewell Lecture at the University of Oxford, 1903).

No piece of History is true when set apart to itself, divorced and isolated. It is part of an intricately pieced whole, and must needs be put in its place in the netted scheme of events, to receive its true color and estimation. We are all partners in a common undertaking, — the illumination of the thoughts and actions of men as associated in society, the life of the human spirit in this familiar theatre of coöperative effort in which we play, so changed from age to age, and yet so much the same throughout the hurrying centuries. The day for synthesis has come. No one of us can safely go forward without it. — WOODROW WILSON, *The Variety and Unity of History* (Address at the World's Congress of Arts and Science, St. Louis, 1904).

A lawyer without history or literature is a mechanic, a mere working mason; if he possesses some knowledge of these, he may venture to call himself an architect.—Sir WALTER SCOTT, *"Guy Mannering,"* c. XXXVII.

CONTINENTAL LEGAL HISTORY SERIES

GENERAL INTRODUCTION TO THE SERIES

"All history," said the lamented master Maitland, in a memorable epigram, "is but a seamless web; and he who endeavors to tell but a piece of it must feel that his first sentence tears the fabric."

This seamless web of our own legal history unites us inseparably to the history of Western and Southern Europe. Our main interest must naturally center on deciphering the pattern which lies directly before us, — that of the Anglo-American law. But in tracing the warp and woof of its structure we are brought inevitably into a larger field of vision. The story of Western Continental Law is made up, in the last analysis, of two great movements, racial and intellectual. One is the Germanic migrations, planting a solid growth of Germanic custom everywhere, from Danzig to Sicily, from London to Vienna. The other is the posthumous power of Roman law, forever resisting, struggling, and coalescing with the other. A thousand detailed combinations, of varied types, are developed, and a dozen distinct systems now survive in independence. But the result is that no one of them can be fully understood without surveying and tracing the whole.

Even insular England cannot escape from the web. For, in the first place, all its racial threads — Saxons, Danes, Normans — were but extensions of the same Germanic warp and woof that was making the law in France, Germany, Scandinavia, Netherlands, Austria, Switzerland, Northern Italy, and Spain. And, in the next place, its legal culture was never without some of the same intellectual influence of Roman law which was so thoroughly overspreading the Continental peoples. There is thus, on the one hand, scarcely a doctrine or rule in our own system which cannot be definitely and profitably traced back, in comparison, till we come to the point of divergence, where we once shared it in common with them. And, on the other hand, there is, during all the intervening centuries, a more or less constant juristic sociability (if it may be so called) between Anglo-American and Continental Law; and its reciprocal influences make the story one and inseparable. In short, there is a tangled common ancestry, racial or intellectual, for the law of all Western Europe and ourselves.

For the sake of legal science, this story should now become a familiar one to all who are studious to know the history of our own law. The time is ripe. During the last thirty years European scholars have placed the history of their law on the footing of modern critical and philosophical research. And to-day, among ourselves, we find a marked widening of view and a vigorous interest in the comparison of other peoples' legal institutions. To the satisfying of that interest in the present field, the only obstacle is the lack of adequate materials in the English language.

That the spirit of the times encourages and demands the study of Continental Legal History and all useful aids to it was pointed out in a memorial presented at the annual meeting of the Association of American Law Schools in August, 1909:

"The recent spread of interest in Comparative Law in general is notable. The Comparative Law Bureau of the American Bar Association; the Pan-American Scientific Congress; the American Institute of Criminal Law and Criminology; the Civic Federation Conference on Uniform Legislation; the International Congress of History; the libraries' accessions in foreign law, — the work of these and other movements touches at various points the bodies of Continental law. Such activities serve to remind us constantly that we have in English no histories of Continental law. To pay any attention at all to Continental law means that its history must be more or less considered. Each of these countries has its own legal system and its own legal history. Yet the law of the Continent was never so foreign to English as the English law was foreign to Continental jurisprudence. It is merely maintaining the best traditions of our own legal literature if we plead for a continued study of Continental legal history.

"We believe that a better acquaintance with the results of modern scholarship in that field will bring out new points of contact and throw new light upon the development of our own law. Moreover, the present-day movements for codification, and for the reconstruction of many departments of the law, make it highly desirable that our profession should be well informed as to the history of the nineteenth century on the Continent in its great measures of law reform and codification.

"For these reasons we believe that the thoughtful American lawyers and students should have at their disposal translations of some of the best works in Continental legal history."

And the following resolution was then adopted unanimously by the Association:

"That a committee of five be appointed, on Translations of Continental Legal History, with authority to arrange for the translation and publication of suitable works."

The Editorial Committee, then appointed, spent two years in studying the field, making selections, and arranging for translations. It resolved to treat the undertaking as a whole; and to co-ordinate the series as to (1) periods, (2) countries, and (3) topics, so as to give the most adequate survey within the space-limits available.

(1) As to *periods*, the Committee resolved to include modern times, as well as early and mediæval periods; for in usefulness and importance they were not less imperative in their claim upon our attention. Each volume, then, was not to be merely a valuable torso, lacking important epochs of development; but was to exhibit the history from early to modern times.

(2) As to *countries*, the Committee fixed upon France, Germany, and Italy as the central fields, leaving the history in other countries to be touched so far as might be incidentally possible. Spain would have been included as a fourth; but no suitable book was in existence; the unanimous opinion of competent scholars is that a suitable history of Spanish law has not yet been written.

(3) As to *topics*, the Committee accepted the usual Continental divisions of Civil (or Private), Commercial, Criminal, Procedural, and Public Law, and endeavored to include all five. But to represent these five fields under each principal country would not only exceed the inevitable space-limits, but would also duplicate much common ground. Hence, the grouping of the individual volumes was arranged partly by topics and partly by countries, as follows:

Commercial Law, Criminal Law, Civil Procedure, and Criminal Procedure, were allotted each a volume; in this volume the basis was to be the general European history of early and mediæval times, with special reference to one chief country (France or Germany) for the later periods, and with an excursus on another chief country. Then the Civil (or Private) Law of France and of Germany was given a volume each. To Italy was then given a volume covering all five parts of the field. For Public Law (the subject least related in history to our own), a volume was given to France, where the common starting point with England, and the later divergences, have unusual importance for the history of our courts and legal methods. Finally, two volumes were allotted to general surveys indispensable for viewing the connection of parts. Of these, an introductory volume deals with Sources, Literature, and General Movements, — in short, the external history of the law, as the Continentals call it (corresponding to the aspects covered by Book I of Sir F. Pollock and Professor F. W. Maitland's "History of the English Law before Edward I"); and a final volume analyzes the specific features, in the evolution of doctrine, common to all the modern systems.

Needless to say, a Series thus co-ordinated, and precisely suited for our own needs, was not easy to construct out of materials written by Continental scholars for Continental needs. The Committee hopes that due allowance will be made for the difficulties here encountered. But it is convinced that the ideal of a co-ordinated Series, which should collate and fairly cover the various fields as a connected whole, is a correct one; and the endeavor to achieve it will sufficiently explain the choice of the particular materials that have been used.

It remains to acknowledge the Committee's indebtedness to all those who have made this Series possible.

To numerous scholarly advisers in many European universities the Committee is indebted for valuable suggestions towards choice of the works to be translated. Fortified by this advice, the Committee is confident that the authors of these volumes represent the highest scholarship, the latest research, and the widest repute, among European legal historians. And here the Committee desires also to express its indebtedness to Elbert H. Gary, Esq., of New York City, for his ample provision of materials for legal science in the Gary Library of Continental Law (in Northwestern University). In the researches of preparation for this Series, those materials were found indispensable.

To the authors the Committee is grateful for their willing co-operation in allowing this use of their works. Without exception, their consent has been cheerfully accorded in the interest of legal science.

To the publishers the Committee expresses its appreciation for the cordial interest shown in a class of literature so important to the higher interests of the profession.

To the translators, the Committee acknowledges a particular gratitude. The accomplishments, legal and linguistic, needed for a task of this sort are indeed exacting; and suitable translators are here no less needful and no more numerous than suitable authors. The Committee, on behalf of our profession, acknowledges to them a special debt for their cordial services on behalf of legal science, and commends them to the readers of these volumes with the reminder that without their labors this Series would have been a fruitless dream.

So the Committee, satisfied with the privilege of having introduced these authors and their translators to the public, retires from the scene, bespeaking for the Series the interest of lawyers and historians alike.

THE EDITORIAL COMMITTEE.

A HISTORY OF
GERMANIC PRIVATE LAW

CONTENTS

INTRODUCTION

CHAPTER I

GENERAL TRAITS OF GERMANIC PRIVATE LAW

BOOK I. THE LAW OF PERSONS

CHAPTER II

NATURAL PERSONS

CHAPTER III

JURISTIC PERSONS AND GROUPS INCAPABLE OF HOLDING RIGHTS

BOOK II. THE LAW OF THINGS

CHAPTER IV

THINGS

CHAPTER V

THE LAW OF LAND

PART I. POSSESSION

CHAPTER VI

THE LAW OF LAND (*Continued*)

PART II. THE OWNERSHIP OF LAND

CHAPTER VII

THE LAW OF LAND (*Continued*)

PART III. REAL RIGHTS

Topic 1. Tenurial Rights

Topic 2. Servitudes

Topic 3. Charges on Land

Topic 4. The Gage of Land

Topic 5. Preëmption Rights

CHAPTER VIII

THE LAW OF CHATTELS

Topic 1. Possession of Chattels

Topic 2. Ownership of Chattels

Topic 3. Acquisition of Title to Chattels

Topic 4. The Law of Chattel Pledges

BOOK III. THE LAW OF OBLIGATIONS

CHAPTER IX

GENERAL PRINCIPLES

Topic 1. Fundamental Conceptions of the Law of Obligations

Topic 2. The Historical Origins of Obligations

Topic 3. The Content of Obligations

Topic 4. Performance and Non-Performance of Obligations

Topic 5. Assignment of Obligations by Obligee and Obligor

Topic 6. Cases of Several Debtors and Creditors

CHAPTER X

SPECIAL FORMS OF OBLIGATIONS

Topic 1. Obligations Ex Contractu

Topic 2. Obligations based upon Torts

BOOK IV. FAMILY LAW

CHAPTER XI

MARRIAGE

CHAPTER XII

CHILDHOOD

CHAPTER XIII

GUARDIANSHIP

BOOK V. THE LAW OF INHERITANCE

CHAPTER XIV

GENERAL PRINCIPLES

CHAPTER XV

INTESTATE SUCCESSION

CHAPTER XVI

TESTAMENTARY SUCCESSION

CHAPTER XVII

SPECIAL RULES OF SUCCESSION IN THE INHERITANCE OF LANDS

EDITORIAL PREFACE TO THIS VOLUME

By Ernest G. Lorenzen [1]

The importance of Huebner's History of Germanic Private Law to the student of legal history, philosophy of law, and comparative law is set forth in such eloquent language in the introductions to this volume by Professors Vinogradoff and Walz as to make any further observations on this point both unnecessary and unfitting. For a general description of the work the following brief quotation from a review in one of the leading German periodicals, "Zeitschrift für Bundesstaatsrecht und Völkerrecht", may suffice: "Huebner's History of Germanic Private Law is a treatise on the private law of Germanic countries the several institutions of which are traced in their development from their origin to the present time. . . . An extraordinary command of the vast literature of the subject and a style, perfect in form and possessing great lucidity, characterize the treatise, which is the only one incorporating the latest investigations in this field." (Vol. IV, p. 519.)

A few data concerning the life and work of the author of this volume will be of interest. Rudolph Huebner was born in Berlin on September 19, 1864. He took a doctor's degree in law at the University of Berlin and was Privatdozent at that institution for several years. He has been professor of law at the universities of Bonn and Rostock and at the present moment occupies the chair of Legal History, German Civil Law, and Public Law at the University of Giessen. Huebner's literary activities have been along the line of Germanic law. His most important contributions in this field before the publication of the present treatise have been: "Die donationes post obitum und die Schenkungen mit Vorbehalt des Niessbrauchs im älteren deutschen Recht"; "Gerichtsurkunden der fränkischen Zeit"; "Immobiliarprozess der fränkischen Zeit"; "J. Grimm und das deutsche Recht." In all of these works Huebner has shown himself to be a follower of Otto v. Gierke and Heinrich Brunner.

The translation of Huebner's History of Germanic Private Law into English was a task beset with the greatest difficulties, which

[1] Of the Editorial Committee; Professor of Law in Yale University.

only a person of great linguistic ability and of the broadest legal training could successfully meet. Fortunately Professor Philbrick possessed all of these qualifications in an eminent degree. He took his Ph. D. at Harvard University, where he specialized in history and political science. Having been granted an honorary John Harvard Travelling Fellowship, he continued his studies in Berlin, Paris, and London. Subsequently he pursued archive researches in Cuba and in Spain. He took his LL. B. degree at Columbia University, and was admitted to the New York Bar. Since 1915 he has been professor of law at the University of California, where he is in charge of the courses in foreign and comparative law and legal theory. Professor Philbrick has addressed himself to his task with great enthusiasm and success, and has spared no effort to make the translation both accurate and readable.

The first edition of the present work was published in 1908. The translation is of the second edition, which appeared in 1913 and brought the history of Germanic Private Law down to date by tracing its development into the Swiss Civil Code, of December 10, 1907.

INTRODUCTION TO THIS VOLUME

By Sir Paul Vinogradoff [1]

The title of Professor Huebner's book is "Principles of Germanic Private Law", and yet it has been rightly included into a collection of works on Legal History. This is in itself characteristic; the fact is that contemporary German law is not only essentially a product of historical development, as indeed all varieties of Law are, but that it was reconstructed and formulated in opposition to another great jurisprudential system — the Roman one — as the outcome of a peculiar national process of legal thought. In this way its positive rules and institutions are liable to be traced to leading ideas which have manifested themselves in a more or less distinct manner in previous history. The learned and talented author himself belongs to a moderate section of the so-called Germanistic school, and may be said to follow O. Gierke in a general way, although he is very careful to notice authoritative opposition, and tries on every occasion to state his conclusions with as much academic impartiality as possible. From the above mentioned point of view the subject commands indeed the greatest interest. It raises questions of the highest importance not only for the practical lawyer and the legal historian, but for the student of jurisprudence. It presents a concrete test for the application of various theories as to the national trend of legal thought, as to the leading distinctions between periods, as to the possibility of a "reception" of foreign law, as to the value of comparative and of analytical study, etc.

I

Let us rehearse briefly the course of the development which culminated in the formation of the system of law laid down in the "Bürgerliches Gesetzbuch", the Civil Code of the German Empire. The threads of the literary controversy need not be followed into more remote antiquity than the beginning of the nineteenth century, when, at the close of the Emancipation War

[[1] D. C. L., F. B. A.; Corpus Professor of Jurisprudence in the University of Oxford; Fellow of the Academy of Sciences of Petrograd. — Ed.]

against Napoleon, the famous conflict of opinion between Thibaut and Savigny led to the formation of the so-called "Historical School of Law." The subject of dispute was the formulation of a general and modern code of law for the emancipated German States which should take the place of that strange figment — "the Common Law of Rome as practised in Germany." Savigny protested against such an undertaking as expressing the conception that law comprised a set of arbitrary rules contrived with more or less skill to meet the requirements of actual life, without any reference to national traditions and to the peculiarities of social psychology of the people who were to be operated upon.

In formulating his own views Savigny, Eichhorn, and the other leaders of the new school came to consider the growth of law as essentially an organic process, akin to the evolution of language, of folklore, of religion, unconscious and half conscious in its most profound currents, but directing the whole of the ostensible life of juridical rules and corresponding rights. From this psychological point of view, sharply opposed to the rationalistic logic of the "Aufklärung" or "age of enlightenment", the Historical School of Law joined hands with the mythological and linguistic researches of a Jacob Grimm, who himself contributed to the work of the lawyers by writing his remarkable "German Legal Antiquities" ("Deutsche Rechtsalterthümer"). What is more, it may be considered as one of the principal varieties of the Romantic movement with its determined opposition to pure intellectualism, to the cosmopolitan violence of the Revolution and of Napoleon's régime. Burke and Wordsworth have given strong expression to the organic, historical teaching of that period as far as Great Britain was concerned. But the application to jurisprudence was mainly the work of German students. English writers were not much affected by the crisis, because in their case there was no danger whatever of a subversion of traditional development: they had rather to face the other extreme; and the rationalistic individualism of Bentham [1] was hailed as a deliverance from the stubborn passivity of an Eldon or an Ellenborough. Thus it was reserved for a late comer like Sir H. Maine to popularize the doctrines of Savigny in England; and, by the time he appeared on the scene, new ideas had supervened which gave the whole problem an entirely different aspect.[2]

[1] As to Bentham's characteristic aversion for historical authority, see *e.g.* Works, VIII, 392, 442.

[2] *Cf. P. Vinogradoff*, "Teaching of Sir Henry Maine" (Oxford, 1904), p. 9.

Let us turn back, however, to the main line of our inquiry. Savigny devoted himself almost entirely to the study of Roman Law. His principal contribution to German legal history consisted in the indirect influence of his History of Roman Law in the Middle Ages, which was intended to show that the reception of Roman doctrines by medieval Europe was by no means the result of mechanical submission and copying, but rather a gradual absorption of rules and examples by the less civilised tribes of Teutonic invaders. The work of the first period of the "Historical School of Law" which has still to be taken into account in the study of German private law is represented broadly in Eichhorn's monumental "History of German State and Law" ("Deutsche Staats- und Rechtsgeschichte") and in his text-book on German Private Law. Eichhorn had to deal with the fragmentary utterances of Germanic legal thought embodied in the legislation and jurisprudence of the numerous German States before their re-union. He was struck by the many points of similarity in these disconnected laws and explained them by common origin — they were for him the various branches of the same tree, which produce the same kind of leaves and fruit because the same sap runs through them all from the common roots and common stem.

Albrecht's monograph on the "*Gewere*" (the Germanic conception of possession) is perhaps the most characteristic book concerning another side of the Germanistic theory. It was written to prove that the treatment of possession in the ancient and medieval law of the Germanic people was fundamentally different from the development of the corresponding doctrine in Roman law. In this way the two systems were contrasted one with the other, not in vague generalities, but in regard to the specific applications of a leading principle of juridical thought. A further link was added to the chain by Beseler in his famous book on "Popular Law and Lawyers' Law", in which the practical common sense of Germanic legal lore was contrasted with the narrow and pedantic treatment of juridical questions by lawyers trained on Roman doctrine. The spirit of popular revolt in which the task was conceived and carried out by Beseler reminds one of the popular hostility against the Doctors of foreign law entertained by the people at large in the sixteenth century. In a sense, though with much greater learning and a wider view of the field, Gierke may be said to follow on the same lines. He is animated by patriotic zeal when he tries to present side by side the three great currents of legal development which, according to his view, dominate the legal thought of Western Europe — the Roman, the Canonistic, and the Germanistic one. He has chosen the law of "Association" ("Genossenschaft") to prove to what extent their leading ideas are different, and how great an importance must be assigned to the Germanic view, with its realistic treatment of the corporate body, thoroughly opposed as well to the Romanesque theory of fiction as to the Canonistic line starting from the idea of a "foundation" ("Anstalt").

In this way we can undoubtedly observe a continuous stream of research and reflection running in the channel of national self-consciousness ever since Savigny imparted the first impulse by his revolt against cosmopolitan rationalism, and, in spite of many modifications of the doctrine, the main object — interpreting details from this view-point of national psychology — is still well to the fore. We must not omit to notice, however, that in German jurisprudence itself strong tendencies of a different kind have found powerful expression and have proved in many respects to be more scientific and more progressive.

I do not mean in this case the criticism of details and the struggle for supremacy on the part of representatives of the Romanistic school, like Windscheid, Bekker, Dernburg. They were bound to take up a more cosmopolitan point of view and they did so; but apart from some success as regards particular points, their opposition has not prevailed against the onslaught of the Germanists, and they barely succeeded in keeping some of their positions on the debatable ground of practical codification. But there is another set of thinkers who deserve greater attention. Their point of departure may be traced to the work of Ihering and Gerber. Ihering holds a great place in the history of nineteenth-century juridical thought, and the evolution of his ideas has been significant of the gradual working out of leading principles which have shaped juridical opinion in Europe. Already in the first stage of his career, culminating in the work on the "Spirit of Roman Law", he took up an attitude that clashed with the views of the Historical School of Law as represented by Savigny, Eichhorn, and Puchta. He laid stress on the technical side of legal method, and contended that the popular notions of justice and equity constituted merely a background for the formation of legal doctrine effected by the activity of legal experts — legislators, judges, pleaders, interpreters of law.

Altogether the historical side of jurisprudence, though of the utmost importance for explaining the present and observing the peculiarities of juridical thought, was declared to be an introduction to another and more important side, facing the problems of the future. Ihering had the right to paraphrase for the use of his theory the famous reflections of Goethe's Faust on the meaning of the Gospel of St. John, ch. I: "In the beginning there was the Word." Surely the true sense requires a different version — "In the beginning there was the Deed." Inasmuch as legal rules are acts conceived as directions for men's conduct, the creative character of law has to be recognised quite as much as its historical origins.

In further elaboration of this idea Ihering came to consider law chiefly as a factor of social evolution. All legal rules are in the last instance attempts to master social problems by means of State compulsion. Regarded from the point of view of the relations between individuals and the coördinating Commonwealth, their object is the recognition and protection of certain interests, and thereby they create rights, — "subjective rights", as they say in Germany. Taking up his stand on the social functions of law, Ihering was necessarily led to formulate three consequential positions of the utmost importance. (1) He entered an emphatic protest against the purely analytical method of dealing with questions of law. He subjected to ridicule and to scornful criticism those of his colleagues who put all their faith in dialectical exercises of subsumption and constructions, reproaching them with living in a fool's paradise of juridical abstraction ("Der juristische Begriffshimmel").[1] As against the barren pedantry of these scholastic exercises, he set the duty of the lawyer never to lose sight of the practical needs involved. As one illustration of the far-reaching significance of this line of thought, I may be allowed to call attention to Gēny's more recent book on the interpretation of law, conceived in the entirely different surroundings of French practice and yet insisting on that very necessity of breaking with purely dialectical methods of interpretation for the sake of the requirements of actual life. (2) A sociological standard had to be set up for the proper direction of juridical activity, and Ihering found such a standard in the conception of social utility. His "Aim of Law" (Zweck im Recht) is to a great extent devoted to investigating the grounds of social coöperation, and the author has spared no effort to make it clear that in fashion, customs, ordinary morality, and

[1] From "Scherz und Ernst in der Jurisprudenz".

ethical theory, as well as in law, societies are working out the conditions of their existence and welfare by educating individuals to adopt and to follow rules of conduct inspired by the aim of social utility. (3) The study of the historical process, as far as it concerns law, has to be freed from the obsession of national peculiarities. While fully recognizing that all juridical problems have to be considered from the historical point of view, Ihering insists that it is not merely the element of tradition that has to be taken into account, but the element of efficiency. As the social aim is the final test of legal rules, it is clear that the latter have to change with circumstances.[1] It would be preposterous to suppose that modern Germany or modern France, or any other modern country, can be constrained to proceed in the track of medieval precedents or of tribal custom. Each age has to shift for itself; and though national character may influence politics and legislation, the principal considerations of a lawyer must be drawn from a lively sense of reality, of the immediate difficulties and requirements of the age.

Gerber, who joined Ihering in editing the "Journal of Dogmatic Jurisprudence", held similar views and expressed them most forcibly in his treatment of public as well as of private law. His writings are also noteworthy in so much as they contained very effective polemical excursions against several concrete points in the teaching of the Germanistic School. He did not admit any special Germanistic source of law in the shape of "autonomous" formation, nor did he recognize a peculiar principle of "Genossenschaft" or a distinctive treatment of real property.[2]

Although Ihering and Gerber did not form a compact group in the same sense as the leaders of the Historical School, their literary influence has been exceedingly great, both in Germany and abroad. In a sense it may be said that Ihering was one of the most prominent initiators of the Sociological School of jurisprudence. In any case his teaching of historical evolution directed towards conscious aims has presented a powerful antidote to the traditional superstitions of the Romantic movement and of its nationalistic sequels. It came at a time when individualistic ideals began to give way on all sides before socialistic aspirations; and, whatever may be our own standpoint in the contemporary struggle of ideas, it cannot be denied that the juridical thought of

[1] See *e.g.* "Geist des römischen Rechts", III, part 1, 296.

[2] *Landsberg*, "Geschichte der deutschen Rechtswissenschaft", III, part 2, p. 784.

the new century has been deeply affected by this socialistic current.[1] Perhaps the most eloquent tribute to the farsightedness and originality of Ihering may be found in the fact that the most powerful representative of Germanistic jurisprudence, Otto von Gierke, has striven to unite the appeal derived from the social aim of a time which has discarded the tenets of individualism with the arguments drawn from national character and ancient folklore.

In spite of this there remains the fundamental divergence of orientation: while one thinker sees in the socialistic bent of German law a legacy of the past, the other looks upon it as an adaptation to the requirements of the present and a promise for the future.

II

Let us now consider some of the arguments marshalled by Germanists for the purpose of establishing their theory of juridical evolution. The main obstacle with which they have had to deal in their endeavours has been the intrusion of the Roman legal system. It has thrust itself right into the midst of the vernacular process; and quite recently it threatened to confirm its dominant position by taking the leading part in Imperial codification. The first question which Eichhorn, Gierke, Huebner, and other Germanists have to answer amounts to this: How is it that, at the critical period when the modern history of Europe started, an independent current of legal thought like the German has had to give way to a system of foreign origin formed in entirely different surroundings?

As regards the process of so-called Reception, a general agreement has been reached, at the close of strenuous investigation. Apart from the various channels through which the higher culture of Rome permeated barbaric Societies, apart from the influence of "vulgar" Roman law insisted upon by Savigny and especially illustrated by the labours of Conrat, apart from the doctrinal influence of the early juridical renaissance of the glossators and postglossators, the Reception of the entire Corpus of Justinian's law by the German courts and universities in the XVth century was clearly a historical necessity. It certainly created confusion and called forth hostility among the common people and in the ranks of the Schöffen. But it was the best means for providing the innumerable political bodies of the so-called Empire with a common law which was abreast of the re-

[1] *Cf. Dicey,* "Law and Opinion", 258 ff.

quirements of a modern capitalistic economy, of extensive trade relations, and of the growing power of territorial sovereigns. Even Gierke admits that the Reception brought juridical progress, especially in the domain of contract relations, a most important branch of law in times of mobilized wealth and frequent commercial transactions.

And yet, it is contended, the sway of a learned judicature trained in the study of the Corpus Juris arrested the development of native juridical thought, favoured pedantic abstruseness, and threatened eventually to stifle attempts at an up-to-date handling of the law. The chasm between Romanistic doctrine and the real life of modern Germany became especially apparent when the regeneration of the German Empire made it possible and necessary to draft a general Civil Code for the great Commonwealth. The conflict between the Romanists and the Germanists was transferred from the pages of textbooks and pamphlets to the meetings of the Commission appointed to elaborate the new law. The drastic events of the concluding years of the nineteenth century are still present to our memory, — the production of the first draft under Windscheid's guidance on the lines of Romanistic doctrine, the indignant protest of Gierke and other Germanists, the revision of the text in the second and final commission with its compromise between the rival sides.

I should here like merely to remind the reader of the most striking literary production of that time, — Gierke's book on the "Entwurf", or Draft, which summarizes in convenient form the principal points of contention between the two schools. Gierke lays particular stress on the pedantic, abstract manner in which legal doctrines were stated and developed in the Draft (*e.g.* the titles on possession). This method seems to him not only to be characteristic of the doctrinaire spirit of professional reflection, but to be explainable by the foreign material severed from real life; it would have been sufficient to turn to the eminently practical treatment of the "Gewere" in German medieval law, in order to endow that chapter on possession with the required concreteness and common sense. The whole aspect of the law of things is vitiated, according to the Germanistic critic, by the one-sided way in which absolute property ("dominium") is insisted upon in the Draft. It is contrary to all the traditions of Germanic law, which always recognised the superior claims of society and abstained from exaggerating the rights of individuals. In the law of persons, again, the Draft does not take sufficient account of the social combinations of individuals in the family, in the relation between master and servant, in the treatment of leases. All these and other kindred subjects are disposed of as if the persons entering into such relations were mere animated counters and their associations casual sums to be dissolved or combined at pleasure. In regard to juridical persons, Gierke reproaches the authors of the Draft with having overlooked the most vital feature of Germanistic juridical thought, the realistic conception of the "Genossenschaft", which is anything but a fiction, is endowed with a will and a personality of its own, and is capable not only of undertaking acts in law, but of assuming the responsibility for them as well in contract as in tort. As regards family law, it is shown that the Draft is guilty of a ridiculous perversion of the conception of the father's power, which appears in the extraordinary light of a substitute for guardianship. Altogether, in the judgment of the critic, the Romanistic production under discussion may serve as a kind of "reductio ad absurdum" of the attempt to build up a Code for modern Germany on the basis of Justinian's antiquated individualism.[1]

III

It is out of the question for us to investigate here the actual course of legal development in Germany in its dependence on Teutonic and Romanistic origins. But I should like to subject at least one important department of legal thought to a more detailed examination. Let us select for this purpose the doctrine of possession. It forms one of the principal parts of the law as to things; it has given rise to animated controversies between leading jurists; and it has been declared by Germanists, following in the footsteps of Albrecht, to embody legal conceptions of a peculiar stamp characteristic of Teutonic legal lore and exerting their distinctive influence up to our own days.

Let us dwell for a moment on the debatable ground which has been the bone of contention between the rival constructions of Savigny and Ihering, the principal German exponents of jurisprudential theory on the subject. It is not necessary to enter into a minute analysis of the subject in order to see the strong and the weak sides of these rival contentions. Savigny, taking his instigation from great Roman jurists, more especially from Paulus, brought into strong relief the element of intention in the

[1] See *e.g.* "Entwurf", p. 19.

idea of possession. It is the conscious assertion of power over a thing which originates possession, not its casual or vicarious detention. The famous expression "animus domini" was not altogether well chosen, as it held itself too narrowly to the notion of "dominium" — property, ownership; but the central idea that to claim possession of a thing is the same as to assert "this thing is mine", does not admit of doubt. Such a claim admits of many variations in kind, and this is the reason why it has been paraphrased in ancient and in modern times in terms wider than that indicated by "dominus" ("δεσπόζοντος", — Theophilus: "animus sibi habendi").[1] Unfortunately Savigny and his School have gone a great deal further; they have surmised that, because the *claim* to possession is a subjective assertion of power, the *protection* of possession is bound to follow on the same lines; and the well-known teaching as to "corpus" and "animus" has been built up in consequence. Besides, they have assumed that their juridical analysis of the Roman doctrine affords a key to a general jurisprudential treatment. Roman lawyers themselves varied greatly in this respect, to peculiar points of view. The Romans themselves did not consistently hold to the same conclusions as regards the position of lessees or of depositaries, while other systems of law started from entirely different distinctions. Ihering had no difficulty in showing this, and he took advantage of the opportunity to put forward what he calls the "objective" standard for granting or denying possession. According to him, it is the protection of certain interests by the State that raises them to a sphere of legally recognised possession, and it depends on considerations of public utility whether the Commonwealth considers the grown-up son, the bailee, or the lessee, worthy or unworthy of such special protection. The fact that the lessee was denied possession and had to content himself with a detention, protected by contract, speaks volumes for the historical setting of the Roman doctrine, which considered him for centuries to be a subordinate client of a householder in whom the power over the estate and its legal protection primarily rested. In his polemical zeal, Ihering carried his contention undoubtedly too far, made rather risky attempts to confute the Roman jurisconsults themselves, and overlooked the importance of the element of intention. He also left entirely out of account the influence of Greek juridical notions, which became more and more

[1] I may remark that Justice O. W. Holmes' account of Savigny's views lays (as it seems to me) too great a stress on its metaphysical connotation.

considerable towards the third century B.C. But in spite of these and other defects, he succeeded in his main endeavour to present in a strong light the historical evolution of possessory remedies in consequence of social needs and aims.

It is natural therefore to connect Ihering's teaching with the movement towards legal reform spreading over Germany in the last quarter of the nineteenth century. His speculations opened the way towards a bold revision of accepted Romanistic doctrines; and it may be said that the modern Germanists went with him part of the way. They brought forward a theory of possession which was derived from medieval sources, but still held good in the legislation of particular States (for example, Prussia), and started from juridical ideas in entire disagreement with those which had obtained in Rome and had been carried over to Germany by the Reception. The central notion of their theory was the "Gewere", defined as the matter of fact expression of real rights.[1]

It was not an equivalent of Roman "possession", because, as Huebner has expressed it, the "Gewere" included a necessary element of "right"; its assertion and defence started from the fact of possession, but tended towards title as the established and recognised centre of a right. This being so, the German law did not develop a system of possessory actions; when, by way of exception, it had to approach the matter in dispute from the side of possession, it did so not by the help of independent remedies, but by means of a preliminary investigation (in cases of disturbance of possession and of ejectment). The other side of the "Gewere" was that, as regards land, it had to materialise in the shape of actual exploitation the taking of "esplees" (as the Anglo-French lawyers used to say); "Gewere" was necessarily a holding for use and profit ("Not und Geld"). This meant, on one hand, that abstract rights could not form the basis of the "Gewere", on the other, that the various forms of exploitation of one and the same plot gave rise to different forms of "Gewere", corresponding to the various titles connected with it. There is disagreement on this point between our German authorities. Huebner formulates conclusions opposite to those adopted by Heusler.[2] But there can be no doubt that, although in case of litigation some forms of "Gewere" had to recede into the background and other forms to sustain the brunt of the legal struggle, there was a kind of ladder

[1] *E.g. Heusler*, "Institutionen des deutschen Privatrechts", II, 9, 14, 21.
[2] *Ibid.*, 25.

of estates in land, giving rise to particular forms of "Gewere", — "ledigliche", "hebbende", "eigentliche", etc. This was the consequence of the feudal splitting up of the solid notion of property. "Dominium utile" and "dominium directum", the right of the lord and the right of the vassal, the right of the Church, of rent-paying tenants, of reversioners, and of persons endowed by curtesy or dower — all these various estates had their reflection in special kinds of "Gewere."[1]

These features present a treatment of real property entirely different from that of the Roman books. Such a treatment was bound to come into conflict with the Romanesque doctrines of the "Common Roman Law" ("Gemeines römisches Recht") and of the first draft of the Civil Code. This conflict did take place, and the law of the revised Code was framed very much on the lines suggested by Ihering and by the Germanists.

Have these modifications to be traced primarily to national peculiarities? What foundation is there for the oft repeated contention that the modern law of possession, as formulated in the Civil Code of Germany, has been inspired by the peculiar juridical conceptions of Germanic notions? Gierke lays stress on the opposition of the Germanic people against the notions of absolute individualistic ownership proclaimed and developed in Roman law. Undoubtedly the "Bürgerliches Gesetzbuch" has carried out certain mitigations in this respect; a clause against "Chikane", or malicious use of property rights with the object of inflicting harm on others, was introduced into the Code after a lively struggle; rights of expropriation by the State were extended and defined in a way which does not conform with well-known applications of individualistic ownership. But yet, in the judgment of Socialistic writers like Menger, the German Code has remained true on the whole to the basis of individualism; and there can be no talk of a radical change of attitude in this respect. Huebner (following Herbert Mayer) sees the traditional element in the publicity required by German law in order to establish a title — an idea which in his view connects the medieval period with the modern; for in medieval times the creation or transfer of rights to land was effected in a popular assembly (*e.g.* in the important case of surrender or "Auflassung") or under conditions of private disposal which gave the transaction notoriety (*e.g.*

[1] Heusler himself mentions the case where the vassal had to sustain his "Gewere" against the lord in spite of the fact that the "ledigliche Gewere" belonged to a tenant of his.

the "sessio triduana", the procedure by a salman, etc.). The modern device corresponding to these antiquated forms and ensuring the same effects is found in the registration of title in the "Grundbuch." The connection seems, however, far from clear, and the analogy of legal consequences as to title is really produced by very different factors. Registration is a method essentially derived from settled conditions under a strong political rule. To some extent it may arise even in early times, as we may gather from the example of Domesday Book with its registration of tenants "tempore regis Willelmi" and "tempore regis Edwardi"; but in such cases the method is applied only in a rudimentary way, and is resorted to under pressure from the strong hand of a William the Conqueror. The transactions in open court or in surroundings ensuring publicity belong to an entirely different mode of social life; though interesting and characteristic in themselves, they do not concern either the traditional unity of Germanic juridical thought or the particular features of a theory of possession. It is difficult to escape the conclusion that, in striving to trace continuous lines of national development, German writers have been sometimes guilty of an uncritical confusion between the effects of national psychology and the results produced by the requirements of consecutive periods or of racial elements working for similar aims.

The rashness of wide-reaching national claims becomes especially apparent when we shift our ground from Germany proper to States in which German invaders as immigrants have played only a restricted part. Take, for instance, the parallels which may be traced between the doctrine of the "Gewere" and that of Seisin in French and in English law. Let us dwell on the latter, as it has been discussed by many leading writers, and a kind of general impression has been formed as to the fundamental identity of methods of treating possession in German and in English law.

This supposed identity does not go very deep, however, when we examine the facts somewhat closely. It is true that the Germanistic guarantee system [1] and the Anglo-French Seisin ("sitting in") system are both derived from the medieval notion of "investitura" — the "clothing" of a right. But the two conceptions, though starting from the "sensualism" (Huebner) of ancient legal lore from its requirement of visible and tangible formality, developed, one may say, into entirely opposite distinctions. While

[1] "Gewere" means literally "guarantee", and might be rendered in modern German by "Gewährschaft."

in England the stress was laid on possessory remedies and the contention as to title was ruled out from the specific procedure as to seisin, on the other hand in Germany "Gewere" was treated as a presumption of title, the possessory remedies remained undeveloped, and the whole procedure was directed to prepare a decision as to title. The influence of that fundamental contrast may be traced in regard to all the principal incidents of the doctrine. While in England the disseisor was protected against everyone but the rightful owner by the very fact of his possession, he had to disclose his title in Germanic procedure. At common law in England the owner himself was not allowed originally to make good his better right by the help of possessory remedies; if he had been guilty of technical negligence or had to face the heir of the disseisor or a purchaser from the latter,[1] possession of the disseisor was originally maintained.

Again, the Anglo-French seisin stands in "loneliness" with its theory that there can be only one person actually seised of a thing. Lawyers had to choose whether they would attribute it to the bailor or to the bailee, and they came gradually to favour the latter. Thus a clear difference is established, both as against Roman law which favours the owner and Germanic law which admits of several "Gewere." The variety of "estates" admitted by English law belongs to another plane of legal relations — it has nothing to do with possession and is based on differences of right.[2] One may add that there was a germ of the notion of concurrent seisins in the opposition between holdings "in dominio" and "in servicio", but this germ was not developed in practice. As for the relation to seisin of rights to land derived from feoffments, it did not follow any clear theoretical principle, but was evolved in the course of a rather intricate development through the practice of the courts.[3]

Altogether the intricacies of the law of possession cannot be unravelled by the comparatively simple expedient of contrasting national traditions and tendencies. It is evident, for example, that both in Roman and in English law the principle of a strong government, resolved to suppress self-help and lawlessness, asserted itself by creating and developing systems of possessory remedies in the interdicts in one case and the assizes in the other.

[1] *Maitland*, "The Beatitude of Seisin", Coll. Papers, I, 415 ff.
[2] *Pollock* and *Maitland*, "History of English Law", II, 104.
[3] *Pollock* and *Wright*, "Possession", 47; *Maitland*, Coll. Papers, I, 369 ff.

On the other hand, the history of German peoples did not leave much scope for such a decided preference for the principle of outward control over things. The popular and collegiate courts kept up a reverence for title and recognised it even when not embodied in actual control.[1] These traits are conditioned by changing states of society. If on one hand, Roman law kept up a very exacting theory of ownership, which balanced, as it were, its energetic protection of possession, English law gradually got rid of its assize (or possessory) remedies in favour of a more pliable system derived in a curious way from a combination between petitory (or title) remedies limited by exceptions (writs of entry) and special rules for regulating relations between landlords and tenants ("ejectio firmae", forcible entry).

It is natural that there is bound to be in all systems a combination of absolute and relative appropriation; of rights rooted in title and of occupation gradually strengthened by lapse of time; of legal security and of substantive justice. The manner in which different systems of law balance and combine these elements may be conditioned to a limited extent by national tradition and psychological peculiarities, but it has mainly to be traced to inferences of juridical logic and to more or less successful attempts to satisfy social needs. Thus we are forcibly brought back to Ihering's view, that the course of legal evolution depends not so much on descent, as on adaptation to circumstances.

I may add that it is not only by studying the intricate theory of possession that we are led to this conclusion: on all the occasions when legal principles have been claimed as peculiar to Germanic psychology, similar considerations may be urged.

[1] Mark the bold fiction of continuous "Gewere" bridging over tortiously interrupted possession.

INTRODUCTION TO THIS VOLUME

By William Emanuel Walz [1]

The development of humanity through the law is dominated by two powerful currents of thought, — Particularism (in our day perhaps better called nationalism) and Universalism. The one aims at strengthening particular nations through the municipal law. The other, Universalism, tries to win over nationalism itself, now plainly indicated as the coming victor in its struggle with individualism, to still wider conceptions of political, economic and racial unity. These wider conceptions are to be realized through confederations and federations, through alliances and understandings, with a final though still unacknowledged view to a world unity. That unity, it is hoped, can be made acceptable through the administration of a law wisely regardful of the true interests of individual nations, — a law more really international than now because made truly universal in its obligations and in its sanctions.

Municipal law dealing with private and public interests has been, is, and will continue to be the great field of struggle between individualism and nationalism, with national sovereignty expressed through laws and constitutions as the final arbiter in all disputes and contentions among citizens. International law is attempting to gain a like sphere for the exercise of its authority. It looks, for its place in the sun, to the good will of the large and small nations of the world. Municipal law compels individual men to yield to the nation their apparent and often their real rights, while international law asks individual nations to surrender their undoubted as well as their doubtful rights to the needs and convenience of humanity itself. Through popular sovereignty, once known in the United States as squatter-sovereignty, through state and national sovereignty, as well as through what German

[1] Dean of the College of Law, University of Maine.

writers have called social sovereignty, it seeks to arrive at that universal sovereignty backed by international public opinion and by international public force without which it is comparatively helpless, — a stumbling block to great and small nations alike.

This great ideal of international law is not to be realized within a century or two; but, even so, success is possible only by studying and following the lessons taught by nationalism in its unending but hitherto victorious struggle with individualism. Within its own limits nationalism has achieved the very ideals of international law: it has secured freedom of trade, a common citizenship, general education, social insurance legislation, and universal military service, — achievements of surpassing value, but all impossible without a previous corresponding conquest of individualism, and still incomplete without being universalized, that is, made subservient to the interests, not of particular men and nations, but to the true welfare of all nations and of all races of men. And yet, moving within strictly national lines and without intending it, the great Latin and Germanic nations have more or less unconsciously brought one to the other whatever blessings go with free trade within national boundaries, with a common citizenship, with general education, with social insurance laws, with universal military service. This unconscious tendency of the times should be made the conscious purpose of all men.

In the pursuit of this great world purpose, what is propounded to every citizen, lawyer and statesman is the fundamental question: How did nationalism through municipal law succeed in making the individual subservient to its greater purposes, so subservient in fact that a man's property and even a man's life appear to himself as nothing compared with the great interests of the State and nation to which he belongs?

It is perhaps not possible to say anything better of this remarkable book, to which these few and inadequate lines serve as an introduction, than that this great question, which the sphinx of philosophy has placed before man, is answered in Professor Huebner's "History of Germanic Private Law" more fully than in any other history of the law that we have seen. It is answered, not in so many words, but by the whole spirit and scope of the work, and not to the superficial reader, but to the open mind that thoughtfully inquires into the causes and reasons of national development as directed by law and legislation. The last stage of world development, the universalizing, socializing and humanizing of individual nations through the law of all lands, the universal law, cannot intelligently be grasped without understanding the process of the nationalizing of the individual through the law of the land. An extremely able study of this process is offered in the present "History of Germanic Private Law", a work now made accessible to the Anglo-American public in a remarkably accurate and excellent translation.

A more individualistic law than the primitive Germanic private law could not well have been found anywhere in the civilized world. The law itself in its beginning was determined by personal and individual ties more or less voluntarily assumed, not by the territorial bounds of a necessary and natural mutual dependence. Necessity, however, soon modified or changed what the individual would gladly have preserved. With the expansion of the Germanic tribes, coerced by pressure from within and without, and with the consequent conquest by them of Europe from the Straits of Gibraltar to the Baltic Ocean, this personal law was gradually supplanted by the territorial law. With comparative peace and prosperity, individualism asserted itself through legal decentralization. Soon there arose written and unwritten laws for the inhabitants of cities, for nobles, priests, merchants, artisans and public officials, and laws for men engaged in mining or in building and inspecting dykes. Local liberty, then as now the strongest feature of public life, found its fullest scope in the customs and laws of associational groups ("genossenschaftliche Verbände") . . . a development crowned by Prince Bismarck, that past master in the art of nation-building, by his utilizing them under the name of trade associations as the main pillars of his wonderful national system of accident, sickness, and old age insurance. Few men have studied the history of the law to better purpose than this wizard in the art of uniting the body and the soul, the form and the spirit of institutions, and thus endowing them with a life all their own and independent altogether of the life and will of the artist himself.

Individualism, from choice but more often from necessity, worked its way to particularism and gradually to nationalism in legal forms the most various: through custom and habit, through usage and tradition, through right, good, ancient practice, for all of which Germanic private law had its appropriate technical terms. Where these did not result in positive law, they produced that vast and most useful by-product of the Germanic law known as "Sittlichkeit", — a mass of ideal conceptions of the legal mind and of daily manifestations of refined business and social life and of political and public good form, not yet ready to be embodied into actual law but desperately striving for the authority that comes from public recognition enforced by statutory enactment. The wonderful possibilities of which this by-product of the law is capable were duly emphasized by Lord Haldane in his epoch-making address before the American Bar Association at Montreal in 1913, — possibilities that contain the promise and the potency of a new world organization along lines that correspond more fully than now not only to the material, political and commercial, but also to the legal, ethical and spiritual constitution of the universe.

The strength and popularity of Germanic private law lay in the fact that it established legal relations, not in the abstract but in the concrete. Delivering twig or clod, turf or sod, hat and glove, touching the altar cloth or the bell rope, then the putting out of the hearth fire by the old owner and the lighting it anew by the incoming proprietor, the "perambulatio" or the common walking of the boundaries, and finally the "exitus" as proof of release of all claims to the land by the former owner; the placing by the widow of her house key or her mantle upon the bier or grave of her husband to free herself from liability for debts; the hand-clasp before witnesses to make binding some feudal, commercial or even social relationship; the mounting on horse-back from a stone fifteen inches high in proof of testamentary and military capacity (a strange and yet not really unreasonable test, even in relatively recent times appealed to, though not actually gone through as custom once demanded, by General Winfield Scott and Field Marshal Count von Moltke when they insisted on the acceptance of their resignations and when each offered to prove by his inability to mount his horse the positive and irrevocable end of his active military career) . . . all these customs brought the good old law home to the minds and hearts of the people, to men and women, to old and young, standing by and seeing the law of the land visibly embodying and renewing itself in every transaction of life. To become truly strong and popular, international law, like the old law, must manifest these dramatic qualities of its predecessor in a far higher degree than it does to-day. It, also, must appeal to the imagination of mankind.

The doctrine of seisin (a word derived from the Old German "saz-jan", German "setzen", French "saisir"), and the publicity connected with it, so graphically described by Professor Huebner, was built up, not on an abstract conception of ownership, but upon the actual, external, visible element of physical control, publicly surrendered by the owner and as publicly assumed by the purchaser. This aspect of the law is treated with great lucidity and in all its aspects, — proprietary, corporeal, incorporeal, feudal, rental, judicial and pledge seisin, as well as seisin by the collective hand, similar to the being seized "per my et per tout" of the Anglo-Norman law. Equally interesting is the author's account of the legitimizing power of an apparent right, such as that of a record title or of color of title in general, both of them rights based on the great principle of publicity. Our American law has built well upon this ancient foundation, going in this respect, paradoxically enough, in advance of the English law by falling back, consciously or unconsciously, upon the ancient principles of a still remoter past.

The individualism that marked the Germanic law in its earlier days, prevented a strict separation of the public from the private law, because the relation of the State to the folk-men was treated from the standpoint of common and almost equal rights rather than from that of a superior giving commands to an inferior. This distinction did not begin to make itself really felt until more modern theories of the State had established themselves through the Hohenstaufen Kaisers in Italy, through the influence of the Roman and Canon law in the territorial courts and in the law faculties of the universities, and last, not least, through the powerful and persuasive example given to Europe by both France and Prussia. That the Germanic rulers, kings when elected at first by the people and then by the electoral college, kaisers when crowned by the pope in Rome, were by this popular and divine authority considered in some way successors to the ancient Cæsars and recognized as such by the Christian world and its great spiritual spokesmen such as Dante; that the Roman law was taught in all the universities of Europe; that in the administration of justice university trained officials gradually replaced unschooled laymen from the people; that the German law had with every century become less of a unit and more of an incoherent mass of territorial usages, customs and laws; that it was not (outside of a few cities) scientifically cultivated anywhere; that there was no powerful central monarchy with a "curia regis" as in England, and no radical legislative activity to correct defects . . . these were the chief reasons why the Reception came and conquered, spreading throughout the length and breadth of the land, with the exception only of Hamburg, Lübeck, Switzerland, and Schleswig, to which lands the jurisdiction of the Imperial Chamber of Justice had never extended.

In the last analysis the extreme individualism of the race was the real cause of the Reception, and a foreign law thus became the common law of the land. This individualism had in course of time developed a maxim remarkable in itself and only too well observed in practice: an agreement between the parties "breaks" the town law, town law "breaks" provincial law, and provincial law "breaks" the common law. Weak though the common law thus was, it was even so the only legal force that in the later Middle Ages united the people in a certain loose community of law. This anarchic individualism was broken by the growth of the power of the territorial princes, especially those of Austria, Prussia, Bavaria, and Saxony; and these in turn abolished the binding force of the common law and established, each in his own territory, a wholly independent legal province or State. Thus this great evil began to work out its own cure by a slow and painful process, that led, as in the United States, to a civil war, giving the final victory to the North as against the South, and to nationalism as against the adherents of individualism, particularism and State rights. With the defeat of Austria by Prussia, with the foundation of a new federation, and, thirty years afterward, with the enactment of the German Civil Code providing for a centralized administration of justice by a Supreme Court sitting, not at Berlin as Kaiser and Chancellor had strenuously desired, but at Leipzig in Saxony as a particularistic Reichstag had voted, German federal law has now in name and in fact become the law of the land and practically "breaks" all State and territorial laws. Thus nationalism has won a complete victory over a narrow particularism that had been responsible for the existence of more than one hundred and twenty different regions of special and independent law in an empire considerably smaller than the state of Texas. At last, through the efforts of Prince Bismarck, the work of the legal profession, and the will of the people, a common civil code prevails throughout the length and breadth of the land, ranking in excellence with Napoleon's Code Civil, generally and justly designated as the most Germanic of the older codes. Paradoxical as it may sound, Napoleon and Bismarck were the great political founders of German unity; and, consciously and unconsciously, their entire life work, especially that of Napoleon, has tended to the subjection of German individualism to the nationalism of to-day.

A Europe, more or less united, is no doubt the next great step in the world's progress. European individualism, chastened and made more reasonable in the severe school of nationalism, may be ready, sooner than we think, for continentalism, even for the formation of a United States of Europe, especially if a Pan-America under the leadership of the United States or a Pan-Asia under Japanese hegemony should promise soon to become realities. The time of the great individualists, beginning with Luther and ending with Voltaire, is indeed gone; but what might be called the great universalists have not yet arrived. The great men of the present century, as were those of the nineteenth, will be nationalists from conviction, universalists only from necessity, men like Bismarck and Darwin, like Wagner and Tolstoy, like Nietzsche and Bergson, — men that realize that the glory of Europe is really based on the plurality of its great nations, that each, in a different degree and by different methods but always in harmony with its own nature, is offering its gifts and contributions to an ever better state of intellectual freedom, disciplined imagination, political liberty, and social progress, a conviction that regardless of wars and rumors of war tends to become more general and more permanent with every century.

The three great currents that have dominated European history and law dominate it still: the great onward sweep of the restless, active, searching, scientific spirit still represented by the descendants of the Franks, Saxons and Allemans, by France, Great Britain, and Germany; the strong and enduring forces represented by the spirit of ancient Greece and Rome, by the Roman Law, the Catholic Church, and the classic arts; and, last not least, the great social movement of modern times, mediating between the old and the new, endeavoring to harmonize through the law, and wherever possible through religion also, the Teuton spirit with the Roman, the North with the South, the East with the West, honor with conscience, capital with labor, the one with the many, the individual with society, tremendous problems calling for the Grand Synthesis of nations and races through law and religion, a movement growing and developing in ever widening and ever higher circles, in vast spiral lines, tending to embrace all mankind and raising it to nobler and more spiritual planes of development. The soul of a nation is like a prism in which the rays of truth break in a specific manner; but all united, and only when united, give the pure white truth, the perfect law. This new and perfect truth can shine out brightly, not in times of stress and storm, but in times of peace and quiet, can in fact be developed only in eras of great institutions such as the "Landfrieden", the King's Peace, the "Constitutio Pacis", the "Treuga Henrici", or else of institutions greater still such as the coming century may bring to bless mankind, "in terra pax hominibus bonae voluntatis", a peace made effective through a law that is not the law of any one man or of any one nation, but the law of all men and of all nations, and therefore the very law of God himself.

To have contributed to this grand coming consummation is the merit of our author; to try to understand his work is the duty of the reader.

TRANSLATOR'S NOTE

THE present volume has profited by the learning of Professor Lorenzen and Professor Wigmore, but its preparation has been left very largely to the translator's own judgment, and he is responsible for any errors it may contain. Great pains have been taken to make the translation as true to the original in both sense and form as a decent regard for English idiom would permit; to find for words "of art" equivalents that carry some intelligibility apart from technical context or knowledge; and, above all, to avoid the use of any expressions of our own law which, though seemingly bearers of light, could mislead the reader into assuming a greater similarity between the institutes of the two legal systems than actually exists. The difficulties of the task will be apparent to any reader of the volume; particularly those offered by institutes such as pledge, land charges, rents, and seisin, whose analysis and history have received much less attention in our own than in German legal literature, and whose terminology is correspondingly richer in the latter. Not every institute of foreign law of which one reads *can* be fitted into our own technical nomenclature. Indeed, in view of the notorious fact that one of the greatest defects of our law is its careless orismology, no apology should be necessary for any honest endeavor to escape from the English and American practice — often productive of grotesque results, and never an aid to clear thinking — of describing foreign institutional development in the peculiar terms that embody specifically Anglo-Saxon experience. The translator has never forgotten that he was dealing with an account of *Germanic* things, and that the greatest obstacle in a reader's way is the difficulty of getting away from English things that he knows too well. Even at best, one is forced to the use of scores of words, such as "reversioner", "dower", "advowson", "occupancy", "chattels", and so on, that never had for Germanic law the precise content which they bear in our own — not forgetting that their meaning in that has varied at different times, and varies to-day from State to State.

Save in a few cases, it has not been necessary to resort to the aid of particularly strange expressions; and in the few exceptional cases where this could not be avoided the expressions adopted are no odder than are scores of those of the Scots law with which American and English lawyers should be fairly familiar. To take an example, the expression "in collective hand" (tenure, ownership, or alienation "in" or "by" collective hand) will be unfamiliar to most readers. Even Mr. Maitland once yielded so far to the English tradition as to employ "joint tenancy" as the equivalent of the German "zu gesamter Hand", although with a caution as to the differences between them (III "Collected Papers", 336). But inasmuch as only one of the two main characteristics of the English joint interest (true, the one most familiar to lawyers and of greatest practical importance in our modern law) belongs to interests "zu gesamter Hand", while in details there are great diversities, the translation "joint" is certainly undesirable. It may be added that the German institute has been very much discussed in other countries, and that in French legal literature it is the custom to do as has been done in the present volume; that is, translate it literally ("en main commune"; see, for example, "Le Code Civil, 1804–1904, Livre du Centenaire", Vol. I, pp. 357–379). The truth is that the history of community and individual ownership, under varying circumstances of time and place, is recorded in primitive and modern legal systems in an extraordinary variety of forms of collective interests, for whose classification and description our own alternatives of joint, common, or several, are totally inadequate. The same is true of the systems of succession and partition associated with such collective interests. Think, for example, of attempting to bring all the junior rights in succession that occur in different parts of the world under the descriptive cover of "borough English"! Such translations, far from being examples of "good English", are merely evidences of parochial thinking.

Finally, with respect to the title of the volume ("History of Germanic Private Law"), which departs somewhat from the original ("Grundzüge des deutschen Privatrechts"), this was deliberately adopted by the Editorial Committee, as better suggesting than does the original title the historical treatment and the wide range of comparative references to various bodies of Germanic law which in fact characterize the work, and which constitute much of its value for students of our own law; although it may be added that throughout the body of the text the greatest care has been exercised in distinguishing between "Germanic" and "German."

LIST OF IMPORTANT WORKS CITED

I. SYSTEMATIC TREATISES.

A. *Written from an older standpoint.*

Eichhorn, "Einleitung in das deutsche Privatrecht" (1823, 5th ed. 1845).

Beseler, "System des gemeinen deutschen Privatrechts" (3 vols., 1847, 1853, 1855; 4th ed. 2 vols. 1885).

Gerber, "System" = "System des deutschen Privatrechts" (1848, 1849; 16th ed. 1891).

Gengler, "Das deutsche Privatrecht in seinen Grundzügen" (1854, 4th ed. 1892).

Stobbe, "Handbuch des deutschen Privatrechts" (Vol. 1, 1871, 3d ed., by *K. Schulz*, 1893; Vol. 2, 1875, 2d ed. 1882; Vol. 3, 1878, 2d ed. 1885; Vol. 4, 1st & 2d ed. 1885; Vol. 5, 1st & 2d ed. 1885).

v. Roth, "System des deutschen Privatrechts" (3 vols., 1880, 1881, 1886; incomplete).

Franken, "Lehrbuch des deutschen Privatrechts" (1894).

Behrend, "Übersicht über das deutsche Privatrecht", in *Holtzendorff's*, "Enzyklopädie der Rechtswissenschaft" (Vol. 1, 5th ed. 1890, 565–609).

B. *Written in the light of the Civil Code or its drafts.*

Gerber, "System des deutschen Privatrechts auf der Grundlage des Entwurfs eines BGB für das deutsche Reich", revised by *Cosack* (17th ed. 1895).

Stobbe, "Handbuch des deutschen Privatrechts", revised by *H. O. Lehmann* (Vol. 2, Part 1, 3d ed. 1896; Vol. 2, Part 2, 3d ed. 1897; Vol. 3, 3d ed. 1898; Vol. 4, 3d ed. 1900).

H. O. Lehmann, "Geschichte und Grundzüge des (deutschen) Privatrechts", in *Birkmeyer's* "Enzyklopädie der Rechtswissenschaft" (1901, 290–353).

Gierke, "Privatrecht" = "Deutsches Privatrecht", in *Binding's* "Systematisches Handbuch der deutschen Rechtswissenschaft" (Vol. 1, "Allgemeiner Teil und Personenrecht", 1895; Vol. 2, "Sachenrecht", 1905).

Gierke in *Holtzendorff-Kohler* = "Grundzüge des deutschen Privatrechts", in *Holtzendorff-Kohler's* "Enzyklopädie der Rechtswissenschaft" (6th ed., Vol. 1, 1904, 431–559).

II. REPRINTS OF SELECTED SOURCES.

Franklin, "Geschichte und System des deutschen Privatrechts, ein Grundriss zu Vorlesungen" (1878, 2d ed. 1882).

Kraut, "Grundriss zu Vorlesungen über das deutsche Privatrecht" (1830; 6th ed., by *von Frensdorff*, 1886).

Lörsch and *Schröder*, "Urkunden zur Geschichte des deutschen Privatrechts für den Gebrauch bei Vorlesungen und Übungen" (1874; 2d ed. 1881; 3d ed., revised by *Schröder* and *L. Perels*, 1912).

Stutz Höngger, "Meiergerichtsurteile des 16n. und 17n. Jahrhunderts zum Selbststudium und für den Gebrauch bei Übungen erstmals herausgegeben und erläutert" (1912).

III. HISTORIES.

Heusler, "Institutionen" = "Institutionen des deutschen Privatrechts", constituting Part 2 of Vol. 2 of *Binding's* "Systematisches Handbuch der deutschen Rechtswissenschaft" (2 vols., 1885, 1886).

v. Amira, "Recht" = art. "Recht" in Part 2 of Vol. 2 of *Paul's* "Grundriss der germanischen Philologie" (1893, 35–200; 2d ed. 1897, pp. 51–222; also published separately).

Cl. Frhr. von Schwerin, "Deutsche Rechtsgeschichte" (Part 3 of Vol. 2 of Meister: "Grundriss der Geschichtswissenschaft," 1912).

Hoops, J., "Reallexikon der germanischen Altertumskunde, unter Mitwirkung zahlreicher Fachgelehrten herausgegeben von—" (thus far 2 parts, 1911, 1912); it also treats in many articles of the history of the Germanic and older German law.

A. *Treatises upon Germanic legal history, particularly:*

Brunner, "Geschichte" = "Deutsche Rechtsgeschichte", constituting Part 1 of Vol. II of *Binding's* "Systematisches Handbuch der deutschen Rechtswissenschaft" (Vol. I, 1887, 2d ed. 1906; Vol. 2, 1892).

Brunner, "Grundzüge" = "Grundzüge der deutschen Rechtsgeschichte" (1901, 2d ed. 1903; 5th ed. 1912).

Schröder, "Lehrbuch" = "Lehrbuch der deutschen Rechtsgeschichte" (1887, 5th ed. 1907).

Hedemann, "Die Fortschritte des Zivilrechts im 19n. Jahrhundert. Ein Überblick über die Entfaltung des Privatrechts in Deutschland, Österreich, Frankreich, und der Schweiz.—Ier. Band: Die Neuordnung des Verkehrslebens" (1910).

IV. TREATISES ON REGIONAL GERMAN LEGAL SYSTEMS.

A. *Systems prevailing within the limits of the present German Empire.*

Dernburg, "Lehrbuch des preussischen Privatrechts und der Privatrechtsnormen des Reichs" (3 vols., 1871; 5th ed., Vol. 1, 1894, Vol. 2, 1897, Vol. 3, 4th ed. 1896).

v. Roth, "Bayerisches Zivilrecht" (3 vols., 1871; Vol. 1, 2d ed. 1881, Vol. 2, 2d ed. and Vol. 3, 2d ed., ed. by *von Becher*, 1897, 1898).

Grützmann, "Handbuch des sächsischen Privatrechts" (2 vols., 1887, 1889).

K. G. Wächter, "Handbuch des im Königreich Württemberg geltenden Privatrechts" (2 vols., 1839, 1842; unfinished).

Boehlau, "Mecklenburgisches Landrecht" (Vol. 1, 1871; Vol. 2, Part 1, 1872, Part 2, 1874; Vol. 3, Part 1, 1880; unfinished).

Roth & v. Meibom, "Kurhessisches Privatrecht" (Vol. 1, 1858; unfinished).

Falck, "Handbuch des Schleswig-Holsteinischen Privatrechts" (5 vols., 1825–1848; unfinished).

Dernburg. Of the supplemental volumes to Dernburg's "Darstellung des bürgerlichen Rechts des deutschen Reichs und Preussens" (6 vols., Vols. 1 & 2 in 3d ed.; Vol. 3, 4th ed.; Vol. 5, 2d ed.—all edited by *Kohler*) there have appeared the following:

Oertmann, "Bayerisches Landesprivatrecht" (1903).
Kisch, "Elsass-Lothringisches Landesprivatrecht" (1905).
Kloss, "Sächsisches Landesprivatrecht" (1904, 2d ed. 1908).
Dorner & Seng, "Badisches Landesprivatrecht" (1906).

v. Buchka, "Landesprivatrecht der Grossherzogtümer Mecklenburg-Schwerin und Mecklenburg-Strelitz" (1905).
Nöldecke, "Hamburgisches Landesprivatrecht" (1907).
Porzig, Strichling, Unger & Böckel, "Landesprivatrecht der Thüringischen Staaten" (1908).
Wolf, "Hessisches Landesprivatrecht" (1910).
Lange, "Landesprivatrecht der Fürstentümer Waldeck und Pyrmont" (1910).

B. *Systems prevailing outside the limits of the present German Empire.*
Unger, "System des österreichischen allgemeinen Privatrechts" (Vols. 1 and 2, 1856, 1859, 4th. ed. 1876, — "Allgemeiner Teil; Vol. 6, 1864, 3d ed. 1879, — "Erbrecht").
Finger & Frankl, "Grundriss des österreichischen Rechts", including:
Pfersche, "Grundriss der allgemeinen Lehren des bürgerlichen Rechts" (1907, 2d ed. 1911).
Demelius, "Sachenrecht" (1900, 2d ed. 1911).
Schuster von Bonnot, "Obligationenrecht" (1899).
v. Anders, "Familienrecht" (1899, 2d ed. 1911), "Erbrecht" (1899, 2d ed. 1911).
Huber, "Schw. Privatrecht" = "System und Geschichte des schweizerischen Privatrechts" (4 vols., 1886–1893).
Erdmann, "System des Privatrechts der Ostseeprovinzen Liv-, Esth-, und Kurland" (2 vols., 1889, 1891; unfinished).
Tuor, "Das neue Recht. Einführung in das schweizerische Zivilgesetzbuch" (1912).

V. HISTORIES OF RELATED LEGAL SYSTEMS.

Viollet, "Histoire du droit civil français" (3d ed. 1905).
Brissaud, "Manuel d'histoire du droit français" (1898).
Zachariae von Lingenthal, "Handbuch des französischen Privatrechts" (2 vols., 1808; 8th ed. in 4 vols., ed. by *von Crome*, 1894, 1895).
Crome, "Allgemeiner Teil der modernen französischen Privatrechtswissenschaft" (1892).
Crome, "Grundlehren des französischen Obligationenrechts" (1894).
Pertile, "Storia del diritto italiano" (2d ed. in 7 vols., 1892–1903).
Nani, "Storia del diritto privato italiano" (1902).
Schupfer, "Il diritto dei popoli germanici con speciale riguardo all' Italia" (4 vols., 1907, 1, 1909).
Hinojosa, "Historia general del derecho español" (thus far 1 vol., 1887).
Pollock and Maitland, "The History of English Law before the Time of Edward I" (2 vols., 1895, 2d ed. 1898).
Holmes, O. W., "Das gemeine Recht Englands und Nordamerikas (The Common Law)", presented in 11 lectures; translated with the author's consent by *R. Leonhard* (1912).
"*Select essays*" = "S. E. in Anglo-American Legal History, by various authors. Compiled and edited by a Committee of the Association of American Law Schools" (3 vols., 1907–09).
Kolderup-Rosenvinge, "Grundriss der dänischen Rechtsgeschichte", translated by Homeyer (1825).
K. Maurer, "Vorlesungen über altnordische Rechtsgeschichte" (5 vols., 1907, 1908, 1909, 1910).
S. J. Fockema Andreae, "Het oud-nederlandsch burgerlijk recht" (2 parts, 1906).

VI. PERIODICALS.

"Zeitschrift für deutsches Recht und deutsche Rechtswissenschaft", ed. by *Reyscher*, *Wilda*, *Besseler*, *Stobbe* (20 vols., 1839–1861).

Z. Gesch. R. W. = "Zeitschrift für geschichtliche Rechtswissenschaft", ed. by *Savigny, Eichhorn, Göschen* (15 vols., 1815–1850).
Z[1]. R. G. = "Zeitschrift für Rechtsgeschichte", ed. by *Rudorff, Bruns, Roth, Merkel, Böhlau* (13 vols., 1861–1879). Continued by:
Z[2]. R. G. = "Zeitschrift der Savigny-Stiftung, für Rechtsgeschichte", ed. by *Bekker, Pernice, Mitteis, Schröder, Brunner, Stutz* (1880– ; thus far 32 vols. in the Germanistische Abteilung).

VII. COLLECTION OF MONOGRAPHS ON GERMAN LAW.

Gierke's "Untersuchungen" = *Gierke*, ed. "Untersuchungen zur deutschen Staats und Rechtsgeschichte" (1878–).
Beyerle's "Beiträge" = *Beyerle*, ed. "Deutschrechtliche Beiträge" (1906–).

ABBREVIATIONS USED IN THE FOOTNOTES OTHER THAN THOSE ABOVE INDICATED

AHGB = HGB = (Allgemeines) Handelsgesetzbuch.
Akad. Wiss. Berl. = Abhandlungen der Akademie der Wissenschaften zu Berlin.
Allg. L. R. = Allgemeines Landrecht (of Prussia).
Allg. öst. G. Z. = Allgemeine österreichische Gerichtszeitung.
v. Amira "Obligationenrecht" = Nordgermanisches Obligationenrecht.
Arch. B. R. = Archiv für Bürgerliches Recht.
Arch. Kult. G. = Archiv für Kulturgeschichte.
Arch. Soz. W. Soz. Pol. = Archiv für Sozialwissenschaft und Sozialpolitik.
Arch. Urk. F. = Archiv für Urkundenforschung.
Arch. öff. R. = Archiv für öffentliches Recht.
Arch. zivil. Praxis = Archiv für zivilistische Praxis.
Arch. R. W. Philos. = Archiv für Rechts- und Wirtschaftsphilosophie.
Amer. Hist. R. = American Historical Review.
BGB = Bürgerliches Gesetzbuch.
Beit. z. Erläut. D. R. = Beiträge zur Erläuterung des deutschen Rechts, begründet von Gruchot.
v. Below-Finke-Meinscke, "Abhandlungen" = Abhandlungen zur mittleren und neueren Geschichte, herausgegeben von v. B., F., und M.
Brandenburg's "Abhandlungen" = Brandenburg-Seeliger-Wilcken, editors, Leipziger historische Abhandlungen.
Brie & Fleischmann, "Abhandlungen" = Abhandlungen aus dem Staats- und Verwaltungsrecht.
Brentano & Lotz, "Studien" = Münchener volkswirtschaftliche Studien.
Brunner, "Forschungen" = Forschungen zur Geschichte des deutschen und französischen Rechts.
Crome, "Bürgerliches Recht" = System des Bürgerlichen Rechts.
Dahn, "Bausteine" = Felix Dahn, Bausteine; Gesammelte kleine Schriften, 6 vols.
Dernburg, "Bürgerliches Recht" = Das Bürgerliche Recht des deutschen Reichs und Preussens.
Deut. G. Bl. = Deutsche Geschichtsblätter.
Deut. Monatssch. ges. Leben = Deutsche Monatsschrift für das gesamte Leben der Gegenwart.
Deut. Litt. Z. = Deutsche Literaturzeitung.
Deut. Z. Kirchenr. = Deutsche Zeitschrift für Kirchenrecht.
Delbrück, Preuss. J. B. = Preussische Jahrbücher.
Dopsch, "Forschungen" = Forschungen zur inneren Geschichte Österreichs, ed. by Dopsch.
EB = Schw. ZGB, EB = Schweizerisches Zivilgesetzbuch, Einführungsbestimmungen.
EG = BGB, EG = Einführungsgesetz zum Bürgerlichen Gesetzbuch.
Ecker's Zür. Beiträge R. W. = Ecker, Hafter, Hitzig, M. Huber, editors: Züricher Beiträge zur Rechtswissenschaft.

Forsch. Br. Pr. G. = Forschungen zur Brandenburgischen und Preussischen Geschichte.
Forsch. D. G. = Forschungen zur deutschen Geschichte.
Gmür's "Abhandlungen" = Gmür, ed., "Abhandlungen zum schweizerischen Recht."
Götting. G. Anz. = Göttingenische gelehrte Anzeigen.
J. Grimm, "Rechtsaltertümer" = "Deutsche Rechtsaltertümer" (1st ed. 1828, 4th ed. 1899).
Hans. G. B. = Hansische Geschichtsblätter.
Hoop's "Reallexikon" = Reallexikon der germanischen Altertumskunde.
Hist. Vj. S. = Historische Vierteljahrschrift.
Hist. Z. = Historische Zeitschrift.
H. W. B. der Staatsw. = Handwörterbuch der Staatswissenschaften.
Heymann, "Arbeiten" = Arbeiten zum Handels-, Gewerbe-, und Landwirtschaftsrecht.
Jenaer Lit. Z. = Jenaer Literaturzeitung.
Fischer, "Abhandlungen" = O. Fischer, ed.: Abhandlungen zum Privatrecht und Zivilprozess des deutschen Reiches.
v. Inama-Sternegg, "Wirtschaftsgeschichte" = von Inama-Sternegg, Deutsche Wirtschaftsgeschichte, 2 vols.
J. B. gem. R. = Jahrbuch des gemeinen deutschen Rechts, I (1857).
Inter. W. Sch. = Internationale Wochenschrift.
Ihering's J. B. = Ihering's Jahrbücher.
Inst. öst. G. F. = Mitteilungen des Instituts für österreichische Geschichtsforschung.
J. B. für Dogm. = Jahrbücher für Dogmatik.
K. Bayer. Akad. Wiss., "Abhandlungen" = Abhandlungen der königlichen Bayrischen Akademie der Wissenschaften, Philosophisch-philologische und historische Klasse.
K. Preuss. Akad. Wiss., Sitz. Ber. = Sitzungsberichte der königlichen preussischen Akademie der Wissenschaften, Philosophisch-historische Klasse.
K. Gesell. Wiss. Göttingen, "Nachrichten" = Nachrichten der königlichen Gesellschaft der Wissenschaften zu Göttingen, Philosophisch-historische Klasse.
Krit. Vj. G. R. W. = Kritische Vierteljahrsschrift für Gesetzgebung und Rechtswissenschaft.
K. Sächs. Gesell. Wiss., "Berichte" = Berichte über die Verhandlungen der königlichen sächsischen Gesellschaft der Wissenschaft zu Leipzig, Philologisch-historische Klasse.
K. Sächs. Gesell. Wiss., "Abhandlungen" = Abhandlungen der phil.-hist.-Klasse der königlich sächsischen Gesellschaft der Wissenschaft.
Kohler, "Gesammelte Abhandlungen" (1883) = "Gesammelte Abhandlungen aus dem gemeinen und französischen Civilrecht" (1883).
Landsberg, "Geschichte"; see Stintzing-Landsberg.
M. G. Cap. = Monumenta Germaniae Historica, Capitularia.
Meckb. Z. Rp. Rw. = Mecklenburgische Zeitschrift für Rechtspflege und Rechtswissenschaft.
Meister, "Münsterische Beiträge" = Münsterische Beiträge zur Geschichtsforschung.
N. Arch. Gesel. A. deut. G. K. = Neues Archiv der Gesellschaft für ältere deutsche Geschichtskunde.
O. R. = Obligationenrecht.
Pollock-Maitland, "History" = Sir F. Pollock and F. W. Maitland, "The History of English Law before the Time of Edward I" (2d ed. 1895).
Schücking's "Arbeiten" = Schücking, ed., "Arbeiten aus dem juristischen-staatswissenschaftlichen Seminar der Universität Marburg."
Ssp. = Sachsenspiegel.
Swsp. = Schwabenspiegel.
S. Ver. Soz. Pol. = Schriften des Vereins für Sozialpolitik.
Schmoller's J. B. = Schmoller's Jahrbuch für Gesetzgebung, Verwaltung und Volkswirtschaft.

Schmoller's "Forschungen" = Schmoller, ed., Staats- und wissenschaftliche Forschungen.
Sch. Wis. Ges. Strassburg = Schriften der wissenschaftlichen Gesellschaft in Strassburg.
Schrader, "Reallexikon" = Reallexikon der indogermanischen Altertumskunde, Grundzüge einer Kultur- und Völkergeschichte Alteuropas (1901).
Schröder, "Lehrbuch" = Lehrbuch der deutschen Rechtsgeschichte.
Schw. ZGB = Schweizerisches Zivilgesetzbuch, — see also EB.
Stobbe, "Beiträge" = Beiträge zur Geschichte des deutschen Rechts.
v. Stengel-Fleischmann, "Wörterbuch" = Wörterbuch des deutschen Staats- und Verwaltungsrechts.
Stintzing-Landsberg, "Geschichte" = Geschichte der deutschen Rechtswissenschaft.
Stutz, "Untersuchungen" = Stutz, ed., "Kirchenrechtliche Untersuchungen."
Thüringisch-sächsische Z. G. K. = Thüringisch-sächsische Zeitschrift für Geschichte und Kunst.
Unter. G. D. Stadtverf. = Untersuchungen zur Geschichte der deutschen Stadtverfassung.
Vj. Soz. W. G. = Vierteljahrschrift für Sozial- und Wirtschaftsgeschichte.
Westd. Z. G. K. = Westdeutsche Zeitschrift für Geschichte und Kunst.
W. B. der Volkswirtschaft = Wörterbuch der Volkswirtschaft.
W. O. = Wechselordnung.
Wörter und Sachen = Wörter und Sachen, kulturhistorische Zeitschrift für Sprach- und Sagenforschung.
Wien, K. Akad. Wiss., Sitz.-Ber. = Sitzungsberichte der kaiserlichen Akademie der Wissenschaft in Wien, Philosophisch-historische Klasse.
Z. Volk. Psy. = Zeitschrift für Völkerpsychologie.
Z. Bergr. = Zeitschrift für Bergrecht.
Z. Vergl. R. W. = Zeitschrift für vergleichende Rechtswissenschaft.
Z. ges. H. R. = Zeitschrift für das gesammte Handelsrecht.
Z. Priv. öff. R. = Zeitschrift für das Privat- und öffentliche Recht der Gegenwart.
Z. schw. R. = Zeitschrift für schweizerisches Recht.
Z. Sav. St. R. G. = Zeitschrift der Savigny-Stiftung für Rechtsgeschichte.
Z. Hand. R. = Zeitschrift für Handelsrecht.
Z. deut. R. = Zeitschrift für deutsches Recht.
Z. deut. Wortf. = Zeitschrift für deutsche Wortforschung.
Z. deut. Phil. = Zeitschrift für deutsche Philologie.
Z. Ver. Lübeck G. A. K. = Zeitschrift des Vereins für Lübecksche Geschichte und Altertumskunde.
Z. Westpreus. G. Ver. = Zeitschrift des westpreussischen Geschichtsvereins.
Z. Ver. Thüring. G. = Zeitschrift des Vereins für Thüringische Geschichte.

A HISTORY OF GERMANIC PRIVATE LAW

INTRODUCTION

Chapter I

GENERAL TRAITS OF GERMANIC PRIVATE LAW

§ 1. **German Private Law before the Reception.** — It is only through its history that one can understand the present-day meaning of the phrase "German Private Law." The decisive fact in that history was the reception of alien legal systems, above all the "Reception" of the Roman law. It was only after, and as a consequence of, the Reception that there was developed the technical conception of "German Private Law" which appropriated the special field proper to it as an independent branch of German legal science.

In the first place, if we look at German private law before the Reception a whole sequence of signal characteristics can be pointed out which essentially distinguish it in form and content from its later form. But in doing this we must never lose sight of the fact that it was subjected during the centuries of the Middle Ages to a continuous development, which led it, with the progress of material and intellectual culture, from awkward, undiversified beginnings to a richer development. At the same time certain features remained stamped upon it to the very end of this period of unbroken growth.

(I) **Disunity of the Law.** — From the very beginning Germanic law was lacking in unity; it was a much disintegrated law. For though, from the remotest time, the Germans were racially distinct, as a "gens tantum sui similis", from Romans, Kelts, and Slavs, and even from their Germanic brothers, they have nevertheless always, like the Greeks, been characterized politically by particularism. The dismemberment of the law was manifested in several respects.

(1) *Racial law* ("Stammesrecht"). — Germanic law, private not less than public, was already a racial law in its earliest recognizable form. For the laws of the individual Germanic racial branches ("Stämme") had originated in and developed upon a basis of common habit and legal conviction, though they nevertheless reveal many variations which, under the influence of external circumstances, might attain considerable importance. According to the old Germanic view the racial law was not only binding upon the members of the racial branch, but was also determinant of all legal relations that arose within the territory occupied by the "Stamm." Men knew no law other than their own: where they could not or would not apply that, there was no law at all. The Burgundians and Lombards, probably also the Visigoths, clung to this principle in the States later founded by them; and among the Franks, also, it prevailed down to the time of the "Lex Salica." In the later Frankish empire, however, there was developed the contrasting principle of "personality", as it is called, which presupposed a recognition of the parity of all the racial branches ruled by the Frankish King, and of their laws. Interpreted in terms of the personality-principle, "racial-

law" was simply the law of the members of the "Stamm." It was applied to them whether resident within or without the territory of their "Stamm": every subject of the Empire carried about with him throughout the Empire the law of his racial branch. Law was determined solely by personal, not by territorial, bonds of mutual dependence.

(2) *Territorial law* ("Landrecht"). — When the rigid frame of the Carolingian monarchy began to loosen, the principle of personal law again gradually disappeared, and the territorial principle took its place in ever increasing degree. Racial law became territorial law. A man was no longer born into the law of his forefathers, but into the law of his home. And once again the law, — henceforth as territorial law, — laid hold upon everything in legal life (with certain definite exceptions) that happened within a given territory. Distinct provinces with variant legal systems were thus formed within the domain of the Germanic law; provinces which, as lands of Frankish law, of Saxon law, and so on, originally coincided with the boundaries of the racial duchies. But while this territorial law, at least in its beginnings, was a unitary law, — a law that prevailed uniformly in all parts of the region throughout which it had validity (although, to be sure, we find, even in the Frankish period, *local* legal growths within the racial domains of Saxons, Anglo-Saxons, Lombards, and Franks), — this condition also came to an end as political dismemberment increased. The great legal provinces marked off by racial settlement split up into increasingly small and numerous districts, within each of which legal development went on independently; because there were everywhere lacking the bases of constitutional law necessary for the enforcement of a uniform (*i.e.* a centralized) law. Franchised districts, principalities ("Landesherrschaften"), and towns detached themselves as independent jurisdictional fragments from the old territory of the racial law. Finally things went so far that every court followed the legal customs of its particular district.

(3) *Bodies of special class and local law*[1] ("Rechtskreise"). — Along with the breaking up of the domain of the territorial law into jurisdictions geographically separate there went on a division — particularly significant for the medieval period — of the originally unitary racial or territorial law itself into various special legal systems for distinct legal classes and districts ("Rechts-

[1] *Heusler*, "Institutionen", I, 23–44.

kreise"). The racial law had originally been supreme over all members of the racial branch in all their legal relations, and the territorial law had enjoyed a similarly unqualified authority within the region in which it prevailed, but this condition of things changed about the beginning of the Middle Ages proper, — or say about the end of the 900 s. The territorial law, which was "pointed out" or declared in the ordinary county-courts by the lay-judges ("Schöffen"), was not capable of keeping pace with the necessities of advancing economic development. Especially in the cities, where trade and handiwork called into existence wholly new legal institutes, men could not get along with a territorial law adjusted to a rural economy. For that very reason, as has been remarked, the cities broke away from the domain of the territorial law as districts of independent law. City law was "a further development of the territorial law upon a more advanced economic plane." But city law within its jurisdiction was the same as the ordinary territorial law within its jurisdiction: namely, a general law that found uniform application to all residents of the district and all local legal relations.

It was different, however, with the detachment from the territorial law of independent bodies of feudal, servitary, and manorial law. This phenomenon, as Heusler has shown, is by no means sufficiently explained by conceiving it as an accompaniment and consequence of the development of the special estates of knights, servitors, and serfs. Feudal, servitary, and manorial law were originally not laws of estates, — *i.e.* peculiar laws of definite classes of the population. They had to do with particular legal *relations*. They had originally a material, not a personal, basis; an objective, not a subjective, character. They were the law of those feudal, servitary, and manorial legal relations which became established between feudal, personal, and manorial lords on one side and their tenants on the other, as well as among the latter themselves, and which found their special nucleus in the feudal, servitary, and manorial courts, wherein they received independent development. In so far as these legal relations were withdrawn from the old (rural) moots that administered the territorial law and were abandoned to the seigniorial courts, the development of the feudal, servitary, and manorial law was a corresponding loss to the territorial law, and was another, and especially weighty, cause of legal decentralization. They constituted independent bodies of law, alongside the territorial and the city law: Heusler calls them "Spezialrechte" ("special" legal systems), as contrasted with the general law applied in the town and rural courts. That this remained the general law is shown by the fact that even those persons who lived in feudal, servitary, or manorial legal relations with a lord were by no means thereby wholly withdrawn from the authority of the territorial law. Serfs were subject to the territorial law for misdeeds which they committed or suffered outside the manorial community, and for those legal arrangements ("Rechtsgeschäfte") which they were permitted to enter into with outsiders. Similarly, the liegeman as respects land held freely, in addition to his fief. Again, the burgher might acquire a manorial holding, and he then became subject, for this, to the manorial law.

This tendency of medieval law to develop particular "Rechtskreise" (bodies of special class and local law) attained as time went on an ever more decided predominance. And the basis of these did not remain purely material. There were added to the law of feudal, servitary, and manorial relations, as new bodies of "special" law, regulations of mines, dikes, the chase and similar matters; but independent bodies of law were developed as well for specific social classes united by blood or by occupation, — as *e.g.* for nobles, princes, merchants, artisans, public officials, etc.

(II) **Relation of Customary and Enacted Law** ("Gewohnheitsrecht").[1] — (1) *Customary law.* — In the earliest times law rested, among the Germanic peoples as elsewhere, upon custom; and differed only slightly from mere habit. It found expression in the judgments of courts; perhaps already, too, in judicial "findings" of law ("Rechtsweisungen"). It may be, of course, that even in primitive times individual public statutes were issued and conventions that established law concluded; such, however, must certainly have been but rare exceptions. After the migrations of the Germanic tribes, it is true, the different Germanic racial branches made comprehensive records of their law. But these so-called folk-laws or "Leges Barbarorum" were, in their original form, essentially written formulations of old customary law. It is true they were frequently made part of royal legislative acts, and also variously modified or supplemented by legislative "novels." Frequently, however, these supplementary laws themselves were not actual public statutes, but only "declarations of legal practice or records of

[1] *Brie*, "Die Lehre vom Gewohnheitsrecht. Eine historisch-dogmatische Untersuchung, I: Geschichtliche Grundlegung, bis zum Ausgang des Mittelalters" (1899), 202 *et seq.*

dooms."[1] Moreover, the folk-laws were never exhaustive legal records; numerous unwritten rules of customary law remained in authority beside them. Even the Frankish capitularies did not sweep aside the customary law. And for private law the whole legislation of the Frankish period had almost no significance whatever.

After the disintegration of the Frankish Empire the folk-laws and the capitularies gradually fell into oblivion, until in the 1000 s they were completely forgotten. Almost no new statutory law appeared until in the 1200 s. Thus the norms of the customary law again became almost exclusively authoritative. Again, the general imperial statutes of the later Middle Ages, which from beginning to end left the private law almost wholly unnoticed, confined themselves, substantially, to the confirmation of actual conditions already recognized by the customary law; or attempted, in rarer cases, to do away with such. The numerous official records of the law made in jurisdictions of the territorial and manorial law, and by associational groups ("genossenschaftliche Verbände"), likewise embodied, for the greater part, old customary law. Only in the cities was a richer legislative activity developed. The private digests of the law, the Sachsenspiegel and its successors, also drew their materials, for the most part, from the customary law.

At least in so far as rules of private law were concerned, the medieval customary law was almost wholly of a particularistic character, and developed within more or less narrow legal spheres ("Rechtskreisen"), partly geographical, partly personal or social. A scientific theory of the customary law was, of course, lacking. Something unstable, which one rather feels than sees, characterized its whole development. Even the current names of the customary law implied at times statutory law: "consuetudo", "mos", "ritus", "lex", "lex et consuetudo", "ius et consuetudo", "pactus", "Gewohnheit" — custom; "Sitte" — habit; "Brauch" — usage; "Herkommen" — tradition; "Recht und Gewohnheit" — what is right and customary; "rechte Gewohnheit" — good and ancient practices; etc. Nevertheless there was a general agreement in the views that prevailed of the essential qualities and significance of the customary law.

The greatest importance was generally attached to its age; to preserve faithfully to coming generations the usage of their

[1] *Brunner*, "Geschichte", I (2d ed.), 424.

fathers, as an inherited treasure, was regarded as a sacred duty. Therefore it was that Eike von Repgow, in the heart-touching words of his rhymed preface, explained that he had not spun out of his own head the law that he there presented, but that "iz haben von aldere an unsich gebracht unse gude vore varen" ("our good forefathers have brought it down to us from olden times"). The requirement that the legal rule must be one actually practised also found occasional expression. Not less insistent were men that the custom must be a good and just one, for as the legal proverb ran: "A hundred years of wrong can never be right" — ("Hundert Jahre Unrecht getan wird nimmer Recht getan"). The influence of the Christian church early attacked legal rules with heathen reminiscences as sinful customs. Only those customs consonant with the Church's law are characterized by the Schwabenspiegel as "good." To the customary law was attributed a force at least equal to that of a public statute; not infrequently, indeed, a yet higher prestige was ascribed to it than to the statutory law, and even the power of nullifying statutes. Inasmuch as the customary law was an actual law, the courts were bound to apply it without question. It was rarely necessary, indeed, to inquire deeply into it, since the judgment-finders were immediately conscious of it. At the same time records were willingly made of it to the end of safely preserving it. This purpose was served by the dooms, especially in the rural districts.

(2) *Enacted law* ("Satzungsrecht"), *public* ("Gesetz") *and private* ("Satzung"). — The legislation of the empire abstained almost wholly from interference with the private law. The slight amount of enacted private law which the entire medieval period produced owed its existence to the autonomy ("Satzungsgewalt", "Autonomie") of unions narrower than the State, — Territory, towns, seigniories, and associations ("Genossenschaften"), — to all of which there belonged in medieval polity an independent enacting power ("Satzungsrecht") for their respective jurisdictions. The law thus produced was itself called "Autonomie"; other expressions were "Willkür", "Einung", "Beliebung", "Ordnung", "Statut" ("self-imposed rules", "agreements", "voluntary agreements", "ordinances", "statutes"). The "Statut" was contrasted with the "Gesetz"; for in the medieval theory of the State only the law "set" ("gesetztes Recht") by the emperor or pope was regarded as true "Gesetz." This contrast of public and private statutes disappeared, it is true, during the medieval period itself, for as soon as

the Territories and the cities developed into political entities the conception of the "Gesetz" was extended to formulations of legal rules that originated in them, and thenceforward the conception of "Autonomie" was applied, substantially, only to the statutes of other groups, especially those of the communes.

(III) **The Content and Form of the Medieval Private Law** show that it was still, on the whole, in an early stage of development.

(1) *Its national genius* it preserved during the greatest part of the Middle Ages. It did not, indeed, remain wholly unaffected by foreign influences, for an acquaintance with the advanced civilization of the old provinces of the Roman empire prompted borrowings of foreign legal institutions. Thus the late Roman documentary system was very early taken over; the usage of testamentary dispositions was gradually introduced on the model of the ancient customary law, etc. But the character of the law, as a whole, was not thereby affected. Alien influences were confined to isolated matters, or acquired authority over special classes of society only, or over isolated portions of the land. And the foreign matter that was adopted was fused completely with the native mass. The German people, especially in its rural strata, — by far its predominant portion, — lived, down into the 1200 s, under a private law practically purely national: the legal materials of the Sachsenspiegel were still exclusively native. It was only after this that the strength of the alien influences began gradually to increase. Needless to say, however, this national law was itself no product developed in absolute isolation. It grew up upon a basis of common Germanic traits of mind; it was developed under economic conditions that were essentially alike throughout the whole of medieval Europe, though these became influential (for the most part) somewhat later in Germany than in the more westerly and southerly portions of the continent. The influences of Christianity and of the Church upon the law were also identical in all occidental countries. Doubtless the intellectual genius of nations is felt within the domain of law, but, upon the whole, legal development depends far more upon economic conditions.

(2) *Its unlearned character* revealed the juvenile stage of its development. It lived, like morality and faith, within the consciousness, or rather within the feelings, of the common man.[1] There was no need yet for scholars who made out of its study an

[1] *v. Amira*, "Recht", 7.

independent profession. Every free member of the community knew how to apply it to the legal transactions of everyday life, and took part, in the court, in its application. In his charming study " Von der Poesie im Recht ",[1] Jacob Grimm therefore rightly compares the old law with the ballad: " the song belonged to no poet; whoever sang it made it more true and more perfect in the singing; just as little did the prestige of the law proceed from the judge, who could not make a new one; the minstrels were guardians of the common property of song, and the judgment finders were entrusted with the office and ministry of the laws." Law was looked upon, not as fortuitous human statute, but as something sacred, to be reverenced, standing above the will of man. Under the influence of Christian doctrine these immemorial ideas were restated in the form that the law comes from God, that God himself is the law; plaints were addressed to God and the judge; the last judgment was painted in the town-halls, to the end of reminding the judges that they should declare the right as representatives of eternal justice and in the name of God. Beyond this, men did not bother their heads about the nature of law. But that men felt, at least instinctively, the many-sided significance of law, the distinction between legal norms ("Rechtsnorm ") and legal rights or authority ("Rechtsbefugnis "), is evidenced by the rich terminology which Germanic languages possess for the conception " Recht." So *e.g.* words like " lagh ", " bilida ", " gizunft ", " êva ", signified rule, norm, law in the objective sense; while, on the other hand, " reht " (" rectum ", M. Lat. " directum ") meant that which is directed (" gerichtet "), brought into harmony with a rule, the appointed social order, the right to act (" Befugnis "), law in the subjective sense.

(3) *Its external form* affords the most striking indication that Germanic law, at least until the culmination of the Middle Ages, still remained in a juvenile stage of development. What Jacob Grimm called the " sensuous element " outweighed by far the abstract, the logical, the conceptual. In this respect also the law was still in the closest consonance with all other aspects of popular life.[2] When we find that the German law of the early Middle

[1] Z. Gesch. R. W., II (1815), 25–99; also in his "Kleine Schriften", VI (1882), 152–191.

[2] Most, and in a certain sense all, parts of the great masterpiece of *Jacob Grimm*, "Deutsche Rechtsaltertümer" (1st ed. 1828, 4th ed. 1899), deal with this sensuous element of the old law. In this work he develops with unrivalled knowledge of the sources and in the broadest possible

Ages, — like the French and the English, but unlike the matter-of-fact Scandinavian law, — was distinguished by an especial affluence of forms and symbols, we must accept this as the result of an already advanced development; for the primitive period seems to have contented itself with few, but clear and simple legal forms.[1] The numerous phenomena that are here in question affect, as Heusler has shown,[2] on one hand the mode of formulating legal rules, on the other hand the form of legal transactions.

(A) *Legal rules* were conceived "plastically", in a "naïvely demonstrative" manner, and expressed "in a way that creates, out of concrete, sensuous forms and phenomena a picture, as original as possible, which, thanks to that quality, remains stamped on the memory."[3] From the same quality the old legal terminology derived its strong suggestion of poetry. It loved alliterative compounds ("Erbe und Eigen", — heritage and title; "hoven und hausen", — homestead and house; "recht und redlich", — right and righteous; "was die Fackel zehrt ist Fahrnis", — whatever the torch devours is chattels); rhymes ("ungehabt und ungestabt", — without keep or staff; "wer darf jagen darf auch hagen", — he who has the right to hunt may also hedge the land); tautologies ("getreu, hold und gehorsam", — true, loyal, and obedient); the negative conclusion ("frei und nicht eigen", — free and not servile). Men were especially prone to express provisions relating to time and space in such a naïve and inexact way as left room for chance in particular cases. It is often declared that something shall be the rule as far as a cock walks, or flies, a cat springs, as a stone or hammer is thrown, as one can reach with a sickle. A law shall endure so long as the wind blows from the clouds and the world stands, so long as the Main flows into the Rhine, etc. If the shortness of a period of time is to be indicated, it is provided that a piece of land may be acquired during the sleep of the king, during the midday nap of the emperor; or so much land shall be acquired as can be ridden round in a certain time on horse or ass, turned over with the plow,

manner the ideas summarily expressed in the essay above cited, "Von der Poesie im Recht." See also *Gierke*, "Der Humor im deutschen Recht" (2d ed. 1886); the remarks of *Heusler* in "Institutionen", I, 45–92; *v. Zallinger*, "Wesen und Ursprung des Formalismus im altdeutschen Privatrecht" (1898); *Borchling*, "Poesie und Humor in friesischen Recht", in "Abhandlungen und Vorträge zur Geschichte Ostfrieslands", X (1908).

[1] *Brunner*, "Geschichte", I (2d ed.), 153.

[2] "Institutionen", I, 65 *et seq.*

[3] *Ibid.*, 65.

or covered with hides. The formulas that interpret how high, heavy, and numerous are the taxes, afford an especial wealth of examples.

(B) Very intimately connected with this naïvely sensuous manner of expression was the *symbolical quality* ("die Plastik") of legal transactions. Germanic law, like all juvenile law, was rich in striking symbols and solemnities, adapted to every event. Its symbols, as Heusler has shown, were imaginal forms created for the purpose of giving visible expression to an abstract event; its solemnities were the exaggeration of essential words and acts into ceremonial allocutions and actions. The things employed as symbols were extraordinarily numerous. The livery of seisin was manifested by the manual tradition of twig and turf or hat and glove, the touching of the altar-cloth or the bell-rope. One who entered into servitude delivered the hair cut from his head and beard. The widow who wished to free herself from liability for debts laid the house-key or her mantle upon the bier or the grave of her dead husband.

The token that occurs most frequently is the staff. According to the exhaustive investigations of von Amira,[1] the walking-staff may be regarded as the "common-ancestor" of symbolic staffs. From it were derived the messenger's pike and the staff of office, the latter very extensively used as the tipstaff and the judge's rod. Emperor, dukes, princes, communal magistrates, the masters of gilds and corporate associations, carried the staff as the symbol of authority. In the private law the use of the staff in legal transactions was of particular importance: *e.g.* throwing it away in renunciation of one's sib and in conveying of land, and the delivery of a staff in the contract of pledge. In the field of mimic symbolry the law made use above all, and in the most various manners, of the gesture-language of the hand, the "most obvious, natural, and simple of signs" (J. Grimm).[2] The handclasp was the usual confirmation of pledges of faith ("Gelübde", —"fides facta") and of contracts. By giving his hand a person

[1] *v. Amira*, "Der Stab in der germanischen Rechts-symbolik", in K. Bayer. Akad. Wiss., "Abhandlungen", XXV (1909), "Abhandlung" no. 1. Compare with this the detailed references of *R. Schröder* in Z². R. G., XXX (1909), 436–451; *A. Schultze* in Hist. Z., CV (3d ser. IX, 1910), 132–142; *Goldmann* in "Deutsche Literaturzeitung" of 1910, nos. 41–42. Also *Rintelen*, "Der Gerichtsstab in den österreichischen Weistümern", in the "Festgabe für Brunner" (1910), 631–648.

[2] *v. Amira*, "Die Handgebärden in den Bilderhandschriften des Sachsenspiegels", in K. Bayer. Akad. Wiss., "Abhandlungen" I, (I Kl.), XXIII, 2 (1905).

gave himself into the power of his lord. The hand was essential to an oath. In making a vow, in accepting a vow, in expressing agreement, in making recompense, the finger was raised; in expressing renunciation it was bent. In actions for the recovery of a chattel of whose possession one had been involuntarily deprived ("Anefangsklage"), the hand was laid against or upon the chattel in taking possession; and similarly in the execution of a legal document. In many cases everything depended upon a correct position of the body. "Various ceremonials in seating oneself ("Sitzriten") were observed in taking possession ("Besitz", 'be-seating') of land, as well as of public offices and seigniories"; and the object, too, upon which one must sit (chair, bench, or earth), and the quarter of the heavens toward which the sitter must look, were exactly prescribed. Much of this palpable legal symbolism that still flourished in the Frankish period was early lost; some maintained itself longer—the symbolism of manual pantomime proved capable, according to von Amira, of producing new variations, in actual practice, so late as the time of the Sachsenspiegel. Its time passed irrevocably with the impairment of the original public character of the popular courts, and with the increase of written procedure; for "writing is the sworn enemy of all [other] sensuous representation."[1] And in the second half of the Middle Ages abstract formulas, written protocols, and registry in books, became increasingly noticeable, in German as in other law. Much that was charming was thereby necessarily lost forever. Jacob Grimm regretfully compares the law of the good old times with that of the new: "in place of its colorfull symbols, bundles of documents; in place of its quick-found judgments, lawsuits lasting for years; in place of its court under the blue of heaven, stuffy record offices; in place of rents in fowl and shrovetide eggs, a bailiff comes to extort nameless tributes in every season of the year."

(4) The older private law was also influenced as respects *its content* by the predominance of the sensory element; for it was characterized by what has been called "pigeon-hole law" ("Rechtschablone") or "casuistic formalism" ("typischer Formalismus").[2] The Germanic people, like others, lacked in the first stages of its history that degree of capacity for abstract thought which is necessary in order to conceive of legal relations as that which they really are; namely as facts, purely and simply, of men's

[1] *Heusler*, "Institutionen", I, 75.
[2] *Ibid.*, I, 49 *et seq.; v. Zallinger*, "Formalismus."

mental life. Men clung to visible and tangible things, and reasoned "a posteriori" from the external facts of the sensory phenomenon back to the inner and intellectual basis. At the same time only those particular sensible manifestations were at first heeded which revealed such facts of men's intellectual life in average or normal cases: which constituted their typical and normal expression. This principle we meet in all parts of the older law, *e.g.* in procedure, where only declarations made and processual acts performed in a definite mode were valid, — "one man one word", "qui cadit a syllaba cadit a tota causa"; and in criminal law, where only the physical consequence was punished. It dominated also the old private law: "the recognition and full validity in practice of private legal transactions were made absolutely dependent upon embodiment in some certain dress of external circumstances; upon being made visible in a definite form."[1] Thus, for example, the law associated capacity for rights and capacity to do legal acts with definite and easily recognizable physical signs. The new born child must have "cried to the four walls" in order to inherit; in order to make a valid testamentary disposition one must be in a condition to mount on horseback from a stone about fifteen inches ("Daumelle") high, unaided and with sword and shield. The law of things was not built up upon an abstract conception of ownership, but upon that of seisin, — *i.e.* upon the actual, external element of physical control, as seen in the usufruct of lands and in the occupancy or physical custody of chattels. What right might underlie this physical control was regarded at first as immaterial; on the other hand, absolutely all rights in things must be clothed in this typical external form. If a *legal tie*, a liability ("Verhaftung"), was to arise from an agreement ("Schuldvertrag") — *i.e.* a "must" and not merely a "should" — there must be established a relation of control capable of a visible physical embodiment; the debtor must furnish his creditor with a legally appointed power either over a person ("Geisel" = hostage, or pledge; "Bürgen" = surety) or over a thing ("Pfand" = pledge). As rights of dominion over things were bound to take the form of seisin, so all relationships of power over persons found their visible expression in the "Munt" (representation) of the power-holder.

The emphasis put upon the visible outward form of a legal relation, the decisive importance attributed to the publicity of

[1] *v. Zallinger, op. cit.*, 6.

juristic acts, served in a remarkable manner the security of legal transactions. Whatever had been declared before the community and confirmed by the communal court, whatever had been registered in public documents or books, everybody could put faith in. One could rely upon the apparent right which a juristic act, formally correct and publicly performed, created; even when that apparent right was not in accord with the positive law. This legitimizing power of an apparent right ("Rechtsschein",—record title, color of title), the so-called principle of "publicity",[1] was in its beginning nothing more than a particular application of the typic formalism peculiar to the old law. But while this was otherwise broken down and discarded within the medieval age itself, the principle of publicity displayed an enduring creative power in the development of the law. The medieval law built upon it its entire law of things, and thereby found it possible, among other things, to develop what is known as the "public faith" of land registers and certain forms of commercial paper; thus laying the foundation of the modern law of those subjects. We have here an important example of the truth that the medieval law was capable, in itself, of transforming the rigid routinism of its primitive period, and of developing out of it freer legal institutes suited to the increasingly complex conditions of social life. It shows that the medieval German, too, was not without an endowment of juristic technic; although, indeed, he could not yet raise himself to an objective standpoint.

Upon the principle of publicity rested also the institute of tacit-preclusion or acquiescent-prescription ("Verschweigung")[2]— the closing of a demandant's mouth by his own prior silence, wherein the medieval law made allowance in striking manner for the necessity of regulating the influence of time upon legal relations. Whoever desired to impugn any state of things as unlawful was required to do so during a definite period after he had received actual notice; otherwise he closed his own mouth by his prior silence and could no longer avail himself of his right. It was very com-

[1] *Cf. H. Meyer*, "Das Publizitätsprinzip im deutschen bürgerlichen Recht", in *O. Fischer*, "Abhandlungen", XVIII, no. 2 (1909); *Naendrupp*, "Rechtscheinforschungen. Heft 1: Begriff des Rechtscheins und Aufgabe der Rechtscheinforschung" (1900). But see also *Hellmann*, in Krit. Vj. G. R. W. (3d ser. XIV, 1912), 117 *et seq.* And also, most recently, against exaggerations of the theory of ostensible right ("Rechtschein"), *Müller-Erzbach*, "Gefährdungshaftung und Gefahrtragung" (1912), 297 *et seq.*

[2] *Immerwahr*, "Die Verschweigung in deutschen Recht", in *Gierke*, "Untersuchungen", No. 48 (1895).

mon for the judge to issue a peace-ban, by which he required all persons having causes of action to make their just demands either immediately (being residents of the jurisdiction) or (being non-residents) within a certain period. As a rule the demand had to be made, in the phrase of the medieval sources, within "a year and a day." By this was originally understood a year plus one day, in the literal sense of the phrase. Later, however, men interpreted it usually as a term of one year plus six weeks, or of a year, six weeks, and three days, — that is they added to the year the interval between two ordinary popular courts for "causae maiores" ("echte Dinge"), and often also the three day term of the court itself.[1] The running of the period was prevented only by actual necessity ("echte Not"); that is, by definite typical reasons for failure to satisfy the requirement: according to the Sachsenspiegel, by imprisonment, sickness, service of God without the country (as on the Crusade), service of the Empire.[2] "Verschweigung" was of special importance in the field of the law of things, where it led to the development of the institute of legitimate ("rechte", — *i.e.* legally sanctioned) seisin (*infra*, § 28). Other examples of its application we find in the preclusion of claims of inheritance (*infra*, § 103), of rights over found articles (*infra*, § 60, III), of lordships and of personal liberty (*infra*, § 13). The effect attributed to the so-called limit of legal memory implies an extension of the principle of acquiescent-prescription. To recognize a condition which had existed time out of mind as sanctified by user, and to accord it the protection of the law, was consistent with the general viewpoint of the old law. Here again it was the appearance of right that possessed legitimizing power, although the origin of the existing state of things was obscured by time.

(5) And finally, it must be pointed out that a conception of private, as contrasted with public, law — such as was already stamped, even though imperfectly, upon the Roman law, and has been developed in modern legal theory — remained wholly alien to the Middle Ages. There was *no separation of private from public law;* each ran over into the other. The reason for this lay partly in a conception, peculiar to Germanic races, of

[1] *Fockema-Andreae*, "Die Frist von Jahr und Tag und ihre Wirkung in den Niederlanden", Z². R. G., XIV (1893), 75–111. *Güterbock*, "Der Prozess Heinrichs des Löwen", Exkurs III: "Die Bedeutung von 'Jahr und Tag'" (1909). *Puntschart*, "Zur ursprünglichen Bedeutung von 'Jahr und Tag'", in Z². R. G., XXXII (1911), 328–330. *Brunner* in "Festgabe der Berliner juristischen Fakultät für Gierke" (1910), 44 *et seq.* and "Grundzüge" (5th ed.), 200.

[2] *Arthur Schmidt*, "Echte Not" (1888).

the relation between the State and the folkmen; which was treated far less from the standpoint of authority and subjection than from that of common and equal rights. It lay, further, in the political, economic, and social conditions of the Middle Ages; which in conjunction with that conception, mutually limiting it and limited by it, made impossible the rise of a State power, either in the sense of the classical imperium or in that of modern political theory, — and thus prevented the appearance of a corresponding public law. Authority and competence under public law assumed forms of private law, as *e.g.* in feudal relations and in the regalities; rights under private law were clothed with public powers, — as *e.g.* those of a landowner over his free tenants ("Hintersassen"); capacity for rights and for juristic acts under the private law was very closely connected with the position a man occupied in the political frame-work of society; and so on. This fact, however, does not hinder one from considering apart the private-law constituents of the medieval legal order; although one must be mindful of their connections with the public law.

§ 2. **The Reception.**[1] — (I) **The Roman Law** maintained itself as a living law throughout the Middle Ages, as the law of the church and as the personal law of the Roman population even of Germanic lands: it also reacted from an early period, as above noticed (p. 8), upon the national legal systems of those Germanic racial branches which came in contact with the world whose past was one of Roman culture. The folk-laws already show traces of this influence; indeed in the Frankish empire of the 700 s and 800 s a universal authority was already ascribed, at times, to the Roman law; and the Carolingian kings declared binding, as that of their predecessors, the legislation of the Roman emperors. One could not, however, speak as yet of any considerable alien influence in Germanic lands within the field of private law. If a few technical names and expressions of Roman legal terminology found their way into documents and legal records, they were nothing more than embellishments drawn from an erudition for the most part quite incomprehensible to its borrowers.

At the turn of the 1000 s and 1100 s, however, the Roman law be-

[1] *v. Below*, "Die Ursachen der Rezeption des Römischen Rechts in Deutschland" (1905, — Vol. 19 of the "Historische Bibliothek" pub. by the editors of the Hist. Z.). *Cf. Stölzel* in Krit. Vj. G. R. W., XLVII (3d ser. XI, 1907), 1–49. See also *Litten*, "Römisches Recht und Pandekten-Recht" (1907); *Vinogradoff*, "Roman Law in Mediæval Europe" (1909).

gan anew a conquest of Europe, and with it was joined the Canon law. A new epoch in European legal history began. No land, save only at first the Scandinavian North, proved capable of resisting this triumphant progress. Yet in no land other than Germany did this invasion of the foreign law lead to a catastrophe for the native law. In Germany alone there resulted a "Reception" of the alien law in a technical sense of the word, and thereby a break in legal development the worst of whose consequences were corrected only after 400 years.

It follows that it would be a misconception if one were to conceive of the Reception merely as a partial expression of that resurrection of antiquity, that "return to the ancients", which remade toward the end of the Middle Ages the whole intellectual life of Europe, and culminated in the Renascence and the Reformation. In England, for example, where there was much more nearly an adoption of Roman legal ideas than in Germany, the national law was spared a "Reception"; an early acquaintance with the "Corpus Juris Civilis" seems rather, "in the manner of a prophylactic inoculation, to have rendered it immune to a fatal infection."[1] The causes of the Reception must therefore have lain in the peculiar conditions of Germany.

(II) **Circumstances that prepared the Way for the Reception.** — Among those circumstances mention must always be made in the first place of the opinion that the medieval Empire was a continuation of the Roman world dominion, an opinion that developed in the period of the Hohenstaufen into a firmly established dogma. In that way, by reasoning peculiar to the Middle Ages and wholly unhistorical and uncritical, men reached the undisputed practical conclusion that the "Corpus Juris" of Justinian was entitled, as "imperial law", to claim direct validity in their own age.

To this evaluation was due the increasing ardor that men showed in the study of foreign, — yet according to that view, after all not foreign, — law; first at the Italian, and then, from the 1400 s onward, also at the German universities, in all of which there was accorded to the Roman law, by about 1500, a recognized and permanent place in the curriculum. To this was added the circumstance that the Canon law which was enforced in the ecclesiastical courts could be thoroughly understood and properly

[1] *Brunner*, in his Berlin rectoral address, "Der Anteil des deutschen Rechtes an der Entwicklung der Universitäten" (1896); "Grundzüge" (5th ed.), 264.

applied only with the aid of the Roman law. In a wealth of popular legal writings, most of them expressly prepared for ecclesiastics and the needs of the ecclesiastical courts, the task was assumed of disseminating a knowledge of the Roman-Canon law. The advance of Roman legal studies was not, however, it would seem, the consequence of an already increased application of the Roman law in the lay courts; for generally speaking, the German law remained intact down to the end of the 1400 s. The spread of scholarly knowledge of the Roman system was in advance of its practical application. The assumption would also be unjustifiable that the preference shown in the service of princes to those particular jurists who were trained in the Roman system was due to the fact that they served such princes as handy tools in their personal absolutistic ambitions; for these endeavors belonged only to a later time. Certainly, rulers did highly appreciate such jurists, and employed them in ever increasing numbers upon their administrative boards; not from political motives, however, but on account of the general superiority of scientifically trained officials as compared with unschooled laymen; and in this preference they made practically no distinction between the doctors of the Canon and those of the Roman law. The truth is rather that the increased scholarly zeal of this last period of the Middle Ages was taking hold of laymen, and impelling them to a study of the Roman law, because the study of this was not forbidden to them, as it was to the clergy. Once they had attained to influential administrative and judicial positions, thanks to the culture thus acquired, it was of course inevitable that they should influence legislation and legal decisions in a Romanistic sense. Yet even that could not have led to an almost unqualified conquest by the Roman law had not other causes even more urgent cooperated.

(III) **The decisive causes of the Reception** lay in the condition of the German law itself. The reproach some have brought against the German law, that it was incapable of an independent evolution to meet altered social and economic relations and the growing need of legal technic; and that men therefore adopted the Roman law for its inherent advantages, for its substantive superiority to the German, is indeed indefensible. For it is contradicted by the fact that precisely in those places where there was the greatest advance in economic and juridical conditions, — namely in the great city communities, — men clung far more tenaciously to the native law than they did in the open country.

And in Switzerland the legal development of modern times has been completed upon a purely Germanic basis, yet the alleged imperfection of the German law has never become evident.

Two other facts, however, were of decisive influence: the disintegrated character of the German law, and its lack of scientific cultivation. Both facts were very intimately connected with the unhappy political history of Germany. The weakness of the central power, steadily increasing through centuries, made impossible the growth in Germany of a powerful supreme court, such as the "Curia Regis" of England and France, which might have given a unitary tendency to the decisions of the lower courts; it made equally impossible any radical legislative activity for the purpose of a coherent development of the law. And the lack of such courts of superior instance in which the native law was practised prevented any professional devotion to it, and still more any scientific instruction in it. "If we except the single feat of that gifted man Eike von Repgow, — which, though indeed not a theoretical work was a juristic work in the truest sense, — we have nothing in the whole medieval literature of legal sources that can even remotely be compared with the contemporary achievements of Italian, French, and English jurists."[1] The significance of this lack of any legal science is shown especially clearly in the example of Italy and England. Just as there developed at Pavia, in the school there established by royal jurists for the study of Lombard law, a national jurisprudence that served as model for the Romanistic jurisprudence of the Glossators by which it was followed, so in England, as early as the Middle Ages, there was developed at the law schools of the Inns of Court a scholarly study of the national law which gave this a greater power of resistance against alien influences. In Germany, likewise, it was in the lands of the Saxon law, which found literary treatment upon the basis of the Sachsenspiegel and a rich development in the practice of influential city "over-courts" ("Oberhöfe"),[2] that the native law succeeded best in maintaining itself against the foreign law. Inasmuch, however, as nothing similar was possible in the Empire as a whole, the acceptance of the alien law necessarily and truly promised a release from insufferable abuses. Men received in it a coherent law, fixed in writing and therefore certain; a law, moreover, whose text had been worked over in detail in an abundant scien-

[1] *Sohm* in Z. Priv. Öff. R., I (1874), 252.
[2] (Compare Vol. 1 of this Series, p. 313. Transl.)

tific literature, and fitted for practical use. This was the reason why it found such rapid entry. It was not the classic Roman law taught by the Glossators, and in many ways useless for another time, but the modernized Roman law of the Post-Glossators, the Italian law, that crossed the Alps.[1] Defects in the external form of the German law, and superiorities in the form of the Roman law, were therefore the decisive causes of the Reception. Certainly the Roman law was superior to the German in many of its rules, especially in the law of obligations; certainly, too, it made possible juristic training to a degree far beyond that possible in the unlearned German law. But by no means everything "received" was good, or better than the native law: on the contrary, many excellent ideas of the latter were supplanted only to be brought again to light much later. Its greatest service, too, — a schooling of men in legal thinking — was really not rendered until in the 1800 s; and perhaps it might have rendered this without any Reception.

(IV) **The Reception was realized** in part directly, through the entry of the Roman system into the administration of justice as a common law; in part indirectly, through the local legislation of the 1400 s and 1500 s under Romanistic influence.

(1) In the process by which *the administration of justice* was subjected to the Roman principles the reorganization of the Imperial Chamber of Justice in 1495 was of primary importance. In this supreme court, which had evolved out of the royal council, doctors of law had long been employed; and they naturally based their judgments upon the alien law. This custom was now made a statutory rule. The Ordinance of 1495 relative to the Chamber obligated both judges and assessors, — of whom half should be men learned in the law, — to decide "according to the common law of the Empire, and, further, according to such righteous, honest, and sufferable ordinances, statutes, and customs of the principalities, lordships, and courts, as shall be brought before it [by litigants]." "The common law of the Empire" meant nothing else than the law of the "Corpus Juris Civilis." This was thereby raised to the rank of a directly obligatory source of law. The regular decisions of the Territorial courts quickly accommodated themselves to the supreme court. And as for those Territories that were exempt from the influence of the Imperial Chamber through "privilegia de non appellando" (*e.g.* the electoral principalities), the courts of the Territorial sovereigns

[1] *Gierke*, "Privatrecht", I, 14.

were themselves soon functioning in the same manner (as *e.g.* in Berlin). And although many courts (as *e.g.* the Municipal "Oberhöfe") resisted the Romanization of judicial law, thus forced from above, their resistance was energetically and triumphantly combated by the Territorial rulers, supported by judgments of the Imperial Chamber and by counsels of university faculties of law, who were likewise champions of the Roman system. Only a very few courts succeeded in permanently escaping from the influence of the Imperial Chamber. Such were those of Lübeck and Hamburg, where the land law, being excluded from the appellate system, remained German. That Switzerland and Schleswig were not wholly unaffected by the Reception was due simply to the fact that the competence of the Imperial Chamber of Justice never extended to those lands.

(2) When the Roman law thus became, as a common law, the supreme rule in the decisions of the courts, what was really involved was an adoption of its rules realized through the medium of custom, and supported by the practice of the Imperial Chamber of Justice. It attained obligatory force through *legislation* in the Territorial legal systems ("Landrechte") and the "reformations" of town law which were issued from the mid 1400 s onward for the purpose of replacing, within the limited area of a Territory or a city, the complex and uncertain native local law by a "set" ("gesetzes") law, unitary and written. The more jurists took part in these legislative activities, the more Romanistic was the result. Only where there were already older legal records fit for use was the fate of the German law better, yet even then this advantage of position was often lost through the folly of the Romanizing practice of the courts.

The result was that the Reception of the Roman law went on with surprising rapidity and ease, almost everywhere in Germany. Its triumph was secure within a few decades. Here and there, indeed, a hostile voice was raised in angry diatribes against the "doctors", — the "Bartolistæ", as Hutten called them. The most of such complaints against the jurists were due, however, to resentment of the rural nobility at their increasing number in the higher official places, and had nothing to do with the foreign law. For that matter, if we except the great imperial cities, which (above all Lübeck) defended with determination their native law, the mass of the nation, of all classes, probably nowhere realized what a revolution was progressing in intellectual life, and what was at stake for German law. Even among jurists, at first, indifference predominated over hostility to the native usages. Astonishing as the fact may seem to us, it warns us not to overestimate the mutual dependence of law and nationality.

§ 3. **German Private Law after the Reception.** — The character of German private law was fundamentally altered by the Reception.

(I) In the first place, **as regards legal unity**, the hopes men had entertained of realizing this through the Reception were speedily and bitterly disappointed. True, men did now possess for the first time, in the alien lawbooks they had received, a common law of authority throughout Germany; and unquestionably this was no slight improvement over earlier conditions, — only this new common law was not identical with any of the native systems, and therefore increased, instead of lessening, the number of sources men had to reckon with. It is also true that the theory came to prevail of a Reception "in complexu", — *i.e.* an assumption that all the glosses of the lawbooks received were also to be applied as rules of positive law. In spite of that, however, the attempt could not seriously be made to base legal decisions exclusively upon the "Corpus Juris." For countless legal relations it contained no rules: such must be decided, as before, according to the native law. That raised, however, the difficult preliminary question, whether or not it was mandatory so to do; and this preliminary question contributed not a little toward increasing the uncertainty of the law. Further, there was attributed to the common law the rank of a subsidiary law only; *i.e.* wherever native rules of law, whether customary or enacted, were in actual force, they took precedence of the alien law. The extremely unequal development which German law had attained in different regions also contributed materially to the patchwork character of legal practice. What was decided in one place by native rules had to be abandoned in another to the foreign law. Even when agreement had been reached respecting the principle in accord with which the various legal sources were to be applied, the above-mentioned preliminary question too often remained a source of doubts. The rule, namely, became gradually recognized that the more special should take precedence of the more general law. Accordingly, in cases where all was not left to the caprice of the parties, the local customs and statutes were to be resorted to in the first place, then the more comprehensive of the provincial and city statutory systems, and only in the last place the common law, — the weakest legal source, lying back of all others. Or, as men were wont to express the rule in a legal proverb: "Willkür bricht Stadtrecht, Stadtrecht bricht Landrecht, Landrecht bricht gemein Recht" ("by-law breaks town law, town law breaks provincial law, and provincial law breaks common law"). In this predominance — theoretical, at least — of local and special law, the persistent decentralization of German law found its clearest expression. At the same time the common law, despite its merely subsidiary force, united all German lands into a certain, albeit loose, community of law, through the uniform administration of justice and legal theory to which it gave rise. In the tangle of German legal organization the science of the common law was thus the only real refuge of legal practice and development.

Even this bond, however, lost in time the power to hold together all parts of Germany. The perdurance side by side of countless legal sources, if reconcilable because of necessity with the loose framework of the Empire, was a condition of things that could not in the long run be maintained in the modern States into which the most powerful of the imperial Territories developed following the 1600 s. That which could not be accomplished for the whole Empire, either through the Reception or otherwise, was realized, at least for some portions of the Empire, by the great codifications effected after painful labors in the 1700 s and 1800 s.[1] The Prussian "Allgemeines Landrecht" (General or Territorial Code, 1794), the Austrian Civil Code (1811), the Saxon Civil Code (1863), as well as the French Code Civil (1804) — which attained authority over great regions in Germany — and its revision for Baden in the Baden Territorial Code (1809), created in their respective jurisdictions a unitary law. The Prussian Code was, indeed, designed to have merely subsidiary authority, in place of the common law, intact primary authority being still preserved to the local and provincial laws, which were to be collected and recorded. But the centralizing forces in the Prussian State were stronger than the intent of the legislator: with few exceptions the provincial laws dried up, as it were, and the Code was treated almost everywhere as the exclusive source

[1] On the history of codification *cf.* *Stölzel*, "Carl Goelieb Svarez" (1885); and "Brandenburg-Preussens Rechtsverwaltung und Rechtsverfassung" (2 vols. 1888). Also "Festschrift zur Jahrhundertfeier des [österreichischen] allgemeinen bürgerlichen Gesetzbuchs" (2 vols. 1911); "Le Code Civil. Livre du Centenaire, publié par la Société d'Études Législatives" (1904); *Andreas*, "Die Einführung des Code Napoleon in Baden", Z². R. G., XXXI (1911), 182–234.

of law. The codes that followed assumed this authority from the beginning. In so doing they broke with the principle of the common law that special law should take precedence of more general law. Supreme authority was thenceforth attributed to the general law of the State; indeed, often no other law was recognized. But great as the advance was that codification brought about in these States, it meant new and heavy loss to the legal unity of Germany. For in wholly abolishing the common law, — to which the earlier Bavarian Code of 1756 had left its subsidiary authority, — the regions of code law abandoned the community of the common law, and became wholly independent legal provinces. The harm resulting from this separation was borne principally by these States themselves, for as a result of their losing connection with the jurisprudence of the common law, their legal development fell into a state of torpor, for which the lego-political benefits of the unitary law thus attained offered no adequate compensation.

Not until the establishment of the present German Empire were those conditions realized which made it possible to extend legal unity throughout Germany. The relative rapidity with which that great task was carried through and the goal achieved which had so often and so fervently been striven for since the days of Emperor Maximilian, and particularly since the Wars of Independence, gave proof that the chief reason why preceding centuries had felt no "call to legislation" ("Beruf zur Gesetzgebung") lay solely in the unhappy political conditions of Germany. During the rule of the North German Confederation a national law, uniform for all the federated States, was successfully established for the most important matters of commercial law by the German Bills of Exchange Act of 1848 and a general German Commercial Code of 1861; and since then the legislation of the Empire, which rests upon authority[1] expressly granted in the Constitution, has created through numerous separate statutes and through the crowning work of the Civil Code of August 18, 1896, a common German private law, which, as imperial law, unlike the old common law "breaks" all State law, in accord with a principle adopted in the imperial constitution[2] and repeated in the Ordinance of Promulgation ("Einführungsgesetz") regulating the Code's adoption.[3] True, the after effects of the old

[1] Imperial Constitution, Art. 4, and imperial statute of Dec. 20, 1873.
[2] Imperial Constitution, Art. 2.
[3] BGB, EG, Arts. 3, 55.

inrooted tendency to particularism have been so far felt that there is still reserved to the States, by the Ordinance of Promulgation, the power to legislate upon a not inconsiderable number of matters, particularly those in any way connected with public law. The Articles (55–152) of the Ordinance here referred to have been justly characterized, with reference to German legal unity, as "a list of dead and missing." Happily, however, these reservations are not very important in comparison with the great body of law unitarily regulated; and in a common legislation, and above all in the centralized administration of justice assured through the imperial court, a firm foundation has been laid for the preservation and further extension of German legal unity.

Switzerland, too, has now unified its private law by a Civil Code of December 10, 1907. This remarkable statute, for the most part the work of Eugen Huber, draws heavily upon the German and the French civil codes, but is based primarily upon the native Germanic law. Inasmuch as this was never affected, as has been seen, by the Reception, but retained its fresh native character, the Swiss Civil Code is "the most Germanic of all codifications of Germanic civil law"; it has been possible to say of it that it is like an improved edition of the German Civil Code.[1]

The present law of Germany is a *general* system of private law. Like the old racial law of the Germanic and Frankish time its authority is equal over all members of the legal community. In this, too, there lay a victory of the forces that worked for legal unity. For although the originally unitary racial law split up in the medieval age into separate systems of town and Territorial law, and peculiar law was developed for the feudal, servitary, and manorial divisions of medieval society (*supra*, p. 3), these legal growths really first attained a sharply exclusive character in the second half of the Middle Ages and later, through their transformation into true laws of status, — the law of distinct estates based upon birth or profession. They maintained their validity in the empire and in the imperial Territories until the disappearance of the old social order. The Prussian "Landrecht" still knew a special law for the estates of nobles, townspeople, and peasants, of civil officials, military officers, etc. But since the principle of the civil equality of all members of the State has been established in Germany, special laws of status have disappeared. Only the law for the higher nobility has been

[1] *v. Voltelini*, in the Allg. öst. G. Z., LXI (1910), 37.

maintained, — an anachronism no longer befitting the present day. This was spared also by the Introductory Act of the Civil Code (*infra*, § 13). On the other hand, though the modern law still enforces peculiar rules for certain professions, — as *e.g.* commercial law for merchants, an industrial law for industrials, etc., — and regulates in a special manner certain kinds of property, — as *e.g.* family fideicommissa and property subject to the peculiar claims of single heirs, — these provisions are no longer to be regarded as laws of privilege such as were laws of status. What is here involved is rather the special regulation of certain legal relations, — as in the case of feudal, servitary, and manorial law, — which, however, remain subject to the general rules of the private law, and are open to everybody.

(II) **The content and the form of the law**, too, took on a wholly altered character.

(1) The most direct and most important result of the Reception was, of course, that *German private law ceased to be a national law.* To the formal contrast of distinct jurisdictions that caused the patch-work of the German legal chart, there was thenceforth added a substantial antithesis in the diverse historical origin of individual legal rules, — the antithesis between the Roman and German elements of the law in force within Germany. The common law was predominantly, indeed almost exclusively, foreign law. Because of the almost total sterility of imperial legislation in the Middle Ages, as also in the modern period down to the dissolution of the Holy Roman Empire, there existed practically no statutory law binding for all Germany; and under the North German Confederation the creation of such a law was made impossible by constitutional provisions. It was, indeed, possible to maintain in theory the existence of a common German customary law, but to translate the theory into practice was more difficult. For in the Middle Ages German customary law was already predominantly local in character (*supra*, p. 5), and in the modern period it did not cease to be so. As opposed to it every advantage lay on the side of the foreign law; for while this could formally claim merely a similar customary authority, by way of compensation it was easy of access to the judge, thanks to its printed form. The native law survived in the main in particularistic legal records alone; though there, one must admit, often with astonishing tenacity. Only in the lands of the Saxon law was there recognized a local, so-called Saxon, common law. This was the old racial law, further developed upon

the basis of the Sachsenspiegel and its glosses, which maintained a primacy over the general common law; a fact that was "of incalculable value in the preservation of the native law."[1] As many of the Territorial systems and town-law "reformations" gave the German law an effective protection, so also the modern codes have in many ways accorded a new recognition to Germanic legal ideas: the Saxon Civil Code least of all, the Austrian more,[2] and most of all the Prussian "Landrecht" and, especially, the Napoleonic Code Civil, which last has been justly called the most Germanic of the older codes. The German law lived on in provincial statutes and customs, for the most part wholly misunderstood, until down into the 1800s. It was badly mistreated by the Romanistic jurisprudence; on the other hand, this was often obliged, in interpreting the alien sources,—primarily under the influence of the law of nature—to give effect, albeit unknowingly and unintentionally, to many ideas of German law.

Thus the private law that prevailed in Germany after the Reception assumed in many respects a peculiar composite character; it was neither Roman law nor German, but a product of both, sometimes happy, but more often an abortion. In order to identify correctly the contributions of the one and the other to the elements of the positive law, and to create from them a modern, internally coherent system fitted to the present day, there was indispensable an insight into the historical development of both systems which was attained only in the 1800s through the Historical School. This task has been since accomplished, and one may well note with satisfaction that the native law has not come off badly in the process.

(2) Although the Reception was directly responsible for a weakening of the national character of the German law the consequences of which were long to be felt, the *transformation of the German law from a popular and unlearned into a learned law* would have resulted without it. For the German law, as well as for that of the other civilized nations of Europe, there had come, at the latest at the close of the Middle Ages, that inevitable moment for every legal system when, to use Savigny's expression, it acquires a scientific character and is left the consciousness of jurists, by whom the people are henceforth represented in their

[1] *Gierke*, "Privatrecht", I, 19.

[2] *Cf. Hugelmann*, "Deutsche Rechtsgedanken im allgemeinen bürgerlichen Gesetzbuche", in Allg. öst. G. Z., LXII (1911), 172–177.

old functions as law-makers.[1] But it was truly a misfortune for German law that there existed in Germany, in the beginning, only "an unspeakably narrow-minded class of jurists." [2] They despised the native law, or haughtily ignored it as compared with the revered "ratio scripta" of the Roman law. With an utter lack of understanding they forced the living institutes of the German law, wherever these had maintained themselves in positive authority, into the categories of the Roman law. Under their pedantic and incompetent hands the German law, once so full of vitality, became an inflexible and esoteric mass of learning, full of subtleties. It was lost to, — it even became in many respects plainly opposed to, — the popular consciousness; and we have not yet succeeded in closing the lamentable breach between them, an evil heritage from the Reception. Measured against this, it was of little moment that the law now completely lost in its professional cultivation the "sensuous" character already partially cast off in the Middle Ages. A few symbols maintained themselves, *e.g.* the handclasp; but they were colorless in comparison with the old ones, and in part they were dragged along without being in the least understood, and were sadly mutilated. The original rich formalism of legal acts often gave way to complete informality; often, too, it was replaced by writing or by judicial or notarial attestation. In the land-law alone men held fast to the old requirements of publicity in juristic acts; developing independently and happily in the elaborate system of land registry ("Grundbuchwesen") the formalistic elements of the old native law, in preference to the principles of the alien system. One must grant that all these losses were inevitable; one must also admit that it was unusually late in Germany before capacity for abstract juristic thought, juristic construction and interpretation, attained the level of an art, — the "ars juris." German jurists came to rival the great Frenchmen and Dutchmen only at a late day. This too may have been an unfortunate consequence of the Reception, which deprived legal science of a sound native basis. The result was strikingly evidenced in a juristic German ridiculously embellished with foreign words. Painful efforts proved necessary to acquire again a worthy terminology, comparable in force and neatness with the best legal monuments of the Middle Ages.

[1] *v. Savigny*, "Vom Beruf unserer Zeit für Gesetzgebung und Rechtswissenschaft" (1814, 3d ed. 1840), 12.
[2] *Brunner*, "Grundzüge" (5th ed.), 265.

(III) Finally, the **relation between customary and statutory law** also was altered in the modern period. This, too, was a development inevitably resulting from altered conditions, especially from political transformations; but it was also materially influenced by the Reception.

(1) Lost to the consciousness of the ordinary man, the law could no longer find its main source in the practice of a customary law, but only in consciously adjusted *enactment.* The modern State, in particular, laid claim in increasing measure to the legal regulation of all relations of life as a task exclusively belonging to it. Thus, law that was enacted or "set" ("gesetzt"), and what is more set by the State, — statute ("Gesetz") in its true sense, — became by far the most important and influential source of law. However, legislative power belonged, as had already been the case in the last part of the Middle Ages, not only to the Empire, but to every lesser political community ("Staatsgewalt").

Relatively to legislation, autonomous enactment sensibly diminished, but without wholly disappearing. The autonomy of town and rural communes was, it is true, almost completely broken by the provincial princes, who sought to assure to the State a monopoly of law-making. Only the sea towns of Rostock and Wismar have been able to preserve down to the present day rights of enactment of the old type. Of course, the right of the communes, conceded to them by the State, in its communal ordinances, to establish legal rules by local statutes, etc., may be called "autonomy"; but the State marked off the limits of this authority. In this sense the churches, and likewise the other corporate associations ("Körperschaften") of public law, possessed large powers of enactment. The privilege accorded to them was, indeed, slight in comparison with the autonomy of the old estates of the realm, universities, craft gilds, etc. The autonomy of the high nobility has survived till today as a remnant of the old law of status (*infra,* § 13).

(2) As regards the *customary law,* the full-grown theory of the Roman-Canon law was adopted in Germany. This was not in itself unfavorable to the customary law; nor can it, therefore, be alleged that the German jurists of the age of the Reception were animated by any particular hostility to the customs.[1] In principle they recognized these as a source of law equal in rank

[1] *Brie,* "Die Stellung der deutschen Rechtsgelehrten der Rezeptionszeit zum Gewohnheitsrecht", in "Breslauer Festgabe für F. Dahn", I (1905), 131–164.

with public and private enactments ("Gesetze" and "Statuten"); indeed, even as superior to these and therefore capable of nullifying them, provided they satisfied the requirements adopted from the alien theory. As such there were demanded: a time-honored, frequent, and uniform practice, resting upon jural conviction, — that is, recognized as binding, — and accompanied by an "opinio necessitatis"; a collective will manifested through such practice; and a rational content. That there was in all this nothing inherently hostile, — not even in the requirement of a rational content,—to customary law in general, and the native customs in particular, is evidenced by the fact that the same requisite was set up by the legal theory of the time for public and private enactments. But in truth this attitude was little help to the German customary law. For though the jurists assumed at first a friendly attitude to the customary law as such, they felt therefore a repugnance the more decided to every particularistic legal system: a repugnance which, as Landsberg has aptly remarked, has animated German jurists of every age, and has steadily opposed the particularistic bent of the nation.[1] And unfortunately, almost all German customary law was (as has been remarked) of a particularistic character. Therefore, when it was demanded that every local law should be strictly interpreted, and proved to the judge by the party pleading it, it was precisely the German customs that were thereby primarily affected. The exceptions to this rule, too, that were permitted in the case of notorious — *i.e.* written — law, profited the native customary law only to a slight extent, because it was usually unwritten. On the other hand, the written common law was — as notorious law — not required to be proved; and when to this rule there was added the theory of a reception of the Roman system "in complexu" (*supra*, p. 22), he who appealed to principles of the Justinian law was conceded a "fundatam intentionem", *i.e.* he did not need to prove the authority of the rule. The prejudice that later prevailed against customary law as such is doubtless to be explained by the endeavors of the States completely to shut off, by legislation, all sources of legal variance and uncertainty, in order to prevent paths painfully cleared from being choked again by weeds.[2] To this end all customs not adopted in public statutes were denied authority. The modern codes, above all the Prussian "Landrecht", also assumed this attitude of hostility to the

[1] *Stintzing-Landsberg*, "Geschichte", III, 1, 55.
[2] *Gerber*, "System" (17th ed.), 29.

customary law. The German Commercial Code was the first to break with this tradition: it declared (Art. 1) that effect should be given after its own provisions to the usages of trade, in preference to those of the general private law, thereby endowing the customary law of merchants with a general supplementary, though not indeed amendatory, authority.. The codes that are today in force, both the Civil and the Commercial, and their respective Ordinances of Promulgation, contain no provisions whatever respecting the relative rank of legal sources. The possibility of free development has thus been restored to the customary law; but particularistic custom will no longer be able to modify imperial law. The Swiss Civil Code expressly imposes upon judges the duty to decide according to the customary law when no rule can be derived from public statute.

(3) As a consequence of the fact that the law had become a learned law, cultivated exclusively by jurists, practitioners, and theorists, there was placed among the sources of the law, beside the statutory and the customary law, a *law of courts and treatise-writers* ("Juristenrecht"); distinguishing, within this, the "judge-made" law that was a product of practice and the conclusions of theoretical jurisprudence. This postulation was, however, erroneous. The administration of the law by the courts, especially the highest, can, it is true, influence in a very decisive manner the further growth of the law; but the authority of judicial decisions is never binding. When expression is given in legal practice to a general sense of what the law is, and a further development of the law is thereby initiated, we have here only a special aspect of the production of law by custom. And the same is true of legal theory. The "communis opinio doctorum" is not a source of law, but a view so represented may be raised to the rank of positive law through statute or through custom. The peculiar turn given by Beseler[1] to the doctrine of "Juristenrecht", by his division of customary law into folk-law and "Juristenrecht", rested upon an inadmissible induction of general concepts from actual legal conditions as they had been shaped in Germany by the Reception. Beseler placed folk-law and "Juristenrecht" side by side because in fact, in Germany, the jurists schooled in the alien law impressed their signet upon the law's development. In so doing he failed to recognize that when German jurists innocently treated in Romanistic fashion

[1] "Volksrecht und Juristenrecht" (1843).

legal relations of everyday German life, though they thereby caused infinite damage to the German law, making out of it in many respects a mongrel thing of Germanic and Roman breed, the result was the same, from the formalistic view-point of a theory of legal sources, as if they had decided according to good old Germanic law. Their "Juristenrecht" was, in great part, nothing other than the "folk-law" of that time. It was the mystical conception "folk" of the Historical School which led to this high esteem for the customary law sprung from the people, and to this contempt for so-called "Juristenrecht." But anyway, the attempt, in practical application of this theory, to apportion the institutes of customary law among these two assumedly independent sources of law, was predestined to failure.

§ 4. German Private Law as an Independent Science.

(I) **Common and Regional Law before 1900.**—Since January 1, 1900, law has been declared in German courts, — if we disregard matters reserved to the legislation of the several States, — according to the Civil Code and the imperial statutes supplementary to it. With it German legal science is today primarily occupied; at the universities it occupies the central position in the curriculum. There is a German private law, a German law that covers the individual's civic life.

Before January 1, 1900, such a law had, as we have seen, never existed for any considerable area. Germany was split up into numerous regions of special law, of which — with reference to their leading legal sources and the mode of their application — more than one hundred and twenty could be counted just before the Civil Code came into effect.[1] In the regions of the common law the "Corpus Juris Civilis" was in force; exclusively in only a very few districts, but generally as a subsidiary law — back of various local statutes and bodies of customary law, Territorial codes, and town-laws; behind the Sachsenspiegel and the common Saxon; law behind the Bavarian "Landrecht" of 1756; and, in Schleswig, Fehmarn, and Helgoland, behind the Jutish code ("jütisch Low"). Just before 1900 about sixteen and a half million Germans were living under the common law. Beside this there were the regions of the Prussian "Landrecht" with about twenty-one, of the French and Baden law with about eight and a half, of the Saxon Civil Code with about three

[1] *Cf.* the legal map in *Stammler's* "Übungen im bürgerlichen Recht für Anfänger", I (2d ed. 1902), and the explanations there given.

and a half, million inhabitants. These codes which made the administration of justice in their respective territories wholly independent, could not under such conditions of mutual isolation become the basis, at least for a long time, of a local legal science of merit equal to that of the common law. The importance of codified law for legal study, therefore, diminished. Even at the Prussian, Baden, and Saxon universities the chief emphasis was put, not upon the courses in the local Prussian, French, Baden, or Saxon law, but upon the Pandects: no training worthy of mention was offered to the law student in the local positive law.

At all the universities, however, there was given a supplementary dogmatic course in German private law along with that on the Pandects; and in legal literature German private law was cultivated as an independent science along with the common and the particularistic regional law.

Our next question, is, how was this possible, and what significance was attributed to such "German" private law?

(II) **The Science of German Private Law, and its Tasks prior to 1900.**[1] A *common* private law, *i.e.* a law proceeding from one source and binding upon all regions politically united in the German Empire, did not exist, or existed only in very few divisions of the law, before January 1, 1900. But of course there had always existed a *German* private law. German law is a product of the German people, which despite its political disintegration has nevertheless always constituted a national unit. German law has grown up upon the basis of common mental traits. The same is true of German law as of the German language. As the beginnings of German law go back to racial varieties of law so do those of the German language to various dialects, and a long time passed before a common German literary language gained dominance over the dialects; nevertheless there existed from earliest times a German speech, and Jacob Grimm could with right give the title "German Grammar" to his celebrated work in which he derived the history of that tongue's development from colloquial dialectic forms. The spirit of the law, like that of the language, was everywhere the same. Frankish, Saxon, Thuringian, Swabian, Bavarian, and Frisian law were only variant forms of *German* law.

[1] *Stintzing-Landsberg*, "Geschichte", I–III, 1, 2 (1880–1910). *Gerber*, "Das wissenschaftliche Prinzip des gemeinen deutschen Privatrechts" (1846). *Gierke*, "Die historische Rechtsschule und die Germanisten" (Rectoral Address, 1903).

When men began, however, to busy themselves scientifically with German law, they were as yet far from ready for the recognition of this fact. Only in the 1800 s did the Historical School, following the course marked by Montesquieu and Voltaire[1], attain to a conscious realization of it. Men sought, therefore, another justification for their labors. As has been remarked (*supra*, p. 25), the Reception had by no means displaced all native law. This maintained itself in numerous local statutes and customary systems, influencing the practical application of the Roman law in the courts, and therefore also its scientific treatment. When there arose in the 1600 s, to use Stintzing's phrase, though not as yet a science of German law[2] at least a German legal science, the material content of this, in so far as private law was concerned, was based upon Roman law as modified by the still living native legal sources. It was therefore designated as "usus modernus Pandectarum", or "praxis iuris Romani in foro Germanico", and otherwise. The representatives of this literature — among others Carpzow, Stryck, Leyser, Böhmer — recognized the continued authority of German legal principles: they explained the existing positive law as a development of the borrowed Roman law produced under their influence, through the medium of custom. In this respect they rose far above the purely mechanical juxtaposition of Roman rules and surviving Germanic rules that had become customary in the 1500 s, — for such Germanic rules had found, of course, only gradual recognition among the Romanists. But only when Conring had destroyed (1643) the fable that the Roman law was introduced by a capitulary of the Emperor Lothair, thus making possible a historical understanding of German legal conditions, could the idea gain headway that in those native legal rules and institutes there was still living the old Germanic law; that they could not, therefore, be fused with the Pandect law, nor explained by this; that they must be investigated as independent growths, and contrasted as an independent system with the foreign law. With this idea men undertook, in the first place, to bring together all available materials of German law, to the end of proving that there existed, — as Schilter (1632–1705), the leading representative of these endeavors, put it, — two common laws in Germany, a Roman and a German; and in order to develop from as great a mass as possible of statutory

[1] *Cf. Kantorowicz*, "Volksgeist und historische Rechtsschule", in Hist. Z., CVIII (3d ser. XII, 1912), 295–325.

[2] *Stintzing-Landsberg*, "Geschichte", II, 24.

German systems the principles common to all. While this scientific movement led by Schilter, in conjunction also with certain endeavors of the Humanists, was primarily concerned with an accumulation of material (it reached its culmination later in the work of Heineccius, 1681–1741), no less a man than Christian Thomasius (1655–1728) undertook to reduce this material to unity, to comprehend it in its historical evolution, and, — as an independent branch of science, created one might say by himself, — to introduce it into university courses and work it over in scientific literature. True, in so doing he followed, like others, the arrangement of the Institutes and Pandects; but, contrary to the practice of his predecessors, he made German, not Roman, legal principles his point of departure; and his avowed object was to prove the limited applicability of those alien law-books. That which Thomasius and his pupil Beyer began, Pütter, and after him Selchow, continued. Pütter (1725–1807) developed as a scientific program the idea that the problem was to find, by a comparison of all particularistic rules, the common legal ideas underlying them all; and Selchow (1732–1795) elaborated this plan in a system that rested upon a hitherto unheard of wealth of sources. But while Thomasius had merely naïvely fitted the individual rules of German law together into a system, the two great Göttingen scholars set themselves thus early the problem which was destined thenceforth to torment the scientific conscience of every Germanist: the question, namely, whether the system thus derived from German legal materials enjoyed the status of actual positive law. Pütter and Selchow both answered this question, with critical moderation, in the negative, claiming for the system they established merely universal theoretical authority as a doctrinal abstraction; for which reason Selchow also declared necessary an exhaustive and painstaking cultivation of the various particularistic Territorial systems. The same question was answered even more decisively in the opposite sense by Runde (1741–1807), whose "Principles of German Common Private Law" acquired a dominant reputation about the turn of the 1700 s and 1800 s. He admitted that the mere coincidence of many single provisions did not suffice to establish the actual authority of the principles therefrom deduced; he derived these, instead, from what he called "the nature of things": whatever followed from the "nature" of a given German institute had in his theory the force of directly authoritative law.

This bold but dangerous attempt to rescue for German private law the character of actual law ("Positivität" — positivism), — which as Landsberg says,[1] unqualifiedly and openly set up as ruler the law of nature in place of the legislator, — collapsed when K. F. Eichhorn applied the principles of the Historical School also to the German law, thereby opening the way for a correct understanding of its historical development and its true condition.[2] In his "German Political and Legal History" (1808–1822, 5th ed. 1843–1844) and in his "Introduction to German Private Law" (1823, 5th ed. 1845) Eichhorn deduced from the history of German law the proof that not one of its institutes existed in isolation; that all of them were controlled by certain cardinal principles, which only historical research could discover and reduce to consistency. In Eichhorn's works there was incarnated for German law that epoch-making advance in the conception of intellectual matters which was introduced by the romantic movement: the awakening of the historical sense. Jacob Grimm unveiled to us in his "Legal Antiquities" the old German and Germanic law in its original primitive form[3]; Eichhorn followed it through the course of its development, and taught men to recognize in its latest stage the result of all its earlier stages. In this broad and grand conception, distinguished equally by historical understanding and constructive power, and beside which the views of even his greatest predecessors of the 1700 s lose all relative importance, lies his immortal merit: in details he went astray in many things, and especially his "Introduction" was soon obsolete. But he had laid the solid basis on which could be gradually erected by his followers of the 1800 s, though often only after violent conflict with the champions of the Romanist views, the science of an independent German law, ever becoming more nearly equal to and worthy of its Romanistic fellow.[4] A long series of other general treatises, complemented and carried deeper by many important monographic researches, followed his "Introduction." Of these unquestionably the most important was the "System of the Common German Private Law" of Beseler (1847–55, 4th ed. 1885), whose chief merit, in Gierke's

[1] *Stintzing-Landsberg*, "Geschichte", III, 1, 452.

[2] *Cf.* with this *Frensdorff*, "Das Wiedererstehen des deutschen Rechts", in Z². R. G., XXIX (1908), 1–78; *Hübner*, "K. F. Eichhorn und seine Nachfolger", in the "Festgabe für H. Brunner" (1910), 807–838.

[3] *Hübner*, "Jacob Grimm und das deutsche Recht" (1895).

[4] The development of Germanic legal science in the 1800 s has now been treated excellently and exhaustively in pt. 2 of Vol. 3 of *Stintzing-Landsberg's* "Geschichte", by the latter. Compare with it the elaborate references of *Gierke* in Z². R. G., XXXII (1911), 341–365.

words,[1] lay in "the rediscovery and requickening of such native legal ideas as had been preserved." As Germanistic scholarship turned its attention in increasing measure toward these ends it became a chief promoter of the efforts directed toward the establishment of German legal unity. It was led to that goal by Gierke. In his far-reaching researches, along the lines marked out by Beseler, in the Germanic law of associations he has gained new victories for German law, has conquered for this in a battle ardently contested the influence due it in the recent codification of the civil law, and has begun to assemble in his great work on "German Private Law" the results of a century of researches.

The scholarly cultivation of Germanic private law has therefore exercised a mighty and practical influence upon the most recent German legislation. Eichhorn, however, and the majority of his followers, insisted upon the old viewpoint so far as to demand that such law should retain the character of a positively authoritative law. This was the view of Mittermaier, Renaud, Walter, Gengler, Franken, Gierke and — these with an approximation to the viewpoint of Rude — Reyscher and Beseler, and of others. Only a minority made bold to defend the contrary opinion, as had Albrecht in an earlier day, and, especially uncompromisingly, Gerber, followed by Stobbe and Roth. For the champions of positivism in this controversy respecting what they called "the scientific principles of German private law" the first and controlling necessity was "the legitimation of their science as one not merely historical or comparative but of positive law";[2] because only then could they believe it of equal rank with the Pandect common law — which was the issue which, though perhaps unconsciously, underlay their theory. As Landsberg very justly remarks, a self-deception was here involved; but "one of the most fruitful of all self-deceptions, and one that was historically nothing less than necessary." Without it, men would not have had for any length of time the courage and persistence necessary for the study of the German sources.

In more recent years some have sought support for this view in the existence of common German customs. Even the Imperial Court ("Reichsgericht") has assumed the positivism of German private law, and has treated its principles as legal rules ("Normen"), though subject to judicial review. Nevertheless,

[1] "Privatrecht", I, 92.
[2] *Stintzing-Landsberg*, "Geschichte", III, 1, 55.

although there have doubtless always existed common German customs, they were never so numerous that a scientific system could be restricted exclusively to them. In fact the systems of the Germanists were by no means restricted to this common customary Germanic law of native origin that was authoritative in Germany; by far the most important matters dealt with by them were particularistic statutes and customs. Out of these they pieced together as full a system as possible, but of course without securing in this an internal consistency equal to that of the system of the Roman private law. The system thus created could not possibly be regarded in the same light as one constructed of materials of a common positive law, as was that of the text books of the Pandect law. No matter what rule the Germanists might fit into their system, and support with more or less numerous precedents from the range of sources at their disposal, it could be made the basis of judicial decision, unless its authority followed from general custom, only when its special applicability was demonstrable. That its place was important in their system of theory, was not enough. In truth, therefore, German private law as a whole, and its scholarly cultivation, found no direct practical application in the courts. Its importance was not, however, on that account slight, even for judicial doctrine; for this German private law, this "hypothetic common law" as men were wont to call it, was an indispensable medium for the interpretation of the individual provisions of the particularistic systems. The study of German law constituted the necessary introduction to the study of the local laws, whose whole content is unintelligible when dissociated from the general development of Germanic legal ideas; it was an indispensable complement to the science of the Pandects.

(III) **The Task today of German Private Law.** — That which before 1900 was the subject of strife is today settled. It is no longer necessary to argue, in an endeavor to establish the positive character of German private law; for it is only in the few cases in which matters reserved to State law have remained without particularistic statutory regulation that it still remains in the same uncertain condition as of old. What is more, it has acquired a totally different status through the recent establishment of German legal unity. The "civil" law ("bürgerliches",—the law that covers the several and mutual rights of citizens) is the *positive* private law of today, and the science of this civil law is today the positive-dogmatic science of a common law. The science of German private law has therefore a propædeutic task. As the system of the pure Roman law must unlock to us an understanding of the Roman elements in our positive system, so the science of German private law should serve as an introduction to the Germanic elements of the present civil law. Disregarding those few matters respecting which one can still speak of a common private law in the old sense, the existing imperial and State law does not fall within the scope of that science, which only leads up thereto, as the end of the national legal development. It endeavors to picture that development in a general way. Heusler's "Institutions of German Private Law" present their subject at the period of its flower in the age of the Law-Books, thus affording as it were a cross-section of it at a particularly important point in its growth, but the present science of German private law follows its growth, and seeks to discover at first hand in the sources of all times and regions in which it was a living law its essential nature. Its task is therefore historical.[1] Yet it is not on that account less important, — no, not even less practical, — than is a dogmatic branch of instruction; "for," as Savigny says, "a legal theory that does not rest upon the basis of thorough historical knowledge, really contributes to judicial practice nothing better than the services of a copyist."[2]

[1] It is a different task which *Gierke* has undertaken to perform in his "Deutsches Privatrecht." His design is to give a detailed dogmatic presentation of the existing private law in so far as this is not of Romanistic origin. On the other hand his "Outline" in *Holtzendorff-Kohler's* "Encyklopädie der Rechtswissenschaft" (6th ed. I, 431–559) has substantially the same plan as that indicated in the text, above; and in the Address cited on p. 33 *supra* (at p. 33) he also declares that academic instruction must lead the student up to the existing law from the Roman as well as from Germanic law. The work of *Cl. Frh. v. Schwerin* cited on p. liv *supra* is a purely historical presentation of the development of the Germanic private law in systematic order.

[2] "Vom Beruf unserer Zeit", 78. Compare also on the value of legal history *Ernst Jacobi*, "Die Ausbildung der Juristen" (1912), 21 *et seq.*

BOOK I. THE LAW OF PERSONS

Chapter II

NATURAL PERSONS

§ 5. **Man as the Holder of Rights: (I) Capacity for Rights** ("Rechtsfähigkeit"). — Our present-day simple and perspicuous arrangement of the law of persons, based on a recognition of every human being as a holder of rights, belongs only to a modern period of civilization. German law, in its beginnings, like other systems, by no means treated all human beings as legally equal. To many classes it utterly denied all legal worth, to others it attributed only a partial worth. Only gradually was this primitive view overcome. With it there disappeared contrasts and distinctions which had once possessed profound significance in social life, above all that division into estates which characterized the medieval world. Even the Christian doctrine of the moral equality of men could not overcome this, — albeit far-seeing spirits like Eike von Repgow recognized the legal equality of all men as a tenet of religion and morality, justifying this by the fact that God had created man in his image and had given salvation to all equally through his martyrdom.[1]

The doctrine of the Law of Nature first carried this view to final triumph. Under the dominance of its ideas serfdom was abolished, the feudal class divisions of society into estates were swept away, and the legal equality of different religious faiths established. The principle of the equality of men or of citizens, which found express adoption in many German constitutions in imitation of foreign models, was established without restriction within the field of private law: every man is a person in the legal sense, a subject of rights, *i.e.* "capable of appearing as the holder and bearer of rights."[2] Hence the modern State, in Germany

[1] Ssp. III, 42, § 1.

[2] *Heusler*, "Institutionen", I, 100.

as elsewhere, banished slavery utterly from its soil, and in the more modern codifications it was explicitly provided that foreign slaves should become free the instant they should set foot within the boundaries of the State. The limitations in this respect still retained in the Prussian "Allgemeines Landrecht" of 1794 (II. 5, §§ 196–199) were abolished by a special statute in 1857.

In this case, therefore, development came, by way of exception, through statutory simplification. Yet it should not be forgotten that this realization of formal legal equality accompanied a steady deepening of economic contrasts, and that culture, particularly, has in most recent times created social divisions which at least equal in actual importance the one-time division between the free and the unfree, — although perhaps, this new contrast is itself about to lose its distinctness.

(II) **Capacity for Legal Action** ("Handlungsfähigkeit"). — In no stage of its development can the legal order ignore certain natural differences between persons. When it has so risen to a recognition of the equality, in principle, of all individuals, it must still treat minors and persons in tutelage otherwise than adults. Formerly sex also made a great difference, but modern times have established to an increasing extent the equality of man and woman in the private law. Sickness, also, was formerly of more widespread legal effect than it is to-day; though law must, under all circumstances, take into consideration diseased disturbances of mental capacity.

These differences in natural qualities and conditions do not destroy legal personality, the capacity for rights; but they do make more difficult any independent participation in legal transactions, or render this wholly impossible: they restrict or wholly do away with capacity for legal action.

§ 6. **The Beginning of Capacity for Rights.** (I) **Birth.** — Germanic law did not, generally speaking, recognize capacity for rights as beginning before one's appearance as an independent human being; in other words, not until after birth. Certain provisions, however, of the Frankish law [1] would seem to indicate that its original theory attributed to the child in womb a capacity for rights in relation to property. Later, however, German law, like other systems, contented itself with holding open to such a child the acquisition of rights that would inhere in it in case it should be born alive, and especially the acquisition of a

[1] *Coulin*, "Der Nasciturus. Ein Beitrag zur Lehre vom Rechtssubjekt im fränkischen Recht", in Z². R. G., XXXI (1910), 131–137.

paternal inheritance,—the actual distribution being delayed until the delivery of the decedent's pregnant widow. The medieval law thus realized an idea which the Roman system first formulated in principle;[1] and though the modern codes adhered to the Roman system,[2] they gave heed at the same time to native legal ideas. We find in them also the provision that a curator might be appointed for the "nasciturus" during gestation. On the other hand the moment of birth was decisive of its social status, nationality, and membership in the commune. However, in case a father lost his nobility during his wife's pregnancy, many legal systems did not let this affect the child.

(II) **Adoption.**[3] — In the primitive law, unlike that of today, the natural fact of birth was by no means sufficient basis for the acquisition of full capacity for rights. Whether the child should be adopted into the family of its father, and thereby become a member of the legal community, depended, moreover, according to Germanic law, upon the father's will. He might expose it, *i.e.* disown it. "The newborn child lies on the floor until the father declares whether he will or will not let it live. If yes, he takes it up, or orders it taken up; it seems that the term for midwife ('Hebamme') comes from this act ('Aufheben')."[4] This adoption ("Aufnahme", "taking up") was the visible recognition of the child by its father.

The right of exposure was gone so soon as the first acts in care of the child had been done. "A child exposed must not yet have tasted anything whatever, a drop of milk or of honey assured it life."[5] In cases of necessity, as *e.g.* after the father's death, the act of offering nourishment might stand in lieu of a formal recognition by the father. The first sprinkling or the first bathing of the child had a like effect according to primitive ideas.

The bestowal of a name, which was a necessary consequence of adopting the new-born child, was taken in hand among the

[1] Digest, Liber 50, Tit. 16, "De verborum significatione", 231.

[2] For example the Prussian "Landrecht", I, 1, § 10: "The natural ('allgemeine') rights of men inure even to children not yet born, from the moment of their conception."

[3] *Konrad Maurer*, "Über die Wasserweihe des germanischen Heidentums", in K. Bayer. Akad. Wiss., "Abhandlungen" (I Kl.) XV, 3 (1880); *K. Müllenhoff*, "Anzeiger für deutsches Altertum", VII (1881), 404–409, also in "Deutsche Altertumskunde", IV (1900), 632–638; *H. Brunner*, "Die Geburt eines lebenden Kindes" in Z[2]. R. G., XVI (1895), 63–108; *Grosch*, "Die Wasserweihe als Rechtsinstitution", in Z. Vergl. R. W., XXIII (1910), 420–456.

[4] *J. Grimm*, "Rechtsaltertümer", I, 627.

[5] *Ibid.*, 630.

Scandinavians immediately after birth, and among the other Germanic races (as among the Greeks and Romans) on the ninth day thereafter, — with which fact seems to be connected the later jocular saying, with reference to the Swabians, that they remained blind for nine days after birth.

When the right of exposure disappeared, under the influence of Christianity, the necessity of a formal adoption of the child into the family disappeared with it.

(III) **The Proof of Birth.** — Birth alive was a precondition to the origin of legal personality. In accord with the formalistic character of Germanic procedural law definite facts were required to be established when the birth of a living child was questioned. According to the South-Germanic systems the proof must be to the effect that the child had opened its eyes and seen the roof-ridge and four walls of the house. In North Germany emphasis was laid upon its filling with its cries the four walls. Often too, a cry of a particular character [1] was required, — *e.g.* in Westphalia one that could be heard through an oaken plank or a wall. It is Brunner's conjecture that this requirement of the child's cry, found in the whole body of Saxon, Frankish, and Anglo-Norman sources, is connected with the fact that the primitive law required the testimony of men, and in critical cases these could give proof of life only as ear, not as eye, witnesses; since for reasons of propriety men were not allowed to be present at the delivery.

Inasmuch as precisely these manifestations of life, and not any others one might choose, were regarded as proofs in the theory of the old law, the legal consequences attendant on a living birth did not follow when these exact facts could not be established, notwithstanding that the child might have lived without seeing or crying.

Only gradually did it become possible to establish the fact of life by other signs, until here too, with the abolishment of formal methods of proof, foothold was gained for an untrammelled judicial estimate of proof. Those manifestations of life that were once exclusively heeded retained thenceforth merely the importance of particularly reliable evidence, as *e.g.* still in the Prussian "Allgemeines Landrecht" (I. 1, § 13), which declared the birth of a child established "when reliable witnesses, present at the birth, shall have clearly heard its voice."

[1] *Brunner*, essay just cited, 64.

(IV) **Viability.** — Now when we consider that the older Germanic sources laid down the requirement of the child's cry; that the West-Gothic law required that a child, in order to inherit and leave property, must have lived ten days and been baptized; and that the bestowal of a name requisite to the acquisition of full capacity for rights must have taken place not earlier than nine days after birth, — it becomes obvious that Germanic law attached legal consequences to the birth of such children only as proved capable of life. Those brought into the world in so premature a state that they could not maintain life, and monstrosities, that showed no human form, were regarded as incapable of having rights. In this sense the Sachsenspiegel, for example, required (I. 33) that the child should be "large enough", *i.e.* born at such a stage of maturity "that it should be capable of living" ("lifhaftich").

Even after the Reception men held fast in the common law, under the influence of the Germanic legal ideas, to this requisite of vitality, interpreting in this sense the expressions of the Roman law, particularly law 2, Cod. "de postumis", 6, 29. Savigny was the first to take the opposite view; nevertheless, in more recent years the older view has again found champions as against the common law. The modern Territorial systems did not adopt the requisite in question, and in this respect they were followed by the present German and Swiss civil codes; only the Code Civil (§§ 725, 906) retained it.

(V) **Registry of Birth.** — The registry of births was in general ill cared for in the Middle Ages. The custom observed since the 400s by the clergy of keeping a register of baptisms died out, to reappear only in the 1400s in the practice of individual bishops, who aimed thereby to make possible the proof of disabilities for marriage. The Council of Trent made the Church's records, as registers of births and marriages, a general institution of Catholic countries, and the church ordinances of the evangelical church devised similar regulations. These church records were then recognized by the State as public documents. For all that these methods of authentication remained imperfect. Baptisms often took place only a long time after birth; the registers were confined to a definite diocese, were often ill kept, and imperfectly preserved; above all, all those persons who did not belong to the recognized Christian churches, — the Dissidents, the Jews; in France, also the Protestants, — were wholly excluded from them.

All these circumstances contributed powerfully to the introduction of governmental registers of personal status. Introduced first into individual Italian cities in the 1300 s and 1400 s, they received in France, through the legislation of the Revolution and the Code Civil (§§ 34 fg.), a universal application that served as a model for later times. Germany followed the French example in the imperial statute on personal status of February 6, 1875, which had been preceded by a Prussian statute, identical in content, of March 9, 1874. In the regions of the French law in Germany registers of civil status had already been introduced with the Code Civil, and had for the most part since then been maintained; only in a few regions, as *e.g.* in Hesse and Hamburg, had they been again displaced by reactionary legislation. Here, and in the other German States until the enactment of the imperial statute just referred to, men contented themselves with increasing the dependability of the church records, with the introduction of similar books in the synagogues for Jews, and with the intrustment to village magistrates or judges of the registration of dissidents and non-Christians.

§ 7. **Determination of Capacity for Rights.** (I) **Natural death** always involved, and in the law of to-day it alone involves, the end of capacity for rights. For purposes of record and for the proof of death, ecclesiastical records served in former times as they did for births; their place was later taken by civil registers.

With regard to the question whether, in case of the loss of several persons under circumstances of common peril, some should be regarded as having died before others, — a question that may be of importance in the settlement of inheritances, — no particular rule seems to have been adopted in most of the older Germanic sources. The modern State systems, with the exception of the Code Civil and a few Swiss statutes, rejected the presumption, taken over from the Roman into the common law, of the decease of certain persons before others, — of parents before children beyond tutelary age, of children under tutelage before parents; on the contrary they generally established a presumption of the simultaneous death of those lost under circumstances of a common peril. To this principle the Civil Code has adhered. The Swiss Civil Code (§ 32) provides the same for all cases in which the time of death of the several persons is incapable of proof, — *i.e.* it does not limit the presumption to death in a common disaster.

(II) **Destruction of Capacity for Rights notwithstanding Continued Life.** (1) *Social Outlawry* ("Friedlosigheit", — "peacelessness") *and Outlawry as Judicial Process* ("Oberacht"). —

The primitive law was far from indissolubly associating capacity for legal rights with physical life, and therefore it could withdraw such capacity from a living person and thereby annihilate his jural existence, his legal personality. This was effected by putting him out of the peace, which was the central idea of Teutonic criminal law, and gave reality to the idea "that he who breaks the peace puts himself outside the peace."[1] Outlawry in its extreme form constituted complete destruction of legal personality; the "peaceless" man lost his place in the circles of his fellows in the sib and folk; his wife became widow, his children were treated as orphans, his property was forfeited, his home destroyed. In time outlawry became less prominent. It retained its place longest in legal procedure, as the ultimate result of contumacy, in the form of judicial process.

(2) *Civil Death.* — While outlawry, even in the form of judicial process, finally disappeared from the law in Germany, there was developed from it elsewhere the legal institute known as civil death; particularly in France where the after effects of outlawry ("forbannitio") united the effects of the Roman "capitis diminutio" and "infamia" with those of Canonic excommunication. So late as in an ordinance of 1670 it was decreed as the consequence of contumacy, quite in the old-time manner; and during the 1700s it was involved in every condemnation to a capital penalty. And although it thereby became a punishment cruel in the extreme and was with justice violently attacked, it was employed freely against the Emigrants in the Revolution, and still found recognition in the Code Civil (§§ 22–23), — though not in the Code Pénal. In the form in which it appears in the Code Civil, — according to which one condemned to civil death lost all his property rights and control of his heritable estate, became incapable of disposing of his property, saw his marriage "ipso facto" dissolved, and could enter into no future marriage, — the institution was adopted in Germany in the regions of the French law. It was adopted, further, by the Baden "Landrecht" and the Bavarian criminal code. However, it had no long-lived authority in Germany. Modern ideas called for its abandonment. It was abolished in France by a statute of 1854, and was also done away with in Germany—in part even earlier than in France, as *e.g.* in Prussia by the Constitution (Art. 10). The present Imperial Criminal Code does not

[1] *Brunner,* "Grundzüge" (5th ed.), 18.

mention it, and has thus wholly done away with it for the entire Empire. English law still knows a "civil death"; it occurs, however, only with extreme infrequency, namely in cases of the still recognized penalty of civil *outlawry*.

(3) *Claustral Death.* — In the Middle Ages those who entered a monastic order or sisterhood were, as the gloss to the Sachsenspiegel put it, "regarded by the world as dead" from the moment of taking vows. An ecclesiastic "unburdened himself", to use again the expression of the Sachsenspiegel (I, 25, § 3), with his entry into the cloister, of the Territorial and feudal law. The English law as early as the 1100 s, and later the French law, therefore explicitly designated him as civilly dead. It is true that this claustral death was a different thing from the institute discussed above, which arose out of the old outlawry. Monks were often enough immersed in worldly affairs, but in the view of the secular law they had no independent will; they were subjected to another's, "which as a matter of religion might be thought of as the divine will, but within the sphere of temporal law was represented by the will of the abbot."[1] Entry into the cloister destroyed, therefore, proprietary capacity; and precisely herein lay the motive for the frequency of monastic vows: they were a favored means of avoiding the partition of family property. With the taking of his vows an ecclesiastic lost the power to dispose by testament of his property; this reverted at once, like the estate of a decedent, to his blood relations, or (as the case might be) to the heirs or legatees already by him appointed. Any further acquisition of property was for him impossible; nor could the cloister inherit for him. These rules of the medieval secular law were followed, among the modern codes, by the Prussian "Allgemeines Landrecht", which declared (II, 11, §§ 1199, 1200) monks and nuns incapable of acquiring, possessing, or disposing of ownership and lesser rights in property. On the other hand the Canon law assumed a wholly different position: it did not in matters of property law nullify the personality of the ecclesiastic; rather, it transferred this to his cloister. This principle was accepted by the common law, and by the Territorial systems other than the Prussian. Limits were very generally set by modern statutes to property accumulations in a dead hand. The Civil Code, by recognizing (EG, 87) the limits placed upon such acquisitions in the State systems, has taken the same position.

1. *Pollock* and *Maitland*, "History", I, 416.

(4) *Enslavement.* — The older law recognized a voluntary enslavement ("obnoxiatio"), and enslavement might also be imposed as a punishment. There was likewise involved in this a destruction of legal personality during life; for persons in bondage were not originally regarded as subjects of rights (§ 13, *infra*). Thus *e.g.* Bracton, an English jurist of the 1200 s, speaks explicitly of the "mors civilis" of slaves, since they are subjected to their lord precisely as the monks to the abbot. Inasmuch, however, as the harsh attitude of the old law was early abandoned and the legal personality of the unfree recognized, there remained in such cases thereafter only a mere restriction upon capacity for rights.

(III) **Presumptive Death and Declarations of Death.**[1] (1) *The Older German Law.*[1] — In the Middle Ages it was a common occurrence that uncertainty prevailed at his home concerning the fate of one who had left his country; for traveling consumed much time and was dangerous, and the possibility of sending messages was slight. Especially one who was compelled to journey over sea as merchant, pilgrim, or crusader, often lost for a long period communication with his home. A prince of Mecklenburg, Henry I the Pilgrim, who had gone to the Holy Land, remained for six and twenty years (1271–1298) in captivity among the infidels; only four years after his capture did the news of it reach his people; afterward, rumors of his death were repeatedly circulated, and only his return finally put an end to uncertainty. In such cases of disappearance, as the Magdeburg and Lübeck laws show, the property of the missing person was delivered to his next heirs, although at first only provisionally; they were bound to give it back to one who returned, and to give security therefor in taking temporary possession. But if the missing person never returned, the possession was unchanged, and so became a definitive inheritance. At what moment the period of uncertainity should be taken to be ended and the death of the missing person to be certain, German law left open for judicial determination in each case, setting up no definite periods. The proof of death was not particularly difficult, because it could be made by the oath of him who averred it; for the medieval law of procedure permitted proof by oath even of those facts which the oath taker merely believed, without having independent knowledge

[1] *Bruns*, "Die Verschollenheit", in J. B. gem. R., I (1857), 90–201, reprinted in his "Kleinere Schriften", I (1882), 48–135; *H. Meyer*, "Vom Rechtsschein des Todes. Ein Beitrag zur Dogmatik der Todeserklärung" (1912).

thereof. Moreover, all definite proof of death could be wholly excused when missing persons, as the Magdeburg "Questions" put it (I, 7, D, 6), "could not in nature have lived longer", *i.e.* when they had already passed the years of a normal age. So long as death could neither be proved, nor assumed with full assurance on grounds of nature, the absent person was regarded as living. And so, for example, the son of the Mecklenburg prince above referred to, when he had attained majority and had taken over the regency for his father, always used the latter's seal in acts of government.

(2) *The Later Development.* — After the Reception the doctrine of unexplained disappearance received a more ordered form through the further development of older German legal ideas and their association with the results of Italian theory and practice. In the first place, fixed periods were introduced, and formal legal presumptions attached to them; and further, an ordered procedure was prescribed as a precondition to official declaration of death.

(A) The periods. — The classic Roman law knew, as little as did the older Germanic law, statutory presumptions of life and death; the judge was permitted to draw from the circumstances an inference of probable fact after an untrammelled weighing of the evidence. On the other hand, the Italian practice, "under the influence of the theory of formal proof,"[1] developed from the assumption (current among the Roman jurists as well) that a hundred years were to be regarded as the extreme age of man the strong presumption that the missing person should be taken to be living to the end of his 100th year of life ("presumption of life"), and from that moment on as dead ("presumption of death"). The former presumption was, however, rebuttable by proof, which in turn was facilitated by further presumptions.

These presumptions of life and of death were adopted in Germany. In the practice of the Saxon courts particularly, especially of the court of lay-judges at Leipzig, the attainment of a definite age was thus treated as decisive. The only change was that under the influence of Leipzig jurists, especially of Carpzow, the limit was lowered, in echo of the saying of the Psalmist, from the hundreth to the 70th full year of life ("Saxon system"). This age then attained a common law authority.

[1] *Gierke*, "Privatrecht", I, 367.

A mode of calculating the necessary period, differing from the Saxon, evidences of which already occur occasionally in the Middle Ages, and which agrees also with the older French customary law, was prevalent in Silesia (" Silesian system "). This emphasized, not age, but the duration of absence, requiring for the assumption of death the passage of a definite period of time since the receipt of the last news, without regard to the age of the person missing. The expiration of thirty years was originally required; later, men were content with twenty, or more frequently with ten years. This method of reckoning was adopted by the Prussian " Allgemeines Landrecht " and by the Austrian Civil Code. Under certain circumstances the two systems were united; for when the missing person was of very great age a shorter period of absence was deemed sufficient, — *e.g.* the Prussian law lowered it from ten to five years for persons above 65 years of age; or it was wholly waived, — *e.g.* at 100 years according to the Code Civil, at 90 according to the Saxon Code. And according to many systems of law the requisite of advanced age was wholly disregarded in cases of exceedingly long absences; as *e.g.*, in Bavarian and French law, in case of an absence for 30 years.

All such periods were much shortened in case the missing person was proved to have been in jeopardy of life, as for example in a shipwreck or a theater fire. Notably after the great wars of 1864, 1866, and 1870–71, special statutes were enacted according to which the death of missing soldiers should be assumed after the running of a short period, or from a definite date in the future. The Swiss Civil Code (§ 34) has derived from these the new and general principle that the death of any person shall be regarded as proved, even though no one may have seen the corpse, whenever he disappeared under conditions that make his death seemingly certain.

The Saxon practice united in a peculiar way the imported presumptions of life and death with the native rules concerning provisional instatement in actual possession, transforming the latter, in analogy to the Roman " cura absentis ", into a so-called " cura anomala ", a peculiar guardianship of absent persons. A " curator absentis " was appointed at the instance of the next heirs for an absent person whose fate began to be doubtful, and thereupon the heritable estate was turned over to them with full powers of administration, subject to their giving security. The time reached to which was attached the presumption of death, the heir received back his security and acquired the inheritance definitively; moreover he was thenceforth treated as though the inheritance had fallen to him at the moment when the "cura" had been instituted ("successio ex tunc"). This antedating of the fact of inheritance was in harmony, however, with the older Germanic law, which knew no succession save in individual pieces of heritable property. It was only because men held fast to this view of the Germanic law, despite the theoretical reception of the principle of universal succession, that they did not at first remark the contradiction between the presumption of life and the antedating of the accrual of the heritage. But later the "successio ex tunc" was abandoned, being replaced by a "successio ex nunc"; that is, that moment was made decisive of definitive accrual of the heritage in which the [absolute] presumption of death took effect. This rule attained a common law authority.

(B) Procedure by citation ("Aufgebotsverfahren"). — The presumption of death originally arose the instant the term had run. But from the middle of the 1700s onward there came to be usual, as a further precondition, a process of judicial summons, which was introduced in view of improved facilities of trade and communication. It prescribed repeated public summonses of the missing person, to be printed in the newspapers. If these remained fruitless the procedure ended with a judicial finding embodying a declaration of death. Such summonses were introduced first into Prussia (1763) on the model of the Saxon practice, and spread rapidly thereafter through the rest of the Empire. The Code Civil, alone, did not adopt them. The procedure was regulated in detail in codes of procedure. It is true that by no means all of these attributed the same legal significance to the final judgment; and that in general the detailed regulation of the whole institute assumed quite variant forms in the different State statutes. A few of these, as the Prussian "Landrecht", the Austrian Civil Code, Thuringian statutes, and a Bavarian statute of 1879, attributed to the judgment a constitutive force; so that the date when such judgment became effective was treated as the day of death, the effects of the declaration of death becoming positive from then onward. On the other hand other statutes treated the judgment as declaratory, so that, in accord with the older Saxon practice, that day was regarded as the deathday on which the legal preconditions of a presumption of death were satisfied, — the day, accordingly, upon which either the requisite age was reached or the necessary period of absence had run. This rule passed over into the common law; it was also adopted by the Saxon Code and by an Austrian statute of 1853.

(C) THE RETURN OF A MISSING PERSON. — By force of a declaration of death the missing person was regarded in law as dead from the date so fixed. But this assumption was rebuttable; news might come establishing another deathday, or the continuance of life; or the missing person himself might return. The effects of the declaration of death had then, of course, to be rescinded. Special difficulties resulted when a spouse left behind had contracted a new marriage. Different legal systems assumed, as to this question, varying positions. The majority, including the Prussian "Landrecht" and the common law, declared the new marriage to be legally existing and the old marriage dissolved. Some adopted the opposite view, that of the Canon law, and declared the second marriage void. A compromise between these two extremes was attempted by the French law, which made the second marriage voidable at the instance of the missing spouse who returned, and also by the Saxon law, which made it voidable by the spouse twice married.

(3) *Final Result of Development.* — The new Civil Code has substituted for the earlier diversities of the law a complete uniformity. The rules adopted by it (§§ 13–19), which are supplemented by the provisions of the Code of Civil Procedure (§§ 960–976) relative to citation-process, have given a common law authority, as regards the essential prerequisites, to what was formerly the Silesian system (§ 14). It expressly adopts the presumption of life (§ 19). It attributes declaratory force to the judicial declaration of death (§ 18). In case of disappearance in war, at sea, and in accidents it establishes abbreviated periods (§§ 15, 16, 17). The presumption of death applies also to the case of marriage. Hence, in case the presumption be unrebutted, the old marriage is to be regarded as dissolved at the moment of presumptive death; but in case the error of the presumption be discovered after the contraction of a new marriage, the latter nevertheless remains valid, for its consummation, — provided it be not void because of bad faith of both of the new spouses, — dissolves the former marriage (§ 1348). Each of the new spouses, however, can impeach the new union if the missing spouse still live (§ 1350) subject to the condition of good faith.

The Swiss Civil Code (§§ 35–38) has established a somewhat variant regulation of declarations of the legal death of missing persons, resembling that of the Code Civil. Such a declaration is made by a judge upon the basis of a petition, which can be presented when five years have passed, either since the peril to his life simultaneously with which the missing person disappeared or since the last news of him, and when the judicial citation has also remained fruitless. Swiss law knows no presumption of continued life. The declaration of death is as in German law, of merely declaratory effect. An existing marriage is not dissolved by such a declaration, in itself, but the spouse left behind may demand its dissolution. The return of the missing person has no influence upon a new marriage (§ 102).

§ 8. **Age.**[1] — Youth and old age are, as has been seen, not merely physical distinctions; they always involve legal differences, also. And the law can take account in various ways of differences of age.

I. **Youth**: (1) *The Older Law.* — (A) Age periods. — In contrast to the later variety of vital periods recognized by the law, men recognized in primitive times only one division: that between maturity and immaturity, "just as they divided the day into halves of morning and evening, corresponding to the ancient assumption of but two seasons of the year, summer and winter."[2] Below this limit stood the minors, those "within or under their years"; they passed it so soon as they came "to their years", — to years of discrimination, of discernment, of self-consciousness, to "anni intelligibiles" or "discretionis"; which coincided with their attainment of puberty. The dooms still maintained, on the whole, this primitive view.

It seems that among the Germans, — as also *e.g.* among the Romans, — no precise moment was originally assigned at which the transition from immaturity to maturity was realized. This took place according to individual development. "The oldest rule is probably one which counted no years, but measured the outward signs of physical power; as the child was judged by its cry, speech, and the blowing out of a candle, so perhaps the man was judged by his ability to swing the spear, or slay the enemy, or in other ways."[3] Nevertheless, the attainment of majority by no means effected, of itself, the removal of all the limitations theretofore placed upon minors. In particular, it did not put

[1] *W. Wackernagel*, "Die Lebensalter, ein Beitrag zur vergleichenden Sitten- und Rechtsgeschichte" (1862); *Stobbe*, "Die Aufhebung der väterlichen Gewalt nach dem Recht des Mittelalters", in "Beiträge" (1865), 1–24.

[2] *Wackernagel*, *op. cit.*, 9.

[3] *Grimm*, "Rechtsaltertümer", I, 572.

an end to paternal authority. On the contrary, this was ended only by a formal declaration of majority by the father; or what was most common, by the son's desertion of the paternal household and establishment of his own. The grant of arms was, rightly considered, no emancipation. Only for fatherless youths was it so; in their case, unless they voluntarily submitted themselves to a further period of guardianship, the grant of arms and majority were coincident. In other cases the able-bodied sons still remained under the authority of the family head. Where there was sex-guardianship, *i.e.* where women were subjected through life to the tutelage of a man (*infra*, § 9), the contrast of minority and majority existed only as to the men.

Among Germanic peoples, however, fixed limits for the attainment of majority were adopted at an early period and thus a free appreciation of each individual case was replaced by a routinary rule, — which, indeed, in this particular matter, the law cannot dispense with, even in its ripest development.

The ages fixed for the attainment of majority, as these prevailed among the different Germanic racial branches, according to earliest reports, were in all cases strikingly early. This is a phenomenon that appears among all undeveloped peoples. It can perhaps be explained by the fact, already referred to, that paternal power was usually continued, and that where that was not the case there might be a voluntary continuance of guardianship; and that, in general, the prevailingly simple conditions of life could not make any great demands upon the maturity of the individual. The earliest date to be found within the whole extent of Germanic legal sources is the tenth completed winter, which is spoken of in the old Kentish law, and which, with the addition of a year and a day, is still to be found in the Ditmarsh law of the 1400 s. Among most of the Germanic racial branches the twelfth completed year of life was the age-division, — it was so with the Salic and Chattish Franks, Frisians, Lombards, Saxons, Anglo-Saxons, Alamanians, probably among the Bavarians, and originally among the Visigoths, Norwegians, and Icelanders. Among others the completed fifteenth year was the limit, as among the Ripuarian Franks, Burgundians, and the later Visigoths (to all of whom, perhaps, the Roman date of puberty of fourteen years served as a model); and also particularly among the West Franks in their later period, among the later Norwegians and Icelanders, and in the "Libri Feudorum."

While these early age-divisions of the primitive law remained in force among a few racial branches,—as in the Saxon Territorial and feudal law, in the law of Groningen, Gelders, and Holland,—the age limit was later raised by most of them. In Germany the limit of eighteen years was widely prevalent. It is found in many town laws (*e.g.* in those of Lübeck, Hamburg, Goslar, Brunswick, Strassburg, and in the Ditmarsh law of 1567), and was established by imperial legislation for the electoral princes in the Golden Bull. Along with it we find the twentieth year, as in Augsburg; and the twenty-fifth, *e.g.* in the Schwabenspiegel (G. 54, 5). In short, a great diversity prevailed regarding the age of majority, and in all lands,—alike in Germany, in the Netherlands and in Italy; while in France and in England the age-limit was variously fixed for different classes, and not infrequently the sexes too were differently treated. A rule prevailing particularly in the Saxon law was peculiar. Here the old limit of twelve years was retained as the beginning of majority, but another was introduced at the end of the twenty-first year, up to which voluntary guardianship remained possible. Heusler justly remarks [1] that there was no inconsistency of principle between this and the other legal systems (mainly of South Germany), for these also recognized the possibility of prolonging the period of guardianship. The difference was that the latter, at an early date, postponed the age of majority to a later year, and therefore did not need expressly to distinguish the second age-limit that became customary in the Saxon law. In Saxon legal phraseology children under twelve years of age were characterized as "under their years", and those between the twelfth and twenty-first years as "under their days"; in which connection Jacob Grimm makes the acute remark [2] that even yet our speech is wont to count childhood by years and old age by days: "we speak of 'years of childhood' and 'days of old age.' . . . Time becomes ever more precious with advancing age, in youth it is unheeded."

However, despite the introduction of an age of majority it remained true that only by the child's desertion of the paternal house,—in the case of sons, by the establishment of their own household; in that of daughters, by their marriage,—was paternal authority displaced. Accordingly, only "free" boys, *i.e.* boys whose fathers were dead, became self-governing as soon as they attained "their years"; otherwise majority merely had the consequence that the father of a grown child, if it wished to leave his house, was no

[1] "Institutionen", II, 491 *et seq.*
[2] "Rechtsaltertümer", I, 571.

longer able to hinder this. Moreover, despite the introduction of a fixed limit to the tutelary period, it was, as before, not infrequently necessary to take note of "the physical probative signs",[1] for "until far into the Middle Ages only the fewest people knew with exactness the year of their birth or even their birthday."[2] Thus the Sachsenspiegel tells us (I, 42, § 1): "if the age of any man is not known, then if he have hair in his beard, and below, and under each arm, it shall be known that he has attained his years" ("swelkes mannes alder man nicht ne weit, hevet he har in dem barde unde nidene under iewederme arme, so sal man weten, dat he to sinen dagen komen is"). As a last means of proof the oath of one who asserted his majority was decisive.

(B) As regards THE LEGAL STATUS OF MINORS, although Germanic law denied them full judgment, the power to distinguish between good and evil, it by no means treated them as lacking all capacity for legal action. On the contrary all persons "under years", even the smallest children, were regarded by it as having such capacity; herein contrasting sharply with the Roman law, according to which "infantes" were without capacity for legal action. To be sure they could not undertake those jural acts for which express self-government was requisite, — *e.g.* acts in court, disposition of their persons, and so on; and further it was possible for them to revoke within a certain time after attaining majority all acts, although such in themselves as they were capable of performing. Heusler calls attention to the fact that the dangers which this rule might in some cases have involved for young persons were lessened by the circumstance that the guardian held the property of his ward, and could thus prevent ill-considered acts; as also by the fact that third parties would certainly hesitate to have dealings with minors, inasmuch as they must expect that the transaction might, after years of uncertainty, be voided by the minor on his attaining majority.[3]

(2) *Development since the Reception.* — While the Reception did not lead to a complete displacement of the native by the Roman rules, it did result in a far-reaching influence of these rules upon the former.

In the first place the period of "infantia" was everywhere interpolated; whereas the English law, for example, has held to the old Germanic view, and even to-day knows, in principle, only

[1] *Wackernagel, op. cit.*, 55.
[2] *Heusler*, "Institutionen", I, 66.
[3] *Ibid.*, 201 *et seq.*

one divisional line between minority and majority. At the same time, even in the older German law distinctions already appeared within childhood: with seven years the child began to learn; the church, too, permitted from seven years onward ordination into the priestly office. But now, in imitation of the Roman law, the seventh completed year of life sharply divided children wholly without capacity for legal action from minors merely limited in such capacity. On the other hand the Roman distinction between "impuberes" and "minores" attained no importance in Germany, all minors above seven years, whether or not they had passed the age of puberty of twelve or fourteen years, being treated alike. Their juristic acts remained for the time in suspense, — as had formerly those of children under seven years, — and bound only the other party; they were incapable of being parties to an action; the privileges of "restitutio in integrum" and the bar of the thirty-year prescription period allowed in their favor, in imitation of the Roman law, were again abolished in modern times. As regards the moment of attaining majority, the Roman divisional period of twenty-five years also attained a common law validity in Germany; the Schwabenspiegel, as already mentioned, had earlier adopted it. Side by side with this, however, the limit of eighteen years maintained common law authority in the case of the high nobility save in Mecklenburg, where it was nineteen, and in a few princely houses in which it was twenty-one. All these rules have remained unchanged as regards the houses ruling to-day, and those dispossessed in 1866, though not as regards the other families of the high nobility. Unlike the common law the Territorial systems held fast to the native age periods. The Prussian "Landrecht" adopted that of twenty-four years. So also the Austrian Code, by virtue of which this age-limit still exists in Austria. In recent years, however, the term of twenty-one years has attained the widest prevalence in Germany, after having earlier found general recognition in France as a result of the Revolution and the Code Civil, and also recognition within the regions of French law in Germany. The close of the whole development was reached in an imperial statute of February 17, 1875, which fixed that period for all Germany. The new Civil Code (§ 2) has also retained it, whereas the Swiss Civil Code (§ 14) makes majority begin with twenty years. Moreover, the newest German law has also retained the period of "infantia" of the Roman law: it treats children under seven years as wholly incapable of juristic acts (BGB, Art. 104, 115,

828, 1), while it attributes to minors of over seven years a limited (§§ 107–111), and under certain circumstances even an unlimited (§ 112–113), juristic capacity. On the other hand the provision is new that paternal authority ends in all cases with majority (§ 1626; similarly, the Swiss Civil Code, § 273).

(II) **Declarations of Majority.**[1] — In view of the early age of attaining majority under the older law, there could scarcely exist any need of allowing earlier the rights of majority. From the 1200 s onward, more frequently from the time of Charles IV, and under the influence of Roman legal ideas, the emperors, the imperial counts-palatine, and Territorial princes had occasionally conceded to individual minors the rights of majority. Along with the Roman period of majority of twenty-five years, there was also received in Germany and in France the institute of the "venia ætatis", though this was substantially modified in the Territorial systems. It could be attained with eighteen years; it was granted either by the Territorial prince or by the court of wards. The latter principle has been adopted by the new Civil Code (§ 3), subject to variant regulations of State law (EG, § 147). Beside this majority, conferred by explicit declaration, many of the earlier legal systems also recognized one tacitly established, namely by marriage. According to them the principle held, "marriage emancipates" ("Heirat macht mündig"), without the husband's powers being thereby affected. This principle attained a common law validity in French customary law; it is found similarly in almost all systems of Dutch law; the English law knows only this form of "venia ætatis." In Germany, where it had remained quite unknown to the rural legal sources, it has fallen more and more into desuetude since the end of the 1700 s; men even disputed whether common law authority was not rather to be ascribed to the opposite Roman principle than to it. According to the new Civil Code an end of minority and guardianship is involved neither in marriage nor in the assumption of a public office (to which similar effects were formerly often attributed). On the other hand, the Swiss Civil Code (§ 14) has raised the old view of the German law again to honor, according acceptance to the principle "Heirat macht mündig" in its original proverbial conciseness.

(III) **Further Age Periods.** — Although the limits of majority, and after the Reception of childhood, were and are by far

[1] *Suchier*, "Geschichte der venia ætatis in Deutschland" (1908) (doctoral dissert. at Halle).

the most important of divisional age-limits, there are a few others that can be of importance in private law, — and save with such we are not concerned. In general the course of development has been to do away with these special divisions and to make decisive in all things the limits of childhood and minority. Capacity for *betrothal* was not attached in the old Germanic law to any definite age. It began according to the Canon and the common law at seven years; according to most of the particularistic systems only later, and in part of these simultaneously with capacity for *marriage*. This last, which to be sure by no means put an end to the parental right of consent, was originally included in the general right of self-control ("Mündigkeit"), and was therefore acquired at an astoundingly early age. Later it was raised in varying manner, — by an imperial statute of February 6, 1875, to the twentieth or (for women) the sixteenth year. On the other hand the new Civil Code (§ 1303) makes such capacity coincident in the case of men with majority, lowering it for women to the sixteenth year, — as the Swiss Civil Code (§ 96) does to eighteen years. Capacity to act as *guardian*, which was once often distinguished from majority, was made to coincide with this in the common law, and this rule has become general German law since the imperial statute of 1875. Capacity to make *negotiable paper* was formerly not acquired with majority, but has ceased to be distinguished from this since the German Bills of Exchange Act (1849). *Testamentary capacity* was very generally associated under the common law with the Roman ages of puberty of twelve and fourteen years. Under the modern particularistic systems it was generally acquired from the fourteenth, sixteenth, or eighteenth year onward. The new Civil Code (§ 2229, 2) gives to a minor of sixteen years capacity to make a will, except in holographic form; he can make testamentary dispositions in the form of a contract of inheritance only with his spouse (§ 2275, 2). The Swiss Civil Code (§ 467) also makes the eighteenth year determinant in this connection, but requires absolute majority for the conclusion of a contract of inheritance (§ 468). Finally, the new Civil Code recognizes a special age-division for the incidence of *tort liability*, inasmuch as it does not recognize such responsibility on the part of children and youths of from seven to eighteen years, unless at the time of committing the harmful act they possess the discrimination necessary to perceive their responsibility (§ 828, 2). Each case is therefore determined upon its merits, even though this cannot be so naïvely done as once, when children under seven years were tested by holding before them an apple and a coin, — if they reached for the apple they could not yet be held accountable for their acts.[1]

(IV) **Old Age.** — The older German law attributed also to old age an influence upon capacity for legal action. "To paganism life seemed nothing without bodily health and full use of all limbs."[2] Accordingly, he who because of his age was no longer entirely sound in body was also regarded as no longer a legal member of the community. In accord with a cruel and widely disseminated primitive custom, belated traces of whose influence are still discernible, as children incapable of life were exposed, so the old were buried alive or drowned. There is no longer mention of such practices among the Germans of historical times; but old people who had attained an age "boven ire dage" (above their days), — *i.e.* had reached sixty years of age, — were freed of many obligations. They were no longer bound to take oaths, since they were no longer able to defend their oaths with arms. They might again put themselves under guardianship, thereby sacrificing their legal independence. Modern law has in general abandoned this view. Nevertheless, even to-day the attainment of old age, — which was taken by the common law to be reached with the seventieth, and in the modern Territorial systems and also in the new Civil Code with the sixtieth, year of life, — does produce certain legal consequences, especially the right to decline the assumption of a guardianship (BGB, Art. 1786, 1. 2; similarly the Swiss Civil Code, § 383, 1).

§ 9. **Sex.**[3] — Although law has been compelled at all times and in all places to place distinctive values upon the different periods of life, the history of human culture shows us that a like compulsion has not been felt as regards the difference, equally fixed by nature, between the sexes. The position of women in

[1] *Grimm*, "Rechtsaltertümer", I, 569.

[2] *Ibid.*, 669.

[3] *Laband*, "Die rechtliche Stellung der Frauen im altrömischen und germanischen Recht", in Z. Völk. Psy., III (1865), 137–194; *Weinhold*, "Die deutschen Frauen in dem Mittelalter" (2 vols. 2d ed. 1881); *Bücher*, "Die Frauenfrage im Mittelalter" (2d ed. 1910); *Dahn*, "Das Weib im altgermanischen Recht und Leben", in his "Bausteine", VI (1884), 161 *et seq.*; *Gide*, "Étude sur la condition privée de la femme", 2d ed. by *Esmein* (1885); *Marianne Weber*, "Ehefrau und Mutter in der Rechtsentwicklung. Eine Einführung" (1907); *Hartwig*, "Die Frauenfrage im mittelalterlichen Lübeck", in Hans. G. B., XIV (1908), 35–94; *Finke*, "Die Stellung der Frau im Mittelalter", in Inter. W. Sch., IV (1910), nos. 40–41; *Fehr*, "Die Rechtsstellung der Frau und der Kinder in den Weistümern" (1912).

the law of the Germanic peoples was, indeed, during a long time, notably different from that of men. A woman was worth less than a man; the new-born child was regarded more highly if it was a boy.[1] But this unequal treatment has more and more given way, at least within the field of private law, until finally to-day in answer to one of the most insistent demands of modern legal consciousness, the equality of man and woman has within that field been fully realized.

(I) **The legal position of woman among early Germanic peoples.** — If we contemplate the conditions of the primitive Germans as they are revealed to us by the oldest direct testimony and as they can be inferred from later accounts, — leaving unconsidered the difficult question as to possible or probable prehistoric relations, — it is evident that the legal status of women, among the early Germans precisely as among other civilized people in the earlier stages of their development, was in striking contrast to the important and highly respected part played by her in economic and social life.

The wife cared, with the husband, for the family. If he drove the plow, it was she who was particularly active in caring for the livestock; she was the housekeeper, she was responsible for the training of the children, she prepared the clothing and the food. And never did the German regard women as mentally inferior; on the contrary he very commonly bowed to women as to superior beings. They were active as priestesses, seeresses, surgeons, and nurses. Yea, despite their lesser physical strength they took part, often enough, as warriors in battle; one need recall to mind only the rôle of women in the marches and battles of the Cimbrians and Teutons, and the Walkyries, the shield maidens, of whom there were historic counterparts in the North as late as in the Viking age. History and saga have tales to tell also of vigorous women rulers. The Germanic ideal of woman, to which they held true through changing times, was on one hand, in the words of a recent Scandinavian scholar,[2] " the blond and radiant woman, bringing to men peace and gentleness ", but on the other hand the warrior woman.

But this high estimate of the female sex, — the account of which by Tacitus, though indeed idealistic, is nevertheless fully confirmed in its essentials by the poetry, religion, and history of the early

[1] *Grimm*, "Rechtsaltertümer", I, 557. *Fehr*, *op. cit.*, 6.

[2] *Alexander Bugge*, "Die Wikinger. Bilder aus der nordischen Vergangenheit", translated by *Hungerland* (1906), 57.

Germans, — by no means accorded with the legal status of Germanic woman.

The family law of the Germans at their entry into history was unquestionably of a patriarchal character, — that is, one that rested upon the power of the family head over the persons belonging to his house, and which was substantially limited to that; and this involved the consequences that not only the daughters of the house but also the married women were subjected to that power of guardianship, and were therefore wanting in legal independence, — or, as it was called, self-mundium or self-representation. But what is more, mature unmarried women (of whom indeed there were probably always but few, for in the eyes of the people of that time a life for women outside marriage had in general no purpose or meaning) and widows were under the mundium of male relations. Women were thus subjected throughout life to the legal authority of other persons. This relation, known to-day as sex-guardianship, must be taken as the starting-point of the historically demonstrable evolution in the legal status of women; for the contrary view, represented by Ficker [1] and Opet,[2] which assumes an original legal equality of women and men rooted in prehistoric conditions of "mother-right", is lacking in conclusive proofs in the sources. Although among the Franks, for example, the independence of women was recognized in many directions, and true sex-guardianship appears not to be found at all in the Anglo-Saxon sources,[3] one must assume that in these racial branches, as among the Bavarians, Burgundians, and Goths, the old conditions had been overcome at an early date. Sex-guardianship was most sharply developed among the Lombards, perhaps because the military character of political organization was with them most strongly developed. The Saxon and Frisian sources likewise show strong traces of the institute. Of the Scandinavian legal systems the Swedish shows sex-guardianship in greatest development.

The reason for this legal treatment of women can only have lain, in the last analysis, in the physical weakness of the female sex, which, in an age when public and private law were not yet

[1] "Untersuchungen zur Erbenfolge der ostgermanischen Rechte" (incomplete, 4 vols. and 2 half-vols., 1891–1904).

[2] "Geschlechtsvormundschaft in den fränkischen Volksrechten", in Mitteil. I. Öst. G. F., 3d "Ergänzungsband", 1890, 1 *et seq.* Also "Zur Frage der fränkischen Geschlechtsvormundschaft", in same, 5th "Ergänzungsband", 1899, 193 *et seq.*

[3] *Pollock* and *Maitland*, "History", II, 435.

separated, was bound to influence the legal status of women in every respect. Despite all Walkyrie ideals Germanic women were generally regarded as incapable of bearing arms, notwithstanding that in case of necessity they had known how to support the men in battle. And since the community was constituted by the totality of arm-bearing persons, they could not be independent members of the community; they were incapable of serving in the army, and therefore also in the courts—for he who would participate in the popular court must be able to bear arms, since the procedural contest might at any moment be transformed into a warlike combat. Consequently, women were excluded from public life; in a legal sense they were but members of a household community, that was represented in external relations by its head. This had prejudicial effects, also, upon their capacity for legal action under the private law. They had originally no capacity for proprietary rights; for according to the legal notions of antiquity, to which representation was unknown, whoever was to hold property was bound also to administer it; that is, he must be able to perform juristic acts, which in turn required capacity to sue and be sued. Inasmuch as a judicial character was retained longest in the case of juristic acts involving realty, the proprietary incapacity of women was also longest preserved in respect to such property. Proprietary incapacity involved incapacity to inherit: "the right to inherit is either denied to all women by the oldest statutes, or is limited."[1] And even after their status in this branch of the law improved, "they were still postponed, for the most part, to men in rights of inheritance, either in that they were excluded by males of equal (if not by those of more remote) degree, or in that they received lesser shares than such; or again, in that they were treated thus, generally, in the distribution of the heritage, or were discriminated against only as respected particular classes of property."[2] Their inferior rights of inheritance lasted longest in respect to real property.

The peculiar legal status of the female sex found visible expression in the fact that the wergelds and bóts of women were, under most of the folk-laws, different from those of men. But only the West-Gothic law assigned to them, in most periods of life, lower tariffs than to the men. The law of the Alamanians and Bavarians assigned them higher sums; and this for the reason, as the Bavarian folk-law put in (4, 29), that they were unable to bear

[1] *J. Grimm*, "Rechtsaltertümer", I, 562.
[2] *v. Amira*, "Recht", 108 *sq.*

arms, "quia femina cum armis se defendere nequiverit"; for which reason this favor was also denied them once they had taken personal part in a combat, "quod inhonestum est muliebribus facere." This thought recurs in the dooms, in whose phrase women who challenge a man to battle "scorn manhood."[1] The enactments of the Lombard king Rothari fixed a sum for killing a matron, woman, or maiden that exceeded by a third the wergeld of a man. In the laws of the Franks and Anglowarns, a wergeld threefold a man's was set upon women of child-bearing age; in the Alamanian law the "mulier" enjoyed double that of the "virgo", doubtless because a woman during her child-bearing years possesses the greatest value to society. On the other hand, the Saxon folk-law distinguished the woman who had not yet borne children by a double wergeld and bót, while it set only the ordinary sums for one that had already borne children. If the pregnant woman was assured a higher wergeld, along with other advantages that were accorded her by many later legal systems, this had its reason in her greater needs of protection. Equal tariffs for men and women are found in the older Frisian sources, whereas most of the more modern ones favor women with higher bóts and wergelds, and some also give special protection to the pregnant.[2]

(II) **The Medieval Development.** — The lifelong dependence of women upon their arms-bearing male relatives could become less complete only as the importance of the sib declined, and an independent State power developed that took into its own hands the protection of the weak; and, moreover, only as the close connection between the capacity for bearing arms and for attending court began to relax. As regards the first requisite, the influence of the Church, which contributed to give prominence to the protective duties involved in guardianship, was certainly important. The restrictions placed upon women's capacity for legal action were thereby mitigated.

Sex-guardianship, though it persisted, as such, for the time being in most parts of Germany, took on an altered character. No longer based upon the inability of women to bear arms, it was transformed into a protection by court, which was manifested only in certain judicial acts which women, because of their ignorance of business, were forbidden to execute, — as *e.g.* the [judicial] livery of seisin. Moreover, whereas the nearest paternal collateral

[1] *Fehr, op. cit.*, 38.
[2] *His*, "Das Strafrecht der Friesen im Mittelalter" (1901), 142.

relative was formerly, by virtue of that relationship, the guardian of an unmarried woman, who was thus subject to a legal wardship, the woman herself later came to choose a guardian, whom the court merely confirmed; and in the end the guardian was not even intrusted with the office once for all, but was chosen only for the particular transaction demanding his co-operation. Thus the institute completely lost, as is readily understandable, its one time importance, and it is therefore not surprising that in many regions it was wholly done away with even in the Middle Ages. This was the case in many parts of Austria, in the domains of the Saxon, Bavarian, and especially of the Frankish law; in France it entirely disappeared as early as feudal times, save for scant traces. In Germany a legal status equal to that of men was accorded, at least to widows, by many legal systems.[1]

An equality of women with men in private and procedural law was by no means realized, however, by this recedence or disappearance of sex-guardianship. It is true that in the course of the Middle Ages women became capable, practically everywhere, of holding land, — indeed, very commonly also of holding fiefs. But in Germany, at least, they nevertheless remained postponed to men throughout the law of inheritance: they were incapable of acting as guardians and of making testamentary dispositions; and their testimony in court was also less highly valued than that of men. Indeed it is a striking fact that many legal systems then began for the first time to assign to them a lower wergeld. The Sachsenspiegel and the Schwabenspiegel laid this down a general principle: "iewelk wif hevet ihres mannes halve bute unde weregelt; iewelk maget unde ungemannet wif het halve bute na deme dat si geboren is" (Ssp. III, 45. § 2). However, these rules of the Law-Books and of other contemporary sources regarding wergeld and bóts had no longer any great practical importance, inasmuch as the penal system of primitive times resting on wergeld and bót soon fell into complete oblivion. In particular, they could not prevent the ever increasing prominence of women in economic life. Especially in urban industries they played a not unimportant part. In many craft-gilds they were received as independent members with full rights of fellowship, *e.g.* as wool weavers and linen weavers and as tailors; this was particularly true of the widows of deceased masters. There even existed craft-gilds consisting of women only; for example, in Cologne,

[1] *Fehr, op. cit.*, 45 *et seq.*

those of yarn-makers, gold-spinners, and silk-weavers.[1] In the second half of the Middle Ages tradeswomen acquired unlimited capacity for legal action. Many town laws—as those of Augsburg, Memmingen, Munich, Vienna, and Prague — even granted them full dispositive powers at an early date; within the scope of their business they might assume independent liabilities and prosecute a case in court; and in order to do so they did not need, if they were married, the consent of their husbands.

(III) **The Modern Development**: (1) *The Restoration of Sex-Guardianship.* — One might expect that the independence gained by women in the Middle Ages could have been developed without difficulty into a complete equality of the sexes in private law. However, within the domain of law as elsewhere, development by no means always takes place in a straight and upward line; not infrequently constraining influences divert it. A striking retrogression set in in this very instance.

That which women had gained in the Middle Ages they retained, it is true, in large measure until into the 1600 s, and the independence of women in trade and industry was practically no longer subject to any limitations whatever. But with this exception, and almost everywhere, sex-guardianship awakened to new life from the 1500 s onward; and this in a form far harsher than that of the older law. The reason for this lay perhaps in a general setting or fixation of culture. The fact that with the collapse of a household regimen men felt misgivings about making women generally independent, particularly when trade was expanding and legal business becoming more involved and difficult, may also have been a contributory cause.[2] The justification for this new sex-guardianship, — " Kriegsvogtei ", "Litiskuratel" (military guardianship, guardianship " ad litem "), as it was called, — could no longer be found in women's incapacity to bear arms. Its justification was found quite in contrast to the views of earlier Germanic and of Roman law, in an alleged defective mental acumen of the feminine sex, whose understanding, as the general Frankish ordinance of judicature of 1618 put it, is " somewhat weak and easily taken advantage of." Moreover, the more detailed development of the institution was aided by the reception of the Roman law, for though the latter

[1] *Behagel*, "Die gewerbliche Stellung der Frau im mittelalterlichen Köln", in *Below-Finke-Meinecke*, "Abhandlungen", No. 23 (1910).

[2] *Huber*, "Schw. Privatrecht", IV, 293; *Fehr*, *op. cit.*, 53 (note 3) denies the alleged revival of sex-guardianship.

knew nothing of such an institute, but recognized merely the guardianship of "impuberes", the rules applicable to the latter were carried over to the "cura sexus." In South and North Germany they were accepted and regulated. It was so in many Swiss town-laws and judicature statutes, in the Territorial law of Würtemberg, in the Saxon Constitutions of 1572, in the law of Bremen, Hamburg, and Lübeck. The Saxon and Lübeck judicial practice became especially influential. Thus every adult woman, unmarried, widowed, or separated, again received a permanent guardian as the curator of her property; a "true steward", whose acquiescence alone gave validity and obligatory force to her processual and business acts. The Roman inhibition upon the assumption by women of obligations of suretyship and "intercessio", — the so-called "benefit" or privilege of the "Senatus Consultum Vellejanum", — also attained a common law authority.

(2) *The Establishment of Legal Equality.* — Although David Mevius, the celebrated commentator on the Lübeck law, lauded the legal system attained by the reëstablishment of sex-guardianship, and keenly regretted that it was not still everywhere in force, its contrast with the rationalistic theories that were then attaining supremacy gradually became too sharp to permit of it being permanently maintained; particularly because the institute had long since been transformed from a legal safeguard for women into an empty form, rather burdensome or even dangerous to them than one affording them protection.

For this reason the German States in which it existed, following the example set by France, proceeded to abolish it. The Prussian "Landrecht", it is true, left standing in certain cases a curatorship over adult married women, and a legal adviser for adult unmarried women (II. 18, § 51); but it laid down, nevertheless, the general principle of the equal rights of both sexes, so far as exceptions did not exist by virtue of special statutes or regulations having the force of law (I. 1, § 24). No repeal was needed in the Austrian Code, since the institute had never been introduced into Austria; as was true also of Hesse, Oldenburg, Nassau, Brunswick, Detmold, Waldeck, and Frankfort, — so that it was a disputed question whether it really possessed a common law authority. In the other States it was done away with in the course of the 1800 s: first of all in Anhalt-Bernburg in 1784, and last of all in Wismar in 1875. In a few Swiss cantons it persisted until 1881. The prohibitions of "intercessio" were swept away by special statutes; in Prussia, for example, in 1869. The

German General Commercial Code and the German Industrial Code recognized the unrestricted capacity of women engaged in commerce and industry to perform juristic acts and to sue and be sued (though it is true the Commercial Code required the husband's consent to the wife's assumption of the status of a tradeswoman), and the German Code of Civil Procedure recognized the full capacity of all women to sue and be sued. Thus there remained in effect in Germany, of limitations upon the feminine sex in private law, only the postponement in inheritance in the case of feudal estates, peasant land-holdings, "fideicommissa" and land-holdings of the high nobility the limited capacity for exercising guardianships; the incapacity within the regions of the French law to take part in family councils; and incapacity for feudal tenure.

German law as it exists to-day has done away even with most of these few limitations. The Civil Code recognizes no difference between man and woman as respects capacity to act as guardian or participate in family councils. Similarly it accords to every woman, to the married woman as to others, unrestricted capacity to perform juristic acts, thereby ending the restrictive rule of the old Commercial Code. It gives to the mother parental powers along with those of the father; recognizes women equally with men as witnesses; and concedes to the male sex a preference in inheritance only in cases involving family "fideicommissa", estates subject to the system of single heirship, and the law of the high nobility. An earlier marriageable age and the rule respecting the widow's year of mourning (§ 1313) have been recognized and continued, and are the sole consequences, the field of private law, of a woman's sex.

The natural differences of sex have thus been reduced to negligible traces in private law, the law of inheritance excepted; and an evolution of a thousand years brought to a close. Man, of whom it was once possible to say that he was the oldest beneficiary of privilege, is no longer to be valued higher by the private law than woman.

§ 10. **Health.** (I) **Physical Health:** (1) *The Older Law.*— As men reasoned in primitive times, a perfect physical constitution was a necessary precondition of full capacity for legal rights and action, for from its lack they inferred mental weakness. And so long as every member of the legal community was bound to be capable of bearing arms, he was in fact prevented by bodily infirmity from participating in legal transactions.

Badly crippled and deformed persons had therefore only a limited capacity for rights. They were, as a proverb preserved by Eike von Repgow says, incapable of inheritance and feudal tenure: " Uppe altvile unde uppe dverge Ne irstirft weder len noch erve Noch uppe kropelkint ", — the puzzling word " altvile " denoting, seemingly, cretins, or children that were bewitched (Ssp. I. 4). Their relatives, however, were bound to care for and maintain them, so that some capacity for rights was after all accorded to these poor creatures.[1]

In the same class belonged lepers: they retained ownership, it is true, in property acquired by them before the appearance of the disease, but were incapable of further acquisitions. Indeed, the malady originally dissolved their marriage. They were compelled to live apart from all mankind, — which requirement was based upon the precept of the Mosaic law (3 Mos. 13, 46); they were incapable of litigation, testamentary disposition, inheritance, and the contraction of liabilities. Their lot improved only with time. The Church interested itself in them; intrusted their care to the bishops; forbade the dissolution of their marriages; founded hospitals for them; and in the beginning of the 1100 s founded a special order, of St. Lazarus, for their support. Leprosy gradually disappeared, beginning in the 1400 s; since the 1600 s it has ceased to be a plague in the greater part of Europe.

The blind, the deaf, and persons without hands or feet, were incapable of inheriting under the harsh theory of the older time, at least in feudal law.

Even persons only temporarily victims of a physical and contagious disease were, as a consequence of the views referred to, obliged to suffer a limitation of their capacity for legal action. In particular, the law denied them unrestricted dispositive power over their property. They were obliged to secure the assent of their legal heirs-apparent for dispositions both of immoveable and of moveable property. Hence the frequent tests of strength that the medieval law prescribed in order to render unquestionable one's unimpaired bodily vigor, and therewith one's unlimited dispositive capacity. A man must be able to swing himself without aid, armed with sword and shield, upon his steed, or turn with the plow a certain piece of land; a woman must be able to walk as far as the church, etc. (*supra*, p. 13). Above all, testamentary gifts from the sick bed, when one was conscious of speedily approaching death, were on this account

[1] *Heusler*, "Institutionen", I, 102.

either forbidden or similarly associated with certain tests of physical strength: for example, a gift was permitted of only so much as the sick person could hand out over the bedstock. In this connection there was the additional consideration, as the gloss of the Sachsenspiegel expresses it (I. 52, § 2), that "wi sin gut vorgift, als he is nicht mehr gebruken ne mach, di vorgift nicht dat sin is, mer gift dat siner erve is" ("he who gives away his goods when he is 'broken' and no longer able, gives away, not what is his, but gives what is his heirs'").

(2) *The Later Law.* — Already in the Middle Ages, however, the idea developed that physical sickness should not, of itself, affect legal capacity; a view to which King Liutprand gave statutory effect,[1] and which was later especially advocated by the church with an eye to the numerous gifts made to it for the good of the givers' souls. The "Kleines Kaiserrecht" (Little Book of Imperial Law) gave expression to it with the striking words: "der sin gut gibet, der gibt das mit dem mut und nit mit dem libe" (2, 36), — "he who gives his goods, gives through his spirit and not with his body."

At the same time these limitations upon the dispositive capacity of persons physically sick, and physical tests, persisted down into modern times in many legal systems, — *e.g.* in the law of Würtemberg, Lübeck, and Lüneburg; and in feudal law, consistently with its military character, the acquisition and inheritance of fiefs was very generally permitted to the ablebodied only. German law in its latest form no longer knows any general influence of bodily conditions in the private law; in case of necessity, only, the decrepit, blind, deaf, and dumb may be placed under guardianship, at their own instance or without such request. The Civil Code (§ 1910) also permits, in such cases, the institution of a curatorship. Finally, specially prescribed formalities exist as regards the juristic acts of the blind, deaf, and dumb.

(II) **Mental Health**: (1) *The Older Law.* — In earlier times insight into the nature of mental ailments and their various degrees was very slight. Typical of the naïve attitude of the old Germanic law is the passage of the Icelandic Gragas according to which he was treated as mentally afflicted who could not tell whether a saddle lay upon a horse properly or reversed, and whether he himself was sitting with his face toward the horse's head or tail. Naturally, then, the treatment of such invalids — who were designated by such expressions as "geck", "rechter dor",

[1] "Leges Langobardorum," *Liutprand*, 6.

"sinnloser man" ("booby", "downright fool", "idiot") — was not in the least determined by medical views. They were regarded as bedeviled, or as criminals; and against them men proceeded with exorcisms and imprisonment. A gentler view finally came to perceive their need of protection, founded hospitals, and, especially, placed them under guardianship; which in turn limited in another way their capacity for legal action.

(2) *The Later Law.* — With the Reception, the Roman distinctions, supplemented by those of the Canon law, found adoption in Germany: insanity ("Wahnsinn"), which renders one incapable of any juristic act whatever, but may be interrupted by "lucida intervalla"; feeble-mindedness or idiocy ("Geistesschwäche", "Blödsinn"), which only in its extreme degrees resulted in complete incapacity for action, and otherwise only in a limited incapacity like that of "impuberes" above seven years of age; finally, mere intellectual limitations which might be considered in individual cases in order to avert prejudicial consequences. These indefinite categories were variously readjusted in the later Territorial systems according to the ability, for the most part scant, of the jurists of each period to utilize in the law the progress of medical science. Most important of these developments was a peculiar judicial process of interdiction, which received its final form in the present Code of Civil Procedure (§§ 645 *et seq.*). Interdiction, so long as it continues, effects incapacity for action without regard to lucid intervals. In addition to interdiction on account of such mental disorder ("Geisteskrankheit") as results in incapacity for juristic acts, the Civil Code, which followed in the main the system of the Prussian "Landrecht", recognizes an interdiction on account of feeble-mindedness which places the interdicted person under the disabilities of infants (§§ 6, 104, 114). Besides insane persons, who are interdicted and subjected to guardianship, those persons are also incapable of juristic acts who are permanently in a condition of morbid mental disorder that renders impossible their free volition (§ 104).

(III) **Prodigality:** (1) *The Older Law.* — The medieval law already knew an interdiction of prodigals, which very generally assumed a form certainly somewhat drastic. For young spendthrifts, especially in the cities, were not infrequently simply locked up for the betterment of their habits, or were banished. Subjection to guardianship also frequently occurred, however; being decreed either at the instance of the next relatives or of the authorities, officially, in order that such persons might not, as paupers, become a burden on the towns. A definite part of his property was customarily left at the free disposition of the ward; in respect to the rest he was incapable of legal action.

(2). *The Later Law.* — The Roman "cura prodigi" was further developed in harmony with older native principles, but without producing a wholly consistent regulation of the institution. The present Civil Code has followed the Austrian, Saxon, and Hamburg law by postulating as an element in the conception of prodigality the condition that the spendthrift expose himself or his family to want, whereas the Prussian "Landrecht" accepted as sufficient an unjustifiable and continual squandering of his property. A person put under guardianship as a prodigal has a limited legal capacity as in the case of an infant (§ 114). The Swiss Civil Code (§ 370), going still farther, has introduced an interdiction on the ground of incompetent management of one's affairs, — the precondition to which is not culpable incompetency (prodigality), but simply bad management.[1]

(IV) **Guardianship of Dipsomaniacs.** — Guardianship of habitual drunkards is an innovation of the present Civil Code. The Swiss Civil Code has also adopted it (§ 370).

§ 11. **Legal Status of Aliens.**[2] — The law not only takes account of the natural differences between men in age, sex, and bodily health; it also assigns a different status to persons on account of certain legal qualities.

In the first place there is a distinction between natives — fellow-members of a commune, state, empire, or race — and aliens.

(I) **The Older Law.** — Primitive man regards foreigners, whom he neither knows nor understands, with the utmost mistrust. And in the earliest times, which as yet hardly knew a friendly commerce of folk with folk or land with land, but almost exclusively conflicts in war, it is true that most foreigners with whom men came in contact were enemies, wrongdoers, exiles, or spies. Aside from these, foreigners hardly crossed the boundaries, unless as beggars or peddlers. Law existed solely for the fellows of the folk or racial branch who felt themselves united, above all by a common tongue. And therefore among the early Germanic races "the earliest antiquity accorded no right to foreigners."[3] And foreigners were to them, at first, those who spoke differently,

[1] *Hedemann*, "Fortschritte des Zivilrechts", I, 73.
[2] *Ibid.*, I, 65 *et seq.*
[3] *J. Grimm*, "Rechtsaltertümer", II, 467.

i.e. the Romans, Kelts, Slavs; also, later, the North German to the South Germanic races; and finally, with the development of fixed constitutional conditions, "all those who were not united by the bonds of a general popular assembly, who did not stand together in sacrificial community and in a close community of law."[1] Only gradually did men come to conceive of those persons as strangers who were not native within a "Land", — that is, within the domain of a racial branch bound together as a legal community, — or within the Empire, — that is, within several such "Lands" subject to a common sovereign;[2] until later, in the Middle Ages, the conception of aliens was made to cover not only the subjects of a foreign State but even persons belonging to another commune. In consequence of the territorial parcellation of government, which eventually threatened infinity, alienage and the law respecting aliens therefore played a very great and troublesome part in actual legal life. Under primitive law foreigners ("Fremden", from "fram" = 'from', 'away'), like slaves, were rightless; for the law of a racial branch, folk, or "Land" in which they were strangers had no application to them, and their own law, attached to them by birth, found no recognition abroad. Thus the conception of the alien, the "Elende" (from Old High G. "alilanti" = Ausländer, "outlander"), ran over into that of "unfortunate" ("Elend" = misery); just as in Latin the "hostis" (corresponding to the German "Gast" = guest) came to mean enemy.[3] The harshness of this viewpoint, which marked the sharpest possible retrogression in comparison with views already practically realized in the Roman world, was, it is true, considerably mildened by the right of hospitage, just as the actual lot of the unfree was better than their legal status (§ 13, *infra*). Out of the hallowed custom of granting to the guest, "to the man coming from away", the protection of a roof, there developed at an early date a legal duty upon whose violation the folk-laws imposed punishments; and Charles the Great later made these still harsher in a capitulary.[4] Such a duty was indispensable in a time when there were no inns or hospices.[5] To the stranger, who travelled ("wandeln", from "wargenga", "wara" = protection) thenceforth under the protection of his host, it secured indirect participation in the local legal

[1] *Wilda*, "Das Strafrecht der Germanen" (1842), 672.
[2] *Wilda*, "Strafrecht."
[3] *v. Amira*, "Recht", 92.
[4] "Capitulare missorum generale", a. 802, c. 27 (M. G., Cap. I, 96).
[5] *Müllenhoff*, "Deutsche Altertumskunde", IV (1900), 328.

fellowship, inasmuch as the host represented him legally. The guest might not dally, it is true, above three days; a longer harborage might all too easily involve dangers for the host, who was also answerable for the stranger under the criminal law.

In time, even aliens who did not put themselves under the protection of a native folk-man also attained a secure status through the fact that the king held it his duty to appear as their protector. This royal protection, which was interposed for their fuller security, and to whose development ecclesiastical influences and Roman practices doubtless contributed, is found among the Anglo-Saxons, Lombards, Franks, and Bavarians. But above all, the establishment of the Frankish empire, in which were united under one supreme authority not alone most of the German racial branches that had lived until then apart but also foreign races, was bound to modify to the advantage of foreigners the views theretofore prevailing respecting them. Through the introduction of the principle of the personality of law (*supra*, p. 2) the laws of all the racial branches and people united in the Empire acquired equal prestige and authority, and "if the Saxon was bound to recognize the Italian as his fellow in the Empire, and a subject of legal rights, why should he deny to the Englishman, to whom he felt himself, after all, more nearly related, what he was forced to concede to the other?"[1] The Frankish king regarded himself as the protector of aliens within his Empire, granting them his own (*i.e.* the Frankish) law, — although in exchange he confiscated their estates when they died; which, be it noted, was not possible under the Lombard law, save in default of sons. By this concession aliens in the Empire were also provided with at least an actual, albeit not unlimited, capacity for rights; they had, for example, a lesser wergeld than the ordinary freemen of the Empire.

But these achievements of Carolingian civilization, like others, were only transitory. In connection with political disintegration, the segregation of Territories and of cities as independent political units, there appeared in the Middle Ages a retrogressive tendency toward an exclusiveness, ever more strictly enforced, against aliens, and an increasing favor to natives, although it did not come again to the point of a complete outlawry of the former.

These ungenerous views gave origin to a series of special legal institutions which played a considerable rôle in the later Middle Ages and down into the modern period.

[1] *Heusler*, "Institutionen", I, 145.

(1) *The Right of Enserfing* ("Wildfangsrecht").—As a consequence of the old idea of the rightlessness of aliens, the local feudal lords treated as their serfs all strange people who remained on their land a year and a day without their original lord following to reclaim them, and without voluntarily subjecting themselves to a native lord,—so-called "Wildfänge", "Wildflügel", "Bachstelzen" ('trapped game', 'wild birds',—*i.e.* men taken up while wandering about in the wilds).[1]

This right, widespread also in France, was laid claim to particularly by the counts of the Rhine Palatinate, on the ground of a regality ("Wildfangsregal") alleged to have been granted to them over all lands of the Frankish law; which claim was the cause of countless and long-protracted feuds and law-suits.

(2) *The so-called "landsassiatus."*—An alien was denied the unconditional right to buy real estate. He was required first to take an oath of allegiance and become a burgher or "Landsasse" (a person settled on the land); that is, to submit himself in all his legal relations to the law of the locality in which the land lay. Possession of land therefore involved a general subjection to the law of the jurisdiction,—the so-called "landsassiatus plenus." Or it might be held sufficient that the alien obligate himself to take his law from the native judge in transactions or actions affecting the possession of land,—so-called "landsassiatus minus plenus." The "landsassiatus plenus", which held sway in Hesse, Bavaria, Würtemberg, Saxony, Mecklenburg, and in some parts of Prussia, owed its origin to the increasing power of the State in the modern period. In Mecklenburg, for example, it was only in the early 1700 s that theory and practice began to develop and apply it, and only in 1853 was it sanctioned there in its full extent by statute, being then done away with in 1873. Elsewhere, it was earlier abolished.

(3) *The Right of Aubaine* ("Fremdlingsrecht", "ius albingii", "droit d'aubaine"). Aliens ("albini", *i.e.* doubtless = "alibi nati") who died in a country could pass their estate to their relatives abroad either not at all or only partially; the local government took possession of the estate of a deceased alien, in whole or in part, as of an estate without heirs. Frederick II, following the example of earlier papal statutes, already forbade this custom by a special imperial statute, the authentic "Omnes peregrini" (c. 10, Cod. 6, 59). Nevertheless it persisted,

[1] *J. Grimm*, "Rechtsaltertümer", I, 452.

and was practised also by feudal lords within their domains; the more excusably because in that imperial statute such abatement was expressly forbidden only to the harboring "hospes."

(4) *The Inheritance Tax* ("Abschoss", "ius detractus," "gabella hereditaria"). — Aliens did not receive in full property given to them by a native's last will, but were bound to suffer a reprise by the local governmental authorities of a tenth to a half.

(5) *The Tax on Emigration* ("Nachsteuer", "gabella emigrationis"). — Emigrants were bound to deliver to the government as a tax a part (one tenth to one half) of the property with which they desired to leave the country.

(6) *The Medieval Law of Wreck* ("Strandrecht", *infra*, § 60), in so far as it involved not only the occupancy of wreck but also the inservitude of the shipwrecked sailor, had its basis in the original rightlessness of aliens.

(II) **Modern Development.** — The increasing commerce of modern times could not permanently endure the fetters of the right of "aubaine." It was done away with first of all in Italy, where this view appeared at an early day in legal theory, and where, in Milan for example, the principle of the equal rights of aliens was declared so early as the late 1300 s. In Germany the town laws, at least, secured from the beginning to the foreigner, the "guest" within the district of the city-law, the same legal protection as to the native. And therefore in the city the estate of a deceased guest was handed over to his heirs abroad without question and without deduction, if they removed thither within a year and a day; only under the opposite conditions did the municipal authorities lay claim to it — as they did also, under the like conditions, with respect to natives. It is indeed true that such guests were later subjected in German cities, as elsewhere, to manifold restrictions. When a burgher left a heritage in movables to foreign residents, a tax was levied; certain articles of inheritance, such as military trappings and the widow's paraphernalia were not even allowed "to cross the bridge"; above all, the acquirement of realty in the city was forbidden to alien residents. In addition there were disabilities upon them in judicial procedure. The aggregate of these principles made up the municipal law of alien residents ("Gästerecht"). Nevertheless, this should not be thought of as derived from the old law of alienage ("Fremdenrecht"); it seems rather to owe its origin to "tendencies toward monopolistic exclusiveness" only gradually gaining authority in the cities.[1]

Still later men were again obliged to introduce ameliorations out of regard for commerce. Outside of the cities, too, the old disabilities upon aliens in time lost ground. For the alleviation of the distress prevailing among their transient population, there were formed in many localities in Germany in the 1300 s and 1400 s, most likely under the influence of the Church, special associations, so-called "Distress ('Elenden') Brotherhoods", which provided for the Christian burial of foreigners and also for their maintenance and hospitage.[2] At an early date, too, the hardships of the right of "aubaine" were mildened for certain classes of aliens; as for example for merchants traveling to fairs and other marts, for diplomatic representatives, and in Italy for foreign students. The treaties between different Territorial rulers that appear at times as early as the 1200 s, and become thereafter more and more frequent, also brought considerable alleviations; in them the compacting parties bound themselves to treat equally the subjects of both, and in particular to afford them safe conduct (treaties of safe conduct and legal redress).[3] But a general and equal treatment of all subjects of the Empire within all its Territories, the old German Empire was incapable of bringing about. The Constitution of the German Confederation swept away for the first time at least the most oppressive limitations by abolishing the "landsassiatus", the inheritance tax, and the emigration tax for all German subjects (Art. 18). The right of "aubaine" between German and non-German States was not affected by this provision, but it also disappeared in most of the States through international treaties or through statutes, — as *e.g.* the Prussian constitution (Art. 11). Thus the principle that the alien stands on an equality with the native, already laid down by the Prussian "Landrecht" and the Austrian Code (though there still broken by exceptions), and demanded among the "fundamental rights" of 1848 (Art. I, § 4), is recognized today in Germany as in most

[1] *Rudorff*, "Zur Rechtsstellung der Gäste im mittelalterlichen städtischen Prozess", in *Gierke's* "Untersuchungen", No. 88 (1907). With which compare *A. Schultze* in Z². R. G., XXVIII (1907), 502–511, and Hist. Z. CI (3d ser. Vol. 5, — 1908), 473–528, on "Gästerecht und Gastgericht in den deutschen Städten des Mittelalters"; *Joachim* in Hans. G. B. XV (1907), 218–236. *H. Meyer* in Deut. Litt. Z. 1909, No. 48; *O. Loening*, "Das Erbrecht der Fremden nach den deutschen Stadtrechten des Mittelalters," in "Festschrift *O. Gierke* dargebracht" (1911), 285–303.

[2] *v. Moeller*, "Die Elendenbrüderschaften" (1906).

[3] *A. Schultze*, "Zum Geleits- und Gästerecht," in Vj. Soz. W. G. IX (1911), 229–237.

other civilized States. France alone still remains an exception, inasmuch as Art. 11 of the Code Civil, excluding aliens from "droits civils", has not yet been repealed. In Germany limitations exist today, generally speaking, only upon the subjects of such States as do not concede to Germans equality with their own subjects. Only a few peculiar rules, respecting aliens, partly of the Empire and partly of the States, are known today to the private law. State law can, for example, make the acquisition of realty by foreign juristic persons dependent upon the approval of the State; aliens are barred from acquiring interests in ships, and are less favored than natives in the law of copyright, trade marks, and trade names; they have no right to reside in Germany; etc. Moreover, according to Art. 3 of the Imperial Constitution, which has established the common nativity of all Germans, only persons from outside the Empire are aliens in the eye of the law. In Switzerland the Civil Code has abolished all older Cantonal limitations upon aliens.

§ 12. **Religion.** (I) **The Influence of Religion upon Private Law, generally:** (1) *In the Middle Ages,* and for the Christian population comprehended in the Catholic church, membership in that church was just as essential a precondition of an individual's legal existence as was his membership in the State. He who stood outside the one ecclesiastical community could not be a member, either, of the secular community of law: from the viewpoint of the medieval-Christian theory of the world, heretics, heathen, and Jews were not persons in a legal sense. Hence it was that the anathema of the Church drew after it the outlawry of the Empire, and he who fell from faith committed in so doing a secular crime, which the German emperor, exactly like the later Roman rulers, threatened with severe punishments.[1]

(2) *Only in Modern Times* and as a result of the schism of faiths, did a change take place in these views and conditions.[2] Not, to be sure, directly. For the Reformers and their followers likewise persisted to the end in the opinion that State and Church constituted an indissoluble unity, and that therefore all subjects of the State must be members of the same church. Although the Protestants were unable to secure dominance over the followers of the old faith, they did attain through the Augsburg

[1] *Eichmann,* "Acht und Bann im Reichsrecht des Mittelalters." ("Görres-Gesellschaft zur Pflege der Wissenschaft im katholischen Deutschland. Sektion für Rechts- und Sozialwissenschaft", Vol. 6, 1909.)

[2] *Rieker,* "Die rechtliche Stellung der evangelischen Kirche Deutschlands in ihrer geschichtlichen Entwicklung bis zur Gegenwart" (1893).

religious peace of 1555, as Augsburg co-religionists, the status of a merely temporarily tolerated sect, and thus an exceptional status as compared with the legal position of the Jews. Alike in the Empire and in the Territories, one exclusive church was recognized, after as before, as the only possible arrangement; but with this difference, that these Territorial churches conformed to the confession of the Territorial ruler, and might therefore be either Catholic or Evangelical. Accordingly, here too membership in the Territorial church remained the first essential to the recognition of legal personality.

The triumph of the modern scientific spirit, which prepared the way for the dominance of the "law of nature", deprived of their foundation these medieval views. Men came to recognize that the State was not appointed to care for the spiritual welfare of its subjects, but merely for the external legal order; the religious confession of its citizens might therefore be indifferent to it, provided only that the faiths thus practised side by side did not disturb the public peace. Religious faith thus lost its former importance for the legal status of the individual. However, it always remained a self-evident precondition that there must be in question a Christian confession, — membership in one of the two Christian faiths recognized in the Empire.

In the peace of Westphalia this view received recognition as a fundamental principle. But although that peace assured to the Catholic and Evangelical estates of the Empire an "æqualitas exacta mutuaque", in contrast with the mere sufferance of the Augsburg Peace, still this meant only a parity of the two confessions as such, and not at all an equality of the individual adherents to those faiths. On the contrary, the peace explicitly confirmed the "ius reformandi" (*i.e.* "exercitium religionis") of the Territorial rulers; that is, their competence to determine, within the limits of action allowed them by the Empire, the religions of their domains, and therefore to declare either one of the confessions recognized by the Empire to be the Territorial church. Those subjects who did not conform to the State church, the Territorial ruler was not bound to respect: he might, as a last resort, compel them to emigrate, though without loss of property (the so-called "flebile beneficium emigrationis"). An exception to the "frightful" principle "cuius regio eius religio", was made only for those Evangelical subjects of Catholic estates of the Empire, and those Catholic subjects of Evangelical estates of the Empire, who in the year 1624 had been in enjoyment of the right of free religious worship. This exception, moreover, did not exist in Austria; which thus was given the opportunity to root out, with every instrument of force, the Evangelical faith widespread within its Territories.

In time the drastic principle of a rigid State church received further ameliorations in practice, especially through recognition of the principle, first applied in Brandenburg, that Lutherans and Reformed need not be affected by a change in the confession of their Territorial ruler. There was thus developed in most of the Territories during the 1700 s a "de facto" situation under which one church was, indeed, still recognized as the Territorial church, but sufferance was assured to the two other churches, as such, and likewise to their members.

The first break, in principle, with the regimen of a State church was made by Prussia, where the concession of religious freedom as freedom of the individual in conscience and confession, the neutrality of the State in confessional questions, and a liberal toleration of sectarianisms, were principles that determined, as unwritten law, the practical ecclesiastical policy as early as the beginning of the 1700 s. They first took the form of written law in the draft of the General Code (1784–85), afterwards in the Woellner religious edict of 1788, and finally in the "Allgemeines Landrecht" (1794).[1] All three Christian churches received the status of recognized and privileged corporations. Every difference of legal status was thereby utterly abolished as between their adherents; and practically the same was true of the other Christian sects, inasmuch as these secured thenceforth the same toleration which had theretofore been enjoyed by the two minor principal confessions under the dominant one. The Prussian legislation was not yet bold enough to extend this toleration and equality of treatment to non-Christians, and to those who adhered to no religious community whatever; it allowed itself to be forestalled in this respect by France, and even by Austria. For as the Code Civil (§ 8) conceded to every Frenchman the enjoyment of civil rights, so the Austrian Code (§ 39) declared positively and explicitly that, aside from certain statutory exceptions, religious differences should have no influence upon civil rights; a principle which, to be sure, in Austria's case remained simply a paper law. The illiberal view of the Prussian "Landrecht" was raised by the Act of the German Confederation to the dignity

[1] *Anschütz*, "Die Verfassungsurkunde für den Preussischen Staat. Ein Kommentar für Wissenschaft und Praxis", I (1912), 183 *et seq.*

of a general German federal law, by the provision (in Art. 16, 1): "Differences between Christian sects shall be the excuse for no difference in the enjoyment of civil and political rights within the States and districts of the German Confederation." Accordingly, the adherents of "Christian sects" — that is, as was officially determined, the three Christian confessions recognized since the Westphalian Peace — were necessarily treated with complete legal equality in all German States; they could no longer be compelled to emigrate, nor be otherwise put at a disadvantage, one with another, in any way. On the other hand the Act of Confederation did not declare how the adherents of other confessions or sects were to be treated; moreover, it left to the individual States complete liberty to determine what churches they would permit within their territory, and what measure of rights they would accord to churches and confessions as such. Most of the confederated States, following the Prussian example, authorized the three confessions recognized by imperial law as churches entitled to equal rights (though Mecklenburg, for example, did not); and all of them maintained the difference between them and other religious societies.

The movement of 1848 first led to the complete abolition of the old restrictions. The "German Fundamental Rights" (Art. III, §.14. 16) declared for the extension of the principle of the Act of Confederation to the extent that not only members of the three recognized Christian sects, but also the adherents of every confession of faith whatsoever, and equally those who adhered to no religious community, should participate as equals in the enjoyment of civil and political rights. Some States gave positive authority to this principle within their territory, — so *e.g.* Prussia, by the second subdivision of Art. 12 of its constitution: "The enjoyment of civil and political rights is independent of religious faith." The North German Confederation and the present German Empire, soon after their establishment, converted this principle into a main pillar of the centralized legal order under them newly realized. First, the Act of Nov. 1, 1867, respecting liberty of domicile, provided that freedom of residence, domicile, industry, and acquisition of realty, should be denied to no subject of the Confederation on account of his religious faith. And thereafter the Act of July 3, 1869, "the fundamental law of freedom of conscience within the German Empire," — the single short paragraph of which statute embodies one of the most important achievements of modern times, — declared in quite general and unqualified terms that "all limitations whatever upon civil or political rights, based upon differences of religious faith, are hereby abolished. In particular, competence to take part in communal and national assemblies and for the exercise of public office shall be independent of religious faith."

Notwithstanding this, certain restrictions were regarded as still existent, — for example the well-known prohibition in certain States of marriages between Christians and non-Christians; but all imperfections possibly still remaining in the law were finally remedied by the imperial statute of personal status of Feb. 6, 1875, and the present Civil Code. Difference of religious faith is today neither an obstacle to marriage nor a ground for divorce or disinheritance. And though adherence to a definite religion or confession can still, by by-laws ("Statuten") or by legal agreements, be made a precondition to the acquisition or the exercise of rights, this is a result of the principle of freedom of contract, and has nothing to do with the earlier statutory inequality, no more than has the provision of the present Civil Code (§ 1779) that in the choice of a guardian regard shall be had to the religious faith of the ward.

The most important result of the statute of 1869 was the establishment of complete legal equality between Christians and Jews.

(II) **The Status of the Jews in Private Law:**[1] (1) *In the Middle Ages.* — The position of the Jews has been a peculiar one from the earliest times. They were not heathen, since they believed in the same God as did Christians, nor yet heretics, persons fallen from the true faith; but persons who held aloof therefrom. But they were distinguished from the Christian peoples among whom they lived not alone by their faith, but also by their race: they were not fellow-countrymen, but, despite their domicile among them, aliens. These two facts were decisive of their legal treatment, but the Jewry statutes of the Middle Ages laid the greater emphasis now on one, now on the other. The fundamental idea, as a consequence of which the Jews were regarded as adherents of an alien confession, inimical to the dominant State religion and against whose influences this was to be protected, came from

[1] *Stobbe*, "Die Juden in Deutschland während des Mittelalters in politischer, sozialer und rechtlicher Beziehung" (1866); *Scherer*, "Beiträge zur Geschichte des Judenrechts im Mittelalter. Erster Band: Die Rechtsverhältnisse der Juden in den deutsch-österreichischen Ländern" (1901); *Caro*, "Sozial- und Wirtschaftsgeschichte der Juden im Mittelalter und der Neuzeit. Band I: Das frühere und das hohe Mittelalter" (1908), — one of the "Schriften herausgegeben von der Gesellschaft zur Förderung der Wissenschaft des Judentumes").

the later legislation of the Roman Empire, to which the legislation of the Germanic States that arose within the territory of that Empire, — the East and West Gothic, Lombard, Burgundian, and Merovingian,—conformed. What was most important, the medieval church also made that view its own. It granted to the Jewish religion as such, toleration, and to its adherents protection of life, property, and religious customs and institutions; but, on the other hand, it pursued with every means the end of protecting Christianity against any possible influence of Judaism. Numerous papal bulls for their protection served to secure the Jews against force; and countless enactments, partly of a precautionary and partly of a more directly protective character, served for the security of Christianity. Thus the Canonic law of Jewry, gradually given form by the Church, which attained authority throughout the Christian world, and in many lands — as *e.g.* France and England, — was embodied also in the legislation of the State, forbade, among other things, marriage between Christians and Jews, and the holding of public offices by Jews; they might not employ a Christian servant, nor reside in all parts, nor accuse or beat witnesses against Christians; they were obliged to wear a dress that distinguished them from Christians; Christians might neither lease nor rent them goods or houses; and other like restrictions.

On the other hand the medieval Germanic law, to which naturally the Church's standpoint was essentially alien, and in which this received even later but a secondary recognition, and which required membership in the folk as a precondition of capacity for rights (*supra*, p. 73), treated the Jews as aliens; that is, as rightless, like the slaves. The law of alienage formed the foundation for the treatment of the Jews in the Frankish as well as in the German Empire of the Middle Ages. Nevertheless, the actual situation of the Jews, like that of the slaves, was not an unfavorable one down into the 1100 s. For in that early period of the Middle Ages they were an indispensable part of the population as the chief middlemen in trade and banking; and rulers therefore exempted them, through the conferment of special rights, from the results of the law of alienage. The Carolingian kings may possibly have already issued patents of protection to individual Jews, though a true law for the protection of the Jews certainly did not then exist.[1] Such a law took body, however, in the

[1] *Tangl*, "Zum Judenschutzrecht unter den Karolingern", in Neues Archiv der Gesellschaft für ältere deutsche Geschichtskunde, XXXIII (1908), 197 *et seq.*

course of the Middle Ages as a result of such patents of protection, which were granted with ever-growing frequency by rulers, and were not only conceded in favor of specific individuals, but in some cities — as *e.g.* in Speier, Worms, Regensburg — were issued from the 1000 s onward in favor of all Jews dwelling therein. The privileges they enjoyed in Worms were extended by Frederick II in 1236 to all the Jews in Germany. This was the first general Jewry law of Germany.[1] The Jews were generally assured in these privileges of protection against riots, protection of their property, exemptions from special taxes, dispositive powers over their property, a status in court as witnesses which as compared with the unfree was a favored one, and also protection of their lives: from which it is evident that without such special royal protection they were rightless; they received the status of royal serfs, of whom the king could fully dispose. In return for the concession of their charters of liberties the Jews were bound to render taxes into the royal exchequer, in recompense for the king's renunciation in such charters of the powers he enjoyed under the alienage law, and which since the Hohenstauffen period had constituted an independent regality, the "Judenregal." Thence came the expression, as a general designation for the Jews, "cameral" or "exchequer" serfs ("servi camere nostre"), which was first officially used in a Jewry statute of Frederick II. In this expression, and in the burdensome tributes imposed on them as a result of this "cameral" serfdom, — tributes collected not only by the kings but also by the Territorial rulers fitted out by them with the Jewry regality, — was evidenced the worsened condition which the Jews had to bear with, following the Crusades; partly because of the increasing sharpness of religious divisions, partly, and especially, in consequence of economic reasons. As the cities grew prosperous, and the Christian city population turned increasingly to trade and came to see in the Jews inconvenient competitors, these lost their one-time monopolistic position in wholesale commerce and moneylending, and were forced to resort to huckstering and usury, and to petty trade in money, second-hand articles, horses, and cattle. The gilds, too, and therewith many trades, remained closed to them; as also, of course, all political rights in State and commune. The hatred of the Christian population found vent in cruel persecutions, and the unscrupulous administration of the "Judenregal" led to ever more extreme legal restrictions. Their liberty of domi-

[1] *Scherer, op. cit.*, 75.

cile was abolished, their emigration without special license forbidden, the property of emigrants and of heirless decedents confiscated. They were arbitrarily pawned and given away, their claims against debtors were annulled or scaled.[1] The Roman Canonic inhibition of marriages between Christians and Jews, the assignment of Jews' claims to Christians (as a " cessio in potiorem "), and limitations upon choice of domicile came to be universally established; so too the limited probative value of their testimony and of their trade books. Even the advantages generally accorded them over Christians, such as their privilege as usurers and receivers of stolen goods (*infra*, §§ 58, 86), had something hateful about them which contributed to the lowering of their repute.

This complete dependence of the Jewry upon the Christian authorities, their " cameral " serfdom, — in view of which it signified little that peace and protection were guaranteed them in national peaces and special charters, in return for cash payments; and the injustice and even cruelty of which did not remain wholly hidden even to the naïve view of the Middle Ages, —men endeavored to explain by a strange historical fable, which the medieval law books adopted ("Sachsenspiegel," III, 7, § 3; "Schwabenspiegel," Text G, 260, 3). The fable ran that Titus had bailed to the imperial exchequer the Jews that survived the destruction of Jerusalem. Their dependence had its true basis in the medieval right of " aubaine ", and it could only lessen when the views that underlay that right had been displaced by others more humane.

(2) *Modern Times.* — This change did not take place until in the last centuries, under the influence of Rationalism. Here also French legislation, which by a decree of 1791 had assured to the Jews all civic rights and made them equals in all respects of other citizens, was of pioneer influence. Within the area in which the Code Civil had authority these principles acquired authority also in Germany; a few of the other German States, also, soon followed this example, as for example Prussia in its Jewry Edict of March 11, 1812. The German Act of Confederation (Art. 16) provided that the Federal Assembly should take under consideration " how the amelioration of the civic condition of adherents of the Jewish faith in Germany might be realized in a manner as uniform as possible, and how, in particular, the enjoyment of civic rights might be secured and assured them in the confederated States in consideration of their assumption of all civic duties;

[1] *Scherer*, 79 *et seq.*

but until then" — the article continued — "the rights already granted the adherents of this faith *by* individual States of the Federation shall be preserved to them." The federal law here promised was never passed. Indeed, some States, as *e.g.* Brunswick, did not scruple to sweep away the betterments realized in the French period, and to introduce again the old, illiberal legal conditions; which result was, it must be admitted, made possible by the calculated wording ("by", not "in") of Article 16. Nevertheless, most of the confederated States resigned themselves in the course of the century to the repeal of the old Jewry statutes. Complete legal equalization was first declared, however, by the federal statute of 1869. The Talmud thereby lost that significance as an actually authoritative legal source which, at least in those States in which the rabbinic jurisdiction had not already been abolished by special statutes (as *e.g.* in Prussia by the Edict of 1812), it had retained in the rabbinic courts that existed for the trial of purely Jewish causes. The German system of judicature, in authority since 1879, no longer recognizes any special Jewish courts.

§ 13. **Status. (I) Status in the Legal Sense.** — Status ("Stand") was originally a social conception. A universal human impulse draws like and like together and calls into existence group-formations within society. Such strata, originally purely social, are doubtless lacking at no stage of human culture. They invariably rest, in last analysis, upon a conviction of the unequal worth of the different elements of society. So long as the mode of life and distribution of wealth are uniform, they are little in evidence. The commonalty, in general still socially homogeneous, usually endeavors all the more strictly to close its ranks to elements that do not belong within its circle. But with rising cultural conditions social grouping increases. The personal merits of individual members of the folk, and descent from such preëminent men, exert a marked influence upon public matters; the growing disparities in the distribution of wealth divide the population into rich and poor; the increasing complexities of occupation lead to a distinction of callings regarded as suitable or unsuitable to men's respective status.

This stratification of the population, in itself merely social, assumes a legal character as soon as the social position of the individual, his membership in one or another group, comes to involve for him definite legal consequences. The relative rank of social classes becomes one of legal status, in that legal preferences are attributed to the higher groups, as such, and to their members, and denied to the lower. Social groups become estates in a legal sense in that certain legal relations are recognized as existent only between the members of a class, thus uniting these in a legal community distinct from non-members. The legal consequences springing from membership in such an estate may vary in nature and extent. Moreover, though the chief significance of the system of social estates lay, in general, within the domain of public law, it also influenced the position of the individual in private law.

The correlation of social estates reflects in its development the general progress of social and economic relations, of which it was an expression. It is subjected to continual change. Side by side with old groupings new and inconsistent ones therefore frequently appear, without being able, at first, to displace the old; and thus there often result peculiar cross groupings. The legal delimitation by no means always coincides with the cleavage lines of social, political, and economic groups. Not infrequently legal distinctions maintain themselves in formal authority in consequence of their relative inelasticity; notwithstanding that they have been left behind in the ceaseless flux of social changes, and have thereby lost their essential justification. On the other hand, the law is generally late in taking cognizance of altered social groupings. Every system of social estates strives toward the utmost possible exclusiveness. To status in a legal sense a strict delimitation is essential. Birth, calling, possessions, operate as segregating factors. Only the estates based on birth are strictly exclusive, for only in them is there a permanent union of equal fellows; they do not necessarily involve a caste-like exclusiveness. For the same reason the occupational and property estates also tend to acquire a heritable character.

(II) **The Old System of Social Estates**: (1) *The general development of the system.*[1] — At the beginning of historical times a homogeneous class of freemen formed the core of the Germanic races. Beside it, — at least according to the view prevailing up to the present day, — the half-free and unfree were subordinate in number and importance. The law of the present day has, with one inconsiderable exception (*infra*, III), brought about a complete abolition of all class differences. In a certain sense it has thus returned to the starting-point of develpoment. But

[1] See for a brief sketch *Seeliger*, "Ständische Bildungen im deutschen Volk" (rectoral address, Leipzig, 1905).

the twenty centuries intervening are filled with a bewildering wealth of class groupings.

Beside the mass of common freemen, among whom the nobility constituted originally a class merely socially preëminent, there existed even in early Germanic times an unfree class separated from the rest of the population in the sharpest conceivable manner. They were not in any sense members of the legal community; not persons in a legal sense, but things. We may therefore say that there was herein embodied no class differentiation whatsoever, inasmuch as the unfree stood outside the legal community.[1] But the unfree might be manumitted, and emancipation usually secured to them half-freedom. Such half-free persons, or serfs ("Hörigen", "Liten", "Aldien"), were capable of rights; but they continued to be marked off from the full freemen by the lack of liberty of domicile.

After the migrations of the Germanic races the contrast between freedom and unfreedom lost definiteness, the unfree securing legal personality and thereby becoming folk-fellows. Besides this, whole classes of the unfree moved upward, as settled rent-paying peasants, into the class of the half-free, which was thus notably increased. Where the old folk-nobility maintained itself against extinction by the kingship, it developed into an estate superior also in law to the commonalty. Thus there were gradually differentiated four blood estates: the noble, the free, the half-free ("Hörige", serfs), and the unfree ("Knechte"). This fourfold legal hierarchy of freedom found visible expression in a scale of varying wergelds.

But development soon went further. Altered economic and political relations led in the Frankish period to a transformation of momentous consequences of this social organization of the Germanic epoch. The accumulation of riches in the hands of great landholders, secular and ecclesiastic, called into being a new aristocracy of wealth, while the royal service created a new nobility of office. Two new classes rose thereby above the estate of the common freemen. They coalesced readily, inasmuch as royal service was rewarded with land, and they wholly or partially absorbed the remnants of the old nobility of blood. The increased wergeld of the royal officials gave them also a higher legal worth. Although it was not yet an estate limited by birth, this aristocracy developed into such an estate — the estate of lords and princes — in the post-Frankish period,

[1] *Heusler*, "Institutionen", I, 161.

as a result of the transformation of powers of public office into heritable rights of lordship over land and people associated with the possession of land. On the other hand many of the common freemen sank into the estate of serfs, and there met the slaves who had risen into it. For whoever was not in a position to protect his own free holding, but was forced to intrust it to a richer man and receive it back as a tenancy for rent, thereby eventually lowered his personal status. And so, here again, possession of land called into existence, first social and economic, and then legal distinctions.

To all this yet another thing was added. The Germanic common freeman had been at once warrior and cultivator of the soil. This ceased to be true in Frankish times. The need of a professionally trained mounted force created chivalry and the estate of knights. This estate of the knightage ("ordo militaris"), too, was at first a purely social fellowship of all men capable of knight service. But as mounted service in war was as dear as it was distinguished, a knightly lineage was very soon added to the requirement of a knightly mode of life, and thereby transformed a professional into a blood estate. The feudal law included in one legal unit all persons of knightly birth and calling, and graded them within this unity in estates, according to their military rank. Distinctions between the status of freedom and of unfreedom in the Territorial law did not affect membership in this estate, notwithstanding that they were the basis of gradations within it. Unfree persons found admission to it, viz. the ministri, — the servitors of the king and the landed aristocracy employed in military service. So long, therefore, as the distinction made by the Territorial law outweighed in importance the unity that prevailed in the feudal law, the knightage was no status in the sense of the Territorial law, and the feudal law was no law of status but simply a "Rechtskreis" (*supra*, p. 3), — the aggregate of the legal rules that regulated the legal relations associated with feudal tenancy. The Sachsenspiegel still shows us this peculiar parallel growth of estates on the double basis of Territorial and feudal law. Ultimately the principles of the latter came to prevail. Persons of knightly birth separated themselves from all other classes of society as a blood estate, recognizable by their peculiar mode of life. But within this knightly or noble class, a unit both in self-consciousness and in law, the distinction between elements originally free and unfree continued to be reflected in a division between a higher and a lower nobility (*infra*, III).

Beside the knightly estate there appeared an estate of burghers and peasants, whose development ran a similar course. Urban occupations, which in the flourishing towns offered abundant support through industry and trade to an ever-increasing stratum of the population, brought within the burghal class the most diverse elements of the Territorial law. The principle "Luft macht frei" ("free town air makes free")[1] wore down the original contrasts and fused the town population into a legal unit, although indeed social differences, often of great sharpness, persisted or first took form within it. The burghal class also became in a legal sense a blood-estate determined by the occupation into which one was born. Within the town law ("Weichbildrecht") it developed its own law of status, and as the citizenry of the State grew later out of the burghal community, so burghal ("bürgerliches") law became the common ("civil") law of the whole nation.

Among the rural population, also, the distinctions of status connected with the original folk organization became obliterated in course of time, although they did not disappear completely, nor everywhere to the same extent. In some regions free peasants maintained themselves on free soil, though henceforth distinguished by their rustic life from their erstwhile fellows of the knightly and burghal estates. Socially, they constituted one class with the half-free and unfree cultivators of the soil. The peasantry lived under complicated tenurial relations: in the West partly bound to the soil, and partly personally dependent; in the eastern colonized regions originally merely bound to the soil, — it was only in the course of the modern period that personal serfdom ("Leibeigenschaft") found in the latter regions its widest prevalence as a new form of unfreedom.

Thus it came about that the organization of the folk as knights, burgesses, and peasants, which had reached perfection in the 1100 s and 1200 s, remained the essential basis of social grouping until the 1800 s, and gradually displaced the older estates based on gradations of freedom. And though these newer estates did not everywhere attain internal homogeneity, they nevertheless did constitute closed blood-estates, which were distinguished from one another by their occupations: military (knightly) life, civic

[1] *Brunner*, "Luft macht frei. Eine rechtsgeschichtliche Untersuchung", reprint from the "Festgabe der Berliner juristischen Fakultät für O. Gierke" (1910).

industry, and rustic field work were mutually exclusive occupations in the law of status. When mercenary troops and modern standing armies replaced the feudal array, the nobility lost their character of a solidary occupational estate, notwithstanding that it continued very commonly the military mode of life, and that in Prussia it was regarded as nothing less than the legal duty of the landed nobility to serve as officers in the army. Especially in the East, the nobles devoted themselves as great landowners to agriculture, and quite commonly entered the higher civil service as well. Moreover, since urban life involved from the earliest times a variety of occupations, many statutes, as *e.g.* the Prussian "Landrecht", treated these smaller occupation groups as "estates", establishing special rules for the classes (called "estates") of officers, civil servants, merchants, artisans, artists, factory owners, etc. There was here, however, no question of estates in the legal sense, since such groups lacked all definite delimitation within the general blood-estate (*supra,* p. 25).

(2) *Equality of Birth.* — Underlying all social organization upon the basis of a blood-status is the principle of equal birth. Only when an estate rests on equality of blood can it constitute an entity, sharply delimited, of equal-born fellows. Since the old estates of the Territorial law were pure blood-estates, the idea of equal birth was in them quite strictly enforced. Complex relations resulted wherever different social factors, each determinant of status, were in play, and led to cross-stratifications of status. In such cases there might result a double equality of birth, if measured by different standards. For example, and in particular, there existed, at the height of the medieval period, beside the equal-birth of the "Landrecht" the equal-birth of the feudal law. For this reason, the doctrine of equal birth had much that was confusing about it, as the glossator of the "Sachsenspiegel" justly remarks (on III, 73, § 1). The consequences of equality of birth in private law made themselves felt in the law of family and inheritance. Only an equal-born member of the estate had the right — which rested on kinship — of exercising guardianship over minors and women. And only between those equal in birth was there a right of inheritance; for as the "Sachsenspiegel" puts it (I, 17, § 1): "Sve so dem anderen ebenburdich nich ne is, de ne mach sin erve nicht nemen" ("When one is not the equal in birth of another, he cannot take the latter's heritage"). Equality of birth played its most important rôle, however, in the law of marriage. Members of different estates could not originally inter-

marry at all; and later they could at best enter into no marriage of full effect. The once unbridgeable gulf between freedom and unfreedom still found recognition in the provisions of certain folk-laws that imposed penalty of death upon free and unfree unions, or, like the Salic Law, declared a woman who contracted marriage with her slave to be rightless ("aspellis"). Others merely punished the free party with the loss of freedom; the Ripuarian folk-law ordered that sword and spindle be offered the free woman who against the will of her kin took a slave in marriage: if she chose the one, the slave was killed; if the other, she herself sank into bondage.[1]

Under the influence of the Church legal validity was given, in general, to all marriages consummated in observance of the prescribed forms, and the quality of legitimate offspring to the resulting issue. But marriages between those who were not class fellows remained unequal marriages. The principle that the husband's status fixed the status of the wife was applied only when the man was the lower born, in which case he drew the woman down to his own estate. On the other hand a woman lower born did not by marriage rise to the higher status of her husband. As regards the children the principle was that they should follow the "worser hand" ("Ärgere Hand"; "le pire emporte le bon"), that is, receive the status of the lower-born; so that a mother several times married might have children of the most different status, according to the status of their fathers. At times, indeed, even in Germany men maintained the principle of the oldest Germanic law, — which moreover was the rule in Roman law, — and allowed a free woman, even though during the continuance of the marriage she necessarily shared the half-free or unfree status of her husband, to transmit to her children her own natal freedom ("partus sequitur ventrem", "le ventre affranchit", "the womb enfranchises"). The question, what marriages should be recognized as of equal status went to the very essence of the medieval law of status and equal-birth. And this not alone in regard to private law. For upon its decision depended not only priorities in inheritance, but also succession to the crown and sovereignty. And with remarkable although intelligible stubbornness men held fast at precisely this point to the old system of estates of the Territorial law, at least in theory; and this even after that had already been wholly displaced by the newer occupational-estates. For example, as late as the year 1383 the

[1] "Lex Ribuaria", 58, 18.

peasants of the Alsatian village of Grosskembs declared — and from the viewpoint of the old free-estate quite unimpugnably — that they were, as free peasants, the "fellows of princes" ("fürsten genoss"), and could "wiben und mannen, on eygen lüt, wo wir wöllent" ("marry, unlike serfs, whomsoever they pleased"); although, as Heusler adds,[1] doubtless not very many peasant-girls of Kembs can have attained a princely throne. As late as 1670 the Imperial Chamber of Justice also regarded the marriage of an earl with a free peasant as a union that did not debase the status and the rights of the children, and the Imperial Council gave practical effect to the same rule down to the electoral capitulations of 1742.

In this newer organization of society in occupational-estates the principle of equal birth was less and less heeded. Only the higher nobility in Germany clung to it (*infra*, III, 2). In the lower nobility, on the other hand, marriages between free burgesses and peasants seem to have been treated as equal as early as the second half of the Middle Ages: "Ritter's Weib hat Ritter's Recht", "knight's wife has knight's law." Only in the 1700 s were the father's rights of status again denied, in some regions, to children of a marriage between a noble and a woman of an ignoble class (a "vilis et turpis persona"). Where the rural population was predominantly unfree, as in eastern Germany, it did not enjoy equal-birth with the knights and burgesses.

(III) **The Modern Development**: (1) *Abolition of Estates.* — The Prussian "Landrecht" could still treat as part of the law the system of estates handed down from the Middle Ages, but with the old absolute monarchy there fell in ruins the system of feudal estates that formulated its social and legal order. Frederick William I and Frederick II attempted to realize the emancipation of the peasants from personal serfdom ("Leibeigenschaft") though without great success. Joseph II made it a fact. Thenceforth, not only was the hereditary dependence of the rural population abolished in all the German States, under the influence of French legislation (in Prussia by the Edict of Oct. 9, 1807), but what was more, as a result of the proclamation of freedom of industry, and the unqualified opening of all callings; forms of land tenure, and public offices to all classes of society, there was established a homogeneous State citizenship, within which legal divisions no longer existed, however much differences of social rank might persist, and all that these practically involved. Where there

[1] "Institutionen", I, 178.

remained in force the system of special law governing particular occupations, — as *e.g.* for military and civil servants, merchants, industrials, laborers, etc., — or where peculiar rules of law persisted as regarded certain kinds of property, — as *e.g.* for "fideicommissa" and peasant holdings, — there was, as has already been mentioned (*supra,* p. 92), no question of rights of status in the old sense. Only the Bavarian Nobility Edict of 1818, still in legal force, reserved to the nobility the creation of family "fidei commissa." It is therefore opposed to the legal order established everywhere else in the course of the 1800 s, and which the Prussian Constitution (Art. 4) laid down in the laconic rule: "No privileges of estate shall be recognized."

(2) *The High Nobility.*[1] — Despite all this, the movement in Germany directed toward the destruction of rights of status has not realized a complete triumph: even the present German law still knows one legally privileged estate, the high nobility.

(A) ORIGIN AND EXTENT. — Within the estate of knights or nobles there was preserved, as already remarked, a remembrance of the unfree origin of the servitary families which in fact constituted the chief element of the knightage. The families of original free origin felt themselves superior to these; all the more so in that they enjoyed, as Territorial princes and estates of the Empire, a political position superior to that of the other knights. Accordingly, they prohibited marriages of their members with women of families descended from the ministri. This highest stratum of the nobility thus segregated itself as a special blood estate within the general estate of the nobility. The Schwabenspiegel (G. 57) — unlike the Sachsenspiegel, which still regarded as equal-born all who were freemen under the "Landrecht" — already distinguished the two noble classes of "semper"-freemen (also known as "Hochfrei", "high-free", and "Edle", "noble") and the ordinary or "Mittel" freemen, and defined the descent necessary for inclusion in the former class by the rule: "ez ist nieman semper fri wan des vatter und mutter und der

[1] *Rehm,* "Modernes Fürstenrecht" (1904); *Hauptmann,* "Das Ebenbürtigkeitsprinzip in den Familien des deutschen Hochadels", in Arch. Öff. R., XXII, (1902), 529 *et seq.*, "Ebenbürtigkeit und Virilstimmen", in *idem,* XXI (1906), 146 *et seq.*, and "Modernes Fürstenrecht", in *idem,* XXVIII (1908), 193 *et seq.*; *G. Meyer,* "Lehrbuch des deutschen Staatsrechts", ed. by *Anschütz* (6th ed. 1905), 266 *et seq.*, and 829 *et seq.*, *Goldschmidt,* "Die Sonderstellung der Mediatisierten Preussens nach dem öffentlichen Rechte Preussens und des deutschen Reichs", No. 81 (1909) of *Schücking's* "Arbeiten"; *G. Bessler,* "Über die Stellung des bürgerlichen Gesetzbuchs Deutschlands zu dem Familienrechte des hohen Adels. Eine Denkschrift" (1887, 1911).

vater und mutter semper fri waren " ("a person is 'semper'-free when his father and mother and their fathers and mothers were 'semper'-free"). This gradation of ranks found particularly clear expression in the fact that numerous cathedral chapters, religious establishments, and cloisters belonging to the free-estate received only members of noble, free-born families, and not descendants of ministri.[1] In time, however, many houses that had a servitory origin rose to the estate of the high nobility, inasmuch as the emperors, from the end of the 1500 s onward, no longer bestowed the earldoms that escheated to them upon the old ruling families exclusively, but also on persons of the lower nobility, who thereby acquired seat and vote in the Imperial Council of Princes or in one of the Colleges of Earls. The bond unifying this estate was therefore not one of kinship but one of a political nature; it was not likeness of descent but a similar position under the public law. And therefore, as was definitely settled in 1654, the emperor could raise to the estate of the high nobility only such houses as possessed or received an "immediate" imperial territory (a territory immediately subject to the emperor) as the basis of their privileges as an estate of the Empire. Merely personal, and therefore temporary, admission (in which connection men spoke of "Personalisten"), or admission solely on the ground of office, as in the case of the Pappenheims, was not sufficient. As little did the bestowal of an imperial princely title suffice, inasmuch as the title borne by the houses that were estates of the Empire ("Fürst", "Graf") was not of consequence, and consequently the difference between imperial princedoms and earldoms, or old and new princely families, was also of no essential significance. Only at the end of the Empire was the requirement of political rule over an "immediate" imperial territory in some cases disregarded, and the continued enjoyment of the personal status of an estate of the Empire regarded as sufficient in favor of a few families (Stolberg, Schönberg, Fugger, Giech), even when their territories were subject to the sovereignty of another estate of the Empire. With the dissolution of the Empire the constitutional basis of the estate of the high-nobility disappeared, and all those of its members who failed to attain sovereignty as princes of the Confederation of the Rhine should by right have lost the

[1] Recently established by *A. Schulte*, "Der Adel und die deutsche Kirche des Mittelalters", Nos. 63–64 (1910) of *Stutz's* "Untersuchungen." Compare the compendious essay of *Werminghoff*, "Ständische Probleme in der deutschen Kirche des Mittelalters", in Z. Sav. St. R. G., Kanon. Abt., I (1911), 33–67.

privileges of status based upon their former position as imperial estates, sinking into the general mass of subjects. The Constitution of that Confederation, however, assured to these so-called "mediatized" members an equality with the princely houses that had been in the past, and had now again become, sovereign; and this guaranty was repeated by Art. 14 of the Constitution of the German Confederation, whose provisions received statutory force and were carried into practical effect by proclamation in the individual States, supplemented by local legislative regulations. There the matter rested. For though all privileges of status were declared abolished in many States (as *e.g.* Prussia, *supra*, p. 94) in consequence of the popular movements of 1848, the reactionary movement of the years immediately following led, here also, to a complete reëstablishment of the legal position guaranteed by the constitution of the Confederation to those rulers who were formerly estates of the Empire. In Prussia the method chosen to effect this was an official proclamation of the Constitution in statutory form.[1] The Civil Code nowhere recognizes in its text the persistence of a law of status variant from the general civil law, but the Introductory Statute (57, 58) has sanctioned the recognition of the high-nobility by State law as a special estate.

At the same time the extent of this single privileged estate of to-day is not great, because entrance to it has been fast closed since the end of the old German Empire, inasmuch as its legal basis, which rested solely upon the Constitution of that Empire, cannot be created anew. To the high-nobility there belong only the German princely houses, — to which the dynasties dispossessed in 1866, the princely house of Hohenzollern, and since 1904 the ducal-principality of Holstein have been in many respects assimilated, — and noble families that were estates of the Empire and were "mediatized" in 1806. Of such families there are at present in Germany and Austria fifty-four, which are further divided into one hundred and eight branches. The peculiar position of the high-nobility in private law is seen in the autonomy it enjoys, and in its principle of equal birth.

(B) AUTONOMY.[2] — Beginning with the 1300s it became

[1] *Cf. Anschütz*, "Die Verfassungsurkunde für den Preussischen Staat. Ein Kommentar für Wissenschaft und Praxis," I (1912), 107 *et seq.*

[2] *Löning*, "Die Autonomie der standesherrlichen Häuser Deutschlands nach dem Rechte der Gegenwart" (1905); *Oertmann*, "Die standesherrliche Autonomie im heutigen deutschen bürgerlichen Recht" (1905); *Schücking*, Art. "Autonomie" in *v. Stengel-Fleischmann*, "Wörterbuch", I (2d ed. 1911), 290–298.

customary in the houses that ranked as imperial estates to formulate in family "statutes" and "compacts" regulations concerning property and family relations; regulations whose common content was directed to the permanent and secure establishment of a firmly grounded dynastic power, and therefore above all else to the prevention of a parcellation of the land. There originated in this way a private law peculiar to the high nobility ("Privatfürstenrecht"). Its peculiarity consisted in the fact that German legal principles which were elsewhere forced to yield to the alien law were maintained intact on many points in this special class law for the high nobility, notably in the regulation of the order of succession. The principles of this "Privatfürstenrecht" had the quality of an objective law binding third parties. No definite form of expression was developed for this right of private enactment. But even in the case of regulations issued of his own motion by the head of the house, the assent of all the living agnates was customarily necessary; only for such assenting agnates and their descendants did the regulations have binding force. The powers of the family head to act for all its members, every agnate possessed within the limits of family law ("Hausrecht") over his particular line of descendants. The right of autonomous enactment was no unlimited legislative power: aside from possibly contradictory rights of the emperor, it was limited by the end it sought, namely the preservation of the "splendor familiæ." The rules of the "Privatfürstenrecht" had primary reference, therefore, to succession, membership in the family, equality of birth, misalliances, dowry of women and provisions for posthumous sons, guardianships, family "fideicommissa", and the like. The noble house itself, regarded as a corporation, has been assumed by many writers — notably by Beseler and Gierke, as well as by an opinion of the college of Prussian crown-syndics of 1876 — to be the subject of this power of private enactment (*cf.* § 43, *infra*). But no convincing reasons exist for this view. One may equally well regard the family head as the subject of such enacting-power, — only he must act in the name, and where it is so provided only with the concurrence, of the agnates; just as a constitutional ruler is a legislator, although he is bound by the coöperation of the people's representatives. At any rate, no common law authority can be ascribed to the principle that a family of the high nobility possesses legal personality. The constitution of the German Confederation in the Article (14) already cited, guaranteed to houses that had been estates of the Empire the continuance of their autonomy in accord with the principles of the former German Constitution; thus binding all the German States, under principles of international law, to the recognition of the "Privatfürstenrecht." With the end of the German Confederation it lost the sanction of international law which it had thus acquired. Since then the "Privatfürstenrecht" and rights of autonomous enactment have rested solely on State statutes regulative of the matter, and can be altered or abolished by State legislation. This condition of the law is recognized in the Introductory Act of the new Civil Code in the provision that the right of autonomy "as respects family regulations and property" shall be enjoyed by houses formerly estates of the Empire in the measure allowed by State legislation (§ 58). On the other hand, it has left the autonomy of the reigning State dynasties intact, and under the guaranty of imperial law (Art. 57).

(C) EQUALITY OF BIRTH.[1] — It is only in the marriage law of the German high-nobility that the principle of equal birth has maintained itself in its old-time strictness. In it, equality of status has remained to the present day the precondition of a perfectly valid marriage. A marriage beneath one's status is a misalliance ("disparagium"), through which the lower-born spouse cannot enter the high-noble status. The lower-born woman, in particular, acquires neither the name nor the arms of the man, nor further claims to property-preferences under the law of his estate and house; and the children, in accord with the medieval principle, follow the "worser" ("ärgere") hand, and therefore, since they too have no part in the rights and property of the house, are excluded, in the reigning princely houses, from succession to the throne. When the consequences of misalliance are contractually regulated, and the claims of the wife and children thereby assured, such a marriage is given the name of a "left-handed" marriage, in reference to the usual form of the ceremony in such cases; and also "morganatic", because merely a morgive is set aside for the wife instead of the otherwise customary dower (*infra*, §§ 94, 95). The left-handed marriage appears to be a development of Germanic concubinage (*infra*, § 99). Developed first in Italy, and there known also as "matrimonium ad legem salicam", it enjoyed validity in Germany

[1] *Abt*, "Missheiraten in den deutschen Fürstenhäusern unter besonderer Berücksichtigung der standesherrlichen Familien", No. VII, 1 (1911) of *Beyerle's* "Deutschrechtliche Beiträge."

after the Reception as an institute of the common law, and as an essential part of the "Privatfürstenrecht" still has positive authority to-day. Outside of the high-nobility it can no longer occur, since it presupposes inequality of status.

Just what, however, are to be accounted the legal requisites of an equal marriage between families of the high nobility is a much debated question. In recent years this has been studied with especially great exhaustiveness, as the result of certain protracted contests regarding succession to the throne in Lippe and Oldenburg. In the light of the latest researches it seems permissible to assume that in the application of the principle of equal birth in these houses, decisive influence has been exercised by their varied historical origins, which has made impossible a customary law controlling without exception the entire estate; notwithstanding that the existence of such has frequently been asserted.[1] The princely houses of old free origin, whether they bore titles of imperial princedoms or imperial earldoms, whether their princely titles were old or modern, clung to the principle, — always adhered to by them in practice, and often embodied in statutes, — that only marriages among their own members, and members of other houses admitted to the estate of the high-nobility, were "equal." And hence the legal rule that only a marriage between persons belonging to the high-nobility is "equal" — a principle often adopted, moreover, in constitutional documents — still holds good to-day for the dynasties descended from these houses and still ruling, as well as for their equals dethroned in the 1800 s. Foreign Christian princely houses, possessing rights of sovereignty recognized in international law, are regarded as equals of German princely houses.[2]

On the other hand, this strict principle of equal birth, which, in particular, denies such equality to the lower nobility, acquired

[1] *Abt*, *op. cit.*, 91 *et seq.*, attacks this view, which is championed by *Hauptmann* (above) and emphasizes the historical origins of the respective houses. Abt assumes for the whole body of the mediatized higher nobility, in marriages with other Germans ("Inländern"), a rule of customary law in accord with which only marriages between high nobles and commoners are regarded as misalliances.

[2] In connection with the well-known plan of a marriage between Prince William of Prussia, later Emperor and King William I, and Princess Elisa Radziwill, the question of the equal rank ("Ebenbürtigkeit") of the princely house of Radziwill was exhaustively discussed, and despite the affirmative declaration of Savigny, K. F. Eichhorn, Lancizolle, and Count Anton Stolberg, was eventually answered in the negative, possibly because the division of Poland had made an end of the actual sovereignty of the Polish princes of the Empire. *Cf. Hennig*, "Elisa Radziwill" (1911).

no authority whatever as regarded the other high-noble families, or at least no common law validity, notwithstanding that the contrary has been asserted by numerous scholars following the example of Pütter,[1] and is even to-day defended by the partisans of Schaumburg-Lippe. The idea of holding marriages with women of the lower nobility to be misalliances was far from the mind of the families of the high-nobility descended from the imperial ministri, since they themselves had formerly belonged to those circles, and had from earliest times taken from them their wives. They practised this custom, moreover, without hesitation throughout the whole of the 1700 s, and accordingly the Imperial Chamber of Justice in a judgment given in 1773 expressed the view, the only view historically justified, that the strict principle of equal birth did not hold for the lower strata of the high-nobility, in which, on the contrary, the equality of the lower nobility was recognized.[2] The electoral capitulation of 1742 also provided that only marriages with non-nobles were unequal under the common law. To be sure, nothing need prevent that in a particular house variant and stricter principles should be regarded as binding by usage, or established in the dynastic law. Whether this were so might be contestable in a specific case; but the common law authority of the strict principle was again rejected by the Imperial Court in its two decisions of June 22, 1897, and October 25, 1905, in the matter of the contested succession to the Lippe throne.

That the doctrine of equal birth, the most important part in practice of the law of the high-noble estate, could still be the occasion at the present day of lawsuits lasting for decades, to some extent alarming and of serious political consequences, clearly shows that the peculiar position of the high-nobility, spared by even the most modern legislation, is an exception contradictory of the most fundamental legal conceptions of modern Germany. And only in Germany and Austria (to be sure, also in Russia) has this strict law of equal birth been able to develop and maintain itself. Neither to the older nor present-day English law, nor to the monarchical public law of the ancient régime in France, was it or is it known. In contrast to the unyielding and fearful attitude of their German class-fellows, — an attitude doubtless explainable only by German provincialism, — the regnant houses of

[1] "Über Missheiraten deutscher Fürsten und Grafen" (1796).
[2] *Anschütz*, "Das Reichskammergericht und die Ebenbürtigkeit des niederen Adels", in Z². R. G., XXVII (1906), 172–190.

those lands did not consider the contracting of unions with their subjects derogatory to their own dignity.

§ 14. **Honor.**[1] (I) **Honor in the Legal Sense.** — Whereas the division of society into estates rests on the attribution to different groups of society of a different legal worth, the legal influence of the conception of honor turns upon the legal evaluation of the individual, whether in his relation to the nation as a whole or to his class-fellows. Like status, honor was, to begin with, purely a social conception. Within social usage there develops, as Heusler shows,[2] a public opinion concerning the respectability of certain conditions, qualities, callings, and the like which denies to persons affected by these the respect otherwise shown to every man as such. They are not regarded by society as of unblemished repute ("voll"). But only he who enjoys unqualified personal repute has "honor"; and since these social appraisements attain in time an influence so strong that the law also must adjust itself to them, legal consequences attach to the lessening or complete denial of social esteem. It is true that the social and the legal conception of honor do not always coincide; and from this there may then result very unsatisfactory conditions. Thus honor became a legal institute, and as such also became more or less determinant of the position of the individual in private law.

(II) **The Older Law.** — Germanic law seems from the beginning to have laid very great weight upon the possession of full honor.

(1) Exact information is lacking as regards *the oldest law.* But when Tacitus ("Germ." 6) reports that one who had cravenly thrown away his shield in battle was excluded from sacrifices and the popular assembly; and when it is declared in the Carolingian legislation, — doubtless in accord with views dominant since the earliest period, — that a wrongdoer condemned to death but pardoned could give no testimony, nor be a skevin, nor clear himself by oath of criminations, but must submit to the ordeal, one may safely assume that the richly developed growth of the medieval law of honor goes back in its foundations into primitive Germanic time.

(2) *The Medieval Law.* — The German sources of the time of the Law-Books, especially the Saxon, are distinguished from the older sources by a great wealth of notices concerning the different

[1] *Budde,* "Über Rechtlosigkeit, Ehrlosigkeit und Echtlosigkeit" (1842); *Schaer,* "Die altdeutschen Fechter und Spielleute" (1901); *Frensdorff,* "Das Zunftrecht insbesondere Norddeutschlands und die Handwerkerehre", in Hans. G. B., 1907, 1–89.

[2] *Heusler,* "Institutionen", I, 191.

varieties of honor, and the legal consequences of their impairment. In this respect they notably surpass those of other countries; so much so that the elaboration of a law of honor, carried into details, seems to have been peculiar to Germany. The lack of a uniform, technical phraseology is here especially inconvenient. Attempts to unite all existing original data into a consistent system have, up to the present, led to no satisfying result: unquestionably differences existed, of time and place, and the use of terms was very unstable. The results of Heusler[1] recommend themselves by inherent probability and a fairly wide basis in the sources, and have been adopted with certain desirable modifications by Amira[2] and Brunner,[3] whereas Gierke[4] adopts views that are in many respects different.

We may disregard "Echtlosigkeit", — *i.e.* complete loss of capacity for rights, originally through being put outside the peace ("Friedlosigkeit", social outlawry) and later through outlawry as judicial process ("Oberacht"), — which still occurs, though only rarely, in the medieval sources. It involved, particularly, incapacity for the contraction of a valid marriage, but had nothing to do, in itself, with "honor"; out of it civil death finally developed (*supra*, p. 46). There were two other varieties of limited capacity for rights whose limitations were due to defective honor, and which were different both in their preconditions and consequences:

(A) "Rechtlosigkeit" (rightlessness), due to dishonorable acts.—This attached to persons who were proved guilty of such acts as made them impossible among reputable men. Here belonged:

(*a*) Those who had suffered condemnation to a *degrading punishment*, that is, a punishment of "head and hand" ("zu Hals und Hand") or "skin and hair" ("Haut und Haar" = "hilt-an-hair"), particularly for larceny and robbery but also for other more opprobrious misdeeds. The decisive thing here was the condemnation, and the notoriety thereby effected; that the punishment may have been escaped by settlement or composition was not considered.

(*b*) Those who had committed a deed which betrayed a *base or depraved disposition*, especially breaches of faith, lost their honor, and therewith their full capacity for rights, even though no condemnation was suffered.

[1] *Heusler*, "Institutionen", 190–199.
[2] "Recht", 91.
[3] "Grundzüge" (5th ed.), 192.
[4] Privatrecht", I, 416–433.

The sources designate both these categories, which in part evidently overlapped, now as "rightless", now as "honorless", without any sharp distinction. The opinion of Heusler[1] that "honorless" ("ehrlose") was the technical designation for the second group, appears to be unfounded. Commonly, too, men spoke of "rightlessness *and* honorlessness" together.

(B) "Rechtlosigkeit" due to personal relations or social callings.—To designate these the sources employ the expressions "Unechtheit" and "Unehrlichkeit" ("illegitimacy", "dishonor").

(*a*) Those *born out of wedlock,* whom "man unecht seget von bort" ("who are called illegitimate by birth", — Sachsenspiegel, III, 28, § 1). In contrast with the generally prevailing principles of Germanic law, but in accord with medieval views influenced by the Church, such persons were denied civil honor, and finally, in consequence of their lack of all family ties, were burdened with complete "Rechtlosigkeit" (*infra,* § 99).

(*b*) Further, those persons who led a dishonorable life in plying an opprobrious or *ignominious trade,* whom "man unecht seget von ammechte" ("who are called illegitimate by trade"), — that is, minstrels in the strict sense; and also "the whole motley and ever restless troop of all those whom men called 'varende' or 'gernde diet' (itinerant or begging people)":[2] jugglers, conjurers, dancers, streetsingers, and itinerant minstrels and poets; vagabond apprentices, students, and priests; itinerant fencing masters, mercenaries, begging gypsies, wandering comedians, and knife-grinders. At the same time distinctions were doubtless made between these different classes; indeed, many of them joined in associations and gilds, and obtained for these legal recognition and independent rights of judicature. Thus arose the various pipers' brotherhoods, the fencers' gilds, pirate-bands, etc. Under the influence of the craft system, trades and callings in themselves dignified came to bear a stigma in society which made their members appear as "unworthy and unclean subjects"; such as shepherds, millers, linen-weavers, tailors, barber-surgeons, jailers, especially the hangmen and headsmen, cloaca sweeps, and gutter scourers.

"Rechtlose" and "ehrlose", as well as "unechte" persons, were excluded from all judicial procedure, — they could not be skevins, judges, witnesses, or spokesmen. They were all both

[1] "Institutionen", I, 196 *et seq.*
[2] *Schaer,* "Die altdeutschen Fechter und Spielleute" (1901), 87.

actively and passively incapable of guardianship, inheritance rights, and rights of feudal tenure. More than this, the "Ehrlosen", since they had sacrificed their religious faith to their infamous conduct, were also incapable of oath and hence could defend themselves only in judicial combat, whereas this was not so of the "Unechten", who at worst were not fellows of thieves and robbers. They were all excluded from public offices, were not received into the crafts, nor ordained, nor buried in hallowed places. Finally, the lesser legal worth of all found expression in the fact that although offenses against them were possible and punishable, — though indeed visited only with relatively slight punishment, — nevertheless, they had no wergeld and were conceded only a simulated bót ("Scheinbusse"). In the case of two classes of "rechtlose" persons this bót was literally a mere semblance ("Schein"), namely in the case of hired champions and their children, who received as bót the glint of a shield in the sunlight; whereas minstrels, and all who had sold themselves, were accorded as bót the shadow of a man. Other classes of rightless persons received an actual bót, but in mockery: *e.g.* to persons who had forfeited their rights through thievery and robbery two besoms and a pair of shears, the implements with which penalties of "skin and hair" were inflicted. Finally, illegitimate children were given a cart-load of hay such as two yearling steers could draw; and unfree wage-earners received two woolen gloves and a dung-fork, — in short, bóts that were of slight value if not exactly derisive. The reason of these remarkable bót-tariffs set forth in the Law-Books[1] we must doubtless seek with Gierke[2] in the inclination of the old law, to give at least something, even though it be an empty form, instead of simply awarding nothing.

(III) **The Modern Development.** — Although the law of honor is dependent in an especially high degree upon peculiarities of national feeling and the degree of general culture, Germany nevertheless adopted with the Roman law its provisions respecting this matter, without of course totally abandoning traditional conceptions and institutes. A vague condition of the law in many respects was here again a necessary consequence.

(1) *The Roman law* in its latest form knew the two institutes of "infamia" and "turpitudo." The former, whose legal

[1] For example, Ssp. III, 45, §§ 8–10.

[2] "Humor im deutschen Recht", 45. See also *Peterka*, "Das offene zum Scheine Handeln im deutschen Rechte des Mittelalters", in *Beyerle's* "Beiträge", No. VII, 1 (1911), 42 *et seq.*

essentials persisted unchanged from the beginning, intervened automatically, either as "infamia immediata" under certain circumstances of dishonorable fact — *e.g.* in dishonorable callings, double marriage, etc. — or as "infamia mediata" in consequence of a judgment passed upon an act punishable by loss of honor. All criminal judgments, and among civil judgments those decreed in "actiones famosæ", involved this latter type of "infamia." On the other hand, "turpitudo" (also called "infamia facti") was the consequence of a judicial decree, pronounced at the discretion of a court in accord with the judgment already passed on the case by public opinion. It was natural, then, once Roman conceptions had come to be applied, to conceive of the "Rechtlosigkeit" of the German law consequent upon a judicial judgment as "infamia juris mediata"; and to call the "Rechtlosigkeit" or "Ehrlosigkeit" that resulted from a dishonorable action "infamia juris immediata." These interpretations, speaking generally, involved for the most part merely formal modifications, the old conceptions remaining substantially in force. True, the consequences of the Roman institutes were quite other than those of the loss of civil honor in Germanic law: evidently there could be no talk in Germany of the loss of the "ius suffragii et honorum", since the common man had long since ceased to possess such a right. In essence, however, it continued to be true that in these cases of "Rechtlosigkeit" the question involved was the loss of all those rights that marked an individual as an equal member within the circle of his fellows; so that the conception of honor naturally came to appear as a special honor determinant of status, although this did not in itself signify any change in essence.

(2) As a result of applying the conceptions of "infamia iuris immediata" and of "turpitudo" ("infamia facti"), "Ehrlosigkeit" due to birth out of wedlock and to dishonorable trade, — so-called "Unechtheit", — was developed into *the institute of infamy* ("Anrüchigkeit"). In the period of the decay of German culture, the spirit of men's minds, — inclined to pettiness, plagued by trade jealousy, and bound in conceit and vanity, — found in this exceedingly unedifying expression.

Bastards, from whom the common law never removed the ill fame due to the stigma of their birth, secured toward the end of the 1700 s, at least in Territorial legislation, a gradual improvement of their situation (*infra,* § 99). They acquired capacity to engage in industry and to become members of the crafts, and the right to churchly burial; and the Prussian "Landrecht" (II. 2, § 602) declared in terms quite general that illegitimate children should have equal rights in the affairs of civil life with those born in wedlock or legitimized. True, it provided in another place (II. 8, § 279) that admittance to apprenticeship should be denied on account of illegitimate birth to no one who had secured legitimation; a concession to the narrow-mindedness of the crafts hardly to be reconciled with the other principle. With this regulation, however, it directly aligned itself with the positive law of the Empire at that time, which had been fixed by a decree of the Imperial Diet in 1731. And yet that decree signified an advance when compared with older conditions. For legitimation had doubtless long sufficed to wipe out the stain of illegitimacy, and to give those legitimized capacity for all public offices and honors; though it had not been able to secure them under all circumstances normal rights of inheritance from parents and kindred. The craft-law, however, had treated legitimatized children as no better than bastards, accepting as sufficient only a legitimation brought about by subsequent marriage, or recognizing only children born after wedlock. The decree of the Diet just referred to first compelled the crafts to abandon their exclusive attitude. Only in the 1800 s was the requirement of legitimation generally abandoned. It is true, that in consequence of the older view of the stain of illegitimate birth, the rule that illegimate children of a noble mother do not inherit her nobility has maintained itself until recent times in the law of some States (*e.g.* in Prussia and Austria), and many contend, in the common law as well; and the law of the Catholic Church still maintains the idea that birth outside wedlock constitutes an "irregularity", denying therefore to illegitimates ordination in her service.

The circle of so-called dishonorable trades was continually widened toward the close of the Middle Ages, and imperial legislation long attempted in vain to make headway against the movement. Even children and grandchildren of persons of such base condition were excluded from the crafts: the drapers' craft of Paderborn hesitated, for example, to receive a burgher because his father had been in youth a minstrel and his wife was a miller's daughter. The Diet decree of 1731 first determined that in future no profession or handicraft should constitute ground for exclusion from the crafts: only in case of hangmen did it permit, through two generations, the rule theretofore practiced. This exception too was narrowed by a decree of the Diet of 1772. The Prussian "Landrecht" and the legislation of most of the other States assumed a like position. Not until the 1800s was the executioner's calling freed of its stigma,—in Prussia by administrative ordinances of 1819 and 1827: a necessary consequence of the introduction of universal military service. His base-condition maintained itself longest in Altenburg, Hamburg, and Schleswig-Holstein.

(3) The law has thus attained at *the present day* a position where it no longer recognizes, save within narrow bounds, any influence of honor in matters of private law. On the other hand it has developed the denial of rights of civil honor into an important institute, as a criminal penalty, entailing also consequences in private law. In the abjudication of all or certain rights of civil honor, decreed as a criminal penalty, one can trace the old "Rechtlosigkeit" due to crime, and the Roman "infamia iuris mediata." It also influences the private law to the extent that it may effect incapacity to assume a guardianship, curatorship, attorneyship, or membership in a family council. Further, persons who are deprived of rights of civil honor may be excluded from associations, trade unions, and general meetings of associations ("Generalversammlungen"); they may not be editors of periodicals, etc.

The old institute of "infamy" lives on in the law of to-day in so far that the lack of civil honor may still have legal consequences, even without a judicial abjudication of the rights of civil honor. When a person is guilty of a dishonorable life his marriage may be dissolved at the instance of his spouse; his parental power may be limited; he may be disinherited; his dishonorable life may become an issue, to his prejudice, before a court or an administrative board, and still further disabilities may be decreed against him as respects his juristic acts. Especially in the modern labor law the principle has been recognized that contracts may be dissolved for lack of honor ("Ehrlosigkeit") in the other party; nobody shall be held to labor longer with another who has revealed himself as a "bad" member of society.[1] Certain further consequences drawn by the earlier law — *e.g.* incapacity during the period of one's imprisonment for the administration of property, incapacity to acquire a "fideikommissum", to hold land by feudal tenure, postponements in inheritance — are no longer of practical importance in the law.

[1] *Hedemann*, "Fortschritte des Zivilrechts", I, 75.

CHAPTER III

JURISTIC PERSONS AND GROUPS INCAPABLE OF HOLDING RIGHTS

§ 15. **Associational Organization in Germanic Law, generally.**[1] (I) **Significance of the Association.** — If we designate by the expression "association" ("Genossenschaft"), with entire generality, unions of several human beings into legal communities of narrower or wider scope, closer or laxer structure, such associations have at all times been numerous and of great importance in Germanic law. A strong associational quality is stamped upon Germanic law from the earliest times. It gives this a character distinct from that of the ancient Roman law. At the same time the fact is not to be overlooked that little is known respecting the actual development of the society and partnership law of antiquity: the scanty rules of the "Corpus Juris Civilis", a meager final selection from a technical literature dealing with a practice that is lost to us, cannot be compared with the superabundant wealth of information that we possess respecting the actual legal practice, unaltered by scientific editing, of the Middle Ages. Nor should it be forgotten that this associational character is not, strictly speaking, a

[1] Of fundamental importance are the great works of *Gierke:* "Das deutsche Genossenschaftsrecht", Vol. 1: "Rechtsgeschichte der deutschen Genossenschaft" (1868), Vol. 2: "Geschichte des deutschen Körperschaftsbegriffs" (1873), Vol. 3: "Die Staats- und Korporationslehre des Alterthums und des Mittelalters und ihre Aufnahme in Deutschland", (1881) — one section of which last has been translated into English with a valuable introduction by *F. W. Maitland* under the title "Political Theories of the Middle Ages, by Dr. O. Gierke" (1900); "Die Genossenschaftstheorie und die deutsche Rechtsprechung" (1887); "Das Wesen der menschlichen Verbände" (rectoral address, Berlin, 1902). See also: *Sohm*, "Die deutsche Genossenschaft", in the "Leipziger Festgabe für Windscheid" (1888); *Fr. Kauffmann*, "Altdeutsche Genossenschaften (gemein und geheim; Bauern, Gesellen, und andere Genossen)", in Wörter und Sachen II (1910), 9–42.

thing exclusively German. It is rather peculiar to all Germanic peoples; likely enough it had its richest development in England.

The political and economic conditions of the Middle Ages everywhere favored its development. While the omnipotence of the State and the slave economy of antiquity were hindrances to a richer associational life, the weakness of the medieval State, the sharp division of population by birth and profession into strata and groups of varied rights, and the impossibility of realizing greater undertakings — such as the clearing of the primeval forests, or the transportation of goods—otherwise than by the united physical power of many individuals, offered strong inducement and even compulsion to the formation of associational groups. State and law were too weak to protect the individual as such; only as a "fellow" ("Genosse"), as one belonging to a union of his equals, could he find the security requisite for his existence. Thus, the practical necessities of life in the Middle Ages led to an enormous wealth of associational groups. But when the modern State later established security of law and commerce, and drew in increasing measure within the domain of its power such important tasks of civilization as poor-relief, the regulation of industry and education, and the like, the importance of those narrower communities of sib and family, merchant gilds and craft gilds, communities of "collective hand", rural associations, etc. disappeared; more especially because to an age of individualistic feeling they appeared to be, for the most part, only belated fetters upon free individual action. It was economic tasks, mightily growing in the modern period, that gave new life to the associational type of organization and brought it to an imposing development, — though truly in large degree in new forms, and for new ends; creating, especially in share companies and other forms of capitalistic associations, instruments of the greatest importance. Since the second half of the 1800 s personal unions of the most varied kinds have spread over the whole world in numbers which, in the opinion of the most gifted modern historian of English law, have far exceeded the relative increase of natural persons in the same period of time.[1]

(II) **Possible Classifications and Viewpoints.** — One who should review this whole rich development, and seek to classify the associational groups created in its progress, might proceed

[1] *Maitland,* translation just cited, XII.

from different points of view. One might proceed chronologically; in which event it would perhaps be found that in the earliest time blood connection, next the rural economic system, and only later still city life, were successively the most active factors in the growth of associations. Again, one might contrast unions adapted to a large membership with those of limited extent. And though fast boundaries are hardly to be recognized, originally, between unions of public and of private law, nevertheless such became settled in time, and the associations of public law, — foremost among them the State itself, but also the commune, ecclesiastical unions, and the like, — come to be distinct from those of the private law. According to their ends, a division would result into such groups as were designed to further the whole legal and economic existence of the individual members, and which therefore involved the entire personality of the individual, and others that pursued more limited purposes. Again, their tasks are either exclusively of an economic character, whether of a barter or money economy, or have reference to more general cultural ends, — benevolent, social, religious; and so on. Some of the most important unions affect the individual independently of his coöperation; so, in particular, those of the family law, but also the commune and the State. Others rest upon voluntary accession, though even this may, under certain circumstances, assume a compulsory character. Many took form in an unconscious process of development of customary law; others were called into existence by consciously creative acts. In some the principle prevails of equal rights for all members; others reveal a hierarchal organization. Some are directed by the wills of the members, which are assembled by the law in the most varied ways into a collective will; others are controlled by a will outside and above themselves.

Now, for purposes of legal appreciation, it is a circumstance of primary significance that the union, as such, may be more or less distinctly independent of its individual members. And accordingly the legal relation of the members to the totality of associates, the legal relation of the members with third persons, and the legal relation of the members among themselves, may assume very different forms. The last stage in the growth of the union toward independence is reached when there is attributed to it, as such, the character of an independent holder of rights, or juristic personality. It then appears as an independent "juristic" or "group" ("Verbands-") person beside the physical persons of its members, and increases by one their number as holders of legal rights.

Germanic and German law both attained to the development of these associational forms with independent legal personality, but this result was only gradually realized. It presupposes advanced cultural conditions, and a nicety of juristic technic that is not present in the youth-time of a race. The understanding of medieval legal development has, indeed, been made particularly difficult precisely at this point, because, with the reception of the Roman law, the fundamental concepts of its law of society and partnership acquired an unqualified ascendancy. Not only was the development of Germanic legal institutions interrupted, but a just scientific appreciation of them was made impossible. Modern research into Germanic origins has effected a change in this respect. It has discovered the ideas dominant in the historical evolution and in the present-day authority of the German law of associations; and above all, it has taught us to comprehend the characteristic differences that distinguish them from the Roman conceptions, which men long regarded as the only ones conceivable. In this connection it has appeared that, as contrasted with the rules of the Roman law, which were logically a perfectly consistent whole but for that very reason indigent in content, the medieval German law produced a great variety of legal communities, distinguished only by slight differences from one another; and maintained them, despite all romanistic attacks, down to the present day.

And so a general survey should here be given of the most important forms in which the Germanic associational type of organization found legal embodiment, before discussing (in §§ 22, 27 *infra*) the fundamental view peculiar to Germanic law and underlying these different embodiments. In so doing the distinction already made between unions possessing independent legal personality and those lacking in such independence, is to be postulated as legally the most important, — while remembering that only in the course of time did this distinction lead to their complete separation. In the case of some personal unions, nuclei for the development therefrom of independent juristic personalities were doubtless present from the beginning. But the legal institute of juristic personality attained perfection, as already remarked, only by degrees, and everywhere only in the second half of the Middle Ages. Accordingly, juristic persons also became differentiated only in course of time, as a legally peculiar group among the numerous associations ("Genossenschaften") of the German law, and consequently it is impossible in this place, — where the problem is to give a general view of the historical development, and of the fundamental ideas reflected in it, — to adopt the view-point appropriate to a dogmatic presentation of the positive law of to-day, or to direct attention exclusively to those unions which were, or have become, juristic persons. On the contrary, we must follow the method of treatment chosen by Gierke[1] and Heusler,[2] and consider here all types of the community ("Gemeinschafts-") law, including those which in the scheme of Roman and modern law and in the new Civil Code, find their place in the law of obligations.

Topic I—Specific Types of Communities in Germanic Law.

§ 16. **The Sib** ("Sippe"). (I) **Origin.** — The oldest type of association, existing already in the primitive Germanic period, is the union of the blood-group ("Geschlechtsverband"), the sib. The sib is "the germ of all associational life."[3] It developed at an early day out of the household community, the patriarchally administered "greater" family, in which the primal-cell of all social evolution among Aryan races is discernible, in this way: that the younger member of household communities thus grown to independence, seceded, by stratification as it were, from the common household and set up their own economic establishments. Inasmuch, however, as these derivative separate families, each of which was under the rule of its founder, maintained intact the bond with the ancestral house, the sib remained beside the separate houses as a group embracing all.

(II) **Associational Character of the Sib.** —The Germanic sib was constituted of a fixed circle of persons related by blood. Since the primitive Germans lived in father-sibs ("Vatersippen"), *i.e.* in sibs that based their kinship solely upon descent from a common tribal male ancestor, the Germanic sib was an agnatic union (*infra*, § 90). Its solidarity depended on the fact that the women belonging to a foreign sib abandoned this by their marriage, and entered the sib of their husband, while no bond of relationship resulted for him and their children with the sib of the wife and

[1] "Privatrecht", I, 456 *et seq.*, 660 *et seq.*
[2] "Institutionen", I, 223 *et seq.*, 252 *et seq.*
[3] *Schreuer*, "Untersuchungen zur Verfassungsgeschichte der böhmischen Sagenzeit" (1902), 59.

mother. In contrast to the house-community, which was organized on a theory of patriarchal power, the sib of the primitive Germans, unlike *e.g.* the Roman "gentes", was presumably from the beginning a union of equal fellows; all adult male members, but particularly the heads of the separate households, being thus regarded. A patriarchal head was foreign to the Germanic sib.

The sib stood at the center of all social and legal relations, played a great rôle in the military and judicial organization, assured its members internal peace, and protected them against attacks from without. It was also an agrarian union, and as such the prototype of the rural associations of the Middle Ages. Already in it we note a special form of collective real rights in land, similar to those developed in the mark-associations (*infra,* § 17) and reflecting its legal solidarity under the law of persons. Thus, when Caesar reports (B. G., VI, 22) that the land had been distributed for cultivation "gentibus cognationibusque hominum, qui tum una coierunt", the "gentes" stand for the agnatic sibs, to which the Gau assigned for common cultivation the land it occupied. Clear indications from a later time of a collective right of the sib in the mark-arable have also been preserved, — for example, the dispute of the "genealogiæ" over the limits of their districts which is treated of in the Alamannic folk-law (81). And like the land, movables also seem to have been the object of collective rights, and indeed in early times of a collective ownership, in the sib.

(III) **Disintegration of the Sib.** — The sib, as a solidary associational group, was bound to disintegrate when cognatic relatives, those connected through women, received legal recognition beside the agnatic (details *infra,* § 90). Many duties theretofore incumbent upon the agnatic sib were then taken over by the kinship ("Verwandtschaft"). This last took a different form in every generation, — in other words, it did not constitute a solidary and exclusive body, — inasmuch as only brothers and sisters of equal birth have the same paternal and maternal kindred. Economic tasks, however, fell thenceforth upon the vicinage-groups based on bonds of locality, in place of the kinship unions of the sibs. A bond of neighborhood here replaced the bond of blood-relationship; the blood-mark was transformed into a vicinage-mark.[1]

With this change there was associated a strong re-emergence of the house-community. The position of the individual house-

[1] *Huber,* "Schw. Privatrecht", IV, 235.

holds and of their heads became the more independent, the more the sphere contracted within which the sib was active. Within the unorganized and non-exclusive body of the kinship there developed, as the narrowest community determinant of legal and economic life, the household. Unlike the sib, this continued to retain in its "pater familias" ("Hausherr", house-master) a monarchical head; yet it might under certain circumstances perfectly well assume an associational character, — namely, whenever the family-members who had been united under one authority continued their common life after the death of the "pater familias."

Thus, the oldest associational group had already become subordinated to new growths at an early day. The further development of community organization from the principles already dominant although not yet wholly distinct in the sib, took place first in the vicinage ("Orts-") associations and in the communities of "collective hand" which were derivative from the house-community. Later progress was due primarily to urban life.

§ 17. **The Mark-associations.**[1] (I) **Origin.** — When the land

[1] Of the abundant literature, see: *Heusler*, "Die Rechtsverhältniss; am Gemeindeland in Unterwalden", in Z. Schw. R., X (1862), 44–144; *v. Miaskowski*, "Die schweizerische Allmend in ihrer geschichtlichen Entwicklung vom 13. Jahrhundert bis zur Gegenwart" (1879); *v. Inama-Sternegg*, "Deutsche Wirthschaftsgeschichte", I (1879, 2d ed. 1909): 96 *et seq.*, 370 *et seq.*, II (1891): 78 *et seq.*, 207 *et seq.*, 274 *et seq.*, III, 1 (1899): 64 *et seq.*, 237 *et seq.*; *Lamprecht*, "Deutsches Wirtschaftsleben im Mittelalter", I (1886), 259 *et seq.*, 384 *et seq.*, 695 *et seq.*, 902 *et seq.*, 992 *et seq.*; *Haff*, "Geschichte einer ostalemannischen Gemeinlandsverfassung" (1903); *Rüttimann*, "Die Zugerischen Allmendkorporationen", No. 2 (1904) of *Gmür's* "Abhandlungen"; *Rennefahrt*, "Die Allmend im Berner Jura", No. 74 (1905) of *Gierke's* "Untersuchungen"; *Schotte*, "Studien zur Geschichte der westfälischen Mark und Markgenossenschaft mit besonderer Berücksichtigung des Münsterlandes", No. 17 (new ser., 1908) of *Meister's* "Münsterische Beiträge"; *Lappe*, "Die Bauerschaften der Stadt Geseke, Ein Beitrag zur Geschichte der deutschen Stadtverfassung", No. 97 (1908) of *Gierke's* "Untersuchungen"; *Haff*, "Die Dänischen Gemeinderechte", Part 1, "Almende und Markgenossenschaft", Part 2, "Die Feldgemeinschaft" (1909), and *cf. v. Schwerin* in Z.[2] R. G., XXXII (1911), 512–14; *Varrentrapp*, "Rechtsgeschichte und Recht der gemeinen Marken in Hessen, Teil I: Die Hessische Markgenossenschaft des späteren Mittelalters", No. 3 (1909) of *Heymann's* "Arbeiten", and *cf. Haff* in Z. R. G., XXX (1909), 386–394, *Rörig* in Vj. Soz. W. G., IX (1911), 200–206, *Rietschel* in Hist. Z., CVII (new ser. 11, — 1911), 119–23, and *Caro* in Hist. Vj. S., XIV (1911), 582–584; *Thimme*, "Forestis", in Arch. Urk. F., II (1909), 101–154; *Haff*, "Markgenossenschaft und Stadtgemeinde in Westfalen", in Vj. Soz. W. G., VIII (1910), 17–55; *Lappe*, "Nordlüner Markenrecht" (1910), and "Das Recht des Hofes zu Gahmen, Zur Geschichte des Hofverfassung des Mittelalters" (1910); *G. v. Below*, art. "Markgenossenschaft" in H. W. B. der Staatsw. VI (3d ed., 1910), 585–587; *Weimann*, "Die Mark- und Walderbengenossenschaften des Niederrheins", No. 106 (1911) of *Gierke's* "Untersuchungen", and *cf. Haff* in Deut. Litt. Z., 1911, No. 48, *Thimme* in

that had been originally assigned to the sibs by the Gau merely for temporary cultivation (*supra*, p. 115) came in time to be held in permanent possession, and finally in ownership, by them, they were thereby transformed into unions of definite local limits which were united physically by the land standing in their ownership, — the mark (" Mark ": signifying originally boundary, or march, later the domain enclosed), — and personally by the bond of neighborhood that had replaced blood-relationship. These unions, which were the mark-associations, ordinarily coincided with the village-communities wherever, as was most commonly the case among the early Germans, settlement took place in that form; the village-communities were, so to speak, the topographic projection of the sibs. In some cases, however, the mark-association was greater in area than the village-community because, for one thing, the Gau did not always allot its whole domain among the blood-groups, but might retain for itself parts of the same as a Gau-mark. These great collective-marks — Gau-marks, and doubtless also hundred-marks — disappeared for the most part, it is true, in the course of the Middle Ages; but in some regions, as *e.g.* in Allgäu, Upper Bavaria, and North Tyrol, they have maintained themselves down to the present day. Again, with the growth of population within the territory of a village settlement, new derivative village communities arose, and this always led to a partition of the arable lands among all such rural communes, but not always to a corresponding partition of the remaining land. In this case, therefore, as in the other,

Westd. Z. G. K., XXX (1911), 447–449, and *Rörig* in Hist. Vj., XV (1912), 407–413; *v. Schwerin*, art. "Allmende" in *Hoop's* "Reallexicon", I (1911), 63–65; *Lappe*, "Eine untergegangene Bauerschaft", Z.[2] R. G., XXXII (1911), 229–246, and "Bauerschaften und Huden der Stadt Salzkotten", No. VII, 4 (1912) of *Beyerle's* "Beiträge"; *Dopsch*, "Die Wirtschaftsentwicklung der Karolingerzeit vornehmlich in Deutschland", I (1912), 333–369. See also *Kauffmann*, article cited above, p. 30 *et seq.*, 35 *et seq.*; also *Sohm*, "Über das Hantgemal", in Z.[2] R. G., XXX (1909), 103, 107 *et seq.* — Questions as to the age, originating causes, and nature of the mark-associations are still sharply debated. The view represented in the text, which is the older and as yet the predominant one, and which maintains the independent primitive origin of the mark-associations, is opposed by another that denies them such character. The former theory was accepted, among others, by Varrentrapp (at least before he allowed himself to be influenced by the assumptions of Schotte, which in my opinion are unsound), v. Schwerin, Thimme, Rörig, and in essentials also by Haff. Its most aggressive opponent is Dopsch; he contends that those marks of which there are reports in the sources of the Carolingian time were not the survivals of an undemonstrable agrarian communism of primitive Germanic times, but the result of the continued appropriation of forest lands, originally lordless, either by manorial lords who were ever becoming more powerful or by free and independent landowners.

the members of various village communities remained united in one mark-association inclusive of their several individual districts.

Although all the land was originally subjected, by its allotment among the neighborhood-unions as mark, to their collective rights, a reduction of the mark was eventually caused by the appearance and growth of individual ownership. All those parcels which passed into the private ownership of individual mark associates, ceased to be part of the mark; and also in the same way isolated pieces of land assigned to individual usufruct. The former included, at first, only house-plots with the yards and gardens surrounding them, but later the arable fields as well. Thenceforth, the meadows and woods, — the so-called "Allmende" ("Allgemein", commons), — constituted practically alone "the mark" or "the common ('gemeine') mark."

Where settlement did not take place in villages, but by individual farms, — as was the case in mountain valleys, and also in many regions of the lowlands, as *e.g.* along the Hellweg in Westphalia, — the Allmende, in the indicated sense of meadow and woodland, was the sole basis from the beginning of the community constituted of the individual settlers. This was known in such localities as the "peasant"-community ("Bauerschaft").

(II) **Legal nature.** — The origin of the mark-associations made them in their very nature economic unions, notwithstanding that their boundaries not infrequently coincided, in the earlier periods, with those of the political administrative districts, the Gaus and the hundreds, and that in consequence of this topographic coincidence there regularly resulted a complete fusion of the two into one communal entity, from one viewpoint political and from another purely economic. The mark-associations had for their exclusive end the advancement of the agricultural interests of the whole association and of each individual associate. These interests, however, were in no way contradictory, for the purposes of the whole were precisely the purposes of the individual associates. The individual associate needed the common land for any ordered prosecution of his own agriculture: he needed the right to pasture over and to cut wood upon it; and so on. And that these usufructuary rights should inure to each associate was for the benefit of all, and therefore of the group. It was these usufructuary rights that inured to each associate as an appurtenance to his individual ownership, — originally in unrestricted measure, and later to an extent proportioned to that of his land (measured by the full-hide), — that embodied the practical value of membership in the association. Inasmuch, however, as no division of the common-mark took place incidentally to the usufruct thus enjoyed by each associate in the entire undivided common, such rights were *collective* rights of usufruct. To be sure, definite pieces of the common might be assigned to individual associates for individual usufruct; but in this case they ceased to be part of the common-mark. And when (as was still true in the Frankish period) the right of "Neubruch", — that is the authority to clear mark-land, especially woodland, and to appropriate its ownership — belonged to the associates, such land-breaks also became the separate property of the improver.

But who was the owner of the mark? To this much debated question no other answer can be given than this: that in the sense of the medieval law the associates in their *entirety* were *regarded* as the owners. This entirety, however, the association as such, was in medieval conceptions by no means opposed to the individual associates as a legally independent and distinct third person. On the contrary it was, as it were, "built up out of them as a personality uniting all: the associates stood as with one part of their personality in the group."[1] The mark belonged to the totality of associates. And the same was true of "collective" chattels ("Gesamtfahrhabe") such as implements, buildings, and breeding stock, — which must always have existed, even though not always in great amount, — and of the property accumulated out of taxes and penal fines. The associates as a body controlled the mark, they determined the economic plan for its exploitation. That this collective right of the association in the mark was a remnant of their one-time collective right in the whole domain, including the arable fields, was shown by the fact that it retained certain supreme powers over the arable that had passed into private ownership. Thus, for example, the individual was bound by the resolves of the commonalty in the cultivation of his arable land. This was the principle of compulsory regulation of the common fields ("Flurzwang"). Again, the whole body had the right to reclaim lands allowed to go to waste; and also a right of escheat in the hides left by heirless members. Indeed, under some circumstances even a new allotment of the arable ("Reebningsverfahren") might be undertaken. With these powers over the mark that inured to and

[1] *Stutz*, "Rechtsgutachten . . . betr. das Recht der Fischerei im Rhein zwischen Rheinfelden und Säckingen" (1900), 11.

were exercised by the associates as a body, were united those of the individual associates. Nor were these in the nature of rights in "alieno solo." They were simply derivative from the collective privileges that pertained to them as a body, and therefore also to each individual; not distinct and separate, but ideal, shares in a collective right, which were united by an associational principle. In the literature of modern Germanic studies this peculiar distribution of powers between the whole and the individual members is designated "associational collective-ownership" ("genossenschaftliches Gesamteigentum", *infra,* § 33). It was the counterpart in the law of things of that bond which united the associates themselves into a whole recognized by the law of persons, and which, while it did not as yet possess, unlike them, a legal independence, nevertheless at least did already represent an entity.

(III) **Organization.** — That the associates were united in a legal entity was manifest in the fact that from the earliest times a definite organization was an essential of the mark-association. For without some organization, however simple, unions consisting of numerous members, such as the mark-associations were from the beginning, could not have continued to exist; though that is of course by no means to be regarded as proof of a legal personality inherent in them from their origin.[1] Special officers of the mark-associations were necessary, however, only in those marks that belonged to a Gau or a hundred; since the officers of the Gaus and the hundreds exercised exclusively political powers. In the village communities the organs of the political commune served at the same time the village mark-association. The supreme administrative organ was the totality of associates gathered in the assembly of markmen, which sat under the presidency of the chief-markman (called "woodward", "wald-grave", "village magistrate", etc.). It regulated the usufruct of the mark and the services imposed on the markmen; judged in cases of waste committed on the mark; elected the mark officials (foresters, field-guards, etc.); and doubtless chose a committee as a permanent supervisory organ. Originally all persons settled within the mark and possessing their own household — "flame and fire keepers ('Flammer und Feurer') behind the mark", — ranked as "full" or "mark" associates, enjoying equal rights. Such were called "Märker", "Erbexen", "villani", "vicini", "commarcani." However, it was a precondition to this that

[1] This is the opinion of *Heusler*, "Institutionen", I, 262 *et seq.*

they should either have descended from a markman or should have been adopted by vote of the community. Inasmuch as the principle of majority rule was still quite foreign to the primitive law, so that resolutions could be taken only by unanimity in the assembly of associates, each associate might raise objections at any time within a year to the settlement of any stranger (as was laid down, for example, in the Salic folklaw).[1]

(IV) **Free, Mixed, and Manorial Mark-associations.**[2] — The mark-association that corresponded to the Germanic agrarian system, consisting exclusively of free and equal fellows and endowed with far-reaching autonomy, lost ground following the Frankish period in consequence of the growth of manors. Fully free ("altfreie", primitive free) village and mark-communes maintained themselves only in Friesland, Ditmarsh, Switzerland, and in some regions of West Germany. On the other hand, wherever ecclesiastical and secular land-lords acquired the possession of numerous hides formerly subject to equal rights of vicinage, and remained at the same time within the union of the mark-associations, their rapidly expanding demesne lands and lands dependent thereon procured them a dominant position within such unions. And since usufructuary rights in the mark were measured by the extent of one's landed possessions, their supremacy was thereby continually strengthened, until finally it came to be an unqualified lordship over the mark and the mark-community, exercised through a bailiff. With this change the mark-community ceased to be free. It had still earlier become a so-called "mixed" mark-community, in which the land-lord became ever more prominent beside the free associates; and its development from that into an "unfree" community was due principally to the frequent entrustment of free hides to landed magnates and the abasement thereby brought about (*supra*, p. 90) in the legal status of the tenants. From the beginning, moreover, unfree mark-associations resulted wherever village communes grew up under manorial law upon manorial estates that had either detached themselves from a union of free mark-associations or had never become part of such. These mark-associations of manorial law ("hofrechtliche Genossenschaften" or "grundherrschaftliche Hofmarkgenossenschaften"), which were especially numerous, and to which by far the most of the dooms refer, were exact

[1] "Lex Salica", 45, 1.
[2] Compare with this, especially, *Varrentrapp*, cited p. 116 *supra*, I, 22 *et seq.*

replicas of the free communities save for the absence of personal freedom. Viewed from the standpoint of the Territorial law, it is true that their members enjoyed neither individual ownership in the plowland nor collective ownership in the mark set apart for them by the manorial lord, for the lord alone was owner of the whole domain. His will was therefore here decisive in a measure even greater than in the mixed associations, in matters concerning the mark; the more so because the office of a chief-markman was regularly conceded him by birth. The manorial law, however, which was being created within these limits (*supra*, p. 3) assured to the associates a usufructuary ownership ("Eigen") in the hide in the sense of *that* law, though not in that of the Territorial law, and a collective ownership of the mark; and it was also customary to concede them an autonomy, as concerned the mark, which was defined and protected by the manorial law. Of course these things remained in a flux of development, and development was possible in two different directions: it might lead to a gradual strengthening of the association's powers and to a repression of the power of the manorial lord, or it could lead to a complete absorption of the former into a fully developed, unqualified sole ownership of the lord. In the course of time there developed in connection with these manorial groups the conception of the "Anstalt" or "foundation" — a personified institution — as a wholly passive body of individuals who found in their lord a center of union (*infra*, § 23).

(V) **Transformations of the Old Mark-association.** (1) *The Commune and Mark-association distinct Corporate Associations* ("Körperschaften"). — As already remarked, the tendency toward a differentiation of the group as distinguished from the associates was already growing in the Middle Ages. Nevertheless, the recognition of the aggregate of fellows as a distinct legal personality, that is as a corporate association in the sense of Germanic law (*infra*, § 22), was first realized, not in the rural but in the city communes. These were similarly developing. "The economic as well as the legal status of a town commune was originally no different from that of the rural commune."[1] It also generally had commons, though these lost their old importance in the larger cities the more agriculture and grazing diminished relatively to trade and industry. At the same time the singleness of ends characteristic of the rural commune disappeared. The varied problems, political, economic, and cultural in nature,

[1] *Heusler*, "Institutionen", I, 306.

whose solution the city was undertaking with the help of its new wealth built up out of the taxes of the residents (and no longer primarily destined, by any means, to the mere usufruct of the residents), made it appear as the instrument of an independent power and will that was plainly detached from the interests of the citizens considered individually. In this way the town grew into a corporately organized political commune with its own recognized legal personality. Now conditions were different in the rural communes in so far that a predominance was always retained in them by economic interests, relatively to which their political aspect was sharply subordinated. Yet in these also the individual began increasingly to feel a distinction between himself and the association quite in contrast with the views of the early Middle Ages.[1] And this, in its turn, influenced the transformation of the village commune of the open country into an independent "corporate association", so that wherever the village commune and mark-association were united in the old way and so long as they remained so, the collective right in the mark inhering therefore in the commune, the collective ownership of the mark, which was formerly only "associational", became "corporate" in character (*infra*, § 33). Here too, however, the economic association ultimately became completely separated from the political commune, so that the village commune and the mark-association appeared side by side as two independent "Körperschaften", which were no longer necessarily of the same personal membership. This separation was connected with changes that took place in the membership of the mark-association.

(2) *Transformation of the Mark-association into an Economic Association of Privileged Members of the Commune.* — Every person in independent possession of a hide who belonged to the association by birth or adoption was originally, as already stated, a "full" associate, and shared as such, by virtue of his right of membership, in the usufructuary rights in the common lands. The ordinary landless hired laborers ("Hintersassen"), the cotters, hovelers, cottagers and the like, settled on little plots without practicing true husbandry; the feudal tenants planted on the lands of others; and, finally, the landowners dwelling outside the mark ("Ausmärker") were associated with the markmen solely for mutual defense ("Schutzgenosse"), and had shares in the mark only indirectly or by special favor. In time, the

[1] *Huber*, "Schw. Privatrecht", IV, 275.

circle of "full" associates came more and more to exclude such communists of lesser privileges, in order to prevent a depreciation of the value of the right of fellowship through the increase in number of those entitled to defense. This was accomplished, in part, by abandoning the requirement of landholding, retaining unchanged only that of an independent household; while the adoption of strangers either took place no more, or only upon payment of high entrance dues. In this manner there originated within the village commune personal associations of families exclusively entitled to the usufruct of the common land, a "blooded village-patriciate." [1] More commonly, however, landed ownership was maintained as a condition of membership, but with the new requirement that every member own either one of the old homesteads endowed with such rights of usufruct or a "full" peasant hide. There were thus formed within the village commune true "real" communes. Finally, in some regions — in Switzerland, Hesse, Ditmarsh — the right of usufruct in the common mark became an independent, heritable, alienable, partible, and accumulative ideal share-right, like a share of stock, which conferred full membership privileges in the usufructuary commune ("Rechtsame gemeinde" or "Nutzungsgemeinde") that was constituted of the totality of such shareholders.

(VI) **Dissolution of the Last Remnants of the Mark-associations.** — Where the result was not the formation of such special agrarian corporate-associations as those just described, into whose collective ownership the one-time common mark passed, this generally fell to the political commune, which by this time was independent. It thus became communal property, in which, however, the usufructuary rights of the communists theretofore entitled to such might continue. These rights were now commonly regarded simply as rights in the property of another, unless they were classed with rights in public streets and squares. Ownership of the commonties also frequently passed to the Territorial rulers, who had often laid claim to a commonty-regality already in the Middle Ages.[2]

Finally, beginning with the end of the 1700 s State legislation undertook a total dissolution of the few remaining remnants of the old mark-associations and the relations of collective ownership incident to them. On the one hand the common fields of

[1] *Gierke*, "Privatrecht", I, 587.

[2] *Wopfner*, "Das Almendregal der Tiroler Landesfürsten", No. 9 (1906) of *Dopsch's* "Forschungen."

arable and meadow, and therewith every restriction reminiscent of the old compulsory regulation of the common fields, were abolished by enclosures; and on the other hand, by the redemption of all statutory rights of usufruct in land, the usufructuary privileges of individuals in common lands were done away with. Above all, the so-called discommon ordinances ("Gemeinheitsteilungsordnungen") that were issued in the different German States in the 1800 s — *e.g.* the Prussian discommon ordinance of June 7, 1821, the Baden commune ordinance of 1831, the Saxon statute of redemptions and discommons of 1832, the Bavarian commune statute of 1834, etc. — swept away the community enjoyment of lands, apportioning the commonties on various principles as individual property among the landowners. In this manner most of the commonties disappeared, particularly in North Germany. In South and West Germany, where the commonties had become for the most part public communal property, and had been thereby subjected to far-reaching restraints on alienation, many old marks continued to exist; and so also in Switzerland. At the present day altered economic views are again more favorably inclined to commonties, and seek to hinder, especially, the partition of the woodlands.

§ 18. **Neighborhood Associations of more Restricted Purposes.** — Beside the mark-associations there originated in the Middle Ages many other associations which likewise had for their end the common usufruct of land, but in lesser measure.

(I) Most nearly related to the mark-associations were **associations for special agricultural purposes.** — They were distinguished from the former by this, that the land held in collective ownership was not a communal mark, and the associates were in no way united as members of a commune. These associations, like the mark-associations, very generally assumed a corporate-like character already in the Middle Ages. Some of these special agrarian associations have persisted down to the present day.[1] Examples are:

(1) *The "farm communities"* ("Gehöferschaften") of the administrative district of Trier: agrarian associations which hold collective ownership over an arable mark. This is divided into a definite number of "lots", "shares", or "plows", which originally corresponded to the number of fully privileged associates.

[1] See *Haff*, "Die Weide-, Forst- und Alpgenossenschaften im rechtsrheinischen. Bayern und das bürgerliche Recht, mit einem Rechtsgutachten", reprint from the "Festschrift für H. v. Burckhard" (1910).

Such associations later denied membership to strangers, and the shares thereby became independent objects of commerce. The arable is periodically distributed anew by lot among the members, in the ratio of the share-holdings. These farm communities have played a great rôle in the investigation of economic and legal history, for Hanssen[1] thought to identify in them the last remnants of the primitive Germanic system of common fields and allotment of arable described by Tacitus. Lamprecht has shown, however,[2] in opposition to this view, that they originated much later. In his opinion, which Hanssen has accepted, they owed their origin to the manorial organization of the 900 s to 1300 s, and go back to the assarts made with the services of manorial serfs, — *i.e.* to manorial tiller-unions ("Betriebsgenossenschaften") on assarts ("Beunden"); associations of cultivators which then, after the decay of the manors, had retained ownership of the fields originally cultivated by them in the service of their lord. It is true, this view has itself since been controverted.[3] In modern times woodland and meadow have become predominant over the arable, and the modern farm communities (of which in 1878 there were still 20 in the administrative district of Trier) have thus become very similar to the "Allmende" corporations alluded to above (p. 124).

(2) The "*Hauberg*" *associations* of the region of Siegen in Westphalia[4] are woodland associations whose property includes so-called "Hauberge", or leafwood copses on the mountain sides. Every "Hauberg" is subjected to a rotation period of sixteen or eighteen years; the district is therefore divided into sixteen or eighteen "hews" or "fellings" — *i.e.* rotation parcels — of which one is cut over yearly, while the others are meanwhile wholly enclosed or used for grazing or as arable. The "hews" or "fellings" vary in area and productive value. All the "hews" of the same "Hauberg" are divided into an equal number of sub-

[1] "Die Gehöferschaften (Erbgenossenschaften) im Regierungs-Bezirk Trier", in the "Abhandlungen" of the Berliner Akademie, 1863; reprinted in "Agrarhistorische Abhandlungen", I (1882), 99 *et seq.*

[2] "Deutsches Wirtschaftsleben im Mittelalter", I, 418 *et seq.*, and art. "Gehöferschaften" in "Handwörterbuch der Staatswissenschaften", IV (3d ed. 1909), 553 *et seq.*

[3] *Rörig*, "Die Entstehung der Landeshoheit des Trierer Erzbischofs zwischen Saar, Mosel und Ruwer. Anhang: Zur Entstehung des Agrarkommunismus der Gehöferschaften", Westd. Z. G. K., "Ergänzungsheft 13" (1906).

[4] *Delius*, "Hauberge und Haubergsgenossenschaften des Siegerlandes. Eine rechtsgeschichtliche und dogmatische Untersuchung", No. 101 (1910), of *Gierke's* "Untersuchungen."

divisions called "Jähne" ("strips"). These strips are measured in terms of an imaginary unit, which furnishes the basis for the allotment of the hews among the associates. The strips are therefore mere quota rights, to which, however, there correspond definite pieces of land in the hew. The number of strips into which the hew is divided is identical with the number of persons having rights in the "Hauberg" as it existed at the time of the introduction of the strip system. By subsequent alienation or inheritance complicated subdivisions were formed. The "Hauberg" system of woodland management has been regulated in recent years by special "Hauberg ordinances" applicable to the Circles in which such woodlands still exist, — Siegen, Dill, Oberwesterwald, and Altenkirchen. A Nassau ordinance of 1804 still serves for the administrative district of Wiesbaden.

(3) The *Alp associations* in Switzerland are to-day purely private associations which, especially in the canton of Unterwalden, practice a community agriculture of the Alps. An Alp is terraced into a certain number of share-rights ("cow-rights", "cow-feeds"), which in turn may be divided down to "quarter-cows" or "hoofs."

(4) In the Middle Ages *vineyard associations* were common which practiced a common cultivation of vineyards, and possessed for this end a corporate-associational organization. Supervision of the vineyards, the police of roads and boundaries, the setting of the slips, and the regulation of the vintage, were the chief objects of associate action.

(II) The **associations developed under the law of waters and mining** were similar to the mark-associations, although no definite piece of land constituted their material basis. These included fishery, dike, and sluice fellowships, and mining associations ("Gewerkschaften"). They will receive further treatment below under the law of things (§§ 40–41).

(III) Finally, mention may be made of the **transportation unions** that arose in the Middle Ages and endured well into modern times. To these belonged the so-called "road-associations" ("Rottgenossenschaften", — roaders' union) of Bavaria and the Tyrol,[1] as well as the frontier "port-associations" of

[1] *Johannes Müller*, "Das Rodwesen Baierns und Tirols im Spätmittelalter und zu Beginn der Neuzeit", in Vj. Soz. W. G., III (1905), 360–420, 555–626; *Stolz*, "Zur Geschichte der Organisation des Transportwesens in Tirol im Mittelalter", in same, VIII (1910), 169–267; *Haff*, "Zur Rechtsgeschichte der mittelalterlichen Transportgenossenschaften", in Z.[2] R. G., XXXI (1910), 253–282.

eastern Switzerland;[1] companies of entrepreneurs which on one hand attended to the maintenance of the Alpine passes, and on the other hand claimed a more or less extensive monopoly of transportation. In the communes having rights of "road" those villagers were members of the road-association, who also shared as markmen in the usufruct of the commonty. The purpose of such roaders' unions was to attend to the transport of goods upon the great roads ("auf der Rod zu fertigen") that led from Ulm through Landeck, Meran, and Trient, and from Augsburg through Innsbruck and Toblach, to Venice. Ports were maintained on the Septimer-road between Chur and Chiavenna (four); on the Splügen-road between Chur and Chiavenna; and on the St. Bernhard-road between Chur and Bellinzona (six). All the "ports" of each highway were organized, and held regular sessions under the presidency of port-magistrates. The roaders' unions were also organized.

§ 19. **The Craft Gilds.**[2] (I) **Origin.** — The craft gilds owed their origin to the increasing prosperity of the medieval cities. They are therefore of considerably later origin than the rural mark-associations, the oldest reports of them being of the 1100 s. And in their case the legal independence of the association as such, and its corporate-like organization, were from the beginning more sharply and more consistently realized.

(1) The opinion, formerly widespread, that the craft gilds were derived from unions of unfree manorial craftsmen ("the manorial theory") is to-day generally abandoned.[3] As little can their origin be traced to the dissolution of a "greater gild" that preceded them. For general *gilds merchant* ("Kaufmannsgilden")

[1] *A. Schulte,* "Geschichte des mittelalterlichen Handels und Verkehrs", I (1900), 372.

[2] *Hegel,* "Städte und Gilden der germanischen Völker" (2 vols., 1891); *Keutgen,* "Ämter und Zünfte. Zur Entstehung des Zunftwesens" (1903); *Frensdorff,* essay cited in § 14 *supra; v. Below,* art. "Zünfte" in W. B. der Volksw., II (2d ed. 1907), 1425–35, "Zur Geschichte des Handwerks und der Gilden", in Hist. Z., cvi (3d ser. 10, — 1911), 268–294, and "Die Motive der Zunftbildung im deutschen Mittelalter", in same, CIX (3d ser., 13, — 1912), 23–48; *Stieda,* art. "Zunftwesen" in H. W. B. der Staatsw., VIII (3d ed., 1911), 1088–1111.

[3] The manorial theory has recently been again adopted, although with changes that are concessions, by *Seeliger,* "Staat und Grundherrschaft in der älteren deutschen Geschichte." (1909), and by *Walther Müller,* "Zur Frage des Ursprungs des mittelalterlichen Zünfte, Eine Wirtschafts und verfassungsgeschichtliche Untersuchung", No. 21 (1911) of *Brandenburg's* "Abhandlungen"; by the latter with the approval of *Schmoller,* in his J. B., XXXV (1911), 2033–36. In criticism of *Seeliger* see *v. Below* in the Hist. Z., CVI (3d ser., 10), as above cited; and in criticism of *Müller,* also *v. Below* in same, cvii (3d ser., 11, — 1911), 591 *et seq.*

of the kind that existed in the Netherlands, Flanders, England, and elsewhere, have, it seems, not been provable in Germany. Yet undoubtedly there existed there also, and at an early day, special gilds of merchants, who traded either in certain wares or with certain foreign market-towns. These gilds of merchants and itinerant traders became less important when increasing security of intercourse made less imperative the need of alliance. Nevertheless, gilds of merchants trading to foreign parts maintained themselves for a very long time, — for example the Association of Herring Fishers in Lübeck; and along with these there were unions of German merchants in foreign lands, such as the hanse of German merchants in Nowgorod, Bergen, Brügge, and London.

(2) *Craft-companies* ("Ämter"). — Contrary to the above theory, the development of the crafts seems to have had its starting point in official market regulations issued by local governmental authorities (Keutgen's theory).[1] From the Carolingian time the control of markets was included among the powers of public officials, or later among those of the city lords, especially the bishops, and they assigned the administration of the trade police and the jurisdiction of the market court either to the regular town magistrate or to a special administrative official ("Kämmerer", chamberlain, custodian). In order to exercise an effective control of the market the sellers were divided into groups of single traders, and separate stands ("Stände") were assigned to them. These groups of artisans and tradesmen were the "companies" ("Ämter" or "magisteria"). They were based exclusively upon the market ordinances issued by the municipal authorities. The local government soon came to restrict itself to a general oversight; it set over the gilds masters taken from the unions, who held the court and (often aided by a committee) exercised the police power.

(3) *Fraternities.* — The essential characteristic of free association, which marked the later craft gilds but was still lacking the craft companies, made progress in the craftsmen's unions as soon as the artisans, united for industrial purposes in the companies created by the market authorities, extended the purposes of those unions beyond industrial matters to social, charitable, and religious ends. This was the more natural because it gave expression to an old Germanic idea, afterward strengthened by Christianity,

[1] The opponents of this theory are indicated by *v. Below* in Hist. Z., cix (3d ser., 13, — 1912), 24, note 2.

that those with whom one stands in close relationship, even though not one of blood, are brothers, and that such brotherhood should be employed in a common cultivation of spiritual interests, — which in those times ordinarily found primary expression in religious and churchly communion. The old Germanic brotherhood was a community of board (hence Mid. Low G. "matschap", Mod. Dutch "maatschapij"), a community of bread ("Kompagnie" from "panis"), a community of the bowl ("convivium"), a gild, — in short "a gathering for festive eating and drinking." Further, it was a fellowship of covenanters ("coniuratio").[1] The craftsmen started from these old ideas and institutions, and the brotherhood ("fraternitas") offered them the institutional type by which to pass from the position of a branch of the municipal administration to that of a free society. The immediate result was an intimate fusion of the very diverse elements that had been brought together in the companies, — freemen and men formerly unfree, native townsmen and immigrants; and which had theretofore wholly lacked all coherence, such as resulted in the mark-association from the earlier relationship of blood. And although, as is readily understood, the local governmental authorities were in no wise friendly disposed to any endeavors of the city population toward union, such tendencies toward religious and ecclesiastical unity must nevertheless have been least unwelcome to them, especially to the clerical authorities. Indeed, they owed their origin, to a great extent, precisely to clerical incitement. Their churchly ends, like their commercial purposes, being of a public nature, the establishment of craft gilds that were to be at the same time fraternities required the authorization of ecclesiastical authority. Moreover, it was not true that every craft gild of later times had necessarily originated in a company: freedom of association was the basis of many of the later crafts from the beginning. Nevertheless, the craft gild as a special type of association is to be conceived of as having originated in a coalescence of company and fraternity.

(II) **Essential nature of the Craft Gilds.** (1) *The Principle of "Gild-coercion"* ("Zunftzwang"). — The craft ("Zunft", from "ziemen", to be fit), a name which was used exclusively in South Germany down into the 1500 s for what were ordinarily called in North Germany "gilds" ("Gilden"), was a union that affected the entire personality of the gildmen, being therein akin

[1] See *Pappenheim*, "Über künstliche Verwandtschaft im germanischen Recht", in Z.[2] R. G., XXIX (1908), 304–333.

to the mark-association. It concerned itself with all their relations, under both private and public law, those that were social and those merely human. For this reason the whole family of an associate, not merely himself alone, belonged to the craft gild. But in the crafts, as in the mark-association, the economic purpose was primary; they were essentially economic associations. From this aspect their most important characteristic was the principle of "gild-coercion", which was already essential in the administrative "companies." "Gild-coercion" meant that definite handiwork or industrial tasks ("Werk") were assigned to each union as its peculiar field of activity and production; and that only its members had the right to exercise these callings and perform such work within the town-limits or the surrounding "banlieue", and to offer there the products of their labor for sale. At the same time, the question was not one merely of handiwork in the true sense; on the contrary the trades of fishermen, tilers, vintagers, and innkeepers were frequently organized as crafts; and various classes of merchants, money-changers, etc., formed gilds, for the most part of great prestige. The medieval view did not distinguish between tradesmen ("Händler") and industrials ("Gewerbetreibende"), but included both under the common conception of the merchant ("mercator", "Kaufmann").

The right to prosecute their respective handiwork or industries inured to the gildsmen collectively; but it was imposed upon them, also, as a collective duty. Especially in the flowerage period of gild and city life the artisans regarded themselves on that account as officials, and men looked upon the craft as an office to be administered with the utmost possible fidelity and conscience. Consequently, not alone the public authorities but the gild itself protected the interests of the public through associational oversight, by means of penalties, price-tariffs, and otherwise. On the other hand, the craft was supposed, from its beginning, to guard and further the interests of its members and realize equality and fraternity among the gild fellowship, to the end that none might sink to the position of a dependent wage-earner, nor raise himself above his fellows by an undue extension of his business. Above all, it should prelude the competition of workers not included in the gild, — who were later known as "Bönhasen" (bunglers).

(2) *Organization.* — From the beginning the gilds possessed a regular organization which was, in substance, always the same. In earlier times it rested upon the craft privileges conferred by

the public authorities; later it was recorded in the gild rolls and further developed as a result of the autonomy conceded to the crafts.

(A) Membership. — Since the essence of the craft gild was an organized community of labor, and since every worker was obliged by the principle of "gild coercion" to enter that organization which corresponded to his calling, the rules concerning memberships constituted the most important part of the gild law. And though even at an early date special circumstances might make the gild a close corporation, — as *e.g.* when all the stalls or shops assigned to a particular industry were occupied, to the last place, — nevertheless acquisition of membership was generally little impeded in early times. Whoever had gone through the preparatory schooling of apprentice and journeyman, had passed his master's examination, and had completed his master-work, and paid certain fees, was taken in, provided he had also become a burgher of the city. For men at first regarded the increase of members as an advantageous strengthening of the gild, economically and politically, not as an unwelcome lessening of their share in the labor market. Only toward the end of the Middle Ages did an increasing exclusiveness come to be dominant.

(B) Organs. — The organs of the gild were those that everywhere recur in German corporations: the assembly of members and the directorate. The former — which, on account of the hour at which it originally always met was also called the morning parley ("Morgensprache") or "breakfast" parley — exercised the rights of autonomy granted to the gild, making decrees relative to the gild-property, and when necessary establishing new by-laws. At the same time it was subject to the oversight of the public authorities, — that is, the town-council; which in Lübeck, for example, was exercised by delegating two councilmen (so-called "morning-parley men") to the gild-assemblies, notice of whose sessions was given to the council. One or several "masters" ("Zunft-", "Amts-", "Gilde-meister") constituted the directorate: they too were subordinated in a definite way to the council, and must take oath to it to take care that the gild should do nothing prejudicial to the common weal of the city. The gild-masters exercised the right of autonomous judicature which, like that of legislation, belonged to the gild: gildsmen who violated the gild ordinances were punished by them, acting as the gild-court, or the wrongdoers were expelled from the craft. Civil controversies of lesser import between fellow craftsmen must be brought before the gild judges for settlement; if outsiders desired to make complaint against gildsmen they must, before applying to the public court, apply to the gild masters for an adjustment. Above the gild-court stood, as a court of second instance, the council or the court of the city's lord.

(3) *Corporate Character of the Craft Gild.* — From the beginning the entire body of gild members, as such, stood opposed to the individual associate in an independence far more pronounced than was originally the case in the mark-associations, and this is explained by the fact, already adverted to, that there was not in the case of the crafts, as there was in the case of those associations, a complete coincidence of the purposes of the group with those of the members. The craft was not from the beginning designed to further merely the interests of individuals; we have seen that it was precisely the older period when the idea was vital that it had ends to fulfill in the interest of the association, the city, and the purchasing public. But though it was thus, as a body, distinct from its members, — possessing, for example, in the seal it used an external sign of this independence, — nevertheless, there was no more realized in it than in the mark-association a total separation of the association, as such, from the physical persons of the members who composed it. In particular, the gild property was not the property of an independent third person; it could not have seemed to the gild fellows a thing wholly alien to themselves. The gild-chambers, the gild-furniture, the capital accumulated by contributions, entrance fees, and penalties, and gifts, served not alone the ends of the association, but also the economic, social, and other purposes of the members. Every associate might, for example, use the gild-houses for his convivial pleasures; each could demand support or loans from the capital of the gild; and so on. These benefits were not, however, indispensable to the gild members in the same way that the usufruct of the commonty was to the markmen; the gild-property was devoted in far greater degree to the whole body as such. It was not merely an associational but a corporate-like associational collective property (*infra*, § 33).

(III) **Decline and Disappearance of the Crafts.** — The organization of industries in crafts continued to flourish, speaking generally, down into the 1500 s, notwithstanding that some abuses manifested themselves earlier. From that period onward the craft system fell into an increasing torpidity and renitence which, in conjunction with the general decline of intellectual culture and material civilization, led finally to complete decay. From remotest times the regulation of entrance conditions to the gild had been, as already remarked, essential to the gild-organization and with good reason, since the crafts were supposed to be responsible for good workmanship. Hence the requirement of the master's examination, and the exhaustive regulation of apprenticeship and journeyman's service. But these institutions were now made over in uncompromisingly monopolistic fashion. "Egoism became supreme in place of public spirit."[1] Membership in the crafts came to be a purchasable thing; members of the gild families were shown preferences formerly unheard of over strangers; the journeyman system, instead of being used to broaden the workers' views, as was so necessary, was developed into a most oppressive fetter. Above all, the requirement of stainless civil honor ("Ehre") was overemphasized to a most unreasonable degree. Illegitimate birth constituted an absolute cause for exclusion, not to be avoided even by legitimation (*supra*, p. 107); which must have seemed the stranger because the other social estates tolerated in this same period decidedly free ideas on that point. It could justly be said that the 1700 s saw bastards climb to the highest honors in State and army, but cobblers and tailors they could not have become in a German town. And equally extravagant was the extension given to the concept of dishonorable industries (*supra*, p. 107).

Thus, precisely because of the craft organization German handicraft continuously declined. In place of seeking the introduction of fresh blood, it timidly shut the way to this. From the proud burgher who had once defended his city in arms, there sprang the jibe-provoking "Spiessbürger" ("piddle burghers", — of parochial outlook and cheese-paring policies) or philistines. The word "gild-spirit" ("Zunftgeist") acquired at that time its unpleasant secondary meaning.

The abuses of the old gild system, which nevertheless found a warm defender only shortly before its complete disappearance in so perspicacious a man as Justus Möser, demanded ever more insistently a remedy. The municipal authorities being too weak to achieve reforms, the imperial and Territorial governments finally intervened. But the endeavors made by these in the 1700 s — the decree of the Imperial Diet in 1731, and the Territorial statutes associated with that (*supra*, p. 107) — failed to bring about any lasting improvement. And thus men finally found

[1] *Frensdorff*, in Hans. G. B., 1907, 61.

themselves compelled in Germany, following the example of France, to do away completely with the crafts in their character of involuntary organizations of city artisans endowed with exclusive industrial privileges. This was done in Prussia by the edict of Nov. 2, 1810, and the statute of Sept. 7, 1811; and the Imperial Industrial Code (" Reichsgewerbeordnung ") of June 21, 1869, accomplished as much for all Germany. In more recent years imperial legislation has again abandoned the principle of unqualified industrial freedom, and introduced anew gild-like organizations. Supplements to the Industrial Code, particularly the statutes of July 18, 1881, and July 26, 1897, once more conferred upon trade unions (" Handwerkerinnungen ") a compulsory character, subject to definite preconditions. These unions of the present-day law are juristic persons, — societies (" Vereine ") in the sense of the Civil Code, — and indeed public corporations (" öffentliche Körperschaften ").

§ 20. **Other Associations without the Bond of Vicinage.** — Just as there developed alongside of the mark-associations other groups bound together by interests connected in some way with landholding, so the craft-gilds were accompanied by numerous other associations which in part pursued industrial ends and in part other purposes, without, however, being consolidated by bonds of vicinage.

(I) **Industrial Associations.** — To these belonged, among others:

(1) *The Minters' Associations.* — In the Middle Ages the " Münzherr ", that is the holder of the regality of coinage, was accustomed to entrust the care of the mint to a corporate association endowed with various privileges known as the " Hausgenossen " (mint fellows), at whose head was a mint-master whom they freely chose. The " Hausgenossen " were originally unfree artisans of the city lord, and the mint-master was chosen from his household servitors. Later both attained a respected position, for in time the indispensable precondition to membership in the minters' association came to be the possession of a fortune, instead of technical skill, its chief task having become the procurement of the necessary minting metal at its own cost and risk. The technical labor was left to servile workers. Thus the minters' association came to imply membership in a corporation of high repute; it obligated the associates merely to a money contribution and secured them in exchange a share in the profits of coinage. This was employed by them principally in the business of money changing.

(2) The minters' association already shows the type, — not yet, to be sure, fully developed, — of a *capitalistic association* ("Kapitalgenossenschaft"). This type has attained in modern legal and economic life an importance far exceeding that of all other personal unions. Modern capitalistic associations are imaginary unions ("begriffliche Vereine") in which a social fund divided into numerical shares constitutes the essential "raison d'être" of a group of persons possessed individually of complete legal independence. According to their form they are in part share companies, in part coöperative ("Erwerbs-") and economic associations, in part mutual insurance companies. Inasmuch, however, as they have been developed, primarily, as products of or in connection with commercial law, it would be superfluous to go further into their nature in this place.

(II) **Associations for Convivial, Religious, and Scientific Purposes.** — As mentioned above (p. 131), the medieval crafts, in addition to their industrial purposes, pursued as brotherhoods religious, convivial, and social ends. There were also at that time many associations that existed exclusively for such purposes. It was precisely the oldest personal unions, based not upon kinship or neighborhood but upon voluntary agreement, that belonged to this category. This was true of the Frankish gilds of Carolingian times, which, like all Germanic gilds based upon the idea of brotherhood, united within a peculiar communal life the religious end of spiritual welfare with the temporal ends of fraternal support and a common table (whence their other name of "convivia"). Then there were the later fraternities founded for special religious or secular ends. The religious were closely connected with the church, their members being admitted without regard to family or social status, and obligated to the practice of pious works and performance of churchly services that they might be assured eternal salvation; the secular secured to their members mutual support and legal aid. Both classes, however, merged easily in each other. Secular gilds for mutual defense ("Schutzgilden") did not play in Germany the same rôle as, for example, in England, Denmark, France, and the Netherlands. The merchant gilds above mentioned (p. 128) may be reckoned among these. On the other hand ecclesiastical brotherhoods were similarly widespread in Germany, at the end of the Middle Ages. In many German cities there were as many as a hundred and more of them, — *e.g.* in Cologne, Lübeck, and Hamburg. The calends-gilds or "calends", so called after the custom of the priests to assemble on the first of the month, were exclusively of the ecclesiastical class. The societies of Beguins or Beghards, which spread to Germany from Belgium and were at times pursued as heretical, were very popular, particularly in North Germany. Originally intended only for women, but later also for men, they often included both in a common household and community of goods, like the kindred monastic associations of brothers living a communal life. Their members devoted themselves, without monastic vows, to industrial labors and pious and useful works.

Among associations for idealistic ends were the universities. That these go back for their origin to Germanic legal ideas, clearly appears from the beginnings of Bologna and Padua, the two type-universities of the Occident.[1] In Bologna the "scholars", *i.e.* the students, grouped themselves in free associations ("universitates"), each of which was divided into a number of compatriotic unions called "nationes." Among these the one of greatest power and prestige was the "natio teutonica", the German student colony. Its archaic, purely Germanic organization shows all the essential characteristics of a Christianized, Germanic frith-gild; this shows us that it was a phenomenon allied to the mercantile hansas, the protective gilds founded by German traders in foreign lands. In Paris the academic union was not composed of the "scholars" alone, but embraced also all the holders of learned degrees, — bachelors, masters, and doctors, — much as is still the case at Oxford and Cambridge; so that there existed there a union comparable to the gilds. The principle of an industrial union ("Innung"), also, was reflected in the fact that the Parisian "studium generale" was divided, at the beginning, not into "nations", but into four "faculties", corresponding to the four learned professions. Later, however, the Italian model was accepted also at Paris, and the entire body of scholars, inclusive of the magistri of the Faculty of Arts (our modern Philosophical Faculty), were divided into four nations, at whose heads stood the rector chosen by the masters of arts. To him the masters of the three higher faculties were compelled finally to bow. The "studium generale" itself, the "University" in the specialized modern sense, thus became a centralized association, and the rector its head. "In this stage of development Paris became the model of the universities established on German

[1] *Brunner*, "Der Anteil des deutschen Rechts an der Entwicklung der Universitäten", rectoral address (Berlin), 15 Oct. 1896, reprinted in the "Deutsches Wochenblatt", IX (1896), No. 43.

soil." The oldest German universities constituted, therefore, "voluntary, self-perpetuating corporate-associations. They possessed, as entities, a quantity of special rights and duties, but above all the usual rights of associations; particularly,— besides the right of public instruction and its consequences — autonomy, judicature, and self-government, the free determination of their own organization and choice of directors and organs, the admission and exclusion of members, and the capacity to carry on trade and to hold property under the private law."[1] Their branches, the individual faculties, formed separate corporations. The associations of the students — the colleges and students' gilds ("Kollegien", "Bursen") — early lost importance in Germany, as compared with England.

(III) Finally, **political ends,** — which were important even in the case of many of the associations already referred to, especially the craft gilds, — might be the essential incentive to union. For example, there appeared in many medieval towns so-called gilds of "ancient burghers" ("Altbürgergilden"), "tavern clubs" ("Stubengesellschaften"), "round-tables" ("Artushöfe"), "Junker clubs" ("Junkerkompagnien"), and commensal and drinking fellowships ("Konstaffeln"); all of which, though dedicated incidentally to the promotion of good fellowship and piety, were chiefly intended to assure to their members, as a body, a prominent share in the town government. Here belongs, for example, the much debated magistrates' club ("Richterzeche") of Cologne, an association of the wealthy persons of the whole city which originated in the second half of the 1100s. It was composed of three classes of members: the two actual burgomasters, ex-burgomasters ("verdienten"), and the officials from whom that office was still to be filled ("unverdienten", "Anwärter"). Their functions consisted in an oversight over the crafts, the administration of the municipal police of trade and industry, oversight of the wine trade, and the conferment of rights of citizenship, — in short, political privileges, whose oppressive exercise drew upon the gild the hatred of the artisans. The public (Cathedral) scales were included among their property.[2] The great town leagues, also, the Hansa and the Rhen-

[1] *Gierke*, "Genossenschaftrecht", I, 438.

[2] *Lau*, "Entwicklung der kommunalen Verfassung und Verwaltung der Stadt Köln bis zum Jahre 1396" (1898), 78 *et seq.* Most recently, *Philippi*, "Die Kölner Richterzeche", in Inst. öst. G. F., XXXII (1911), 87–112; *Seeliger*, "Zur Entstehungsgeschichte der Stadt Köln. Kritische Bemerkungen im Anschluss an H. Keussens 'Topographie der Stadt Köln' (1910)", in Westd. Z. G. K., XXX (1911), 463–505, 485 *et seq.*

ish City League, were of associational character. The knightage was organized in numerous unions of corporate character. These associations of knightly covenanters ("Eidgenossenschaften"), such as the widespread Order of the Lion, the Order of the Mace in Swabia, and the Stellmeiser of the Mark of Brandenburg, played an important rôle, particularly in the 1300 s. While all these political associations possessed only transient importance and sooner or later fell apart, the various alliances, compacts, and treaties of peace out of which the Swiss "Eidgenossenschaft" arose developed into a unitary political community ("Gemeinwesen"). Finally, the estates represented in the imperial Diets, — usually the clergy, the nobles, and the cities, — were organized in the Territories into corporate estates of the realm.

Not only the individual estates ("Ständekorpora") or "curiæ" ("Kurien") as such, but also all of them collectively (the "Landschaft"), possessed such corporate character. These corporations were inconsistent with the conception of the modern State: only in few Territories were they able to withstand, down into modern times, the advance of that idea. The Empire, in its old form, also recognized political corporations of the same kind: unions ("Vereine") of the electoral princes, princes, and counts of the Empire; the colleges, "curiæ", and benches of the imperial Diet; the corporately organized imperial knights of Swabia, Franconia, and the Rhine Province, — who did not enjoy the privileges of estates of the Empire; the corporations of the Catholic and Evangelical estates of the Empire; and the Circles of the Empire.

§ 21. **The Communities "of Collective Hand."**[1] **(I) The Medieval Law.** (1) *Nature of these Communities.* — Besides the associations that were by their very nature so organized as to confer upon the entire body of members, as such, more or less independence apart from the individual members, the medieval law also knew personal unions which, because they included and were calculated for only a relatively limited number of members, showed no such corporal independence. Neverthe-

[1] *Max Huber*, "Die Gemeinderschaften der Schweiz auf Grundlage der Quellen dargestellt", No. 54 (1897) of *Gierke's* "Untersuchungen"; *Georg Cohn*, "Gemeinderschaft und Hausgenossenschaft", in Z. Vergl. R. W., XIII (1898), 1–128; *Dübi*, "Die Gemeinschaften zur gesamten Hand im deutschen und schweizerischen Recht. Ihre Forderungs- und Haftungsverhältnisse", No. 40 (1910) of *Gmür's* "Abhandlungen"; *Fehr*, "Die Rechtsstellung der Frau und der Kinder in den Weistümern" (1912), 147–167.

less, in their case also there was equally recognized a sphere of common rights distinct from the spheres of individual rights of the persons interested, and the holder of those common rights, namely the associated individuals as a body, constituted a legal entity. In their case also, therefore, a community will was operative within the union, and the aggregate membership appeared to the world as an entity endowed with capacity for rights and action. That this entity, however, was not at all regarded as something different from the members individually, was shown in the fact that it was active only through the *collective* action of all the co-holders of the rights held by the community. The associates ("Genossen") or commoners ("Gemeinder," the term usual in this connection) must clasp hands, and then, as with collective hand ("zu gesamter Hand", "communi", "communicata manu") perfect the juristic act. Only so, in unison, could they exercise the right pertaining to them collectively. The individual could not in any way exercise it alone, not even with limitation to the partial interest pertaining to him individually. From this form of common action this species of personal union derived its name. "The unitary nature of action by collective hand lies in this, that rights and duties are realized only through common action, action by one without coöperation of the others being impossible."[1] It was not impossible, it is true, under given circumstances, to grant to one of the "commoners" authority to act at the same time for the rest. And therefore there was quite possible, in the case even of these personal unions, a certain internal organization that corresponded to the apparent solidarity which they presented externally; they showed what we are accustomed to call a certain "corporate" element.

(2) *Origin.* — The communities of collective hand had their roots in the Germanic law of the family. Their point of origin was the Indogermanic institution of the household-community (*supra*, p. 114). Just as the family-members united under the potestas of the house-father constituted a community of which he was the representative, to which community belonged the allotted lands as the collective property of the house, so among the primitive Germans it was a widespread practice that the grown sons, instead of dividing the heritage after the death of their father, should continue to hold the inherited estate "in collective hand", that is in a common household, in order, by thus living together, to maintain the family estate in as com-

[1] *Heusler*, "Institutionen", I, 226.

pact a form as possible. Such greater "house associations" ("Hausgenossenschaften") or associations of commoners ("Gemeinderschaften"), which might include even grandchildren or more remote descendants, are explicitly attested in the folk-laws of the Lombards, Alamanians, Bavarians, and Franks. The Saxons, Frisians, and Anglo-Saxons knew them, also, as did the original East Germans (Burgundians), and equally the Scandinavians. The Latin texts designate the commoners as "coheredes", "comparticipes", "consortes"; an old German translation of a Carolingian capitulary that is preserved to us already uses the common medieval expression "Ganerben", that is co-heirs.[1] These communities of collective hand of the family law persisted down to the end of the Middle Ages, and locally down even to present times, — though of course not everywhere as an institute occurring, as it once did, equally throughout all classes of society, but only as one occurring in sporadic forms.

(3) *Specific Types.* (A) THE PEASANT COMMUNITIES OF COLLECTIVE HAND. — Within the peasant estate communities of collective hand were widely spread throughout the Middle Ages in South and West Germany. Though they have even to-day by no means wholly died out in these regions, they have nevertheless gradually grown rarer, for the most part retreating into Switzerland. They played a great rôle there in the 1500 s and 1600 s, as well in the Burgundian as in the Alamanian districts. Even to-day they are there still alive in the popular consciousness. In the Zürich Code of 1853–55 they were capitally regulated. The new Swiss Civil Code, continuing the traditional development of the law, classifies them exhaustively from a socio-political viewpoint. These peasant communities existed for the most part among brothers and sisters and their descendants, but almost always among individuals of equal rights, and consequently not among parents and children. The last, at any rate, was only exceptionally the case, and was explicitly excluded in the legal systems of many regions because inconsistent with parental powers.[2] Such communities were marked, throughout, by the old characteristics of the family law. However, they did not originate solely by force of statute as a consequence of the death of the heritor but might be also established by contract. The latter was the case, particularly, with the very numerous communities that existed among serfs, especially among those of

[1] M.G., Cap. I, 380.
[2] *Fehr*, work just cited, 147–149.

ecclesiastical houses, which were formed for the purpose of avoiding the necessity of paying the tribute due on the death of every serf; tribute being paid only on the death of the eldest commoner, who represented the community. The commoners or share-holders (" Geteilten ") usually lived in communal household, in joint profit and loss; in the words of the sources, they lived " in einem Mus und Brot " (" with common pap and bread "). The community generally extended to the entire heritage; in addition to which the individual members might of course possess separate estates, — the property of the wife a man took was, for example, so regarded. Shares existed only in the ideal sense; any separate disposition of the same was impossible. Externally the community of collective hand appeared, as of old, only in the common act of all its members. But the eldest male member was usually, nevertheless, the representative of the community: as it is put in a doom of Einsiedeln, the eldest brother might " undertake to attend the courts, and to represent the other brothers who remain at home " (" zu den gerichten gan und die anndern brüder, so daheimen beliben, versprechen ") ;[1] and so too the eldest was alone liable to death duties. If a commoner died, his children took his place ipso facto; if he died without descendants, there was originally benefit of survivorship in favor of the remaining commoners, to the consequent exclusion of such heirs of the decedent, whether equally near or more distant, as did not belong to the community. In some legal systems, however, such benefit of survivorship was in time weakened in favor of the heirs. The community was readily dissolvable; in particular, dissolution could be demanded in case of the loss (" Wegfall ") of any members. Indeed, in some places the commoners possessed a right, exercisable at any time, to give notice of withdrawal. The dissolution of a community in consequence of the complete partition and consequent satisfaction of the rights of the individual commoners out of the family estate theretofore held in common (" Tod- ", " Grund- ", " Realteilung "; partition by death, real partition), was known as " Watschar " (from " swascara " — more exactly " twas-scara ", " propria portio "). In later times partition was made more difficult. Partition was made upon the basis of the relations existent at the moment of division (" ex nunc ").

(B) Co-heir communities of knights. — Such institutions

[1] *Grimm*, "Weistümer", I, 152. *Cf. Huber*, "Schw. Privatrecht", IV, 253. Fehr, *op. cit.*, 159 *et seq.*

were not kept up, nor did they originate, independently, in the burgher classes. Crafts and other associations in the cities were evidently so numerous that the need of communities of collective hand could not there be felt; and besides, it was in the cities that the community forms of the *commercial* law (hereafter referred to) later found their widest distribution. But among the knightage the co-heir communities played an important rôle. They too preserved the principle of the old family community, although in somewhat different manner than did the peasant communities of collective hand. Of these last, as already remarked, a communal household continued to be, under all normal circumstances, the necessary foundation; for a vital consciousness of family solidarity could not survive, in them, a "real" partition. On the other hand, the feeling of solidarity and the regard for family fame was stronger in the exclusive classes of the upper and lower nobility. In these, therefore, men did not shrink from divisions of the common household, notwithstanding such division could be carried through only with inconvenience to knights who were accustomed to rather pretentious needs. When, as was frequently the case, the partition was merely one of usufructs, not affecting the preservation of the substance ("Mutschierung", "Örterung", as contrasted with "Watschar"), solidarity was easily preserved. Equally so wherever the castle-garth afforded sufficient room to assign to the individual co-heirs their own buildings, farms, and towers. Burg Eltz in the Moselle valley and the Schwarzburg in Thuringia are examples of such "Ganerben" castles.[1] But even where a partition of substance was made, the principle of "collective hand" was preserved in the co-heir community. Notably in the so-called "castle-peaces" ("Burgfrieden") or "family unions" ("Stammvereine"), — compacts by which relations of co-heirship could be established among non-kindred, and in which we see the prototypes of the later "fideikommissum" settlements,[2] — it was customary expressly to regulate inheritance by the principle of collective hand; so that in the absence of near kindred the share of a decedent passed to the other co-heirs by survivorship. Further, the shares were inalienable, or alienable only to a limited extent; a partition could be had only with the consent of all. Consequently such relations, when protected, persisted for long periods, and might assume a corporate character, as in

[1] *Piper*, "Burgenkunde" (3d ed., 1912), 571 *et seq.*
[2] *Brunner*, "Grundzüge" (5th ed.), 242.

the case of the so-called "castle communities" ("Burggemeinwesen"), which outlived centuries. Moreover such collective relationships were not based solely upon contractual unions, but very often upon collective feoffments.

(C) Herital fraternities. — It was chiefly among the nobles of the knightly class, especially the class of imperial knights, that co-heir communities were a favored type of the community of collective hand. Among the high nobility there were formed for the same ends from the 1300 s onward so-called "herital fraternities" ("Erbverbrüderungen"), in which the principle of collective hand found similar embodiment, although in a still weaker form. These involved a purely formal union: the different houses associated in the fraternity acknowledged mutually the use of the coats of arms and titles of their various seigniories, arranged mutual recognition tributes, and doubtless each accepted homage from the subjects of all. But the government of their domains remained entirely separate. At the same time the principle of collective hand was evidenced in the fact that dispositions relative to territories received into the fraternity could be made only with collective hand; and that on the extinction of one of the fraternal houses its possessions escheated to the other members of the fraternity. Examples of such herital fraternities are the Saxon-Hessian "Erbverbrüderung" of 1373, to which Brandenburg acceded in 1457, and which was last renewed in 1614; and the Wittstock Compact of 1442, renewed in 1752, which gave Brandenburg rights of succession — not mutual — in Mecklenburg.

(D) Unions under public and international law. — These "Erbverbrüderungen" were predominantly political in character, and this was true in still more pronounced degree of many unions under public and international law. At the same time, these are only very loosely connected with the communities of collective hand. Here may be included the real unions of international law; further, joint governments, common bailiwicks, joint rights of judicature and of advowson, as well as the common seigniories of the old Swiss Confederation of the Thirteen Places.

(E) The marital community of collective hand. — Finally, a form of community of collective hand that appears in all Germanic lands and in all classes of society, was the marital community of collective hand ("Eheliche Gesamthand"), which controlled the legal relation of husband and wife wherever the idea of the husband's guardianship was supplemented in the field of property law by the idea of the "Genossenschaft", and the law of marital community of property built up upon that double basis. The community of collective hand between the spouses was often extended to the recognition of a community of goods between the surviving spouse and children. (As to this see details below under Family Law.)

(II) **The Modern Development.** — Personal unions of collective hand either remained or became of great importance for modern German law, and even for the law of to-day. It is indeed true, as already remarked, that the peasant communities of collective hand have disappeared in Germany save for scanty vestiges: the co-heir communities of knights have wholly disappeared, and the herital fraternities have been completely divested of their slight content of private law. On the other hand the marital community and the "continued" marital community of goods have persisted in various legal systems. Some, as *e.g.* the Prussian "Landrecht", regulated the herital communities ("Erbengemeinschaften") as communities of collective hand. Others, as *e.g.* here again the Prussian "Landrecht", gave effect to the same principle — either unconsciously or under the influence of conceptions of the Law of Nature — in regulating the *general* law of societies or partnerships ("Gesellschaftsrecht"). But it was of still greater importance that the principle remained (or again became) dominant in commercial law. Beyond a reference to the literature[1] of that subject it need here be only briefly remarked that not only the commandite partnership, and in peculiar degree the ship partnership ("Reederei"), but above all that particular form of mercantile partnership which is recognized in our law to-day as the typical form, namely the mercantile partnership of unlimited liability, are based upon the principle of collective hand. The question may be left unanswered whether the unlimited partnership goes back in origin — as many reasons indicate to be at least probable — to co-heir communities of collective hand in which the sons of a merchant continued the business of their father. Equally without discussion must the question (variously answered) remain, whether in medieval Germany, and especially in the world of trade dominated

[1] See: *K. Lehmann*, "Lehrbuch des Handelsrechts" (2d ed., 1912), 280 *et seq.; Hacmann*, "Beitrag zur Entwicklung der offenen Handelsgesellschaft", in Z. ges. H. R., LXVIII (3d ser. IX, 1910), 439–482; LXIX (3d ser. X, 1911), 47–92.

by the Hansa, the unlimited partnership had already been adopted to any considerable extent before contact with the law of Southern and Western Europe.[1] At all events, the Germanic principles of collective hand were adopted in the Italian and French legislation of the 1500 s and 1600 s, which regulated the unlimited partnership in a sense which, especially in France, was decisive of its later development. They were thence brought back, through the old Commercial Code, to Germany, thereby acquiring importance as models for the law of the present Civil Code (below, § 25).

Topic 2 — Practical and Theoretical Results of German Legal Development

§ 22. **General Principles of the German Law of Associations.** — If one takes a general view of the legal ideas that have controlled the development of associational organization in German law, one notes first of all a contrast, which was present from the beginning, between associations proper ("Genossenschaften"), which included a great number of members, and communities dominated by the principle of the collective hand ("Gemeinderschaften"), whose organization was adapted to a smaller number of participants.

(I) **Associations proper and Corporate Associations.** (1) *Associations.* — These unions, which were ordinarily relatively large, went through an evolution that gradually brought to full development certain nuclear principles which, though already present in them from the beginning, were at first undeveloped. In the oldest form of such unions that can be denominated associations in the strict sense ("Genossenschaften"), — namely in the sib, and especially in the mark-associations of the early Middle Ages, — there was, indeed, already recognized a certain independence of the entire body, as distinguished from its members; but it was one of which contemporaries were as yet scarcely conscious. It gradually became manifest, however, and with increasing definiteness. It found clearest expression in those localities where the commune appeared, in contrast with its members and their separate economic interests, as a group

[1] *Keutgen*, "Hansische Handelsgesellschaften, vornehmlich des 14. Jahrhunderts", in Vj. Soz. W. G., IV (1906), 278 *et seq.*, 460 *et seq.*, 567 *et seq.*; *K. Lehmann*, "Hansische Handelsgesellschaften", in same, VIII (1910), 128–136. *Stein*, "Zur Geschichte älterer Kaufmannsgenossenschaften", in Hans. G. B., XVI (1910), 571–591.

impelled by its own political purposes. This was earliest true of the urban communes. But the rural communes followed the same development, and likewise the purely economic unions; and this was true of these last alike when they had existed independently from the beginning beside the village commune as a complex of mark-associations, and when they were only gradually differentiated, in varied forms, from the political communes.

(2) *Corporate Associations.* — Wherever such a process of differentiation took place, and a group-entity as such made its appearance in legal life as the locus of an independently active will, the "Genossenschaft" (association) had developed into a "Körperschaft" (corporate association). It was characteristic of such corporate associations of Germanic law that the group ("Verband") was on one hand regarded as an independent entity endowed with its own legal personality, — a collective person composed of the physical persons of the associates, and possessing a collective will, which was formed through the formal fusion of all individual wills; but, on the other hand, the abstraction which men already needed for the mere *conception* of a collective personality unembodied in a definite physical being, was not carried so far in medieval law that men would have recognized in this entity to which independence was so far attributed, a subject of rights wholly distinct from the individual associates, and into legal relations with which the associates could have entered only as with a wholly alien person. Therefore, and in particular, the usufructuary rights of the associates in the property belonging to the group were not regarded as rights in the property of another. On the contrary all possible rights in the association property appeared as apportioned between the group and the individuals, and this in such manner that the right of disposing thereof inhered essentially in the whole body, but the rights of usufruct therein inhered in the individuals. This view reflected the peculiarity of the German concept of ownership. A corporate collective personality behind which the plurality of associates is in no way hidden, found its counterpart in the law of things in a corporate collective property (*infra*, § 33).

As collective personalities, an organization was essential to the corporate associations; but no other or greater organization than the older associations already possessed. In this way it became possible to conceive of a unitary will, although in the constitution of this the majority principle, by which the greater body of persons was enabled to bind the lesser, did not find absolute recognition until a late day.[1] The corporate organs, through which it exercised its autonomy in enactments, judicature, and administration, were everywhere the general assembly of members and a directorate consisting of one or several persons. The directorate represented the "Körperschaft" (the corporation of Germanic law) in its external relations; but it sometimes happened that in certain cases special representatives were named, as for example in lawsuits. Here again, however, the old view long made itself felt that the group, that is all the members together, must appear before the court, in order to bring complaint, be impleaded, take oath, and so on; and special privileges were besought and granted by which representation by a few members was recognized as sufficient. So, for example, in a lawsuit which the city of Göttingen prosecuted in 1383, 278 burghers were obliged to appear before the Territorial Court; only in 1385 was it provided by charter that two councilmen and four or five worthy burghers should thenceforth act as representatives of the city. In 1443 the town of Lauingen was similarly summoned before the Veme in the person of her 88 burghers above 20 years of age.

In consequence of the legal personality of the corporation it was regarded as capable of holding property, and therefore also as possessing capacity to inherit. All the varieties of medieval corporations that have been discussed, and equally the still older types of association, were owners alike of immoveable and of moveable property: commonties, herds, agricultural and industrial implements; buildings in town and country, food supplies, stocks of goods, capital funds, etc. And they might equally well possess, as corporations, real rights of all kinds, and obligational claims.

From the corporation's capacity for rights and action the medieval law logically deduced the rule that it might also commit torts; in other words, it had delictual capacity. But here again the characteristic regard shown at once for the group and for the individuals composing it, found clear expression. For the consequences of a violation of law committed by a corporation, — *e.g.* the pronouncement of an unjust doom, the choice of an inefficient official, the breaking of a contract, the punishment of alien subjects contrary to law, etc. — might fall either upon the corporation as such or upon the individual associates, and either in the form

[1] *Cf.* the Ssp., II, 55.

of an obligation to give damages or as a penalty. It was not rarely the case, in the medieval period, that villages, cities, communes, whole countries, as well as other corporations, were proscribed by vehmic right, outlawed, or excommunicated; that their corporate property was confiscated, and their corporate rights taken away. And such punishments — as outlawry, ban, proscription, razure of the town — came home to every individual in a very near way. But aside from that, when the city was bound to pay damages execution was possible, in case of necessity, against the persons and private property of all the burghers. That is, although men found it possible to distinguish between city or village and the citizens or villagers, and to conceive of the council or local governing authority as an *organ* of the commune, nevertheless, in cases of *obligations* of the commune under the property law, not only the communal property but also all the commune members, or at least the councilors, were regarded as liable. Not infrequently, in the establishment of city schools, the council expressly made the individual burghers co-obligors. Conversely, the whole association was originally liable for the delinquencies and contractual obligations of the individual associates; though this view, it is true, was more and more abandoned, speaking generally, even in the Middle Ages. At least the cities thenceforth admitted their liability for the contractual obligations and delictual liabilities of their burghers only when the city denied the creditors of these a legal hearing, or otherwise protected the wrongdoers, thereby making their debt its own.[1]

Most of the corporations of the Middle Ages originated as a product of customary law. Mark-associations and communes existed from the earliest times, and gradually assumed associational and corporate character quite in the natural course of development. Other corporations, however, originated in consciously creative acts. Such acts often proceeded from the State or from the local superior authority; manorial lords formed manorial communes and mark-associations; kings and princes established cities or conferred the privileges of town-law upon older settlements; city lords called craft companies into being and consented to their conversion into gilds; and so on. Many other associations, however, owed their existence to voluntary union, that is, to an establishment by virtue of compact, as was true of the protective gilds and brotherhoods, — and indeed the

[1] *Gierke*, "Genossenschaftsrecht", II, 772.

impulse of voluntary union was essential to the craft gilds. As these varied modes of origin show, the Middle Ages knew no general, invariant legal rules that applied in all cases to the process by which associations and corporations were formed. As a matter of fact the principle of voluntary corporate organization was of wide prevalence. It is true that the local authorities claimed the right to dissolve personal unions that appeared to them dangerous, and that general prohibitions of gilds and fraternities were consequently repeatedly resorted to from the Carolingian period onward for political reasons, although without lasting effect. But at all events the view was unknown that an existing personal union, recognized as such, needed any special act of the State as a prerequisite to the acquisition of legal personality. On the contrary this was inherent in all corporate, and in lesser degree in all other, associations.

(II) **The Communities of Collective Hand.** — The "Gemeinderschaften", unlike associations proper ("Genossenschaften"), originated in the house community, and not in the sib, and they continued to the end without independent legal personality. The principle of collective hand by which they were controlled always remained distinct from the associational and corporate bond. It is true, however, that this contrast first appeared in full clarity when the corporate association had everywhere been developed out of the older and looser association. Thenceforth, the community of collective hand could be contrasted, as a type of union lacking legal personality, with the corporation as a personal union endowed with individual legal personality. But despite this fundamental and principal unlikeness, there was no sharp division between the two types in actual life, so that under some circumstances the one might pass over into the other, — as was the case, for example, with many co-heir communities of knights that gradually acquired a corporate character (*supra*, p. 143). The reason for this fact, peculiar to medieval law and springing from its scant liking for clean-cut and exclusive formulas, lay in the following qualities (already mentioned) of those two varieties of personal unions. The corporate association involved as little as the association proper a complete absorption of the individual associate in the entity of the union: on the contrary the right of the whole was restricted by the individual rights of the associates. There resulted from this, despite the recognition of the totality as an independent legal personality, an approach to the principle of collective hand, to which was essential an *exclusive* regard for the individual commoners and the absence of any fully developed entity embracing them. On the other hand, in the case also of the community of collective hand, although this remained a mere legal relation among several individuals, it was nevertheless possible to unite these participants into a group recognized by the law of persons and to bind their separate wills "associationally." For the principle of collective hand merely signified that the united commoners were the holders of the collective right; that no one of them possessed even a distributive power of disposition, in proportion to his share, over the community property. In that respect, however, the community of collective hand approximated a corporate organization, although without passing over into it. Moreover, a certain organization, and notably the conferment upon one of the commoners of representative power, was also by no means impossible in its case.

In these forms of association, corporate association, and community of collective hand, the medieval law had devised a regulation of associational unions which was closely adjusted to the rich expression of the social life of the time, and excellently adapted to its needs, and one which rested throughout upon sound and simple conceptions. Undoubtedly it was susceptible of further development, and would have presented no difficulties to a thorough scientific elaboration and systematic treatment. But the reception of the alien law made all that impossible.

§ 23. **The Reception of the Alien Law and the Renascence of Germanic Law in Theory and Practice.** (I) **The Corporation Theory of the Alien Law.** — With the Reception the romanistic corporation theory, as it had been constructed in medieval Italy upon the basis of the rather barren Roman sources by the Civilians, Glossators, Post-Glossators, and Canonists, — an elaborate structure of ideas influenced in many parts by Germanic legal conceptions, — attained a dominance at first unlimited. Unfortunately, the Roman-schooled jurists of Germany lacked understanding for the Germanic elements of that theory, and the native law was in danger of dying in the bonds of alien legal concepts. For the fundamental concepts of the alien law were diametrically opposed to those of the Germanic law. Its distinction between juristic persons and other forms of personal unions, as well as its classification of juristic persons, contradicted theretofore familiar conditions and conceptions.

(1) "*Universitas*" *and* "*Societas*." — The Roman-Italian law

arranged personal unions under two categories that were in the sharpest contrast, notionally, with each other:[1] that of the "universitas" and that of the "societas."

(A) The "UNIVERSITAS", or corporation in the narrow sense, ("Korporation") is a collective person, or group entity, endowed with legal personality. It is entirely independent of, and is sharply distinguished from, the members of the corporation. The property of the corporation is not the property of the corporation members; these can have rights in it only as in an alien thing; but no distributive or share rights therein based upon such membership. The claims and obligations of the corporation are not claims and debts of its members.[2] In a law suit the corporation is an independent litigant party; its members are not parties. Acts of the members neither give rights to nor impose obligations upon the corporation as such, unless when those members are formally empowered to act as its representatives. The corporation is organized for all time; a change in the content of its membership has no effect upon the existence of the corporation. In Roman law, the Roman State and, particularly, the commune were regarded as such "universitates." Private societies ("Vereine"), though many such existed, played only a subordinate rôle.

(B) Unlike the "universitas", the "SOCIETAS" or partnership ("Gesellschaft") was no subject of rights, but merely a legal relation between the partners. The partnership is therefore, as such, without capacity either for rights or action, and consequently is incapable of holding property. There is therefore no partnership property that can be distinguished in any manner from the private property of the partners. If the partners accumulate property through contributions or otherwise, it belongs in shares, distributively, to the individual partners. Each partner can at any time require the dissolution of the partnership relation, and has a claim, then, to his share as a partner. The partnership is a legal relation that exists exclusively between

[1] For the contrary view see *Mitteis*, "Römisches Privatrecht bis auf die Zeit Diokletians", I (1908), 342–347. He attempts to establish the existence in the Roman "universitas" of traces of the associational idea, declaring it possible "that the inflexible corporation concept of the classical period was merely the result of a long evolutional process which may perhaps have started with a group-concept quite as full of germinal vitality as that of the Germanic law."

[2] According to *Mitteis, op. cit.*, 345, this principle, ascribed by dominant legal theory to the Roman law, is also not in point: "Expressions such as 'quod universitati debetur singulis non debetur' express merely the formal unity of corporations in relations with third parties, and leave quite untouched the question as to the nature of the internal bond."

the persons who join in the partnership contract; every change in the membership theoretically dissolves the partnership. Moreover, the Roman "societas" exacted of the individual not even the slightest sacrifice of his existence as a separate personality.[1]

(2) *Nature and Species of Juristic Persons.* — Under the influence of Christianity, the later Roman law came to recognize as corporations, besides group-persons ("universitates personarum"), so-called "universitates bonorum." That is to say, it assumed that property segregated by juristic acts inter vivos or mortis causa, and dedicated as an "endowment" ("Stiftung") to a pious or charitable purpose ("pia causa", "pium corpus"), could itself be an independent holder of rights and duties. But it was not from the scanty rules of the Roman law that the Canon law developed the doctrine, — dominant in medieval and in modern times, — of the "foundation" ("Anstalt") and the endowment as independent legal personalities. The conception of the "foundation" as an immortal person, endowed with special property, created for special ends, and subjected to an external will, found a prototype in the ecclesiastical theory of the church, which men conceived of as an establishment ordained of God, organized from above, and endowed as an independent holder of rights. The legal concepts of foundation and endowment passed, however, from the Canon into the German law. The latter had developed in the localized property of the proprietary church, or in certain parts thereof—namely the benefice, the church lights, and the church-buildings ("Fabrikvermögen")—a peculiar ecclesiastical type of a special estate ("Sondervermögen," § 27 *infra*). And though the statutes of the Church relating to advowsons later swept away the element of ownership which was the basis of this, they nevertheless recognized this special estate as an independent endowment. "It was not out of the endowment of the old Roman law, with which connections had for centuries been broken, but from Germanic roots, that the personality of the foundations and endowments of the ecclesiastical law directly grew, — and mediately, the foundations and endowments of the private law. But of course this development was furthered by the revival of legal science."[2] Finally, as re-

[1] *Gierke*, "Genossenschaftsrecht", III, 41.

[2] *Stutz*, art. "Kirchenrecht", in *v. Holzendorff-Kohler*, "Encyklopädie", (6th ed. 1903), II, 809–972, 860, and "Das Eigenkirchenvermögen, Ein Beitrag zur Geschichte des deutschen Sachenrechtes auf Grund der Freisinger Traditionen", in the "Festgabe O. Gierke dargebracht" (1911), 1187–1268, 1263 *et seq.*, especially 1267 *et seq.*

gards the nature of the juristic person or corporation, the fiction-theory, only suggested in the Roman sources, attained complete elaboration and undisputed dominance. Men were agreed that the "universitas" was, indeed, a person; but equally that its personality rested on a legal fiction, that it was an insensible and invisible thing without body or soul, cognizable by reason only. True, men remained uncertain as to the relation between conception of this "persona ficta" and that of the aggregate of individuals. The idea appeared that an artificial holder of rights had been created out of nothing. This idea was opposed to the other and more Germanic idea, according to which the fiction consisted only in regarding the aggregate of individuals as a personal entity separate from the members.

(II) **The Reception of the Alien Doctrines.** — After attempts had been made from the 1300 s onward to interpret the German law of associations in terms of the doctrine of the alien law, this was finally adopted by German jurisprudence at the beginning of the 1500 s. In this movement the Imperial Chamber of Justice took the lead, and the judicial-opinions of the university law faculties, and the counsel-practice of individual scholars powerfully coöperated. Legislation next passed under the same influence. But at first, of course, the influence of native conditions and ideas continued to be felt at many points, and even in the final elaboration of the common law they retained a not unimportant influence.

In particular, the conception of the foundation was now for the first time put forward in contrast to the Roman concept of the corporation ("Korporation"). And it was just here that connection could be made with old Germanic conditions. For the German law too, as above pointed out (p. 121), had known from the earliest times relations of power and dependence in which a mass of dependent persons were united about a lord who was their common superior. Above all, the growth of national sovereignty and of the modern State that sprang therefrom, became of decisive importance. Men came to regard the national sovereign, as such, — the ideal entity, outliving changes of dynasties and time, of a governing group ("obrigkeitlicher Verband") ruling over a particular country and attached to a particular ruling house, — as the bearer of supreme governmental rights and duties; as an invisible person, although, indeed, without other physical embodiment than the person of the Territorial ruler, and therefore identified with him, or at least with the ruling house. These were theories of secular content which harmonized with the above-cited Canonistic theories, and which eventually found additional and important support in the political theory of the antique world with which men were then making acquaintance. There was thus developed, within both State and Church, a like conception of the foundation. And this was now applied, following the Canon law, to endowments established by private persons, which were left unconnected with State and Church save that to both of these there was attributed a general power of oversight over such endowments. The contrast between " Anstalt " and " Körperschaft " thenceforth retained fundamental importance. The corporate association represented an aggregate of persons (" Personengesamtheit ") conceived of as a holder of rights directed by the collective will resultant from the formal fusion, in prescribed manner, of the several individual wills. On the other hand, the " foundation " was not based upon the will of a majority, but was subjected to an external will from above, be it that of a ruler or superior in whom the foundation is integrated, or that of the founder, who remains permanently active in his private endowment. In the development of the concept of the foundation and in the classification under it of the State, of ecclesiastical establishments (" Institute "), and of endowments, one may well recognize an extension, reasonable enough from the standpoint of Germanic law, of the doctrine of collective personality.

The same cannot be said of the extension to corporate associations of " foundational " elements, and the transformation of many corporate associations — for example, universities — into " foundations." But this reflects the growing tendency of the time to break down the self-imperium (" Selbstherrlichkeit ") of the medieval " Körperschaft "; [1] a tendency which ultimately, under the lead of the law of nature, united politics and jurisprudence in an endeavor to destroy all independent corporate life, and to set in its place an all-powerful State, sweeping away the corporate-concept along with that of the foundation.

The " Körperschaften " of the German law were treated outright as " Korporationen " in the sense of the common law theory. They were regarded, therefore, as fictitious persons. Accordingly, since as non-existent beings they could not act, representatives must be appointed for them. And so men came, in Germany also, to class juristic persons with infants and insane persons,

[1] *Gierke*, "Privatrecht", I, 461.

who can likewise participate in legal transactions only through representatives recognized by the statutory law. This arrangement passed over into modern codes. True, capacity to hold property was conceded them as a matter of course; but delictual capacity, in the strict sense of the Roman law, was denied them. The sharp division between juristic persons as such and their members, — a division which was flatly contradictory of the native law, — was advocated as at least the sole institute that satisfied the needs of theory; but of course this could not be fully established by statute. Similarly, the Romanists demanded the introduction of the Roman concession theory of incorporation. In fact most of the Territorial systems of law took this view, and associated the attainment of juristic personality with an express act of recognition by the State. Whether this principle also acquired a common law authority remained, it is true, in dispute. At all events, it was in complete contradiction to the native tradition. Moreover, men were constrained to do away with it as regarded certain classes of corporations and to introduce for these the freer principle of normative preconditions.

As the "Körperschaft" was subjected to the corporation-concept of the alien law, so the principles of the Roman "societas" were applied without qualification to the relationships of collective hand of the German law; and there was doubtless involved in this a violence to the native law still more incomprehensible. Precisely here, however, the alien doctrine proved incapable of forcing into its categories the forms of the living German law. The types of partnership of the commercial law, particularly, escaped from its control at a comparatively early date; and in the regulation of partnership law the legislation of the 1700 s was compelled to make many concessions to Germanic ideas (*supra*, p. 146).

(III) **The Renascence of the Native Law.** (1) *In Legal Theory.* — So long as the associational ("Vereins") life of Germany was prostrate in consequence of its general political and economic decline, and so long as the literary and legislative activity of the jurists was directed, in more or less naïvely rationalistic manner and with an entire lack of historical discernment, toward an adjustment of legal theory to the needs of practical life without much regard to logic or principle, the unsatisfactory state of the law of associations was not urgently apparent. But it was bound to become so when the associational type of organization wakened to new life at the beginning of the 1800 s, and modern historical and doctrinal research showed that the existing law was neither in agreement with the Roman sources nor itself presented a consistent system. The more zealous the Romanists were to establish the principles of the pure Roman law as the only ones entitled to recognition, the more insistent was the opposition thereto on the part of the Germanists. It was the great achievement of the associational theory, — as this was first formulated by Beseler,[1] and then elaborated, in particular, by Gierke,[2] who chose this in a special sense as his life work, — that it finally cleared the way for an understanding of the German law, taught men to realize the peculiar genius of this, and helped it to a revived authority.

The "association-theory" ("Genossenschaftstheorie") in the ultimate form given it essentially by Gierke, showed that the two Roman categories of "universitas" and "societas" did not suffice to make intelligible the types of the Germanic law of associations. It offered in their place the contrast developed in the sources between corporate association and association in communities of collective hand in the senses above explained, and proved that the wealth of forms in German law was explicable only by the possibility which it afforded of assimilating the corporate association to the community of collective hand through a recognition of the separate rights of the members, and the community of collective hand to the corporate association by regarding the commoners collectively as constituting a composite entity recognized by the law of persons, and by the recognition of a special social property ("Gesellschaftsvermögen"). It showed that the German law had developed in the "Körperschaft" its own peculiar conception of a collective-person ("Gesamtperson") distinct from the physical members. This collective person of German law is not, like the Roman "corporatio" ("Korporation"), a fictitious person; nor can it be understood through the principles of appointed funds for special purposes ("Zweckvermögen"), or by making the beneficiaries ("Destinatären") collectively the subjects of the common rights, — nor did these theories even fit the Roman law itself.

The "Genossenschaftstheorie" pointed decisively toward the conclusion that the collective person possessed an actual existence in all the forms in which it was manifested; hence it necessarily sought to deduce from general principles of legal philosophy a

[1] First in his "Lehre von den Erbverträgen", I (1835); later in the writings cited on pp. 31 and 36 *supra*.
[2] In the writings cited on p. 110 *supra*.

solution of the difficult problems of the nature of juristic persons and the possibility of a collective will. Granting that it may, in this endeavor, have fallen to some extent into all too abstract and nebulous refinements; granting also that it may well have left unduly in the background the indisputable fact that such collective person, through its very lack of a natural basis, must always remain essentially different from the separate individuals composing it, and that after all it is the individual human beings for whose sake all human unions exist, not vice versa, — still, it sharpened our sight for discernment of the fact that juristic persons, even though not sensible to sight and handling, share this lack of physical existence with *all other* juristic facts and concepts. And as we nevertheless ascribe reality to property or to an obligational relation, so too the State, the commune, the society, the endowment, are real; not merely fictional. We are compelled in our juristic thinking to group together certain phenomena and processes of social life under the category of juristic persons, — that is of legal personalities, — that correspond to no individual human beings. The discernment of this fact of legal theory, which became of essential importance in the theory of the State, was an achievement of ideas developed in Germanic law.[1]

(2) *In Positive Law.* — After the "Genossenschaftstheorie" had won increasing influence in the administration of justice and had received recognition in many imperial statutes, notably those of the commercial law, it was adopted by the present Civil Code as the basis of the law of the society ("Verein") and of the partnership ("Gesellschaft"). The Civil Code no longer knows a "persona ficta"; it concedes to juristic persons not merely capacity for holding property, but also — as it does to physical persons — situs, name, civil honor, etc.; it ascribes to them capacity for action, and also — here again like the old Germanic law — delictual capacity.[2] It is true, however, that because of political misgivings a general introduction of the principle of free association, such as is realized in the English law for example,

[1] The Germanistic theory has recently been sharply attacked by *Hölder*, "Natürliche und juristische Personen" (1905). One may well approve the repudiation of certain exaggerations and one-sided views of the Germanists. Still more radical is *Binder*, "Das Problem der juristischen Persönlichkeit" (1909). See also *Otto Mayer*, "Die juristische Person und ihre Verwertbarkeit im öffentlichen Recht", in "Staatsrechtliche Abhandlungen, Festgabe für Laband" (1908), I, 1–94.

[2] *Cf.* herewith *Fleiner*, "Institutionen des deutschen Verwaltungsrechts" (1911), 137 *et seq.*

has not been ventured; the concession-system being retained to a considerable extent beside that of normative requisites.[1] On the other hand, the Swiss Civil Code has adopted the principle of complete freedom of association and endowment. Societies (" Vereine ", — " associations " in the French text of the Code) with economic ends do require registration in the commercial register (§ 61); but the steps to such registration, " instead of leading through strict normative conditions expressive of anxiety and distrust, are completely free ": so soon as the corporation is organized it is empowered to demand registration. And " societies that are devoted to an end neither political, religious, scientific, artistic, charitable, social, or otherwise non-economic, attain personality so soon as the will to exist *as* a corporation (" Körperschaft ") is discernible in their by-laws " (§ 60). As species of juristic persons, the German Civil Code (which, be it remembered, regulates only those of private law) sets beside the society (" Verein ") — which corresponds to the corporate association (" Körperschaft ") of the old German law — the endowment (" Stiftung "); that is, a " foundation " (" Anstalt ") with a legal personality that is created by the will of a private person. Finally, the principle of collective hand has been made by the Code the basis, not only of the marital and continued marital community of goods and the community of heirs, but also — what is most important — of the ordinary partnership of the private law (§§ 705–740). In so doing it assimilated this to the unlimited mercantile partnership, following the example of the Prussian " Landrecht." The ordinary mercantile partnership of the private law of to-day constitutes, like the old community of collective hand, an entity in which are bound together the individual associates, and which, without actually possessing independent legal personality, has the appearance, particularly in relations with third parties, of a solidary and self-sufficient body. It can have its own social property, which, as a separate estate distinct from the private estates of the partners, belongs to these in collective hand. Similarly, partnership obligations are possible that are not at the same time private debts of the members, and for which these are liable in collective hand.

Thus, within the law of associations, a triumph great almost beyond expectation has been vouchsafed to Germanic legal science, both in theory and in positive law.

[1] *Hedemann*, "Fortschritte des Zivilrechts", I, 39–52.

BOOK II. THE LAW OF THINGS

Chapter IV

THINGS

§ 24. **The Concept of Things. Rights in Things.** (I) **The Legal Concept of Things.** — (1) The law applies the expression "*thing*" ("Sache"), in its primary and most important sense, to that which also in common speech is called a "thing", — namely "the impersonal corporeal pieces of the outer world."[1] In so doing it lays down as its basis the view of practical life, without

[1] *Zitelmann*, "Das Recht des bürgerlichen Gesetzbuchs. Allgemeiner Teil" (1900), 76.

endeavoring to adhere to the categories of natural science. "Sache", thing, is not equivalent to "Naturgegenstand", or natural object. It is corporeal things, therefore, that are primarily the "things" of the law. As the Romans said, "res quæ tangi possunt"; and without doubt Germanic law also had as its point of beginning this narrowest conception of a thing.

(2) Just as the Roman law, however, already set "res incorporales" beside the "res corporales", so in the Middle Ages and later men had resort to the legal concept of *incorporeal things*. To the Romans rights were incorporeal things. They included under the general concept of "res" (= "Vermögensbestandteil", *i.e.*, any portion of property) both "res corporales" and "res incorporales." But while thus classifying things as corporeal and incorporeal they nevertheless made corporeal things identical with "res quæ tangi possunt", and thereby violated, it must be admitted, logic. For corporeal things, as such, are not regarded by the law; they do not, as such, concern "property", — but only in so far as legal rights are attached to them; in other words, to be accurate, again as "res incorporales" only. It was different with the medieval view, which, though itself by no means above criticism in its theory, was highly characterized by imaginative lucidity. The value of a corporeal thing, — of a piece of land or an animal,—lies in the economic utility that it possesses for him who is the holder of rights in it. And so here also men came to identify the right with the thing. Men regarded not alone the land but also the right in it, whether ownership or another usufructuary right, as a thing; namely, an incorporeal thing. The modern codes have gone even further than this medieval view, extending it from rights in things to all rights whatever. The Prussian "Landrecht" (I. 2, § 1. 2), for example, described as a thing "whatever can be the object of a right or of an obligation, including the acts of men, and equally their rights in so far as these can constitute the objects of other rights." Nevertheless the extension of the "thing-concept" beyond corporeal things has been in recent times definitively abandoned. The new Civil Code (§ 90), following the precedent of the Commercial Code, understands by "Sachen" corporeal things only. At the same time it applies its rules concerning corporeal things to whatever other objects can be property, namely to property rights; so that, as to these, the category of incorporeal things continues to be necessary.[1]

[1] *Gierke*, "Privatrecht", II, 3.

(II) **Rights in Things** ("Sachenrechte"). (1) Rights attaching to corporeal things are called *real* ("dingliche") *rights*. Their content constitutes the law of things. In so far as a corporeal thing is the immediate object of such real rights, and in so far as they secure to the person entitled thereto a direct control over it as against the world, — although perhaps only in the negative sense that he can prohibit interference with it by strangers, — they stand opposed to personal rights, which merely subject the will of a particular person, in a particular respect, to the control of him who is entitled thereto.

This division of all property rights into the two classes of real rights and personal rights, — a division basic in the Roman as in modern law, — was not unknown to the medieval law. It, too, knew the concept of real rights, although here again, for reasons easily understood, no theoretical development of the conception was realized. The existence of the category of real rights has been denied by some scholars (Laband, Stobbe), but without reason. For, as Heusler has shown in reply,[1] the medieval law conceived of all rights that assured actual control over things — or, in the vernacular, "seisin" ("Gewere", — § 28 *infra*) — as a group of rights distinct from all others. Every right that was evidenced by seisin was a real right; and every action that relied upon seisin of a thing was a real action. It follows that the field of real rights was not one of hard and fast boundaries, as in the Roman law; but that every right that assumed the form of seisin thereby became real. Whereas personal rights are effective only against definite obligors, real rights are rights "in rem" ("absolut"), that is are effective against everybody. This was as much the case in medieval times as in Rome and among ourselves to-day. Where such effect was lacking, as for example when no action was allowed against a third person to the owner of a movable pledged or bailed, it was precisely because the seisin essential as the basis for a real action was there lacking, and only the possibility of a personal action against the other party to the contract existed (*infra*, § 58).

(2) The extension of the thing-concept, as defined above, to rights of permanent usufruct led logically to the recognition of the existence of real rights *in* such usufructuary rights, considered as incorporeal things. For these real rights ("Gerechtsame") might equally well in the medieval view be the object of seisin. Thus men arrived at the conception of *rights in rights*. This was another ex-

[1] "Institutionen", I, 384 *et seq.*

tension little satisfactory to legal logic, but it was perfectly adapted to the extension of the law of things, as demanded by the increasing needs of economic life, to incorporeal things. It led in this case to a blurring of the sharp line maintained in Roman law between the law of things and the law of obligations.

(3) A similar confusion was that which men called a "ius ad rem" ("Recht zur Sache"), which was independently developed, in different aspects, in both feudal and Canon literature in the 1200 s.[1] It eventually passed over into modern codes, and notably into the Prussian "Allgemeines Landrecht." The term was coined by the feudists to designate the legal status of one who had been invested with a fief but had not yet received physical possession. Had it been remembered that the acquisition of real rights, through investiture, lay in the seisin of the fief, there could have been not a moment's hesitation in ascribing to one so invested real rights in such a fief, — a "ius in re." The Italian feudists, however, who were under the influence of Roman ideas, were disinclined to recognize such rights as arising otherwise than through the giving of actual possession. They therefore regarded the right of one invested but not yet instated in possession as merely a "quasi-real" ("relativ-dingliches") right, and called it — in contrast to the fully potent "ius in re" — a "ius ad rem": a right of the vassal against the lord of the feud to be put into possession. Like the feudists, the Canonists went astray when they designated as a "ius ad rem" the legal relation that resulted from papal procurations and expectancies. As in one case the fief, so here the benefice, led to a like treatment; which is easily explicable, since in the fief as in the benefice there appeared the contrast of symbolic investment and actual instatement in possession. It was a Germanic legal concept which in both cases stood in the way of a complete divorce, such as existed in the Roman law, of the real juristic act from the obligatory contractual act giving rise thereto, and which produced in its conflict with the Roman "ius in re" the concept of the "ius ad rem"—"impelled thereto, in the case of the Canon law, by the interest of the papacy in its benefices, which were spreading throughout the world."[2] In the later law, most clearly in the Prussian "Allgemeines Landrecht", there grew out of this fact the assumption of a right to the *surrender* of a thing, which was good not only against the contract party obli-

[1] *Heymann*, "Zur geschichte des jus ad rem", in the "Festgabe O. Gierke dargebracht" (1911), 1167–1185.
[2] *Heymann*, *op. cit.*, 1184.

gated to such transfer, but also (at least to some extent) against all third persons: out of which personal right to a thing there arose through an actual instatement in possession a real right in the thing. To our law in its latest form this superfluous fore-stage of the real right is unknown.

§ 25. **Immovable and Movable Things.** (I) **The law of Land and law of Chattels.** — Corporeal things are divisible with regard to their natural qualities into immovables and movables ("Liegenschaften", "Fahrnis"). The law can in very great part, although never wholly, disregard this natural difference, and give to its principles so general and abstract a form as to be equally applicable to both classes of things. This the later Roman law did. Not so the legal system of the Middle Ages, which, on the contrary, converted the natural contrast into a legal distinction of primary importance. As regards possession, acquisition of ownership, real rights, the law of pledge, of family estates, and of succession, it subjected immovables to legal rules different from those applying to movables. Indeed, one may say that it knew no law of things, but that there existed a double system of law: one for immovables, another for movables; besides the law of land, an independent law of chattels.[1]

The reason for this was not that from time immemorial a higher economic value had been attributed to land than to movable objects of property. In times of primitive culture that knew as yet no individual rights in the soil, a man's wealth consisted of his charger and weapons, cattle herds and slaves, chests of golden ornaments, and vesture. Although such objects did not, after possession and ownership of land by individuals had taken form, on that account lose their intrinsic value, there was soon developed that economic and social order, peculiar to the Middle Ages, which made possessory relations to land the basis of the legal, political, and economic status of the members of the folk, and of their class divisions. Herein, the medieval law envisaged differently than did the Roman the facts that lands are indestructible parts of the State domain; that they are the basis of the social existence of whole families through generations, and may therefore serve not alone the individual but society generally as well.[2] During the continuance of an agricultural economy legal traffic affected only their use; not, as in the case of chattels, their substance. The

[1] *Cosack*, "Lehrbuch des deutschen bürgerlichen Rechts", I (3d ed., 1900), 136.

[2] *Herbert Meyer* in *op. cit. infra*, p. 172, at 279.

legal relations associated with land owed their origin and elaboration to a more modern stage of historical development than did those associated with chattels, which go back to the most primitive conditions of society; but they eventually received, thanks to their importance, an elaboration all the richer. As "the great interests of the nation, the conditions of independent existence and of political freedom, revolved about possessory relations to land as an axis", so the medieval legal order worked most creatively within this same field, and in the shaping of the law of real property accomplished "a feat of the first order in the way of harmonious legal construction, consistent down to the smallest details." [1]

When movable capital became prominent in the cities, and personal status there became for the first time independent of the possession of land, — for the new wealth of the cities by no means necessarily rested, in its origins, upon accumulated ground-rents, — the different treatment of land and chattels was intentionally maintained. In the interest of the security so essential to legal transactions in land, and which Germanic law had developed under primitive conditions, men gladly abstained from copying the Roman law in assimilating the possession of land to the trafficability of merchandise. While the English law has preserved to the present day the old Germanic view, and among all the legal systems of western Europe has developed it most inflexibly,[2] in Germany the difference in the legal nature of immovables and movables was to a considerable extent abandoned, at least in the common law, in consequence of the Reception. For that very reason, however, the particularistic legal systems clung all the more firmly to the contrast, and from them it passed with renewed vitality into the great codes of the modern period, into numerous modern statutes, and, finally, into the most recent legislation of the Empire. The result has been justly characterized as a "triumphant progress of Germanic ideas." [3]

(II) **The Delimitation of the Two Classes of Things.** — (1) *Immovables* ("liegendes Gut") are, of course, in the first place lands ("Grundstücke", "Liegenschaften", "terra", "res", "possessio", "proprietas", "hereditas", "eigen", "erbe", etc.). But they also include, besides "Liegenschaften" proper — that is definite portions of the earth's surface, — whatever is connected

[1] *Heusler*, "Institutionen", II, 12.
[2] *Vinogradoff*, "Zur Geschichte der Englischen Klassifikation der Vermögensrechte", in "Festgabe H. Brunner dargebracht" (1910), 573–577.
[3] *Gierke*, "Privatrecht", II, 5.

with the soil organically, as for example trees, or mechanically, as houses; and which could therefore be regarded, equally with the land, as imperishable objects. Of course these things could be so classified only from the time when they actually became immovable. Like the simple tents and huts of primitive times which men took down, after exhausting the land they had put under cultivation, in order to erect them again at another place, the wooden houses that were common in all parts of Germany down into the 1200 s, and in many places, especially in North Germany, until the 1500 s and later, were regarded as movables. On the other hand stone buildings, — at first churches and town-halls, then the houses of rich patricians and stone castles of the knights, were surely always regarded, not only popularly but in law, as immovables. This was equally true of places where goods were sold ("Verkaufsstätte"), such as merchandise-shops and butchers' stalls, from the moment a building was solidly erected, — *i.e.* not merely for a time but for all time, — upon a definite plot of land. On the other hand, structures which were erected merely with a view to their being later taken down, such as market booths, summer theaters, and (under some circumstances) windmills, were in earlier times reckoned, as they are still to-day, among movables.

(2) As opposed to immovables, *movables* ("Fahrnis") — "bewegliches" or "fahrendes" ("fahren" in the old and wider sense of "ire", "moveri"; *cf.* "fahrender Schüler"), or "treibendes", in the North also "loses", "greifbares Gut" — were things removable from place to place, and whose economic nature was unaffected by such change of locality. In the legal terminology of France and England the term "chattels", — "cateux" (literally "Viehhäupter", head of cattle), "catalla", "capitalia", — was employed, because cattle were the typical form of movable property. To chattels belong those things which were the earliest objects of individual property: arms, clothes, ornaments, utensils, the booty of the chase, above all cattle; and also slaves. The Schwabenspiegel gives this definition: "Waz varende gut heizet, daz suln wir iu sagen. Golt, silber und edel gesteine, vie, ros unt allez, daz man triben und tragen mac—": "We shall now tell you what is called 'varende Gut': gold, silver, and precious stones, cattle, horses, and everything that one can drive and carry" (G. 144, § 3). Or, to put it in a general way, animals and all inanimate things not firmly fixed to the soil.[1]

[1] *Gierke*, "Privatrecht", 11.

(3) However, the medieval law did not rest content with making this natural distinction between land and chattels a legal one. On the contrary, it sometimes classified tangible things under the law of land or of chattels from a technically legal standpoint, with conscious disregard of their natural properties. Such was the case when the rule was established that all wooden houses should be regarded as chattels, without regard to their natural immovability, — which in later times was doubtless generally unquestionable. This point of view found expression in the maxim, " Was die Fackel verzehrt, ist Fahrnis ": " Whatever the torch consumes is a chattel." Indeed, the legal qualities of movable property could be attributed to immovables at the caprice of individuals. Such " mobilizing " (" Entliegenschaftung ", " de-realty-izing ") was practised particularly in Lübeck in the 1200 s, 1300 s, and 1400 s, in order to give to " Erbgut ", a heritable estate that could be transferred only with the common consent of the heirs, the character of " Kaufeigen ", property which one could buy and hold as his own; in other words, in order to release it from the bonds of the family estate and subject it to the free control of the owner. In the later law of Lübeck all such restricted heritable property was treated by the law as movable; that is it could be freely conveyed by legal act " inter vivos ", — though it could not be bequeathed. In the law of France and Baden the legal transaction of " mobilizing " or " chattel-izing " (" ameublissement ") has continued down to the present day.

More common in Germany was the " demobilizing " or " realty-izing " (" Verliegenschaftung ") of chattels. A very ancient instance is the treatment of settled slaves, — the " servi casati ", — who were regarded as "pars fundi" and therefore shared the legal fortunes of the land they cultivated. Such movable creatures as fish in ponds and wild game in the forest are even now treated by the Austrian Code as immovable property so long as they remain in freedom. Again, particularly costly chattels of an estate, — such as jewels, articles of gold or silver, art-collections, libraries, stocks of goods; also the movable property brought with her into the marital community by a wife, and the capital realized from the sale of lands, — were quite commonly declared by statute to be immovables, in order to fetter the transfer of such objects. This continued to be true of modern legal systems; and even in our present law such a "de-mobilization" (" Immobilisirung ") occurs in the case of larger vessels: they are movables, but in many important respects, and especially as regards acquisition of title and mortgaging, they are subjected to the principles of the law of land.

(4) How deeply medieval law was influenced by the contrast of land and chattels is seen in the fact that it applied that distinction also to *incorporeal things,* little applicable to the latter as those natural properties would appear to be. Nevertheless such a result was natural enough. As has been already remarked (*supra,* p. 161 *et seq.*) rights in things were conceived of as themselves things, and it was therefore easy to regard rights in lands as immovable things, since they, like the lands themselves, were the source of permanent usufructs. This was the result in the case of servitudes and land charges ("Reallasten") appurtenant to land, which were treated as actual land; so also in the case of powers ("Befugnisse") of the public law, such as judicial jurisdiction, bailiwicks, regalities, rights of ban, liberties of coinage, and customs franchises; indeed, even in the case of the general right of sovereignty. This "real-izing and realty-izing" ("Verdinglichung und Verliegenschaftung") of rights was, as has been justly said, "the most medieval part of the medieval law."[1] These rights also secured permanent usufruct, and were objects of seisin; they applied to definitely limited territory; they resembled, extremely, real rights in land. Down to our days such rights have been treated as immovables, and have therefore, to give an illustration, been provided with separate leaves in the land register. The present Civil Code recognizes, in this category of rights, only heritable building rights (1017), but others have been reserved to the law of the individual States (heritable leasing rights, rights of hunting and fishing, etc.). In this case the *permanency* of the economic use was determinant of the legal view-point; in other cases this was determined by the inquiry whether the particular thing in which the rights in question so inhered as to make it appear the holder thereof, was a movable or an immovable thing. The former, which as a rule secured to the owner of a dominant tenement definite privileges ("Befugnisse"), — so-called "subjective real rights" (*i.e.* "Realrechte"; *cf. infra,* § 27) — were regarded as immovable things; while all rights secured by commercial paper ("Wertpapiere"), negotiable or non-negotiable, were regarded as appendants to movable things, and were treated as such themselves. Finally, there was still another division, — though indeed

[1] *Pollock* and *Maitland,* "History", II, 148.

one by no means entirely exact, — resulting from the physical character of the respective objects by which the content of such rights was determined. From this point of view real rights in land were reckoned among immovable things; although an exception existed in the common law and in modern State legislation in the case of mortgage rights, which the present Civil Code (§§ 1237 *et seq.*) also places among movables. The same is true to-day of mining shares. Real rights in chattels, on the other hand, were treated according to the principles of the law of movable property. Legal claims were similarly treated. Rights to demand the delivery of a piece of land or its usufruct are immovable property; rights to demand the delivery of chattels — especially of money, rights established by litigation, and in general any rights whatever that do not involve the delivery of a thing, are movable property.

§ 26. **Things of Limited Trafficability.** — (I) There are things to which the ordinary law of property cannot in its full extent be applied, for the reason that "they are **dedicated to a special end** ('Zweckwidmung') which should be protected in the public interest."[1] This dedication causes an "objective constraint" ("objektive Gebundenheit") which is shown in a greater or less restraint upon alienation.

In the German law, as in other legal systems, this phenomenon has been known since early times. It could not be otherwise. The great military roads, the streams that facilitated commerce, the communal woods, etc., existed either in the interest of the public or of large bodies of associates, and for that very reason could not be surrendered to individual ownership without regard for such purposes; nor be made the object of any and every legal transaction, — such, for example, as rights of pledge or of "legitimate" ("rechte") seisin.

It is true that in the Middle Ages a rational conception and scientific development of these relations was nowhere attained. On the other hand, the Roman doctrine of the "res extra commercium" was likewise incapable of satisfying actual conditions that were in many respects new. Only in very recent years has a satisfactory theory been established from the viewpoint of the ends they serve ("Zweckbestimmung", — appointed ends). Various groups of such things of merely partial trafficability are to be distinguished, therefore, with reference to the nature of the end

[1] *Zitelmann*, "Das Recht des bürgerlichen Gesetzbuchs. Allgemeiner Teil" (1900), 85.

they serve; and in accordance with this the degree of their transferability is also determined.

(1) *So-called "Public" Things or Property.*[1]— Among these are to be reckoned:

(A) Things dedicated to a COMMON USE ("Gemeingebrauch"), the "res publico usui destinatæ" of the Roman law. Such dedication may be either to the common use of all, that is of the public, — as for example public rivers (*infra*, § 40), the sea-shore, lakes, canals, harbors, streets and ways, squares, bridges, parks, letter-boxes, public toilets; or to the use of a greater or smaller group of persons, the use not being dependent upon a special admission to such group, — for example market halls, the books of a public library, the treasures of a museum. A particularly important category of the second class is constituted of things dedicated to religious ends, the "res divini iuris" of Roman law: namely, things intended for religious service (churches, chapels, synagogues, "res sacræ") and burial grounds ("loci religiosi"). Though the "res divini iuris" in earlier and in modern German law are the object of ownership, and not "res nullius", the historical explanation of this fact is found in the law relating to the Germanic "proprietary" ("Eigen-" —) church.[2]

(B) Things which are dedicated to the PUBLIC SERVICE and which therefore serve ends of general utility, precisely as do those named above under (A) notwithstanding the fact that they cannot be the objects of common use: as for example city walls, fortifications, public buildings and their furnishings, etc.

On the other hand, things held by public juristic persons as their individual property do not fall under the category of "public" things: such are lands of the State and of smaller political entities ("Gemeinden", communes), money in public treasuries. And the same is equally true of undertakings prosecuted by such persons as private undertakings, — for example city gas-works or electric plants.

Public things always were and still are the property of the State, of communes, of religious societies, etc. Such, at all events, was the doctrine that finally acquired supremacy in the common law and equally in most of the particularistic systems, and which Keller and Ihering vainly sought to overthrow in the famous con-

[1] *Biermann*, "Die öffentlichen Sachen" (1905); *Otto Mayer*, "Der gegenwärtige Stand der Frage des öffentlichen Eigentums", in Arch. öff. R., XXI (1907), 499–522; *Fleiner*, "Institutionen des deutschen Verwaltungsrechts" (1911), 282–290, 295–309.

[2] I owe this remark to a friendly suggestion of U. Stutz.

troversy concerning the fortifications of Basel. There was no agreement, it is true, as regarded public rivers (*infra*, § 40). And the French law, with its theory of the " domaine public ", rested upon a totally different basis. But this ownership, which — save in the French law — is to be regarded as private ownership, does not confer the powers thereby ordinarily implied. So long as such things are dedicated to their respective purposes they may not be dealt with in a way inconsistent therewith, and rights that are repugnant to the advancement of such purposes cannot attach thereto. The present Civil Code has made no essential changes in the earlier law. It contains no particular provisions concerning the matter, since the question what things are public is one to be decided by the public law.

(2) Things devoted to particularly appointed ends include, further, things dedicated to the *burial of the dead*, the corpse itself and the objects buried with it; which according to older conceptions were regarded as the property of the dead, and were given him for his service beyond the grave. One must doubtless assume to-day an ownership by the person who buries him, which ownership is bound by the special purpose.[1] Here, it may be noted, transferability is even more limited than in the case of public things.

(II) " **Res Communes Omnium.**" — Those portions of nature which are beyond all human influence, and are consequently permanently exempt from all legal control,—the "res communes omnium " of the Roman law; as the sun, moon, stars, the high sea, the free air, running water, and the like, — do not belong among things of limited trafficability. They are not in a legal sense " things " at all. Similarly, the living human body is not a thing; for it lacks the essential characteristic of the legal conception of things, namely impersonality.

(III) " **Res Nullius.**" — But so-called ownerless things or " res nullius ", — as for example wild animals, — are undoubtedly things in the legal sense, for they are intrinsically quite capable of a legal control like that over other things; they are only de facto temporarily outside legal relations. Unoccupancy is unknown, moreover, to many legal systems, as for example the French; ownership of such things being attributed to the State.

§ 27. **Individual and Composite Things.**[2] (I) **Simple Things**

[1] *Zitelmann*, *op. cit.*, 86.

[2] *Kuntze*, "Die Kojengenossenschaft und das Geschosseigentum" (1888); *Kohler*, "Zur Lehre von den Pertinenzen", in *Ihering's* J. B.,

and Component Parts. — (1) Just as the subjects of rights in legal transactions are ordinarily single or individual persons ("Einzelpersönlichkeiten", "Personenindividuen"), so the objects of rights in legal transactions consist primarily of *simple or individual things* ("Einzelsachen", "Sachindividuen"). They are regarded by the law as units, notwithstanding that they may consist, physically, of more or less numerous parts. Simple or individual things in the legal sense exist not only where the organic processes of nature create distinctive individual things, as animals; but also wherever a thing in the commercial sense exists. Accordingly, utensils, clothing, things in bulk ("Mengesachen", such as piles of corn), and for the same reason parcels of land are, for example, treated by the law as simple things.

(2) The *component parts* ("Bestandteile") of simple things are therefore not themselves things in a legal sense, but merely parts of a thing. From the standpoint of the law they do not themselves exist; rather, they constitute, with the principal thing ("Hauptsache") an actual economic, and legal whole. At the same time things are not "individual" in the same strict sense as are persons. By division, where such is possible, individual things can become several, parts of things can become independent things, and independent things may by combination become mere parts. Even to parts of things there can be attributed a certain legal distinctiveness. Of these principles the medieval law affords various examples.

(A) Buildings might stand in the ownership of another than the owner of the land. This principle is doubtless an echo of those primitive conditions in which houses that were not yet firmly attached to the soil were regarded as chattels, and consequently did not constitute component parts of the land (*supra*, p. 166). But it maintained itself long beyond that early period. The house that the medieval burgher built upon the plot of land given him in tenancy ("leihen") by the town lord became the builder's property; he could sell it, bestow it as a morgive, etc. Similarly, according to the account of the Sachsenspiegel the wife be-

XXVI (1888), 1 *et seq.*; *Schröder*, "Über eigentümliche Formen des Miteigentums im deutschen und französischen Recht" (1896); *Martin Wolff*, "Der Bau auf fremden Boden, insbesondere der Grenzüberbau nach dem Bürgerlichen Gesetzbuche für das Deutsche Reich auf geschichtlicher Grundlage", in *O. Fischer's* "Abhandlungen", XVI, No. 2 (1900); *Herbert Meyer*, "Die rechtliche Natur der nur scheinbaren Bestandteile eines Grundstücks", in "Breslauer Festgabe für Dahn", III (1905), 269–301.

came owner of the house that was erected upon the husband's land with the timber for house and fence which her husband had given her as her morgive (I. 20, § 1, 2). That the German law, in other respects, — that is where the natural characteristics of the structure were not involved, — treated the building as a component part of the land, thus recognizing as did the Roman law the principle that "superficies solo cedit", is proved by the law of the proprietary church. These proprietary churches, like all other churches, were bound to have a stone altar firmly attached to the soil, and the lordship of the soil below the altar, the right to the soil, disposed also of the church.[1] The old rule, derived from the character of primitive wooden buildings and inconsistent with the principle "superficies solo cedit", maintained itself in some localities after the Reception. It subsisted, for example, rather widely in Switzerland and in Schleswig-Holstein; was expressly recognized under the Prussian "Landrecht", the Code Civil and the Baden "Landrecht"; and is not unknown in the English law.

In the same way that the old German law treated cases in which another than the landowner erected a building and acquired the property therein, it treated the closely related cases in which not houses, but other structures and works that were annexed to the soil of another, were involved. The butcher put up shambles on the ground floor of the house he rented, the brewer buried in or affixed to the walls heavy kettles and pans: evidence of the former exists particularly in Frankfort and Breslau, of the latter in Lübeck. Nor were these fixtures ("Werke") regarded as component parts, because, unless the building itself was specially devoted to the purposes of that trade, they did not serve the economic ends of the building but the personal ends of the respective craftsman or tradesman, securing to him a permanent use. They were therefore treated, quite in analogy to the primitive wooden houses, as independent pieces of land: they could be mortgaged, conveyed, and entered in the city register ("Stadtbuch") in the name of their owner, and thus made the object of a land rent. The exceptional position which the Civil Code assigns (§ 95) to so-called merely "apparent component-parts" ("scheinbare Bestandteile")[2] must be regarded as a recognition and further development of these growths derived from Germanic law.[3]

[1] *Stutz* in the contribution cited on p. 153 *supra* to the "Festgabe für O. Gierke", 1250.

[2] *Zitelmann, op. cit.*, 79.

[3] *H. Meyer, op. cit.*, 295.

(B) From the 1100 s onward we already find extremely widespread in German towns so-called "STORY" or "ROOMAGE" OWNERSHIP ("Stockwerks-", "Geschoss-", "Gelass-", "Etageneigentum"), — ownership of the individual stories of a building. Houses were horizontally divided, and the specific parts so created — the stories, floors, and cellars — were held by different persons in separate ownership; this being associated, as a rule, with community ownership of the building site and the portions of the building (walls, stairs, roof, etc.) that were used in common. Notwithstanding that this peculiar legal institute was totally irreconcilable with the alien law of the Reception, it remained part of the law, — not, however, of the common customary law, for which reason the Prussian "Landrecht" and the Austrian and the Saxon codes refused to recognize it. It was preserved as a particularistic legal institution in many localities, even in the face of statutory prohibitions, especially in Bohemia and South Germany: in Salzburg, Munich, Würzburg, Regensburg, in Württemberg (to a quite extraordinary extent, according to Kuntze's reports, in Wildbad), Sachsen-Meiningen, Frankfort, and above all, with extraordinary vitality and in many cases down to the present day, in Switzerland. It has also been expressly recognized by the Civil Code. A particularly clear example, illustrating the law as it stands to-day, is afforded by the contract concluded in 1901 between the municipality of Freiburg i. Br. and the Edifice of the Holy Virgin, a cathedral-building endowment at Freiburg, for the purpose of determining the legal relations existing between them; by which contract it was agreed that the cathedral, together with the spire, should be registered as the property of the cathedral-building endowment; but, as to the construction plant ("Münsterbauhütte"), that the property of the yard and lower story should be registered as in the building-endowment, and that of the second story and roof as in the city; which was accordingly done.[1]

The Civil Code, however, recognizes the Roman principle according to which fixtures, as component parts of land, necessarily follow the land surface; and has therefore not recognized independent property in building-stories. The Roman principle applies to entire buildings when they are actually component parts, and so holds also as to their stories. On the other hand, the Civil Code has recognized continuance of property in building-

[1] *Stutz*, "Das Münster zu Freiburg i. Br. im Lichte rechtsgeschichtlicher Betrachtung" (Address, 1901), 35, 36.

stories existing at the time it became effective (EG, § 128). The Swiss Civil Code has taken the same position (§ 675, 2; EB, 45).

(C) Finally, the medieval law attributed to the PRODUCTS OF THE SOIL — trees, grain, fruits — a separate legal existence; often treating them, even before their severance, as chattels. Another than the owner of the soil might therefore have the right to harvest them (*infra*, § 62). In the State systems, as for example in the Prussian "Landrecht", this view has been preserved. The possibility, not infrequently admitted, of a separate mortgaging of fruits, which has also been recognized in the imperial Code of Civil Procedure (§ 810), was a consequence of the same principle.

(3) The modern law has for the first time sharply distinguished the conception of the *component part* ("Bestandteil") from related legal institutes, and recognizes as a component part "that which can exist without alteration of its nature only in union with another definite thing, and finds in this its indispensable support and preservation."[1] The component part is therefore absolutely subject to the legal fortunes of the whole. The Civil Code has gone farther than this, and has placed beside what it designates as "essential" component parts (§ 93), — which correspond to those of the common law, and share like those the legal status of the entirety, — so-called "non-essential" component parts. These are likewise only parts of a whole, and not themselves specific things in a legal sense, but at the same time they can themselves be the object of special rights, because they can be separated from the whole without the destruction or essential change of either. Non-essential component parts are, for example, the surface portions of a piece of land, and the units of a mass of goods ("Warenmenge"), as the liters contained in a cask of wine. The concept of non-essential component parts was unknown to the earlier German law. Unlike the German Civil Code the Swiss Code has adopted a uniform concept: according to its definition a component part of a thing is "that which according to the usage of the locality is essential to its existence, and cannot be separated from it without destroying, damaging, or altering it"; all such parts belong to him, as owner, who holds the property in its entirety (§ 642).

(II) **Composite Things** ("Sachverbindungen"). (1) **Principal Thing and accessories.** — Although the medieval law recognized, in various cases, independent rights in the component parts of

[1] *Regelsberger*, "Pandekten", I (1893), 367.

a thing, this involved — when judged from the standpoint of modern theory — a confusion of the two conceptions of component parts and accessories, which at that time were not differentiated. The law of to-day, however, draws a sharp line between the two. For whereas the part merges in the principal thing ("Hauptsache"), loses its individuality, has no longer as such a legal status, and has forced upon it the legal quality of the whole, the accessories or appurtenances ("Zugehör", "Zugehörigkeit"; "Neben-", "Hilfssache"; "Pertinenz") retain their independent quality as things. They stand to the so-called principal thing in a relation, however, by virtue of which the legal fortunes of the latter also influence them. The accessory quality of a thing depends upon its appointed economic purpose, which is to augment the utility of the other thing with which it is connected. In so far it serves that other or principal thing. All these characteristics the Civil Code enumerates in its definition of accessories (§ 97). With it agrees substantially the definition adopted by the Swiss Civil Code (§ 644, "Zugehör").

A sharply-defined conception of appurtenance was lacking in the older Germanic as in the Roman law. On the other hand, accessories played from the very earliest times a far more important rôle in Germanic law than in the Roman, or in the law of to-day. The modern concept of pertinence is only a faint shadow of the old Germanic concept of appurtenances, which — with most immediate and particular reference to land — had a far wider range of application in practice and an incomparably greater importance than to-day. The appurtenance relation appears in the old law as nothing short of a universal formula with which results were obtained, at least approximately and for practical purposes, which we attain to-day only with far more artificial creations.[1] It appeared in the following applications:

(A) The most important appurtenance relations were those in which CHATTELS WERE APPURTENANT TO LAND. In the case of rural lands these included all objects that served the management of the estate, the entire stock of the estate, especially the utensils, cattle, provender, manure; everything that, in the phrase of the old documents made a "mansus vestitus", everything that constituted the "integritas" of an estate, including the serfs permanently settled upon the land. All this the landlord needed for the utilization of the estate; his seisin of the estate covered, therefore, all such objects.

[1] *Stutz's* essay in "Festgabe für O. Gierke" (1911), 1188.

In the case of buildings the old sources laid greatest stress upon the close connection into which chattels were brought with the house. An oft-repeated maxim and definition ran, that all should belong to the house that was " earth-, wall-, rivet-, or nail-fast." No distinction was here made, as is seen, between component parts and appurtenants. But here also it was necessary, in addition, that the objects thus firmly affixed should be intended to serve the economic ends of the principal thing, and not merely as it were the use of the temporary possessor; for in this event they would be, even according to the present Civil Code, only "apparent component parts." On the other hand all accessories did not need to be firmly affixed, — as for example storm windows, utensils to extinguish fires, cabinets, tools, the armor and weapons that must be kept in the house, the artillery in forts, etc. As already mentioned (p. 167), these movable accessories, which despite their legal union with the land did not lose their inherent chattel qualities, were by many legal systems assimilated to land, and themselves subjected to the principles of the land law. Among modern codes it was so with the Code Civil (" immeubles par destination "), and in less degree with the Prussian "Landrecht." The idea has disappeared from our law in recent years. According to the Civil Code an accessory is always a movable thing, and cannot even be a non-essential component part of a principal thing (§ 97). In other respects the Civil Code follows the old Germanic law (§ 89, Z. 2) as regards accessories of rural estates (" Landgüter "). In the case of buildings, on the other hand, all firmly affixed objects are component parts, and what is more essential parts (§ 94, 2); so in particular machines, according to the holding of the imperial court. This interpretation of the law leads, it must be confessed, to the gravest inconveniences, inasmuch as it makes impossible a reservation of title by the vendor of machines. It would accord with the view of the Germanic law to classify machines with "*apparent* component parts."[1] According to the Civil Code the conception of accessories is applicable only to such loosely attached machines and implements, as belong to a building that is permanently adapted to an industrial enterprise (§ 98, Z. 1).

(B) CHATTELS APPURTENANT TO CHATTELS occur in the modern as they did in the old law, as *e.g.* cabinet keys and furnishings of ships.

[1] *Krückmann*, "Wesentlicher Bestandteil und Eigentumsvorbehalt" (1906).

(C) Lands treated as appurtenant to other lands, on the other hand, were a peculiarity of the older law which has been abandoned in modern times. In the pertinence formularies of medieval documents the house, the homestead ("Hofstätte"), the estate ("Hof"), the virgate ("Hufe"), etc., are designated countless times as the principal things, as accessory to which are then enumerated the "campi", "agri", "prata", and the shares in the common lands ("Allmende"), — the "marchis", "viis", "silvis", "aquis aquarumque decursibus", etc. Similarly the commonty, apportioned and unapportioned, was regarded as accessory to all the individual estates in the village, or to the whole village conceived of as a unit. The estates dependent upon a manor were equally regarded as its appurtenants. These manifold relations of dominant and servient lands disappeared with the decline of the medieval economic and social order. The treatment of particular dependent estates ("Nebengüter"), outlying farms ("Vorwerke"), etc., as appurtenants of the principal estate, and of yard and garden as appurtenants of the house, persisted alone down into modern times. The Civil Code, however, has declined to recognize such relations, because the conception it has created of non-essential component parts here interferes: the surface portions of a piece of land can, as such and in relation to it, be made the objects of special rights.

(D) Rights as appurtenances. Finally, it was natural for the older law to carry over the quality of pertinence from corporeal to incorporeal things, or rights. As remarked above under (C), along with the allotted portions of the commonty the rights of user in the common march belonged among the appurtenances of the individual holdings. This of itself was a common illustration of the treatment of rights as appurtenants. We meet another no less common and important instance in the so-called real rights ("Realrechten"). There existed in the Middle Ages countless rights which were attached to, inherent in, definite pieces of land. He who was the owner of certain land possessed by virtue of that fact membership rights in a political or economic fellowship ("Genossenverband"), or certain industrial privileges; or else, a point particularly characteristic of the medieval period, rights of a public character — rights to taxes, rents, seigniorial rights, official powers, political privileges. Even the rights and dignities of the members of the diets ("Landstandschaft") and of the estates of the Empire ("Reichsstandschaft") were ordinarily dependent upon the possession of certain lands. When the paternalistic constitutional arrangements of the Empire were done away with, these real rights of the public law, which the Reception had left in the main unimpaired, were for the most part swept aside. On the other hand such real rights have maintained themselves down to the present day within the field of private law — *e.g.* industrial rights, rights of ban, chase, fishery, and membership; real servitudes, charges on land, preferential rights of purchase (" Näherrechte"), etc. The Civil Code itself recognizes, among real rights, servitudes, land charges, and real rights of sale; besides these there are many regulated by State law. In Mecklenburg the political real rights of eligibility to the local government and the diet are still, as in the Middle Ages, associated with the ownership or tenancy of a manor.

Whereas real rights in the older law were appurtenants, the present Civil Code classifies them under component parts.

All the principles mentioned above, which German law had already developed at an early period in regulating appurtenants, are most lucidly explained by the results of U. Stutz's latest researches regarding the property of the proprietary (" Eigen- ") churches, drawn from the " traditions " of Freising of the 700 s and 800 s.[1] As these documents show, the establishment of proprietary churches occurred regularly in the following manner. The founder, — after the ground had been prepared, the church built, and the altar erected, and the dedication of the church had taken place, — made a tradition as to the church, and only after that was the property conveyed to the bishopric of Freising. In this act of tradition there was involved a creation of pertinence (" Pertinenzierung "), " a dedication: in purpose, and as regards at least part of the revenues in actuality, a delivery of property for ecclesiastical purposes." [2] The accessories with which church or altar were furnished included the furnishings of the church, the parsonage, the roadway; also rights to the ecclesiastical revenues, especially the tithes, besides those of a purely temporal nature. All these appurtenants were dependent upon or accessory to the principal thing, and that was the church, or to be more exact its great or high altar. Such a creation of appurtenances was " no legal transaction, but simply a legal act." [3] " It did not pass ownership; this remained where it had been. No subjective right was by it either

[1] "Festgabe für O. Gierke", 1187–1268.
[2] *Ibid.*, 1254.
[3] *Ibid.*, 1253.

destroyed, created, or conveyed, for only *one* holder of rights took part in the act. Only the objective relations are changed. The founder undertakes a shifting of his property rights: portions of his property heretofore disconnected are brought into dependence upon each other. The altar, or as the case may be the church edifice, becomes a central object upon which the rest of the property thereto conveyed depends."[1] "Moreover, these proprietary churches, with their property, could in turn themselves be accessories; namely, of a manor or great estate."[2] When the law respecting proprietary churches was later replaced by a law of advowsons, the remnants of these old manorial and other proprietary churches were preserved as ecclesiastical ("dingliche Patronate"); and since the latter had now themselves become subjects of legal rights, the right, in place of the thing, became an appurtenant. Rights of presentation are still known to the law as real-rights of public law.

(2) *Composite things* ("Gesamtsachen", "Sachinbegriffe"). In composite things there is not, as in relations of pertinence, a principal and a subsidiary thing. There are several independent things, which, in accordance with custom or commercial practice and as a result of the common end they serve, habitually constitute a unity; though they need not necessarily appear in such a form. We have to do here with collections ("Zusammenfassungen") of several corporeal things, whether individually ascertained or fluctuating units. Such are corporeal group-things, which have been familiar to Germanic law from the earliest times, — cattle herds, the stock of an estate, a stock of goods, dowry, warriors' accouterments, etc. But the law went further and made such aggregates of incorporeal things: there are incorporeal group-things. It thus became possible to deal with the entire property of an individual as a unit, and to develop manifold forms of special property ("Sondervermögen").

Both of these forms of group-things played an important practical rôle in legal life already in the Middle Ages. And the conception was to be of extreme importance in the future.

Just as untold numbers of Christians, in pious zeal, formerly gave all their goods and chattels to church or cloister at their deaths, or as the entire property of a wife could pass into the seisin of her husband under the marriage property law, so the later law has known similar things. This was true of the Prussian "Landrecht"; and under the Civil Code, as well, an entire

[1] "Festgabe für O. Gierke", 1242.

[2] *Ibid.*, 1255.

estate, or a definite part thereof, viewed as an entirety or aggregate, may be the object of succession, usufruct, and community.

The important concept of special property (" Sondervermögen ") appeared, among other places, in the separation of the allodial and the feudal estates, and of the trading capital of the merchant and the capital of shipping partners (" Reeder ") from their other property. Like the principle of pertinence and in closest connection therewith, it found at an early day particularly clear expression in the law of the proprietary church. When the lord or proprietor of such a church transferred certain lands, chattels, and rights that were portions of his free property, to another part of his property which was " bound ", because grouped about the altar dedicated to religious service and bound to this by the pertinence relation, he thereby created within his estate, considered as a whole, a separate estate, which in contrast to his free property, appeared bound not only by a special purpose and dedication, but as a property mass of a peculiar legal character, namely, as church property. Not in the sense of an ecclesiastical allodium (" Eigengut "), since it remained in the ownership of the church's proprietor; but in the sense of a holding devoted at least primarily to the use and profits of the church. It was therefore subject to ecclesiastical restraints on alienation; that is it could no longer be released from its objective and real connection with the church and the altar: it no longer stood immediately, but only mediately, in the ownership of the lord.[1] The Freising documents speak explicitly of a person's " church property " (" Kirchenvermögen "), for they contrast " possessio " and " res ecclesiastica " with "possessio secularis" and "alia hereditas." Thus, "as the older German and the present-day maritime law have distinguished property on land ('Landvermögen') and at sea ('See-', 'Schiffsvermögen'), or in the more ancient mining law mining from town property, so the lord of a proprietary church possessed, besides his secular or 'burghal' property, spiritual or 'church' property. This consisted of the church — an ecclesiastical enterprise conducted by him, as it were, under the firm-name of the Lord, — with its furnishings and ornaments, the land belonging thereto, and the rights of usufruct and revenues thereto attached." [2] In the modern period the delimitation of a special partnership estate, particularly the special estate of an

[1] *Stutz* in "Festgabe für O. Gierke", 1254, 1262.
[2] *Ibid.*, 1267.

unlimited partnership, from the other property of the partners, has become of especial importance. A separate estate recognized in the law of today is the "railway unit" ("Bahneinheit") of the Prussian statute of August 19, 1895.[1]

The scientific literature of the common law developed from these phenomena of legal development the doctrine of the "universitates rerum", which were divided into "universitates facti", or complexes of corporeal things (lots, heaps, groups), and "universitates iuris", or artificial complexes of incorporeal property rights ("Vermögensinbegriffe"). This theory was successfully attacked as inconsistent with the Roman sources. An attempt was made to prove that the whole concept of group-things ("Gesamtsachen") was vicious, since simple things alone were conceivable as objects of rights. This "atomistic idea"[2], however, did not prevail. Both corporeal and incorporeal group-things must be recognized even under the present law, although the Civil Code does not explicitly mention the concept. These corporeal things-aggregate ("Sachinbegriffe") could and can be subject, as units, to a unitary right of ownership, usufruct, or pledge; the individual corporeal things remain, however, at the same time, independent objects of rights.

No similar rules of law have been formulated for incorporeal things-aggregate; but that a unitary right may exist in them, as incorporeal things, is not impossible.

[1] On the concept of special estates ("Sondervermögen", "Sondergut") see also *Zitelmann*, "Sondergut nach deutschem Internationalprivatrecht", in *ibid.* 255–284, 255 *et seq.*

[2] *Gierke*, "Privatrecht", II, 51.

CHAPTER V

THE LAW OF LAND

PART I: POSSESSION

§ 28. **The Medieval Seisin of Land.**[1] **(I) General Course of**

[1] *Albrecht*, "Die Gewere als Grundlage des älteren deutschen Sachenrechts" (1828); *Laband*, "Die vermögensrechtlichen Klagen nach den sächsischen Rechtsquellen" (1869); *Heusler*, "Die Gewere" (1872); *Huber*, "Die Bedeutung der Gewere im deutschen Sachenrecht", in the "Berner

Development. — Nowhere do we find more sharply marked than in the law of things that feature which above all others characterized the Germanic medieval law; namely, the endeavor to give a tangible embodiment to legal relations that actually existed only in the human mind. All real rights, ownership as well as rights of more limited content, rights in land as well as rights in chattels, appear in a visible form, in the dress of a so-called "seisin" ("Gewere"). Seisin was therefore, in fact, the basis of the medieval law of things.

This "sensuous" character was here also, originally, merely the expression of a naïve attitude of mind, which could recognize a right in a thing as present only where there was some visible relation between it and the person entitled thereto. Within the domain of the law of things, and especially within that of the law of land, the prominence given to the "sensuous element", to the formalism that demanded for every right a physical form perceptible by the senses, was of the greatest value in the later development of the law. It rendered possible a formulation of legal rights in the soil capable of adaptation to the highly complicated economic gradations of the time; and it afforded a security to transactions affecting land that could scarcely have been maintained by a more abstract regulation.

In the law of land, therefore, the fundamental ideas of the older law were not abandoned, but on the contrary were retained and further developed. The modern German land-registry law is a further development and perfection of principles that were first actually applied in the medieval seisin of land.

The power of the medieval Germanic ideas that once governed the law of seisin has continued to be felt down to the present day, notwithstanding that that conception, as an independent legal

Festschrift für Halle" (1894); *Gierke*, "Die Bedeutung des Fahrnisbesitzes für streitiges Recht" (1897); *Herbert Meyer*, "Entwerung und Eigentum im deutschen Fahrnisrecht" (1902); *Alfred Schultze*, "Gerüfte und Marktkauf", in "Breslauer Festgabe für Dahn", I (1905), 1–63; and "Publizität und Gewährschaft im deutschen Fahrnisrecht", in *Ihering's* J. B., XLIX (1905), 159–186; *Herbert Meyer*, "Das Publizitätsprinzip im deutschen bürgerlichen Recht", in *O. Fischer's* "Abhandlungen", XVIII, 2 (1909); *Naendrupp*, "Rechtscheinsforschungen, Heft 2: Die Gewere-Theorien" (1910); *Bückling*, "Die Wechselwirkung gewererechtlicher und fronungsrechtlicher Elemente im Liegenschaftsrechte des deutschen Mittelalters", in *Beyerle's* "Beiträge", VI, 2 (1911); *Herbert Meyer*, art. "Besitz" in *Hoop's* "Reallexikon der germanischen Altertumskunde", I (1912), 261–265. — *F. W. Maitland*, "The Mystery of Seisin" (1886), republished in "Select Essays in Anglo-American Legal History", III (1909), 591–610. *A. G. Sedgwick* and *F. S. Wait*, "The History of the Action of Ejectment" (1886), *ibid.*, 611–645; *O. W. Holmes*, "Das gemeine Recht Englands" (1912), 208–249.

institute, has long since disappeared. But only within the most recent years has this direct and simple line of development been understood. Unusual difficulties had to be overcome before the nature and importance of seisin became plain. Often as the medieval sources mention seisin, they naturally nowhere give a succinct statement regarding it, and the isolated passages bearing upon the question in documents and legal monuments are often difficult to understand and contradictory. Since Albrecht's celebrated monograph the problem of seisin has been the center of investigations in the history of German private law. Following his contributions, those of Laband and Heusler, especially, have cleared the way. It is only the very recent investigations of Huber, however, which have been accepted by Gierke, Herbert Meyer, and Alfred Schultz, that have resulted in a clarification which may be safely regarded as the definite solution of at least the principal riddles.

(II) **The Term "Seisin"** ("Gewere"). — The substantive "gewere", "gewer", "were", Old High G. "giweri" ("giwerida"), technically used in medieval legal terminology, is derived from the verb "wern", which goes back to the Gothic "vasjan", Old High G. "werjan", A. Saxon "verjan", and means "to dress" or "clothe"; corresponding, thus, both etymologically and essentially to the Latin "vestire", "investire", which is used in the Latin sources in its place. Accordingly, "clothing" ("Einkleidung") is also the meaning of the substantive "gewere"; which is rendered with "vestitura", "investitura" in Latin.

From this derivation it follows that "Gewere" has nothing to do with "Wehr", "Gewehr", — defense, weapon ("were" = "arma", from the Gothic verb "varjan"; "wern", = "prohibere", "defendere"); nor with "Gewähr", — warranty ("were", "gewere" = "præstatio", "cautio", "Garantie", from the verb "wern" = "præstare").

The expressions "wern", "vestire", "gewere", "vestitura", found their first known application in designating the *act* by which the control over a piece of land was conveyed in a legal manner. This act (which will be discussed more fully in § 34 *infra*) was regarded as the clothing or vesting of the transferee with the thing, the piece of land. The *result* produced by such investiture was also designated by the same word; so that thenceforth the actual control itself over the thing was known as seisin or investiture ("Gewere", "investitura"). And inasmuch as the expression was also extended to the control over chattels, and also was applied to those cases in which the control of a thing had not been acquired by transfer from or investiture by another, but was original, it came to have a general meaning nearly equivalent to the modern term "possession" ("Besitz").[1]

(III) **The Requisites of Seisin.** — If we now look at the law of seisin of land in the form in which we meet it at the time of its ripest and widest development, — namely in the age of the Law Books, — our first question must be: when is there seisin according to the medieval sources?

Two requisites must have been satisfied, as a general rule, if seisin was to be recognized: two requisites which remind us, at least, of the essentials "corpus" and "animus" of the Roman "possessio." The cases in which these two requisites were present, the normal and uncontested cases, may be designated, to follow modern writers, as cases of corporeal ("leibliche") seisin. Along with these cases there were a few others in which one of the two requisites was lacking, but in which the sources none the less recognized seisin. These are the cases known to modern scholars as incorporeal ("ideelle") seisin. Their explanation has given very great trouble. We will discuss first the former.

(1) *Cases of Corporeal Seisin.* — (A) The first requisite was that of ACTUAL CONTROL. He who is the master or dominus ("Herr") of a thing has it in his seisin, has seisin in it. From the naïvely-sensuous viewpoint of the Middle Ages, however, the visible sign of dominion over a piece of land was its economic enjoyment ("Nutzung"). Everybody can see who derives the profit from an estate; who, as the sources say, holds it "for money and profit" ("in Nutz and Gelde") and exploits ("utbort") it. That person, therefore, had the seisin.[2] There were, however, very different forms of economic usufruct. The case in which the owner of a landed estate cultivated it himself or by his servile dependents was by no means the ordinary one in the Middle Ages. It happened countless times that the landowners let out their lands under various forms of tenancy ("Leihe"). With respect to them, the enjoyment ("Nutzung") lay in the services, rents, and taxes, that were rendered them by the tenants. On the other hand, vassals, holders of benefices ("Benefiziaten"), renting tenants ("Zinsleute"), usufructuary lessees ("Pächter"), etc., farmed

[1] The French and the English law derived their technical terms equivalent to the German "Gewere" from the Old G. verb "sazjan" (Latinized, "sacire") = to set, put in possession: "saisine", "saisir"; "seisin."

[2] "Richtsteig Landr.", 26, § 6.

the land themselves, and so enjoyed the profits directly. There resulted from this a circumstance particularly characteristic of the medieval law, — the possibility and the exceedingly common occurrence of plural seisins; beside the superior seisin of the full owner, who had surrendered his estate to another for cultivation and received from the latter produce from the land, the seisin of the renting-tenant who enjoyed the immediate usufruct.[1] To designate this immediate seisin the expression "pure" ("ledigliche") seisin was used, while the designations "possessory", "common", or "simple" ("hebbende", "gemene", "blote") seisin were equally applicable to all cases of usufruct.

(B) In addition to the physical requisite of actual control, that of enjoyment comparable to the "corpus possessionis" of the Roman law, the medieval law demanded also a peculiar MENTAL RELATION of the usufructuary to the thing. If a lord gave his estate for management to a steward, who of course was bound to deliver the whole produce to his master, no seisin was conveyed to the steward. And as little to a servile tenant ("Knecht") who worked on the estate for the lord: if the tenant was ousted, this was after all only an injury to the seisin of his lord. Evidently it never occurred either to the steward or to the servile tenant to conduct himself otherwise than as the mere instrument of the lord, — as a "servant in possession" in the sense of the present Civil Code. They did not assert an independent right in the land. But it was precisely this — the assertion of a real right to a thing — that must be added to physical control if there were to be seisin. In the case of a rentaler ("Zinsmann"), on the other hand, the usufruct of the estate was conveyed by a legal act from the owner to the rentaler; and in the case of an heir the possession of the deceased owner descended upon his death to such heir according to the rules of the laws of inheritance. Both could justify physical control, therefore, by real ("dingliche") rights, ceded to them or otherwise acquired: in the case of both the exercise of objective dominion might appear as the exercise of subjective rights.[2]

There was yet another peculiar circumstance connected with this necessary assertion of a real claim. Suppose that in consequence of a gift of land a lawsuit resulted, as was often the case. The donee, often a church, demanded of the donor delivery of the land, and in an action against him charged him with unlawful possession ("malo ordine possides"). The donor replied to the

[1] "Sächs. Lehnr.", 14, § 1. [2] *Gierke*, "Privatrecht", II, 191.

complaint that he had retained for himself a life estate in the land. If judgment was rendered in favor of the plaintiff, it would be a decision that the defeated donor, who had theretofore enjoyed physical control and had believed himself entitled thereto, had in truth not been so entitled. Nevertheless, he was regarded as having seisin up to the moment that the error of his assertion, its inconsistency with the positive law, was shown; that is until the pronouncement of the judgment of the court against him. His seisin was lost only through the judgment. He might still retain his actual dominion. From this it follows that it was not absolutely necessary that every assertion of a real right should correspond, under all circumstances, to an objective legal right. Or more exactly, no preliminary inquiry was made whether it so corresponded or not. The identity of the subjective right claimed and the objectively existing right was assumed throughout, pending evidence to the contrary. Seisin could therefore be attributed, pending further evidence, to one who set himself up as heir without being such. On the other hand, so soon as doubt was thrown upon such alleged right by one's opponent, he must prove the same, if he wished to defend his seisin. If he could not do so his seisin was lost. The mere allegation of a purely subjective right, such as was the Roman " animus domini ", was therefore insufficient: the will of the person seised must have " absorbed ", as Huber puts it,[1] an element of objective right. The right alleged must be consistent with the objective right, if he were to be secure when obliged to defend his seisin against attack.

It follows from what has been said that this will, so constituted, was in no way directed toward the possession of the thing in question as by an owner. This was a further and obvious difference as compared with the Roman "possessio", because to this there was ordinarily essential besides the "corpus" an "animus domini",—*i.e.* the will to possess the thing as owner; for which reason the possession of an owner was regarded in Roman law as the normal case of " possessio." In the medieval law, on the other hand, it was sufficient if there was a will to control a thing upon the basis of any legal right whatever; so that he who claimed a right and was minded to take the profits from the land as usufructuary lessee ("Pächter"), pledgee, etc., had the seisin. This could not be otherwise, inasmuch as the medieval law, as we have seen, allowed a plurality of seisins in the same piece of land,—proprietary, feudal, rental, or pledge seisin. This gradation of dif-

[1] *Huber, op. cit.*, 42.

ferent seisins one upon the other was the legal expression of the manifold actual possessory relations to the soil that were peculiar to the Middle Ages. We meet it in France, in Germany, and in England. It is true that the sharp definition of all these distinctions was only gradually attained in the case of tenancies held under feudal, servitary and manorial law. This was because in their case,—at least as regarded the Territorial law, and consequently also in the ordinary courts,—only the lord of the vassals, servitors and serfs was at first regarded as the owner, possessed of the seisin of the land let; whereas for tenants seisin had a legal existence only under the feudal, servitary, and manorial law, because recognized as such in the feudal, servitary, and manorial courts alone. Only gradually did the relations of the feudal, servitary and manorial law find recognition in the ordinary courts of the land ("Landgerichten") and only then did such rights of tenancy receive also the character of seisins, albeit limited seisins, under the law of the land ("landrechtlich"). In the Territorial law, however, there had also existed several seisins beside or above one another whenever lands were let as free fiefs—heritable, for life, or for years; or rights to life rents created, trust relationships established, the property of wards given to guardians, etc. For example, in the early Frankish "affatomie" one who for lack of relatives entitled to inherit desired to appoint an heir, conveyed his property to a fiduciary, the "Salmann", and conferred upon him a seisin therein in order that he might turn it over to the selected heir after the death of the testator. So also in the numerous cases in which the donor of property given to a church or cloister retained a life-interest or usufruct, and therewith the rental seisin ("zu Leiherecht"); but on the other hand recognized the ownership of the chosen institution by giving a nominal rent; the acknowledgment of rent, in any mode whatever, being a means frequently adopted for the creation of seisin.[1] So also in the case of freeholds of inheritance, of precaria for definite periods, of numerous leaseholds for years, etc. Wherever, as in such cases, multiple seisins existed, they were the expression of rights in the economic returns of a single piece of land simultaneously inherent in several persons.

(2) *Cases of Incorporeal Seisin.* — Besides the ordinary cases of seisin of lands thus far discussed, which united both requisites and indicia of the seisin-concept, namely actual control (user) and the assertion of a real right underlying this, there existed, as already

[1] "Swsp." (G), 22.

mentioned, a few others in which one of those two characteristics, namely physical dominion, was absent; notwithstanding which seisin was assumed to be present according to the uniform testimony of the medieval sources. Such cases are classed together by modern students as cases of "ideal", "juristic", or "incorporeal" seisin. Since Albrecht these have been the subject of various attempted explanations. These cases were the following:

(A) Release or surrender ("Auflassung"). This was the legal act by which the transfer of a piece of land was ordinarily effected in the Middle Ages (see § 34 *infra*, for details). It conferred seisin upon the grantee though no instatement in physical possession, or investiture, took place. Accordingly, he might thenceforth take forcible possession of the land himself, or in case the release had been made in court might accept a judicial induction. But he already had the seisin from the moment of the surrender.[1]

(B) Judgment of court also conferred seisin upon the person held to be entitled thereto. By force of the judgment the seisin passed directly from the losing party who had theretofore held it, to the successful party; and he too might thereupon, and without further warrant, reduce the land to his physical control.

(C) Inheritance passed the seisin of lands directly from the testator to his heir: the testator by his death "abandoned" the estate, and "released" it to his heir; or, as men said in the Netherlands, had "opened the door." Hence the legal proverbs that characterize this leading principle of the Germanic law of inheritance: "the dead man makes the living his heir", "the dead man seizes the living", "the seisin of the dead man descends to the living" ("Der Todte erbt den Lebendigen", "le mort saisit le vif", "saisina defuncti descendit in vivum", — *cf. infra*, § 103). And this was true even when a stranger had acquired physical dominion over the land by force, after the death of the testator. Such a stranger had no seisin, inasmuch as his assertion that he was entitled thereto proved false (*supra*, I, B). This defect was more material than that of physical control, which did not prevent seisin by descent.[2]

(D) Disseisin ("Entwerung"). — Finally, seisin also continued when a person in the enjoyment thereof had been put out of possession by forcible or otherwise illegal disseisin. The one thus forcibly dispossessed was regarded as still in possession, and the

[1] Sächs. Lehnr., 39, § 3.
[2] Sächs. Lehnr., 6, § 1.

act of violence as a circumstance without prejudice to his seisin:[1] "one of the strongest of legal fictions in the face of actual conditions, and one of the proudest expressions of the power of right against all attacks upon its sacred character and its inviolability."[2]

The reason why the medieval law assumed seisin in these four cases notwithstanding that actual control was lacking, — because it had either (as in cases *A*, *B*, and *C*) not yet been acquired, or (as in case *D*) had been lost, — one may now, thanks to the light of Huber's and Gierke's researches, venture definitely to state. As will be later explained in more detail, legal relations to the soil were subjected from the earliest period of the Middle Ages to requirements of publicity, in accordance with Germanic legal notions. Like the primitive apportionment of the common arable to individuals by lot, all legal transactions in lands were later performed in public. The legal relations of the inhabitants to the individual pieces of land were assumed to be, and were known to everybody. One and all found expression in seisin; every seisin was based upon an act of vesture, "investitura"; and this act was a public one. Every seisin rested "upon the force, sanctioned by law, of an appeal to common knowledge."[3]

How great was the importance attributed to the visibility of the conferment of seisin, was shown by the custom, peculiar to the older law, of the so-called "sessio triduana": in those cases, in which a donor received back the usufruct of the land of which he made a gift, so that there was no recognizable external change of legal relations, the donee, after the ownership and therefore the proprietary ("Eigen-") seisin had been transferred to him, was bound to move onto the land, and there exercise for three days actual dominion. If, after the expiration of this period, the donor again entered, his altered legal status, namely the transformation of his proprietary into a rental seisin, had nevertheless been made apparent.

A judicial release of seisin perfected without investiture, a judgment of court declaring the seisin, and likewise an inheritance of seisin, had, as regards publicity, exactly the same value as an investiture. The only difference was that in the case of release, court decree, and inheritance, only the fact which was the *cause* of the change of rights was made visible, but in the case of investiture the altered *conditions produced* by that change, as well. But this difference was immaterial, for even in investi-

[1] Schwäb. Lehnr., 96. [2] *Heusler*, "Gewere", 269.
[3] *Gierke*, "Fahrnisbesitz", 3.

ture the decisive thing was the public nature of the voucher. And, finally, in cases of violent dispossession an event was involved which, when land was in question could but rarely be screened from publicity; so that such public breach of right could not, in itself, have the effect of destroying the right. There was therefore good reason for disregarding, in these cases, the requisite of actual control, and for ascribing seisin to one who did not enjoy such control.

(E) In addition to these four cases of incorporeal seisin, there were still a few OTHER CASES in which, according to the theory of the sources, seisin was present, notwithstanding that after it had been so created and made evident by an act publicly performed, there was an absence of every other external token of seisin. Though the superior proprietary seisin of the lord usually received expression in dues and services, cases occurred in which the proprietary seisin of the grantor was, at least temporarily, wholly subordinated, and did not even continue to be recognized by a nominal rent. Gierke speaks [1] in such cases of "dormant" ("ruhende") seisin. This existed in the dower ("Leibzucht") that was set apart for a woman when she married, but which became available only after the death of her husband; in the usufruct which a donor reserved to himself, it might be for life, in the land he gave away, without making provision for a rent in favor of the donee, who, through a gift perfected by judicial surrender had acquired ownership and seisin; likewise when a debtor gave land in gage to his creditor, thereby conveying to him the pledge-seisin therein, leaving his own proprietary seisin thenceforth wholly without external indicia, pending redemption. In such a case the owner had, in the language of the sources, simply the reversion ("Anfall"); that is, upon the elimination of that other seisin which barred him, his own seisin, till then existent but invisible, immediately revived.

Similarly in the case of a so-called seisin in expectancy ("anwartschaftliche Gewere"), — a seisin conveyed upon a condition, upon the happening of which it should first become effective, or upon the happening of which it should determine. For example, when a "donatio post obitum" was made, the donee acquired seisin immediately by means of a present transfer taking the form of release with investiture; therefore there was no need, after the donor's death, of the additional act, no need of an induction into possession; but the seisin acquired legal effect only with the

[1] "Privatrecht", II, 200.

happening of the condition (here precedent), — namely, the death of the donor. And similarly, and above all, in the case of the seisin of a pledgee, who was given a junior gage in land (*infra*, § 53).

It is true that cases of incorporeal were distinguished from those of dormant and expectant seisin in their effects. The latter forms were without any effect until the happening of the event which determined another person's corporeal seisin, which had temporarily kept them in the background. With the happening of the condition they acquired against all third parties the absolute validity of a corporeal seisin. An incorporeal seisin, on the other hand, was effective from the instant of its creation, but in all cases it was effective in but a single very definite respect. It assured to him who enjoyed it, in particular cases, simply a legal right as against one who had released the seisin, or one who was judicially decreed to give investiture, or one who was not an heir, or a disseisor; that is to say, a right against persons who had retained, or who had acquired corporeal seisin or physical dominion, but not against strangers to the seisin. As against such third parties those persons who held the physical dominion were regarded as entitled to retain possession. Such incorporeal seisin was therefore also known as "relative." It prevailed only as against a corporeal seisin which, at the outset, had existed simultaneously with it. We are thus led to the consequences of seisin.

(IV) **The Consequences of Seisin**: (1) *Its Defensive or Vindicative Aspect* ("Defensivwirkung" = Huber, "Wirkung der Rechtsverteidigung" = Gierke), in protection of actual possession. As we have seen, it was the rule that every seisin was a cloak for a real right in land. Only in those exceptional cases in which the law recognized an incorporeal seisin, was it otherwise. But the medieval law took account, at first, of the typical cases only. From seisin men implied a right embodied within it. The actual circumstances of possession were regarded as "prima facie" evidence of a legal right. It was therefore forbidden to disturb such possession by force, *i.e.* otherwise than by way of judicial action; and every person who enjoyed seisin was allowed to defend himself against such disturbance by self-help, and in case of necessity by the use of force. In the capitularies, in the Territorial Peaces ("Landfrieden"), in the town laws, as well as in the Law Books, it is repeatedly declared that no one may be disseised, unless it be by law when "broken" by a judgment after just complaint.[1] Such a protection of the actual possessory status was indispensable to the preservation of the peace of the land.

It is true, as we have seen above under (III), that the legal basis presumed to underlie every case of actual possession might be questioned; the seisin could be attacked by an action at law. Against such an attack in the courts the seisin must be defended "with the weapons of the law"; a reliance upon actual possession was no longer sufficient. If a defendant in actual enjoyment of seisin wished to succeed, he must prove now, in addition to the fact of possession, the rightfulness of his seisin; and if such a right were also claimed by the plaintiff, his better right. If he failed in this, then his seisin was "broken", for the absence was revealed of the supporting right theretofore assumed in his favor. But — and here the advantage that was given by actual dominion, by seisin, was seen also in the case of an action at law — his status was that of a defendant; which, according to Germanic procedure signified that he had the advantage of proof, he "stood the nearer to" the proof. In the Germanic law of procedure it was regarded as an advantage to go to the proof; whereas in the Roman law of procedure that party was regarded as procedurally favored who could wait until his opponent brought proof of the right he asserted. The position of defendant was therefore always the more favorable — in the Roman law because he did not need to prove anything, and in Germanic law because he, and not the complainant, had the first right to make proof. Seisin, then, secured to him who enjoyed it the rôle of defendant in a lawsuit about to begin, and thus the advantage of proof.[2]

As the court records of earlier times clearly show, this lawsuit was always begun, when the plaintiff lacked the seisin, with an averment in his complaint that the defendant possessed wrongfully ("malo ordine possidet"). Perhaps a relative of the donor alleged that a usufruct had been appointed to him in lands given to a church; and after the donor's death, from which the usufruct was to date, he brought action against the church, which had taken possession of the estate and denied his right. And thus the contest and the proof turned throughout upon the point whether the defendant had or had not been entitled to the enjoyment of seisin. Against the naked allegation of the plaintiff the defendant defended himself with his oath, swearing that his seisin

[1] For example the Sächs. Lehnr., 38, § 4. In England this rule was adopted even in the Magna Charta of 1215.
[2] Schwäb. Lehnr., 10 b.

had been rightful. If the plaintiff appealed, himself, to a right existing in his favor, then the defendant must prove the right which he on his side asserted. The attack upon the seisin was therefore, in truth, an attack upon the right that was manifested in the seisin. The trial, therefore, made form and substance identical. The protection first accorded to actual possession as such thus became a protection of the underlying right, since it made it easier for the person having seisin to establish his right. But this protection accorded to seisin found application not only in cases of corporeal, but also in those of incorporeal seisin: it was precisely here that the great practical importance of "relative" seisin appeared. The particularly frequent case of forcible dispossession was the most important in this connection. The seisin of one forcibly disseised was (as has been remarked) considered as continuing notwithstanding that his physical dominion had been actually destroyed. In order to have the benefit of this assumption it was incumbent on him, in the first place, to establish the fact of the forcible disseisin, which was required to be done by two witnesses. Thereupon the seisin of which he had been deprived was awarded to him by a judgment commanding its present holder to put the disseisee again in enjoyment thereof. If now the defeated holder of the corporeal, albeit defective, seisin — who was either the disseisor himself or his legal successor — made claim on his part to a right, the advantage of the defendant's position, the advantage of proof, remained nevertheless with the disseisee as in ordinary cases, notwithstanding that he was the formal plaintiff. True, this advantage was his only for a limited time: he must bring action within a year and a day against the disturber of his seisin. Otherwise he lost his rights by silence and the defective seisin of the disseisor was cured of its defect; so that if the disseisee should still demand of him possession, the disseisor, and not as before the disseisee, could make effective in his favor the advantages of seisin, — that is would be the nearer to the proof. This limitation as to time upon the effect of a relative seisin is explained by the purpose it was to serve; namely, to put an end as quickly as possible to violent interferences with actual possession. If, however, the complaint was brought within the proper period, then evidently the decision of the court upon the fact of the disseisin alleged by the disseisee and subjected to proof, — a decision turning upon a pure question of fact, and commanding that the plaintiff be reinstated in the seisin, simply and solely because he had it before, — established at the same time the proper procedural relation of the parties in the contest about the right itself. It was, as it were, a medial judgment in the suit, which itself turned upon an issue of right. Not infrequently effect was given to the judgment by an actual surrender of the seisin to the disseisee in accordance therewith, so that the latter received not only the procedural advantages associated with seisin, but at the same time reacquired the seisin itself. In many instances the trial must then have come to an end; namely, whenever the disseisor was not himself in a position to assert and prove a legal justification for his act. Otherwise the suit would go on.

If the action ended with the return of the seisin to the disseisee following such a medial judgment, it appeared as if only the questions of fact, as to the enjoyment of seisin and the act of disseisin, had been passed upon; and if the action was continued after actual reinstatement of the disseisee, the procedure fell, formally, into two distinct parts in the first of which the question of fact was adjudged, and in the second the question of law. In reality, however, those cases in which the action ended with reinstatement following a judgment that commanded restitution were merely "uncompleted actions, which had been abandoned during a preliminary stage of the proceedings touching the right to possession during the trial."[1] And the other cases, where further litigation followed the reseisin, were but simple actions in which for the present only the position of the parties had been determined; the result being the same when no actual reinstatement in seisin took place, but the action was continued without it in accordance with the relation of the parties which was prescribed by the medial judgment. For all that, the Germanic law came near to the introduction, in these cases, of a special possessory remedy; a procedure such as the Roman law had perfected in its possessory interdicts, and through which the issue of possession is directly regulated and a usurped possession reëstablished, every inquiry into the right to possession being intentionally left over for a special suit. Unlike the German law, the Anglo-Norman and the French law did develop distinctive possessory actions, — the former as early as the 1100s, the latter in the 1200s, — particularly the so-called "querela novæ dissaisinæ": actions that originated in the inquisitorial powers of the Frankish kings and the inquisitorial procedure developed in the royal court, and which therefore continued to be decided, not in the ordinary

[1] *Laband*, "Die vermögensrechtlichen Klagen nach den sächsischen Rechtsquellen" (1869), 189.

courts, secular and spiritual, but in the ducal and royal courts. The absence in Germany of similar organs, which might have guaranteed even to the man of lower degree a prompt possessory protection as against great landholders, made impossible there a similar development. It was the influence of the alien law, and especially that of the Canon law, that first led to similar results in Germany.

As for the other cases of incorporeal seisin, if one who enjoyed such seisin relied for his defense upon the fact of livery, of judicial adjudication, or of inheritance, and had established such fact, the rôle of defendant was assured also to him, and the advantage of proof; and by the proof of such fact there was simultaneously shown his better right, and the absence of right underlying the mere physical seisin of his contestant, — so that the question of law was decided at the same time with the question of fact.

The distinction between the two appeared, on the other hand, more sharply in those cases where both parties relied for their defense upon seisins of equal rank; as when, for example, in boundary disputes between two neighbors each of them alleged that he had been seised of the land; or when two landlords contested an estate which neither would surrender to the other, each claiming to have the seisin, having received rent from the rentaler. Whereas in earlier times accident would seem to have been decisive in such a case, — accident in the sense that he who first brought his action acquired "ipso facto" the position of a defendant in an action concerning seisin, — *i.e.* the advantage of proof, — it appears from the sources of the time of the Law Books that the judge then inquired, which of the parties had done acts that must be regarded as enjoyment of the lands, or, as the case might be, which could point to earlier acts of such character. If, however, nothing definite could be determined in this respect, then the neighbors were heard. If the inquiry still remained without results, then resort was had either to the expedient of a public partition of the disputed land, so that each party must thereafter appear as plaintiff with reference to the piece that had fallen to his opponent, or else matters were left to an ordeal. In such judgments, again, the same as in judgments for restitution in cases of disseisin, we have to do, not with the termination of an independent possessory action, but merely with a settlement, in accord with a medial judgment, of one part of the litigation. For in this case as in that, and as in all the cases referred to in which seisin is defended against an attack at law or a court asked to protect a seisin already interfered with, the defense alike of actual and of ideal seisin was based, not upon the assertion of the naked fact of its enjoyment, but always and directly upon the assertion of a right — or as the case might be, the better right — to the land.

(2) *Its " Aggressive " or " Creative" Aspect* (" Offensivwirkung " = Huber, " Wirkung der Rechtsverwirklichung " = Gierke) in the establishment of possessory rights. As we have just seen, a relative seisin gave him who relied upon it and proved his allegations the favored position of a defendant, who might prove his right against the plaintiff's attack. At the same time it displayed its aggressive force. Thanks to the favored procedural standing that it conferred upon one who enjoyed it, it was superior to every corporeal seisin that opposed it; it " broke " such seisin unless this was supported by an independent right. The person who had such incorporeal seisin could bring an action, relying upon it, and enjoy as plaintiff those benefits of proof which ordinarily inured to a defendant only.

The same was true, as already explained, in case of forcible dispossession. The disseisee could try, in the first instance, to reinstate himself by his own power in possession of the land; for the intruder's physical control, because resting upon a breach of right, had as against him no right to protection. If, however, that attempt failed, or was in the nature of things impossible, and the disseisee brought an action for reinstatement in the seisin, then his incorporeal seisin, which by assumption was continuous, secured to him the advantage of proving the interference with his right, thereby securing a judicial restoration of his seisin through a retransformation of an incorporeal into a corporeal seisin.

So also in the other cases of incorporeal seisin. He upon whom such a seisin had fallen, by livery, adjudication, or inheritance, might first attempt by self-help to reduce the lands to control. If he was hindered in so doing by one who had a corporeal seisin, then, in case seisin was adjudicated to him by decree of court or awarded to him by judicial livery, he could immediately demand a judicial induction into possession by executory process. He was, indeed, bound to bring action against the occupant, but here again, — because he could rely upon the incorporeal seisin, — he enjoyed the position, favorable from the standpoint of procedure, of one having seisin. If, for example, the heir found the estate in the hands of a stranger, he would bring an action against the abator on the basis of his (incorporeal) seisin of inheritance, which enabled him to prove at once his character as heir. Once such proof was made, the corporeal seisin of the abator was "broken." Only when the latter could oppose to him an independent source of right or title, — for example the fact that he had bought the land in controversy from the heritor before his death, — did the demandant's incorporeal seisin fail to break the defense, for in such case the right of the occupant proved to be older, and consequently better.

With dormant and multiple seisins the case was similar. Either of the co-existent seisins empowered its holder to make upon the other an attack by way of legal action, which would "break" the latter if there appeared in it a physical control inconsistent with the demandant's right.

In the same way a proprietary seisin could "break" the immediate (usufructuary) seisin dependent upon it. Suppose, for example, that lands were let at a rent by the owner to a peasant as tenant for life, and after the tenant's death his heir remained on the land and refused to surrender possession; or that the question was one of a lease for years, and despite the expiration of the term the tenant did not vacate. Here also, if the owner brought suit against the actual occupant on the basis of his proprietary seisin, the advantage of proof lay with the plaintiff, for the corporeal seisin of the defendant had become wrongful.

The result was the same when the owner possessed only a dormant seisin, — for example because he received no rent. If the seisin of the owner who had let lands for rent, or of a pledgor who had given to his creditor a pledgee's seisin in a piece of land, had been violated, — let us say, in that the holder of the immediate seisin (the rentaler, the pledgee) had conveyed or re-pledged the lands to a third person, — the holder of the superior seisin (the owner) could turn the "aggressive force" of his proprietary seisin against any third occupant, and "break" his physical control. For here again there came into play the effect of the principle of publicity applicable to all legal relations to land. Since the lease, or the pledge had been effected by a public act, "it was perfectly well known within the community and the whole jurisdiction of the court who was occupying lands as owner, and who as rentaler or pledgee; and if not known, the fact could everywhere be ascertained."[1] The corporeal seisin of the third person, also, was therefore defective, since it lacked the one essential requisite of seisin, the possibility of alleging an objec-

[1] *Huber*, "Die Bedeutung der Gewere im deutschen Sachenrecht" (1894), 12.

tively existent real right; and it was therefore bound to yield to the undefective seisin of the owner. And whether the seisin of the owner was a visible, or only a dormant or expectant, seisin made no difference in the result.

(3) *Its "Translative" Action, or effect of passing rights* ("Translativwirkung" = Huber, "Wirkung der Rechtsübertragung" = Gierke). Since every possible real right in lands found expression, as has been shown, in a seisin, the conveyance of every such right necessarily assumed the form of a transfer of seisin. Seisin was therefore "inevitably a precondition to, and the sufficient legitimation of, the conveyance of every right in land." Even seisins of inheritance could arise only upon condition that the heritor had had seisin in the land inherited.

Incorporeal, dormant, and expectant seisins possessed in the same degree as corporeal seisin the power of transferring to one who acquired them the rights that underlay them. It is true that inasmuch as the former classes themselves were lacking in the element of physical control, such control could not be conferred upon the grantee by their transfer. He did acquire, however, the right embodied in those forms of seisin; so that for him also there resulted from such a transfer an incorporeal, dormant, or expectant seisin in his favor, and this had the same effect thenceforth, as to him, as it had had before in favor of his grantor.

In the case of a corporeal seisin we have seen that there was always a possibility of its being imperfect or defective, in that the assertion of an objectively existent right might be opposed to the actual facts. If such a defective seisin was conveyed from its holder to another, it retained its defect, as a matter of course, in the hands of the transferee. True, the defect was not necessarily visible; it became so only when one with a better right attacked such defective seisin. Until then the appearance of right spoke for the grantee, as before for his grantor; and until the defect was taken advantage of he was also protected by the law against strangers, as the holder of the right apparently embodied in the seisin.

Under some circumstances, however, the defect might be cured in the hands of the transferee, so that the apparent right became, as to him, transformed into an actual right. This leads us to the institute known as "rechte" seisin.

(V) **Legitimatized or Citation Seisin** ("rechte" = "rightful" — *i.e.* judicially sanctioned — seisin). — As was shown above (pp. 195 *et seq.*), the mere running of time was capable, in certain cases of defective seisin, of creating a right where there had been before a lack of right. For if one forcibly disseised did not within a year and a day proceed, in reliance upon his incorporeal seisin, against the holder of the corporeal seisin, then the corporeal seisin, which was as such defective because of the breach of right, was transformed into a legitimate ("rechtmässige") seisin, in favor of the disseissor and every later holder. The defective origin was wholly overcome by the fact of physical control exercised through a year and a day; for the disseisee had forever estopped himself by silence. Here, however, there was no question of a legitimatized seisin, — "rightful" seisin in the technical sense; although the latter also arose from prescription ("Verschweigung", acquiescent preclusion).

In citation seisin the question was never one of curing an unlawful possession based upon violent disturbance of another's right; on the contrary, it presupposed a perfectly lawful seisin, — indeed, always originally, and as a rule even later, — a seisin created by judicial release.

This citation seisin of lands, — which we meet with in fully developed form "toward the end of the 1000 s or in the first half of the 1100 s in France, in Germany, in Northeastern Spain, in England, and in Flanders; and whose existence in the first half of the 1000 s we may infer, for Germany from documentary evidence, and for France from the Franco-Oriental and the Norman-Sicilian systems of law", — had its origin (as is shown by the recent researches of Brunner,[1] which confirm the older studies of Sohm [2]) in the legal institutions of the Frankish Empire. It was evolved in the course of the 800 s: "doubtless in the first place as a privilege of the king that originated in connection with the tacit-preclusion period ('Verschweigungsfrist') of a year and a day, which had been applied under the 'missio in bannum regis' in execution proceedings since the capitulary of Ludwig I of 818–819." Just as in those proceedings a year's stay was left open to the outlaw within which to release his land from the royal power, after the running of which period the preliminary outlawry of his goods ("Fronung") became a definite confiscation, so in the case of a judicial release of seisin notice was given that all outstanding claims against the estate must be presented within a certain period, under penalty of acquiescent preclusion. Parties present in court were required to do this immediately; others,

[1] *Brunner*, "Luft macht frei" (*supra*, p. 91), 38–46.
[2] In Z.[2] R. G., I (1880), 53 *et seq.*

within a year and a day, — that is, according to the later interpretation (*supra*, p. 15) within the period covered by three regular ("echte") and three bidden ("gebotene") folk-courts, or one year, six months, and three days. Claims that were not presented within such time were thereby barred; whereas, aside from judicial publication and ban, claims were ordinarily barred only after thirty years. Whoever, after such judicial ban, retained unchallenged seisin for a year and a day, gained thereby the "rechte" or judicially sanctioned seisin.[1]

This carried with it important procedural advantages in his favor. According to early Frankish law, as it long maintained itself in the Netherlands, — and quite in accordance with the origin of the institute, — in case an attack should nevertheless be made upon his seisin he needed simply to oppose to the complaint an allegation of the fact of his unchallenged possession during one year; or in case such allegation were denied by his opponent to prove such fact. In other words, he need not enter upon a discussion of the question of right at all; he could, in this respect, simply refuse to answer the complaint. It is true that the medieval Saxon law, which brought the institute of judicial seisin to its fullest development, showed many departures from this simple rule, and particularly one according to which the defendant, after proving by witnesses his unchallenged possession for one year, swore by his own oath to the rightful basis of his seisin, therewith repelling the demandant's attack. According to Heusler[2] the explanation of this fact may be that the period that determined the legitimacy of the seisin had come to be differently reckoned. The important question was no longer whether the seisin had been challenged during the first year after its inception, but whether it had been so challenged during the year last prior to the bringing of the action. This last could easily be proved by witnesses, but the fact of quiet possession during the first year could not be proved so readily if, — as was usually the case, — many years had passed since the establishment of the seisin. For this reason the defendant was allowed, in such case, to make his oath. These variations of the Saxon law showed an emancipation from the old historical basis of the Frankish peace-ban; and this was apparent also in the fact that the preliminary requirement of a livery perfected before the court was later abandoned, — citation seisin being recognized as possible whenever the seisin had originated in a visible act. Thereafter the period of a year

[1] Ssp., II. 44, § 1.

[2] "Gewere", 107.

and a day was no longer strictly maintained, but was arbitrarily varied. The institution gradually fell into confusion, which was increased still more by classing it with that other institute, mentioned above, by which a seisin wrongfully acquired was validated after a year and a day; with which, however, it had originally nothing to do. At an early date the influence of alien law also made itself felt in this connection; for the Schwabenspiegel already accepted, as regarded land, the Roman usucapion periods of ten and twenty years. All these transformations, which brought about the eventual decay of the institute,[1] are to be explained by the circumstance that judicial release of seisin became ever more rare, especially in South Germany.

(VI) **Seisin of Incorporeal Things.** — Inasmuch as the medieval law, as shown above (p. 161), applied the law of land not only to land itself but also to incorporeal things, — such as existing rights to land, and all other independent interests in land ("liegenschaftliche Gerechtigkeiten") — it was logical to assume a seisin in them, in other words a seisin in rights ("Rechtsgewere"), which conformed in every respect to the principles of seisin in material things, and which might therefore, like the latter, take the form of corporeal and incorporeal, feudal, rental, pledge, or judicial seisin. As a practical matter, it made no difference whether the holder of the real right, — for example a lessor, — was regarded as having a seisin in the right to collect the rent, or a seisin in the land out of which the rent was payable that was outwardly expressed in the right to the rent. As a general rule, probably in all cases where seisin involved actual occupancy of land, this right was regarded as seisin in a material thing, whereas in other cases of real rights men spoke preferably of a seisin in the right rather than in the thing, — for example, in cases of rights to rent ("Zins"), annuities ("Renten"), land charges, and rights in "alieno solo" ("Grundgerechtigkeiten"). Alike in private and public law a peculiar significance came to attach to this concept of seisin-in-rights in the case of those real rights in gross ("liegenschaftliche Gerechtsame") that related to definite lands but did not include the immediate usufruct thereof. Such were the usufructuary regalities, rights of ban and judicial execution, perquisites ("Gerechtsame") of office, and political privileges (*e.g.* a privileged status in court): in short, all rights that could be the subject of *tenure*.

[1] Compare with this "Rechtsfall 3" in *Stutz*, "Höngger Meiergerichtsurteile des 16. und 17. Jahrhunderts" (1912), 12–15.

(VII) **Common Qualities of Medieval Seisins.** — If one compares the leading features of the law of seisin brought out in the preceding pages, it becomes manifest that it was an institute of literally universal importance. It is to be remembered also that the seisin of chattels rested upon the same bases (*infra*, § 57), notwithstanding that its elaboration was different in details, and that it was precisely in this difference that the distinction between the law of land and of chattels, so important in the Middle Ages, found expression. With regard to the end it was designed to serve seisin must be put alongside the Roman "possessio" and the modern concept of possession, — although it is distinct from both. It was "the form under which real rights were defended, acquired, and transferred." There existed no real right that could not have been represented in the garb of seisin, and every real right was recognized in the form of seisin only.[1] It was neither mere actual dominion, nor a condition corresponding to ownership and protected by the law in the interest of ownership; it was neither a right to the possession, nor, as Albrecht believed, an independent real right to "represent" a thing in court.[2] It was, on the contrary, a form-concept. Its most important function, aside from its effect of passing rights, lay in its service as a formal legitimation in the enforcement of the real right that was assumed to lie back of it, but which it was necessary to look to only when questioned.

The reception of the Roman-Canon law, coupled with a lack of understanding for the consistency and practical utility of seisin, threw the foundations of that institute, at first, into confusion. In the end, however, the fundamental idea that characterized it, — the embodiment of real rights in a form visible to, and therefore binding upon, all — has gained renewed recognition in the modern system of land registry.

§ 29. **Influence of the Alien Law of Possession.**[3] — The doc-

[1] *Huber, op. cit.*, 20.

[2] *Albrecht*, in his "Gewere", 125, makes the generalization: "If for the concept of seisin, which was treated as a right to represent a thing in litigation, we seek an equivalent that brings it nearer to our present law, we find such available in the concept of materiality or 'thinglikeness' ('Dinglichkeit'). Seisin is that which gives real ('dingliche') effect to the relation of a person to a thing; that is, which is the basis of a real action or a defense against the real action of another." *Gierke* aptly remarks ("Privatrecht", II, 194, N. 30) that by this assumption of an independent real right to represent a thing in litigation, as existing alongside of real rights that themselves give no right of action, seisin is transformed into a special real right in a material sense.

[3] *v. Savigny*, "Das Recht des Besitzes" (1803; 7th ed., by *Rudorff*, 1865); *Bruns*, "Das Recht des Besitzes im Mittelalter und in der Gegen-

trine of seisin was unable to hold its own against the intruding alien law. The alien law before which it had to yield was not, however, the pure Roman law of "possessio." It was rather that law which Italian theory and the practice of legists and canonists had developed out of the Roman, following the lead of the Canon law. The classical Roman system was built upon assumptions of underlying social conditions quite different from the actual conditions of medieval life. It was therefore natural that a theory and judicial practice which had to serve the conditions of their time, and consequently to adapt the classical Roman law to those conditions, was controlled by the influence of Germanic legal views that had sprung from those conditions. In the feudal law; especially, there prevailed "the absolute cult of the Germanic theory of seisin."[1]

This Germanization or medievalization of the classic Roman law was continued in Germany. The Italian-Canon law of possession taken over at the Reception suffered still further transformations in German courts and statutes, the result of which was to make it conform still more nearly to old native institutions. The legislation of the Territories, particularly, and above all the great modern codifications, preserved many elements of Germanic law.

All the same this did not alter the fact that in place of the old law of seisin there had entered into the common law of Germany an essentially alien law of possession, so that the very name of seisin wholly disappeared. Unlike the former doctrine of seisin, this new common-law doctrine of possession, a mixture of antique and medieval ideas, was far from being clear and logical; and this mainly because the older common-law theory, without any understanding for the fragments of the native law and without historical insight into the antique law of the "Corpus Juris", attempted as best it could to fasten the old and new mechanically together. It was the Historical School of the 1800 s that first undertook, under the leadership of Savigny, to clear the pure Roman law of alien blemishes, and to bring the classical law, thus theoretically restored, into exclusive supremacy in judicial practice. In the latter undertaking it did not succeed, for the influence of the particularistic systems was the stronger; and in the end these prevailed also in the drafting of the present Civil Code.

wart" (1848); "Die Besitzklagen des römischen und heutigen Rechts" (1857).

[1] *Heusler*, "Gewere", 298.

Before we proceed in the following pages to point out in their chief features the mutations of the old doctrine of seisin, we must first of all remark that the Germanic distinction between the law of lands and the law of chattels came to an end, in principle, with the Reception. The new-made "Roman" doctrine of possession applied equally to all sorts of things; and that now became the rule in Germany, though not indeed in so absolute a form as that which ultimately prevailed at Rome. This was prevented, in particular, by the development of the registry-system in the law of land. The result was that the form or mode of possession, as well as the provisions for protecting possession, remained different in the law of land and the law of chattels, — an important after-effect of the old theory of seisin. Because of these facts it will be necessary, in the following discussion, to continue the separate treatment of the two classes of things with reference to the points indicated, and to consider first lands, exclusively. What we have to say in the following account of them holds good, however, in other respects, of movables.

(I) **The Concept of Possession.** — The "possessio" of Roman law was itself not merely the physical occupancy ("Innehabung") of a thing, — mere detention that stood in contrast to possession. But possession, in Roman law, did presuppose under all circumstances actual physical control. To this, the "corpus", there must be added a will, the "animus possidendi"; though it is true that as regards the nature and significance of this, unanimity never was attained in the Pandect theory. Where it was lacking, the Roman law denied the protection otherwise accorded to possession, namely the possessory interdicts. The normal case of possession was the possession of an owner, — possessory dominion ("Besitzherrschaft") exercised with an "animus domini." This conception of possession was the same for movable and immovable things.

(1) *Seisin and Possession.* — As has been shown in preceding pages (§ 28), seisin was the "dress" of things in Germanic law: every real right must appear within that covering. It was foreign to the Roman law, "possessio" being as just remarked normally merely the outward form of the right of ownership, but the idea of seisin was nevertheless not abandoned. However, in consequence of the development of the modern system of land registry, which was associated with the treatment of the incorporeal seisin created by livery, this "publicital" function of seisin became separated in the law of land from the element of physical control,

and passed over into the register-entry. The entry was thenceforth "the legal vesture of the land." In the law of chattels, on the other hand, the seisin of the old law, and its legal significance from a substantive viewpoint, have lived on in the "possession" of the modern law. There was thus perpetuated a distinction, in this respect, between the law of land and the law of chattels that was unknown to the Roman law. In the land-law, in consequence of the prevalence of the registry system, the significance that formerly attached to possession came to attach exclusively to the book-entry; whereas in the law of chattels, after as before the Reception, possession exercised upon the substantive law, as respects the protective remedies accorded to it, the consequences peculiar to the former law of seisin. In the same way, possession played no part in the conveyance of land and the establishment of rights therein. According to the registry system, as will be later explained, a mere book-entry suffices to transfer rights in land; whereas in the law of chattels,—in agreement with the Roman law, — the modern possession took over the "translative" function of seisin. The "public faith" ("öffentliche Glaube") of the register realized, far the more completely, the idea of the old law that the actual circumstances of possession should give rise to a presumption of rightfulness in their favor. But this also holds good only for the land law. In the case of movables simple possession, in the sense of actual physical control, suffices in the modern law; as did once incorporeal seisin, to establish the right of the occupant.

(2) *Elements of Possession.*—Possession was attributed in Roman law to no one besides the owner save to a pledgee, a "precario-habens" (permissive possessor), and a stakeholder. These were exceptions to its general rule which were known in the common-law theory as cases of "derivative possession", and which are doubtless to be explained upon grounds, not of theory, but of social and historical conditions. It did not, on the other hand, attribute possession to the depositary, commendatary, mandatary, hirer ("Mieter"), and lessee ("Pächter"). Nor did it accept the Roman law in this matter. On the contrary the attempt was made to attribute the character of "juristic" possession to every kind of physical control that rested upon an independent right; and to deny this, as did the old law of seisin, only in those cases where such control was exercised in another person's name. It was sought to reconcile this doctrine with the Roman law either by putting in place of the "animus domini" required by the prevailing theory the wider term "animus rem sibi habendi", or by ex-

tending the cases of "derivative" possession. Similar attempts, grounded upon the law of seisin, were made by the codes.

The Prussian "Landrecht" went farthest in this respect. Alongside of a "perfect possession" that corresponded to the old proprietary seisin, and which alone was covered by the Roman "possessio", it put an "imperfect possession" that included every form of detention, other than that of an owner, that was accompanied by an intent to exercise a right for the detainer's own benefit. Thus the Prussian "Landrecht" recognized, besides the possession of an owner ("Eigenbesitz"), an independent possession ("einen eigenen Besitz") of a lessee, hirer, usufructuary, etc.; and regarded only cases of user ("Verwaltung") in the exercise of another's right as cases of a dependent "detention" ("unselbständige Inhabung"), — though according possessory protection even to the latter as against third parties. The present Civil Code has brought the evolution to an end in perfect harmony with the old Germanic law. It has, it is true, wholly abandoned the physical indicium of usufruct ("Nutzung"), characteristic of the old law: every independent physical dominion — along with that of the owner and of all persons entitled to enjoyment, that of a custodian, a guardian, etc. — is "possession" (§§ 872, 868). Only a dependent administrative-custody ("unselbständige Verwaltungsinhabung") is no possession (§ 855); in this case the person having control is a "possessory-servant" ("Besitzdiener") of the possessor. The Swiss Civil Code has gone still farther in recognizing outright all actual control over a thing as possession (§ 919).

(3) In close connection with all this was the recognition — quite irreconcilable with the classic Roman law — of *multiple possessions of the same thing*. The Italian jurists had already found themselves compelled to recognize this characteristic product of medieval life; and had striven to bring it into harmony with the classic sources by employing the concepts of "naturalis" and "civilis possessio", and superior and subordinate ownerships. In Germany, also, the law remained after the Reception decidedly upon an indigenous basis. The recognition of classes of "independent" possession, besides proprietary possession, was precisely and primarily designed to make possible such co-existence. Here again the new Civil Code has gone back to the old law even more completely than did the codes that preceded it. Its "mediate" possession (§ 868) is the old proprietary seisin; its "immediate" possession, subordinate to the former, the old immediate seisin of

rentalers, vassals, etc. And though, in the case of mediate possession it omits the requisite of physical user, one may regard this, with Gierke,[1] as a continuation of the old "dormant" seisin. In the Swiss Civil Code (§ 920) the "independent" possession of an owner corresponds to the "mediate", and the "dependent" possession of one to whom a thing has been transferred for the purpose of conveying a limited real or personal right corresponds to the "immediate", possession of the German Code. Thus in the law of to-day there is again possible, as was the case in the Middle Ages, a gradation of several "possessory dominions" ("Besitzherrschaften"): below the proprietary possession of the owner other independent ("Fremd-") or tenurial ("Lehn-") possessions of the most varied sorts, — for example, those of owners, usufructuaries, usufructuary lessees ("Pächter") and sub-lessees ("Afterpächter"). In what respects the Civil Code has gone, in this matter, even beyond the medieval law, recognizing the possibility of multiple possession in the case of chattels, will be indicated in connection with the law of chattels (*infra*, § 57).

(4) As respects *possession of rights*, the prevailing tendency in the Middle Ages to assimilate legal relations to things had already led (as noted *supra*, p. 201), to an application of the seisin-concept to all rights in any way associated with particular pieces of land; and this even when such rights necessarily lacked the element of usufruct which was required in other cases. The tendency of this principle was bound to be absolutely contrary to the Roman law, for this, aside from a few special cases, recognized a so-called "iuris" or "quasi possessio" in the case of servitudes only. At the same time, seisin of rights was classified without scruple under the Roman concept of "quasi possessio", thus completely transforming this. The Canon law, especially, stretched the concept beyond all limits: it recognized quasi-possession in all rights of lordship — over churches, in ecclesiastical offices and dignities, in the benefices associated therewith, in advowsons, and even in the mutual rights of husband and wife. Germany followed the Canon law in this respect. The term "possession", — which the adjective "quasi" of course no longer fitted, — was extended to cover all rights, including rights in movables, and claims; only rights under the family-law, or at least the marital-possession, ("Ehebesitz") of the Canon law, were excepted. The Codes, too, treated either all rights of permanent enjoyment (so the

[1] "Privatrecht", II, 220.

Prussian Code) or all trafficable incorporeal things whatever (so the Austrian Code) as equivalents, as regarded possession, of corporeal things. On the other hand the present Civil Code has at last "heedlessly broken at this point the thread of German legal development",[1] inasmuch as it concedes possessory remedies for the protection only of real, and restricted personal, servitudes; recognizing no possession of rights in other cases. The Swiss Civil Code, however, makes the actual exercise of the right equivalent in the case of real servitudes and land charges to the possession of a thing (§ 919, 2).

(II) **Acquisition and Loss of Possession.** (1) *Original Acquisition of Possession.* — The common law as well as the Territorial systems adopted the principle that in order to acquire possession actual physical custody ("corpus") must coexist with the will-to-possess ("animus"). The requirement of actual physical custody was set up by the common law, following the Roman, as an absolute principle, even with reference to land. This made the acquisition of possession by judicial surrender of seisin and decree of court impossible. Consequently, the cases of incorporeal seisin disappeared from the common law, which in its law of possession maintained simply the old doctrine of corporeal seisin. On the other hand, wherever the land-registry system was developed the consequences of seisin based upon release and judgments were transferred to the book entry; most distinctly in the Austrian law, which in its so-called "Tabular" or "book" (*i.e.* registered) possession recognized a special kind of possession. With respect to the possessory animus, the common law also rejected, as already indicated (p. 208 *supra*), the narrow Roman view, and adhered to the old theory of seisin. In the law of to-day, on the other hand, the element of will is taken into account, but only to the extent that a corresponding will-to-possess must, under some circumstances, accompany an actual reduction to physical custody.

(2) *Derivative Acquisition of Possession.* — The other Roman principle — that all acquisitions of possession are original, and in particular that even in the case of "tradition" there is merely a sequence in time, but no succession — was rejected. On the contrary, "original" acquisition resulting from a unilateral physical reduction to custody was placed alongside of "derivative" acquisition that came into existence by a transfer of possession. This un-Roman conception, which dominated the older

[1] "Privatrecht", II, 226.

common law and the systems of Territorial law, has been adopted also by the new Civil Code and by the Swiss Civil Code.

The transfer of possession is a juristic act.

(A) This juristic act may sometimes consist in a CORPOREAL DELIVERY. Originally, this was an indispensable requisite, as well in medieval as in Roman law, for every acquisition of possession. However, as explained above (*supra*, pp. 189 *et seq.*), the medieval land law abandoned this requirement in cases of incorporeal possession. And even the Roman law disregarded it under some circumstances (depositing something in the house of the acquirer, posting of a guard by the acquirer, delivery of a key, delivery of documents of title, putting identification marks upon a thing, a declaration of tradition in sight of the object to be conveyed, "traditio brevi manu", "constitutum possessorium"). This concurrence, which at best was only superficial, had already been seized upon in Italy for the purpose of developing the theory of the so-called "traditio ficta", that is a transfer of possession by mere words and tokens without corporeal delivery; which theory was then carried to Germany and adopted in the Law Books.[1] Certain cases of this "traditio ficta" used in contrast with "traditio vera", — in particular the tradition of keys and deeds, — were designated as "symbolical" tradition, with inaccurate reference to the old forms of transfer in the Germanic land law. This was, however, a complete confusion, historically, of entirely distinct principles of Germanic and Roman law. The clarified Romanistic jurisprudence of the 1800 s showed the inconsistency between such a concept and the Roman sources. It was consequently abandoned, and is not recognized by the new Civil Code. At the same time, however, under the general principles of that Code the requirement of delivery ("Übergabe") is satisfied by handing over that which, according to popular understanding, is the means of assuring physical control over the thing to be delivered; for example, a key. Similarly, the marking of wares, which according to medieval notions was a peculiarly effective means of satisfying the requisite of a visible notification of change in their control, can be regarded under the present law, also, as equivalent in effect to an actual delivery. The Swiss Civil Code gives expression to this idea in the general provision that possession is transferred, not only by delivery of the thing itself but also by delivery of the means of procuring control over the thing to be delivered (§ 922). Peculiarly important in modern commercial

[1] *Biermann*, "Traditio ficta" (1891).

law, yet likewise rooted in old Germanic law, is the delivery of wares by manual delivery of mercantile papers relating to them (bills of lading, carrier's receipts, and warehouse receipts and dock warrants).

(B) Beside the transfer of possession by physical delivery (or its substitute) stands TRANSFER PERFECTED BY JURISTIC ACT, which, provided certain preconditions are satisfied, passes possession by a "possession-contract" ("Besitzvertrag"), in other words, by a mere declaration of will. The principles of the Roman law have come to control this mode of transfer, and also dominate the regulation by the Civil Code of agreements for the transfer of possession.

(3) As already explained (*supra*, p. 190) seisin of lands passed by inheritance directly to the heir, as incorporeal seisin. Such *seisin by descent* stood in the sharpest contrast with the principles of the Roman law of possession and inheritance. Nevertheless it had already been retained in Italian theory under the name of "possessio civilissima"; and in Germany, the Roman law was likewise unable to dislodge it. Many statutes and many writers recognized it. Most of the modern State systems, also, either provided explicitly that the heir should acquire the inheritance only by a special reduction to possession, — as did the Bavarian "Landrecht" and the Saxon Code; or contained no explicit provision whatever, — like the Prussian "Landrecht" and the Austrian Code. This abandonment of the old native law in Germany itself was all the more striking because almost all of the modern codes outside of Germany, and notably the Code Civil (to be sure there was doubt as to the meaning of its provisions, the Baden "Landrecht" being clearer), retained the principle of inherited possession. It was only with the Civil Code that a return was made to original Germanic law (§ 857). Not only has it recognized the transfer of possession by inheritance, but it has applied this to all things; not merely to lands. The Swiss Civil Code has taken the same stand (§ 560, 2).

(4) As regards *positive prescription* ("Ersitzung"), it has already been explained (*supra*, pp. 200 *et seq.*) that this was unknown to the medieval law, although citation ("rechte") seisin played a similar rôle in the case of land. With the Reception of Roman law its doctrine of usucapion was adopted in Germany. Wherever the land-registry system attained predominance, however, the possibility of acquiring possession in lands by the mere running of time wholly disappeared; although in many local systems,

e.g. in the Austrian, there was introduced "a positive prescription upon the basis of the book-entry reminiscent of judicial seisin" ("Tabularersitzung").[1] Citation seisin, on the other hand, lived on without a break in the so-called "possession annale" of the French law, which gives a possessory remedy solely for the protection of a possession undisturbed during one year. The present Civil Code has wholly done away with any ordinary positive prescription of rights in land, admitting an exceptional one in certain cases only (§§ 900, 927). The Swiss Civil Code recognizes an ordinary positive prescription in favor of one who has been unjustifiably registered in the landbook as owner, and has possessed the land in good faith, uninterruptedly and without challenge, for ten years (§ 661). It recognizes also an extraordinary prescription after an uninterrupted and unchallenged possession for thirty years whenever the land has not been entered in the register, or its owner does not appear therefrom (562).

(5) In accordance with the principles that regulated its acquisition, *loss of possession* necessarily resulted, from the Reception onward, from the cessation of actual control. The Italian jurists, however, had earlier insisted upon the fiction, peculiar to the seisin theory, that one who was forcibly disseised of land did not cease to "possess", but retained at least provisionally the (incorporeal) seisin. As we shall see in the next section (§ 36), this Germanic idea was of great importance in Italy in the transformation of the Roman possessory actions. In Germany, too, where with the Italian concept of possession there was adopted the Italian doctrine relative to the protection of possession, the fiction was for a time adhered to; the theory being followed that the disseisee "possessionem solo animo retinet." Indeed, this theory was even extended to chattels. In more recent times, however, this after-effect of the old incorporeal seisin disappeared, along with the whole medieval scheme of possessory actions. In the law of chattels, the distinction between voluntary and involuntary loss of possession retained a decisive importance even after the Reception (as will be shown later, § 57); and thus it continued to be true in the modern and in the present law that the effects upon the positive law of protecting possession are different and more limited in the law of chattels than in the land law, a regulation totally at variance with the Roman law of the Reception.

(III) **The Protection of Possession**: (1) *The Roman Interdicts.* — As we have seen, German law knew no independent, no special,

[1] *Gierke*, "Privatrecht", II, 265.

protection of possession, and no special possessory action. The lawsuit upon the issue of seisin became, in its trial-stage, a contest with regard to the right embodied therein. Only the mere beginnings were established of a procedure designed to regulate solely possession. The special protection of possession that was independently developed in the French and English law was first adopted in Germany with the alien system,—and then in a form by no means clear.

In sharpest contrast to the German law, the Roman had carried through "with great clearness" the protection of possession as such, without regard to its rightfulness or lawfulness. In its possessory action prosecuted upon the basis of the so-called possessory interdicts derived from the prætorian law, possession and its disturbance, or ouster therefrom, constituted the exclusive cause of complaint. Pleas based upon a right in the thing itself, so-called petitory pleas, were absolutely excluded. Moreover, the interdict procedure served to fix the rôles of the parties in the trial of title that followed; for, with respect to the latter, the victor in the possessory action either gained for himself, or made himself secure in, the position of defendant of which he had been deprived, or his claim to which had been contested; and could now wait to see whether the dispossessed demandant could succeed in proving a better right than his own to the thing contested. But both actions, later distinguished as "possessorium" and "petitorium", remained wholly distinct.

The Roman law knew two possessory actions, according as the question involved was one of damages for past disturbance or of security against a threatened disturbance of possession, or a question of regaining possession after ouster. The first purpose was served by the so-called "Interdictum uti possidetis"; for the originally co-existent "Interdictum Utrubi" for movables had disappeared before the Justinian codification. It was an "Interdictum retinendæ possessionis." By means of it, a present possessor, that is one who at the time of bringing action was in actual possession, demanded protection against disturbances that had already taken place or were threatened. He succeeded, however, only when he had not himself gained possession by a wrong done in some way to his opponent. He must not possess, as against him, "vi, clam, precario." If such proved to be the case, he was himself condemned to give back possession to the defendant he had sued (hence called "iudicium duplex"). The "uti possidetis", therefore, could be used also by one who had been dispossessed " vi, clam, precario ", in order to regain the possession which his opponent had so procured " vi, clam, precario." The interdict served here, exceptionally, as an aid in the reacquisition of possession. If both parties alleged possession, the interdict served to determine the disputed facts regarding possession, and thus the rôle of defendant in the trial of title.

The " Interdictum Unde vi " was an " Interdictum recuperandæ possessionis." It was available to one who had been forcibly dispossessed of land, and compelled the dispossessor to deliver up possession.

(2) These institutes of the classic Roman law suffered, first in Italy and later in Germany, *important changes.* It is not difficult to recognize in these the influence of seisin, which was still exercising its dominance over men's minds, unbeknown to them.

(A) The fact just mentioned, that the Roman law, under certain circumstances, already attributed to the " Uti possidetis ", which originally served merely to defend possession, a restitutive function,—namely, in favor of one who had lost possession " vi, clam, precario ", thus according a protection that extended beyond the "Interdictum Unde vi" (which had reference only to land and violent dispossession in the proper sense) was plainly in entire agreement with the assumption, familiar to medieval jurists since the days of seisin, of an incorporeal seisin that continued to exist in the disseisee. The interdict was thenceforth used for the protection not only of corporeal but also of incorporeal seisin (to use the terminology of Germanic law). In other words, a disturbance of possession was assumed where the Romans had seen ouster, and would therefore have permitted the " Interdictum Unde vi " alone; and the result of this was wholly to obliterate the line between disturbance and ouster, so that the difference between the " Uti possidetis " and the " Unde vi " was, at least practically, abolished. This was, moreover, as Heusler points out,[1] a natural result of the actual conditions of medieval possession, which differed so greatly from the Roman. If, for example, an isolated collection of tithes was to be prevented, this could be regarded equally well as a disturbance of the possession of the tithe-owner or as a disseisin of the right itself to the tithes.

But there was a further Germanistic muddling of the Roman law. The "Interdictum Uti possidetis" was based, as above remarked, directly and exclusively upon the fact of possession at

[1] "*Gewere*", 312.

the moment action was brought. This fact alone needed to be proved. If both parties relied upon possession, the court had to decide which side had actually enjoyed it at that time. This also, as Heusler remarks,[1] fitted Roman conditions, especially "the aedes, the present possession of which was open and manifest." But it was not adapted to possessory relations as developed in medieval civilization, — not, for example, to lands that were scattered among the estates of any number of lords (think of the landed possessions of a rich church or cloister!), and still less to all kinds of real rights in gross ("Rechtsamen") which were quite unknown to the Romans. For this reason, when both parties alleged any usufructuary ("hebbende") seisin, the medieval law, as above pointed out (page 196), fell back upon the *older* seisin. There was developed from this in Italy the presumption that such elder seisin was also the present seisin; and therefore proof was required, at the outset, of the older, but not of the present, seisin.

Finally, the influence of the seisin-concept was also seen in the fact that instead of adhering to the original function of the "Uti possidetis" as a purely possessory remedy, the question of right was drawn into the suit in Germanic fashion, and petitory pleas allowed; although the Glossators were not friendly to this mixture of "possessorium" and "petitorium."

(B) The "INTERDICTUM UNDE VI" was subjected to changes no less radical than those suffered by the "Uti possidetis." From it the Canon law developed what was later known in Germany as the action of spoliation. The name implies the historical origin. The Pseudo-Isidore had laid down the rule in a number of the decretals he forged, that a bishop who had been driven from his see and robbed of his power and property, and against whom a criminal action was brought, need not make answer to the charge until the Church's power should have restored to him everything: the "exceptio spolii" should be available to him — although this was not merely a dilatory plea, but at the same time an action directed against the possessor of the object of which the complainant had been despoiled, for the return of the impropriated possession. "Certainly", says Savigny,[2] "nobody could have foreseen less than the forger himself who concocted these letters of Roman bishops that from one of their passages there would one time be derived a wholly new system of law relating to possessory remedies, and indeed of possession itself." That resulted from the celebrated "Canon Redintegranda", which Gra-

[1] "Gewere", 311.

[2] "Besitz", § 50.

tian included in his Decretals (c. 3, C. 3, q. 1). Upon this Canon the canonists based an independent action, the "condictio ex canone", or, as it was called in France, the "Redintégrande." It extended the scope of the "Interdictum Unde vi", in that it was applicable also to chattels; in being available not only against actual "vis" but also against any "iniusta possessio"; and in being directed not only against the dispossessor but also against every third party in possession. And although these extensions constituted, in truth, essential improvements as compared with the Roman "remedium recuperandae possessionis", yet here too there resulted, in time, from the 1300 s onward, a complete obscurement of the Roman foundation. As in the case of the "Unde vi" so in that of the "Condictio ex canone", the plaintiff was originally bound, in accordance with its character as a mere possessory remedy, to establish the fact of ouster or spoliation. But in this action, as in the "Uti possidetis", the rule was, as it were, "smuggled in"[1] that the plaintiff should show his elder possession, and that from this there must then be inferred the "iniustitia" of the defendant and the illegality of his possession, until proof of the contrary. The consequence was that a distinction between the two actions, — the "Uti possidetis" as transformed, and the "Unde vi" as extended to serve as an action of spoliation, — was thenceforth quite impossible. Both actions, peculiar hybrids of Roman and Germanic ideas, united what the Roman law had consciously and sharply distinguished: disturbance of possession and ouster, possession and right. These were, therefore, themselves incapable of mutual delimitation.

In this way the medieval Italian procedure had deprived the Roman possessory action of its simple character. It had become cumbersome and slow. This caused the introduction of a new procedure, a so-called "summariissimum", which concluded with a judgment preliminary to the "possessorium."

(3) *Possessory Remedies of the German Law.* — These complicated actions were now introduced into Germany. The "Uti possidetis", mixed in Italy with elements of seisin, was developed by the theorists into a so-called "*possessorium ordinarium.*" As such it "almost became a petitory action founded upon a better right of possession."[2] This action had to be brought in cases of disturbed possession; or as men said in the 1500 s, "umb Irrung des Besitzes" (on account of disturbance of possession), without

[1] *Heusler*, "Gewere", 319. [2] *Gierke*, "Privatrecht", II, 247.

distinction between immovables and movables. At the same time men also clung very fast in Germany to the notion, derived from the old law of seisin, that a violent dispossession does not destroy legal possession. The *spoliation action*, which found equal application to all classes of things and which received the broadest possible interpretation in its application, remained the remedy for all those cases in which the plaintiff had been deprived of his possession, not by an act of violence, but in some other wrongful manner, or simply against his will. In cases of violent dispossession it was concurrent with the "possessorium ordinorium." Inasmuch as the spoliation action was confined to the issue of ejectment and admitted of no pleas of title, — *i.e.* was given a possessory character, — it actually served, in cases of dispossession, mainly as a possessory process preliminary to the petitory "ordinarium." In cases where the facts of possession were doubtful the "summariissimum", which was also received into Germany, served as the possessory remedy. In the Prussian law, for example, it was the sole action, aside from the purely petitory "ordinarium", for the protection of possession. It was characterized by certain peculiarities of procedure that aimed at prompt results; but certainly without permanent success, for Savigny relates that he took part in a suit that lasted twelve years, and in which the "ordinarium" might easily have lasted fifty, and the "petitorium" a hundred years!

Recent imperial legislation has completely swept away this rubbish. There are no longer any special possessory actions, the possession being protected by means of the ordinary civil procedure. The functions of the old "summariissimum" are now performed by provisional orders. The actions for the protection of possession that are allowed by the new Civil Code, and which are based either upon a dispossession or an interference with possession, alike of movables and immovables, are pure possessory actions. Pleas of right to the possession are barred, and reserved to the petitory proceeding. Every possessor is protected, not merely the owner. As all possession, even of land, presupposes under the existing law actual physical control, there is no longer anything analogous to the one-time protection of incorporeal seisin. As regards land, however, the registry system applies.

§ 30. **The Land-Registry System.**[1] — (I) **The Medieval Law.** — Already in the early Middle Ages there became prevalent in Ger-

[1] *Randa*, "Die geschichtliche Entwicklung des Instituts der öffentlichen Bücher in Österreich", in Z. Priv. öff. R., VI (1879), 81–119; *Aubert*,

many, along with the late Roman system of diplomatics, the custom of employing written notes or memoranda to give greater security to legal transactions which were especially important or which were designed to have permanent effect; and especially, therefore, in the case of transactions relating to land. The churches and cloisters, in particular, not only began to keep copy-books in which they gathered together copies of instruments executed in their favor, but also conveyance-books in which were entered in the form of a register original notes of conveyances of land. Whether these private conveyance-books of the great seigniories became the model for the public "town-books" that began to appear from the middle of the 1100 s on, is doubtful. It is more probable "that the institution of town-books or registers, once developed in a particular city and region, spread from such a point, in other words from town to town."[1] In this process the development of municipal chanceries and of the office of town clerk was certainly of material influence. The town clerk was often himself brought from abroad, and brought with him into his new position the chancery practices elsewhere observed. Inasmuch as it had become customary from the 1000 s onward, and in many places a necessity, to carry out in court legal transactions affecting land (*infra*, § 24), such acts came to be performed in the cities, especially in those of North Germany, before the town-court or, later, before the town council; which tribunals habitually

"Beiträge zur Geschichte der deutschen Grundbücher", ed. by *Doublier*, in Z². R. G., XIV (1893), 1–74; *Rehme*, "Das Lübecker Oberstadtbuch" (1895); "Zur Geschichte des Münchener Liegenschaftsrechtes", reprint from "Festgabe für H. Dernburg" (1900); "Geschichte des Münchener Grundbuches" (1903); "Über das älteste bremische Grundbuch (1438–1558) und seine Stellung im Liegenschaftsrechte" ("Stadtrechtsforschungen, 1er Teil", 1908); "Über die Breslauer Stadtbücher, Ein Beitrag zur Geschichte des Urkundenwesens, zugleich der städtischen Verwaltung und Rechtspflege" ("Stadtrechtsforschungen, 2er. Teil", 1909); *K. Beyerle*, "Die deutschen Stadtbücher", in Deut. G. Bl., XI (1910), 145–200; *Kleeberg*, "Stadtschreiber und Stadtbücher in Mühlhausen i. Th. vom 14. bis 16. Jahrhundert nebst Übersicht über die Editionen mittelalterlicher Stadtbücher", in Arch. Urk. F., II (1910), 407–90; *Redlich*, "Die ältesten Nachrichten über die Prager Stadtbücher und die böhmische Landtafel", in Inst. öst. G. F., XXXII (1911), 165–71; "Die Privaturkunden des Mittelalters", in *v. Below* and *Meinecke's* "Handbuch der mittelalterlichen und neueren Geschichte", "Urkundenlehre" by *Erben, Schmitzkallenberg* and *Redlich*, Part 3 (1911), 181 *et seq.*; *Weiss*, "Zur Geschichte des Realfoliums und des Hauptbuchsystems in Österreich", in "Festschrift zur Jahrhundertfeier des allgemeinen bürgerlichen Gesetzbuchs", II (1911), 509–549; *Rehme*, "Zur Geschichte des Grundbuchwesens in Berlin", in "Festschrift für Gierke" (1911), 525–587.

[1] *Beyerle, op. cit.*, 183. To the same effect, *Redlich*, "Privaturkunden," 191.

made notes of them — at first very brief — for preservation. From these official registers there were developed the town registers. They appear earliest in Cologne where, in the Martin's parish, there is to be seen a protocol of as early a date as 1135 or thereabouts, drawn up by skevins upon great sheets of parchment, concerning the acquisition of real rights in lands. This example was soon followed by other parishes of the city, save that they, instead of fastening together loose sheets ("Schreinskarten", — shrine sheets), used books, in such a manner that each quarter of every parish had its special press-book. From Cologne the practice spread rapidly to Andernach and Metz. In the 1200 s such town-books soon spread over the whole of North Germany, particularly to those cities that belonged to the Magdeburg and Lübeck groups of town law; in many of which places (Stralsund, Rostock), the keeping of loose sheets similarly preceded the keeping of books. Originally, all legal transactions made known to the officials were entered in these books in purely chronological order, without regard to their content; and this whether they were of private or of public character, and whether they referred to lands or to chattels, to sales, pledges, gifts mortis causa, the creation of annuities, etc. Later, however, different books were in many places opened for the different classes of transactions, in the interest of greater clearness. Thus, for example, a special inheritance book ("liber resignationum") was separated from the book of debts, pledges, and annuities ("liber obligationum et censuum", "liber impignorationum et reddituum"). And so with others. At the same time the limitation of the books to single municipal divisions, as already adopted in Cologne, found extensive imitation. In Hamburg, for example, each parish was given its own books; in Munich they were given to the four quarters of the inner and the four quarters of the outer city; in Danzig, to the old and to the new town. In the Cologne press-books, moreover, the practice was begun as early as the 1200 s of bringing together in the same part of the book all entries relating to one piece of land, thus making possible an easy examination of the same. In this manner there originated the arrangement of "real" folios, which were probably first utilized in Danzig: the books were arranged according to streets and pieces of land, and each piece of land was given a special sheet (or a number of sheets), which made manifest, so far as possible, its complete legal status.

In the open country the model of the town books was not

generally followed during the Middle Ages. The rural books of that period were in the main mere lists of the charges and taxes imposed upon individual peasant holdings. The sole exception was the development as early as the 1200 s in the lands of the Bohemian crown (Bohemia, Moravia, and Upper Silesia) and in Poland of the institution of land-tablets ("Landtafel"), known as the "jewel" of those lands. It is a disputed question whether this was based upon the national Slavic law or due to the influence of the German law. The registers ("land-tablets") in Prague, Brünn, Troppau, and Jägerndorf, — which have continued to exist without essential change down to the present time, and have served as the model for the system of land registers introduced at the end of the 1700 s into the other lands of the Austrian crown, — were already land registers in the modern sense; for an entry in them was a precondition to the legal validity of land transactions.

This principle received frequent recognition also in the medieval German town laws. Many made the transfer of ownership dependent upon registration; notably the law of Lübeck and Bremen, and probably also that of Hamburg, Hanover, and the Mecklenburg group of towns. Others prescribed the requirement of registration for the creation of rights of pledge and other real rights; for example those of Munich, Vienna, Greifswald, and Hamburg. In this manner the book entry, which was originally merely evidence of the conclusion of a legal transaction effected by the declarations of the parties, became itself the validating act. It thus took over the functions of seisin: it became the form in which were expressed all legal transactions involving land.

(II) **The Modern Development.**—The institution of land registers was powerfully promoted by the Reception. According to the Roman principles that were taken over into the common law, even transactions in land could be consummated without special forms and without official coöperation. At the same time the regional legal systems for the most part adhered or returned to the traditional institutions; although there was almost everywhere a more or less extensive adaptation of these to the Roman system. On the other hand, in very recent times, for the most part before 1900, the registry system has again received general recognition and consistent application; first in State law, and finally, through the new Civil Code and the Imperial Land Registry Ordinance of March 24, 1897, as general German law. In Switzerland, also, the land registry system has been introduced without qualification by the Civil Code.

The modern statutes, it is true, adopted at first different viewpoints, thus introducing conditions of greatly varying character.[1] They differed particularly in that some had adopted the mortgage registry system and others the land registry system proper. Where the mortgage registry system prevailed the books were primarily designed to give security for credit based upon land ("Realkredit"). Acquisition of title was not dependent upon entry in the register; only he who wished to place a hypothecary charge upon his land was required to be a registered owner; that is, registration was essential only for the creation of a hypothec. Such was the view, notably, of the Prussian Hypothec Ordinance of December 20th, 1783, and of the Prussian "Landrecht." It was adhered to until the year 1900 in Baden, Bavaria to the right of the Rhine, Alsace-Lorraine, Rhenish Hesse, parts of Mecklenburg, Saxe-Meiningen, Saxe-Weimar, Schwarzburg-Rudolstadt, and Württemberg; and until 1895 by Hamburg and Frankfort o. M. Yet even within most of these regions, registration of title generally offered greater security, and might even be required under penalties (*e.g.* in Frankfort).

More and more, however, the land registry system proper came to predominate; in most regions again in the form of single land registers which included a record of all real rights. Only in relatively few legal systems (Nassau, Baden, Frankfort, Hamburg, Hesse, Meiningen, and Württemberg) were special land registers prescribed in addition to mortgage books. The pure land registry system made even transfers of title by juristic act dependent on a book entry. In such cases, therefore, the registers also afforded information regarding the condition of title. Among the States in which this system was practised were Saxony, since the statute of November 6, 1843; Mecklenburg, whose legislation, — especially the revised Town-Book Ordinance of December 21, 1857, and the act relating to the hypothecation of crown lands of Schwerin, of January 2, 1854, — was very influential in the development of the modern law; and finally, Prussia, with its important statutes of May 5, 1872 (the Title Transfer and Land Registry Acts).

These Prussian statutes have been adopted as the basis of the new imperial legislation. The present land register is therefore designed to give publicity to all legal rights in land in so far as these are subject to the requirement of registration; and that is the case in by far the great majority of instances. Only a few

[1] See the detailed table in *Stobbe-Lehmann*, II, 1, 104–167.

legal relations — possession, the rights of usufruct of husbands and parents, rights in lands not subject to registry, etc. — lie outside the purview of the land registry law. And only such changes in real rights as arise independently of any legal agreement to that end (as for example acquisition by inheritance) can be acquired or created without registration. This rule is in harmony with the earlier Prussian law. On the other hand the earlier statutory systems of Saxony, Hamburg, Lübeck, and Mecklenburg required registration under all circumstances, carrying to an extreme the idea of the old law that legal rights were created by the act of entry. From this they deduced the further consequence that wherever a formally correct, but materially incorrect, entry or cancellation had been made, no regard might be paid to the substantial right contradicting it; and that a person thereby injured should be given only a personal claim for restitution of his right or for damages. In contrast to this view the majority of other legal systems required, as a condition precedent to the efficacy of registration, a valid real ("dinglicher") juristic act (the principle of substantial — "materielles" — consensus); which in cases of conveyance of title and imposition of charges must consist in an agreement of the wills of the parties concerned — in other words, in a real contract. This rule also has been adopted by the Civil Code. In the Prussian law, and in the other legal systems related to it, the so-called "public faith" of the land register has therefore quite another meaning than in those systems which recognized the unqualified formal validity of the book-entry. For the latter attributed to the registry the power, under some circumstances, of producing effects destructive of a substantial right. A third person acting in good faith should according to their view be protected; he should be able to rely absolutely upon the register. If a person entered into a legal agreement with another party who was improperly registered, the semblance existing according to the register should have exactly the same effect in his favor as if it were not a mere semblance; in other words, the same effect as if the basis of substantial right supposedly underlying the entry, but actually absent, were in fact present. It is true that according to the Prussian law negligence excluded good faith, and that the public faith of the register protected only such third persons as had acquired rights for value. Both provisions have been abrogated by the present Civil Code; which here again, however, followed the Prussian law in other respects. It denies protection only in case of actual bad faith, and treats rights that have been acquired gratuitously the same as those acquired for value. This public faith of the land register, thus established in the modern law, is therefore capable, under certain circumstances, of creating a purely formal right that may not coincide with substantive right.[1]

Finally, as regards the physical arrangement of the register, most modern statutes have adopted as their general rule the system of real folios, and have admitted personal folios only as exceptions, namely for regions of particularly disintegrated holdings, and when no confusion is to be feared therefrom. The national Code has followed the same rule. It was usual to divide the real folios, — as in Prussia, for example, — into a title-sheet and three subordinate parts, the first being devoted to a record of proprietary transactions; the second, of perpetual charges; and the third, of hypothecs and land charges. This regulation of the internal arrangement of the land-book folios has been left, under the Civil Code, to State legislation. Prussia, for example, has retained its old registry system with some few alterations. There are also special registry officials, whose training has been similarly left to the State law; the local courts (" Amtsgerichte ") serve, for the most part, as registry offices. An important innovation made by the new and formal law of land registry is found in the fact that whereas until its adoption there was only a secondary liability on the part of the State (as in Prussia, Bavaria, Mecklenburg, and Hamburg), or no liability whatever (as in Württemberg, Hesse, and Nassau), for negligent or intentional violations of duty on the part of the registry officials, responsibility for damages rests, since the adoption of the new system, exclusively upon the State or other political body in whose service the official acts (Land Registry Ordinance, § 12), the right of the State to save itself harmless at the expense of such officials being, of course, left unaffected thereby.

[1] *Gierke*, "Privatrecht", II, 320.

CHAPTER VI

THE LAW OF LAND (*Continued*)

PART II. THE OWNERSHIP OF LAND

§ 31. **The Concept of Ownership. (I) The Medieval Law.** (1) *Antiquity of the Concept and of its Designations.* — The concept of ownership as the fullest right that one can have in a thing,[1] as "a right directed to the dominion over a thing as an entirety",[2] was known from the earliest times not merely to the Germanic law of chattels but also to the Germanic land law. "Eigen", a substantive participle of the verb "eigan" = "haben", to have, is a word of the common Germanic stock that was applied to lands to indicate that they belonged to somebody; that they were objects "had" or held by somebody. In the Latin sources use was made of the expressions "dominium", "proprietas", "proprium." It was a favorite practice, also, to enumerate exhaustively in the documents the different powers that an owner enjoyed. The German words "Eigenschaft" and "Eigentum" first appear in the 1200 s; the earliest authority for "egindum" occurs in a Cologne archival document of 1230.

(2) *Ownership and Real Rights.* — The conception of ownership, however, had not, by any means the sharp definition in the medieval land law which is familiar to us in the Romanized modern law. In particular, it was not in principle dissociated from and opposed to restricted real rights. The reason for this lay in the forms of the actual economic relations of that time, upon which the growth and form of legal ideas was dependent. As has been mentioned (*supra*, p. 115) individual ownership in house and homestead had certainly been developed at an early day; in the arable land, on the contrary, only after the period of the tribal migrations; while in the case of the commonties ("Allmende") the old collective ownership has been dissolved only in very recent years. Moreover, even after the development of individual ownership the old communism continued to influence the rights of associations, of neighbors, and of kin. To all this was added the development of land tenancies, which led to a wide distribution of the economic produce (rents and profits) of the soil among different persons, and made exceptional the union of all rights of enjoyment in one hand. It must be remembered that until far into the Middle Ages the value of land lay solely in such produce; its utilization in exchange played almost no rôle whatever.

This is the explanation of the fact that the conception of a general legal and physical control, of a general right of control

[1] *Brunner*, "Grundzüge" (5th ed.), 197.
[2] *Gierke*, "Privatrecht", II, 347.

without more definite description, constituted for a long time the final and the central idea in the medieval land law. This idea of a right of control capable of varying limitations and gradations without being thereby affected in its essence, was for a time quite sufficient to classify such legal relations to the soil as actually occurred. They all appeared solely as degrees, differing in their content, of the one universal fact of a physical dominion over, and directed to the usufruct of, a material thing; all of which rights, moreover, were equally visible under different forms of seisin in lands. From the naïve medieval point of view which concerned itself solely with the economic produce of the land, the right of ownership of one who had received a piece of land as a gift, and who, under the Germanic law of gifts, was not allowed, without the assent of the giver, either to alienate or to pass it by descent, was not essentially different from the right of him in whose favor there was created a usufructuary right in a piece of land. Just as little did it make any tangible and practical difference, whether the limitations imposed upon the usufructuary rights of the occupant of land originated in mutual adjustment through legal forms, or, as might be the case, through the rights of the association, of neighbors, or of the kin, and so on, above mentioned. Hence it was that men did not scruple to employ such expressions as "dominus", "res sua", "proprietas", "Eigentum", and others, in reference, similarly, to one who possessed merely a limited right of usufruct, of dower ("Leibzucht"), of holding lands by descent as a rentaler, or of pledge. The Sachsenspiegel still calls him to whom "dat gut to horet" the lord or master of the thing, whether he had the ownership or enjoyed only a limited real right in it.

Gradually, however, and already in the Middle Ages, there came about a refinement of the point of view. Just as proprietary seisin had been contrasted with the various cases of limited physical seisin, so men learned to distinguish the right of ownership from other real rights. Especially in the case of feudal and manorial tenures the right of the landlord ("proprietas", "allod")[1] was contrasted from the beginning, even in terminology, with the right of the tenant ("precarium", "feudum"). It is indeed true, as has been already remarked (*supra*, p. 189), that the Territorial law did not at first give the least consideration to the right of feudal, servitary, or manorial tenants. On the contrary this found recognition at first solely within the special boundaries

[1] *v. Schwerin*, art. "allod" in *Hoop's* "Reallexikon", I (1911), 65.

of the feudal, servitary, and manorial law: namely, as "Eigen" or ownership in the feudal, servitary, or manorial sense, and it was limited by the landlord's supreme right of control in a manner not very unlike that in which ownership under the Territorial law was limited by the superior power of the State. Later, however, the Territorial law also recognized these rights of tenancy as independent rights in things, just as it had itself long since developed its own peculiar tenancies, both free, peasant, and burghal.

The distinction between the right of ownership and a limited real right (rights of tenancy, of usufruct, of pledge, of dower, etc.), thus marked out and later everywhere enforced, nevertheless never caused the essential unity of all rights of control in lands to be lost sight of. The right of ownership which corresponded to proprietary seisin, — namely, that right which was directed to the control of a thing in all respects, — was distinguished from real rights that appeared in forms of limited seisin only in its extent, its contents, and its purpose, and not in its essence. It remained a real right along with other real rights, and these were, to use Gierke's apt expression, nothing else than "splinters of ownership that had become independent."[1] The number of these real rights could be increased at will, since every element that entered into the right of ownership was capable, in principle, of such a segregation. All rights that could assume the form of seisin were therefore real rights; and so, for example, the right of a lessee and hirer, the right of a guardian in his ward's property of which he was seised, and so forth. Nor was even a physical seisin requisite in all this, for those rights that were expressed in a mere juristic seisin thereby acquired the character of materiality ("Dinglichkeit" — "thinglikeness"), — for example, reversionary rights in land, or to shares in the produce of land.

For another reason there could be no talk of a contrast, in principle, between rights of ownership and (lesser) real rights; namely, because the idea of the limitability of the right of ownership was retained, and regarded as consistent with its nature. Landed ownership existed in manifold gradations: besides an ownership or holding that was full, genuine, free, direct, and so on, and which included within itself all those rights of control that were recognized in the state of economic culture and under the actual circumstances which then prevailed, there existed the "ownership" ("Eigen") that was encumbered, liable to rent,

[1] "Privatrecht", II, 359.

etc., and which was restricted within more or less sharply defined limits by the co-rights of other persons. And a fixed boundary between this qualified or lesser ownership and limited real rights did not exist, at least in an economic sense.

(3) *Ownership and Physical Control.* — The concept of physical control over things, out of which there were only gradually developed (another illustration of the rule that legal institutions are only gradually differentiated) the distinct conceptions of the right of property and of restricted real rights, was evidently a more comprehensive concept than these, in so far as the ideas of ownership and control still existed unsevered within it. The original unity of public and private law clearly appeared in it; and the expressions "dominium" and "dominatio" (also "ditio") which are used in the documents, designated at once a relationship of control in the most general sense, the nature of which was by no means necessarily peculiar to the private law, and ownership in the proper sense.[1] The right that pertained in the earliest times to groups, large and small, in the districts that they occupied, was in the same way a right of political dominion and a private legal right of property; and wherever such a collective right persisted, as in the commonties, it long preserved this double character. Neither did the individual rights in the soil that later developed wholly merge in a simple right of property, if only for the reason that they remained the basis of the individual's legal status, and, in particular, determined his personal status. The most potent cause of this confusion of concepts of public and of private law was the development of feudalism, which in fact was based precisely upon this union of seigniorial power and landed ownership in the hands of the land-lord. Inasmuch as rights in land were subjected, as incorporeal things, to the principles of the law of things (*sŭpra*, p. 168), — which now attributed ownership to them, as it had formerly attributed seisin to them, — every right of lordship that related to a definite territory could be treated as the result of a real right in the soil; which fact eventually led in Germany to the theory of the "dominium eminens" of the State, and in England to the assumption of a supreme ownership in all land inhering in the king. The extension of the ownership concept to incorporeal things was retained; but the separation of lordship from property in the sense of private law was begun at the end of the Middle Ages, first of all in the cities, although without attaining to a complete

[1] *Stutz* in "Festschrift für O. Gierke", 1228.

emancipation from the old views, which long remained alive in the institutions of the paternalistic State.

(II) **Influence of the Reception.** — The Roman conception of ownership was of a different nature from that of the medieval law. According to the Roman law, ownership was an unlimited legal power. But it is a mistaken view, albeit one widely held, that this legal power was "a dominion without limitations or duties, abandoned to individual caprice." Moreover, the Roman law, like the German, was originally not blind to the social implications of landed property. It was only in the imperial period that the ownership concept suffered a transformation in an absolutistic sense; yet even then the limited character of ownership was never denied, and no confusion ever resulted between public and private legal rights. The acute insight of the Roman jurists perceived, however, the contrast in principle between that right of ownership which confers, in and of itself, full legal control (notwithstanding that it might be a limitable, and frequently enough was actually a limited, right), and those "iura in re aliena" which were in their nature merely limited powers, and of which only a small number were known. Upon this contrast they built their entire law of things: ownership and real rights of usufruct were not, as in the medieval law, essentially identical, but were powers fundamentally different in their nature.

This distinction between the two conceptions was adopted with the Reception; though to be sure it proved impossible to realize in practice the clearness of the Roman division. At the same time the absolutistic element in the Roman idea of ownership was gladly accepted in Germany; because, however opposed it might be to native habits of thought, it could be made serviceable to manifold necessities and ambitions. It was the influence of the natural law doctrines of the 1700 s, and especially of the ideas that triumphed in the French Revolution, that gave origin to the ownership concept of the modern common law, which first introduced that exaggeration of individual interests above those of society which has been mistakenly ascribed to the Roman law. It found expression in the formula, which was adopted even in modern codes (as for example in the Prussian "Landrecht" and the Code Civil), that ownership is an absolute and unlimited power.

The acceptance of the Roman idea of ownership, since this conferred power exclusively pertaining to private law, has unquestionably facilitated a desirable segregration of those elements of ownership which were derived from public law, and had theretofore clung to it; and has, in so far, furthered endeavors directed toward the destruction of the paternalistic and feudal order of society. On the other hand, the exaggeration of the individualistic view, and the treatment of all real usufructuary rights as Roman "iura in re aliena" has led to grave evils, and, in particular, has in many places completely deprived the lower rural population of their property rights. These evils have been lessened by the circumstance that remnants of the native legal institutes and ideas have everywhere retained vital influence. Most local legal systems preserved the fundamental division of landed and chattel ownership, the recognition of a graduated and limited ownership, a wealth of real rights in addition to ownership, and, above all, the extension of the concept of ownership to rights, — which last, moreover, has been given such broad meaning that in the Prussian and in the Austrian codes, for example, there is talk even of the "ownership" of contractual claims.

The new Civil Code has adopted, in its essentials, the conception of ownership that was held by the common law. At the same time the native law continues to be felt in many ways; for example, in the wide scope of the limitations upon ownership which are recognized, and in the greater number, although now again definitely limited, of real rights. It has been preserved to even greater extent as regards matters reserved to State law. With the rule of the Civil Code (§ 903) that the owner may dispose of a thing as he chooses, so far as the statute law and the rights of third parties do not forbid, and that he can exclude others from all interference therewith, the Swiss Code (§ 641) agrees.

§ 32. **Divided Ownership.** (I) **Conditions of fact.** — The peculiarities noted above (p. 227) in the land-holding relations of the Middle Ages, — namely, the distribution of the produce of the land among several persons entitled thereto, which was becoming the rule, and the consequent peculiar conception of the right of property as a form of physical dominion distinguished only in extent, and not in essence, from other limited rights, — naturally led to a conception of *ownership* as partitioned out among various persons whose rights were of varying strength, and who were therefore not equals but arranged in a hierarchy: a conception which from the standpoint of the Roman law was quite impossible. Here again the development of distinct bodies of class and local law ("Rechtskreise") was of great influence. For inasmuch as the vassals and the serfs possessed, in their respective feudal and rental holdings within the limits of the feudal and manorial laws, approximately the same privileges that freemen enjoyed in their holdings under the Territorial law, they could perfectly well be regarded as owners, if not according to the Territorial law, at least according to the feudal and manorial law; and their rights, as feudal and manorial proprietorship, could be contrasted with the ownership of the landlord under the Territorial law. When their legal status was also recognized, later, under the Territorial law, men clung to the old view, and spoke of ownership as divided between the lord and the usufructuary; they spoke as if the same land might be of many lords or of many liegemen.

(II) **The Legal Theory.** — These actual conditions and views, — which were natural products of the medieval system of landholding, and were especially closely related to the fact that that system was bound together by the principles of feudal law, — were first brought within the formulas of a legal theory by the Glossators, in Italy. They employed in their theory the concepts and terms of the Roman law, without remarking what violence they did to these. But since their doctrine nevertheless harmonized with the actual conditions of the time, it quickly acquired great influence despite its inconsistency with the sources, and maintained itself down into modern times.

From the fact that, because the emphyteuta and the superficiary exercised a physical dominion that nearly approached ownership, the Roman law gave them, not it is true a proprietary action proper, the "rei vindicatio directa", but a corresponding "utilis rei petitio", the conclusion was drawn that the "actio directa" was based upon a "ius directum" and the "acto utilis" upon a "ius utile." The owner would therefore have a "dominium directum", and the emphyteuta and the superficiary a "dominium utile." There came thus to be recognized two "dominia", although of different strength, over the same object. And very soon these conceptions were carried over into feudal relations: to the feudal lord was ascribed the "dominium directum", to the vassal the "dominium utile" in the fief. This terminology seemed the more natural because the word "dominium" was already used in association with the German words "Fug" (privilege) and "Recht" (right, law) in order to characterize that position of lordship which, under the feudal law, was occupied not merely by supreme lords but also by their vassals, as mesne lords ("Aftervasallen"), over their liegemen.

The lower tenures were next interpreted in the same way, and finally, in all cases where ownership and real rights of usufruct existed in one piece of land, men came to speak of "dominium directum" and "utile", or of "over" (superior) and "under" (subordinate) ownership.

The Italian doctrine found its way into Germany in the Middle Ages. It finally acquired an unqualified dominance in legislation, in the courts, and in legal literature. The Prussian "Landrecht" and the Austrian Code undertook to give it new life by ascribing to the "over"-owner so-called "Proprietät", the right to the substance of a thing, and to the "under"-owner at once a co-ownership in that "Proprietät" and an exclusive ownership in the usufruct.

In the meantime, however, the real foundation of these ideas had been removed, and they were thereby condemned to disappearance. Already in the Middle Ages there had set in in the cities a movement which ultimately led to an almost complete abolition of "over"-ownership, and assured to the "under"-owner, who had theretofore enjoyed mere rights of usufruct, the whole ownership, as this was understood in the private law. Modern agrarian legislation has swept away the last traces of the old "over"-ownership. This is the reason why the Code Civil had not a word to say of this whole institution of divided ownership, which sprang from a medieval-feudal legal order that it no longer recognized. The new German Civil Code, following the Saxon, has likewise done away with it (by failing to adopt it), save in so far as continued existence was guaranteed by the Code (EG, §§ 59, 63, 184) to the slight remnants that had been preserved down to present times in the legal systems of the States; as for example in fiefs, family "fideicommissa", and peasant holdings. Moreover, the future creation of divided ownership has been especially forbidden by statute in a number of German States, as for example by the Prussian constitution.

That the whole doctrine was irreconcilable with the concepts of the classic Roman law was shown by the German Romanistic jurisprudence of the 1800 s, although, of course, that did not prove that it had no excuse for existence.

§ 33. **Community Ownership.** (I) **The Medieval Law.** — Even after the development of individual ownership in land, there lived on in the medieval law, as an after-effect of the collective ownership of the soil that earlier existed, the idea of collective rights in the soil inherent, at the same time and in the same degree, in various persons. This idea was richly developed under various forms. The chief of these forms were the following.

(1) *Ownership "in Collective Hand"* ("Eigentum zu gesamter Hand"). — (A) PURE FORM. — In all personal groups controlled by the principle of "collective hand" (*supra*, p. 140 *et seq.*) there existed a collective right of the group members, which right acquired its peculiar features from this community of the private law, resting upon an original or a still continuing family unity. It found characteristic expression in two rules that have already been referred to. The one was that no one of the co-owners could dispose, by himself alone, of either the whole or any part of the common property, whether by act inter vivos or upon death. On the contrary, only all the co-owners, acting together "as with one hand" ("mit gesamter Hand") could dispose either of the whole or of a part. And although the right of the individual might be regarded at the same time as his share or quota in the collective property, — and in truth a community, whether in an entire estate or in a single piece of property, is not easily conceivable apart from shares of individual shareholders,[1] — nevertheless he enjoyed no dispositive power over such share, but was absolutely bound in relation to it by the common will of all.[2] Only when the bond that joined the members into a legal group disappeared, could the idea of *shares*, till then inactive and inconspicuous, become effective[3]: the co-owner who abandoned the group had a claim to a quota corresponding to his co-right, which had until then been undifferentiated.

The other rule that characterized ownership "in collective hand" was this, that the estate left by a decedent member of the community was not lost to the community, but accrued to the other commoners, — save that there was generally allowed to the children of the dead member their lawful share of the inheritance: they were received in his stead into the community, with a right in expectancy to such a quota. With this exception survivorship took place in favor of the remaining commoners, who continued by themselves the collective-hand relationship. Although such communities of collective hand were generally intended for permanent existence, indivisibility of the collective property and indissolubility of the union were by no means of

[1] *Heusler*, "Institutionen", I, 238.

[2] The Sächs. Lehnr., 32, § 3, lays this down, accordingly, for collective feoffees.

[3] *Gierke*, "Genossenschaftsrecht", II, 928.

their essence. But of course the right to partition might, in individual cases, be excluded; either by contract, as was often true of the co-heirship of knightly orders, or by the nature of the personal group, as in the marital community.

(B) Weaker forms. — Since the "collective hand" was simply and solely a principle of law, the application of this principle, however, being dependent upon the nature of the union in which the commoners were associated, it followed that legal institutes were possible which represented a weakening of the pure principle. The pure form was present wherever there was undivided administration of property, as in the peasant communities and in the marital community. But wherever, as in the case of co-heirship in the knightly orders, the common household was abandoned and a distribution of holdings made for separate usufruct ("Mutschierung"), collective control was continued solely with respect to the substance of the property, and community ownership found expression solely in the requirement of common disposition thereof. In the possibility that existed of entrusting one of the co-owners with the representation of the rest, thus permitting him to dispose of it in the name of all, there was involved another weakening of the principle. Finally, the personal union might be entirely dissolved, within the group, and an ideal share assured to each individual in accordance with the "quota principle" (*infra*, under 3). In this case the former unity of the group continued externally only, — as for example in its relations with a feudal lord: as against him the collective tenants were regarded as a unit, and upon the death of one of them his share did not become free of the group and pass to the lord, but accrued to the surviving commoners.

(2) *Ordinary Collective Ownership* ("Gesamteigentum"). — Another form of community ownership was the collective ownership developed in the sib, and later (and especially) in agrarian associations. In agreement with the gradually sharpening differentiation, already discussed (*supra*, pp. 140 *et seq.*), of the group as opposed to the fellow members, it appeared in an older and in a younger form.

(A) Associational collective ownership ("genossenschaftliches Gesamteigentum") in the common march of the old mark-association was located, so long as such an association was not regarded as a juristic person, in the whole body of associates and in the individual associates. The essence of this collective associational ownership lay in this, that a part of the powers included in the rights of ownership inhered in the entirety of the fellows as such, while the individual associates were permitted to exercise another part as members of the group. Thus the group, as such, had the power of disposing of the commonty, — the communal assembly determining the uses to be made of it by vote of the majority, — and exercised, as such, certain rights of usufruct in it; the communal officials, for example, were paid their salaries out of its produce. The produce of the commonty was primarily devoted, however, to the benefit of the individual associates and the satisfaction of their special economic needs. To this end they enjoyed rights of usufruct in it (right of pasture, of estovers, rights to clear land, etc.) which were originally unlimited, but which later, out of regard for the interests of the group, were restricted. Rights of ownership in the collective body, as such, and rights of ownership in the members of the group, occurred, therefore, in unison; and both in the apportioned and (particularly) in the unapportioned lands. This collective ownership was neither the purely corporate ownership of a juristic person, nor a mere co-ownership of individuals by shares; but, as Gierke has shown, contained within itself the germs of both. It was therefore the exact counterpart, in the law of things, of mark and village associations in the law of persons.

(B) CORPORATE COLLECTIVE OWNERSHIP ("korporatives Gesamteigentum"). — Wherever the association ("Genossenschaft") became a corporate association ("Körperschaft, — *supra*, p. 140), the associational property became a quasi-corporate property. But this made no essential change in the character of the collective ownership. For despite the corporate bond between the fellows, the objects included in the corporate property were not therefore things "foreign" to them as individuals; their separate rights, here also, were not limitations upon, but were results of, the corporate ownership. Afterwards as before, the rights that inhered in them as members of the juristic person were united with those that inhered in the group, as such, into a collective right, whose content was ordinarily apportioned between the individuals and the group in such a way that the latter received dispositive and administrative powers and the former rights of usufruct, wholly or principally in the form of shares representing distinct rights.

Inasmuch as ownership in collective hand and the old associational ownership, although of diverse origin, rested upon the same principle, — such a union of the co-owners as was recognized by the law of persons being a pre-condition of both, — it was possible in later times to class them together as different forms of the same type, and as such to contrast both of them with corporate collective property.

(3) *Co-ownership by Shares.* — Finally, the medieval law also recognized (although it was probably not widely distributed) that form of community ownership which is represented for each individual co-owner by an independent "quota-right", upon the strength of which he is entitled to dispose of his ideal share by pledging it, by charging it with annuities and the like, by alienating it freely, and by devising or bequeathing it; as well as to demand partition or distribution at any time. But here again only the whole body of co-owners were capable of dispositive acts affecting the whole thing. Such a simple co-ownership often occurred among heirs. It was applicable to houses (a person possessed the half or the third or fourth part of a house), to other realty, and to sea-going ships held by several shipowners in co-ownership by shares. In the last case any co-owner could demand the dissolution of the associational relation through what was called "putting a value on the ship": that is, he must indicate a sum for which he was ready either to abandon the ship to the other co-owners or retain it alone.

(II) **The modern development.** — (1) *The Reception and the Older Germanic Theory of Collective Ownership.* — Unlike the medieval law the Roman knew only a "condominium pro partibus indivisis", or co-ownership by separate ideal shares ("Quotenprinzip") such as had already found adoption in the German law, and the exclusive sole ownership of a juristic person beside which the rights of the corporate members in the social property could exist only as "iura in re aliena." Here again, after the Reception, the chief endeavor, at first, was to bring these two Roman categories to undisputed dominance, and to arrange under them the wealth of forms of community property developed in the native law. The futility of this undertaking finally became apparent. After a vain endeavor to piece out the Roman concepts with "modifications" by institutes peculiar to the German law things went so far, toward the end of the 1600 s, that a native theory was opposed to the theory of the Roman law, — "the first conscious attempt at independent construction" to be found in Germanic jurisprudence.[1] The

[1] *Gierke*, "Privatrecht", II, 377.

newly devised concept of "collective ownership" was first used to explain the marital community of goods,[1] collective-tenancy, co-heirship, and the mark-association. In the end, the Roman concept of co-ownership was placed beside it as a general concept of equal rank. But however much men thus endeavored to satisfy practical necessities, and however quickly the new concept spread, especially in the law of nature (most of the modern codes were influenced by it), its theoretical basis remained no less questionable. When it was construed as a "condominium plurium in solidum" men overlooked the inconsistency of such an assumption with the Roman concept of ownership which they had, in other respects, retained; and when others discovered in the union of collective owners a collective person, a "persona moralis" in the sense of the common law, they shut their eyes to the fact that there were involved in different cases wholly different groups, and therefore also different collective rights.

These obscurities proved fatal to the theory. The Romanistic jurisprudence of the 1700 s was indefatigable in proving beyond contradiction the inconsistency with the Roman sources of the conception of collective ownership theretofore taught; it was made the object of ridicule, and was rather generally abandoned, even by Germanists.

(2) *The Increasingly Wide Occurrence of Community Property as an actual Legal Institute.* — In the meantime, however, the forms of community property developed by the German law, far from disappearing, had found an increasingly wide acceptance that was of the utmost significance.

(A) OWNERSHIP IN COLLECTIVE HAND maintained itself, as has already been remarked (*supra*, p. 144), in the marital and the continued-marital community, and was also extended outright to the community right of co-heirs; for example in the Prussian "Landrecht", which, like the Bavarian "Landrecht" and the Austrian Code, closely assimilated co-ownership to ownership in collective hand. But above all it was retained in the commercial and admiralty law, in which it had already found application in the Middle Ages. The partnership estate of an unlimited mercantile partnership was owned in collective hand by the partnership (which was not made a juristic person although recognized as a unity) and the partners, who were entitled to share rights therein. It was the same with the limited partner-

[1] *Justus Veracius*, "Libellus consuetudinum principatus Bambergensis" (1681).

ship. Ship-partnership property ("Reedereivermögen") also shows that union of ownership by a group, as such, and the members as individuals, which is characteristic of ownership in collective hand.

(B) Corporate collective ownership, as contrasted with the Roman institute of ownership by a juristic person, was very generally maintained, on the one hand, in the legal relations of agrarian associations; and, on the other hand and especially, in the capitalistic associations ("Kapitalgenossenschaften") of the mining law based upon shares in the company property, and still more in commercial share companies ("Aktiengesellschaften") and the like.

(3) *The Present Law.* — The Germanic theory of associations (*supra*, p. 157), through its investigation of personal groups in the Germanic law, made possible, at the same time, an understanding of the concepts of the law of things that underlay them; and also taught men to recognize, both in the community ownership of partners held in collective hand and in the collective ownership of the Germanic corporate associations ("Körperschaften"), forms of collective right which differ both from the co-ownership of the common law and from the sole ownership of the juristic person recognized in the common law. In this way that theory made it possible, not only consciously to retain thenceforth the extensions of the ownership concept developed in German law, wherever they had persisted (even though not understood) in practice, but also to secure for them still wider application through legislation. Besides the simple co-ownership by undivided shares recognized by the present Civil law (BGB, § 1008) and the ownership of juristic persons that was derived from the Roman law, corporate collective ownership exists today under imperial law in the partnerships of the commercial law, which are endowed with juristic personality, and, particularly, under State law in trade unions. Ownership in collective hand has not only been retained in the new Civil Code in the marital and continued-marital community of goods (§§ 1438, 1492 *et seq.*, 1519, 1549) and in the herital community (§ 2032), but, what is most important, has been made the basis of the partnership of the private law (§ 718 *et seq.*). There exists in such a partnership, in contrast to the bare co-ownership of the Roman partnership, a separate partnership estate held by the partners in collective hand. Moreover, ownership in collective hand continues to be recognized in the case of a ship partnership, and may

continue to appear in special institutes developed in the law of the individual States (EG, §§ 164, 181.2). The Swiss Civil Code, also, recognizes two forms of community property; namely, co-ownership by undivided shares (§§ 646–651) and collective ownership (§§ 652–654). The latter it defines, — something which the German Code has thus far refused to do, — in the sense of the Germanic law, declaring: "whenever several persons who are united in a community by contractor in obedience to the command of law, hold the ownership of a thing by virtue of such community, they are collective owners, and the right of each extends to the whole thing." It further provides that the rights and duties of collective owners are determined by the rule by which their community is regulated; that in cases of doubt a unanimous vote is requisite to the exercise of ownership; and that no right to partition, or to dispose of an undivided share, can be exercised during the continuance of the community.

§ 34. **The Acquisition of Ownership by Contract.**[1] — The appearance of individual ownership in the soil was a necessary precondition to any frequent application in practical life of land conveyances by juristic act. Such conveyances, like all other juristic acts, were associated in Germanic medieval law with definite formalities, and were dominated, as were all other dealings in land, by the principle of publicity. The German law has always clung steadfastly to these requirements.

(I) **The Oldest Law.** — (1) *The Original Single Act performed upon the Land.* — In the oldest Germanic law the contractual alienation ("Veräusserung") and actual transfer ("Übereignung") of land were both effected by a single act that was performed upon the land itself. Like every contract relating to property rights, it was a real contract (*infra,* § 71), a non-credit trans-

[1] *Stobbe,* "Die Auflassung des deutschen Rechts", in J. B. für Dogm., XII (1872), 137–272; *Sohm,* "Zur Geschichte der Auflassung" in Festgabe der Strassburger Fakultät für Thöl (1879), 79 *et seq.*; *Brunner,* "Zur Rechtsgeschichte der römischen und germanischen Urkunde", I (1880); *Beyerle,* "Grundeigentumsverhältnisse und Bürgerrecht im mittelalterlichen Konstanz", I (1890); *Goerlitz,* "Die Übertragung liegenden Gutes in der mittelalterlichen und neuzeitlichen Stadt Breslau", in *Beyerle's* "Beiträge", I. 2 (1906); *Otto Loening,* "Grunderwerb und Treuhand in Lübeck", No. 93 (1907) of *Gierke's* "Untersuchungen"; *Dyckerhoff,* "Die Entstehung des Grundeigentums und die Entwicklung der gerichtlichen Eigentumsübertragung an Grundstücken in der Reichsstadt Dortmund", in *Beyerle's* "Beiträge", III. 1 (1909); *Böckel,* "Die Grundstücksübereignung in Sachsen-Weimar-Eisenach. Zugleich ein Beitrag zur Rechtsgeschichte Thüringens", No. 109 (1911) of *Gierke's* "Untersuchungen"; *Wissmann,* "Förmlichkeiten bei Landübertragungen in England während der anglonormannischen Zeit", in Arch. Urk. F., III (1911), 251–294.

action, in which, when it was bilateral (as for example in sale), the mutual performances, — payment of the purchase price and delivery of the land, — were simultaneously rendered. This act was performed in public, that is to say in the presence of witnesses; who, if they were boys, had their ears boxed and pulled as an aid to memory.[1] Nevertheless, even in this oldest stage of development there are two theoretical elements that must be kept apart, although they were still united in what was outwardly a single act, and only later became sensibly separate. These elements were:

(A) The agreement to alienate: that is to say, the formally perfected contract, following any preliminary negotiations, for the transfer of ownership; in other words a real contract in the sense of the present private law,[2] — a declaration of will intended to effect an immediate transfer of physical control, and at the same time an obligatory contract by which a legal duty was imposed to proceed (and that at once) to the act of delivery. In the sources we find used to designate this transaction the expressions "sala" (Old High G. "sala", Mid. High G. "sale", "salung", from Gothic "seljan"; Old Norse "selja", A. Saxon "sellan" — English "to sell": = "tradere"), and "traditio"; and so too it is customarily called to-day (Sohm, Brunner). These names were also used, however, to designate the entire act; and "traditio", "tradere", were employed to designate its second part alone.

(B) The delivery of the land: the clothing with possession, — the "giwerî", "giwerida", "vestitura", "investitura" of the sources (*supra*, p. 185). Since the transfer of a piece of land could not be realized as a physical fact, as could that of a movable thing, by manual tradition,[3] it was made visible by symbolic juristic acts. These acts served to express two things: the clothing of the acquirer with the seisin of the land, and the abandonment of seisin on the part of the alienor.

The former consisted in the alienor's taking a piece of the land suitable for manual delivery (clod, turf, twig, sod, door post, bell-rope, or altar-cover) from the land, and laying it in the hand or in the lap of the acquirer. In addition to this there was very often also handed over an object, — such as a glove, "Andelang" (= perhaps pot-hook)[4], spear, knife, or hat, — symbolical of

[1] "Lex Ribuaria", 60, 1.
[2] *Brunner's* "Grundzüge" (5th ed.), 197.
[3] *Brunner*, "Urkunde", 273.
[4] *E.g.* according to *Goldmann*, "Der Andelang", No. 111 (1912) of *Gierke's* "Untersuchungen", who derives the word from Romance roots.

physical control; and this latter may originally have been the form that gave efficacy to the contract of conveyance. This investiture was called, inasmuch as it had to be performed upon the land itself, corporeal or real.

The release of seisin was realized by the alienor's actually going off the land ("exitus", "exire") in a legally formal manner. Among the Salian Franks he must spring over the hedge with a stick in his hand, after delivery of the turf. With these formalities there were associated other acts indicative of a change of control: a common walking of the boundaries, putting out the hearth fire and lighting it anew, the sheltering of guests by the acquirer, sitting down upon a three-legged stool, and others. The formal vacation ("evacuatio"), renunciation ("abdicatio", "resignatio"), or abandonment ("Verlassung", later "Auflassung"), was doubtless always accompanied by formal speech. The Saxons, from the earliest times, made this with the finger crooked in accord with a definite rule; and this has in places persisted to the present day, — renunciation with "finger and tongue", "curvatis digitis." Among the Franks there appeared at an early day, in place of a legally formal "exire", the "exitum se dicere", "facere", "se absacitum facere", and others; that is to say, in place of an actual vacation of possession a contract for such vacation.[1] This was concluded as a formal contract, a little staff ("festuca") being thrown into the lap of the feoffee ("festucam in laisum iactare"), or, as later became usual, handed over. Hence the whole contract was designated as "exfestucatio", "werpitio", "laesowerpitio" (medieval "Verschiessen", = "to shoot").[2] This abandonment with "haulm and mouth" spread from the Frankish domain to that of all the other Germanic racial branches with the exceptions of the Saxons and the Frisians.

(2) *Investiture away from the Land.* — The requirement that the conveyance should be perfected upon the spot must have proved burdensome in many ways as transactions involving land increased. But it was long maintained intact where the number of such transactions was relatively small, even in smaller urban communes (as Constance). It was not indispensable, because not only the contractual agreement but also the acts that made visible the change of possession, namely the delivery of pieces of the soil and of symbols of dominion and the renunciatory declaration, could in fact be performed exactly as

[1] *Brunner's* "Grundzüge" (5th ed.), 197.
[2] See *v. Amira*, "Stab" (*supra*, p. 9), 147 *et seq.*

well off the land. Thus, beside the conveyance with corporeal or real investiture, performed upon the land itself, there appeared an incorporeal investiture that took place off the land.

(A) Release in court. — Such incorporeal investiture was earliest applied in the form of a judicial release, at first exclusively in the king's court but later in the popular courts also. The party who was condemned to vacate possession made to the victorious litigant, in accordance with the court's judgment and before the court, an immediate investiture ("revestitio") and renunciation of seisin ("Auflassung", "exfestucatio"). Inasmuch as this judgment did not necessarily presuppose an actual suit at law, but could also be secured through a collusive action, an instrument had here been found which, like the Roman "in iure cessio", could be made to serve as a voluntary conveyance of ownership;[1] an instrument that was valuable, because he who acquired the land also received, in the judicial record of the release thus made, documentary evidence of peculiar strength.

(B) "Investitura per cartam." — Still more important was the combination of Germanic investiture with the "traditio per cartam" developed in the vulgar Roman law, which required nothing more than the delivery of the conveyance deed ("carta"): this perfected at once the contract of alienation and the transfer of ownership. This form of conveyance found wide acceptance in the Frankish empire, owing especially to the influence of the church. But not only was it associated with a subsequent corporeal investiture: it was also, — and this by far most commonly, — transformed in peculiar manner into an incorporeal investiture. Small portions of the land and symbols of control were handed over at the same time as the deed. For this purpose the "carta", still unexecuted, was laid upon the ground beside the piece of turf, and then (often after pen and inkwell were laid upon it) was raised with the turf from the ground; whence the phrase, common among the Franks, Alamanians, Bavarians, and Burgundians, "cartam levare", of which we hear the echo in our expression "eine Urkunde aufnehmen" — to "raise" a document ["levy" a fine]. At the same time a renunciatory phrase was spoken; among the Saxons with fingers bent as the rule prescribed, and among the Franks and

[1] *Brunner*, "Urkunde", 275. See also *Peterka*, "Das offene zum Scheine Handeln im deutschen Rechte des Mittelalters", in *Beyerle's* "Beiträge", VII. 1 (1911), 21–32.

other racial branches that followed them in this respect, with manual tradition of the "festuca", which not infrequently was fastened to the deed.[1] In this manner the conveyance forms of the old popular law and the Roman deed were united organically in one institute.[2] Like the Roman "traditio cartae", the "investitura per cartam" could be performed at any place, for example in the church; the Ripuarian folk-law originally stood alone in requiring judicial character.[3]

This "investitura per cartam", like the original Germanic conveyance, was a single act, combining at the same time and place the contract ("sala") and the delivery ("investitura"). It was only after a capitulary of 818–819 permitted a "traditio cartae", for the good of the conveyer's soul, outside the county where the thing was located, allowing the promised investiture to take place later on the spot, that the "sala" and the investiture become distinct. Only in this exceptional case did the "traditio cartae" continue to have real effect, by itself, as a "sala" concluded according to legal forms, despite the temporary lack of investiture. In other cases it remained true that only "sala" *and* investiture together conveyed right and possession; incorporeal investiture was sufficient only when united with the judgment of the court or with a "traditio cartae", for it secured to the acquirer, precisely as did a real investiture, not only the real right but also, as against the alienor, seisin in the land (in the sense of the medieval law, the incorporeal seisin). The real vacation of possession that followed upon the incorporeal investiture was of no effect upon the legal relations of the parties. It simply established the accomplished fact, as against third parties, of the alienee's seisin; in particular, it alone prevented the acquisition of seisin by a third party through one year's possession (*supra*, p. 201). Although a real effect was generally denied to a delivery of a deed without a simultaneous delivery of the symbol of investiture, such delivery being only rarely recognized (at least in Germany) as itself investiture, yet from the beginning of the 800 s the mere delivery of the symbol of investiture without a "carta" *was* regarded as a valid form of investiture, even away from the land. It is possible that this was a consequence of the decay of culture that set in after the later Carolingians.[4]

[1] *Tangl*, "Urkunde und Symbol", in Festschrift für H. Brunner (1911), 761–773.

[2] *Brunner*, *op. cit.*

[3] "Lex Rib.", 59, 1.

[4] *Schröder*, "Lehrbuch" (5th. ed.) 292.

(II) **The Medieval Law.**—(1) *Relaxation of the Old Forms.*— In the post-Frankish period of the Middle Ages the conveyance retained essentially its old form, save that the old formalities were relaxed, that the symbolism ceased to be a living form, and that a deed as a symbol of tradition fell very soon into complete disuse. Yet even after that period, and until well into the period of the Law-Books and often until a time far later, and in South as well as in North Germany, the two (or, if one counts separately the two elements that entered into investiture, the three) acts of the primitive law can be still distinguished: first, the real juristic act, the old "Sala", the gift, renunciation, "donatio", etc.—still frequently associated with the delivery of a symbol of dominion (now the glove), but also frequently consummated by mere formal declaration (known in Breslau as "resignare", "ufgeben", "ufreichen"); second, the investiture, seisin, execution—likewise still given sensible form by the employment of the old symbols (turf and twig), but also perfected in this period by mere handclasp; third, the act of renunciation—the release of the Saxon law, known in the South German town laws and also in Breslau, a town of Magdeburg law, as "entziehen", "verziehen", "sich verziehen" ("to remove")—still expressed in the regions of French law in the form of the "exfestucatio", "werpitio", but elsewhere usually effected like the gift merely by formal words. In time, however, many further changes came about.

(2) *Increasingly Judicial Character.*—From about the 1000 s onward it became in Germany a custom, and in many places a requisite, to make conveyances of land with the coöperation of the court, and therefore ordinarily at the place where the court met, in other words in the major folk-court ("echtes Ding"). Different causes contributed to this result. As has been already mentioned, there were cases even in the Frankish period in which seisin was surrendered on the basis of a judgment given in court, following either an actual or a fictitious suit, and which furnished the alienee with evidential security in the testimony of the court and the judicial record. It now became possible to attain the same advantages without any litigation whatever (whereas in England, for example, collusive suits as a means of conveyance lived on until 1833):[1] for in the medieval law a judgment might issue, upon requisition of the acquirer, without any precedent suit, confirming his right and the legality of the conveyance. What was still more important, there was united with the judgment

[1] *Brunner*, "Urkunde", 288.

a summons (connected with the Frankish "missio in bannum") by which the right of the acquirer was assured against any possible adverse claims of third parties. Upon summons thrice repeated by the judge to enforce such claims, persons within the jurisdiction must bring them at once; if this was not done then the judge laid a peace upon the land, thereby not only cutting off any later impeachment by such parties, but at the same time imposing upon persons outside the jurisdiction the obligation of making objections within a year and day; if this was not done their claims were barred by prescription ("Verschweigung", "tacit preclusion"). After the passing of such period the seisin of the acquirer gained by surrender in court was transformed into a citation ("rechte") seisin (*supra*, p. 201).[1] Finally, because the requisite of publicity was best satisfied by a conveyance in court, the rapid and widespread use of judicial surrender is sufficiently explained by these advantages associated with it. Also important, however, were certain circumstances associated with the constitution of the courts (namely, the control exercised by the court's lord over transactions involving lands, which were the basis of the obligation of court duty, and the control exercised by the counts and town authorities over the possession of lands subject to the obligations of paying taxes and court duty),[2] as well as the example of the feudal and manorial conveyances that were associated with the feudal and manorial courts. In the time of the Law-Books the effectuation of conveyances in court was not only the rule, but in many places was absolutely necessary, especially within the regions of the Saxon Territorial law, in the towns of the Magdeburg group of town laws, and later throughout the whole domain of the Saxon common law, as well as in Switzerland.[3] The place of the court was often taken by the town council.

(3) *Registration.* — In many regions, especially in South Germany, surrender in court again lost ground from the 1300 s onward. To this retrogression there contributed the decay of the rural courts, the increasing importance of official certification by seal, — which could be performed by every notary, and indeed in many places (*e.g.* Zürich) by any burgher, — and the beginnings of the influence of the alien law. On the other hand it received in other regions a further development that was of the greatest

[1] *Fehr*, "Fürst und Graf im Sachsenspiegel", K. Sächs. Gesell. Wiss., LVIII (1906), 1–99, 50 *et seq.*

[2] *Cf. Fehr* in Z[2] R. G., XXX (1909), 278 *et seq.*

[3] Ssp., I. 52, § 1. Swsp. (W), 349. "Rechtsbuch nach Distinktionen," I. 45, § 1.

importance for the future. The custom, especially common in North German cities, of entering in public and official books all transfers of land that were consummated and confirmed before the town court or the town council (*supra*, p. 219), had the natural result that the entry in the public book took the place of the documents formerly made out for the parties concerning the transaction in court, as the official evidence that at once attested and gave security to the transfer of ownership. Indeed, it has been shown that already in the Middle Ages the book entry became in some cities the essential and consummative part of the act of transfer.[1] Wherever this was the case, as *e.g.* in Lübeck and Bremen, and alike in the cities and even earlier in the rural districts of the lands of the Bohemian crown, the mere ceremony of surrendering seisin gradually lost its independent importance, and finally wholly disappeared: the transfer of ownership was perfected by the registry that followed the contractual agreement; and even judicial seisin was associated with the book entry. The act of registry, from being mere evidence, had thus become the consummative act; and the principle of the modern law of land registry had thus already been completely realized. At the same time the old summons of adverse claimants, and the imposition of the court's peace, remained in practice. This was so, for example, in Breslau, where the summons persisted until the end of the 1700 s, being given at first through public warning by the officials who executed the judgments of the county courts ("Froneboten"), later through public posting as well, and after 1787 by edicts, advertisements in the newspapers, and the summons of all interested parties by commission; while the laying of the court's peace was effected by the delivery of a judicial possessory patent ("Besitzbrief") which produced at the same time the consequences of judicial seisin.

(III) **The Development since the Reception.** — The course of development, thus far logically progressing, was injuriously interrupted by the reception of the Roman law, which rested upon bases wholly different. According to the Roman law the conveyance of lands as well as of movables was effected by informal delivery of possession; in the case of the "constitutum possessorium" and the "brevi manu traditio", the tradition did not require even a corporeal delivery. The coöperation of a court and the official registration of transactions in lands was to it unknown, for it attached no importance to the publicity of such transac-

[1] *Gierke*, "Privatrecht", II, 281.

tions. And the rules of the Roman law became, — aside from the feudal law, which maintained the institute of investiture, — the common law of Germany. This common law, however, proved incapable of achieving complete supremacy, and even of holding its ground in more than a few districts of Germany. The particularistic legal systems preserved more or less perfectly, or returned to, the native principles; although not indeed without manifold changes, and combination with the alien rules. "There thus originated a confused wealth of variant systems."[1] They may be classified in the following groups.

(1) *Delivery associated with Formal Contract.* — Even of those legal systems that adopted the Roman principle only very few (*e.g.* the revised Mecklenburg Hypothec Ordinance for Rural Estates, of October 18, 1848), made the change of attributing the transfer of ownership exclusively to the informal act of tradition. Most of them required, in addition to the tradition, a contract of alienation concluded in a definite form. Indeed, the contract was required to be of judicial character: the parties must bring it to the knowledge ("insinuieren") of the judge, and cause it to be confirmed ("konfirmieren"), that is registered in the records of the court. In this connection there was imposed upon the judge the duty of making a far-reaching and substantial test of the transaction. In most, although not in all, legal systems, the observance of the prescribed form was a necessary precondition to the validity of the contract, and so to the efficacy of the tradition. This was true of Electoral Hesse, Brunswick, the code of Solm, a few Saxon statutes, and others; also of the French and some of the German cantons of Switzerland from the 1500 s onward.

(2) *Delivery associated with Registry.* — Doubtless the most extensive group was constituted of those systems which, though they recognized the transfer of ownership by tradition after a precedent and formal contract, nevertheless required registration in public books for the full transfer of all rights involved in ownership. In particular, they granted solely to the registered owner the right to create pledge or other charges requiring registration; he alone acquired a perfect ownership. There existed here, therefore, the possibility of a double ownership; of a true or substantial ownership which passed by mere tradition, in accord with a contract of alienation formally correct, and a formal or "book" property which was acquired only by registration in the land or mortgage-book, and which, when no tradition had taken

[1] *Gierke*, "Privatrecht", II, 282.

place, was in truth *no* ownership, but a mere dispositive power under the rules of the registry system. The Prussian law, as based upon the "Allgemeines Landrecht",[1] was an illustration of this system until the year 1872. It required the precedent contract to be written, and in order to prevent so far as possible a conflict between the substantive and the formal right, the owner was compelled, from 1783 to 1831, under statutory penalties, to register his title in the land-book (so-called "Zwangstitelberechtigung", "title by right of compulsory registration"). To the same system belonged, until 1900, the law of Bavaria to the East of the Rhine, which required the contract of alienation to be concluded before a notary, and the law of Württemberg, which required a written contract.

(3) *Release in Court* ("gerichtliche Auflassung"). — The form of conveyance developed by the native law, — namely, a release or surrender of seisin in court, with or without subsequent registration, such registration being either a mere record or an essential to and the consummative element in the act of transfer, — maintained itself in the Saxon common law, in many systems of town law, and in some of the Territorial systems. The Saxon common law, however, attributed certain effects to the tradition, also; so that, here again, there resulted a possibility of two kinds of ownership. The acquirer received possession by title of natural right ("titulirter Besitz"), or "dominium naturale", upon the strength of the mere tradition, whereas release of seisin, even without registration, created what was called "dominium civile." This resulted from release by the alienor to the judge and enfeoffment of the acquirer by the judge (so-called "allodial" investiture). Bremen also was contented with a declaration of conveyance judicially attested. On the other hand, the law of Lübeck,[2] Hamburg, Berlin, and Munich, as well as the Hanoverian and Mecklenburg legal systems, and some Territorial systems, required surrender in court with subsequent registration. In the Austrian land-"tablet" system the act of registry remained the act that created rights, and this principle was elevated to the rank of a general rule in the Austrian Code.[3] Also in Switzer-

[1] Allg. L. R., I, 10, § 1: "The derivative acquisition of property in a thing requires, in addition to the necessary title thereto, the actual delivery of the same." § 6: "Nevertheless, whoever desires to dispose of land by transactions in court must cause to be . . . registered in the mortgage-record the property-right therein which he so acquires."

[2] *Rev. Lüb. R.*, III, 6, 1, 2.

[3] *Öster. G. B.*, § 431: "It is necessary for the conveyance of ownership in immovable things that the transaction of conveyance be entered in the

land the old judicial "Fertigung" was preserved in many places, particularly in the rural districts of the cities and in the common domains of the German cantons; but it was transformed into a "means of official protection for inexperienced subjects", and often treated as a binding form of contract.[1]

(4) *Transcript System, or the System of the French Law.* — In France, where only a few bodies of customary law in the North (the so-called "coutumes de nantissement") held to a form of conveyance in court that corresponded to the German "Auflassung", there had developed as a common law of the "coutumes" (as distinguished from the German and Roman systems) the principle that ownership was transferable by mere contract without tradition. This doctrine was borrowed from the Italian doctrine of "traditio ficta"; which also acquired authority in Germany in the "usus modernus Pandectarum" (*supra*, p. 215). It was accepted by the Code Civil.[2] A so-called transcript, that is, a written copy of the contract entered in a judicial register, — which in the systems of Northern French law just referred to was obligatory, — was required by the Code only in certain cases, as for example in those of gifts. But it was later raised to the position of a general and essential requisite by a statute of 1855, in that the validity of the title acquired, as against third parties, was made dependent, thenceforth, upon it. In this form the French law retained authority in Alsace-Lorraine until 1900; in the other regions of French law in Germany the rule of the Code Civil had, for the most part, been similarly altered from the beginning (so in Baden and Hesse).

(IV) **The Latest Stage of Development.** — In the 1800s, in consequence of the renewed vitality shown by the land registry system, the principles of Germanic law gained that ascendancy in respect to conveyances of land which they already enjoyed in other matters. Wherever they had continuously maintained their authority, or had already been reintroduced, they were now, in many States, extended and affirmed by modern statutes. This was true, above all, of the modern Mecklenburg statutes already referred to (*supra*, p. 228, — the Town-book Ordinance of 1829,

public books appointed for that purpose. Such entry is known as 'incorporation' ('Einverleibung') or 'intabulation' ('Intabulation')."

[1] *Huber*, "Schw. Privatrecht", IV, 710.

[2] Code Civil, Art. 1583: "The sale is complete between the parties, and the title has passed, in law, to the vendee as respects the vendor, from the instant that they have agreed upon the thing and the price, even though the thing may not yet have been delivered nor the price paid."

the Wismar Town-Book ordinance of 1838, the revised Town-book ordinance of 1857, the Hypothec Ordinance for crown lands of 1854); further, in the Hanse towns, in most of the minor Saxon States, in the kingdom of Saxony (statute of 1843 and Civil Code), and in Austria (statute of 1871). In the same way, in many legal systems of German Switzerland "entry in the land-book acquired all the importance of the tradition of a piece of land, so that the ownership of such could be conveyed by it and by it alone."[1] Within the regions of the "tradition" and "transcript" systems the elements of Germanic law were also strengthened by modern legislation,—as in Bavaria, Württemberg, Brunswick, and Hanover; in some of them, indeed, it went over completely to the Germanic system, as for example in Hesse-Darmstadt. But of greatest importance was the Prussian legislation, which established new regulations in place of those of the old Territorial law in the statutes of 1872 (*supra*, p. 222), which were drawn up after long preparations. In normal cases of voluntary conveyance they required release and registration.[2] The release, which therefore replaced the tradition of the Territorial systems, results from the oral declarations simultaneously made before the appropriate registry office: by the registered owner that he assents to the registration of the new acquirer, and by the latter that he desires such registration. This new release of the Prussian law was therefore an "abstract" legal transaction, for it based the acquisition of title upon the naked declaration of a will to convey, regardless of all reference to the transaction that underlay this.[3] With this change the Prussian law returned to the old Germanic principles; and this, not alone in that a real contract concluded in a definite manner again became, in the form of a release, an essential part of the act of conveyance, but also in the further fact that the real ("dinglich") juristic act was thenceforth separated from the precedent transaction that created the legal duty to perform under the law of obligations. And as the medieval law required investiture in addition to the "Sala", so the Prussian system required registration in addition to release. For while many other legislative systems (*e.g.* those of Lübeck, Hamburg, the Kingdom of Saxony, certain Mecklenburg statutes)

[1] *Huber, op. cit.*, 711.

[2] Prussian Act regulating acquisition of title ("Eigentumserwerbsgesetz") of May 5, 1872, § 1: "In case of a voluntary alienation, property in land is acquired solely through the recording of the title-transfer in the land-book, following a release."

[3] *Dernburg*, "Lehrbuch des preussischen Privatrechts", I, § 240.

attributed outright to the registration the power to create and to destroy rights, the Prussian statutes permitted transfers of title by release only when united with registration in the land-book; herein agreeing with the old law, which recognized such a creative force in the registry only in exceptional cases, and following the Austrian law and the majority of modern systems. The statutes of 1872, which were originally issued only for the regions of the Territorial law, were gradually introduced throughout the entire Kingdom; last of all in the Rhine Province in 1888 and 1896, in Frankfort o. M., in the former landgraviate of Hesse and in the districts formerly belonging to the grand-duchy of Hesse in 1895, and in Lauenburg in 1896. In Helgoland and Nassau alone they acquired no validity. They served, further, as a model in a number of other German States: Oldenburg, Koburg-Gotha, Anhalt, Brunswick, Waldeck, Lippe, Schwarzburg-Sondershausen, Schaumburg-Lippe.

But what is most important, the principles of the Prussian law have passed over in all essential points into the new Civil Code and the German Land-book Ordinance. Here again, therefore, the restoration of legal unity signified at the same time a victory for native legal ideas. In Switzerland, too, these have been universally established: the Swiss Civil Code requires registration in the land-book under all circumstances (§ 656) for the acquisition of ownership in land, and official record of every contract designed to convey ownership (§ 657).

§ 35. **Acquisition of Ownership otherwise than by Contract. (I) Occupancy.** — The oldest mode of acquiring ownership in land was by occupancy ("Aneignung", "Okkupation") of ownerless or conquered land; so-called "Landnahme." Undertaken by the entire folk or by the larger divisions in which this was organized, such occupancy resulted in a collective ownership by the folk ("folk-land"); out of which there developed, in time, as has been already shown (*supra*, p. 115 *et seq.*), a collective ownership of the sib and of the mark-association, and finally individual ownership. Wherever a monarchy arose, the land so occupied fell to the king as the representative of the folk ("Königsland", royal demesne), and the rule of law took form that the king possessed the right of occupancy over all land that had no lord. The unlimited right that had originally inhered in the mark associates of laying hold of wild land, particularly the primeval forest, by clearing it, suffered a material restriction. Only as regards the commonties were they still permitted to exercise it; either freely, or else within such limits as were set by the association. Beyond these, clearings required thenceforth the approval of the king. From the royal right of *occupancy* of ownerless lands, which was thus recognized, in Germany as early as in the Carolingian period, and which the king exercised by means of ban, there developed a regality in the soil of the country ("Bodenregal"). This passed during the Middle Ages, along with other regalities (*infra*, § 38), to the Territorial princes; and its influence continued to be felt after the development of the modern State in the rule, thenceforth frequently recognized, as for example by the Code Civil (*supra*, p. 161), that the ownership of all otherwise ownerless land is in the State. Most of the regional legal systems retained this regality. On the other hand a few, including the Prussian "Landrecht" and the Saxon Code, again relaxed the principle, returning to the old view that the State enjoys merely an exclusive right of occupancy in ownerless lands. The present Civil Code has also adopted this rule (§ 928), thereby definitely rejecting the Roman principle of free occupancy of ownerless land which had been received as common law in Germany. In comparison with this right of occupancy inhering, in principle, in the fisc, little attention is merited by those few cases, preserved intact by the Introductory Statute to the Civil Code, in which it can still be exercised by private persons, — as for example by the commune according to the town law of Munich, and by the possessors of manorial estates according to the Silesian law regulating the right of pasturage. Moreover, in accordance with the principle of land registry, the acquisition of ownership itself results, at present, only when the person entitled to occupancy causes himself to be registered in the land-book. The viewpoint of the Swiss Civil Code is somewhat different, inasmuch as it treats ownership, in cases of occupancy, as originating before registry, but gives the acquirer the right of disposing of the land only after registry (§ 656, 2); moreover, it leaves to cantonal law the regulation of the occupancy of ownerless land, which it classes as an exercise of sovereignty (§ 664).

(II) **Positive Prescription.** — Positive (acquisitive) prescription was unknown to the older German land-law as a mode of acquiring ownership. For judicial seisin, which performed in many respects the functions of that principle, itself rested upon a presupposed acquisition of ownership already perfected. With the Reception there was of course adopted the Roman-Canon doctrine of usucapion, of which, moreover, earlier traces can be recognized in the folk-laws. This not only became the common law, but penetrated as well into many of the regional systems. According to that doctrine, land could be acquired by "ordinary" usucapion upon the basis of possession in good faith and with color of title ("title of natural right") in ten, or as the case might be twenty, years; and by "extraordinary" usucapion upon the basis of possession in good faith during thirty years. The persistence of native legal customs, however, was shown by the fact that the Roman periods of prescription were not everywhere retained, but were frequently replaced by the Germanic period of a year and a day, or united with the same (the Saxon common law for example required 31 years 6 weeks and 3 days); and moreover the entire institute contradicted the system of land registry. Hence it is that many modern statutes or legal systems have absolutely done away with positive prescription as regards all lands that are registered in the land-book, — as for example the Saxon Code, the law of Hamburg and Lübeck, of Brunswick and of Mecklenburg; while others, as the Prussian Act of 1872, exclude it as against a registered owner. Only a few—*e.g.* certain statutes of Mecklenburg and the Austrian Code—have recognized such a prescriptional title as capable of registration. The present German Civil Code has repudiated any and all prescription contradictory of the contents of the land-book. On the other hand, following the example of the Austrian Code and a Hessian statute of 1852, it has adopted (§ 900) what is called "tabular" or "book" usucapion: whoever has been wrongly registered in the land-book for thirty years as the owner of a piece of land, — that is, without having meanwhile acquired ownership, — and has been at the same time the exclusive possessor of such land, acquires the ownership thereof, regardless of good faith or of any further title. Further, in place of positive prescription it has introduced (§ 927) a mode of acquiring ownership that was unknown to the earlier law, namely that of citation ("Aufgebot"). Whoever has had a piece of land in his exclusive possession for thirty years, may demand the institution of a citation-procedure against the owner, and if the owner is excluded from rightful claim thereto as the result of this citation procedure, the possessor can then require the registration of himself as owner. Similar provisions are to be found in the Swiss Civil Code, save that it has reduced the period for acquisitive prescription by one wrongly registered (so-called "ordinary" usucapion) to ten years (§ 661).

(III) Still other cases in which title is acquired otherwise than by contract are acquisition by **inheritance**, and acquisition by a declaration of the State's will. According to Germanic law, from the earliest times, the former was perfected by the sole fact of death, and has therefore generally been regarded as needing no registration even under the law of land registry (*cf.* the chapter on inheritance, *infra*). Under the latter belonged the **judicial adjudication** of the older law, which was sometimes the truly consummative element in the institute of release ("Auflassung"), as for example in what was known as allodial investiture (*supra*, p. 250); and in the modern law, among other institutes, the adjudication of property to the highest bidder in forced sales in **execution proceedings** (regulated today for the whole Empire by the imperial act concerning forced sales and sequestration in execution proceedings, of March 24, 1897). Another class of cases belonging here is that in which ownership is acquired by expropriation.

(IV) **Expropriation.**[1] — This we may more particularly consider.

(1) *History.* — In expropriation we have to do with an interference by the State with landed property (rarely with any other right in things) which is taken by the State, subject to compensation, for the purpose of applying such things to an end required by the public welfare.[2] Expropriation is a legal institute that was unknown both in antiquity and, although indeed for other reasons, in the early Middle Ages, and which owed its appearance to the rise of the modern State. So long as associations on the one hand, and Territorial rulers on the other hand, enjoyed powers of a "real" nature that restricted the private ownership of individuals in the interest of the whole community or of the sovereign power, there were lacking the preconditions necessary to expropriation. This made its first appearance in the cities. Indeed, the community as an independent holder of rights was there first developed, its legal relations to its members being purely those of public law.

The earliest cases in which a true expropriation was exercised come therefore from the legal life of the cities. Expropriation of landed property by municipal authority, against compensation, for the purpose of erecting walls, towers, and fosses, occurred in Italian cities as early as the 1100 s and from the 1300 s onward in Germany; at first only in individual cases (*e.g.* an expropriation

[1] *Grünhut*, art. "Enteignung" in H. W. B. der Staatsw., III (3d ed., 1909), 955 *et seq.*; *Layer*, "Prinzipien des Enteignungsrechts" (1902); *Schelcher*, art. "Enteignung" in *v. Stengel-Fleischmann*, "Wörterbuch des deutschen Staats- und Verwaltungsrechts", I (2d ed., 1911), 717–730.

[2] *Gierke*, "Privatrecht", II, 464.

for the laying out of a public canal through the Tullner Feld near Vienna) and later in accord with general regulations. Thus, different town-laws gave to the council authority to cause a house to be razed in order to prevent the further spread of fire (Lüneburg, Breslau, Munich), or to remove any house whatever within the limits of the municipal jurisdiction in case of the urgent need of the community (as in an ordinance of Schaffhausen of 1380). This idea found special application, later, in mining law and in the dike-law: the mining ordinances from the 1400 s onward imposed upon land-owners the duty of conveying to anybody desirous of opening a mine upon their land the land necessary for that purpose, in exchange for proper compensation. From the time of the Glossators jurists were solicitous to establish a principle that would cover such interference by the State in private ownership; a principle difficult to reconcile with the Roman law. In this the Law of Nature first succeeded, owing to its deeper insight into the nature of the State. It traced such interference back to that general power of sovereignty recognized by men in the interest of the common weal which was set up by Hugo Grotius, the founder of the doctrine, and which was called "ius eminens", and later "imperium"; and to this power of the State it fixed sharp limits, under the determinant influence of Montesquieu, by recognizing in theory the inviolability of ownership, by requiring under all circumstances a "iusta causa", and by giving to the dispossessed owner a claim for full damages. These principles were first put in practice in France. The right of expropriation within these limits was recognized in the Declaration of the Rights of Man, and in the constitutions of 1791 to 1852. Of epoch-making importance was a statute of March 8, 1810, which first laid down the rule that expropriation might be decreed by judicial authority only, "and which constitutes the true basis of all modern legislation upon this subject, at once as regards its spirit and its principles."[1] In Germany the doctrines of the Law of Nature had earlier found adoption in the great codes, namely in the "Landrecht" of Bavaria and of Prussia, and in the Austrian Code; they were later laid down in most constitutions.[2] The further elaboration of the law of expropriation

[1] *Grünhut*, article just cited, 627.

[2] For example the Prussian constitution, Art. 9: "Property is inviolable. It can be taken away or limited solely for reasons of public welfare and in exchange for prior compensation, — which even in pressing cases must be at least provisionally settled, — in accordance with statutory provisions."

which acquired extraordinary importance, especially as regards the development of railroads, was effected by special statutes, for which French legislation afforded the model. While these statutes at first attributed expropriating power to the State for definite and occasional purposes only, later statutes regulated the entire institute comprehensively, and with attention to theory. This was first true of a Hessian statute of 1821; it was followed by Baden in 1835, by Bavaria in 1837, and by others. In Prussia there was passed a general act upon the subject, of June 11, 1874. Many other German States have passed acts modeled upon this, and many others have, like Hesse, replaced their older by more modern statutes. Inasmuch as the right of expropriation crosses the limits between private and public law, it has been preserved by the Introductory Statute of the present Civil Code (EG, § 109) to State regulation.

(2) *General Features of the existing Law of Expropriation.* — Although the legal nature of expropriation is much disputed, Gierke[1] has conclusively shown that if rightly considered it is not a juristic act, and so not at all in the nature of a forced sale, but a proceeding of public law, a unilateral declaration of the will of the State involving effects in private law. By this proceeding there is perfected a transfer of a private right, ordinarily that of ownership, from a person dispossessed thereof to one who acquires it without any prior acquisition of the thing by the State; and there is established an obligatory relation, in the sense of private law, between such person dispossessed and such acquirer, but not between the latter and the State. Expropriation is permissible only when it is required by an undertaking in whose realization there is involved a public interest. The decision of the question whether that is the case, whether there exists a case proper for expropriation, is made either directly by special statute, or, as is usual in modern law, by an administrative act of government declaring the preconditions generally established in the statute to be satisfied in the particular instance in question. Only the State can expropriate, is expropriator. But it is true that he in whose favor expropriation is made, to whom the so-called right of expropriation is given, is commonly also called the expropriator; this may be equally well either the State itself or any other person (the "entrepreneur"). The "entrepreneur" receives a subjective right which, although founded upon a public act, is directed to the acquisition of a private right, and which we may, with

[1] "Privatrecht", II, 464 *et seq.*

Gierke, class among personal rights. In a very great majority of cases the object of expropriation is the ownership of land, which may be taken by expropriation either in whole or only in part; but every other limited real right, even the right of an ordinary or of a usufructuary lessee, can be expropriated. Expropriation takes place only with compensation to him who is deprived of property, for which compensation the " entrepreneur " is responsible. The compensation must be full. In its calculation the value of the thing to be conveyed is taken as the basis; namely, the value which it has objectively (market value) and to the individual owner, — not a possible ideal value or affection value; and in such calculation account is taken of the damage which the owner suffers in consequence of the conveyance, including prospective profits thereby sacrificed. A specially regulated administrative procedure has been introduced for the enforcement of expropriation. According to the Prussian statute, and to most others, its first step is the identification of the object to be expropriated; and this upon the basis of a map (" Feststellungsplan "), which in case reclamations are made by interested parties is tested by the evidence of witnesses. In most cases it is thereafter definitively defined by administrative decree. In the absence of an agreement of the parties, the damages are next fixed; again, as a rule, by decree of the administrative officials; but from this decree an appeal is allowed in all cases to the courts. Finally, the procedure is ordinarily ended by a formal judgment of expropriation rendered by the board. This completes the transfer of the real rights involved, without any entry for that purpose in the land register. But, since an error is thus introduced into the register, there must be a correction, which is usually effected at the instance of the board.

§ 36. **General Restrictions upon Ownership. (I) Source and Classes of General Limitations upon Ownership.** — Notwithstanding that ownership assures the fullest control of a thing recognized by private law, no legal system can permit an unqualified exercise of such control in the case of land; for a piece of land does not constitute a world in itself. The medieval law, in adopting as a part of its concept of ownership the essential quality of limitability, gave particularly sharp expression to this idea from the earliest times—an expression sharper than that given it in the later Roman law, although, as has been mentioned, it was by no means unknown to the Roman theory. To this was added the fact that the after-effects of original collective ownership persisted for a very long time in the Middle Ages, and, after private ownership in land had been developed, resulted in restrictions upon landed ownership in favor of the family, of neighbors, of associations, of lordship, and of the State (*supra*, p. 227). Thus in the older law a manifold restriction of ownership in land was the rule; and a complete transformation of the economic and social bases of the legal order was necessary before the principle of freedom derived from Roman law could be given as full practical effect in relation to ownership of land as in the case of other property. By no means all limitations were, indeed, in this way done away with, or their creation made impossible for the future; but they were henceforth (what they were not before) exceptions to the general rule.

We are here concerned solely with limitations that exist for all times, by force of a rule of law, a statute, or of customary right, and not with such as are agreed upon between the parties by contract. They protect either the interest of the public or that of definite individuals as against the owner; they may therefore be designated, in those cases in which,—to use modern terms,—they find expression in rules of public law, as *limitations of public law;* and in those where they give rise to real rights of individuals in the land of others, as restrictions of private law. It must, however, be noted, that in protecting individual interests the public welfare may be furthered at the same time; and that, in particular, these two points of view became distinct only very late in the course of their historical development. Above all, the so-called regalities were a mixture of elements of public and private law; for they clothed sovereign rights, which restricted landed ownership in definite respects, in the cover of private privileges.

(II) **Restrictions in the Public Interest.** — (1) In the older law numerous limitations were imposed, in the common interest, *upon the dispositive powers of owners.* Alienations, charges beyond a definite amount, and above all partitions, were frequently prohibited, many estates being required to be treated as impartible ("geschlossene"), as contrasted with lands subject to unrestricted charging and alienation ("'walzende' Grundstücke", "Wandeläcker"). Impartibility was of course inconsistent with the Germanic law of inheritance (*infra*, §§ 43, 44, 105). Nevertheless, even in early times the lords of manors succeeded in establishing prohibitions of partitions; moreover, no feudal tenant whatever might alter the "body" of the land he held. Later, impartibility, especially of rural lands, was either preserved or newly introduced by State legislation in the general interest of the country. But free partibility of all estates was recognized by the State in the course of the 1800 s.[1] At the same time, in order to put a check upon the minute division of landed holdings, at least formal impediments to partition have been quite commonly introduced by legislation in very recent years. For example, in the case of lands subject to a rent-charge ("Rentengüter") such provisions of State law have been left in force in Prussia by the new Civil Code (EG, § 119, Z2).

(2) Other restrictions imposed in the public interest compel an owner, *in the exercise of his rights of ownership*, either to refrain from certain acts, or to suffer certain interferences with his rights, or to perform certain positive acts.

Thus rural landowners were bound from the earliest time by the compulsory regulation of the mark arable ("Flurzwang"); and the place of this was later taken, quite commonly, by State legislation that controlled the agricultural activity of individuals.[2] In modern times agriculture has been freed from such restrictions; yet even to-day the police power exercised over agriculture may interfere, in the public interest and in definite respects, with private management, — *e.g.* under the imperial Act of July 6, 1904, relative to the phylloxera.

A police power over buildings already existed in medieval cities; at the present day restrictions of municipal building-codes play an important rôle. To these must be added limitations upon landed ownership necessitated by military interests, examples of which likewise exist in medieval systems of town-law. Those subject to imperial legislation are regulated to-day in the Act concerning fortification-zones of December 29, 1871, and in the Acts of 1868, 1875, 1878, 1887, and 1898 relative to military burdens. Here belong, further, those limitations that result from the police of industry, those resting upon the imperial control of telegraphic communication, and especially all those restrictions that are to be regarded as outgrowths from earlier regalities

[1] See *e.g.* the Prussian Edikt of Oct. 9, 1807, § 4: "The possessors of urban and rural lands and estates ('Güter') of all kinds, which are in nature alienable, ... are entitled, subject to the rights of creditors thereby secured and of persons holding preëmption-rights, to partition liens ('Radikalien') and appurtenances, and, generally, to make partial alienations, and co-owners shall therefore be entitled to a partition among themselves."

[2] Compare, for example, the Prussian Allg. L. R., II, 7, § 8: "Every occupant of land ('Landmann') is bound to conduct economically the cultivation of his land, if necessary for the satisfaction of common necessity ('Nothdurft')."

(*infra*, § 38 *et seq.*). Finally, whenever circumstances of necessity demand, the modern State claims the right to exercise extensive police powers that interfere seriously with landed ownership.

(III) **Restrictions imposed in the Interest of Private Individuals.** —(1) *Upon Dispositive Powers.* — The land ownership of the old law derived its special character, in which it so sharply differs from the law of to-day, from the fact that only exceedingly few landowners could dispose with complete freedom of their land. Rights of individuals or of groups, which they were bound to respect, stood in the way. In the case of alienations, partitions, charges, and testamentary dispositions, members of the family, conventional co-heirs, and members of herital-fraternities, members of the mark, and feudal and other land-lords, had rights of co-operation or of assent, rights in expectancy, rights of co-alienation ("Beispruchsrecht"), rights of preëmption ("Näherrechte") and of option ("Vorkaufsrechte"), rights of escheat, and the like, which limited the dispositive powers of the owner. And though these rights ultimately became less important, they nevertheless persisted for a long time, and even to the present day in the case of estates subject to blood restrictions ("gebundene Güter"); developing even in modern times some peculiar institutes, such as family "fideicommissa." These have also been assured continued existence by the Introductory Act of the new Civil Code.

(2) *Upon the exercise of the rights of ownership.* — As regards these, aside from such general and self-evident rules, explicitly laid down in the German (§ 226) as in the Swiss Civil Codes, as that no right may be exercised for purposes of chicane, special attention must be given to restrictions imposed by rights of vicinage (*infra*, § 37).

Statutory restrictions upon the enjoyment of ownership existing in favor of private individuals have often been called "Legalservituten." The expression is, however, inexact; for there is not involved in them any true servitude, notwithstanding that they ordinarily have the same content as servitudes. Rights that are thus created in interested persons by restrictions upon the ownership of another, cannot properly be conceived of as independent real rights in the land of the latter.[1]

§ 37. **Restrictions imposed by Rights of Vicinage.** — Limitations upon ownership due to the rights of neighbors have had a rich and varied development in German law. Owing to their

[1] *Gierke*, "Privatrecht", II, 418.

close connection with general economic conditions they were affected only to a very slight extent by the reception of the Roman law. Even in the law of the present time the native principles are for the most part preserved. The Civil Code has regulated in a uniform manner, and in essential agreement with the earlier law, some few restrictions of vicinage, — the discharge of inhibited matter, buildings and other improvements, threatened collapse of land or structures, excavations, "over-hang" and "over-fall", projecting buildings, ways of necessity, and mutual rights in questions of boundary. It has reserved further regulations to the State law (EG, § 124). The Swiss Civil Code has taken a similar position.

The most important restrictions of this class (for restrictions based on vicinage in mining and in water law *cf.* §§ 40 and 41 *infra*) are the following:

(I) **Ways of Necessity.**[1] — The obligation of a landowner to afford his neighbor ways and passage, for agricultural purposes, was directly connected with the old agrarian system, the three-field method of cultivation, and the compulsory regulation of the mark-arable that originated in primitive collective ownership. The old legal sources prescribed exactly when and for what reasons the mark-associates must grant each other "ways and by-ways." Often a duty of compensation was also prescribed ("wer den Weg fordert, soll ihn mit Garben belegen," "he who asks a way shall pave it with sheaves"). With the right of way there was associated another limitation, which likewise served agricultural purposes. This was the so-called "Pflugwenderecht" ("Anwende-", "Kehr-", "Tretrecht"). It obligated the owner to permit his neighbor to swing his plow and turn his ox upon the other's land. The right of enjoying ways of necessity, which in such extension was unknown to the Roman law, persisted as common customary law, was adopted by modern codes, and has been regulated by the new Civil Code (§§ 917, 918) in accord with the old law. This "Tretrecht" persisted in some of the regional legal systems, and still exists in State law (*e.g.* in Bavaria east of the Rhine). The Swiss Civil Code has added to ways of necessity springs and conduits of necessity (§§ 694, 691, 710).

(II) Likewise known only to the regional legal systems was the so-called "**hammer**" or "**ladder**" **right** ("Hammerschlags-"

[1] *Buch*, "Der Notweg im römischen und älteren deutschen Recht. Ein Beitrag zur Lehre von den Notrechten und den Eigentumsbeschränkungen" (Breslau Habilitationsschrift, 1909).

"Leiterrecht"); namely, the right of a neighbor to enter upon adjacent land or erect scaffolding thereupon in order to make repairs in his own house. Related to this was what was known as "**shovel-right**" ("Schaufelschlagsrecht"): the right of the possessor of a mill to enter upon his neighbor's land through which the mill stream ran, in order to cleanse the waters. These rights, also, were preserved in the particularistic systems and thus continue to exist.

(III) **Rights of "Over-hang" and "Over-fall."** [1] — (1) *Rights of Over-hang* ("Überhangsrechte").—Wherever a tree, bush, or vine projects with its branches, twigs, or roots over or into the land of a neighboring landowner, there results a conflict between the right of the owner of the tree and the landowner's rights of control over the air above and the earth below the surface of his land. The German law has always emphasized primarily the rights of the owner of the tree, and has therefore given him the right not only to fell the tree, but also to cut off its projecting branches in so far as he can do so from his own land.[2] The neighboring landowner, on the other hand, did not need to suffer such encroachment of twigs and roots upon his close. In addition to a right of action against the owner of the tree for its removal, he might, in exercise of the right of self-help, cut off and appropriate all encroaching twigs and roots found within his close. In this connection rules are often given, in the manner of primitive law, concerning the formalities to be observed in such cutting.[3] Many sources declared explicitly, however, that actual damage must have been caused by the over-hang.[4] Only exceptionally was it required that the landowner should first demand of the owner of the tree that he remove its branches; and likewise only exceptionally, that the landowner should deliver to the owner of the tree the wood so cut, or share it with him. The modern law, which is here in complete disagreement with the Roman, has retained these principles. The new Civil Code has likewise adopted them (§ 910): a landowner may, in case of such trespasses by branches or roots, cut them off and keep them; the branches, however, only after the occupant of the adjoining land has been required to do so, and has not removed

[1] *A. B. Schmidt*, "Das Recht des Überhangs und Überfalls", no. 21 (1886) of *Gierke's* "Untersuchungen."

[2] Ssp., II, 52, § 1.

[3] "Benker Heidenrecht" (a Westphalian doom), Art. 20; *Grimm*, "Weistümer", III, 42.

[4] Ssp., II, 52, § 2.

them within a definite period allowed him for that purpose. The same is provided by the Swiss Civil Code (§ 687, 1).

(2) *Rights of Over-fall* ("Überfallsrechte"). — German law gave to a landowner the right to appropriate the fruits that fell upon his land from over-hanging branches projecting from an adjoining close. This was known as "Anriss" or "Abriss" (the right of "pickings"). As men then said, "whatever falls in a neighbor's yard is his"; and even when this was a consequence of the tree-owner's having shaken his tree, the rule was the same.[1] The right was justified by the argument that a neighbor, who had suffered the damage of an overhanging branch, as for example through the shadow it had caused, should also have the benefit of it: "he who drinks the bitter drop shall also taste the good." In this form the right of "over-fall" passed into many modern statutes. Very often, however, the landowner was given not only the right to appropriate fruits that had fallen, but also permission to pick the fruit that hung from the branches penetrating his close. This was true of the Saxon common law, and was adopted by the Prussian "Landrecht" and the Austrian Code. On the other hand, many legal systems prescribed a division of the "pickings" between the owners of the tree and the land, — among others the French and the Swiss. The new Civil Code has regulated the right of over-fall in agreement, for all practical purposes, with the older German law, giving to the neighbor the ownership of all fruits falling upon his land, provided he has not himself shaken the tree. But it has at the same time set up the fiction, theretofore unknown, that such fallen fruits shall be regarded as the fruits of the adjoining land from the moment of their falling (§ 911). More simple is the provision of the Swiss Civil Code (§ 687, 2), according to which a landowner who suffers the trespass of branches upon lands cultivated or over-built, has a right to the fruits ("Anries") growing upon them.

(IV) As respects the **improvement of his land**, an owner was subjected by German law to manifold restrictions in the interest of his neighbors. The older legal rules were, in part, later adopted in police provisions of modern building codes. Under this head come the following rules:

(1) *Window Rights and Rights of Light.* — Numerous German legal systems forbade a landowner to open windows looking out upon a neighbor's yard, and from which anything could be thrown or poured upon the same; as likewise to shut off by building the

[1] Gloss to the Ssp., II, 52.

access of light to existing windows of his neighbor. Such provisions have frequently been adopted in modern statutes (*e.g.* in the Prussian "Landrecht"). These retain their authority as State law alongside the new Civil Code, which itself, like the Roman law, knows no such restrictions.

(2) The provisions contained in many older as well as modern statutes forbidding the erection in the immediate neighborhood of a boundary of *disagreeable or dangerous structures,* such as privies, stalls, dung-pits, kilns, straw-ricks, bee-hives, and the like,[1] has been extended in the new Civil Code to a prohibition expressed in general terms (§ 907, 1).

(3) The provision, occasionally occurring, forbidding any building whatever immediately at the boundary, was justified in the older sources by the reason that no *eaves-trough* might empty upon a neighbor's land.[2]

(4) Many legal systems contain a prohibition against planting trees, shrubs, or hedges, or digging springs, directly upon the *boundary.* It was required that the boundary be left entirely clear. Wherever structures or plantations exist upon or near the boundary line, many legal systems have assumed a community ownership, and usually an undivided ownership. The new Civil Code, on the other hand, has adopted the view-point of the Roman law and declared (§§ 921, 923) for a mere community of usufruct, leaving room, however, in the case of fruit and forest trees for the provisions of State law (EG, §§ 122, 183). Special and exceedingly varied rules formerly prevailed relative to the use of party walls.

(5) *Encroaching improvements* ("Grenzüberbau").[3]—As a landowner was bound to regulate his conduct within the limits of his own land with regard to the interest of his neighbors, he was all the more strictly forbidden to cross the boundary with structures or plantations ("Anlagen"). His neighbor was not bound to suffer a projecting building; he could require the removal of such part of the structure as was erected upon his land or projected into the air above it. Nor was encroachment permitted even where the adjoining land was not subject to private ownership. The prohibition of such buildings belonged, therefore, among restrictions imposed in the interest of public intercourse. And this was doubtless the point of departure in the law's development.

[1] Ssp., II, 51, § 1. [2] Ssp., II, 49, § 1.
[3] *Martin Wolff*, "Der Bau auf fremden Boden, insbesondere der Grenzüberbau", in *O. Fischer's* "Abhandlungen", VI, 2 (1900).

For this reason the burgrave was empowered in many cities (Strassburg, Regensburg, Worms, and Cologne) to ride through the streets with his lance or staff of office crosswise, and to require the removal of all projecting structures that he struck ("Stangenrecht", "Recht der Räumung"; — "staff-right", "right of ouster").[1] Many town-laws later prohibited the building of projecting stories, so popular in medieval cities.[2] Many other legal systems provided, however, that a neighbor must suffer a projecting building, once completed, if he had not protested upon receiving notice from its owner, or even without such in case of notorious construction; he had closed his own mouth by silence. This principle, which was inconsistent with the Roman law ("superficies solo cedit"), was retained in the Territorial systems, and was extended in some of them (the Prussian "Landrecht" and the law of Württemberg) by the further rule that a house owner who built upon a boundary in good faith acquired ownership in the surface of his neighbor's land so overbuilt, subject to compensation for its value. The Civil Code has adopted this principle along with a peculiar extension (§§ 912–916): the owner of the land built upon is obliged to suffer the projecting portion of the building, which remains in the ownership of his neighbor; but he receives from his neighbor in return damages in the form of a money rent, which is a charge upon his neighbor's land even without registry in the land-book. Here again the rule of the Swiss Civil Code is at once simpler and in more exact agreement with the earlier law (§ 674, 3): whenever a projecting building is erected without right, and the injured party, notwithstanding that this ought to be manifest to him, does not protest in due time, the real right in the building or the ownership of the soil may be assigned to the party so overbuilding, provided he acted in good faith and circumstances otherwise justify, in return for proper compensation to the other party.

[1] *Rietschel*, "Das Burggrafenamt und die hohe Gerichtsbarkeit in den deutschen Bischofstädten während des früheren Mittelalters", no. 1 (1905) of the Unter. G. D. Stadtverf., 331 *et seq.* *Cf. Seeliger*, "Studien zur älteren Verfassungsgeschichte Kölns", K. Sächs. Gesell. Wiss., XXVI, 3 (1909), 109 *et seq.*; *Sander*, in Hist. Vj. S., XIII (1910), 77 *et seq.*

[2] *Goethe*, "Wahrheit und Dichtung", Bk. 1, Absatz 14: "In Frankfort, as in many old cities, it became customary in erecting wooden buildings, in order to gain room, to take the liberty of building out over the street not only the first but also the upper stories; the result of which was of course to make especially narrow streets somewhat gloomy and forbidding. Eventually a law was passed that whoever erected a new house might build only the first story out beyond the foundation, and that the others must be vertical." Goethe's father found a way to evade the law.

(6) We may class here also the prohibition of "*spite-*" *structures,* already found in many of the medieval town-laws, and which is covered to-day by the general prohibition of chicanery. Likewise the duty, imposed upon the owner in modern statutes, of preserving his buildings and his land in such a *condition that no damage shall result* therefrom to his neighbor, for example by their collapse or by undue excavation. Both of these are regulated by the Civil Code in harmony with the earlier law (§§ 908, 909).

(V) The most important practical restriction imposed to-day upon ownership by the rights of adjoining landowners is the obligation of an owner to suffer upon his land what are called "discharges", that is, certain "indirect physical effects due to the **discharge of matter or the transmission of vibrations.**"[1] Satisfactory rules relative to this subject were unknown in the Roman law. But the principle is to be found in some of the medieval town-laws, inasmuch as they designated certain industries as "insufferable", which a neighbor was therefore not obliged to put up with. This view, which grew into a definite customary right, has been given statutory force by the Civil Code (§ 906): the right — which belongs in principle among the privileges of ownership — of repelling all external interferences with one's land, has its limit wherever interferences are involved which are either inappreciable or are produced by such a use of another piece of land as is usual with land in similar situation. Supplementary provisions are contained in the Industrial Code (§ 26). The Swiss Civil Code (§ 684, 2) forbids, for the same reason, all harmful encroachments by smoke or soot, disagreeable vapors, fumes, or odors, noises or vibrations, that are not justified by the situation and nature of the land, or by local usage.

§ 38. **Restrictions originating in Regalities, generally.** — A series of important restrictions upon landed ownership resulted from the widespread medieval institute of the regality. By the expressions "regalia", "iura regalia", the earliest technical use of which is found in the Concordat of Worms of 1122, men designated from the 1100 s onward all those profitable rights of sovereignty, originating in public or in private law, which inhered in the king as the holder of supreme power, and which permitted him either to monopolize the administration of the law within a definite territory (the fundamental meaning), or out of the plenitude of his power to permit such administration by others.[2] In

[1] *Gierke,* "Privatrecht", II, 420.
[2] *Fehr,* in Vj. Soz. W. G., VII (1909), 375.

consequence of the patrimonial conception of sovereignty the profitable character of these rights was chiefly emphasized; that is, their availability within the rules of the law of property through sale, pledge, or lease. In this connection no distinction was made between rights of sovereignty proper, — for example executive power, military power, and judicature, rights to customs and of coinage, — and the mere property rights of the king in lordless land, in things belonging to the public, and even in the private property of the subjects, which he had possessed ever since he had come to represent the public interests in place of the organized folk. The possibility thus created of alienating these rights in exchange for political concessions or for financial considerations, was made use of in the most lavish manner by German rulers, especially from the Hohenstaufen onward, to the permanent damage of the crown's power. Thenceforth the regalities, in so far as they were not included in the original powers of the dukes of the German racial-branches, — as was the case, for example, with the coinage regality,[1] — passed in increasing measure into the hands of the Territorial rulers, the cities, and the manorial or feudal landlords. All this found recognition as regarded the electoral princes in the fundamental statutes of the Empire, namely in the Golden Bull of 1356 and, later, in the electoral capitulations and the Westphalian Peace. The movement was completed in many cases not by way of law but by way of usurpation. Objects of regalities were, above all, the mint, tolls and customs, markets and castles, safe conducts and protection (*e.g.* of merchants, Jews, and foreigners), goods of heirless decedents and confiscated goods, lordless estates, the sea-shore, rivers, roads, fishing, the chase, forests, mines, salterns, treasure trove, certain trades, the right of military ban, and rights of judicature. In Germany no general definition of the objects and matters subject to regalities was ever made. This was done, however, for Italy by the motley catalogue of the Roncaglia "constitutio pacis" of the emperor Frederick I of 1158;[2] and this, after being embodied in the "libri feudorum" (II, Feud. 56), became with the Reception of the Lombard feudal law the common-law basis of the theory of regalities in Germany. From the 1700 s onward jurists and cameralists made numerous attempts to develop a theory of the regalities.

[1] *Menadier*, "Das Münzrecht des deutschen Stammesherzogs", in Zeitschrift für Numismatik, XXVII (1909), 158–167.
[2] M. G., Constitutiones, I, 244.

Their chief endeavor in so doing was to extend these as far as they possibly could (they got as far as four hundred), seeking thereby to support the sovereignty of the Territorial princes, at once against the Emperor and the Empire and against the estates of their respective realms. A conceptional division of the regalia was also attempted between "regalia maiora", that is rights of sovereignty proper, and "regalia minora" which were certain incidental financial rights, profitable and alienable; a distinction which, though lacking to be sure in any distinct principle, nevertheless became established doctrine, and as such passed over, for example, into the Prussian "Landrecht." Only when a maturer insight had made clear the political character of sovereignty, and the dissimilarities between it and privileges of private law, did men attain to any adequate limitation of the regality concept. They then abandoned entirely its application to political rights of sovereignty, applying it thenceforth solely to the exclusive rights of the State in the exercise of certain economic activities, especially the exclusive occupancy of certain objects and the exclusive prosecution of certain trades; rights which persisted down into modern times only in scanty number.

In this sense the regalities still belong to the existing law as "profitable rights which by force of a rule of public law inhere exclusively in the State, whereas their content is regarded, 'in se', as a privilege of private law."[1] Aside from the right of the fisc to ownerless goods which is recognized by the Civil Code (§ 928, 2), and which can be connected at least historically with the corresponding old regality (*supra*, p. 253), the regalities have been reserved to State law (EG, § 73). In addition to industrial regalities (which cannot here be considered) there still occur in isolated cases, as so-called manorial regalities, those of mines and salterns, of the chase, fisheries, amber, rafting, ferrying, and milling; a regality of treasure trove also still exists. As regards roads, forests, and dikes, however, the right of the State has been weakened into the general right of sovereignty which it enjoys over everything, whether or not a regality be present. From the earliest times the most important regalities in their relations to landed ownership have been those of woodlands and of hunting, of rivers and of fisheries, of roads, mines, and salterns; and this remains true of the law to-day, even in those cases where regalities have as such been abolished, being weakened into a political sovereignty over forests, waters, and mines. It is there-

[1] *Gierke*, "Privatrecht", II, 399.

fore advisable, following the example of Gierke, to discuss here the law of forests and hunting, of waters and fisheries, and of mining.

§ 39. **Restrictions originating in the Regalities of the Forest Law and Hunting Law.** (I) **The Forest Law.** — The forests, which at the beginning of historical times and until far into the Middle Ages covered Germany far more thickly than at the present day, were only gradually subjected to human control and thereby converted into objects of ownership. Doubtless only small pieces of woodland were occupied, at first; the great clearings which in the course of the Middle Ages opened to cultivation the entire woodland area began only after the end of the age of tribal migrations. As a result of this original occupancy the woodland passed into the collective ownership either of entire racial branches ("Volkswald", folk-wood), or of mark-associations ("Markwald", mark-wood). Here again the king took the place in the Frankish empire of the organized folk: the old folk-wood became a royal forest, and the king, moreover, assumed the right to appropriate to himself, as lordless land, all those woodlands which were neither commons of mark-associations nor private property of individual landowners. Such woodlands were set apart as forests ("forestae", which is doubtless to be derived from "foris", "foras") by royal ban, the special object of which was to retain to the king as an exclusive right the chase in these extensive woodlands.[1] Besides the royal forests and the mark-woodland, we find early evidences of private woodlands, which originated in clearings made by individual landowners. These were greatly extended from the 700 s onward by gifts of royal forest of enormous areas to secular magnates, churches, and cloisters, as well as by their sale and gage, later, to princes and cities. In this way the one-time wealth of forest standing in the ownership of the king or the crown continued to shrink, down to the 1300 s. The growth of mark-woodland also contributed to increase the private woodland of the great landowners when the rights originally enjoyed therein by the members of the mark through their collective ownership of the communal woodland were undermined. This took place, partly because of the general loosening of the mark system, the land-lords settled within the mark

[1] *Thimme*, "Forestis. Königsgut und Königsrecht nach den Forsturkunden vom 6. bis 12. Jahrhundert", in Arch. Urk. F., II (1909), 101–154. Compare with this *Uhlirz* in Deut. Litt. Z., 1909, No. 13; *Philippi*, "Forst und Zehnte", in Arch. Urk. F., II (1909), 327–334; *Baist*, "Forestis", in Z. Deut. Wortf., XII (1910), 235–237.

arrogating to themselves as over-markmen the over-ownership in the mark-woodland; and partly because the kings, in the exercise of their right to establish hunting preserves, afforested not only the royal and the lordless woodlands but also the woods, and the lands lying between them, of the mark-associations and private individuals. All this was accelerated by the development of Territorial sovereignties. As the king had made use of his right of ban to the damage of all others who had woodland rights, so the Territorial princes now laid claim, within their respective Territories, to the right of afforestation. Indeed, from the middle of the 1300 s onward they claimed the forests outright as their property, especially those of the mark-associations, so that the usufructuary rights of the markmen thenceforth appeared to be mere servitudes in the property of another, for which they were even commonly compelled to render tribute. Only in the case of the noble landowners did they proceed more considerately. Thus, in the interest of hunting privileges of manorial lords and Territorial princes, the peasants were crowded out of the woodland, which had once been their property and of the greatest value to them. No wonder that this produced a bitterness which, in the words of Jacob Grimm,[1] "has in it something imprescriptible"; in the Peasants' War it was one of the chief complaints. From the 1500 s onward men made use of the idea of regality in order to justify in legal theory the extensive rights claimed by the Territorial princes in the woodlands within their States. The consequence of this was that there was thenceforth no necessity of continued afforestation, since the rights of usufruct and occupancy inhered in the Territorial princes by virtue of the regality, even in the woodlands of noble owners and in the few communal woodlands that still existed. It is true that their forest regality was never exercised in Germany without restriction, because of the resistance of the estates of the realm; but the general right of sovereignty over the forests that was implicit in the regality was used to subject the entire administration of the woodland to a jealous oversight on the part of such rulers, and to regulate them by forest ordinances, partly in the general interest of forestry, but sometimes in the interest of the hunting privileges enjoyed by the Territorial princes. Such forest ordinances were issued in especially great number in South Germany (the oldest is one of Württemberg of 1515). They were the continuation of products of an older forest legislation. Similar results had

[1] "Rechtsaltertümer", I, 346.

already been aimed at in some of the folk-laws, — for example, the "lex Ribuaria" and "lex Baiuwariorum", — in occasional provisions of imperial statutes, and especially, later, in manorial enactments (*e.g.* a forest ordinance of Maursmünster of 1184, and a doom of 1383 concerning the forest preserves of Dreieich). Especially after the havoc wrought by the Thirty Years' War the forest statutes of the different States assumed as a special task the improvement of forestry; but the limitations imposed by them, in harmony with the tutelary character of the State's activity in that age, were often of such extent that the owners hardly remained masters of their woodlands. Thus, for example, the Prussian "Landrecht" (I, 8, §§ 83 *et seq.*) threatened the owners of private woodland with penalties for waste, and compelled them to observe the instructions of the State police as respected restrictions upon cutting.

These ideas were abandoned in more modern times, following the example set by France. The oversight of the State over private woodlands was greatly lessened or entirely done away with; the latter was the case, notably, in Prussia (edict of September 14, 1811). However, here as in other departments of government a reaction set in against the individualistic view which regarded the woodland simply as an object of private law. In Prussia the freedom of private woodlands was, in general, maintained; whereas in other States, for example in Baden and Hesse, the consent of the State was made requisite for the clearing even of private woodland. On the other hand, in Prussia also the woodlands of communes (*e.g.* the "hewing-" hills in Siegen) and of public institutions were subjected by a statute of August 14, 1876, to a certain, although not a stringent, State oversight; and likewise, by statute of March 14, 1881, community woodlands, the partition of these being restricted at the same time. The oversight of the State under the Prussian law is intended merely to insure such exploitation of the woodland as will not endanger its permanence, but in some States such oversight extends further, in that any plan for their exploitation must be approved by State officials (*e.g.* in Bavaria), or else the actual administration of communal woodlands is entrusted to governmental overforesters (as in Baden and Hesse). Finally, the Prussian statute of July 6, 1875, although it has thus far proved of but slight practical importance, introduced greater restrictions (for which compensation was given) in the case of what are known as "Schutzwaldungen" ("protected woodlands": those whose conservation is regarded as especially necessary to society), — similar provisions exist in Bavaria, Württemberg, Brunswick, and Alsace-Lorraine; and at the same time authorized the compulsory establishment of forest-associations, — which provision has likewise been imitated in some other States, as *e.g.* in Brunswick. The Introductory Act of the New Civil Code gives effect to these laws (§ 83). The Swiss Civil Code has applied the idea of compulsory community as a general principle. Under conditions which it indicates in detail, it permits (§ 703) a majority of landowners to compel coöperation by the minority in common undertakings for the good of the woodland which could not be accomplished without such coöperation. Such compulsory communities may be formed not only for purposes of afforestation but also for the correction of the course of streams, drainage and sewage, the opening of roads, and consolidation of holdings.

(II) **The Hunting Law.**[1] — The right to hunt was most intimately associated in Germany from the earliest times with the ownership of land.[2] Wherever private ownership was developed, the landowner had the exclusive right of hunting over the land he owned. Where the woodlands were the collective property of mark-associations, only the mark-associates had the right to hunt over the common mark and to appropriate the wild game (right of "freie Pürsch"). In time the right of hunting became dissociated from the ownership of land: there was developed a right of hunting upon the land of others.

The earliest cause of this result was the creation by the Frankish kings of forest reservations by royal ban ("Bannforsten", *supra,* p. 271). They not only afforested the woodlands that were lordless, and those they owned themselves, — thereby penalizing poaching in such hunting preserves with the punishments of the royal ban, which were more severe than the penalties of the popular law, — but also extended their forest laws and game ordinances over woodlands that constituted portions of common marks, and even over such as were objects of private ownership. In this manner they abolished within such districts the hunting privileges theretofore enjoyed by mark-associates and individual

[1] *v. Brünneck,* Art. "Jagdrecht" in H. W. B. der Staatsw., V (3d ed., 1910), 564 *et seq.; Frommhold,* "Über das Jagdrecht", in *Ihering's* J. B., LIII (1908), 188–212; *Ebner,* "Die Grundbegriffe des Jagdrechts", in Beit. z. Erläut. D. R., LV (1911), 535–575, 737–750.

[2] *R. Schröder,* "Lehrbuch" (5th ed.), 547, and *Thimme, op. cit.,* 116, are of the contrary opinion, namely that the hunting law originated in the right of appropriating wild animals.

landowners, reserving these either for themselves or for those ecclesiastical and secular magnates to whom they granted exclusive privileges of the chase. How sharply opposed this withdrawal of hunting privileges was to the inrooted popular consciousness of right is seen in the fact that even in the Sachsenspiegel the memory of free hunting rights is still alive.[1]

But even outside of the royal forests hunting rights were ultitimately segregated from the ownership of land. This was a consequence of the increasing organization of the folk in occupational estates, and of the idea, which in consequence came to be generally predominant, that the chase was an occupation fit only for persons of a knightly mode of life, the higher clergy being regarded in this connection as the equals of the nobles. It is true that the cities, — particularly the imperial cities, — and their burghers often retained unlimited rights of hunting in the woods belonging to the city mark, or at least a limited right of hunting. On the other hand, as respects the peasants such rights were everywhere either wholly denied them or materially limited, and this as regarded both the common marks and lands that were the private property of peasants. They were, for example, permitted only the rights to hunt ignoble ("niedere") game, or to hunt only upon condition that they use upon their own tables the game which they should kill, and not for sale, etc. Finally, in the 1400 s and 1500 s their right of hunting, in so far as they still enjoyed any, was everywhere taken from them by ordinances of the ruling princes, upon economic grounds or for purposes of rural police.

From the 1400 s onward the hunting rights of landowners were still further limited, those of noble landowners as well as others, by the claims which the Territorial rulers asserted to a hunting regality throughout the entire extent of their domains, just as they had previously laid claim to a forest regality (*supra*, p. 272). The right formerly granted them by the kings to set apart forest preserves they now extended beyond such reserves, usurping the right to forbid to other persons the right of hunting anywhere in their domains; that is to say, as a general rule, granting such rights only by way of special privileges. Maximilian I, for example, a passionate and reckless hunter, did not shrink from using any means to acquire the exclusive privilege of chase in his earldom of Tyrol, as the Territorial lord. As may readily be understood, he was thereby plunged into violent conflict with all others who

[1] Ssp., II, 61, § 1.

held similar privileges. In other regions, also, resistance was made to these efforts of the Territorial rulers. The estates of the realm succeeded in establishing the rule that the regality in question (which in some Territories, as *e.g.* Mecklenburg, was wholly unknown) should be recognized, in general, only as regarded noble game, — that is, stags and wild boars; whereas "ignoble" game (hares, partridges, and roes) or "ignoble" and "ordinary" game (roes) were reserved to the nobles and the clergy. On the other hand, the Prussian "Landrecht", which extended throughout the kingdom the Slavic-Polish law of Silesia, did establish a general regality, permitting the exercise of no hunting rights whatever except under licenses granted by the Territorial ruler. Not only where a regality was lacking, but equally where such existed, manorial lords continued to enjoy hunting privileges upon the estates of their dependent peasants, frequently in the form of a servitude associated with the demesne which secured to the lord of the manor either an exclusive or only a so-called "common" right of hunting ("Mitjagdsrecht"). Again, such rights might be enjoyed by several persons in the same way and in like measure; that is, as though by ideal shares ("Koppeljagd"). It was only infrequently that vestiges of the old rights of mark-associations persisted, in the form of hunting rights enjoyed by the inhabitants of a city throughout the municipal domain, or by villagers over the communal fields ("freie Pürsch").

Even under this form of the hunting law, the rights of chase permitted over the land of others, hunting services ("Jagdfronden"), and the damage caused to the fields by immoderate stocking of the preserves, were a sore oppression to the rural population. The law was done away with in Germany beginning about the middle of the 1800 s. Here again France had led the way with such legislation. In accord with the principles laid down in the Fundamental Rights of 1848, every right of hunting upon the land of others, and likewise the right of pursuit onto the land of others were everywhere finally abolished by legislation in the different States; in Prussia and in Bavaria without, and in the other States in return for, compensation. Only in Mecklenburg does the manorial right of hunting upon the land of others still exist to any great extent. In the same way the regality of hunting was entirely done away with; but the supreme control of the State over hunting ("Jagdhoheit") was reserved, and thus it is able to fix closed seasons for the protection of game, and prescribe the manner in which hunting rights shall be exercised. As to this last, the rights of landowners upon their own estates were in many States (for example Prussia and Bavaria) originally left entirely unrestricted, which was going further in this respect than the Frankfort Fundamental Rights. This rule, however, soon proved to be very harmful both politically and economically; and in consequence there has come about in such States since 1850 a change in legislation: the Prussian hunting law ("Jagdpolizeigesetz") of March 7th, 1850, and most recently the hunting ordinance ("Jagdordnung") of July 15th, 1907; the Bavarian statute of June 15th, 1850; and similar statutes in Baden, Saxony, Hannover, Württemberg, and other States. The principle was adopted that the right of hunting must be inseparably united with the ownership of land, — which was a return to the starting-point of the law's historical development; but the exercise of hunting rights was made dependent upon certain qualifications, some personal, others of landownership. As regards the first, the procuring of a hunting license was required, and its issuance can be denied to such persons as it is feared may abuse it. As regards the latter, only those landowners whose estates amounted to a certain area were permitted to exercise the hunting rights to which they would, as landowners, be "prima facie" entitled. This amount is in Prussia approximately three hundred acres ("Morgen"), — according to the Hunting Ordinance of 1907 such a private hunting district must have an area of at least seventy-five hectares; in Bavaria it is two hundred and forty "Tagewerke" (land that affords a day's labor) in the lowlands, and four hundred in the highlands. All other lands are included in community hunting-districts, within which the exercise of hunting rights belongs to a "hunting association" constituted of the owners of the lands so united. This, however, is represented in most States by the political commune, or by its official organ the communal administrative board, which exercises hunting rights in the name and for the account of the associated landowners. Under the Prussian Hunting Ordinance of 1907 a "hunting director" has charge of the administration of the association, and this director is the president of the commune. In some States (Bavaria, Württemberg, Alsace-Lorraine) the right to hunt is always required to be exercised through lessees; other statutes (as those of Prussia and Saxony) leave it to the individual's choice whether the game shall be disposed of by lease, or shot by official huntsmen, or left undisturbed. In the case of leases a definite maximum number of lessees is prescribed (in Prussia ordinarily not more than three). These rules have also done away with the right of "freie Pürsch": the communes must likewise either lease their hunting rights or exercise them through an official huntsman. The old distinction between noble and ignoble game has also disappeared; the right of hunting now extends indifferently to all animals that are allowed to be hunted at all. Which these shall be is determined by State legislation, ordinarily after an exhaustive enumeration; this is the case in Prussia (under the Game Protection Act of July 14th, 1904, and now by the Hunting Ordinance of 1907), Bavaria, and Saxony.

The hunting law has been reserved, generally speaking, to the States (EG, § 69). It is only as regards damage done by wild game that the Civil Code has laid down certain rules (§ 835) which are a development of the earlier Prussian Game Protection Act of 1891. This imperial ordinance, however, "is of little importance, as compared with the State hunting laws",[1] the Introductory Act of the Code having left undisturbed the existing rules of State legislation (§§ 70, 71, 72) and authorized the issuance of new ones. The Prussian hunting ordinance of 1907, for example, regulates exhaustively the subjects of compensation for damages done by wild game and prevention of such damages. Such provisions were unknown to the older law. Only after the full development of the hunting regality were any great number of them issued; and from that time on their sphere of application was materially restricted, inasmuch as the right of hunting was permitted (in principle) to all landowners. Since that time an obligation to pay damages has existed, generally speaking, only in the case of lessees of hunting rights as against landholders not entitled to those rights. The Civil Code fixes a uniform minimum measure of compensation in such cases. It also prescribes which animals shall be compensated for by damages, — wild boars, red deer, damine buck, roe deer, and pheasants; but not hares. Nevertheless, these as well as other animals are subject to State legislation determining what damage shall be compensated for, who is entitled to damages, and who shall pay them — as to the last, the person entitled to the hunting privileges, in case the landowner has not himself the right to hunt.

[1] *Dernburg*, "Das bürgerliche Recht, des deutschen Reichs und Preussens", II, 2, § 397.

§ 40. **Restrictions Originating in Regalities of the Law of Waters, Fishery, and Dikes.** (I) **The Law of Waters.**[1] — (1) *The Older Germanic Law.* — German law has always given particular attention to the fact that inland waters are not so well fitted to serve private needs as they are to serve needs that are primarily those of the public. The land that was permanently covered with water was, like the forests, originally subject to the collective ownership of the folk; and all waters, in so far as they were capable of utilization, were subject to the common user of all members of the folk. The permanent assignment of definite districts among the smaller groups of the mark-associations, and the appearance of private ownership of land, resulted in a variant legal treatment of different waters. In this connection their size was of fundamental importance.

(A) Larger waters, navigable by ships and serving commerce between land and land, so-called PUBLIC RIVERS ("flumina publica"), remained, like the military roads of the land ("viæ publicæ"), the property of the whole community, and therefore subject to everybody's use. But in this case, as with the forests, the old ownership of the folk was displaced by that of the king as the representative of the folk, that is of the Empire. Thenceforth the great arteries of trade, alike of water and of land, were called roads of the king or the Empire. For a long time, however, the old popular view persisted that they had not therefore ceased to be objects of common user: this still found sharp expression in the Law Books.[2] But the kings early put forward another claim. From the rule that the greater waters were royal,[3] they deduced the right personally to dispose of the profits therein. They, too, were "afforested" by them; though here they were of course not interested, as in the case of game, in excluding other persons from the usufruct, but only in a fiscal exploitation thereof by grants to such persons. There thus resulted a regality of public waters.

[1] *Geffcken*, "Zur Geschichte des deutschen Wasserrechts", Z². R. G., xxi (1900), 173–217; *Peterka*, "Das Wasserrecht der Weistümer" (1905); *Aström*, "Über das Wasserrecht in Nord- und Mitteleuropa" (1905); *Kloess*, "Das deutsche Wasserrecht und das Wasserrecht der Bundesstaaten des deutschen Reiches" (1908); *Stoerk — E. Loening*, article "Gewässer" in H. W. B. der Staatsw., IV (3d ed., 1909), 836–847; *Kloess*, "Die Rechtsstellung der Quelle und des Grundwassers nach deutschem Recht", in Beit. z. Erläut. D. R., LIV (1910), 296–313; *Moll*, "Zur Lehre von den öffentlichen Sachen", in same, 313–354; *Fischel*, "Zur Reform des Wasserrechts" (1911).

[2] Ssp. II. 29, § 4; "Landrecht" of Görlitz, 34, § 1.

[3] Thus, Ludwig the Pious declared in a document of 816: "Siquidem cujuscumque potestatis sint littora, nostra tamen est regalis aqua."

The "stream regality" ("Stromregal") included the right to impose taxes upon every private use of reserved ("gebannten") waters by vessels of whatever kind, as well as by harbor structures, ferries, bridges, mills, etc. Of course, the kings could grant freedom from such taxes.[1] Inasmuch as the bed of such streams was the property of the Empire, islands that were built up within them fell to the Empire or to subjects endowed, as its grantees, with supreme rights over the stream, as was decided by an imperial doom of 1294.[2] As this same doom shows, rights of safe-conduct and of towing, and particularly rights of judicature over the stream, were also included in the regality. This did not belong to the Territorial rulers who controlled the banks, but was independently disposed of by the Empire.[3]

This regality over streams remained longer than other regalities in the control of the Empire. It was only from the second half of the 1300 s onward that the power of the Territorial rulers came more and more to control the rivers at the expense of the Empire. At the same time sporadic applications of the crown's regality are to be found down to the end of the 1400 s.

(B) Smaller waters within individual marks, so-called PRIVATE WATERS ("aquæ aquarumque decursus"), which were not supposed to serve any larger purposes of intercourse but merely the necessities of neighbors, usually passed, like roads and byways ("viæ convicinales"), as parts of the mark commonties, into the ownership of mark-associations, by which they were administered, remaining free to the use and profit of the mark-associates alone; whereas waters upon lands not yet under cultivation were subject, as lordless domains, to the king's right of appropriation. With the appearance of private ownership in land, many waters fell immediately into the exclusive ownership of individual landowners. This was true of springs, brooks, and ponds, as well as of water diverted by canals; such cases, however, were of slight importance both in law and in fact. On the other hand, the king soon came to exercise his rights of reserva-

[1] Thus, for example, Frederick I declared the Rhine a "libera et regia strata", the Main a "via regia" free of customs dues.

[2] "Curia Norimbergensis", an. 1294, c. 1 (M. G., Constitutiones, III, 487).

[3] For example Frederick I gave Lübeck in 1188 jurisdiction over the Trave from Oldesloe to the sea; in 1890 the Imperial Court, acting as an arbitral court in a suit between Lübeck and Mecklenburg brought before the Bundesrat, confirmed Lübeck's sovereign rights over the lower Trave on the strength of this grant, thereby settling definitely a dispute centuries old. *Schröder*, "Landeshoheit über die Trave", in "Neue Heidelberger Jahrbücher", I (1891), 10 *et seq.*

tion ("Bannrechte") over the waters of the mark commonties as he had earlier done over their woodlands. He thus withdrew their usufruct from the public, and either reserved this to himself or conveyed it to ecclesiastical and secular magnates to whom he made gifts of lands. These magnates acquired in this way the same exclusive private ownership over such waters as they had already gained over the woodlands. Moreover, wherever and however manors were constituted there eventuated private ownership. At the same time, as many dooms show, by no means every kind of user of such waters was reserved to the landowner alone, even in manors and manorial marks; the dependent markmen might also draw water, bathe, water animals, and often also fish therein. As contrasted with mark-communes that had remained free, the only difference was that the land-lord, like the king, was in a position to reserve rights of ban, especially the right to lay taxes, and also to reserve to himself, in such measure as he pleased, particular rights of usufruct. However, with the decline of the free marks and with the growing economic supremacy which landed magnates (as chief markmen, or otherwise) were acquiring therein, the difference between free and unfree marks almost disappeared, in respect to water rights the same as in other matters. Not only that, but the free associates of the mark were often enough actually no longer in a position to utilize the waters otherwise than for ordinary fishing; they were obliged, if only because of economic conditions, to abandon all other modes of usufruct to the lord of the manor. This condition of affairs received legal recognition, and led to a right of ban over private waters on the part of manorial lords and Territorial rulers that corresponded to the stream regality of the crown. Thus the Middle Ages ended with the law in a condition that was the very opposite of the originally unrestricted right of public user. Had an undisturbed development of the law been possible, there might perhaps have been gradually evolved from the regality of the Territorial princes a regulation of water rights which should once more have given heed to public interests, and thereby increased authority to the old Germanic idea that water is a common property of the folk. Such a result, however, was made impossible by the Reception.

(2) *The Modern Law of Waters.* — The Roman law of waters, which was adapted to the peculiar geographical and economic conditions of Mediterranean lands, could not be accepted unchanged in Germany. But many principles were borrowed

from it that were inconsistent with the native law, particularly the distinction, which was totally different in the Roman and German law, between public and private rivers. The consequence of this was an extremely incoherent and patchy restatement of the modern law of waters, which proved increasingly incapable of satisfying the greatly increased necessities of water traffic that were created by modern industry. The law of waters is another branch of the law which is not regulated by the Civil Code, but is reserved to State legislation (EG, § 65). It is thus that authority has been retained by the modern statutes which have been issued in almost all the States. Nevertheless, it cannot be said that legal uniformity has been realized even within the individual States. In Prussia, especially, there does not exist in a single part of the law of waters, down to the present day, legislation entirely uniform for the whole kingdom. Bavaria, Saxony, Baden, Hesse, and other States, are better situated in this respect. A draft of a general law of waters was, however, presented to the Prussian Diet in December, 1911, and has a prospect of realization.[1] The most important statutes to be considered in this connection are: the Prussian law of February 28th, 1843, regulating the use of private rivers, and that of April 1st, 1879, concerning "stream associations"; the Bavarian Water Act of May 28th, 1852, which has recently been displaced by the Act of March 23rd, 1907; the Saxon statute of August 15th, 1855, supplanted by that of March 12th, 1909; the Württemberg statute of December 1st, 1900; the Baden statute of June 26th, 1899; and the statute of Alsace-Lorraine of July 2nd, 1891.

(A) Public rivers under the Roman law were streams that were never dry; in other words, constantly flowing streams. This conception, inapplicable to German latitudes, was replaced in the common law, in accord with the older German law, by the category of "navigable" rivers, — *i.e.* navigable by ships or rafts ("schiff- und flössbar"). But even these fall within the category of public rivers only in so far as they are navigable, whereas the Roncalian Constitution counted also among them "flumina ex quibus fiunt navigabilia."

For the most part the principle has been recognized that ownership in a public river (that is in the bed covered by it, since the

[1] *Holtz*, "Die Neuordnung des Wasserrechts in Preussen", in "Vorträge und Schriften zur Fortbildung des Rechts und der Juristen", V (1912).

flowing water, which is "res nullius", cannot be the object of rights) belongs to the State. This is the rule of the Prussian "Landrecht",[1] and of the Austrian, Saxon, Bavarian, and French systems. On the other hand, according to other legal systems, and notably the common law, a public river is regarded as ownerless, a "res communis omnium"; and a mere right of sovereignty therein is attributed to the State, corresponding to the old regality. The question was a much disputed one in the common law. Where ownership is in the State, islands that form within the stream naturally belong to it as provided by an imperial doom of 1294: the Prussian "Landrecht" stands alone in refusing to draw this logical consequence of State ownership. However, the difference between the two theories is not important either theoretically or practically. For, as on one hand an extensive public user of public rivers exists even where the State is the owner, so on the other hand a river is not given over to unrestricted public user even where it is regarded as a "res communis omnium", the public user being restricted in many respects in the interest of the State. While unlimited public user exists as regards certain uses and profits, — such as drawing water, bathing, watering animals, swimming, and the gathering of ice, often also the removal of stones, gravel, and shingle, — these being allowed to everybody without question, others, such as navigation and rafting, are subject to the observance of restrictions imposed by police statutes of the State, or else to the payment of taxes imposed by the State by virtue of its sovereign rights, as is the case with fishing rights under State regulations. Finally, particular species of usufruct, more extensive than ordinary rights of public user, may be granted by the State to individuals upon their petition, notwithstanding that the public user is thereby restricted in favor of such grantees. These species of usufruct still constitute in many places the objects of special regalities. So, for example, there still remains a logging regality as respects unrafted logs, a regality of ferriage, a regality of milling, in certain regions also an amber regality (in Pomerania and West Prussia as regards amber found on the seashore and in the sea, in East Prussia also as regards that found on the land). Similar special licenses by the State are also commonly required, in the

[1] Allg. L. R., 14, § 21: "Public and military roads, streams navigable by nature, the sea shore, and harbors, are common property of the State." True, the effect of the expression "common property" ("gemeines Eigentum") is disputed; the Reichgericht has declared against State ownership.

interest of public user, for the erection of permanent irrigation works upon adjacent lands, conduits, hydraulic works, baths, and the like.

(B) In the case of PRIVATE RIVERS the Roman law attributed unrestricted private ownership to adjacent landowners. This principle, however, was applied only to such streams as were dry at times in the summer, so that it scarcely involved any damage to the public interests. In Germany, on the other hand, the principle was maintained that private rivers include all those that are not navigable either for vessels or for rafts. Even when men had become willing to discard the restrictions based on the power of manorial lords and Territorial rulers, it was impossible to apply to such streams the principles of the Roman law (principles, moreover, which were in part much controverted) and treat them like other objects of private ownership. On the contrary it was always recognized, and in many of the more modern Territorial statutes was expressly declared, that such streams should also serve the public, albeit in another and more limited manner than public rivers. The only waters to which this principle was held inapplicable were those surrounded by land individually owned, such as ponds, lakes without outlet, springs, brooks, cisterns, and the like. And even as regards many waters privately owned, such as medicinal springs and drinking waters, a special public protection and official oversight have been introduced into modern legislation, in order to maintain their output for the common good of the State (*cf.* the Prussian "Quellenschutzgesetz" of May 14th, 1908). This idea underlies the exhaustive regulation of the law of springs in the Swiss Civil Code (§§ 704–712).[1] In view of such provisions adopted in the public interest, it may be said that all streams are public, under the present as under the older German law, but some are such in a greater degree than others.[2] As a matter of fact, at least one German State, namely Baden, has followed this view, which excellently expresses the law's historical development and satisfies modern necessities, to its logical consequences. In its excellent Water Act of 1899, all natural waters are declared to be public property; those which are navigable for ships and rafts being the property of the State, and others the property of the communes. The same is true of Austria, of most of the Swiss cantons, and of Italy. On the other

[1] *Fleiner*, "Institutionen des deutschen Verwaltungsrechts" (1911), 300.

[2] *Cosack*, in *Gerber's* "System" (17th ed.), 90.

hand, all waters are regarded as private property in Norway and in Finland. In other Germanic States the rule of the Roman and the common law has for the most part been accepted and maintained: namely, that the riparian landowners along private rivers are owners thereof to the thread of the stream, and therefore also of islands newly formed therein. It is only in the law of the provinces on the French side of the Rhine and in the Saxon law that even private rivers are regarded as ownerless.

The private ownership of riparian landholders, however, secures them no exclusive rights of usufruct. On the contrary certain kinds of user are open to everyone's enjoyment, even in the case of private streams; this is true of bathing, washing, drawing water, watering animals, and at times also of boating and the gathering of ice. Of course, the riparian owners enjoy, in respect to such common user, a natural monopoly, for they do not need to allow third persons access to the shores of which they are the owners. The common user of the stream by those who are not riparian landholders is therefore practicable only where a public road adjoins the river. Moreover, the freedom of user inhering in riparian owners, as such, is also subjected to restrictions imposed by the State in the interest of the public and of other riparian owners. It is an accepted principle that such owners shall use their rights moderately or normally ("pfleglich"); the statutes contain numerous detailed provisions upon this subject. Thus, for example, each adjacent landholder is authorized to use half of the water flowing by his land, but it is made his duty to cause no back water, flood, or marshy overflow; he must return to the river-bed water which he diverts therefrom; he must not permit the entry into the river of certain harmful substances, — on which subject the principles of the Civil Code (§ 906) must now control in cases otherwise doubtful; he may not rob lower riparian owners by diverting water in excessive amount for improvements, but must leave them the full flow to which they are entitled; he must also permit them to make use in certain ways of the banks, as *e.g.* for tow-paths; and he must maintain the bank in proper condition; and so on.

In view of these very diverse rights of usufruct, which may easily give rise to disputes, many modern statutes have provided for the organization of so-called "stream-associations" ("Wassergenossenschaften"), in which all interested landowners are united and compelled to submit to resolutions of the majority. Particularly influential in this field was the Prussian act of April

1st, 1879, which was based upon French models; there are similar statutes in Hesse (1899), Baden (1899), Württemberg (1900), Bavaria (1907), and Saxony (1909).[1] These stream-associations, which connect historically with associations for the watering of meadows that existed under the older law, are either constituted by voluntary contract, — this class alone being recognized to-day in the French and Prussian law, — or, like all those of the Bavarian, Saxon, and Baden law, are "public", that is, compulsorily organized at the instance of the public authorities. All are "real" ("Real"), rather than personal, associations. The public class unite in themselves "the qualities of corporate associations of the public law and those of juristic persons of the private law", while in the voluntary class the former character is lacking.

(II) **The Law of Fisheries.**[2] (1) *The Older Law.* — We have remarked under (I) *supra* that the starting point of the German law of fisheries was the principle that the right to fish belonged to every member of the folk, as regarded the greater streams and lakes, and to every markman as regarded the water-commons of the mark-associations. Fishing in the open sea, of which nothing more need here be said, has always been free, and is so to-day. When a "stream"-regality had developed in navigable waters, the rights of fishery in these, as "banwaters", also became a regality of the crown. The king could either exercise them himself or convey them to the Territorial princes; in later times they were generally regarded as regalities of the Territorial rulers, and in many cases were conveyed by them to manors, cloisters, communes, mills, etc., in return for rents or services. By the acceptance of the Roncalian Constitution this view was very considerably strengthened. At the same time the old principle of free fishery was maintained intact in the case of public waters.[3]

As regards the water-commons of mark-associations, the right of free fishery was maintained much longer than that of free hunting,

[1] *Anschütz*, art. "Wassergenossenschaften" in the H. W. B. der Staatsw., VIII (3d ed., 1911), 615–627; *G. Sehling*, "Die preussischen Wassergenossenschaften, zugleich ein Beitrag zur Lehre von den öffentlichen Genossenschaften", no. 28 (1912) of *Brie* and *Fleischmann's* "Abhandlungen."

[2] *Stoffel*, "Die Fischereiverhältnisse des Bodensees", No. 13 (1906) of Gmür's "Abhandlungen"; *Zollinger*, "Das Wasserrecht der Langeten", No. 17 (1906) of the same series; *Winiker*, "Die Fischereirechte am Vierwaldstättersee", No. 24 (1908) of the same.

[3] Compare the passages from the Ssp. and the Görlitzer "Landrecht" cited on p. 279, *supra*. Also, for example, the franchise granted to Parchim in 1225 by Prince Heinrich Borwin: "pisscatio per omnem provinciam communis et libera est cum sportis et hamis et retibus, exceptis soli sagenis."

since the princes and manorial lords attributed much less value to fisheries than to the chase. But in the case of fisheries, also, legal distinctions were nevertheless introduced, — based upon the different classes of fish or the mode of their capture, — which corresponded to the distinction between noble and ignoble game.

Fishing in ponds, lakes, and in other closed waters of private ownership was always regarded as an exclusively private privilege.[1]

(2) *The Modern Law.* — As a consequence of the reception of the Roman law the law of fishery in *public waters* was not altered, since it made no practical difference whether fishing rights in these should continue to be regarded as a regality or as "property" of the State. In either case, private individuals desirous of exercising rights of fishery in such waters were obliged to have a special governmental license. Wherever free ("wilde") fishery continued to exist, — as for example in the French law, which assured to everyone the right of line fishing in smaller streams and public rivers, or (as respects other modes of fishing) in special districts or particular rivers, — it was abolished by more modern fishing laws (as *e.g.* by the Prussian Act of May 30th, 1874), and conferred in most cases upon the communes.

As regards fishery in *private waters* the principle has become established in modern State legislation that it exists in favor of riparian landholders; and therefore to the thread of the stream when the two shores belong to different persons. Every person who exercises fishing rights must observe in so doing the police regulations prescribed by the State; under many statutes he must also, as in Prussia, give notice to the administrative board that oversees the fisheries, and procure from it a license, which he must always carry with him when fishing. If the independent exercise of fishing rights by riparian landholders appears to be detrimental to an economical utilization of the waters, the State may prescribe, as in Prussia, the organization of "fishery associations" ("Fischereigenossenschaften").

The extent of "fishing" rights has been variously defined. Usually the right to take clams and other aquatic products is unrestricted; but pearl fishing is in various States (Bavaria, Saxony) a regality.

(III) **The Law of Dikes.**[2]—The law must not only provide for the apportionment of usufructuary rights in waters, but also for

[1] Ssp., II, 28, § 1, 2.

[2] *J. Gierke*, "Geschichte des deutschen Deichrechts", I (1901); *Anschütz*, art. "Deichwesen", im H. W. B. der Staatsw., III (3d ed., 1909),

guarding the land against dangers with which they may threaten it. Their user is for the profit of the public, and therefore all persons interested therein should contribute to the charges necessary for their assurance against such dangers. Even in early times German law gave expression to this idea in its regulations of dikes. Forces tending toward associational organization found here a fruitful field of action. The dikes along the sea coast and in the lowlands of the greater rivers were originally constructed by voluntary colonizing associations ("Siedelungsgenossenschaften") as a preliminary to the original settlement of marshy districts, and later by communes, after the settlement of the diked land thus created, for the better security of their economic interests. From the end of the Carolingian period onward, particularly in the 1100 s and 1200 s, there appeared, in addition to the old communal dikes built by associations ("genossenschaftliche Gemeindedeichungen"), others constructed by ecclesiastical and secular lords, churches, cloisters, and cities, usually in connection with great colonizing enterprises, and upon the basis of land grants given for enclosure. But dikes continued to be erected by individual "dike-lords" ("Deichbauherren"), or by free peasant communes, or by "dike-unions" ("Deichverbände"), that had nothing to do with such colonial settlements.

While the oldest dike associations were those of communes, either free or manorial, — that is, of associations that coincided with communes, — this was not true of the "dike-unions", in the narrower sense, that were later most common. Such associations originated, for example, when settlements were made upon lands outside existing dikes, and the old communes united with the new in the erection of a new dike, without any political fusion of the old and the new communes; or when a redistribution of charges was undertaken within the dike association of an existing commune, and these were laid upon some only, and not upon all, of the landowners. The medieval dike unions ("Deichverbände", "Deichachten", "Koogen") were originally associations ("Genossenchaften") in the sense of the older German law but they frequently developed at an early date into corporate associations ("Körperschaften"), and at times assumed the form of communities of collective hand. They may be characterized as "autono-

462–481; *J. Gierke*, "Chrene cruda und Spatenrecht", in Z² R. G., XXVIII (1907), 290–341; "Die Verspatung", in "Festschrift für H. Brunner" (1910), 775–805; "Das Boezemrecht (Busenrecht)", in "Festschrift für O. Gierke" (1911), 1090–1137; *Hermes* (*Holtz*), art. "Deichwesen" in *v. Stengel-Fleischmann's* "Wörterbuch", I (2d ed., 1911), 550–554.

mous compulsory associations of public law, with a territorial basis."[1] In their fully developed form they were "special" communes, communal unions that existed for the particular purpose of dike regulation. They were compulsory associations, because no person settled within the dike could free himself from the burden of its construction or maintenance ("Deichlast"). This burden, however, rested as a public real charge upon the lands involved, — "kein Deich ohne Land, kein Land ohne Deich": no dike without land, no land without dike. It was customary to assign to every associate or more exactly to every piece of land, a section of the common dike ("Pfand", "Kabel", "Los") for maintenance ("Pfanddeichung"). Only extraordinary burdens were charged upon all the members jointly ("Kommuniondeichung"). Whoever failed to discharge his duties in respect to the dike thereby renounced the ownership of his land. This was the "Spatenrecht" ("spade-law") in the "objective" sense: the dike overseer responsible for the execution of the work sank his spade into the section of the dike assigned to the unwilling or incapable associate, — "wer nicht will deichen, muss weichen," "who will not dike must give way to another." On the other hand, a person unable to maintain his assignment could voluntarily renounce both land and dike, and in this manner withdraw from the dike association. This was "Spatenrecht" in the "subjective" sense: he himself sank the spade into the dike in a particularly prescribed manner reminiscent of the old Salic Chrencruda.

The organ of the dike association as such was a general assembly of the members. Its administrative business was conducted by special dike officials known as "dikegraves", who were aided by special judges, juries, and subordinate officials.

After the close of the Middle Ages the organization of the dikes was fundamentally altered. The dike associations fell under the police power and oversight of the Territorial rulers and their administrative boards, which gradually claimed a right to regulate and oversee them and to name their officials. In this manner the dike associations lost their autonomy, and their legal status as juristic persons under the private law; the ownership of the dikes themselves was attributed to the State, and later there was also attributed to it a special dike regality. Thus, in the course of the 1600 s and 1700 s, the dike associations were transformed from self-governing bodies into State institutions ("Staatsanstalten")

[1] *Anschütz*, article just cited, 463.

for the apportionment of maintenance charges ("Lastenverteilungssozietäten").[1]

In the 1800s there became manifest a reversal of tendencies that could be called a "regeneration of the associational idea."[2] This found particular expression in the Prussian Dike Acts of January 28th, 1848, and April 11th, 1872. As a result of this change the care of the dikes has again been entrusted to self-governing dike unions, subject of course to public statutes, and under the oversight of the State; the details of such associations being regulated by State statutes of a common type.

In other German States also (Hesse, Oldenburg, Anhalt, Bremen, Hamburg) statutes exist regulating the dike administration. Where this is not the case, those general rules of law apply which regulate protection against flood ("Wasserschutz").

Closely associated with the dikes there frequently existed from the earliest times, drains and sluices; their maintenance was charged upon an association of the landholders whose land they drained. Such associations ("Sielachten"), which were particularly numerous along the North Sea, occurred, and still occur, in connection with dike associations, but also independently. They are always regulated similarly to the dike associations, and in their case also the duty of maintenance rests upon the lands included in the union.

§ 41. **Restrictions originating in Regalities of the Law of Mines and Salterns.** (I) **Mining Law.**[3] (1) *History.* (A) THE MINING REGALITY. — The right of mining was originally included, like

[1] *Anschütz*, article just cited, 466. [2] *Ibid.*, 467.

[3] *Achenbach*, "Das gemeine deutsche Bergrecht", I (1871); *Arndt*, "Zur Geschichte und Theorie des Bergregals und der Bergbaufreiheit" (1879); *Ermisch*, "Das sächsische Bergrecht des Mittelalters" (1887); *Opet*, "Das Gewerkschaftsrecht nach den deutschen Bergrechtsquellen des Mittelalters", in Z. Bergr., XXXIV (1893), 218 *et seq.*; *Zycha*, "Das Recht des ältesten deutschen Bergbaus" (1899); "Das böhmische Bergrecht des Mittelalters auf Grundlage des Bergrechts von Iglau" (2 vols., 1900); *Bernhard*, "Die Entstehung und Entwicklung der Gedingeordnungen im deutschen Bergrecht", XX, 7 (1902) of *Schmoller's* "Forschungen"; *Arndt*, "Noch einmal der Sachsenspiegel und das Bergregal", in Z². R. G., XXIII (1902), 112–122; "Einige Bemerkungen zur Geschichte des Bergregals", same, XXIV (1903), 59–110; *Zycha*, "Über den Ursprung der deutschen Bergbaufreiheit und deren Verhältnis zum Regal", in same, 338–347; *Arndt*, "Zur Frage des Bergregals, Eine Replik", in same, 465–475; *Sehling*, "Die Rechtsverhältnisse an den der Verfügung des Grundeigentümers nicht entzogenen Mineralien" (1904); *Zycha*, "Zur neuesten Literatur über die Wirtschafts- und Rechtsgeschichte des deutschen Bergbaus", Vj. Soz. W. G., V (1907), 238–292, VI (1908), 85–133; "Über die Geltung des Berg- und Salzregals in Mecklenburg, Gutachten den Grossherzoglichen Ministerien der Justiz und des Inneren erstattet von der Juristen-Fakultät der Universität Rostock", in Meckl. Z. Rp. Rw., XXVI (1908), 165–191; *Westhoff*, "Geschichte des deutschen

the other rights we have considered above, in the private ownership of land, although in periods of primitive culture landowners were as yet incapable of utilizing this privilege. The mark-associations did not devote themselves to mining, nor is there any evidence of small free-landowners who devoted themselves to such enterprises. On the contrary, after the destruction during the age of the migrations of the mines that dated from the Roman period, the conditions necessary for such undertakings were first realized, to any considerable extent, under the manorial administration, and by the union of stronger economic forces which it made possible. At the end of the Carolingian period and in the centuries following, exploitation began of the great mining districts in the Alps (in Tyrol, Salzburg, and Switzerland), in Swabia and Franconia, in Bohemia, in the Harz mountains, in Saxony, and in Silesia; and all these mines passed into the ownership, either of the royal treasury, or of ecclesiastical and secular landlords. In this oldest period none but purely private enterprises existed. The metals, and therefore also their extraction, were regarded as appurtenances of landed ownership, like the ordinary usufruct of the soil for agricultural purposes; the landlord merely paid a rent in metal (a tithe) to the king, and this royalty might be in turn alienated by the crown. We are probably justified in regarding this tribute as historically connected with the mining tax of the Roman law, which, — in accord, on this point, with the original Germanic view, — recognized no other holder of mining privileges than the landowner, and no other fiscal right of the crown in the mine than the tithe.

In the 1000 s and 1100 s, however, there was developed out of this bare right of tribute, — which might be designated as the first and oldest form in the evolution of the mining regality, — a practice of the crown of conveying mining rights to landowners, which practice was justified by the king's claim of title to particular minerals. This was the second form of the mining regality. Thenceforth mineral deposits were classed as "iuris imperii", in the sense that their enjoyment was dependent upon the consent of the crown. This consent, however, was given only to him who could formerly have exercised mining privileges without it: the

Bergrechts", ed. by *Schlüter*, in Z. Bergr., L (1909); 27 *et seq.*, 230 *et seq.*, 357 *et seq.*, 492 *et seq.*, LI (1910); 93 *et seq.*, 217 *et seq.*; *Zycha*, rat. "Bergbau", "Bergbautechnik und Betriebsgeschichte", "Bergrecht", in *Hoop's* "Reallexikon", I (1912), 248–254, 256–259; *Silberschmidt*, "Die Entwicklung der Gewerkschaft", in Z. Hnls. R., LXXI (3d ser., XII, 1912), 193–266.

landowner.[1] In this way there was developed for the first time a regality in the strict sense. As Zycha remarks, the main cause of this change may have been the fact that the land-lords early endeavored to free themselves from the payment of the mining tithe, and for this purpose turned to the crown, which, in the privileges it granted them, assured them the entire produce of the mines, including the tithes. There resulted from this an idea that the king had full power to dispose of unmined metals; an idea which it was also attempted to support by citations from Roman legal sources. Like other regalities, that of mining soon passed into the hands of the Territorial princes, who thenceforth conveyed to landholders the right of mining upon land they owned or held as tenants, just as the king had formerly granted them these rights directly. Upon their own domains, the Territorial rulers sometimes prosecuted mining on their own account.

In the hands of the Territorial rulers the mining regality received in the course of the 1200s a great extension of content, thereby entering its third stage of development. It was now transformed from a right to the substance of all precious metals into a general right of sovereignty over the mining industry, which was subjected to public regulation as respected the mode of exploitation, its legal basis, and its product. The mining industry thus became actually separated from the ownership of land, after having already become legally dissociated therefrom in consequence of the requirement of the issuance of mining licenses by the lord who held the regality. Mineral deposits were thenceforth granted to their discoverer to this extent, that the Territorial rulers permitted anyone to open and exploit mines, under their oversight, even upon the land of others. The regality was thenceforth generally exercised in this form, as a license to prospectors ("Finder-Beleihung"), both by the king and the Territorial princes. The Golden Bull granted it in general terms to the Electoral Princes. The struggle for the mining regality was thus finally decided in favor of the Territorial rulers; the Peace of Westphalia made an end of the Empire's claim to the regality even in theory. From that time onward it was treated by the common law as included in the sovereignty of the individual States. It extended from the beginning to all metals, whereas the Roncalian Constitution, issued for Italy, mentioned only silver pits ("argentariae").[2] With respect to other metallic products no rules were established

[1] *Zycha*, "Recht des ältesten Bergbaus", 31.
[2] *Cf.* No. 2, p. 269 *supra*.

in the common law; although in many places, collieries (which we first hear of in connection with Wurmrevier, near Aachen, in the 1300 s) seem to have been subject to the regality from the beginning. (As to salt deposits compare (II) *infra*.)

With this third form of the regality there was very closely associated the origin of so-called "free" mining.

(B) FREE MINING ("Bergbaufreiheit"). We have seen that down into the 1200 s the landowner alone was privileged to open mines upon his land; it was only necessary that he should secure from the lord who held the regality the grant of an express authority to do this. If a stranger to the land wished to mine he was obliged to secure the permission of the landowner, who retained a "stewardship" ("Vogtei") over the enterprise, and as the holder thereof issued regulations, exercised a general oversight, collected produce, and exercised rights of judicature over the miners. In this form we still find mining rights associated with the ownership of land in the Sachsenspiegel.[1] A tendency had already set in, however, which carried the development further. It was associated with the customs of manorial mining concessions ("Bergfreiungen"). With the great increase in mineral production that took place at the end of the 1100 s, it became more and more usual for the landowner in whose soil it was conjectured metals might be found to grant to all experts who wished to try their fortune the right of opening prospect-pits (grants of "Schurf und Bau") within a certain area — hence called a "gefreiter Berg", a "free" or "franchised" mountain, in return for a definite share of the output.[2] What was thus originally permitted voluntarily in isolated cases, soon became a general right; the idea that mining should be free upon the land of others, which had thus made its appearance in such "free" or open-mining districts, was applied to "unfree" soil, and thus special and local mining concessions ("Bergfreiungen") were transformed into a general privilege of free mining ("Bergbaufreiheit"). The interests of the miners worked in the same direction, for after the exhaustion of open districts they were obliged to seek employment elsewhere; and the like was true of the interests of the Territorial rulers as holders of the mining regality, since to them the utmost increase of the mining industry was desirable for financial

[1] Ssp., I. 35, § 2. *Cf. Edgar Schmidt*, "Die Stellung des Sachsenspiegels zum Bergregal" (Breslau dissertation, 1910).

[2] [All the mines were in the mountainous regions, whence the German terminology. Ed.]

reasons. As a result of these changes the regality came to be exploited in the manner above indicated: the Territorial rulers granted the right of mining directly to those who petitioned it, without the intervention of the landowner, placing the prosecution of the industry under their own oversight, and collecting royalties upon the output. The "stewardship" of the landowner became thenceforth of negligible importance; he retained only the right to a certain fraction of the product, and at times, as in Bohemia and Moravia, a share in the royalties collected by the State. The principle of free mining was first fully developed in the oldest mining law of Freiberg, of the early 1300s.[1]

(C) Modes of exploitation.—The original form of working mines was seigniorial ("herrschaftlich"). The land-lords, the king, the ecclesiastical and secular landed magnates, worked their mines either independently by their unfree dependents under the oversight of special household servitors ("Ministerialen"), or leased them in return for money rents or other dues. This seigniorial form of exploitation was later displaced, however, by co-operative ("genossenschaftlich") working. This was the outcome wherever a community of laborers originally unfree gradually acquired rights of possession and exploitation in scattered lodes by associational union, thereby exchanging a purely personal relationship to the mine-owner for a material connection with the mine. Under some circumstances the same thing happened suddenly, as *e.g.* where the working of the mine was entrusted by contract to a gang of miners newly arrived in the district. The material basis of the associations formed in this manner was ordinarily a single shaft. All the members were actual miners ("Gewerken"); and no longer unfree, but free, laborers. In the beginning they were theoretically entirely equal among themselves. Soon, however, a technical and social classification became evident among them. Labor and contributions of capital were distinguished. The beginning was marked by so-called "cost contracts" of the associates, who were originally all manual laborers; only a portion continued to work, while another part, by assuming the obligation of a regular money contribution (known as "Kost"), furnished the capital indispensable in a more developed stage of mining. Again, it often happened that certain portions of a mine were leased by the "Gewerken" to poor laborers known as pitmen ("Lohnhauer") in exchange for a share of the product ("Lehnschaften", "holdings"). It

[1] *v. Inama-Sternegg*, "Wirtschaftsgeschichte", III. 2 (1901), 150.

also happened that leases were made to capitalists, who, in exchange for a certain sum of money, received the right to settle and work with hired laborers, and to appropriate to themselves either the whole or part of the produce. Once these legal institutes were developed, a distinction was made between the whole body of those employed in the mine, — the so-called "mine-commune" ("Berggemeinde"), — and the narrower group of the "Gewerkschaften" or "Gewerken",— within the entire body. Those persons were regarded as members of the latter who possessed a mining-share ("Bergteil"). There was here no question, however, of a physical share, but (doubtless from the beginning) only of a freely alienable and heritable ideal share-right, corresponding to the modern "Kuxen." The right of the "Gewerken" in the mine was an ownership in collective hand; but even the oldest associations of workmen-shareholders ("Gewerkschaften" in the old sense) already possessed a definite organization in their assemblies, so that their development into corporate associations was easily possible. The labor associations ("Arbeitsgenossenschaften") of the mining law were thus transformed in the course of the 1200s and 1300s into capitalistic associations ("Gewerkschaften" in the new sense). This development was furthered by costly tunnel-mining (so-called "Erbstollen"), which demanded large capital, as well as by the growing practice of leasing large pitfields in place of the former practice of letting single shafts, with consequently increasing efficiency of exploitation. It was completed toward the end of the 1400s in the so-called job contracts ("Gedingeverträge"), which originated in Saxony and displaced the old "Kostverträge", "Lehnschaften", and "Teilmieten." The first exhaustive provisions of these "Gedinge", — the labor contracts between the individual miners and the "Gewerkschaft", — are contained in the mining ordinance of Schneeberg of 1479, which was preceded by various other ordinances. Beginning with the ordinance of Annaberg of 1509 there became established in such contracts an invariable form which continued to prevail in Germany for three centuries following, and the principles of which remained, for the most part, in force until supplanted by the Prussian mining laws of 1860 and 1865. These "Gedinge"-ordinances regulated the normal labor contract of the mining law as a piece-work contract; they sought to assure a just protection to the interest of the laborers by precise provisions concerning the form and substance of the contract, the coöperation of the mine officials in its conclusion, and the giving out of the work. In this process a great mass of ordinary manual wage-earners appeared beside the "Gewerken", and the transformation of the "Gewerkschaften" into capitalistic associations was completed.

(D) The Shareholders'-unions ("Gewerkschaften") of the older law. — The "Gewerkschaft", as it existed from the 1400s down to the middle of the 1800s, was already a form of union very nearly related to the modern share company. According to the better view it possessed the qualities of a corporate association; only the Prussian law treated it as a mere co-ownership. In mining operations in which a relatively large number of persons (namely, more than eight) were concerned, it was obligatory to form a "Gewerkschaft"; whereas, when the number was less than eight, and either all or part of these carried on the mine themselves, it was possible to adopt the form of an ordinary partnership. When a "Gewerkschaft" was established the shareholders ("Gewerken") were bound in the first place to meet the expenses of the opening and installation of the mine. For this purpose the mine was divided into a definite number of ideal share-rights ("Kuxe"), — according to the older usage one hundred and twenty-eight, — which were then taken by the "Gewerken", although one might be interested to the extent of a larger, and another to the extent of a smaller, number. In proportion to the number of shares so acquired by him, each associate shared in the expenses of operation, made contributions while the mine gave no returns, and shared in profits as soon as such were realized. These "Kuxe", which, as ideal capital-shares ("Wertanteile") in the property of the mining union, corresponded exactly to modern commercial shares ("Aktien"), and which, like the latter, assured to the "Gewerken" not a direct common control of the mine but only a relative share in its associational control, were treated as immovables, which could be divided, alienated, and pledged by their owners. They were registered in a mine-book ("Bergbuch") similar to a general land register; alienations and pledges were realized by transfers and entries in the transfer book ("Gegenbuch", "Berggegenbuch"). Actions of partition were impossible. The general organ of the union was the shareholders' ("Gewerken")-assembly. Outwardly, the union was represented by a miners'-committee ("Grubenvorstand") or a special representative. Quite commonly such an agent was at the same time known as the lessee ("Lehnsträger") of the mine, to whom the State granted rights of judicature over the mining district.

(2) *The Modern Law.*—(A) MODERN MINING LEGISLATION.—The mining law in the form developed in earlier centuries proved to be inadequately adapted to the enormous development which the mining industry experienced in the 1800s. The principle of "free" mining, in the sense above explained, compelled the State to grant the right of mining to every solicitant who satisfied certain general and definite requirements. But it did not hinder the State from making exceptions to those conditions, especially so-called "district" concessions ("Distriktsverleihungen") by which the mining regality of a large district was granted to particularly favored persons ("Standesherren"), who thereby acquired in such districts the exclusive privilege of mining. The Territorial rulers, moreover, were not bound to respect, as regarded the mines worked directly for their own fisc, the conditions that had been developed in favor of free mining. Moreover, the management of the mining regality had finally resulted in an almost exclusive control of the mining industry by public officials; the shareholders' unions had nothing left to do beyond administering the physical property of the mine. "This system of official mining with foreign capital ("Direktionsprinzip") was perhaps developed in its purest form in the rules of the Prussian Territorial Law."[1] The high taxation of the mines was a considerable impediment to free exploitation (the Prussian "Landrecht" still maintained the fiscal share at one-tenth of the gross output).

The production of the mines, which especially in the case of coal and iron increased in undreamed-of measure, needed, as contrasted with this system, self-government, free competition, and unrestricted speculation.[2] Following the example of French legislation (statutes of 1791 and 1810) all the German States introduced regulations of the mining law upon an entirely new basis. Oppressive taxes were moderated or wholly done away with (in Prussia by the Act of July 14th, 1893); the control of exploitation was put in the hands of the mine owners (in Prussia by Acts of 1841 and 1860); and almost everywhere the mining regality was abolished,—although subject to the maintenance of a supreme control of mining by the State ("Berghoheit") which is exercised through special administrative officers. This last was accomplished for all the Prussian States by a general Mining Act of July 24th, 1865. This statute, which was later introduced into the territories shortly thereafter added to Prussia, and into Waldeck,

[1] *Gierke*, "Genossenschaftsrecht", I, 975.
[2] *Dernburg*, "Bürgerliches Recht", III, § 141.

and which has been supplemented and amended by a series of emendatory acts (among others by those of 1873, 1892, and 1905, as well as by the Prussian ordinance of 1899 promulgating the new imperial Civil Code) has attained an epoch-making importance. Most of the other German States have followed Prussia in their mining legislation and have copied it: Brunswick 1867, Saxe-Meiningen 1868, Saxe-Coburg-Gotha 1868, Bavaria 1869, Reuss j. L. 1870, Altenburg 1872, Alsace-Lorraine 1873, Württemberg 1874, Anhalt 1875, Hessia 1876, Baden 1890, Birkenfeld 1891, Schwarzburg 1894, Lübeck 1895; the Saxon law of 1868 also follows it in essentials. Thus the Prussian Act of 1865 is the basis of a general law of mines which, in essentials, prevails throughout Germany, notwithstanding that this branch of the law has been reserved to State legislation (EG, § 67). It is true that in very recent years a momentous reversal of tendencies has appeared. In order to hinder the unrestricted exploitation by private enterprise, and especially by powerful partnerships, of mineral resources indispensable to the public, particularly coal and salt, some States (notably Prussia, but also among others Hamburg) have returned to the principle of the old regality, — see the Prussian Act of June 18th, 1907, and the Hamburg Act of June 25th, 1906.

(B) Leading principles of the present mining law. — (*a*) "*License*" ("verleihbare") *Minerals.* — The laws of the different States upon this subject provide in detail which minerals are withheld from the landowner and reserved to exploitation under the mining law. Ordinarily these are the most important metals; that is, — in addition to gold and silver, — iron, zinc, lead, copper, and manganese; also pit coal, lignite (not, however, in the kingdom of Saxony, nor in the Prussian territories formerly belonging to the kingdom of Saxony) and graphite; also, in many cases, petroleum and naphtha; finally rock salt and salt-wells (as to which compare (II) *infra*). On the other hand, precious stones, saltpetre, gypsum, marble, granite, and other stones, were ordinarily left to the landowner. The former class of "license" or "concession" ("verleihbare") minerals were not allowed to be dug or prepared for the market otherwise than subject to the mining laws. The license for this purpose can only be secured by concession of the State. Thanks to its sovereignty over mining, therefore, the State creates all concrete mining rights.[1] This right is not exactly ownership in the minerals while yet unbroken,

[1] *Crome*, "Bürgerliches Recht", III, 445.

nor in their deposits, notwithstanding that in many statutes use is made of the expression "mining properties." On the contrary it is a usufructuary right: the exclusive authority to appropriate the minerals that may be found in a certain piece of land. This usufructuary right, however, does not substantially restrict the rights of landed ownership, because the authority to utilize for mining purposes the space beneath the surface of the earth is not included within ownership of the surface as such. The landowner must, therefore, himself procure a license for mining in case he desires to prosecute it upon his land; and for the same reason the wrongful removal by third persons of minerals that have not yet been mined is neither larceny nor embezzlement, but an independent delict, namely a trespass upon a licensed right of occupancy.

(*b*) *Right to Prospect* ("Schürfrecht"). Unless "concession" minerals have been accidentally discovered, the first step toward exercising a mining right is the opening of so-called "Schürfe" (costean pits), — that is, a systematic search for mineral. The landowner himself has authority to prospect without going further. But third persons may prospect upon the land of others, although only with the consent of the landowner or by authority of a license issued by the Mining Board. This permission may be denied only for definite statutory reasons, namely, only when the place in question is one where such prospecting is prohibited, or when decisive reasons of public interest are opposed. Aside from such cases there is therefore unrestricted freedom of prospecting. Damages must, however, be given to the landowner, and ordinarily in advance; and he may demand security. He may also appeal to the courts against a resolution of the Mining Board by which a right of prospecting has been granted, and equally as regards the amount of damages awarded him. This state of the law, theretofore existing, was altered, as regarded certain minerals, by an amendment of 1907 to the Prussian Mining Law. According to it the right to search for pit-coal (save in the provinces of East Prussia, Brandenburg, Pomerania, and Schleswig-Holstein), rock salt, salts of potassium, magnesium, borate, along with other salts and salt springs occurring in conjunction with the foregoing, belongs to the State alone throughout the kingdom. As regards these minerals, prospecting is therefore permitted only to the State or to persons whom it specially empowers. For, under the statute, the right to search for and to procure the salt may, and that to search for and procure coal must, be conveyed to individuals; except that certain fields of pit-coal are reserved to the State.

(c) *The Claim* ("Mutung"). — If a prospector has discovered mineral, he must present to the Mining Board a written petition that the right may be granted to him to take the mineral from a certain district ("Felde"). This petition is known as a "Mutung" (a warning notice). Of several claims for one and the same mineral in the same field the earliest in date takes precedence; on the other hand, the rights of one who has discovered the mineral before such claimants take precedence of all their claims, — he enjoys "das Alter im Felde" ("seniority in the field"), — provided he presents his own claim within a short time after his discovery. This is true, however, in case of an *accidental* find of mineral, only as regards the owner of the land, or another person who accidentally finds one "concession" mineral in a mine he is working for another mineral: all other persons must have prospected under official license in order to enjoy precedence upon the basis solely of a prior discovery.

(d) *The Lease* ("Verleihung", grant). — After the formal claim there follows the grant or concession by the Mining Board of the ownership of the minerals within the mine ("Bergwerkseigentum"), which is accomplished by the delivery of a documentary grant. This creates in the grantees an exclusive right to mine the minerals so conveyed within a claim of definitely indicated extent and form. It is "an extended right in the nature of real property" ("ein ausgedehntes Immobiliarrecht"),[1] which, like every other right in land, may be registered in the land-book, and requires such registry in order to be of full effect against third persons. This entry is made upon a separate sheet of the land-book; either on motion of the Mining Board after the grant, or at the instance of the grantee, who may be called upon by the Board to take the necessary steps in the matter. The Mining Board is obliged to make such concessions as are petitioned for whenever the statutory requirements are satisfied. But the claimant has no right of action against them to compel a grant.

(e) *Rights and Duties of Mine Owners.* — Mining rights are treated by the statute as immovable property. They are alienable and heritable like the ownership of land; therefore a person entitled to such rights can convey them by real agreement ("Auflassung") and registry in the land-book; he can also charge them, and (particularly) mortgage them.

[1] *Crome*, "Bürgerliches Recht", III, 449.

A person may exercise his mining rights in such manner as he may desire. However, the Mining Board, by virtue of the State's sovereignty over mines, exercises a supervisory police power. Therefore a plan of exploitation must be submitted to it for approval. In the main, mines are worked underground; the mine owner may, however, demand that the landowner permit him, in return for compensation, to make use also of the surface, in so far as this may be necessary for proper exploitation; and in case of disagreements the Mining Board decides between them. Under such circumstances the mine worker receives, therefore, either a servitude (*e.g.* one of way) or a superficies (perpetual building right). When the user of the surface continues for a long time the landowner may demand that the mine owner, instead of a bare usufruct, shall acquire the ownership of the land. The mine owner can also acquire similar rights of usufruct in lands outside his mining claim. For the working of a mine underground no damages can be demanded by the landowner, because he himself has no right (since the earlier share-rights of the landowner have been done away with) to the exploitation of minerals found beneath his land. The person entitled to mining rights is bound to give damages only for what are known as "Bergschäden"; that is, trespasses which injure the landowner in those uses which he is legally entitled to make of his land. Heritable adit privileges ("Erbstollengerechtigkeiten") have no longer been granted since the statute of 1865.

(*f*) *The Modern Mining Company* ("Gewerkschaft"). — The act of 1865 gave a new form to the mining company. This was chiefly because the right which every shareholder ("Gewerke") formerly possessed to pledge his share deprived the company itself of the possibility of making an independent pledge of the entire mine, in order to procure the credit desirable for an increase of production.[1] The association in its new form is, however, as contrasted with the older law, only a secondary form. When the shareholders are numerous other forms of union may be chosen as desired, — the society ("societas") of the Roman law, the partnership of the Germanic private law, the share company, or the limited partnership of the commercial law, or others; and, on the other hand, when they are few in number, a "Gewerkschaft" may be formed, — under the Prussian law two, under the Saxon three, persons suffice for its formation. The status of a juristic person has been clearly and explicitly attributed to the

[1] *Dernburg, op. cit.*, § 152.

modern mining company. The mining property therefore belongs to it, as a person, and not to the individual members of the union. It is most nearly related to the share company of the commercial law ("Aktiengesellschaft"). Like the "Aktie", the "Kux" is a document that represents a right of membership; both are rights in the nature of movable property ("Mobiliarrecht"), — and no longer (as once) shares in immovable property which were therefore themselves immovable. Under the private law of to-day the "Kux" is no longer a thing ("Sache"), not even a movable thing, as it still was under the Prussian Mining Act. In Prussia also the earlier conception of the mining law has accordingly been altered by the Prussian ordinance promulgating the imperial Civil Code: it is no longer said of such shares that they have the qualities of movable things, but that they belong among movable property. The "Kux" is distinguished from the "Aktie" by the fact that it always purports to be personal, and never bearer, paper; and that it has no fixed face value, but purports to convey only a certain quotal share, — the number of such shares being no longer, as formerly, one hundred and twenty-eight, but one hundred or one thousand. The "Kux" is freely alienable (its conveyance requires a transfer in the share register, "Gewerkenbuch") and is also freely pledgeable. But "the pledge of the 'Kux' no longer has anything to do with the pledge of the mine; the latter requires an act of the union, the former is the act of the individual shareholder and affects only his right of membership. Accordingly, the rights of mortgagees of the mine take precedence of the rights of pledgees of the 'Kux.'"[1] As a further distinction between "Kux" and "Aktie" the older legal rule has been maintained that the members of the company are not freed from obligation so soon as they have paid the subscriptions for which they have made themselves responsible, as are the shareholders of the "Aktiengesellschaft", but are liable for supplementary levies ("Zubussen") so long as the exploitation of the mine requires these. The organization of the company has remained, generally speaking, that of the earlier law; its organs are the shareholders' meeting, and a board of directors or other representative.

(*g*) *The Legal Status of the Miners.* — In earlier times ordinances issued by the State regulated, in the most important points, the legal relation between the miners as wage earners and the "Gewerken" as "entrepreneurs"; but the legislation of the mid-1800 s

[1] *Crome, op. cit.*, 460.

adopted the principle of contractual freedom, refraining from all provisions of that nature, and "introduced for the mine owners full control of their mines and unrestricted management in their exploitation." [1] Especially was this true of the Prussian statutes of 1860 and 1865. In more recent years, however, a series of compulsory regulations have been issued, — partly in the form of imperial law in the Industrial Code and its amendments, and partly as State law, — concerning labor contracts between mine owners and their employees regarding wages and notices of quitting, the regulation of work, and other matters. In Prussia the amendments of June 24th, 1892, and of July 14th, 1905, to the Mining Act are particularly to be considered, — prohibition against mine operating abuses ("Wagennullens"), etc. The miners, who became united in local organizations at an early period, are obliged to-day to join the miners' unions ("Knappschaftsverein"). These are usually juristic persons, and are included, as such, under the modern system of industrial insurance.

(II) **Law of Salterns.**[2] — This portion of the law has developed similarly in many respects, and differently in many others, from the mining law. Here also the right of the landowner to the products of his own land was the starting point of development; here also it was upon the manors that great works were developed (such as Reichenhall), already in the Carolingian period, to meet the demand for salt. In addition to such seigniorial workings there were early developed, as in the case of mines, associational types of exploitation. These were particularly complicated, for from the beginning a great number of persons were interested in the salterns, or possessed of rights in their produce. Beside the land-lord, who remained the owner of the salt spring, there were other landed magnates (cloisters and secular lords) who had acquired ownership in the salt-cotes or boiling houses; further, the salters themselves, who had rights in the basins either as lessees or as owners, and, finally, third persons possessing rights to demand salt that was obtained, that is, customers of the saltern. In the second half of the Middle Ages the "panners", the persons who controlled the salt basins, succeeded in acquiring a dominant position in the associations that were formed of all these interested persons. In the course of this development the "panners",

[1] *Dernburg, op. cit.*, § 154.

[2] *v. Inama-Sternegg*, "Zur Verfassungsgeschichte der deutschen Salinen im Mittelalter" (1879); *Burmester*, "Der staatliche Salzgewinnungsvorbehalt im gegenwärtigen deutschen Gesamtrechtssystem", in Arch. öff. R., XXIII (1908), 71–122, 209–241.

exactly as in the case of the "Gewerken" of the mining law, developed from laborers originally generally unfree into capitalist salters, whose rights passed by inheritance as property, and who left to ordinary laborers the technical labor of the boiling; and the associations of salters ("Pfännerschaften") acquired the character of capitalistic unions. They were corporately organized; their shares, ordinarily one hundred and eleven in number, and which corresponded to the "Kuxe", were called "pans" ("Pfannen"). In addition to these salters'-associations there were also individual lords who were the owners of salterns and were known as "Salzherren", "Salzbeerbte", and "Salzjunker." In the meanwhile, as in the case of the mining regality, a salt regality had developed, which, like the former, passed to the Territorial rulers, and this led in their hands to a comprehensive public oversight of the salt industry, and also (herein differing from the mining law) to a State monopoly of the salt trade. This monopoly was abolished by an imperial statute of October 12th, 1867. Wherever a salt regality became established, — which, according to the best opinion, was probably as generally true as in the case of the mining regality, — there also developed in the salt wells the principle of free mining ("Bergbaufreiheit"). This was true of the Prussian law until the amendatory statute of 1907 above referred to, by which the old system was abolished. Since then, prospecting for rock salt, for potash, magnesium, and for borates, as well as other salts occurring in the same deposits and for salt wells, has no longer been free to everyone, but only to the State and to persons by it empowered. In many of the States a regality was maintained in the sense that the mining of salt is permitted to the State alone (as in Saxony, Bavaria, and Baden, among others); in other States it has been reserved to the landowners (as in Hannover), and this has not been altered by the act of 1907.

§ 42. **Restrictions upon Alienation due to Co-rights of Relatives** ("gebundene Güter"). — (I). **Rights in Expectancy and of Co-alienation.**[1] — (1) *Rights in Expectancy* ("Wartrechte"). — The most important restriction to which an owner's dispositive power over his property was subjected resulted from the collec-

[1] *Fipper*, "Das Beispruchsrecht nach altsächsischem Recht", no. 3 (1879) of *Gierke's* "Untersuchungen"; *Adler*, "Über das Erbenwartrecht nach den ältesten bairischen Rechtsquellen", no. 37 (1891) of the same; *Brunner*, "Beiträge zur Geschichte des germanischen Wartrechts", in the "Berliner Festgabe für Dernburg" (1900); *Ficker*, "Untersuchungen zur Erbenfolge", V. 1 (1902), 164 *et seq.; Frh. v. Freytagh-Loringhoven*, "Beispruchsrecht und Erbenhaftung", in Z². R. G., XXVIII (1907), 69-102.

tive rights which once existed, both in land and in movables, in favor of household communities and (in still earlier times) of the sibs. The collective right of the members of the household, — who with reference to all household property constituted a community of collective hand, — made it impossible for the head of the community, the house-lord ("Hausherr"), to dispose of the collective estate by his individual act. Gradually, however, his position became a freer one, and at least a limited dispositive power was in time conceded him. On the other hand he continued to be bound by so-called rights in expectancy.[1] A right in expectancy in its oldest form, as it appears in a great number of Germanic legal systems, permitted a decedent to dispose freely of only a certain part of his property, the free portion ("Freiteil"; "Freiteilsrechte", — legal systems of this class). On the other hand he could not deprive of the remaining portion the heirs who were entitled to expect it. Such rights were usually attributed only to sons, but at times, in the absence of such, also to daughters; in other words, to the members of the household community in its narrowest form. In order, however, to make use of his power over the free portion, the decedent was originally bound to have made a partition of the remainder among his sons; only in time was this requirement allowed to lapse, — a capitulary of Louis the Pious abolished it for all the folk-laws of the Frankish Empire.[2] The amount of the free-portion, which he was free to dispose of either entirely as he pleased or, in the earlier period, at least to churches and cloisters for the good of his soul ("Seelgabe"), was variously fixed in different legal systems. Some of them measured the free-portion by "head-rights", with reference to the number of heirs entitled to rights in expectancy ("Kopfteilsrechte", — "per capita systems"); so that, for example "the father who had only one son could dispose of one half, if he had two sons of one third, and if nine sons of one tenth, of his property."[3] This was true of the Lombard and Bavarian law, probably of the Alamannic and Thuringian, and also of many

[1] *Ficker* regards the right in expectancy ("Wartrecht") as having been introduced only later in place of an original freedom in dispositive powers, because it is impossible, in view of the great diversity of its later development, to ascribe to the right in expectancy a common or primitive Germanic character; but this conclusion must be a "petitio principii" for any one who does not accept his highly artificial theory — which is certainly wholly devoid of convincing proof — of the interrelations and derivations of the various Germanic legal systems.

[2] Cap. legib. ad. 818–819, C. 9 (M. G., Cap., I, 282).

[3] *Brunner*, essay just cited, 5.

Swedish as well as of the Danish systems. Other legal systems, on the other hand, made the free portion a fixed fraction, — a half, a third, a fifth, or a tenth, — of the property, or of certain goods; the number of those possessed of expectant rights being disregarded. This was the rule of the law of the Salic Franks and of the Frisians, also of the West Gauls and Burgundians ("Freiteilsrechte", with fixed quotas). The purpose of the right in expectancy in this oldest form was, therefore, on one hand to prevent a decedent from harming the next heirs by any disposition of the heritage, and on the other hand to make possible at least a limited dispositive power upon his part. As may readily be understood, the Church, in particular, sought to support the latter.

(2) *Rights of Co-alienation* ("Beispruchsrechte"). — A more modern form of restriction imposed by blood relationships upon dispositive powers was the so-called "Beispruchsrecht." This, unlike the older right in expectancy, which was one of substance, was a formal right of coöperation in dispositive acts, and according to Brunner's supposition [1] it probably goes back to the ownership that once existed in the sibs, instead of originating, like rights in expectancy, in a collective ownership by the members of a household. It was particularly developed in the Saxon law. In the "Lex Saxonum" we already find it expressed with the utmost clearness; [2] in the age of the Law Books it was still full of vitality; [3] and rights of free portion were finally merged in it. It applied to lands only, not to movables. It existed in favor of the next heir only, not in favor of other relatives; the former, however, enjoyed it even though he stood in no community of collective hand ("Gemeinderverhältnis") with the alienor, and equally without regard to the question whether or not he was damaged by the disposition in question. It applied, moreover, only to alienations inter vivos and charges; and not, as did rights in expectancy, to gifts inter vivos and mortis causa. In consequence of this right of co-alienation the validity of a conveyance was dependent upon the consent of the next heir ("Erbenlaub"), and the effect of such assent was to bind him in nowise to impeach the transaction so approved.

Only in this way could an alienation be made unimpeachable. In default of the assent of the heir he might, within a year and

[1] *Brunner*, "Grundzüge" (5th ed.), 240.
[2] "Lex Saxonum", CC. 62–64.
[3] Ssp., I, 52, § 1; Goslar "Statut.", (S) 26, (Z) 37–42 (Kraut, § 70, n. 13).

day, impeach the conveyance as void. His right of action was based on the idea that in consequence of the invalid alienation the land became his property at the instant of such alienation, precisely as if the alienor had died; wherefore he could demand its redelivery even from third persons. In other words, he possessed a *real* right in expectancy ("dingliches Anwartschaftsrecht"), which was transformed by the unlawful alienation into ownership; or, in the sense of the medieval sources, into an ideal seisin in the nature of a herital seisin ("Erbengewere").

(3) *Weaker Forms.* — The idea embodied in rights in expectancy and co-alienation, — namely, that property, and especially landed property, upon which depended the legal status of a family, must if possible be preserved to it intact, — gradually became less prominent. It was always inconsistent with one of the leading principles of the Germanic law of inheritance, for this recognized no right of primogeniture, nor any other rule of single succession to the inheritance, but divided this among heirs of like degree (§ 105 *infra*). The danger here involved was of course one that did not affect the many estates subjected to tenurial relations ("Leiherechte"); and communities of collective hand, and coheir communities continued beyond the death of the heritor (*supra*, pp. 139 *et seq.*), were also able to maintain themselves against it through many generations. It was by no means everywhere, however, that such community relationships either persisted or were organized. And, aside from this consideration, the interest of landowners in possessing unlimited dispositive power over their property, which grew with the rising commercial value of land, demanded increasing recognition, and broke down more and more the old restrictions. In the systems of town law it was only inherited lands ("Erbgut"), — that is, land whose ownership was acquired by inheritance, — that remained, generally speaking, subject to rights of co-alienation; whereas lands acquired by purchase ("Kaufgut", "Gewinnland") were subject to the free disposition of their owner. But although in some cities (Lüneburg, Stade, Bremen, Hamburg, Lübeck) a special law long existed for such herital lands, the principles regulating their disposition were by no means uniform. Neither their definition and extent nor the number of heirs entitled to claims thereon, was uniformly regulated. The heirs sometimes possessed a revocatory right in the sense of the older right of co-alienation, and sometimes a mere right of preëmption ("Vorkaufs-", "Näherrecht", — *infra*, § 55). In the Hansa cities the conception of

herital-lands was totally transformed in the course of the 1500 s: the owner acquiring full dispositive powers "inter vivos", although obliged to leave to the next heirs the undiminished and total value of his immovable and movable property; the right of the heirs being thus transformed into a limitation upon testamentary disposition and a peculiar right of obligatory portions ("Pflichtteile").

In all other regions the right of co-alienation was regularly weakened in the same manner into a right of preëmption. Indeed, many legal systems, possibly under the influence of the Roman law, went so far as to give the owner a right to deal with his property with entire freedom. In the regions of the Swiss law, for example, certain metaphors were common to the effect that "one might tie his property to the tail of a dog", or "hang it on a wild horse", or "throw it in the brook."

§ 43. **Same. — (II) Entailed Family-estates of the Greater Nobility.**[1] — The old idea of a "family" estate ("Familiengut") retained vitality only among the different classes of the nobility. To some extent it assumed new legal forms. The nobles recognized the danger to their position of social and political power which was threatened, particularly from the second half of the 1200s onward, by the partitions of family possessions that were occurring in enormous number under the Germanic law of inheritance. It was to meet this danger that the many contractual co-heir communities were established of which we have already spoken (*supra*, pp. 142 *et seq.*). But "the tendencies of legal development ran increasingly from a community to an individual basis."[2] It was recognized that only the development of a fixed law of primogeniture could arrest the partition of family estates.

Such a fundamental change in the traditional law, involving a restraint upon landed ownership, only the greater nobles were able to attain in full degree, and the imperial knightage in lesser measure. By virtue of the autonomy that had been preserved to them, the greater nobility created for themselves, either through dynastic statutes ("Hausgesetze") or by way of customary practice, a special law for the entailed

[1] *Zimmerle*, "Das deutsche Stammgutssystem" (1887); *H. Schultze*, "Erb- und Familienrecht der deutschen Dynastien des Mittelalters" (1871); *Frommhold*, "Zur Lehre vom Stammgut, Familienfideikomiss und Familien-Vorkaufsrecht", in "Festschrift für O. Gierke" (1911), 59–88, and supplement in Z². R. G., XXXII (1911), 337.

[2] *Rosin*, essay cited below in *Ihering's* J. B., XXXII (1893), 336.

estates of their class which was governed by identical rules and was everywhere recognized; so that what had formerly been recognized in the case of all land now constituted an exceptional law for them alone.[1] This restraint upon landed ownership affected only entailed estates ("Stammgütter"; "bona aviatica", "stemmatica"); side by side with which, of course, there might, and very frequently did, exist free allodial property. "Stammgüter" are family holdings inherited from ancient times, the legal qualities of which can be given to newly acquired land only by express dedication, unless the estate has already been in the family for two generations. Such entailed estates are inalienable. They are inherited agnatically, and since singular succession has been generally introduced they remain undivided, in accordance with the system of primogeniture. No disposition whatever can be made of them which affects their substance, or involves their renunciation, or changes the order of inheritance, without the consent of all agnates. In case of unauthorized conveyances, the alienor forfeits his rights exactly as under the old law of co-alienation, and the members of the family who are entitled to rights in expectancy (not merely the next heir) can immediately demand from any third person the land so alienated, by means of a revocatory action ("Revokationsklage").

The question, who should be regarded as the owner of entailed property, considering this as a distinct estate ("Sondervermögen"), has been much debated. The view accepted by the majority of Germanists, and defended in particular by Beseler[2] and Gierke,[3] is that the family of the greater nobility constitutes a corporate association with its own legal personality, and, as such, is the owner of the property of the house. The head of the house at any moment enjoys, therefore, merely an irrevocable individual ("Sonder-") right of possession, management, and usufruct; while the agnates, as members of the "Körperschaft", also possess irrevocable individual rights, in the form of rents or appanages ("Apanagen", "Paragien"), to a share in the enjoyment of the property. Such an artificial theory (which Stobbe, Heusler, Cosack, and others have rejected) seems, however, unnecessary. Neither is it permissible to draw from such expressions as "house-property", "property of the royal house",

[1] *Cosack* in *Gerber's* "System" (17th ed.), 135.

[2] "Die Familie des hohen Adels als corporative Genossenschaft", in *Grünhut's* Z. Priv. Öff. R., V (1878), 540-556.

[3] "Die juristische Persönlichkeit des hochadligen Hauses", in same, 557 *et seq.*

and the like, the conclusion that the house is an independent holder of rights; the unlimited partnership, for example, also possesses its own estate without being a juristic person.[1] Nor does the fact that the houses of the greater nobility have created autonomously their special law of entailed and household ("Stamm- und Haus- ") estates lead to this conclusion (*supra*, pp. 97 *et seq.*); for it makes no difference whether the qualified character (" Gebundenheit ") of the estates rests upon autonomy, — *i.e.* upon private enactment, — or upon consensual agreements (*infra*, § 44). On the contrary, it is more in accord with the principle of restrictability which is essential to the Germanic conception of ownership (*supra*, pp. 259 *et seq.*) to attribute to the head of the house the ownership of the family estate; although, indeed, an ownership restricted by the special end to which the family estate is appointed, and by the real rights in expectancy held by the agnate members.[2]

§ 44. **Same. — (III) Family Trust-entails** (" fideicommissa ").[3] — (1) *History.* — The lower nobility was unable to secure for itself the power of private enactment which enabled the

[1] *Cosack* in *Gerber's* "System" (17th ed.), 136.

[2] *Rehm*, "Die juristische Persönlichkeit der standesherrlichen Familie, Denkschrift im Auftrage des Vereins der deutschen Standesherren verfasst", no. XI (1911) of the Sch. Wis. Ges. Strassburg, also rejects the theory of Gierke and Beseler as respects the older period; but he contends that in the 1800 s there was developed in legal practice and by the application to the high noble house of constitutional conceptions of the State, a common law of status for princely houses to the effect that such a family of noble status ("standesherrliche Familie") is as such a juristic person, to which belongs, in the absence of other provisions, the family property ("Hausvermögen"). A number of recent dynastic statutes ("Hausgesetze") have in fact laid down express provisions to this effect. Whether the analogy with the State is decisive in other respects, and whether from such expressions as the family-head "represents" the dynasty, he "exercises" its property rights, etc. a conclusion can soundly be drawn that the dynasty possesses legal personality, still appears doubtful. But at any rate Rehm shows that the course of development in modern times has been toward the development of the juristic personality of such families, which finds expression in dynastic statutes, in the legislations of the different States, and in the decisions of the courts.

[3] *Rosin*, "Beiträge zum Recht der revokatorischen Klage bei Familienfideikommissen und hochadeligen Hausgütern", in *Ihering's* J. B., XXXII (1893), 333–469; *v. Reibnitz*, "Familienfideikommisse, ihre wirtschaftlichen, sozialen und politischen Wirkungen" (1908); *Gierke*, art. "Geschichte und Recht der Fideikommisse", in H. W. B. der Staatsw., III (3d ed., 1909), 104–116; *Conrad*, art. "Die volkswirtschaftliche und sozialpolitische Bedeutung der Fideikommisse", in same, 116–124; *Krause*, "Die Familien-Fideikommisse von wirtschaftlichen, legislatorischen, geschichtlichen und politischen Gesichtspunkten" (1909); *Sautier*, "Die Familienfideikommisse der Stadt und Republik Luzern", no. 39 (1909) of *Gmür's* "Abhandlungen"; *Kunsemüller*, "Zur Entstehung der westfälischen Fideikommisse" (1909); *Ramdohr*, "Das Familienfideikommiss im Gebiet des preussischen allgemeinen Landrechts" (1909); *Beyerle*, "Ein Beitrag zum deutschen Fideikommissrecht", in *Ihering's* J. B., LVIII (1911), 1–100; *Martin Wolff*, art. "Fideikommisse", in *v. Stengel*-

greater nobility, by the end of the 1300s, to subject family estates to statutory restrictions; but they endeavored to accomplish the same ends by means of consensual agreement and entails ("Stammgutsstiftungen"). Such entails, which appeared sporadically in Germany from the 1000s onward (there are evidences of them among the Anglo-Saxons even in the 700s), and whose purpose was to keep lands inalienable in the male line of the first acquirer, first became widespread in the 1500s, and especially so following the Thirty Years' War. By that time they were recognized as the most effective means of guarding the maintenance of the "splendor familiæ" against the dangerous principles of the Roman law of inheritance. The example of the Spanish majorate, with which men became acquainted in this same period, was also of some influence; it was imitated as a foreign fashion.[1] Inasmuch, however, as the lower nobility could not rely upon autonomy, or a private nobiliary law created with its aid, these entails could be made secure only by bringing them within one of the categories of the Roman law. It is remarkable that in Germany, as elsewhere, following the example of the Spaniards and Italians, an entail theory was now quite generally adopted by jurists schooled in the Roman system, the basis of which was the Roman "fideicommissum quod familiæ relinquitur", notwithstanding that this was a totally different institute, superficially combined with certain ideas of the feudal law, particularly that of a "successio ex pacto et providentia maiorum." The work of Phillipp Knipschild, syndic of Essling: "Tractatus de fideicommissis familiarum nobilium" ("von Stammgütern" — 1654), was epoch-making in this connection, determining the entire theory down into modern times. In this form, as developed by the jurists of the 1600s (whence it is known as "Juristenrecht", *supra*, p. 31), the institute of family "fideicommissa" passed over into the common law. It was adopted also in the legislation of the different States, although these generally regulated it in closer conformity with the Germanic law; this was true of the Bavarian and of the Prussian "Landrecht", and the Austrian and Baden codes.

Owing to political and economic causes the institute encountered in the modern period violent opposition. Repeatedly it seemed

Fleischmann's "Wörterbuch", I (2d. ed., 1911), 780–783; *Noack*, "Zur Entstehung des Adelsfideikommisses in Unteritalien, Eine sozialgeschichtliche Untersuchung", I, no. 113 (1911) of *Brentano* and *Lotz's* "Studien."

[1] *Cosack* in *Gerber's* "System" (17th ed.), 138.

destined, in Germany as elsewhere, to complete decay. In the regions to the west of the Rhine it completely disappeared during the supremacy of the French law, after having been earlier abolished in France by a Revolutionary statute of 1792 and later by the Code Civil. The French example was soon followed in some other German States, *e.g.* in Bavaria in 1808. However, the older law was everywhere reëstablished in the first period of reaction following 1815; in the Rhineland by a cabinet order of February 25th, 1826. On the other hand, the institute was attacked with augmented violence in the course of the movement of 1848, and some States actually abolished it in toto, in accord with the principle of the "German fundamental rights" ("Grundrechte"); most notably Prussia, by Art. 40 of its constitution. The reaction that soon set in anew made it impossible to carry into effect these provisions, and they were in turn repealed by special statutes (in Prussia by one of July 5th, 1852). Thus, with the sole exceptions of the Bavarian Palatinate, Alsace-Lorraine, Oldenburg, and Frankfort o. M., the institute has everywhere been preserved down to the present time; indeed, in very recent years it has been applied to an extent extraordinarily increased as compared with earlier periods, despite the considerable economic losses resulting therefrom (particularly the displacement of small peasant holdings), which become ever more disastrously apparent.[1] The Civil Code, in codifying the German law, not only abstained from creating a systematic law of fideicommissa, but did not even touch the institute. On the contrary it declares that the provisions of State law concerning family fideicommissa and entailed estates shall remain unaffected by the Code (EG, § 59). Since the enactment of the Civil Code, however, the law of "fideicommissa" has been subjected to revision in different States; most thoroughly in Saxony by an Act concerning family rights in expectancy of July 7th, 1900, and in Mecklenburg by ordinances promulgating the imperial judicature acts and the Civil Code. In Prussia, however, the intention of "unifying" and "reforming" the hitherto patchy system of the law has not yet been realized; a project of a comprehensive statute upon the subject was submitted to the Diet in 1903, but was afterward withdrawn.[2] In

[1] Compare on this, for example, *Max Weber*, "Agrarstatistische und sozialpolitische Betrachtungen zur Fideikommissfrage in Preussen", in Arch. Soz. W. Soz. P., XIX (new ser. I, 1904), 503–574; *L. Brentano*, "Familienfideikommisse und ihre Wirkungen" (1911).

[2] *Cf. Martin Wolff*, "Die Neugestaltung des Familienfideikommissrechts in Preussen" (1904).

Saxe-Coburg-Gotha the creation of new family fideicommissa and, in the main, the extension of existing ones, was prohibited by the statute promulgating the Civil Code. The Swiss Civil Code has prohibited their creation, but has permitted entails to meet the expenses of the education, establishment (dowries, etc.), or maintenance of family members, or for other similar purposes (§ 335).

(2) *Legal Principles.*—(A) CREATION OF FIDEICOMMISSA. — A fideicommissum is created by a declaration of the donor's will given either inter vivos or mortis causa. This declaration is required at least to be written; and wherever there exists a system of land registry, — that is, at the present day, everywhere in Germany, — it acquires effect against third persons only by entry in the Land Book. By provisions of State law, official coöperation is frequently required; not merely a judicial publication or confirmation, but also the assent of the State government. This is true in Prussia, for example, in the case of fideicommissa yielding a net income in excess of 30,000 marks, and in Mecklenburg in the case of all family fideicommissa whatever. Although the fideicommissum originated as an institute of the nobiliary law, modern statutes have generally authorized their creation by any person. In the Bavarian law alone the fideicommissum is still a privilege of the nobles, since according to it fideicommissa can only be created by nobles and for the benefit of noble families. The last is also true in Baden under the sixth constitutional edict of 1807.[1]

(B) THE OBJECT OF A FIDEICOMMISSUM can only be a permanent and profit-yielding thing, — in other words, lands and, according to the law in some States, capital secured by lands; also, according to many others, other corporeal collective-things, such as jewels, art collections, and libraries. Generally, a definite minimum value is necessary; in Prussia, for example, a net income in the case of landed estates of at least 7,500 marks, and in the case of pecuniary fideicommissa a capital investment of at least 30,000 marks.

(C) OWNERSHIP AND REAL RIGHTS OF HOLDERS OF FUTURE INTERESTS ("Anwärter"). — According to the theory of fideicommissa in the common law, the temporary possessor of the estate is regarded as its owner, herein agreeing with the theory of entailed and house-estates of the greater nobility; although he is bound by the real rights of those entitled in expectancy ("Anwärter") as well

[1] *Dorner* and *Seng*, "Badisches Landesprivatrecht" (1906), 407.

as by the special end to which the estate was appointed. The regional systems, on the other hand, generally adopted another viewpoint. Some of them assumed a collective ownership of the occupant and the holders of future interests; others, notably the Prussian and the Austrian, ascribed to the occupant a usufructuary or "subordinate" ("Unter-") ownership, and to the family, as such, a "superior" ownership. But these are theories which, where they are not expressly recognized by statute, may be disregarded, for it is inconsistent with the Germanic law to recognize either the family, whether of the greater nobility or any other, as a corporate association. The temporary occupant has the right to possession, management, and usufruct under every legal system. The other members of the family have an irrevocable real right in expectancy, which is manifested particularly in a power of oversight, and of coöperation in certain juristic acts, and also in certain privileges of individual usufruct, such as redemptions ("Abfindungen"), maintenance, and rents.

(D) Alienation and charging. — The qualified character of an estate subject to a fideicommissum consists, primarily, in its inalienability. A conveyance by the occupant is null. Exactly as under the old law of co-alienation and entailed estates, he thereby forfeits his own right; the holder of the next future estate is immediately entitled to bring an action to revoke the conveyance. And although the prevailing practice of the common law gives him this right only in cases of dynastic succession ("Sukzessionsfall"), this must, as explained by Rosin, be regarded as incorrect.

Not only the conveyance but also the charging of the substance of an estate subject to a fideicommissum is invalid. This invalidity, however, can ordinarily be established by a holder of a future interest only when his right to possession has accrued.

Whoever assents to alienations or charges thereby loses his right to void them. But according to the common law such consent binds only the person consenting, not his heirs, unless they be allodial heirs of the occupant of the fideicommissum. On the other hand, the regional legal systems recognize conveyances and charges made with the assent of the family. In Prussia an effective declaration of the family will is made in a family-council ("Familienschluss") which constitutes the organ of the holders of future interests as an associational group. (Statutes of February 13th and March 5th, 1855.) Some legal systems demand also the consent of a curator, and confirmation by a court or by the State government.

Under all legal systems certain charges are permitted as so-called fideicommissum debts; they are treated after the analogy of feudal obligations ("Lehnsschulden"; *infra,* § 48). It is only as to these that successors are bound; but in doubtful cases only with the fruits of the estate, — whence the possibility of so-called income-hypothecs.

(E) SUCCESSION UNDER FIDEICOMMISSA. — A fideicommissum is inherited according to the principles of law which regulate special succession in a "universitas iuris" ("Vermögensinbegriff"). "Each holder of a future estate succeeds according to the principle of a 'successio ex pacto et providentia maiorum' under a right conferred upon him directly by the donor, and entirely independently of his predecessor in the possession."[1] The right of one who holds a future estate is never forfeited by an act of his ancestors, nor affected by their incapacity. The descendants of the last occupant may charge themselves with the fideicommissum, unlike the rule of feudal succession (*infra,* § 48), and reject an allodial heritage. In doubtful cases (*i.e.* in the absence of specific rules) legitimate descent from the body of the first acquirer of the estate, male sex, and inclusion in the agnatic line are preconditions of capacity to inherit. The donor can, however, establish any other rules at will; for example, nobility, ancestral nobility, or a qualified ancestral nobility (qualified, that is, according to the provisions of the entail, "stiftsmässig"),[2] or descent from an equal marriage. He may even omit the requirement of male sex. The order of succession may itself be variously appointed (*infra,* § 115).

(F) TERMINATION. — A fideicommissum is terminated, aside from the destruction of its object, if the family entitled to it becomes extinct. The qualified character of the estate then ceases, "ipso facto"; it becomes the allodial ("free") property of the heirs of the last possessor. The donor, however, may himself have provided for such a contingency, and, in particular, may have provided for some particular cognatic succession to be observed after the extinction of the male line. According to most of the regional legal systems, although not according to the com-

[1] *Gierke,* art. cited just above, 111.

[2] *Rauch,* "Stiftsmässigkeit und Stiftsfähigkeit in ihrer begrifflichen Abgrenzung, Ein Rechtsgutachten, zugleich ein Beitrag zur Geschichte des deutschen Adelsrechts", in "Festschrift für H. Brunner" (1911), 737–760; *Schreuer,* "Stiftsmässigkeit und Stiftsfähigkeit", in Arch. B. R., XXXVII (1912), 1–77; *Frh. v. Dungern,* "Zur Frage der Stiftsfähigkeit", in Z. Priv. öff. R., XXXIX (1912), 227–248.

mon law, the alienation of particular parts of the fideicommissum, as well as the destruction of the whole, is possible in other ways: according to the Prussian law in family council; and, elsewhere, also by concurrent declaration of the existing members of the family, with the assent of a curator and subject to confirmation in court or by the government. Finally, any particular fideicommissum, or the entire institute, can of course be abolished by statute.

CHAPTER VII

THE LAW OF LAND (*Concluded*)

PART III. REAL RIGHTS

TOPIC 1. TENURIAL RIGHTS ("Leiherechte")

§ 45. **Peasant Tenures** ("bäuerliche Leihen").[1] (I) **Tenures ("Leihen") in general.** — It was characteristic, above all other things, of the medieval law of land that numerous and exceedingly various tenurial rights existed side by side with ownership. They originated in the Frankish period, and their growth was coincident with the rise of great seigniorial estates, as a result of which possessory relations of land, which must be assumed to have been originally uniform, were more and more altered. Undoubtedly a considerable part of the forms of landed tenure of the late Roman law was borrowed in this process. But not only were these much altered, but all landed tenure acquired a far greater importance than it had possessed in antiquity. The economic and social, indeed the entire political life of the early Middle Ages, was legally embodied in relations of landed tenure. These relations finally led, through a feudalization of constitutional law, to a complete disintegration of the State; but, on the other hand, their wide prevalence was followed by highly beneficial consequences of an economic and social nature. It was they which made it possible "for new strata of the population to attain a share, guaranteed by law, in the produce of the national industry; that is, above all, in the possession of land."[2] And thus they led to a "division of ground rents" which made impossible the appearance of "that contrast between latifundia and pauperism" which was so fateful through a long part of antiquity.[3]

Although sprung from a common root and dominated by the same ideas, tenurial relationships acquired, in the course of their

[1] *v. Schwind*, "Zur Entstehungsgeschichte der freien Erbleihen in den Rheingegenden und in den Gebieten der nördlichen deutschen Kolonisation", no. 25 (1890) of *Gierke's* "Untersuchungen"; *Wittich*, "Die Grundherrschaft in Nordwestdeutschland" (1896); *Brunner*, "Der Leihezwang in der deutschen Agrargeschichte" (address, 1897); *Rittschel*, "Die Entstehung der freien Erbleihe," in Z². R. G., XXII (1901), 181–244; *Th. Knapp*, "Gesammelte Beiträge zur Rechts- und Wirtschaftsgeschichte vornehmlich des deutschen Bauernstandes" (1902); *Seeliger*, "Die soziale und politische Bedeutung der Grundherrschaft im früheren Mittelalter, Untersuchungen über Hofrecht, Immunität und Landleihen", K. Sächs. Gesell. Wiss., "Abhandlungen", XXII. (1903); *Wopfner*, "Beiträge zur Geschichte der freien bäuerlichen Erbleihe Deutschtirols im Mittelalter", no. 67 (1903) of *Gierke's* "Untersuchungen"; "Freie und unfreie Leihen im späteren Mittelalter", in Vj. Soz. W. G., III (1905), 1–20, IV (1906), 190–194; *Opitz*, "Die Arten des Rustikalbesitzes und die Laudemien und Markgroschen in Schlesien", no. 73 (1904) of *Gierke's* "Untersuchungen"; *Hartmann*, "Bemerkungen zur italienischen und fränkischen Prekarie", in Vj. Soz. W. G., IV (1906), 340–348.

[2] *Franken*, "Privatrecht", 168.

[3] *Brunner*, "Geschichte," I (2d ed.), 303.

development, a varying meaning in the case of different classes of the population. As peasant tenures, urban building-tenures, and feudal fiefs, they were shaped into special legal institutes. These three types of tenure we will now consider separately, beginning with rural (" ländliche ") tenure and its development into peasant tenure.

(II) **Tenancies at Will and Benefices. Tenures of Higher and Lower Orders.** (1) *Precarious Tenures.* — The development of the medieval law of landed tenure (" Bodenleihe ") north of the Alps was evidently associated with the " precarium " of the Roman law, which existed in Gaul from the earliest times side by side with the heritable lease and leases on shares, and which had been specially developed by the Church. It is true that in this process the precarium suffered changes " which approached a complete transformation of its legal nature ",[1] and assimilated it in substance to the usufruct of the late Roman imperial legislation (Leo, Justinian). The Roman " precarium " was originally a tenancy at the will of the lord which conferred upon the tenant neither a real nor a contractual right. It was, however, always possible, — and in later times became the rule, — to make the tenancy from the beginning one for a definite period. Indeed, it was customary, following the analogy of the Roman lease for years, to make it for a " lustrum " (five years). True, the lessor was not thereby bound for that term; but since, as a matter of fact, he did not often exercise his right of revocation, but on the contrary often renewed the lease at the expiration of the term, it became a practice of the customary law that the " precario habens " possessed a right of usufruct during the period so set, in return for which he gave to the " precario dans " a certain rent or service, and which he forfeited by a failure to render such dues. It was an old Roman custom that the " precario habens " should petition in writing permission to occupy the land. This petition (" epistola precaria ", " precaturia ", in Italy later known as a " libellus ") acquired in time the character of an acknowledgment of possession. In the case of precaria granted for a certain time and irrevocable during such period, there appeared along with it a document which was prepared by the lessor such as was customary in ordinary leases. In this document the lessor formally assured the tenant in his rights; it also was known as " precaria ", but often, as distinguished from the former documents, " præstaria ", " epistola præstaturia ", " commendatitia."

[1] *Brunner*, "Geschichte", I (2d ed.), 289.

Inasmuch as decisive importance was laid, in the Frankish Empire, upon the visible fact that a petition was employed, it was possible to regard as precaria all those leases in which such a document was made use of. A precarium was thenceforth any tenancy which resulted from a petition. There were thus included under this elastic category leaseholds of very different nature. There were revocable precaria, — tenancies at will; precaria granted for a definite period, — the life of the tenant, or for several lives (usually three, — those of the tenant, his sons, and grandchildren); and heritable precaria. The corresponding dues imposed upon the tenant were also various; they might be money rents or rents in kind, tithes, or plow-work ("Fronden") and other services. Under some circumstances rents were very low and intended only to give expression to the claims of the lord as owner ("Rekognitionszinse", nominal rents); also there might be lacking any counter payment whatever. The estates which were thus let in tenancy might of course be of very different extent; also, they might retain an independent character, or they might be a part of the economic system of a manor. In the latter case the tenurial relation affected, sooner or later, the personal position of the tenant (*infra,* (III)). In many cases, especially in the case of such tenancies as were created by ecclesiastical foundations ("Anstalten"), lands were involved which before the creation of the tenancy had been the property of the tenant: he made a gift of the land to the church, reserving to himself at the same time a usufruct for life; by means of a reconveyance the donor acquired a tenancy for life in the land, the ownership whereof had passed, by the gift, to the Church. As distinguished from these juristic acts which have been known since Albrecht's time as "precariæ oblatæ", there was involved in so-called "precariæ datæ" a simple lease of land that had not before been included in the property of the tenant. When a person gave his land to the Church in order to receive it back immediately along with other lands or to receive in return other lands alone, as a leasehold estate, the tenancy was known as a "precaria remuneratoria"; which resulted, therefore, from a combination of "precaria oblata" and "precaria data."[1] "Precariæ datæ" became less prominent in time, owing to the efforts of the Church; this seems to be the explanation of the fact that in the 800 s the expression "precaria" became restricted to "precariæ oblatæ" and "remuneratoriæ." Thenceforth the

[1] *Brunner,* "Geschichte", I (2d ed.), 307.

precarium was simply a tenancy that resulted from a gift of land on the part of the lessor in connection with a precedent gift of land on the part of the tenant. At the same time a petition ceased to be an essential element of a precarium.

(2) *Benefices.*[1] — In the Frankish period the precarium leasehold was designated, in accord with the usual terminology of the late Roman period, the "beneficium" of the lessor; and this word was used, the same as the word "precaria", to designate both the relation of tenancy and the land held in tenancy. "Beneficium" and "precaria" were therefore, originally, expressions of identical meaning; although the word "beneficium" had from the beginning a wider application. It was not merely employed to designate all tenancies, including those which were not precarious, but was extended also beyond the field of leaseholds generally, and could, for example, be employed to designate the transfer of ownership in land: notably, the land grants of the Frankish kings were included under the category of the "beneficium." For, although a restricted ownership was created by them in the donee so long as only *crown* land was involved, the donee, from the time that the Frankish rulers began to lease confiscated *church* lands to magnates of the kingdom for military purposes, acquired what was essentially a right of tenancy, because of the inalienability which was a fundamental quality of lands belonging to the church. Such gifts of ecclesiastical lands, made by Charles Martel and his successors, were originally known as "precariæ verbo regis", "verbo dominico." The later and more limited conception of the precarium could not be applied to such grants, because these never followed a precedent gift or service on the part of the tenant.

In time, however, even the wide meaning of the word "beneficium" was also narrowed. Men began to distinguish classes of higher and lower tenure, with reference to the purpose of the tenancy and the nature of the services imposed upon the tenant. Only those which, in consequence of the greater extent of the land held in tenancy, involved no economic dependence of the tenant upon a seigniorial demesne, — even though they might be charged with rents in favor of such, — and particularly those which from the end of the Frankish period permitted or required military service from the liegeman ("vassal tenures"), were thenceforth

[1] *K. Lehmann*, art. "Beneficium" in *Hoop's* "Reallexikon", I, 245. Compare also *Dopsch*, "Die Wirtschaftsentwicklung der Karolingerzeit", I (1912), 205 *et seq.*

regarded as "beneficia." With these there were contrasted, as "lower" tenures, those which obligated villeins ("Hintersassen") to labor services upon the demesne and to the payment of rents and tributes of a rustic ("bäuerliche") character.

(III) **Free and Unfree Tenures.** — We have already adverted to the fact that lands given in tenancy were sometimes drawn within the economic system of a manor, and sometimes not. The former class constituted, along with the demesne, a solidary complex of estates ("Gutsverband"); for such manorial villeins ("Hufenbauer") the lord's demesne ("Fronhof") was the centre of economic and social life. Over them stood a bailiff or other manorial official ("Fronhofsbeamte"); they were all united in an association, the legal incidents of which were determined by manorial law. Those holdings ("Leihegüter"), on the other hand, which were not thus drawn within the manorial system, stood in no intimate relation with a lord's demesne, notwithstanding that the tenants thereof might render rents to a land-lord ("Leiheherr"), or even be obligated also to render labor services upon his land. In particular, such tenants were in nowise dependent upon a lord or his officials. Foremost among tenures of this second class were the precaria. They were free tenancies; and this for the reason that the lessor ("Leiheherr") and tenant were regarded, as respects the relation of tenancy between them, as parties equal in rights and subjected in common to the general law of the land, such tenancies being included within the jurisdiction of the county ("Grafen-") court. The personal status of the tenants remained unimportant in this connection; even those personally unfree could receive precaria and be settled under free tenancies upon the land. Compared with these those other tenures by which land subject to the direct usufruct of the lord (the demesne) was let to villeins ("Hintersassen") were unfree tenures, for they were subject to the manorial law, that is to the law of tenancies within the manor that was administered in the manorial court of the landlord (*supra*, p. 4). Here too the personal status of the tenant was not at first regarded, for the manorial law was originally no law of status for manorial serfs ("Hofhörige"). In consequence, however, of the tendency of the law, already referred to, to assimilate even personal relations to things, there took place at the height of the Middle Ages a projection of villeinage upon such dependent tenements. The consequence of this was that thenceforth every person who acquired lands within the manor ordinarily became thereby a serf ("Höriger ") of the land-lord, and also became subject to the manorial law. And therefore manorial tenures finally came to be unfree not only because they were subject to the jurisdiction of the manorial court and not to that of the ordinary courts of the land, but also because they usually involved, although not always, the unfreedom of the tenant, — his personal dependence, and his dependence in private law. In the earlier part of the Middle Ages it was customary, upon the greater manors, to group together a number of dependent virgates (" Hufen ") as an economic unit (" Villikation ", villa) and place them under a special manorial official, the " villicus " or bailiff (" Meier ", " maior "), who was charged with their administration. Later it was not uncommon for the bailiff to lease the entire villa from the lord.

(IV) **Leaseholds for Years and of Inheritance.** — Most manorial tenements were let, from the beginning, to serfs or unfree persons who lacked the right of free domicile, being bound to the glebe. The practice therefore naturally became established, as to such tenements, that the lords, — who as knights felt a pressing necessity for the labor of villeins, — should grant vacant peasant holdings to the able-bodied descendants of the dead tenants. This practice gradually found legal recognition, at least under the manorial law; and there thus originated a legal claim on the part of the tenant to the inheritance of such manorial lands.

Even earlier, before unfree tenancies, generally speaking, acquired a heritable character, this was acquired by the free tenements. These free leaseholds of inheritance, such as attained widespread occurrence from the 1100 s onward in rural regions and especially in the cities, and which greatly checked the growth of manorial tenures, originated in the Frankish precaria, — that is, in tenancies which had been free from the beginning, — and not in earlier manorial tenancies. The precaria were for the most part leaseholds for life (" Vitalleihen "); but at an early date they showed a tendency to become heritable. In the case of " precariæ oblatæ ", which were by far the most numerous, it was customary for the donor, for example, to reserve a usufruct not only to himself but also to his wife, and even more frequently to his children. If in such cases the second or even the third generation were made grantees along with the donor, it was a natural step, upon the death of the lessee, to grant the escheated lands to his next heir; and, still later, to extend the tenancy from the beginning to the next heir, and finally to all the heirs in perpetuity, of the tenant. These heritable tenancies, developed from the precarium, served as models for the free leaseholds of inheritance that were newly introduced in the 1100 s and 1200 s. Their extension to rural districts was favored by various circumstances.

Just as it was earlier customary to make leases of freshly cleared woodlands in return for a heritable rent, in order to have them cleared (" Waldhufen ", assart-virgate), so a free tenancy of inheritance, — known as " Gründerleihe ", " colonial-tenure ", — was the favored form in which the colonization of Eastern Germany was realized. The German colonists were granted heritable holdings as freemen by the founders of marks or villages, and, aside from a nominal rent paid to the owner of the land (*i.e.* to the Territorial princes or to ecclesiastical or secular magnates) in recognition of their title, were subject only to public taxes and services which left entirely unaffected their personal status. The favorable situation of these colonists in Eastern Germany reacted in turn upon the position of the peasant population in the older parts of Germany, and caused a recedence of manorial types of tenancy. To this end the decay of the manorial organization also contributed. It is true, however, that heritable leaseholds did not everywhere take the place at once of the older free tenancies; for example, this was not the case in Northwestern Germany.

In Lower Saxony the manorial lords broke up the villas (" Villikationen ") upon their manors, because, with agriculture becoming increasingly productive while the old manorial charges remained unaltered, they were advantageous only to the peasants, and no longer sufficiently so to the lords. The villeins of the manorial demesnes were therefore freed; a number, usually four, of the older virgates (" Lathufen ") were united into a larger peasant holding; and this was then leased to one of the four tenants, while the three others either remained upon the land as cottagers or cotters (" Köter ", " Kossäte ") upon little house-plots, or emigrated to the cities or to regions under colonization. Such peasants, who were thus provided with new and larger holdings, received them in the beginning as leaseholds for years after the manner of the tenancies that had formerly been customary with the bailiff-lessee of the manor (" zu Meierrecht "). Along with a betterment in the personal position of the tenant at law, there was therefore here involved a weakening of the real right.

There were thus developed in Germany, during the Middle Ages, as in the other countries of Europe, many forms of peasant tenure which continued to exist for a long time beside one another. Along with shorter or longer leaseholds for years, — such as persisted, for example, until after the Middle Ages in the Hessian colonial-tenures ("Landsiedelleihen"), in tenancies of marl-right ("zu Mergelrecht"), and in the older bailiff system ("Meierrecht"), — and along with the unfree tenures subject to manorial law, there existed heritable leaseholds that assured to the tenants, through generations, the full economic produce of the land, and did not affect their freedom. On the whole, the development down to about the 1300 s was characterized by a growing betterment in the legal status of the tenant; that is by a strengthening of his real rights. For all leaseholds conferred upon the tenant a real right in the land, a leasehold seisin ("Leihegewere") based upon an investiture realized in accord either with the manorial or the general Territorial law. The proprietary seisin ("Eigengewere") of the feudal lord, on the other hand, was manifested in a right to certain dues (money rents, reliefs, fines for alienations, etc.) and services, which in consequence of the projection of most tenements upon the land acquired the character of real charges (*infra*, § 51); in the right of escheat in case of failure to render rents or services, often also in case of bad management; and in the requirement of the lord's assent to alienations.

(V) **The Modern Development.** — (1) *In Eastern Germany.* — In a great part of Germany, especially in the colonized regions, there became evident as early as the 1300 s a reactionary movement, which was strengthened by the Reception. From the beginning, knights were settled, along with peasants, upon the lands conquered from the Slavs; and they were granted feudal estates ("Rittergüter") as a reward for military services (which they alone rendered) by the land-lords, by the Territorial princes, or by their greater vassals. These feudal holdings, which were at first of slight extent and therefore cultivable by the personal followers of the knights, were situated in the midst of the peasant holdings; the knights were originally simply neighbors of the peasants, and possessed no seigniorial privileges whatever over the peasant land. The Territorial rulers, however, in consequence of their increasing political impotence and financial necessities, gradually and in increasing measure ceded all their rights of sovereignty to the holders of these feudal estates, who played the leading rôle in the Territorial Diets. At the same time the knights found it possible, either by way of law or of force, to extend and unify their holdings, originally scattered among the virgates of the peasants, at the expense of the latter. In this manner there resulted a fusion of land-lordship, jurisdictional powers, and feudal possessions, out of which sprang the "Rittergut" of Eastern Germany: a solidary seigniory in which the lord of the land was sovereign in place of the State, and whose inhabitants became his private subjects. The more the nobility were forced into agriculture as a calling, in consequence of the appearance of mercenary armies and of a class of learned civil officials, the greater was their endeavor to enlarge their demesne ("Gutsland") at the expense of the peasant holdings. For this reason the holders of such seigniories strove to do away with the traditional relations of heritable tenure that stood in the way of their designs, in order to worsen the conditions imposed in new leases, and thus weaken the possessory rights of the peasants; to increase the services imposed upon these; and thus to acquire the labor necessary for the working of their enlarged estates. To all this was added the fact that the nobles, by abolishing these heritable leaseholds freed themselves at the same time from the obligation to re-lease them; and so managed to effect in ever increasing measure, especially after the havoc of the Thirty Years' War, what was known as "Bauernlegen" (evictions); that is, they confiscated the peasant land in order to enjoy the direct usufruct thereof and to work it by dependent labor. In this connection the reception of the Roman law was to some extent detrimental to the peasants;[1] because the jurists did not understand the complicated types of peasant tenure in the German law, and preferred to classify them under the Roman category of leases for years, which did not recognize a real right in the lessee. In these regions, therefore, not only did the one-time free peasant population sink to personal unfreedom, but the peasant holdings were absorbed in increasing measure by the seigniories, in consequence of the abolition of the old forms of tenancy. This calamitous development was attacked with energy in the 1700 s by the government in most of the greater Territories. The extinction by anyone of peasant or cotter holdings was prohibited throughout the kingdom of Prussia by an edict of Frederick the Great of August 12th, 1749, — following repeated earlier efforts toward the same end, particularly by Frederick William I; and the Prussian "Landrecht", — directly

[1] This view is disputed by *S. B. Fay*, "The Roman Law and the German Peasant", Amer. Hist. R., XVI (1911), 234–254.

attacking the result of the historical development, — provided that the number of peasant holdings should neither be diminished by eviction nor by joinder, and that landlords should care for the due tenancy of existing village holdings ("Stellen und Nahrungen"). This new compulsory leasehold tenure, originating in a principle of public police (which is reminiscent of the compulsory lease of offices in the medieval administrative system)[1] did not protect the peasant but the peasant land. It forbade the landlord to take land for his individual usufruct, thereby restricting in considerable measure his ownership, if measured by the concept of ownership then prevalent in the common law, transforming it into a sort of "superior" ("Ober-") ownership. These measures of the Prussian Crown had such great significance because they effectually checked what was perhaps the strongest force tending to evictions of the peasantry, namely, the technical improvement in the cultivation of great seigniorial estates that began about the middle of the 1700 s. They prevented any such decisive destruction of the peasant class as took place at that time in Holstein, Mecklenburg, and Swedish Pomerania, — oligarchies where "the peasant holdings melted together like snow before a springday sun."[2]

According to the varying outcome of the conflict between the various inconsistent interests, the possessory and leasehold rights of the peasants in Eastern Germany assumed various forms.

In a few regions the view attained predominance that the peasant possessed a usufructuary or "subordinate" ownership in the soil.

More frequently the rights to heritable rents ("Erbzinsrecht") which had earlier existed, in the colonization period, were transformed into so-called heritable "Lassbesitz" (tenancy by sufferance). This relation was akin to the older "rental-lease" ("Zinsleihe"); but unlike that, it obligated the tenants ("Lassiten"), not to the payment of rents, but to considerable labor services which the lord found necessary in the exploitation of his great estate. Such an estate was solidary ("geschlossen"), as the interests of the lord required; that is, it could not be divided, but must pass to a single heir, — for the most part only the nearest relatives had rights of inheritance.

Most widespread of all was the non-heritable "Lassgut." After the Thirty Years' War, especially, most holdings were re-

[1] *Brunner*, "Leihezwang", XVII.
[2] *Th. Knapp*, "Gesammelte Beiträge", 375.

tenanted in this manner exclusively. The "Lassit" (villein) had either a non-heritable right of usufruct for life, — which in fact was usually inherited, — or a revocable usufructuary right, terminable at any moment.

Finally there also existed peasant leases for years.

The effect of all these tenancies was to make the peasant dependent by birth and to bind him to the glebe; to subject him, not only personally but also "dinglich", that is as a result of his relation to the land, to the lordship of the landowner. In the case of all of them, of course, he was deprived of any power of disposition over the land upon which he was settled; such a "Lassgut" (villein) estate, so long as it was not absorbed in the lord's demesne, constituted a solidary aggregate of incorporeal property rights ("Vermögensinbegriff") which the peasant could not partition.

(2) *In the Rest of Germany.* — In Lower Saxony, that is in Northwestern Germany, the most common form of tenancy was the fee-farm lease made to bailiffs (a lease "zu Meierrecht"). It was transformed by the legislation of the 1500 s and 1600 s from a lease for years, which it had originally been, into a heritable right to the usufruct of another's land subject to the obligation to manage the same with proper regard to the economic conditions of the peasantry, and to render therefrom certain annual dues, — usually a "Meierzins" (fee-farm-rent), a low rent which was a real charge upon the estate. The bailiff had no ownership except in the buildings and the stock of the estate. Since the right of usufruct was conditioned upon competent management, personal incompetence entitled the lord to cancel the lease ("Abmeierung"); and sales to, as well as inheritance by, inefficient landlords were forbidden. This led to the development of two special legal institutes, the "interim-farm" ("interim-management", "Interimswirtschaft") and the "parent's portion" ("Altenteil"). During the minority of the next heir an interim manager was appointed, who was charged with the administration of the estate during the so-called years of wardship ("Mal-", "Meier-", or "Regierjahre"). This manager was ordinarily the second husband of the bailiff's widow. His management was based upon a special and independent real right. After the expiration of the heir's period of wardship, the manager was bound to deliver to him the land, thereupon receiving, by virtue of such real right, exactly as did the possessor of a peasant holding who renounced it on account of age, the so-called parent's portion, which was a

right for life to maintenance, — *i.e.* to a free dwelling and certain natural products (" Naturalreichnisse ").

Such a fee-farm (" Meiergut ") could not be charged by the bailiff nor reclaimed by the lord; and for the one as for the other it was impartible. A bailiff-holding also, like the heritable " lassitic " holdings (" Lassgüter ") of the East, constituted a solidary estate; and this solidarity, which was strictly enforced by legislation, had the consequence, here also, that succession was limited to one heir. This was the so-called " single " or " preferential " heir (" Anerbe "). Unlike the rule of succession which prevailed in the case of entailed estates of noble families, and family fideicommissa (*supra*, p. 313), the other children possessed no right to compensation from such a preferential heir, because the estate was not the property of the farmer (" Meier ").

In Middle and Southwest Germany, with the exception of Old Bavaria, heritable leaseholds for money rents (" Zinsleihen ") were most common, except where peasant ownership subject to rents (" zinspflichtiges Eigentum ") was recognized. No solidary feudal estates were developed in these parts of Germany; on the contrary, the old manorial system continued to exist with the open-field system as its basis (" Streubesitz "), and certain dues as its essentially exclusive support. The possessory rights of the tenants were therefore, in these regions, very much more favorable, generally speaking, than in the East. It is true that this advantage had a reverse side: there was far less solidarity of the peasant holdings; only slight restriction, or none, existed upon their free partition inter vivos and mortis causa.

(VI) **Modern Agrarian Legislation.** — The enfranchisement of the peasant has been realized in the German States since the end of the 1700s (*supra*, p. 94). The purposes of this movement included, along with the abolition of the personal servitude of the peasants and the assurance to them of full political rights, the destruction of all charges upon peasant holdings and the transformation of all baser possessory rights into unqualified ownership.

In Prussia,[1] — after the crown had transformed all non-herit-

[1] *G. F. Knapp*, "Die Bauernbefreiung und der Ursprung der Landarbeiter in den älteren Teilen Preussens" (2 vols., 1887); *Aubin*, "Zur Geschichte des gutsherrlich-bäuerlichen Verhältnisses in Ostpreussen von der Gründung des Ordensstaates bis zur Steinschen Reform" (1910); *Skalweit*, "Gutsherrschaft und Landarbeiter in Ostdeutschland", in *Schmoller's* J. B., XXXV (1911), 1339–1366; *Mauer*, "Das Schicksal der erledigten Bauernhöfe in den östlichen Provinzen Preussens zur Zeit der Bauernbefreiung", in Forsch. Br. Pr. G., XXIV (1911), 249–255.

able "Lassbesitz" holdings of peasants upon the crown lands ("Domänenbauern") into heritable holdings as early as 1777, — the great reform statutes were introduced by the celebrated edict of October 9th, 1807, which (to mention only one provision) declared free to everyone the acquisition of peasant holdings, thereby doing away with the conception of the peasant holding as a piece of rural land that presupposed a certain personal status in the possessor. Following this, the edict of November 14th, 1811, provided that not only those peasant holdings as to which there already existed a qualified right of inheritance or at least an obligation on the part of the lord to renew the lease to the heirs of a deceased tenant, but also estates held under less favorable tenancies, should be converted into the free unlimited property of the possessor, subject to compensation to the lord, at the instance of either of the two parties. Of course, in the absence of statutory provision to the contrary, the peasants could not be prevented from thereafter selling their free holdings to their former lords. The compensation was so adjusted that the possessors of heritable "Lassgüter" were required to cede to the lord a third, and the possessors of non-heritable "Lassgüter" and peasant lessees for years a half, of their land. The cost of enfranchisement and of the conversion of the leaseholds into ownership was therefore a diminution of the peasant holdings by a third or a half. There was herein involved an abandonment, — inconsistent with the older policy of the State, yet perhaps with that qualification justifiable, — of the principle of compulsory leasehold renewals formerly imposed upon the lords. The declaration of May 29th, 1816, went even farther in this direction. It restricted the applicability of the preceding rules to holdings that had been registered in the land-book, and were capable of furnishing certain statutory team labor ("spannfähig"). All smaller holdings, although not so convertible into normal statutory estates ("regulierbar") were abandoned either to confiscation by the lord or to conversion into pure leaseholds. It is true that the Compensation Act of March 2d, 1850, endeavored at that late day to cure this defect in the declaration of 1816: it extended the character of "Regulierbarkeit" (quality of being regularized) to every "Lassgut" holding, and imposed a measure of damages, not as before in land, but in money. The Declaration of 1816, however, and the far-reaching renunciation which it contained of the principles of compulsory lease renewals imposed by the State, had the consequence that a great number of peasant holdings had meanwhile disappeared, being taken over into the lord's estate, so that the statute of 1850 found only a relatively narrow field of application; a fact which is not the least among those responsible for the scarcity of labor at the present day, in certain regions.[1]

As in Prussia, so also in the other States of Germany the old types of tenancy were for the most part abolished in the course of the 1800s, especially in consequence of the movement of 1848; the peasant rights of usufruct being in some States completely allodialized and their re-creation prohibited, and in others declared redeemable, either generally or with the exception of particular classes. Only a few States allowed the older forms of tenancy to continue, so far as they still survived (estates subject to heritable rents, heritable leaseholds, fee-farms, etc.: "Erbzins-", "Erpacht-", "Meiergüter"), or made their conversion into ownership dependent upon a voluntary redemption. The new Civil Code has not done away with such relationships, spared by the State law. It does forbid, however, as many State statutes had earlier done, the new creation of heritable tenancies. The Introductory Act of the Code (§ 63) makes an exception to this principle in the case of heritable leasehold rights ("Erbpachtrechte") in those States in which they still exist. But even in many of these States, as for example in Hesse and in the Thuringian principalities, the future creation of new heritable leaseholds has been prohibited by the State law. Only in the two Mecklenburgs and in Lübeck are heritable leases expressly recognized and regulated. The same is true of lands subject to rent charges ("Rentengüter") in Prussia (*infra*, § 52).

§ 46. **Urban Leaseholds.**[2] (I) **The Older Law.** — Leaseholds under town law were developed as free tenancies. There was lacking in them the personal dependence of the tenant upon the lessor which was essential to a great part of the peasant ("bäuerlich") tenancies, as also to feudal tenure. In most cities the lands upon which the burghers erected their houses were conveyed to them by the town lord, not in rent-free ownership but as leaseholds. Such a tenancy was a heritable right: the urban leasehold was a free and heritable leasehold. These free heritable leases of the towns, like those of rural regions, owed their origin to the free precarious tenures of the Frankish period. Indeed,

[1] *Brunner*, "Leihezwang", 22.

[2] Compare the literature cited for § 45 *supra* and § 52 *infra*. Also *Schreiber*, "Die Geschichte der Erbleihe in der Stadt Strassburg i. E.", in *Beyerle's* "Beiträge", III, 3 (1909).

no legal difference whatever existed between the heritable leaseholds of the towns and of rural regions. It is true that in the cities such leaseholds were not only earlier developed than in the country, but attained a far more general dissemination than was possible under rural conditions; for, as we have already mentioned (*supra*, pp. 329 *et seq.*), many other forms of tenure had either persisted or been newly formed in rural districts, at least in the older parts of Germany. In the colonized regions of the East, however, the free heritable lease was at first the generally prevailing form of tenancy, even among peasant tenements. At the same time, despite these special conditions in Eastern Germany, the free heritable leasehold was regarded as peculiar to the town law, and was therefore known simply as "Weichbild", "Weichbildrecht", "Burgrecht": town or burgage tenure. Like the rural "colonial"-lease, the heritable urban leasehold was originally one granted by the founder of a town ("Gründerleihe"). After the district intended for the town had been divided into a number of building lots, as nearly as possible of equal size, the settlers received from the town-lord, on the basis of a general privilege issued by him, a heritable and alienable real right in the building lots assigned to them, in return for which they were bound to render to him, in addition to the public services to which they were obligated as burghers, a certain rent ("census arealis", "Wurtzins", "Freizins"). This was for the most part of slight amount, of no significance except as a recognition of the lord's title, and therefore involved no personal dependence of the citizen. In place of these original "founder"-leaseholds there appeared later, in the course of the city's further development, private heritable leaseholds. These were granted, not by the town-lord· but by private landowners, and therefore created between lessor and tenant a relation under the private law alone. Unlike the founder-leaseholds, which always had exclusive reference to land, such leaseholds often existed in the houses, baths, booths, and stalls thereon erected, and also in gardens and vineyards. In the case also of these private heritable leases the tenant was bound to render a fixed rent of slight amount, to maintain the house in good condition if it was included in the leasehold, and to make good all damage out of his own means.

In time the lessor's ownership in the land sank to a mere right to rent, a right which was a real charge upon the land; whereas the tenant, in addition to the ownership of the house, now acquired the land, also, as his own, subject to the charge resting thereon in favor of the owner of the rent. In this manner there originated the institute of the capitalistic "purchase-rent" ("Rentenkauf" — *infra,* § 52).

These building-leases completely disappeared, almost everywhere, already in the Middle Ages. In their place there was developed the non-usufructuary or occupancy lease ("Miete") of buildings and dwellings. But these ordinarily gave the lessee a real right, in accord with the fundamental idea of the medieval law of seisin, and were therefore not destroyed by a sale of the house ("hur gat vor gop", — *infra,* § 84).

(II) **The Modern Development.** — The Roman law of heritable building rights, the superficies, — also known as "Platz-", "Zimmer-", "Keller-", and "Bodenzinsrecht": rights of "ground", "room", "basement", — was adopted into the common law, with only slight changes, at the time of the Reception. The regional legal systems also adopted it, although they treated it very differently; some of them conceiving of it as a case of divided ownership (Bavarian "Landrecht"); others, as a sort of real servitude (Prussian "Landrecht"), or as a variant form of personal servitudes (Saxon Code), or as a usufructuary ownership of the surface of the soil (Austrian Code).

The new Civil Code recognizes the heritable building right of the common law (§§ 1012–1017) as the single heritable usufructuary right in a thing that is possible under the imperial law, and at the same time has wholly withdrawn it from State regulation. Only existing superficies have been left unchanged. This real right of the present day, because it refers in most cases to buildings, may be regarded as having replaced the medieval building lease ("Häuserleihe"). But it has a broader content, for it is equally applicable to any other structures, — walls, towers, bridges, railways, tunnels, cellars, etc.; and, moreover, in order to promote the better use of the structure, can be extended to land which is not necessary for the building proper, such as a yard, garden, entry-way, and the like. The restriction to a part of the building, which was formerly possible, has, on the other hand, been done away with; and likewise its creation in the case of other improvements than building structures (as plants, "Pflanzungssuperfizies").

§ 47. **The Fief: the Feudal Law of Medieval Germany.** (I) **The Feudal System generally.** — The most important tenurial relation ("Leiheverhältnis") of the medieval law was tenure ("Lehn") in the technical sense. Hardly another institute of the law equalled in importance the tenancy ("Leihe") of the feudal law, since in Germany most lands and in England and France all lands were subject to feudal bonds ("nulle terre sans seigneur"). But the feudal law was not merely a part of the law of things, nor a part only of the private law; in it was most clearly expressed the inseparability of the public and the private law. Through centuries it determined the nature of great portions of the jural life of the country; indeed, the whole of medieval civilization acquired its peculiar stamp from the feudal structure of State and society. How far this affected the ideas of medieval men is seen, for example, in the widely imitated lyric poetry of the troubadours of Southern France, who sang of love as a feudal relation between the lovers. Originating in the Frankish Empire in a union of vassaldom and the "beneficium" ("Benefizialwesen"), the feudal system spread from the Frankish law into most of the countries of Christendom, and brought about what we know as the feudalization of the medieval States. In this place we have to consider the system from the side of the private law alone. It was constituted partly by general statutes of the Territorial rulers, and partly by compacts between them and their vassals; and was further developed by administration in the feudal courts. Because of its wide-reaching importance it was developed with particular care. "The German feudal law is the richest part of the rich field of the German law of things."[1] Aside from this practical development it also found exhaustive theoretical treatment at an early day. In the different Mirrors of the medieval law it was presented side by side with the general Territorial law, — in particularly striking manner by Eike von Repkow. His Saxon law of feudalism "may well challenge, in the fullness and clearness of its content and in the beauty of the presentation, every other legal record."[2]

A brief preliminary sketch must now be given of the classical feudal law of medieval Germany.[3]

(II) **Specific Principles of the German Feudal Law.** — In the beginning the expression "Lehn" (fief), equally with the corresponding Latin term "beneficium", designated relatively colorless tenancies ("Leihen") of the most various kinds (*supra*, pp. 321 *et seq.*). In the sense of the feudal law when fully developed the

[1] *Sohm*, in Z. Priv. Öff. R., I (1874), 247. [2] *Ibid.*

[3] *Homeyer*, in his edition of the "Sächsisches Lehnrecht", has given a detailed and systematic presentation of this: "Des Sachsenspiegels zweiter Teil nebst den verwandten Rechtsbüchern" (Vol. 2, 1844), 201–634.

"Lehn" was opposed, along with the technical expression "feudum" (usually derived from "faihu" = "Vieh" = cattle, money, property; also derived, however, from Old High G. "fehon" = to use; also regarded as Keltic), to the allod (= "alodis", from "al" = all, and "od" = ownership).[1] It was distinguished from all other tenures by its peculiar relations of service and fidelity between lord and tenant. This personal relation retained throughout the Middle Ages a very special importance. In course of time, however, the real element became predominant, even in the case of feudal tenure; and thus there originated the idea, — an idea inconsistent with historical development, — that this bond of personal fidelity was a consequence of the possession of the fief.[2] As Heusler has finely remarked,[3] "the relation between lord and man preserved a moral elevation that was essential to the task which the feudal law was called upon to perform. Lord and man stood infinitely nearer to one another socially and politically than land-lord and peasant; the duty of the vassal was a nobler one, and in consequence of its political aspect was an immediate condition of the existence of the feudal lord; its basis was not a mere economic interest, as in the case of peasant tenures, but one which affected also the tenant's personal individuality. There was not merely a gift of a fief, balanced against certain precisely defined services as equivalents of each other; the relation involved a mutual bond of fidelity and homage, which extended not merely to positive action but also, negatively, to the exclusion of all prejudicial or directly harmful conduct", the violation of which might have as its effect the forfeiture of feudal rights. As for the lord, it was the basis, in particular, of his claims to feudal services, military services, and attendance at his court: "the former including service under arms, for periods not exactly determined, in the field; the latter, attendance at the seigniorial residence or court, and especially suit to the feudal court of justice."[4] The vassal had a claim, in turn, upon the fidelity of his lord, and in particular a claim to security in his feudal rights; although, indeed, the lord (unlike the vassal) was not bound to assume these obligations of fidelity under oath. Since the fief was originally granted to the vassal to the end that he might with its help fulfill the services imposed upon him, and above all military obligations, it was a "Rittersold", a knight's hire.

[1] *v. Schwerin*, art. "Allod" in *Hoop's* "Reallexikon", I (1911), 65.
[2] *Heusler*, "Institutionen", II, 161. [3] *Ibid.*, 162. [4] *Ibid.*, 163.

Anything whatever which yielded a permanent income or produce could be granted as a fief; and although only lands — that is possession of land, including *e.g.* castles — were originally granted as fiefs, certain rights also later became the object of feudal tenures; namely, those that secured a permanent user or an assured income, such as various regalities and real-charges (rights of mill, coinage, customs, tithes), and above all public offices (dukedoms, earldoms, judicial offices, bailiwicks, etc.). The first tenant could, with certain exceptions, subject the fief in turn to a sub-infeudation.[1]

On account of the military character of the fief ("Lehn") as distinguished from other tenancies generally ("Leihen"), only men of knightly status and capable of bearing arms possessed full feudal capacity, active and passive ("Heerschild"). For this reason Jews, outlaws, and excommunicants could under no circumstances be granted fiefs; they were absolutely incapable of feudal relationships. Burghers, peasants, ecclesiastics (with the exception of the princes of the church), women, and corporate associations could be enfeoffed only by the grace of the lord ("per gratiam domini"); and even then they must appoint a so-called "bearer" or holder of the fief ("Lehnsträger") who occupied the position of vassal in relations with third persons, especially the lord, — whereas the seisin remained in the vassal whom he represented. Such tenants were capable only of a relative feudal capacity.

The creation of a fief was accomplished by the act of investiture, which was composed of two parts, corresponding to the personal and the real elements of the feudal relation. Of these the first was the commendation: before the assembled vassals, and with his hand in his lord's, the new vassal swore fidelity to his lord, and confirmed it with a kiss, promising to be true, faithful, and obedient. This was known as swearing or doing homage ("homagium", "hominium", "Mannschaft", "Hulde"). After this followed the second step: the giving or letting ("Leihe") of the object of the fief. It took the form of a symbolic investiture under the law of things (*supra*, p. 242), being performed by the lord's delivery of a symbol of investment accompanied by a simultaneous oral declaration of intention to convey; that is to say, "with hand and mouth." The symbols used included those otherwise customary in livery of seisin, — the staff, twig, glove,

[1] *K. Lehmann*, art. "Afterlehn" in *Hoop's* "Reallexikon," I (1911), 40 *et seq.*

or hat,—but especially a sword or a spear; in the case of secular principalities a flag ("Fahnlehn"), and in the case of ecclesiastical principalities a ring and staff down to the time of the Concordat of Worms, and thereafter a scepter. The ceremony was concluded by the manual delivery to the vassal of a deed of enfeoffment ("Lehnbrief"); and to the lord, of an acknowledgment or counter-deed ("Lehnrevers"). An investiture was necessary not only for the creation of a new fief, but,—inasmuch as the right of the feoffee existed only so long as his relation of vassaldom to the feoffor continued,—whenever there was a change in the person of the lord (a succession to the crown or in the family of the lord) or of the vassal ("Mannfall"). In such case the vassal who was entitled as heir to succession in the fief, or to recognition by the new lord, was bound to give notice ("muten", "sinnen") within a year and a day of his desire for a renewal of the fief.

Feudal investiture was preceded by a contract of feoffment, and frequently,—as earlier in the case of the Frankish precaria,—by a conveyance of the fee upon condition of its reconveyance as a fief ("feudum oblatum"). It included the two elements, common to the law of things, of an alienation ("Sala") and an investiture; but not any "resignatio" or release ("Auflassung") in the older sense,—for the good reason that the lord by no means completely abandoned his rights in the land, but on the contrary retained his ownership of the fief and the corresponding proprietary seisin ("Eigengewere"). The vassal, on the other hand, received, as a consequence of investiture and in accordance with the general rules of the law of things, not only a real right in the land, but, in the absence of a provision to the contrary, the seisin also; namely the feudal seisin ("Lehnsgewere"). In case of an enfeoffment without immediate investiture and livery of seisin, men spoke of feoffment by contract ("Lehen unter Gedinge"). In this case the vassal acquired only a personal right against the feoffor. This form was chosen when lands were to be conveyed which at the time were still in the feudal possession ("Lehnsbesitz") of a third person, whether a particularly designated holding ("geliehenes oder benanntes Gedinge"); or that holding, among several of the same lord, which should first become vacant,—in other words, a deed of an undetermined reversion ("Anwartung", "Anwartschaft", "unbenanntes Gedinge"). Although the feoffment conveyed to the tenant no immediate seisin in the land, in the case either of the direct or the reversionary deed, nevertheless the right of the feoffee was different in the two cases. In the case of conditional feoffment of a definite holding the feoffee acquired the seisin, precisely as an heir, immediately upon the death of the present possessor; but in the case of a feoffment of a reversion the estate reverted first to the lord.

This real right in the estate, which was thus conveyed to the vassal by the feoffment, was of great extent and of varied content. He alone could dispose of its profits; he could also create in it sub-feuds. Only dispositions of the substance of the land, particularly alienations and pledges, he could not affect without the assent and coöperation of the lord, — it was in this connection that the real right remaining in the lord most frequently appeared in practice. Conveyances without the lord's assent were void, and involved forfeiture of the fief by the vassal. The lord, it is true, might "das Gut lassen" ("abandon" the land), *i.e.* eliminate himself by conveying all his rights to another; but the position of the tenant could not thereby be worsened. And therefore alienations by the lord to one of another class ("Ungenosse"), and partitions of the estate, were forbidden. On the other hand, according to the theory of the Law-Books the consent of the vassal's heirs was not yet essential to a conveyance. Such consent became necessary only from the time when a right of inheritance in the fief was recognized in the vassal's sons and later issue. Originally no such right existed; on the contrary, the feoffment was only for so long as the feoffor and the feoffee should live. Inasmuch, however, as the fief came to be employed even at an early date primarily for military purposes, in consequence of the need of mounted vassals, it became customary for the heir of a deceased lord to reconvey the fief to the occupant, and that the lord should not deny to the son of his dead liegeman a renewal of the fief. "From the 1100 s onward the fief was treated, in the absence of express provision, as heritable; in other words, there was developed under the private law a compulsion of re-feoffment ("Leihezwang") which brought about the heritable character of the fief."[1] Along with this compulsory re-feoffment of the private law there was added a similar one of the public law in the case of public offices that became feudal holdings. The lord was bound to refill by feoffment any feudal office ("Amtslehen") the holder of which died without heirs. This was a principle which, in consequence of its application to secular principalities that became fiefs (that is to "flag-fiefs"), had the most

[1] *Brunner*, "Leihezwang", 7.

baleful political consequences; for it made futile in Germany the hope of such a growth of royal power as resulted in France and in England from the confiscation of the great crown fiefs. As regards the ends served by the fief under public law in the organization of the army and the civil service, the principles of the Germanic law of inheritance were inapplicable, since they divided the heritage between the heirs of equal blood. The consequence was that special rules of feudal inheritance were developed which differed from the general law of inheritance in lands. Of course only persons capable of feudal services could be feudal heirs; those absolutely incapable were therefore wholly excluded, and those who were under relative incapacity were bound to satisfy the conditions which made enfeoffment possible, — such, for example, as the appointment of a holder of the fief ("Lehnsträger"). Not only this, but even as to persons capable of feudal service the right was much more limited than in the general law of the land ("Landrecht"). Only the vassal's son seems originally to have been conceded a right of succession under the German feudal law; later the right was extended to all the issue of the last occupant. On the other hand, the other descendants of the first tenant, as well as all ascendants, were excluded. However, these rules were modified, at an early day, by particular agreement in special cases. Women, notably, were accorded rights of succession.

In case of the presence of several heirs of equal rank the lord did not originally need to enfeoff more than one; in return, the others could demand compensation from the fee ("Allod"). From the 1300s onward, however, he was bound to enfeoff the heirs, if they demanded it, in collective hand. Enfeoffment in collective hand was at first the sole form of the German feudal law for the community ("gemeinschaftliche") enfeoffment of several vassals. As required by the general rules of ownership in collective hand (*supra*, p. 139), such feoffment was realized by the tenants' laying their hands in those of the lord and grasping together the symbol of investiture he extended. In relation to him they constituted but one person; but they were bound, upon demand by him, to designate one of their number upon whom he could depend for the due performance of feudal obligations. They received the fief in undivided possession and enjoyment. From the 1300s onward, however, partititions of the usufruct, accompanied by abolition of community management ("Mutschierungen"; *supra*, p. 143) became increasingly common. The collective feoffees could dispose either of the entire fief or of portions thereof only by an act of collective hand. Upon the death of a tenant who left no children capable of feudal services, benefit of survivorship prevailed in favor of the others. Along with this collective feoffment of the German law there was also developed, as early as the Middle Ages, in Germany as elsewhere, a co-feoffment in undivided shares ("Mitbelehnung zu Bruchteilen") similar to the Italian "coinvestitura."

During the minority of a vassal a feudal wardship distinct from the wardship of the Territorial Law was recognized. The lord himself was ordinarily the feudal guardian. As such he took the profits of the fief (the so-called "Angefälle"); but he could also let these out along with the wardship. The origin of this wardship of the feudal law "goes back to a temporary right of escheat ('Heimfallsrecht'), which was not destroyed by the development of the heritable character of the fief and assured the lord compensation for the damages he suffered through the loss of feudal services during the continuance of the tenant's minority."[1] In time the rule was developed that the lord was bound to convey the feudal wardship (*i.e.* of the body) to the guardian of the fee ("Allodialvormund"), even though the latter might be his vassal, upon demand and re-feoffment.

If a vassal died without feudal heirs, and if neither a feudal contract ("Gedinge") nor sub-feuds existed, the fief escheated to the lord. Moreover, the vassal could at any time dissolve the feudal relation of his own motion by a release of the land to the lord or by a renunciation of homage. On the other hand, if he was guilty of a felony (from Old Norse "fel", "felo", Old High G. "fillo" = criminal, wretch), — that is, if he was guilty of a breach of feudal faith, a refusal to perform his feudal services, a conveyance of the fief, or a failure to give due notice, — or if he was guilty of any other dishonorable action, the lord could reclaim the fief from the vassal by judicial action; and according to the earlier and stricter law this would bind also the feoffee's heirs. Similarly, the lord might forfeit his rights by a breach of faith, a denial of the tenant's rights, or by dispossessing the tenant, etc. In these cases the estate fell to the vassal, and he passed it to his heirs released from all feudal obligations; but the lord retained the right of escheat.

§ 48. **The Modern Feudal Law.** (I) **The Common Law.** — (1) *The Lombard law* was received as a common and subsidiary law

[1] *Schröder*, "Lehrbuch" (5th ed.), 425.

in feudal relations beginning with the second half of the 1400 s, notwithstanding that the German feudal law had itself reached a mature and rich development. The evident cause for this was that the Lombard book of feudal law, the " Liber " or " Consuetudines feudorum ",[1] had been embodied in the " Corpus Iuris Civilis " as a so-called " decima collatio novellarum ", and therefore shared the fortunes of that Code. Moreover, the Lombard feudal law had been developed by Italian theorists upon the basis of the feudal statutes of the emperors Konrad II, Lothar III, and Frederick I, and the differences between it and the German could easily be harmonized. At the same time the existing sources of the native feudal law maintained their local authority in the face of the new common law; especially in the regions of the Saxon law the old practices continued in many important matters. The common feudal law was on one hand further developed in a unitary sense by theory, which cultivated it zealously as a special branch of legal science; and on the other hand it was supplemented in a particularistic sense by the feudal statutes issued, even in modern times, in many of the imperial Territories. Among these statutes the most noteworthy are an edict of 1764 of Electoral Saxony, and the comprehensive feudal legislation of the Prussian " Landrecht," which, in Suarez's words, constituted " a ius feudale universale in the philosophic sense "; that is, a subsidiary common feudal law supplementary to the Lombard systems. These were followed by the Baden Feudal Act (" Lehnsgesetz ") of 1807, and the Bavarian Feudal Edict of 1808.

(2) *Variant Institutes.* — The common feudal law was distinguished chiefly in the following respects from the older German law.

Movables, provided their substance or their value was assured of permanence, and money (the profits of an assured capital) were recognized as objects of feudal tenure.

The requirement of the personal presence of lord and vassal in the act of investiture was allowed to lapse; only a few State statutes retained it.

Under the influence of the Lombard law there were developed from the forms of feoffment by contract (" Gedinge ") recognized in the German law, — either of definite lands or of undetermined reversions, — the two institutes of feudal rights in expectancy (" Lehnsanwartschaft ") and feoffments in reversions (" Eventual-

[1] See, on its origins, *K. Lehmann*, "Das langobardische Lehnrecht" (1896).

belehnung "). These became of great importance in the history of the imperial Territories, inasmuch as they determined dynastic succession to the throne in case of the extinction of a Territorial dynasty.

Feudal rights in expectancy were granted either in a particular fief (" exspectativa feudalis specialis ") or in the first fief which should escheat (" exspectativa feudalis generalis ") or in any fief whatever (" exspectativa feudalis indeterminata "). They secured to the holder of such future estate, without any investiture, a contractual right against the lord to investiture upon fulfillment of a condition. This right was inherited, according to the rules of succession of the private law, by those heirs of the expectant who were capable of feudal services; and the corresponding legal duty of the lord descended to his successors. Of several rights in expectancy the oldest took precedence, without distinction between special and general rights.

The feoffment of a reversion (" Eventualbelehnung "), on the other hand, like the old " donatio post obitum ", involved an immediate investiture, either of a definite fief when it should escheat or of the first one that should fall vacant; it therefore conveyed immediately to the grantee a real, — albeit a qualified, — right in expectancy (" Wartrecht "). The instant the condition was fulfilled the right of the feoffee became unqualified; he did not need to seek a new feoffment. Such rights of feoffment in a reversion were also heritable by the heirs of the two parties, and according to the rules of feudal succession.

When a feoffment in a reversion conflicted with a right in expectancy the former took precedence. Among several feoffments in a reversion the earliest had preference.

As for feoffments of several persons, in many regions the principles of the Lombard institute of co-feoffment (" coinvestitura ") were adopted. These were totally different from the principles of the Germanic institute of collective hand, and secured to each vassal an ideal quotal-share in the fief. In such enfeoffments there was no benefit of survivorship among the co-feoffees; on the contrary they could not receive a share of a deceased liegeman unless they otherwise possessed a right to inherit from him, by reason of kinship or a contract of investiture in a particular fief.

Unlike the German law, the Lombard feudal law recognized tenurial relations originating in extinctive prescription (" Verjährung ") in those cases where one had possessed a fief for thirty years with good faith in both parties, and had rendered feudal services from it (so-called "feudum informe"). This principle passed over into the common feudal law and into many of the modern regional systems, the period being reduced in the practice of the common law to ten or to twenty years. Still later statutes repudiated the institute.

The real rights of the lord and of the vassal were classified by theorists under the concepts of "superior" and "subordinate" ownership (*supra*, p. 232 *et seq.*). As regards restrictions upon alienation by the vassal, imposed in the interest of the lord, the strict view of the German law was preferred in the common law, the original and more favorable viewpoint of the Lombard law having already been abandoned, on this point, in the feudal statutes of Lothar III and Frederick I. On the other hand, the common feudal law required, for conveyance, not only the consent of the lord but also the consent of the agnates and of co-feoffees and feoffees of reversions ("Eventualbelehnten"). These also possessed a revocatory action in case of an improper alienation; not, however, one unlimited as to time, such as the lord originally possessed, but one available within a prescriptive period of thirty years. If the lord reclaimed the fief by means of a revocatory action it remained in his hands only so long as the alienor and his descendants capable of feudal service might live. After their death the rights of the agnates and of co-feoffees and feoffees in the reversion became effective. In addition to a right of revocation the feoffor and his successors possessed the feudal preferential right of purchase ("Lehnsretrakt", "retractus feudalis"), which was unknown to the classical feudal law of Germany, and by means of which they could reclaim the land from any third person subject to repayment of the purchase price. Whereas the Lombard law conceded to the issue of the alienor neither a right of revocation ("Retraktionsrecht") nor a preferential right of purchase ("Retraktrecht"), both of these were conceded to them in various particularistic systems, and in the practice of the common law; others of the regional systems, on the other hand, restricted the right of preferential purchase, or totally abolished it while conceding other remedies in its place.

The theory of "feudal liabilities", — that is liabilities "of the fief" ("Lehnsschulden"), — was first developed in the theory of the common law. Feudal liabilities were distinguished, in it, from those liabilities which bound only the allodium of the vassal (to whom the fruits of the fief belonged), and which were always inherited by his descendants, but by his agnates only when they were his universal successors. Feudal liabilities were liabilities assumed in the interest or for the improvement of the fief. They passed with this to successors in possession, who thereby became responsible for them only to the extent of the fief's value, and not, or at least only secondarily ("debita feudalia subsidaria"), with the allodium; they were not a charge upon the fee of the heir.

Feudal liabilities imposed by law ("debita feudalia legalia") included, in the first place, those contracted by the first possessor in order to acquire the fief for himself and his family, and to increase its extent; these feudal debts passed only to such possessors of the fief as derived their possession from the feoffment of the first possessor, — whence they were "debita feudalia respectiva", as contrasted with those that were "absoluta", which last were effective against everyone who acquired the fief. They included, further, debts which were contracted to maintain the feudal estate in its original extent or condition or for the redemption of the rights of co-heirs; also, later, hypothecs imposed upon the land with the consent of the lord and the agnates; and also certain statutory obligations of the successors in the fief. Examples of the last were the living ("Alimentation") allowed by the common law to needy persons next in expectancy, but who were excluded from succession because of bodily defects; costs of burial, support ("Unterhalt") and dowry allowed in the regional systems to needy daughters; and dower ("Leibgedinge", "Wittum") allowed to widows. In addition to these, still other debts could be declared liabilities of the fief with the consent of all living agnates and successors thereto ("debita feudalia consensuata"). Among feudal debts belonged also the so-called "constitutum feudale" ("Lehnsstamm"); a capital permanently invested in a feudal fief the rents from which were inherited according to the feudal law.

The rules regulating succession to the fief differed in especial degree from those of the older German law. Unlike this, the Lombard law conceded a right of inheritance in the fief not only to the issue of the last possessor, but also to his "agnates", his collaterals of the male line; although this was accorded them only so far as they were descendants of the first acquirer, — *i.e.* only to persons to whom the fief was "feudum paternum." To be sure this could be altered, "per gratiam domini", to the extent of conceding a right of succession to collateral kindred who were not descendants of the first acquirer ("feudum novum ex iure antiqui concessum"). This alien law was received in Germany.

From the contractual extension of the rights of collaterals, mentioned above, there was developed in Mecklenburg the right of so-called "Reversal"-cousins: that is, cousins who were appointed successors in deed of feoffment upon the basis of the "Reversalen" of 1621. It was only in the countries of the Saxon law that men clung to the native view, recognizing rights of inheritance in the "agnates" only when the feoffment was made to them collectively; the institute then becoming, in such cases, "a mere substitute for agnatic succession." [1]

The order of inheritance under the feudal law was essentially a special succession in a feudal estate, distinguished from the allodium as a "special" estate; [2] in doctrinal literature it was frequently conceived of as a so-called "successio ex pacto et providentia maiorum", — by which was meant that the feudal heir was not the heir of the last possessor but of the first acquirer.

These different principles of feudal and allodial succession, — and also escheat, or the bankruptcy of the vassal, — might make necessary the separation of the fief from the fee. For this reason, and in case a simple real partition could not be made, special rules were developed regulating the institute of feudal partition. The special guardianship of the lord over a minor tenant disappeared at an early day. Such an institute was unknown also to the common feudal law. Only in some of the particularistic systems do we find a special feudal guardian; he acts as the holder of the fief ("Lehnsträger"), whereas the administration of the fief is incumbent upon the guardian of the allodium.

Finally, as regards the termination of the feudal relation, all other causes thereof became in the modern period progressively less important in comparison with contracts or statutes which abolished feudal lordship ("Allodifikation") and statutes that completely abolished feudal relations generally.

(II) **The Decay of the Feudal Law.** — As early as the second half of the Middle Ages there set in a decay of the feudal system which continued uninterruptedly through the following centuries. True, the feudal character of the imperial Territories was maintained until the dissolution of the old Empire, — an indication of its weakness, [3] — but feudalism was forced to yield step by step before the strengthening conception of the modern State. Grants were no longer made of public powers and of rights of sovereignty as feudal holdings; these were made, instead, the basis of State

[1] *Gierke* in *Holtzendorff-Kohler*, 500.
[2] *Ibid.*, 502. [3] *Ibid.*, 497.

offices. Feudal military service, once the leading feature of the entire institute, lost its importance owing to changes in the mode of conducting war with the appearance of mercenary and standing armies. The protection which the lord was bound to give his vassals lost its value with the growth of a general State citizenship. The feudal supremacy of the Territorial princes grew into a State sovereignty, and subjection to the feudal power of another than the ruler of the State no longer appeared reconcilable with the latter's position. Wherefore, even in the time of the old Empire, the Territorial rulers began to redeem seigniorial privileges and undertake the allodification of fiefs. Among others, Frederick William I of Prussia, who by a statute of January 5th, 1717, ordered the abolition of all nobiliary and villein ("Bauer-") tenures and feudal rights of judicature ("Schulzenlehn") in exchange for a money compensation; a statute which, to be sure, was only slowly and incompletely enforced. The only exceptions were crown-fiefs and heritable feudal offices ("Erbämterlehn"); "feuda extra curtem" (fiefs situated outside the kingdom), and reversionary ("beanwartschaftete") tenures. The purely private side, also, of the feudal law "shrank to a special law of particular estates"; it became "for the most part a mass of principles derived from abandoned premises." [1]

Before the disappearance of the Holy Roman Empire feudal relations had come to be, in fact, "a long-since antiquated system, whose material basis had lost all vitality, and which was filled with countless details elaborated with theoretical subtlety, and therefore correspondingly provocative of controversy." [2] The rickety structure collapsed as soon as it was touched by the ideas of the French Revolution.

In France the feudal régime including all feudal tenurial relations ("Lehnswesen") had been swept away by the Decree of the National Assembly of August 4th, 1789. The principles of the French statutes were introduced into all those parts of Germany which were then a part of France; and after the end of the French occupation they were only in part repealed. This is the reason why in those regions, for example in Alsace-Lorraine and in the Prussian Rhineland, the feudal order is completely antiquated and forgotten: with reference to them one can speak of the feudal law only in a historical sense.

But even in most of the other parts of Germany a fundamental

[1] *Gierke* in *Holtzendorff-Kohler*, 497.
[2] *Franken*, "Privatrecht", 274.

change, although not so radical, was effected in the course of the 1800 s, especially in consequence of the revolutionary movement of 1848 and the demand made in the Fundamental Rights of that year for the abolition of all feudal relationships. Tenure, so far as it existed under the public law, was everywhere abolished; the feudal supremacy of the "superior" owner, and therewith the restrictions upon alienation and powers of retractive purchase which existed in his interest, ceased absolutely to be observed. Moreover, a further step was taken toward the allodification of all land by forbidding the creation of new fiefs. In Prussia, the "Landrecht" had still recognized that right, subject to the approval of the sovereign, but the constitution of January 1st, 1850, provided in Article 40: "The creation of feudal holdings . . . is forbidden. Existing fiefs . . . shall be converted into free ownership under statutory provisions." Only in the case of crown fiefs, *i.e.* those granted directly by the king,[1] and "feuda extra curtem" was a "temporary" exception made (Art. 41). These principles were given effect in statutes of March 2d, 1850, and June 5th, 1852. The first abolished throughout the kingdom the "superior" ownership of the feudal law and all the rights directly derived therefrom, without compensation, but with the same exceptions of royal and foreign fiefs. The second provided that existing fiefs should be redeemed under statute. The result of this was the extinction of the rights of holders of future interests in the fiefs ("Lehnsanwärter"), subject to money compensation, in so far as existing fiefs were not converted into family fideicommissa. Special statutes were later issued in different provinces of the Kingdom for the enforcement of the Act of 1852.

A similar development took place in almost all the other German States, including Bavaria, Württemberg, Saxony, Baden, and Hessia. Everywhere the fief was transformed into an institute similar to a family fideicommissum. With reference to these rights the rules derived from the old conception of "subordinate" ownership, — feudal order of succession, rights of agnates, feudal alienations, feudal partitions, and feudal debts, — still retain authority. Only in a few States does the feudal law, as such, still exist: in Mecklenburg,[2] Lippe, Waldeck, Reuss ä. L.

[1] These include in Prussia the Silesian principalities of Sagan, Oels, Troppau, and Jägerndorf, the principality of Krotoschin in Posen, the fiefs of the "mediatized" princes and counts of Stolberg, Wittgenstein, Hohen-Solms, Solms-Braunfels, and Wied.

[2] In Mecklenburg-Schwerin there are still 390 feudal tenants ("Lehnsbesitzer"), as compared with 557 owners of allodial estates; in Mecklen-

In so far as remnants of the feudal law do still exist their regulation has been reserved by the Civil Code to State law (EG, § 59).

TOPIC 2. SERVITUDES

§ 49. **Servitudes in General.** (I) **The Older Law.** — The conception of servitudes ("Dienstbarkeiten", "Servituten") as an independent group of real rights was unknown to the Germanic law in its original form. It was only through the Reception that it acquired importance in the legal life of Germany. The Roman servitude was a real right of usufruct existing in a thing belonging to another. It was a predial servitude when this usufructuary right served the interests of land, a personal servitude when it served those of a person. Servitudes were originally the only "iura in re aliena" of the Roman law; pledges, emphyteusis, and superficies first appeared later. Personal servitudes remained few in number and restricted to certain definite types: "ususfructus", "usus", "habitatio", and "operæ." Servitudes, including the emphyteusis and superficies, were the only form in which the Roman law could apportion the usufruct value of a thing ("Gebrauchswert") between several holders of rights therein.

Under the totally different conditions of fact and law prevailing in the Middle Ages, the rich development of tenurial ("Leihe-") rights and the numerous real rights and restrictions upon ownership which remained from older collective ownership solved in a far more comprehensive manner the problems with which servitudes were created to deal in the Roman law. At the same time, there also existed in the Middle Ages legal relations based upon juristic acts ("Rechtsgeschäfte") which resembled the Roman servitude, and by which limited rights of usufruct were created in rural and urban lands as special and peculiar rights in things belonging to others, distinct from ownership. Such rights could be given any content at will; and could be created in favor of lands, of individuals, or of groups; nor did men scruple to recognize the alienability and heritability of such rights. To this was added the fact that the idea of ownership merely for life gradually lost vitality. The Sachsenspiegel already contrasted ownership, not

burg-Strelitz 58, as against 22 allodial owners. However, the Mecklenburg fiefs, along with many other peculiarities, have always been peculiar in that, when not freely alienable and chargeable, they are "feuda impropria", and are therefore very like allodial estates. See *v. Buchka*, "Landesprivatrecht der Grossherzogtümer M.-Schw. und M.-Str." (1905), 129.

with the conception just referred to, but with a lifelong right to maintenance ("Leibzucht"), as a limited independent real right of usufruct; for example, the "Leibzucht" of a surviving spouse in the property of his or her deceased fellow.

Thus the German law, also, did succeed in developing its own real rights of usufruct in the property of others; but these rights were neither sharply distinguished conceptionally from its many other privileges of usufruct nor did they, as compared with the latter, play anything like so important a rôle as did the servitudes of the Roman law.

(II) **The Modern Law.** — With the reception of the Roman law acquaintance was made with its simple servitude concept, and an effort was made to apply this to the usufructuary rights of the native law. Here too, this process was not realized without violence to the German law; and here too the result was a theory which neither exactly conformed to the Roman nor did justice to the German law. The assumption of a peculiar "servitus iuris germanici", as one different from the Roman, was nothing else than a confession of embarrassment. Peculiarities of the German law were forced, for the most part, within the rules of the Roman servitude, as regarded their nature, origin, and termination.

(1) With reference to the *nature of servitudes,* there were classified under that concept:

(A) The PRIVILEGES OF MARKMEN in the commons AND OF THE LORD in the land let to his free tenants, which were derived from old relations of community and lordship. From the standpoint of the Roman law this was wrong, for it had always strictly enforced the principle "nulli res sua servit." It was therefore regarded as a peculiarity of the German law of servitudes that there was no place in it for the Roman rule. There resulted from the system of land registry, as a further exception to that rule, an owner's ("Eigentümer") servitude, similar to the proprietary hypothec (*infra,* § 54).

(B) In the second place, there were known to the older native law many BURDENS UPON LANDS that obligated the occupant of lands to positive acts; this was true particularly, of LAND CHARGES ("Reallasten"; *infra,* § 51). The Roman law, on the contrary, restricted the content of the servitude to a sufferance (of another's act) or an abstention (from acts on one's own part), — "servitus in faciendo consistere nequit", — inasmuch as it was only a right to the use of a thing and not a right against a person; and only unwillingly made an exception in favor of the "servitus oneris ferendi." The Germanic view, however, made impossible the consistent application of the Roman principle. Servitudes were recognized which involved positive actions on the part of the obligee; provided such was not the predominant element of the servitude, but merely one supplementary to another main obligation, — *e.g.* the obligation to maintain in condition a way in connection with a servitude of way. The obligation ("Last", charge) to permit the continuance of an existing structure in favor of another person was no longer regarded, as it was in the Roman law, as an exception.

(C) In the Roman law there were, as already remarked, only four types of PERSONAL SERVITUDES. In Germany the law was not restricted to these, but continued after the Reception to recognize as such any right of usufruct whatever, whether a predial or a personal servitude. Nor were the other limitations of the Roman law accepted in any greater degree, — namely, that real ("Grund-") servitudes were only such as secured an advantage in the user of the dominant tenement, and not a personal advantage to each temporary occupant thereof (*e.g.* a permission to paint upon the servient tenement), and that personal servitudes were strictly confined to the person of the individual thereto entitled, and so could neither be conveyed nor inherited. This unlimited content of the servitude concept, which characterized equally the common law and the regional systems, completely burst the servitude concept of the Roman law. Even limitations upon industry, and rights of execution and of ban were recognized as servitudes.

The new Civil Code has returned, for the first time, and as regards most of the points above referred to, to the theory of the pure Roman law. Only the owner's servitude has, at least, not been wholly excluded by it; similarly, it has retained obligations to perform positive acts (§§ 1021–22), while it has rejected (§ 1090) the restriction of personal servitudes to definite types. Among personal servitudes it has developed "Niessbrauch" (profits without user) into an entirely independent institute, which is regulated in essentials by the Roman rules. The corresponding usufructuary rights ("Nutzungsrechte") of the Germanic law continue, in part, to exist in the Civil Code in the "Nutzniessung" (rights of management and user, true usufruct) of the family law; and partly in special usufructuary rights whose regulation is reserved to state legislation; for example, rights to the parents' portion ("Altenteilsrechte"). The Swiss Civil Code contains an elaborate regulation of rights of management and usufruct. It also recognizes owner's servitudes.

(2) The rules concerning the *creation of servitudes* were similarly modified, in many respects, by the influence of native legal principles.

(A) As regards servitudes that were generally created BY JURISTIC ACT, the older Germanic laws required for their creation execution in court; and, in the cities, frequently entry in the town-register. These forms, however, were unable to hold their ground save in a few localities. So too in modern land-registry statutes the entry of real servitudes has seldom been made an indispensable requirement, although it is such under the Austrian Code and in the greater part of Mecklenburg. A few legal systems based at least the effectiveness of the servitude as against third parties upon registry. But most of them entirely excepted real servitudes from the compulsion of registry (Prussia). In the common law, also, according to the best opinion, a simple and formless agreement was sufficient. In this point the Civil Code has returned to the old Germanic principle: it requires registration of every real servitude that is created by a juristic act (§ 873). The same is true of personal servitudes existing only in connection with lands, as well as of a usufruct that is created in land (§ 873); but such a usufruct in chattels is created by a transfer of possession. Therefore, the bequest of a usufruct, which often occurs, and which under the older Germanic law immediately gave rise to the usufruct, now conveys merely a claim for its creation.

(B) Servitudes arising BY ACQUISITIVE PRESCRIPTION ("Ersitzung") did not exist in the older Germanic law. However, aside from the idea that everything that had existed as a right ("zu Recht") since immemorial time is therefore a legal right ("Rechtens"), the principle of judicial seisin (*supra*, p. 201) applied: whoever had exercised a servitude for a year and a day thereby acquired that favored status in litigation which resulted from judicial seisin. The Roman law recognized a servitude acquired by positive prescription, the precondition of which was an uninterrupted and rightful legal possession, exercised in good faith for ten or twenty years. This acquisitive prescription was adopted in Germany, although it was modified at many points by (*e.g.* as regards the prescription period) the particularistic systems. Wherever, also, a land-book system existed men clung to this institute; where compulsory registration prevailed, such possession was for the most part recognized as at least sufficient title to justify registration. On the other hand, the Civil Code has excluded the acquisitive prescription of unregistered servitudes, while recognizing such prescription of registered servitudes ("Tabular"-prescription) exactly as in the case of ownership and all other registered real rights. Similarly, the Swiss Civil Code; although, to be sure, this also recognizes in this connection an extraordinary prescriptive acquisition without registry, — namely, when the land charged therewith is itself not entered in the land-book (§ 662).

(C) Whereas the older Germanic law recognized STATUTORY SERVITUDES (for example, in many legal systems a surviving spouse had a right of usufruct for life — "Leibzucht" — by rule of law, in the property of the deceased mate) the Civil Code has done away with all statutory pure profits ("Niessbrauch": "ius fruendi" only), while permitting the continuance of certain statutory rights of use and profits ("Nutzniessung": "ius utendi" and "ius fruendi"), which, as already mentioned, represent the continuation of the ancient rights of lifelong maintenance ("Leibzuchtsrechte") just mentioned. The Swiss Civil Code also recognizes certain statutory rights of use and profits, the registration of which is alone necessary in order to make them effective against third persons claiming in good faith.

(3) *Termination.* — One consequence, already adverted to, of the Germanic view was that the union of the dominant with the servient tenement did not necessarily cause the destruction of the servitude (owner's servitude). The modern law of servitudes recognized an extinctive prescription of servitudes exactly as it recognized an acquisitive prescription; and these are still recognized in the Civil Code as resulting from registry in the land-book ("book"-prescription), and even, under some circumstances, as against the register itself (§ 1028, pars. 1, 2). On the other hand, the Swiss Civil Code allows a termination of servitudes under no circumstances except by cancellation in the land-book (§ 734). Termination of such servitudes by conveyances has played an important rôle; this method was introduced in modern agrarian legislation in the interest of agriculture. A number of types of real servitudes have been thus abolished, with compensation to their holders.

§ 50. **Particular Servitudes.** — A number of rights of usufruct that played an important part from the earliest times in the economic life of the Germanic people were subjected at an early day to careful legal regulation, especially in the dooms. Many of these were elaborately treated later in the servitude theory of the common law, and in many cases were still further developed by modern statutes.

(I) **Pasture Servitudes ("Weidegerechtigkeiten").** — (1) *Rights of pasture* ("Weide-", "Hutrechte", "Hütungsgerechtigkeiten") usually rested, in early times, either upon the share-rights of the markmen in the common meadows or upon the seigniorial rights of manorial and other land-lords ("Grund-" and "Gutsherren") in the land of the communes and of villeins dependent upon them. Other rights of pasture were only exceptionally recognized. Only in later times did it become more frequent to create independent rights of pasturage ("Hutgerechtigkeiten"); the special regulation of such rights was usually accomplished by means of so-called "Weiderezesse" (meadow-regulations). The influence of the Roman law continued to be slight. The rules of the native law retained authority, and it was possible to unite them with the Roman concept of servitudes only in an artificial manner (*supra*, p. 351).

The legal sources that deal with pasture rights contain detailed provisions concerning the kind and number of cattle that may be pastured. The number is ordinarily measured, after the manner of primitive laws, according to the number of "head" that could be wintered: "if the cattle cannot be wintered they shall also not be summered" ("was nicht erwintert wird an Vieh, soll auch nicht gesommert werden"). They also regulate the manner of user, — which must be "sparing", and with regard for the land charged; the time of pasturage, — for example, "the cows shall be driven ('schürgen') on St. Jürgen from the meadows"; the privilege of the owner of the servient land to undertake changes in its cultivation; etc.

(2) *Pasture communities* ("Weidegemeinschaften") existed in particularly great numbers, as was natural in view of the historical development. The privileges of the members of a mark or village commune or of the later special agrarian associations to drive their cattle upon the common lands (that is the "Hütungsrechte"), were derived from ancient associational and manorial relations. So long as the ownership of such lands had not passed to a corporate association ("Körperschaft") distinct from the members, and so long as the rules of the Roman corporation had not been applied to such corporate associations, such a privilege

was inconsistent with the Roman rules, and led to the rejection, as already mentioned, of the rule "nemini res sua servit"; for the common meadow was certainly no "res aliena" as against the members. The same was true as regards rights of pasture that landlords were accustomed to reserve to themselves in land let to peasants. In such cases legal theory spoke of a "ius compasculationis simplex."

The right of co-pasturage ("Mithut", "ius compascendi") often granted to the owner of the servient land was a peculiar institute of the pure Germanic law. On the other hand, when several persons possessed at the same time a right of pasturage upon the same holding ("ius compascui"), and when, as was frequently the case, a mutual right of pasture ("Koppelhut", "ius compasculationis reciprocum") was granted to both lord and tenant, there were involved rights in "re aliena."

(3) Very often there was associated with rights of pasture a *right of sheep-run* ("Schäfereirecht"), — that is the right to keep a herd of sheep under one's own shepherds; and also the right to name the shepherds of a common herd ("Schäfereistabrecht"). The *right of faldage* ("Pferchrecht"), — that is the right to demand the folding of the sheep upon certain lands in order to manure them, was a corresponding right on the part of the owner of the servient lands.

(4) Rights of way were also ordinarily associated with privileges of pasture. This was known as a *right of drift* ("Triftrecht"), — that is the right to drive cattle over the land of another. Such rights of way, like all others, were generally regulated, as to details, in a manner which varied in many respects from the Roman rules.

Rights of pasture have been restricted in modern times; and some statutes have forbidden their new creation.

(II) **Wood-botes** ("Waldgerechtigkeiten"). — These also originated in ancient associational and manorial relations, and their establishment as independent rights by juristic acts was recognized only at a later period. They included:

(1) Rights to make use of the wood: either as rights of *estover* ("Holzungsgerechtigkeiten"), — house-bote, fire-bote, or for other purposes, — or as rights to gather windfall ("Windbruchs-", "Holzleserechte"), and others.

(2) Rights to make use of the *leafage* ("Streurechnungs-", "Laubsammlungsrechte": the right to collect the leafage, rights of litter).

(3) Rights to make use of the *forest fruits,* especially the right of mast ("Mastgerechtigkeit"), a right of pasturage in the woodlands; further, rights to gather beechnuts and acorns, to pluck bilberries, etc.

(4) Rights of user in the *forest soil,* such as the right of grazing, of tar-boiling, and of charcoal-burning.

Recent legislation has not been favorable to forest rights. In the interest of forestry they have been regulated by the State, and to a great extent abolished. In very recent years a contrary tendency has become noticeable, since the importance of such rights to the poorer population has come to be more highly appreciated.[1]

(III) Of the remaining real servitudes that may occur, **water rights** ("Wasserrechte"), — rights of conduit, rights to take water, and rights to water animals, — have been regulated in modern times in close conformity, for the most part, with the rules of the Roman law. These rights, and also **building servitudes**, although these last are already to be found in the medieval cities, played a lesser rôle than in Rome, because the elaborately developed rights of vicinage sufficed in most cases that arose.

Topic 3. Charges on Land ("Reallasten").

§ 51. **Real Charges, in general.**[2] (I) **Concept.** — Land charges are charges upon land, or recurrent dues ("Leistungen"), of a positive nature, which are rendered from the land as portions of its economic produce to the person entitled to the charge. They are distinguished from servitudes, in the sense of the Roman law, by the obligation of a positive act. They assure to the person entitled to them a limited real right. Such rights in land charges belong among the most important real rights in lands that have been developed in Germanic law. According to the nature of the object rendering them, and according to the extent, the time of accrual, and the continuance of the charge, we speak of services, dues in kind, and money rents; unilateral and mutual or bilateral charges; fixed and variable charges, — the last, for example,

[1] *Gierke,* "Privatrecht", II. 675.

[2] *Duncker,* "Die Lehre von den Reallasten" (1837); *Renaud,* "Beitrag zur Theorie der Reallasten" (1846); *Gerber,* "Zur Theorie der Reallasten", in J. B. für Dogm., II (1858), 35 *et seq.,* VI (1863), 266, and in his "Gesammelte Abhandlungen", 213 *et seq.*; *v. Schwind,* "Die Reallastenfrage", in *Ihering's* J. B., XXXIII (1894), 1 *et seq.*; *Pflüger,* "Über die rechtliche Natur der Reallasten", in Arch. f. zivil. Praxis, LXXXI (1893), 292–328.

those which are rendered on marriage or as death duties; perpetual and temporary charges.

(II) **Historical development.** — Land charges, which were unknown in the law of antiquity, were called into existence by the social, economic, and political conditions of the Middle Ages.

(1) *Relations of dependence,* in part personal and in part economic in nature, *recognized by the private law* between the owners of land and their villeins, constituted one of their roots. Slaves and serfs who cultivated manorial virgates given them as holdings, and equally freemen who received land for cultivation under one or another form of tenancy, were bound to render in return various services and dues, plow-work ("Fronden"), dues in kind, and money rents. In time it came to be immaterial whether these payments rested originally upon personal unfreedom, or represented payments by freemen for the cession of usufructuary rights. The nature and the amount of the payment were alone important in determining the degree of the dependence. And since both of these were ordinarily firmly fixed, such payments came to be closely associated with the lands whose occupants were obligated to render them. The lands, as such, and no longer the status of the occupant, were determinant of the payments: different payments were due from a "mansus servilis" than from a "mansus censualis" or a "mansus ingenuilis." The lands and the charges resting upon them were permanent, and eventually their character reacted upon the legal status of their successive occupants.

(2) Labor services and other dues were not due merely to the owners of the land, as such, from their villeins and rent-paying peasants. The State also claimed certain services, — for example military service, suit of court, the finding of horses for royal officials, and the like; and collected taxes, such as the military tax laid upon those subjects who were unable personally to fulfill their military obligations. The same was no less true of lords of courts and bailiwicks, who gradually developed from State officials into local sovereigns with independent powers of government and taxation; that is, into Territorial princes. Finally, the same was also true of the church, which claimed the tithes of every piece of land, no matter by whom it was cultivated. Unlike the obligations we have just named above under (1), the obligations we are now dealing with involved what would be called in modern terminology *obligations of a public nature.* But it was peculiarly characteristic of the Middle Ages that there was no

boundary between rights of public and of private law. Consequently, these dues owing to the State or to private holders of sovereign rights, were assimilated to private rights; they too came to be regarded as charges upon the land that rested upon its temporary occupant. Thus, they might easily become confused with obligations of the first class; especially because they frequently had the same substantive content, and because the great landowners frequently developed into Territorial princes.

The reason why these obligations were so closely connected with the soil and were thus projected upon it, lay in the prevailing system of agriculture. There was as yet no personal credit worthy of mention. Since property still consisted, for the most part, of land, direct liability attached to the land. It was the land, rather than the person, that was regarded as charged, as obligated, as liable.

(3) The wide prevalence of landed charges explains why this legal institute was utilized, even during the recedence of an agricultural economy, in the creation of real charges of a new kind which appeared in the cities; in other words, within the special fields of the incipient money economy. This was the institute of the "*Rentenkauf*" ("purchase-rent"), a capitalistic rent or annuity by means of which capitalists assured themselves of permanent return in the form of rents rendered periodically as interest for a capital sum invested. In these transactions the association with relations of manorial or economic dependence, which was peculiar to the older real charges, was already notably less prominent. The same was true of many other independent charges for which the form of land charges continued to be retained, — for example, in parents' portions ("Altenteilsrechten," p. 329 *supra*), widows' annuities, etc.

(4) *From the 1500 s onward* the development of land charges, which had until then been unchecked, ceased. Manorial rights were deprived, in time, of their private legal character under the law of things, assumed a purely public character, and were thenceforth subjected exclusively to the public law (State and commune taxes, charges for roads, charges for dikes, ecclesiastical dues, etc.). In the seigniories, which continued to spread, especially in eastern Germany, the services of rural wage earners were more and more utilized along with the plow-services required of villeins in the cultivation of the seigniorial estates. Still other means were created by the necessities of credit. At the same time most of the older land charges were, at first, continued. It was the agrarian

legislation of the modern period, which had as its end the emancipation of rural holdings, that first abolished such charges to any considerable extent. As a matter of fact, they were generally abolished only in the regions of the French law; but in most of the other parts of Germany many special charges were totally abolished, — notably plow-services, — and many others were declared redeemable. In general, also, the creation of new perpetual charges was forbidden. Nevertheless the institute, as such, has not disappeared except in the regions subject to the Code Civil. Indeed, in very recent years, it has acquired renewed importance in the creation of so-called "Rentengüter" — estates subject to land charges that are very generally perpetual — and has also been adopted in the Civil Code. The Introductory Act thereof also left unchanged existing land charges (§ 184), as well as provisions of State law regarding the redeemability, conversion, or limitations both of servitudes and of land charges (§ 113). In Switzerland land charges, aside from annuities ("Renten"), remained in three cantons only; but the Civil Code has adopted the land charge ("Grundlast") despite violent opposition in the French cantons, and has regulated it in common with servitudes. Unlike the German Civil Code (§ 1105), however, it has in this connection (§ 782) recognized as land charges, not only periodical but also single renders ("Leistungen").

(III) **The Nature and Content of Land Charges.** — (1) *The Older Theories.* — Land charges presented the greatest difficulties to legal science from the moment it began to busy itself with their theory. It was precisely here that its efforts were least successful, because the forms of the Germanic law could not be forced exactly into the Roman categories. The countless attempts made to explain land charges have represented three tendencies, the endeavor being made to classify them either as contractual claims, or as real rights, or as mixed rights partly obligational in character and partly rights under the law of things.

(A) When conceived of AS A CONTRACT CLAIM, — a view which found expression as early as the 1600 s, — land charges were classified by the older theorists (Zarpzow, Schilter, Mevius, and others) as ordinary obligations associated with a pledge-like liability of the thing; in other words they were regarded as contractual claims secured by a hypothec. In order to make this relation more intelligible, resort was had by modern theorists (*e.g.* by Kohler) to the Roman conception of an "actio in rem scripta." Even this view, however, was unable to explain "how an obligation ostensibly personal changes its holder with a change in the possession of the land";[1] also, it overlooked the fact that in the case of a land charge there is but a single legal relation, and not, as in the case of a hypothec, an obligational claim and also a right of pledge. The theory which regarded land charges as obligations to an indefinite obligee, likewise proceeded from the assumption of a personal obligation; such obligations, incumbent upon the successive possessors of a definite piece of land, were designated by Gerber "Zustands-"obligations (determined by the *condition* or situation of the land). This construction, however, although it had many supporters (*e.g.* Stobbe), leaves completely out of account the Roman concept of an obligation which it purports to accept as its basis; for the Roman obligation is inconceivable in the absence of a personal obligor. The concept of an obligation, moreover, proved to be useless for the further reason that there is in a land charge nothing like the cancellation or release which is essential to an obligation: an obligation is satisfied by performance, — by payment of the debt; but this is by no means true of a land charge. And though, finally, to avoid these difficulties, the charge was even explained as a series, merely physically associated, of distinct individual payments arising under various circumstances (Mitteis, also von Schwind), this was, in fact, "the very acme of violence in dissimulating the phenomenon that actually exists."[2]

(B) Those theories which explained the land charge AS AN INSTITUTE OF THE LAW OF THINGS rested on a sounder basis. These theories regarded the personal obligation as at most "an accessory element", laying emphasis upon the real right in the land. It is true that the widespread view, especially common in older legal theory, that land charges are servitudes (servitudes, of course, of the German law, consisting "in faciendo") merely avoided the difficulty in the problem, explaining one unknown quantity by another equally unknown. When a peculiar real right to recurrent services was later substituted for the "servitus in faciendo", or the real character ("Dinglichkeit", "thinglikeness") of such right was derived from an original right of control over the land, no very great advance was made toward a solution of the problem. Nor can more be said of the theory, — which would have satisfied the naïve view of the Middle Ages but is inadequate to the needs of modern theory, — that the land itself, conceived of as a person, is the obligor, and its temporary occupant merely

[1] *Gierke*, "Privatrecht", II, 705. [2] *Ibid.*, 707.

his representative (Duncker). It was far more nearly correct to ascribe to the person entitled to the charge an additional real right in the individual payments; though the manner in which this view was developed by Renaud, originally made it appear applicable to those cases only in which natural or money rents were rendered, and not where services were rendered.

(C) The ECLECTIC THEORIES sought to cure the imperfection of the two preceding theories. Some authors, in their desire to save the land charge, rejected in toto the distinction between real and personal rights, or devised transition concepts of subjective-real rights and real-obligational rights (Eichhorn, Reyscher, Pflüger, and others): constructions which necessarily remained unclear and contradictory because based upon concepts of the Roman law, notwithstanding that the correctness of their basic principle was revealed by the historical study of Germanic law (*infra*, §§ 53, 68). Finally, many have attributed a mixed character to land charges because of the fact that such a charge is, as a whole, a real charge upon the land, whereas the obligation to make any particular payment is a personal debt of the occupant (Wächter, Walter, Roth, and others).

This last has doubtless been the theory most widely accepted. It also was unsatisfactory, for it endeavored vainly to distinguish the two classes of rights; a right to a land charge is, broadly considered, nothing else than a right to the individual payments. Nor was there any advance toward a complete explanation when others emphasized, as the most important element in such charges, either the obligation or the real right; adding to the obligation, in the first case, a real right in the land, and to the real right, in the second case, an obligational relation to the occupant (Cosack, H. O. Lehmann, Dernburg, Landsberg, and others).

(2) *The Modern Theory of the German Law.* — A solution of the problem was first offered by the theory which Gierke[1] has recently laid at the basis of his researches, following the lines earlier indicated by Renaud, Gengler, Arnold, and H. O. Lehmann.

It must be noted, in the first place, that in the Middle Ages, when the institute of the land charge was full of vitality, the rights of one entitled to such a charge were conceived of as real rights. They gave him a right of control over the thing which originally appeared as the result of ownership of the land or of some authority under the public law. Like all other real rights, land charges

[1] *Gierke*, "Privatrecht", II, 710 *et seq.*

were clothed in the cover of seisin, either of the estate itself or of the right to the render of the rent; and, like every other right embodied in seisin, the right to a land charge was created by a real juristic act, registered in the land-book, and protected by actions based upon the seisin. Now, land charges existed and still exist, as already mentioned, in the form of recurrent dues, distinct in nature, which under the medieval law were rendered by the possessor cultivating the land in his own right, and according to the later law and the law of to-day by the owner (or in some cases the "subordinate" owner), out of the land and to the person thereto entitled. That such person possessed a real right in the land itself, according to the original theory of the Germanic law, in all those cases where a part of the fruits of the land were rendered to him either in kind or in money, — that he enjoyed, in other words, a seisin in the land, follows directly from the general principles of the Germanic law of land already discussed (*supra*, p. 186 etc.). The same is true today, however, of land charges in the nature of services, however great may be the difficulty of reconciling these with the older theories based upon the law of things. We must conceive of a piece of land, with all its economic organization, as a whole; as a solidary landed estate ("Grundvermögen") whose products and whose usufructuary value include not alone the fruits it yields but also the labor-force available upon it, through whose employment the person entitled to the charge receives the profits due him in the form of payments either in money or in kind ("Abgaben") or in services. The portion of produce or of labor services deliverable to the holder of the right curtails the estate of the possessor. We thus attain a conception of the land charge which is uniformly applicable to all its forms; namely, one of a real charge resting upon the land ("Grundstück") or upon the landed estate ("Grundvermögen") of the possessor, and a corresponding real right in the person entitled to the charge. "Corresponding to the right of the person entitled to the charge to receive, is a duty to perform, which, as a passive element of the estate in the land, rests upon the latter's temporary occupant or owner, and may be designated as a 'real obligation' ('dingliche Schuld,' real debt)." [1]

The conception of a real obligation, which at first blush appears to contradict the principle (always recognized, of course, in the Germanic law) that only a human being can be an obligor (*infra*, § 68), nevertheless results necessarily from the Germanic concept

[1] *Gierke*, "Privatrecht", II, 711.

of liability ("Haftungsbegriff"). Every liability presupposes (*infra*, § 68) the existence of an obligation ("Schuld"): that is, the legal duty of some human being to render some performance. Wherever something is liable there must exist some sort of an obligation. In the case of an "Obligation" there rests upon the obligor, personally, a legal duty; the right of the obligee to receive, corresponding to his duty to perform, is enforceable against him personally whether such personal responsibility originate contractually or in some non-contractual circumstance. In the case of a "dingliche Schuld", on the contrary, it is not a person, as such, who is bound to perform and for whose performance somebody or something is liable, but rather a person who is determined by his ownership of particular land subject to a charge. The temporary owner of this land is the obligor; it is solely his real relation to this land, expressed in his ownership, which makes him the obligor. Unless, therefore, a personal obligation exists, in addition to the real obligation, the obligor's duty cannot be enforced by a personal action against him, but only upon the ground of a real right in the land existing in favor of the obligee.

The "dingliche Schuld", therefore, has a necessary complement — necessary to the person who is obligee — in a "real liability" of the land (*infra*, §§ 54, 69). "A real charge is a right of usufruct secured by the liability of a thing."[1] In other words, the land that is charged is liable to the person who holds the charge for the individual performances as they become due. This idea lay at the basis of the medieval phraseology; as *e.g.* that the virgate "gelded" ("zinsen") the land, was "geldable" ("zinsfällig"), etc. The new Civil Code, — which, it may be remarked, recognizes land charges only in the form of dues in money or kind ("Abgaben"), — and the Swiss Civil Code as well, are therefore entirely in accord with the old law in classifying the institute among limited real rights in land.

Under the medieval law, the person entitled to the charge could satisfy himself for any unsatisfied payment, out of the land and the chattels found thereon; and, indeed, in the case of certain ground rents ("Grundzinsen"), even by distraint by way of self-help. In the more modern law the liability (warranty, "Verhaftung") existing in his favor, which came to be enforceable solely by way of judicial execution, extended to the same things that were liable for the claims of mortgagees. With this step the land charge acquired a character akin to mortgage rights

[1] *Gierke*, "Privatrecht", II, 712.

("Grundpfandrechten"). Nevertheless it remained primarily a usufructuary right, which directly attached to the utility value of the land; whereas mortgage rights are primarily merely rights warranted by a thing, and only as a last resort become the basis of a claim to the land so liable.

Inasmuch as the land charged is liable to the holder of the charge for payment of the debt, the real debt rests upon the possessor or owner, at any moment, of the land. From this the older law drew the correct conclusion that the land was also liable, in the hand of each legal successor, for unsatisfied payments that had become due in the time of his predecessors. To be sure, this was not true of plow-services, for one could owe them only while one possessed the land, and only at the moments when they were demandable; no later payment was possible. Nor was it possible in the case of tithes, which the person entitled thereto was bound to take from the current harvest, and which, in case he neglected to do so, were not delivered in the future. But it was true of all rents in kind and in money; and although the liability of the land for such overdue rents was later, for practical reasons, customarily limited to a definite number of years, modern statutes usually clung to the other view, which alone is consistent with the nature of the land charge. More recently, however, it has been erroneously, and for the first time, abandoned in legal theory. The new Civil Code has followed the older law. Not, however, the Swiss Civil Code; for it provides that each render shall become a personal debt upon the termination of three years after it becomes due, the land not being liable for it thereafter (§ 791, 2).

The real debt and the real liability, and the corresponding real right in the holder of the charge, are the essence of a land charge. And the purpose of the institute was thereby perfectly satisfied in the older law. For the liability of the land gave to the holder of the charge a sufficient security; and from the viewpoint of an agricultural economy the only sufficient security possible. There was no need to make its temporary occupant personally liable in addition; that is, to subject his other property, as well as the land, to attack by the holder of the charge. Consequently, the element of personal liability by the possessor was totally lacking in the land charge of the older law. This is seen most clearly in the fact that the occupant of the land could free himself from liability for overdue payments by renouncing the estate: the charge remained upon the land, though now ownerless (*contra:* Gobbers, and Wopfner). At the same time, in the case of particular charges and under certain circumstances, a personal debt of the occupant was early recognized. This was the case, notably, when the real liability of the land for accrued payments was limited to a relatively short period; for the right to the charge would otherwise have become completely useless at the expiration of such period. The more modern statutes have adhered in principle to the old viewpoint, recognizing only exceptionally a personal obligation. The new Civil Code has recognized for the first time a personal liability of the landowner, side by side with the real charge, for payments accruing during the continuance of his ownership. (Not, to be sure, in the case of the annuity-charge — "Rentenschuld"; — which, however, it does not include among land charges, — *infra*, § 52). That such personal liability is not, however, an essential element under the present law is evident from the Code's recognition (§ 1108) of the possibility of its exclusion. Only in cases where a personal liability exists, — which *may* be, but *need* not be, the case, — does the content of the land charge include an obligational in addition to the real element which, under all circumstances, is essential to it. The land charge is distinguished by this fact from the hypothec, in which the relation of personal liability is theoretically the primary right, and the real right only accessory thereto. The Swiss Civil Code, unlike the German, bases the land charge upon the pure principle of a real ("Sach-", "thingal") liability (§ 782, 791, 1); but, as already mentioned, it permits the transformation of the real into a personal liability after the expiration of three years (§ 791, 2).

(IV) **Creation.** — (1) The older charges upon land were very commonly created *by rule of law*, either of custom or of enactment. In the modern law the latter ordinarily occurs only in the case of dues ("Leistungen") under the public law, which, however, can no longer be regarded as land charges in the true sense.

(2) The older law required for their creation *by juristic act* a release ("Auflassung") and also, often, entry in the land-book. While the common law, under the influence of Roman legal views, permitted their creation by simple contract or testamentary disposition, some of the regional systems have clung to the requirement of registration or judicial confirmation. Modern legislation has likewise required registration either for their creation (Austria, Saxony) or at least in order to make them effective against third persons (Prussia). The new Civil Code permits the creation of land charges, as of all other rights in land, only

by a real agreement ("Einigung") and registry in the land-book (§ 873).

(3) *Acquisitive prescription* of land charges was unknown to the older Germanic law, — save that it recognized, here also, a plea based upon immemorial possession. Aside from this, it recognized only judicial seisin. In the common law the problem of acquisitive prescription remained a disputed one, but in the end an extraordinary prescription in thirty or forty years was generally recognized. The regional legal systems, for the most part, went further, introducing also an ordinary prescription (Prussia, Austria). On the other hand, acquisitive prescription has again either been entirely abolished or at least made more difficult under the modern system of land registration. It is not recognized by the Civil Code.

(V) **Conversion** ("Umwandlung") is a change of the land charge of such a nature that another form of render ("Leistung") is substituted for one formerly existing. It may either be "Fixation", — that is, the conversion of a charge quantitatively indefinite into one quantitatively definite (as *e.g.* the substitution of a money rent in place of tithes); or redemption ("Adäration"), that is, the conversion of an existing charge in services or dues in kind into a money rent. Conversions of this class may be effected by juristic act of the parties; but they have been most frequently accomplished through legislation.

(VI) **Extinction.** — As already stated, a land charge is not destroyed by the abandonment, by the holder of the land, of the land liable therefor; and it is as little destroyed by the extinction of the family who possess the land. Again, acquisition of the land by the owner of the charge merely excludes the possibility of its formal payment; it does not destroy the charge as such. The Civil Code (§ 889) so holds, in accord with the older law; whereas in modern law — at least in the case of unregistered charges — merger ("Konfusion") had been regarded as sufficient to terminate the charge. On the other hand, land charges are extinguished:

(1) *By rule of law*, by the destruction of the land or by the disappearance of the person entitled to it. A land charge of a qualified nature or created for a definite period is extinguished by the incidence of a condition subsequent or the expiration of the term.

(2) *By juristic act*, — a unilateral renunciation by the person entitled to the charge being in general sufficient, under the Civil Code, when followed by cancellation in the land-book

(§ 875). Charges upon land can be specifically abolished by juristic act.

(3) The claim to any individual payment may be lost under all circumstances *through extinctive prescription.* But the right to the charge as a whole cannot so be lost where there exists a system of land registry; save that in case of wrongful cancellation there results a so-called negative prescription of the land-book ("Buchverjährung", § 901). Particularly important under the Civil Code is destruction as a result of a procedure by citation (§ 1112). In the case of unregistered land charges extinctive prescription was recognized by the common law and by most of the regional systems.

(4) The mode of extinction which has played by far the most important rôle historically is that of *statutory provision.* We have already remarked under II that modern legislation, following the example set by France, has endeavored since the beginning of the 1800 s, and particularly since 1848, to abolish land charges, so far as possible, in the interest of the peasantry. A whole series of them were abolished outright, including all charges connected with "patrimonial" rights of judicature and seigniorial police; also, hunting services ("Jagdfronden"), and all charges akin to taxes. As regards others, compensation from the public treasury was provided for in many statutes. Most other land charges, — save those of a temporary nature, such as elders' portions, — were made redeemable by special statutes adopted in all the German States with the sole exception of Mecklenburg. All perpetual land charges were required to be redeemed upon conditions set by these statutes; as respects other charges, the owner of the land and the person entitled to the charge were given the privilege of demanding redemption under the statute. For these latter the statutes prescribe a special redemption procedure. This amounts to a conversion of the charge, when not already payable in money, into a money rent, the redemption sum being a certain multiple of the rent. The State lends its aid in the redemption by paying to the holder of the rent the capital sum involved, generally in the form of interest-bearing obligations of the State ("Rentenbriefe"), and collects the rents in turn from the obligor, in addition to a certain premium required for amortisation. This redemption-premium has the effect, after it has been paid for a series of years, of extinguishing the rent, thereby accomplishing the ultimate release of the land (Prussian statutes of June 27th, 1890, and July 7th, 1891).

§ 52. **Particular Land Charges.** (I) **Plow-work and other Manorial Services** ("Fronden", "Dienste"). — These originated, as already mentioned, partly in old relations of serfdom and partly in seigniorial privileges under public law. After the beginning of the modern period they increased greatly in number and acquired renewed economic importance in consequence of the development of seigniories in Eastern Germany. Only those services, however, that were based upon obligations under the private law retained to the end the character of land charges in the true sense.

The services owed might be of the most varied character. A distinction was made between definite or indefinite services (the latter first became general in the 1600 s), ordinary and extraordinary services, manual services (the person obligated was bound to perform manual labor, but not to furnish anything except the necessary implements) and team services (furnishing in these cases oxen and implements). The performances need not be rendered in person, but were required to be rendered gratuitously.

The agrarian legislation of the 1800 s abolished in most States all forms of plow-work and other services. Where services can still be registered as land charges they are either limited in duration or redeemable under the statutes.

(II) **Ground rents** ("Grundzinsen", "census"). — These appeared in countless forms and species from the earliest period of the Middle Ages. These were land charges that involved the payment of regularly recurrent rents ("Leistungen") of definite amount. Originally dues in kind exclusively, they were later rendered in the form of money rents. Payments in kind were made in the fruits of the soil, but also in fowl, wax, honey, wine, beer, etc. With reference to the part of the tenement charged, men spoke of "garden-fowl" ("Gartenhühner"), "chimney-fowl" ("Rauchhühner"), "hearth-money" ("Herdgeld"), "pasture-tax" ("Wurtzins"); and so on. The time and place of render resulted in such names as "lattice-rent" ("Gatterzins", — a rent collected at the gate or barrier; it disappeared later and was replaced by the "Bringzins", a rent required to be "brought"); "Easter-fowl", "Shrovetide-fowl", "Easter eggs", "Whitsuntide lambs", "Martinmas-geese", "nuptial-fowl", and the like. Rents overdue were in many cases increased by penal interest, — to the extent of duplication in the case of the so-called "sliding-interest" rents ("Rutscherzinsen"). Continued default resulted in the escheat of manorial holdings to the lord of the rent.

The old ground rents of this class have disappeared in modern times. The principles of the medieval law are no longer applicable to the redemption rents substituted in their place (*supra*, p. 367).

(III) **The tithe** ("decima"). — This was a payment of a definite quota, usually the tenth part, but often also the eleventh, twentieth, or sixtieth part, of the yearly harvest of the land. It appeared chiefly in two connections: as a lay or secular and as an ecclesiastical tithe; the former being collected from the earliest Middle Ages by secular land magnates and by the crown; the latter being claimed from an early period by the church from all believers, upon the basis of certain Biblical passages. Although supported in their efforts by the Frankish State, the church was unable, in the long run, to establish generally the obligation of the church's tithe and a prohibition of the secular tithe. The ecclesiastical tithes therefore became, also, a tribute under the private law; which, while it served the ends of the church, accrued to it only by virtue of a special legal title. Moreover, the person of the temporary holder of the rent was not of decisive importance in the conception of the ecclesiastical tithe, but only the mode of its original creation. According to the content of the right, there were distinguished:

(1) "Decima universalis" and "particularis", according as the tithe affected an entire field and all the arable plots and vineyards included within it, or merely individual pieces of land therein. In the first case a tithe was collected also from newly cleared land, as an "assart-" ("Neubruchs-", "Rott-") tithe.

(2) "Decima generalis" and "specialis", according as the tithe was paid in all or only in special products of the soil.

(3) "Decima prædialis" and "decima carnium", predial tithes and blood (or "animal", "flesh", or "living") tithes, — the former consisting in fruits of the field, the latter in animals or animal products (horses, cattle, swine, sheep, eggs, milk, malt, or honey).

(4) Greater tithes and lesser tithes; the former collected upon corn and wine, the latter from the produce of fruit trees and gardens (fruit, vegetables, and the like).

As a rule the collection was so made that the lord of the tithe was notified of the harvest day; and then he himself or his tithe collectors undertook the enumeration of the heaps of corn, sheaves, sacks, or tubs, in the order in which they were garnered in the field.

As a result of the modern legislation of the States, including that of recent years, — *e.g.* the Prussian statute of March 2, 1850, — all tithes have been declared redeemable, and some of them (the lesser tithes, assart tithes, and the blood tithes) generally abolished; the new creation of tithes being prohibited.

(IV) **Capital rent ("Rente") and purchase-rent ("Rentenkauf").**[1] — Both in Germany and also in France, Italy, and elsewhere, there were widely prevalent in the later Middle Ages a special class of ground rents known as "redditus annui", "Gülten", "Gelder". These were capital rents ("Renten"). They owed their origin to the increasing prosperity of urban life; whence they were also known as rents "of town law" ("Weichbildsrenten"; in Lübeck "Wiboldsrenten").

The transition from the older ground rent to the capital rent was made by the so-called "soul-rent" ("Seelzins"). This rent, paid as a "Seelgeräte" to replenish the sacred vessels and vestments ("Geräte") used in the church's offices, — that is, for masses said on the deathday of the donor, — was laid upon a house or land. The donor created it by imposing upon the temporary possessor of the land (usually himself, but in case of an endowment mortis causa one of his heirs) a yearly payment to an ecclesiastical house, which assumed in return therefor the performance of spiritual services. This was done either by the donor's conveying the ownership of the land to the church, receiving it back as a leasehold subject to an obligation to pay the rent, or by his reserving the ownership to himself or his heirs and conveying to the church merely the right to the rents with which he charged the land in perpetuity. These "Gülten", "Zinsen", were already true "Renten."

In the 1300 s there appeared, finally, the true, the annuity or money interest ("Rente"); the yearly payment for money capital loaned to another. Increasing commerce increased in the cities the

[1] *Arnold*, "Zur Geschichte des Eigentums in den deutschen Städten" (1861); *Rosenthal*, "Zur Geschichte des Eigenthums in der Stadt Würzburg" (1878); *Gobbers*, "Die Erbleihe und ihr Verhältnis zum Rentenkauf im mittelalterlichen Köln des XII–XIV Jahrhunderts", in Z². R. G., IV (1883), 130–214; *Rehme*, "Die Lübecker Grundhauern, Ein Beitrag zur Lehre von den Reallasten" (1905); *Winiarz*, "Erbleihe und Rentenkauf in Österreich ob und unter der Enns", no. 80 (1906) of *Gierke's* "Untersuchungen"; *Fr. Beyerle*, "Die ewigen Renten des Mittelalters", in Vj. Soz. W. G., IX (1911), 401–406 (with reference to *v. Stempel*, "Die ewigen Renten und ihre Ablösung, Zur mittelalterlichen Kirchengeschichte Deutschlands", 1910, Leipzig dissertation).

demand for capital. Houseowners, in particular, required it for improvement and extension of their dwellings and work-buildings. On the other hand, as early as the 1300 s many burghers, especially the greater merchants in German cities (*e.g.* Lübeck), had accumulated in trade considerable capital which they were desirous of profitably investing. The only form of secure investments theretofore available had been the acquisition of land: it was possible to buy a piece of land and then to lease it for a "Zins", — preferably under a heritable lease. Of course, as time passed, constantly decreasing importance was laid upon the "superior" ownership that resulted in such cases to the lessor, since the purpose of the transaction, as for him, consisted simply in the receipt of a permanent and secure income. This inconvenient form of the heritable rent-lease ("Zinsleihe") was therefore abandoned. In place of it, it became customary for the capitalist to pay a certain sum directly to the owner of a piece of land in return for the promise of a capitalistic rent ("Rente") from the latter. This rent was at first frequently rendered in natural products, such as small grain, corn, or wine; but from the 1300 s onward it was ordinarily rendered in money. This transaction was the "Rentenkauf" or purchase-rent, an annuity contract. It satisfied perfectly the needs of both parties, the landowner's need of capital and the capitalist's need of income, and therefore gave a powerful impulse to economic progress. Its increasing adoption was also furthered by the circumstance that the church's prohibition of interest ("Zins", — *infra*, § 86) was no impediment to its collection; on the contrary, it was possible to maintain that prohibition only because the "Rentenkauf" fulfilled the economic function of an interest-bearing loan.

This capitalistic rent which was sold by the owner (the debtor, the "Gültmann") out of his land in return for a sum of money paid him by the creditor (the rent-lord or "Gült-" lord, "Rentner") was a charge upon the land. But it was distinguished from the older land charges in an important respect; for it had no connection whatever with any relation of dependence, personal or real, but on the contrary was created by an independent legal transaction, as "a land charge of a purely private nature whose elements were taken exclusively from the law of property."[1] This acknowledgment of a rent, however, involved a limitation upon the owner's estate, in the interest of the holder of the rent, which was characteristic of land charges. Indeed, the charge was

[1] *Gierke*, "Privatrecht", II, 754.

conceived of "as the conveyance of an incorporeal portion of landed property";[1] and it was treated, as the German law of things required, as an incorporeal immovable thing, a seisin in which was held by the recipient of the rent. On account of its character, which was assimilated to the qualities of land, such a rent could only be created by release ("Auflassung") and registration. To these requirements there was early added the execution of a public document, — the rent-deed ("Rentenbrief", "Gültbrief"). This was often treated as commercial paper, the transfer of the paper, accompanied by a corresponding informal contract, sufficing for the alienation and pledging of the rent. Although the amount of the rent was originally determined by free agreement, there was developed at an early day (and in this connection for the first time) a fixed relation between capital and interest; that is, a fixed rate of interest. The purchase price, from being originally very high, sank generally speaking to a sum twenty times that of the rent; in other words, the rent amounted to five per cent of the purchase price, or with 100 guldens of capital one could purchase a yearly rent of five guldens. This was established as the maximum legal income by the imperial police ordinances of 1530 and 1577.

Like other land charges, the annuity charge ("Rentenschuld") was distinctly real in character; and, indeed, to a particularly marked degree. It was paid by the temporary owner, even when he had known nothing, at the time of acquiring the land, of the rent with which it was charged. Of course he was also liable for unsatisfied payments accrued in the time of earlier possessors. Since the creditor's security lay in the permanent value of the house, the houseowner required the consent of the annuity holder to any disposition which could endanger its value. In case payment was not duly made the creditor possessed a right of distraint ("Pfändungsrecht") against the chattels he might find upon the land. If these were insufficient for the complete satisfaction of his claim, he could go against the land, — and against this alone. It was conveyed to him by means of a special execution process.

The sale of the "Rente" involved, in theory, a definitive conveyance of the rent regarded as an incorporeal part of the land. In theory the rent was perpetual. If the parties or their legal successors desired to rescind the transaction, the owner of the land was bound to repurchase the rent he had sold. Such a repurchase, — that is, such a redemption of the rent, — could

[1] *Gierke*, "Privatrecht", II, 754.

therefore originally be accomplished only by contract. At an early day, however, such redemption was commonly made easier to the debtor by giving him, at the time the annuity was created, the right of repurchase.

In this manner he could redeem the rent at any time by repayment of the purchase price. In many cities, and still later in some of the Territories of the Empire, the right was ultimately given to the debtor by statute to redeem the rent by payment of a capital sum, even without any contractual pre-determination of its amount. The imperial police ordinances of 1548 and 1577 made this the rule of the common law. On the other hand, the older law of rents knew absolutely no right of redemption-notice on the part of the creditor; as late as the 1500 s the statutes of the Empire expressly prohibited such a right; its creation by contract was also forbidden, save that it was permitted in one exceptional case, namely, default) by the imperial Recess of 1600.

All this, however, could not prevent a considerable change in the old institute after the Reception. The endeavor to make such rents freely redeemable made futile all statutory fetters; in the 1600 s it became permissible and usual to concede a right of redemption-notice to the creditor, also. This step, alone, accomplished much toward approximating the capitalistic rent to the loan ("Darlehn") secured by a hypothec. And this process was carried still further when its character as a purely real debt was disregarded at a very early day, a liability being imposed, first upon other lands, and later upon all other property whatever, of the debtor ("Fürpfand"). With this change the "Rentenkauf" was completely transformed into an interest-bearing loan secured by pledge. And when the Canonic prohibition of interest lost effect there was no longer any reason for retaining it as an independent legal institute. In its place there appeared the modern hypothec, in which, however, "the elements derived from the 'Rentenkauf' remained more or less vital." [1]

At the same time the capitalistic rent ("Gült", "Rente"), retained, here and there, its old independence. This was true in many parts of Switzerland, and of the "Ewiggeld" (perpetual-geld) of Munich. The latter was only abolished in 1900 by the Civil Code; the numerous "Ewiggelder" then existing have been converted into annuity charges ("Rentenschulden"). [2]

[1] *Gierke*, "Privatrecht", II, 763.

[2] *Lippmann*, "Das Ewiggeld in München" (Erlangen dissertation, 1910).

Inasmuch, however, as neither the earlier State law nor the present imperial law excludes the creation of "Renten" as perpetual land charges ("Reallasten"), but on the contrary have abolished only irredeemable perpetual "Renten", the rent charge ("Rentenbelastung"), which has best satisfied the credit necessities of landowners, has recently acquired increased importance. The redemption rents mentioned on page 367 *supra* are rent charges ("Rentenlasten") in the old sense. But, above all, there belong here the estates subject to a rent charge ("Rentengüter") that have been introduced in very recent Prussian legislation: the purchase price of these is not delivered at one time in a single capital sum, but as a rent which is imposed upon the land as a real charge, and which is to be extinguished in a certain time by amortisation. (See the statutes referred to on pp. 367, 370 *supra*, as well as the Mecklenburg Act of May 24, 1898.)

Finally, the Civil Code recognizes a special institute known as the "Rentenschuld", — a limited annuity-charge. This, accordingly, is not classed by it among "Reallasten", but is treated as a special form of the land-debt ("Grundschuld"; *infra*, p. 393).

Topic 4. The Pledge of Land

§ 53. **The Older Germanic Law of Land Pledges.**[1] (I) **Concept.** — A right of pledge ("Pfandrecht") also conveys a real right in the object pledged.

One consistent legal concept underlies the Germanic law of pledge from the beginning and in all its later forms of development. This is the idea of liability ("Haftung"), such as it has been revealed to us by modern researches in the sources of Germanic law. It will be more carefully considered below (§ 68) in the introduction to the chapter on the law of obligations; beyond a reference to that discussion, it is only necessary in this place to point out a few important matters.

[1] *v. Meibom*, "Das deutsche Pfandrecht" (1867); *Franken*, "Geschichte des französischen Pfandrechts, I: Das französische Pfandrecht im Mittelalter" (1879); *Kohler*, "Pfandrechtliche Forschungen" (1882); *v. Schwind*, "Wesen und Inhalt des Pfandrechts" (1899); *Egger*, "Vermögenshaftung und Hypothek nach fränkischem Recht", no. 69 (1903) of *Gierke's* "Untersuchungen"; *Kapras*, "Das Pfandrecht im böhmisch-mährischen Stadt- und Bergrechte", no. 83 (1906) of *Gierke's* "Untersuchungen"; *Hazeltine*, "Die Geschichte des Englischen Pfandrechts", no. 92 (1907), of *Gierke's* "Untersuchungen"; *O. Gierke*, "Schuld und Haftung" (1910), 26 *et seq.*; *cf.* § 68 *infra*; *Caillemer*, "Les formes et la nature de l'engagement immobilier dans la région Lyonnaise (Xe–XIIIe siècles)", in the "Festschrift für H. Brunner" (1911), 279–307.

"Haften" means "einstehen", to give security or warranty, — namely, for the performance of legal duty or obligation ("Schuld"). The obligee requires a security that no harm shall come to him, under any circumstances, from the transaction into which he has entered with the obligor. To this end a liability is created. This is accomplished in various ways. In this place we are concerned only with the case where a definite thing is subjected to the liability. This thing, whether it be a piece of land or a chattel, is made liable ("verhaftet") to the creditor, in order that he may have recourse to it in case the obligation be not performed. It is "settled", "exposed", "pawned" ("gesetzt", "ausgesetzt", "versetzt"); it is the pledge ("Einsatz"), like the wed of the formal contract ("Wettvertrag"). Thence the terms "wadium", "Wette", "Weddeschaft" — the "vadium", wed; words which are derived from the old verb "vidan", "to bind", and express the idea that the object pledged is bound or "entangled" ("Verstrickung") in the interest of the creditor. The pledge is bound by the "settlement" ("Satzung"). It is only freed from this restriction when the debtor has paid his debt; that is the redemption of the pledge.

The Germanic law of pledge was therefore originally a law of liability. And, further, it originally involved merely liability of a thing ("Sachhaftung"). Only in this form did it exactly express the Germanic conception of a pledge right. The creditor had recourse exclusively against the thing pledged. With other property, and with the person of the debtor, he was not concerned. But he received a real right in the pledge.

These are the common and central principles of the whole Germanic law of pledge. At an early day, however, the law of chattel-pledge and of land-pledge (gage) were differently developed. At this point we have only to speak of the former. Nor are we concerned with any other than the "given" ("gesetzte") pledge; that is, that which was created by contract or which rested upon statute. Germanic law knew, in addition to this, a "taken" ("genommene") pledge, the distress by self-help; but this we shall consider only later, in connection with the chattel-pledge.

(II) **Early Stages of Development. Conditional Conveyances. The Proprietary Gage.** — In the earlier stages of its development the law had only a clumsy form by which to make land liable to a creditor. Practically no credit existed during the continuance of an agricultural economy poor in commerce. Security for a debt could therefore be created only by giving to the creditor some object of value, which, in case the debtor failed to satisfy the debt, might serve as a final and complete substitute for the defaulted payment. Moreover, a conveyance of ownership was the only legal form the Germanic law originally possessed that could be made use of in this connection. The oldest form of a gage of lands was the proprietary gage ("Eigentumspfand"); regarded from the standpoint of the later development, it might be called a preliminary stage in the law of land pledges, properly speaking. But, as already stated, the land so conveyed served as the equivalent of the defaulted payment only in case of the non-payment of the debt; in other words, only upon condition that the debtor failed to redeem the pledge. The ownership in the land gaged was therefore only conditionally conveyed to the creditor; seisin was given him only by a conditional investiture, which was realized by preference "incorporeally", by delivery of a deed. This legal form, comparable with the old-Roman "fiducia", appears in the Germanic systems of the continent in the period of the folk-laws; it was also common in the Anglo-Saxon law.

The condition attached to the investiture might be expressed as one either subsequent or precedent. The condition subsequent was more usual: the ownership of the pledgee was to be extinguished in case the debt should be paid. This transaction remained in common use even after the appearance of more mature types of pledge. It took the outward form of a sale subject to a reservation of repurchase: the debtor transferred (sold) the land to the pledgee in exchange for a sum of money he received as a loan, and to secure which the pledge was given; by repayment he repurchased the pledge. But although the transaction was often conceived of in this manner, and actually developed later into a sale subject to repurchase ("Verkauf auf Wiederkauf"), nevertheless it was always distinguished from a sale by the fact that the pledgee could not, like other purchasers, resell the thing on his own account. In the less usual case of investiture subject to a condition precedent the alienor (the pledgor or debtor) said, in effect, to the alienee (creditor, pledgee): if I do not keep my contract, — if I do not pay the debt within a definite time, — it shall be considered that I have sold this land to you by delivery of this deed, and as of its date.[1]

Aside from this less common form, which did permit the debtor to remain temporarily in possession of the land, the proprietary-gage, based upon a transfer of seisin, involved great disadvantages

[1] *Brunner*, "Forschungen" (1894), 621.

for the pledgor. Not only was he exposed to the danger that his creditor might receive a piece of land of greater value than the debt, but he was frequently not in a situation to give the conveyance, — for lack of the consent of his kindred (*infra*, § 55) or of his lord (*supra*, p. 326) that was required in alienation, — in which cases he was compelled to renounce securing credit. As time passed, therefore, the proprietary-gage became less usual, except as it was tranformed into a sale subject to repurchase.

(III) **The "Older" Form of Land-pledge or Usufruct Gage** "ältere Satzung", "Nutzungspfand"). — Inasmuch as the value of lands in an agricultural age consisted solely in their product, it was a natural step to give these to the creditor as security, without attempting to alter the rights of ownership. Hence arose a usufruct-gage, known in legal literature as the "older" pledge ("ältere Satzung"), — the "engagement" of the French law. The grant of the profits to the pledgee was accomplished, in accord with the general principles of the medieval land law, by a transfer of the seisin to him from the owner of the land pledged. This was the seisin "ut de vadio", "as of gage" ("pfandliche Gewere", "Satzungsgewere"), which was the cover of an independent real right in the land; namely, a pledge right. The transfer of seisin was accomplished in a formal manner prescribed by law; ordinarily before the court or city council and with the consent of the heirs, but — in this respect like the investiture of the feudal law (*supra*, p. 338) — without release. The pledgee, as the holder of the physical ("leibliche") seisin, the seisin "ut de vadio", collected the profits of the land.

(1) Moreover, it was a rule in all Germanic lands that he collected them for his own exclusive use, in place of interest upon the money loaned the debtor. Such a gage was therefore known as an "*interest-gage*" ("Zinssatzung"), and also a *perpetual-gage* ("Ewigsatzung"), because the continuance of the right to the profits depended only upon the repayment of the capital, which was often not at all contemplated. It was particularly common not to repay the sum borrowed upon pledges of sovereign rights, especially in the case of so-called "Reichspfandschaften" (pledges of imperial privileges): kings and princes who were in need of money were not at all disposed ever to repay the sums they received (usually from the imperial cities). In case of an interest-gage, therefore, the usufruct granted to the pledgee did not diminish the capital of the debt, for which reason this form of

pledge was known in France as a "mortgage", and in England as a "mortuum vadium"; it was an "unabniessendes" gage, a gage unlessened by the usufruct. The Church forbade it, as being a violation of the Canonic prohibition of usury (*infra*, § 86). It was sought to lessen the prejudice to the debtor which it might very easily involve by a provision that in case the profits amounted to more than a certain interest upon the loan (usually the rate of 10 per cent. was adopted), the creditor should either be restricted to a portion of the profits or obligated to pay interest, in his turn, to the debtor (the owner) upon the excess profits taken. In such cases the relation between the parties approached a lease ("gepachtete Satzung", pledge-lease).

(2) Along with the interest-gage ("mortuum vadium") there was also employed in Germany, although much less frequently than elsewhere, the so-called "*live*"*-gage*. In the French law, on the contrary, this was the more common. In the "live"-gage the profits collected were reckoned against the capital debt, thus effecting gradually its extinction, whence the German name "dead" "dead"-gage ("Totsatzung", "dotsate"); whereas the French law spoke in this same connection of a "vifgage", and the English of a "vivum vadium", because the pledge did not lie as though dead but exercised a living effect. The Church favored the "vivum vadium."

Seisin "ut de vadio" ("Satzungsgewere") created in the pledgee merely a heritable and assignable right of usufruct, not a right to dispose of the substance of the land. The dispositive power over the title remained, with the ownership, in the pledgor. His proprietary seisin was, it is true, in complete abeyance, save in those exceptional cases in which interest ("Zins") was granted to him by the pledgee. The pledge relation was ended only by redemption, the repayment of the sum loaned, the satisfaction of the debt, — at least in the case of the "mortuum vivum" (interest-gage); it alone released the land from the bond of the pledge and permitted it to pass again into the seisin of the owner. In the absence of definite provisions the debtor had the right of redemption at any moment; on the other hand, the creditor had no right to demand redemption.

(3) If no redemption took place, the pledge relation simply continued. However, as the land passed immediately to the creditor, in the case of a proprietary-gage subject to a condition precedent, upon default in payment in accord with the contract, so also the usufruct-gage ("ältere Satzung") might be associated

with a conditional conveyance. In this case it assumed the character of a *forfeiture-gage* ("Verfallpfand"). The forfeiture-gage was especially dangerous for the debtor; for no account was taken of any difference between the value of the land pledged and the amount of the debt. The surplus value of the land, if any, accrued to the creditor without further formality.

(4) Hence the forfeiture-gage was replaced in many legal systems by the *sale-gage* ("Verkaufspfand", "Distraktionspfand"). In this the creditor generally possessed no right of alienation, but he might repledge the gage, and was also permitted to sell the land under a judicial power after precedent warning to the debtor, and to apply the purchase money thus realized to the satisfaction of his claim. But in this case he must deliver to the debtor any surplus realized.

The sale-gage, as compared with the forfeiture-gage, represented a mode of satisfying the creditor that corresponded to more developed economic relations. For the sale of the pledge offered advantages only as transactions in lands became more common.

In the case of the forfeiture-gage, as just stated, the excess value of the land accrued to the creditor alone; but the reverse was also true — namely, that he alone suffered from any possible loss due to deterioration or destruction of the pledge: "if the value of the land did not amount to the debt, he was obliged to drink the bitter drop since he had already enjoyed the sweet."[1] This fact shows that there was involved in the usufruct gage a pure case of real liability ("Sachhaftung"): the land pledged was the sole security of the creditor, and he could proceed against it alone. If perchance he was to have a right of action against the person or the other property of the debtor this must be expressly agreed upon. The obligation to return any surplus value above the debt therefore represented a relaxation of the principle of real-liability.

(IV) **The Hypothec: the "younger" Form of Land-Pledge, or Execution Gage.** — It might happen even in the case of the usufruct ("older") gage that the pledgee reconveyed the seisin of the pledged land to his debtor, the owner: he allowed him to remain upon the land and to dwell in the house he had pledged, or granted him a feudal seisin, a trustee's seisin ("zu getreuer Hand"), or a hirer's ("Miets-") seisin, — and contented himself with collecting from the debtor in exchange a rent ("Zins"), which might well be to him of as much economic value as the direct usufruct of the

[1] *v. Amira,* "Obligationenrecht", I (1882), 206.

property. Moreover, there were cases in which it did not appear desirable to convey the seisin "ut de vadio" immediately to the creditor, because it was still uncertain whether a debt would arise at all, or of what amount. The owner might, for example, give security for a warranty he had assumed to the pledgee. In this case the creditor could not demand immediate security ("Deckung"); he was content if the land was put in pledge by the conveyance to him of a mere right in expectancy.

Thus there existed various reasons for creating or recognizing gages of lands even without the conveyance of a pledge-seisin. This new idea, embodied in such transactions, was of the greatest value, for it first made it possible to free the gage of land, even in theory, from the necessity of a transfer of possession, which remained at the best onerous enough to the debtor, although not in the same degree as the conditional conveyance that was formerly required.

This new idea was first triumphantly established in the flourishing cities, where it created an institute of pledge law resting upon wholly new foundations. This was the so-called *execution* or "*younger*" *gage* ("jüngere Satzung", "Fronungspfand"), — the "obligation" of the French law. In it there were applied to new purposes certain procedural rules derived from great antiquity. In the oldest stage of the law no means of judicial execution was known; if a debtor did not fulfill his legal obligations, he could be proceeded against only through distress ("Pfändung") of his goods by his creditor, and outlawry from the community. It was only later that distress by public authorities (execution) was introduced; first in the case of movables, and then, in the Carolingian period, also in the case of lands. Execution against lands was modeled after the fashion of the old outlawry, which had affected not only the person but also the land of the outlaw. "In this outlawry of land the king found a means of satisfying the lack that was felt of an execution against immovables, the outlawry being made effective only so far as was absolutely necessary for this purpose."[1] The entire estate of the defaulting debtor (obligor), movable and immovable, "was laid under the ban of the crown, was definitely confiscated after the expiration of a year and a day, and, so far as the claim of the creditor who invoked the executory process made it necessary, was applied in satisfaction thereof."[2] This was the so-called "Fronung", — also designated, in the Frankish sources, "missio in

[1] *Brunner*, "Geschichte", I (2d ed.), 409. [2] *Ibid.*

bannum regis", — the importance of which in the origin of judicial seisin has already been discussed (*supra*, p. 201). Its effect was "a provisional subjection to the satisfaction of the claim" ("Beschlagnahme"; modern, levy on execution).[1] The possessor was deprived of the possession of the land; he lost the right to dispose of it. He could, however, redeem the estate from the ban by payment of the sum owed within a year and a day. As the next step, such executions against land in favor of creditors became free from their old association with the law of procedure, and were developed as a part of the law of pledge. It became possible for the debtor to make a pledge of lands in such manner that he himself retained the possession and the profits while conceding to the creditor, in case of forfeiture, the rights of a creditor "who had obtained a judgment for the debt against his debtor, and for execution against the land."[2] From this time on the debtor's estate was regarded as bound by judicial levy; "it was in judicial custody ("kummer", "besatz") for the creditor's benefit."[3] In this manner both parties were far better served than by the older usufruct-gage. The debtor remained in possession, yet the security afforded to the creditor was one entirely sufficient. For inasmuch as the land was regarded as judicially levied upon, he only needed, in case of default, "to take the second and remaining step in the process of judicial execution";[4] that is, to secure satisfaction of his claim from the estate by means of judicial execution. This newer form of gage was therefore also designated an *execution-gage* ("Fronungs-", "Exekutionspfand"). We can readily understand that this form of pledge was especially common in the cities, notwithstanding that it was by no means peculiar to the town law, and did not by any means wholly displace there the older or usufruct-gage. For one thing, since the creditor renounced any immediate delivery of the object which was his security it presupposed relatively advanced conditions of credit; and these developed, of course, earliest in the cities. Further, the occupant of an urban house, who generally possessed only the house in which he worked, and not several acres of land, was in no position to transfer portions of his property to a creditor, as a rural landowner commonly could, without being thereby compelled to abandon his means of livelihood. Finally,

[1] *Brunner*, "Geschichte", II, 458.
[2] *Brunner*, "Grundzüge" (5th ed.), 219.
[3] *Schröder*, "Lehrbuch" (5th ed.), 745.
[4] *Brunner*, *op. cit.*

as a rule the capitalist was no longer better served by a conveyance of the profits; the security that was assured him sufficed. For these reasons the execution-gage really appeared "as a form of pledge happily adapted to urban relations." [1]

This more modern form of gage was created by definite legal formalities which guaranteed publicity The parties made their declarations before the court or the city council; this was followed by the ban proclaimed by the authorities, and thereafter the gage was registered in the public records. Here also there was no release of seisin ("Auflassung"). In some localities the only necessary formality was the delivery of a document declaratory of the pledge, — the "house" or "inheritance" deed ("Haus-", "Erbebrief").

According to the better view, the execution-gage, like the usufruct-gage, gave the pledgee a real right in the land pledged, as the skevins of Magdeburg took occasion expressly to declare in answer to a case submitted to them.[2] Of course it is to be remembered that inasmuch as neither the ownership nor the right of usufruct was conveyed to the creditor, his right could not be evidenced in any actual physical seisin in the lands.[3] He did receive, however, as a result of the public character of the act by which the pledge was created and which made his right visible, a seisin in expectancy (*supra*, p. 193) in the estate; at the same time he also received, in accord with the earlier view of Germanic law which we have already discussed, "a present seisin-of-rights ("Rechtsgewere") in the right of pledge accorded to him." [4] That he actually possessed a real right in the estate is shown by the fact that in case the debtor alienated his estate notwithstanding the ban that had been laid upon it, thereby lessening the pledgee's right, the latter could make his right good against the new acquirer for a year and a day; or, as in the Magdeburg law, could demand the cancellation of the conveyance and the return of the estate to the debtor's possession. For this reason the owner was originally forbidden to made any alienation whatever of a pledged estate without the consent of the creditor, — in the absence of such provisions, he was in a position to do so, since both the property and the full physical seisin in the thing

[1] *Stobbe-Lehmann*, II, 2 (3d ed.), 122.

[2] To the question who has the "besser gewere", he to whom the land is pledged in the "hedged" folk-court or the pledgor, "ab er nu wol blebe in deme erbe", the answer is: "wirt eyme eyn erbe vor gerichte gesaczt, der hat eyne rechte gewere doran", — "Magdeb. Fragen", I, 6, 8.

[3] *Gierke*, "Privatrecht", II, 820. [4] *Ibid.*

("Sachgewere") remained in him. Later, even the right of alienation was conceded to him; but this had its reverse side in the creditor's right to follow the land, above adverted to. In time there was deduced from the fact that the ownership remained in the debtor the conclusion that he could pledge the same estate repeatedly; which was of course impossible in the case of the usufruct-gage. As in the case of the purchase-rent ("Rentenkauf"), the value of the land was conceived of as divided into several parts, of which each was liable for one claim only. A later gage covered that portion of the value which had remained uncovered; and therefore the right to satisfy the earlier gage was necessarily prior. The only requirement was that the debtor should, in such a case, give an honest notice as to the number of charges that already rested upon the estate. It was precisely in this possibility of repeated pledges that there lay the chief advantage of the execution-gage as compared with other forms of pledge.

The satisfaction of the creditor's claim upon default in payment of the debt was always realized in the case of the execution ("newer") gage with the coöperation of the public authorities; that is, by execution, which the creditor could henceforth initiate of his own notion. This execution might proceed as in the case of a forfeiture-gage; and in earlier times it very often took place in this manner. In such case the creditor was first invested with the physical seisin in court; thereupon the owner was notified by judicial citation to satisfy the debt within a period stated; and after the expiration of such period without performance the ownership was judicially declared to be in the creditor. Soon, however, it became usual, first in South and then also in North Germany, to treat the execution-gage as a sale-gage; that is, a judicial sale of the land was had, and the creditor was satisfied out of the purchase price realized. The excess, if any, was delivered to the owner.

Originally, in the case of the execution as of the usufruct-gage, the land pledged was alone made liable to the creditor's rights. He therefore ran the danger of its destruction; and this was expressly provided by the town law of Medebach, for example, in case of a conflagration.[1] A liability continuing thereafter could only be created by a pledge of faith ("Treugelöbnis") on the part of the debtor. An innovation pregnant with consequences occurred, already in the Middle Ages, when many legal systems assured to the creditor a statutory right to go against the debtor's

[1] "Stadtrecht of Medebach" (1165), c. 13.

other property in case he could not fully satisfy his claim from the land pledged. It was a change inconsistent with the character of pure real-liability originally characteristic of the Germanic law of pledge.

On the other hand, when pledge rights were accorded to the creditor, from the end of the 1100 s onward, in the whole property of the debtor, immovable and movable, as well as in property he might acquire in the future, — although not so commonly in Germany as in Latin countries, — this by no means involved, originally, a right of pledge in the nature of a real right. On the contrary, such transaction merely conveyed to the creditor, generally speaking, a right to distrain the property in case of the debtor's default, without a precedent action, and either by way of self-help or judicial execution. True, there might be developed from them an actual real right of pledge; as seems to have been done in Lübeck, for example, by drawing up an exact inventory of the specific property of the debtor. These prepared the way, also, for the spread of the general hypothec of the Roman law.

The execution gage had a certain similarity with the purchase-rent ("Rentenkauf", *supra*, pp. 370 *et seq.*). Of course there existed between the two transactions important economic and legal distinctions. The latter served the ends of permanent investments; the execution-gage was intended to secure a temporary credit. No independent personal liability existed in conjunction with the rent charge (" Rentenlast "). On the other hand, there were present in both the usufructuary right remaining in the owner of the land charged with the rent or the pledge right, and the satisfaction of the creditor by a forced sale. Toward the end of the Middle Ages, however, the changes, already discussed, in the original law of rent led to an assimilation of the two institutes in very many respects. Owing to the fact that the capitalistic rent (" Rente "), which was redeemable by the debtor, also became subject to notice of redemption, and to the further fact that in the case of the purchase-rent the supplementary pledge (" Fürpfand ") subjected the landowner's other property to the creditor's claim, the rent-charge acquired the character of a redeemable contractual claim (" Forderung ") secured by gage of land. Thenceforth, land subjected to a rent-charge was also known, itself, as a sub- (" Unter-") gage. At the same time, it became usual to unite interest-bearing loans (" zinsbare Darlehen "), which had theretofore been given only in the form of purchase-rents, with the gage of land; and since the land was also liable for the individual payments of interest, the consequence of this was that these could be regarded, like the capitalistic rent ("Rente"), as payments owing out of the land itself. In this manner the line between the two institutes became ever less distinct. If this process, thus tending to their union, could have proceeded uninterruptedly, German law would probably have reached independently a law of land pledge capable of satisfying the needs of modern times. But this development was interrupted by the reception of the Roman law of pledge, and painful labor was necessary before the ideas implicit in the execution-gage and the annuity again acquired authority, and displaced the pernicious elements of alien law.

§ 54. **The Modern Law of Land Pledges.** (I) **The Adoption of the Roman Law of Pledge.** — The medieval law of gage ("Grundpfand"), in the form which it finally assumed, especially in the execution-gage, was based upon sound foundations and gave perfect security to creditors, yet, notwithstanding this, the decidedly inferior Roman law of pledge was adopted in Germany, — a particularly significant example of the uncritical admiration of everything alien to which Germans are prone.

The Roman law of pledge in its final form, which alone need be considered in connection with the Germanic law, recognized, substantially, but a single form of pledge: the hypothec. This could be created equally on movable and immovable things, by informal agreement or testamentary disposition. Since neither change of possession nor any public creative act whatever was necessary, no safe form of real credit was possible: nobody could know whether his right of pledge had been rendered valueless by prior hypothecs or made invalid by an imperfect ownership in the hypothecator. The result of this was that in order to procure credit it was necessary to pledge the entire estate, present and future; that is, to give a "general" hypothec conveying a right of pledge in each specific thing owned by the debtor. In addition to this there existed numerous statutory hypothecs that were tacitly created and canceled, most of which were in character "general" hypothecs. Among various rights of pledge the oldest had priority, in theory; but this rule did not apply to the numerous forms of privileged or special rights of pledge, such as that enjoyed by a wife in the estate of her husband because of her "dos." Moreover, so-called "public" or "quasi-public" rights of pledge created by the observance of certain formalities had priority over all others. Finally, the hypothec was wholly accessorial in character; that is, it was intended to secure a personal claim, upon whose existence it was therefore dependent. In this respect it was quite different from the ideas of the Germanic law. The enforcement of the pledge, — namely, by taking possession of or by selling it, — was accomplished without any judicial coöperation whatever.

To be sure, these rules of the alien law were unable completely to displace the native. Many of the latter remained in authority. But, for a time, they were ill adjusted to the Roman system which had become the common law of Germany. The result in the first period after the Reception was an extremely confused and unsatisfactory condition of the law, which is reflected in the statutes of the 1500 s and the 1600 s.

In many respects, it is true, there was merely a continuation of a movement that had already led to transformations of the old Germanic concepts and institutes in the last centuries of the Middle Ages, in entire independence of the alien law. We are here concerned primarily with the following points:

In general the pledge without transfer of possession became most common, the foreign name "hypothec" becoming usual to designate it. This institute, however, had already in the Middle Ages become the most common form of pledge, in the form of the execution-gage. The usufruct-gage, that is, the possessory-gage, held its place for a time beside the more modern form, mainly because men could support it by an appeal to the related institute of the alien law, the antichresis; but in the end it disappeared, save for slight traces, from legal life. The forfeiture-gage was completely abandoned. Moreover, the Roman prohibition of a "lex commissoria" made its defense impossible from the viewpoint of modern theory. The pure form of real liability occurred only rarely. In general the creditor was permitted to go against the other property of the debtor. Various rights of pledge in the same thing were everywhere permitted.

In other respects, however, the adoption of the Roman law of pledge constituted a direct break with the earlier development.

This was true, in the first place, of the adoption of the informal creation of a pledge; although in many places (as *e.g.* in Switzerland) and by way of exception, such adoption might also be due to a desire to do away with official participation in such transactions, as a burdensome matter and one offensive to feelings of personal independence. However, the traditional and formal requisites, — namely, a legal act before a court or a city council followed by registration in the land-book, or some other judicial or official publication, — were doubtless only rarely wholly abandoned. It certainly was exceptional, thenceforth, to treat them as the sole means of pledging land; this occurred only in a few systems of town law (*e.g.* those of Munich, Nordlingen, Lübeck, Bremen) that clung with unusual tenacity to the old law. Most of the regional systems recognized, indeed, the creation of informal pledges; but they also recognized the continuance, beside these, of the types of the Germanic law, and even attributed to these a preferential effect similar to that of the Roman "pignora publica", though such preference was recognized only in a few legal systems as against statutory and privileged rights of pledge.

Further, one of the most pernicious transformations ever suffered by the Germanic law of land pledges was involved in the widespread adoption of the statutory "special" and "general" rights of pledge, totally unknown to the Germanic law, and the "preferential" pledge rights of the Roman system. Included in these were the special statutory hypothecs of landlords in the farming-stock ("invecta et illata") of the hirer ("Mieter"); of a lessor in the fruits of the leasehold; the general hypothec of the wife, based upon her "dos", in the property of her husband, and of children in the property of their parents, and of a ward in the property of the guardian; the general hypothec of the fisc based upon its claims for taxes, to which was added a similar hypothec for penal fines, and likewise one for "piæ causæ"; etc. Of course all this necessitated detailed provisions concerning the rank of these various rights of pledge. As a result the old Germanic principles of publicity and "speciality" ("Spezialität") were completely abandoned. Certainly it would be wrong to suppose that these unsound conditions of the law of pledge are to be ascribed exclusively to the reception of the Roman law, for we have seen that certain tendencies toward approximation to the alien system had begun to be felt before the Receptions; and the history of the modern French law of pledge shows us that the old Germanic concepts of liability and pledge, when logically applied, are themselves capable of leading to "the same close relation between personal and real credit, the same revival of personal and property liability, and the same general hypothecs and statutory rights of pledge" as existed in Germany after the Reception.[1] And if a strong reaction followed in Germany, and

[1] *Stutz* in Z.[2] R. G., XXVII (1906), 428.

not in France, the cause of this may possibly have been that the development of the law of immovable pledges in the common law so exaggerated conclusions harmful to credit as to make their evil tendency more manifest than where an uninterrupted development fused the old with the new conditions.

(II) **Return to the Principles of the Germanic Law.** (1) *Modern Hypothecary Legislation.* — In consequence of the dismemberment and confusion of the law of pledge that was caused by the Reception, it became necessary for legislation to interfere, especially in the greater cities. In this process Germanic principles were given increasing prominence, although quite unconsciously Modern hypothecary legislation began in the 1700 s. Many earlier statutes, however, had already introduced reforms in matters of detail; for example, the Constitutions of Electoral Saxony, of 1572. Among the statutes of the 1700 s those of Prussia are particularly notable: the ordinance concerning hypothecs and bankruptcy of February 14, 1722, — which was followed by the important supplementary procedural ordinance of 1724, — and the hypothecary ordinance of December 20, 1783; which, in their essential content, were adopted by the "Allgemeines Landrecht", thus becoming authoritative for the later period. The legislation of the 1800 s was based upon the foundations thus laid. So, for example, in Bavaria (1822), in Württemberg (1825), and in Saxony (since 1843); and, as already mentioned, in a particularly independent manner, in Mecklenburg, in its revised hypothecary regulations for feudal estates of October 18, 1848 (*supra*, p. 249), and the revised town registry regulations of December 21, 1857 (*supra*, pp. 223, 251), which have served as models for other statutes. The flood point of this legislation is marked by the great reformatory Act of 1872 in Prussia. The two statutes of May 5th, — the one a Land-Book ordinance, and the other an act regulating the acquisition of ownership (*supra*, pp. 223, 253), — which followed the Mecklenburg statutes at many points and were eventually introduced throughout the kingdom save in Nassau and Helgoland, were not only copied in succeeding decades by a number of other German States (among others by Oldenburg and Brunswick) but also served as the main basis for the regulation of the law of pledge in the Civil Code. The unitary regulation of the law of pledge in the Swiss Civil Code embodies principles of Germanic law similar, in part, to those of the German Code, and in part expressed in peculiar and independent forms.

(2) *The Chief Principles of the Modern Law of Pledge.* — The re-Germanizing of the law of pledge thus effected was not at all uniform in details, but it was nevertheless dominated by a few common and fundamental tendencies, which appear most clearly in the following points:

(A) THE PRINCIPLE OF PUBLICITY, which as we have already stated had been wholly abandoned by only very few legal systems in favor of the Roman law, was once more made a cardinal principle. A beginning in this direction was made by the procedural ordinance of Electoral Saxony of 1724, but it was first completely realized in the Prussian "Landrecht" and in the Austrian Code. The modern system of the land-book cannot be reconciled with any mode of creating hypothecs other than by registration. Entry in the land-book, in other words a legal and formal act in the sense of the medieval law, was thus made the sole means of creating a hypothec and determining its rank; and therefore statutory and passive rights of pledge necessarily disappeared. Thenceforth the statute conferred merely a right to the creation of a pledge ("Pfandrechtstitel"), by virtue of which the person entitled to it could demand registration of the hypothec. And further, since only the date of the entry was henceforth important in fixing the priorities of hypothecs, preferential rights of pledge necessarily disappeared. The Swiss Civil Code, also, has given effect to the principle of publicity; but not without exceptions, for it still recognizes statutory pledges. Indeed, it permits the cantons to create such statutory pledge rights, without entry in the land-book, as security for claims under the public law, — such for example as for tax claims, or for sewage improvements; and further, it even recognizes statutory pledge rights for costs incurred in precautionary measures taken by a pledgee by way of self-help in order to preserve the pledge from damage; and also for outlays by the creditor for the preservation of the pledge. In other cases even the Swiss Code merely creates a right to registry in the land-book.

(B) THE PRINCIPLE OF "SPECIALITY" ("Spezialität") was resurrected along with the principle of publicity. Rights of pledge in lands were recognized only in definite pieces of land, — the general hypothec being discarded. It was a further consequence of this principle of "speciality" that every pledge right charged the land with an obligation to pay a definite sum of money; although, of course, the rules as to the manner by which the charge should be paid might be various, in consequence of the different varieties of pledge rights. The land-charge ("Grundschuld"), — to mention only the final rule adopted by the new Civil Code, — must always be for a fixed sum of money; the same is generally true of the hypothec, but not necessarily so (not in the maximal-hypothec, "Höchsthypothek"); the annuity-charge ("Rentenschuld") involves a fixed money rent. In essentials the Swiss Civil Code embodies the same principles; it likewise recognizes "maximal" hypothecs.

(C) The principle of legality ("Legalität") was developed by modern legislation from the element of official coöperation required by the medieval law in the creation of pledges. According to the older theory (which is expressed for example in the Prussian Hypothecary Regulations of 1783 and also in a series of statutes of the first half of the 1800 s) this principle signified at least a judicial examination of the validity of the juristic act upon which the pledge was based, although no longer an examination of the sufficiency of the pledge, — so-called "substantive" ("materielle") legality. On the other hand, the more modern statutes, particularly those of Mecklenburg and the Prussian statutes of 1872, limited such judicial examinations to the determination of the outward and formal correctness of the declaration of the parties' will, — so-called "formal" legality. This last has been adopted by the law of the present day.

(D) The principle of invariable priorities ("feste Pfandstelle"). It followed from the form of the Roman common law of pledge, which was copied in this respect by the French law, that when several rights of pledge exist in one piece of land and one of them drops out, the junior pledges, that is those later created, each advance ipso facto by one degree; exactly as when one of several books lying upon one another is withdrawn, and the upper ones fall into different places by force of gravity.[1] The owner of the land is powerless to affect the matter. If he wishes to create a new pledge, he can assign to it only the lowest rank, after all the others. It follows that every right of pledge covers the entire value of the land.

On the other hand, Germanic law proceeded from the idea that every pledge right covers a quite definite and permanently limited part of the land's total value; and it was possible to apply this idea with entire consistency in a system of pledge rights based upon land registry. Each pledge right acquires, by entry in the land-book, an exactly defined position; a fixed rank deter-

[1] *Tuor*, "Das neue Recht", 478.

mined by the date of registry. No change of priority can take place; if a prior pledge right is cancelled the result is a vacant place, "an empty compartment in which the owner is free to put whatever he may later desire." This system of the "vacant rank" ("leere Pfandstelle") of the Germanic law has become an essential characteristic of the pledge rights of the present law, along with the land-book system. The German and the Swiss Code have alike given it effect. With this change it became logically possible to recognize the proprietary hypothec, which has also been adopted by both Codes.

(E) It was not alone the formal requisites for the creation and continuance of rights of pledge in land that received, in consequence of the introduction of the principles referred to, a form which gives a Germanic character to the modern hypothecary law; the same was true also of its content. The principle of the PRIMARY OR INDEPENDENT CHARACTER ("Selbständigkeit") of pledge rights was again recognized. It is true that in Germany, as elsewhere, the hypothec was at first merely a right securing a personal debt for which the debtor was only personally liable; this was due to the influence of the Roman law. The result was the disappearance from the pledge law of the pure principle of real liability that had entered the law in the execution-gage. This change was also connected with the fact that the separation of the concepts of legal duty and liability ("Schuld" and "Haftung", — *infra*, § 70), peculiar to the Germanic law, was abandoned. Now, as Gierke has made clear in his fundamental discussion of the Germanic law of pledge, there was associated with the hypothec the idea of a "real" obligation derived from the law of the purchase-rent ("Rentenkauf"): "this idea was inherited by the hypothec from the purchase-rent when the latter was displaced by the hypothecary loan for interest."[1] In other words, land that is charged with a pledge right is liable for a debt that is inseparably united with the ownership of such land, exactly in the same manner as the land-charge produced a real debt that was imposed upon each successive owner of the land (*supra*, p. 362). From this real debt there resulted a credit right in favor of the pledgee which had every appearance of a right in the land itself, and for that reason existed as against any temporary owner. To be sure, this idea, and with it the improvement of the hypothecary law accomplished by its fusion with the law of real charges, has acquired complete accept-

[1] *Gierke*, "Privatrecht", II, 834.

ance only in the most recent law.[1] But the tendency in this direction, and away from the rule of the Roman law, nevertheless appeared in the earlier hypothecary statutes.

In the first place, though the hypothec was generally still treated as a purely supplementary right, some of them, as for example the Prussian "Landrecht" and the Bavarian Hypothecary Act, separated it from the personal claim to the extent of forbidding, as against bona fide assignees ("Zessionäre"), pleas that were allowed to the owner against the first pledgee (the "Zedenten") because of the obligational relation. This refusal was based upon the principle of the "public-faith" of the land-book. In this case the real right, which could be acquired only by a third person who purchased the hypothec in good faith, was separated in the hand of such third person from the personal relation of debtor and creditor, to which he was not a party.

This tendency was further strengthened by the introduction, above referred to, of the proprietary hypothec, which was first recognized, — in the "Rescript" of August 11, 1802 (as "supplement, § 52" of the Prussian Landrecht) — in those cases where hypothec and ownership became united by inheritance or as the result of a juristic act. Still later there was also recognized a hypothec which when paid by the owner was not by such satisfaction destroyed, but on the contrary passed to the owner himself; and indeed, in the end, even though the personal relation of debtor and creditor was extinguished by such satisfaction. The creation of a pledge right in favor of the owner from the beginning was first made possible in the Mecklenburg law. This could be done there because the Mecklenburg law freed the pledge right at the same time from the subsidiary character attributed to it in the common law theory, declaring the hypothec to be an independent real charge upon the land, and applying to it as such the Germanic principle of pure real-liability. Its complete separation of the hypothec from the personal debt, — which, although it co-exists with the pledge right (which certainly presents no theoretical difficulty) does not in the least affect the latter, — was manifested in the fact that the causa ("Schuldgrund"), as for example a loan, was not entered in the land-book along with the amount ("Posten") of the hypothec. The consequence of this was, although the law-makers themselves were probably hardly conscious of this result of their acts, that the old Germanic law of pledge was again revealed in all its purity: the land alone

[1] *Stutz*, art. just cited.

is liable to the creditor; only from its products can he seek satisfaction of his debt.

The example set by Mecklenburg was followed in the Prussian statutes of 1872, although not as the government originally intended. Instead of conceding an independent character to all pledge rights whatever, the merely relatively independent hypothec theretofore existing in the Prussian law was retained, the Mecklenburg hypothec being introduced beside it, and the name "land-debt" ("Grundschuld") given to the new institute to distinguish it from the older type. The expectation that this "Grundschuld" would displace the earlier hypothec in legal practice was, however, not realized; the hypothec has remained the far more common form of land pledge.

The Civil Code has also adopted both forms, the hypothec — in theory an accessory right, in fact a very independent one, and, like the earlier Prussian hypothec, entirely separated under some circumstances from the obligational claim — and the "land-debt", which both in theory and in fact is entirely independent thereof. A sub-variety of the land-debt under the system of the present Civil Code, is the limited annuity-charge ("Rentenschuld"), which is distinguished from the hypothec and from other forms of land-debts by the fact that its basis is not a debt for a loan of capital, whether interest or non-interest bearing, but a recurrent money rent; which, however, can be registered only together with a fixed redemption sum. There has been again revived in this the old purchase-rent ("gekaufte Rente"), which had also finally become redeemable (*supra*, p. 373).

(F) Following the Reception the forfeiture-gage disappeared. But the regional legal systems, not content with prohibiting the forfeiture clause in conformity with the Roman law, clung to the principle that the creditor was entitled to a sale only when made with the coöperation of the court; a principle which was in harmony with the native law but inconsistent with the Roman. Under modern legislation JUDICIAL EXECUTION has become the exclusive means by which the creditor can secure satisfaction of his claim.

(G) When pledge rights had been made independent there resulted the further possibility of making them assignable, "thus 'mobilizing' the land in the form of value-shares of NEGOTIABLE CHARACTER."[1] This also is a result of the pledge-concept of the Germanic law. Already in the case of rights to rents ("Renten-

[1] *Gierke, op. cit.*, 835.

recht") documents were often executed which, as already mentioned (*supra*, p. 372), were treated as commercial paper; their delivery, when associated with an informal contract, sufficed for the alienation or the pledge of the right to the rent. In this way, for example, the perpetual-rents ("Ewiggelder") of Munich were created from the 1300 s onward; namely by public deed ("Verbriefung") and gradually even by private deed, or — if the parties so chose, which was relatively rare — by entry in the land-book. This was the starting point of the documentation of pledge rights that has been developed in the modern law. Along with registry in the land-book it became usual to prepare and deliver a *hypothec deed* ("Hypothekenbrief"). But new legal effect was now attributed to this by legislation. While it had merely the significance, according to some statutes, of a public evidential document, the earlier Prussian legislation attributed to it the character of a "legitimizing" ("Legitimations-") document, possession of which sufficed as authority to assign the hypothec and to enforce it. The statutes of 1872 left this quality to the hypothec deed, but, on the other hand, raised the *land-debt deed* ("Grundschuldbrief") to the rank of perfect commercial paper, whose manual delivery is indispensable for the transfer of the charge. The new Civil Code treats the normal deeds which it prescribes for hypothec and land-charge as commercial paper, but it recognizes *security* ("*Sicherungs-*") *hypothecs*, unlike *commercial* ("*Verkehrs-*") *hypothecs*, only when registered, — that is, as "*book*" ("*Buch-*") *hypothecs;* and permits land-charges and annuity-charges to be made out to bearer.

Like the German Code, the Swiss Civil Code recognizes three different kinds of pledge rights in land: the "Grundpfandverschreibung", the "Gült" and the "Schuldbrief." But these correspond only in part to those of the German Code. The "Grundpfandverschreibung", or the security-pledge ("Sicherungspfandrecht"), is like the German security hypothec decidedly accessory in character; it does not represent an independent land-value, and is not intended to be trafficable, nor is it embodied in commercial paper. The "Gült" corresponds to the German land-debt ("Grundschuld"); like this, it is "abstract" in nature, but, unlike the German Code, the Swiss Code attributes to it under all conditions the quality of a land-charge, and has attempted by various provisions to strengthen its character as a real security. Finally, the "Schuldbrief", which stands midway between the security-pledge and the negotiable land-debt ("Gült"), differs in most of its qualities from the corresponding form of pledge of the German Code, namely, the commercial-hypothec ("Verkehrshypothek"). It includes a personal liability on the part of the debtor and is embodied in commercial paper, but, like the "Gült", has the general character of an "abstract" obligational claim.

TOPIC 5. PREËMPTION RIGHTS ("Näherrechte")[1]

§ 55. **Preëmption Rights in general.** (I) **Conception.** — By the term "Näherrecht" (also known as "Zug-", "Losungs-", and "Retraktrecht"; right of retractive purchase, of redemption) there is understood such a real right existing in the land of another as empowers the holder of the right ("Näherberechtigte", "Nähergelter", "Retrahent") to demand that the land be transferred to him when it has been sold by the owner to a third person; subject, always, to the condition that the person entitled to such retractive right of purchase shall make good the purchase price to the owner, — in other words be substituted in the purchase contract for the third person purchasing the land.

(II) **History.**[2] — The right of preëmption, in particular the oldest and most important of statutory "Näherrechte", the next heir's right of retractive purchase ("Zugrecht"), is in origin "a weakened remnant of, or a derivative from, the heir's right in expectancy under Germanic law",[3] of which we have already spoken as one of the restrictions upon ownership based upon a one-time existence of collective family property (*supra*, p. 304 *et seq.*). As we have there stated, the heir's right in expectancy, in its more modern form of a formal right of co-alienation, became a real right in expectancy in the land of another; a right which became independent upon a sale of the land by the owner, thereby securing to his relatives entitled to it a real claim, effective against any third person, for the delivery of the land. Thanks to this right in expectancy the heirs, by refusing consent, were able to prevent any gift ("Vergabung"), though wholly gratuitous, as well as any sale of the land outside of the family; and also, by

[1] *Laband*, "Die rechtliche Natur des Retracts und der Expropriation", in Arch. civil. Praxis, lii (1869), 151 *et seq.*

[2] The view adopted in the text, which is the prevailing one, is disputed by Ficker, who denies any close relationship whatever between rights in expectancy ("Wartrecht") and rights of preëmption ("Näherrecht") and attributes the greater antiquity to the latter. *Cf.* p. 305, *supra.*

[3] *Gierke*, "Privatrecht", II, 785.

bringing a real action based upon their formal right of co-alienation, could rescind a sale already made. But the harshness of these rights as against the landowner early led to the result that this requirement of the heirs' consent was disregarded, — at least in cases of necessity when only a sale of his estate could save him, — and a mere prior or preferential ("Näher-") right accorded them; that is to say, a right to acquire the land first themselves, by purchase, thus securing the owner against any claims for damages on the part of third persons. For some time the heirs' rights of co-alienation and retractive purchase existed side by side, as is shown for example by the manorial law of the bishopric of Worms.[1] But inasmuch as "the interest of the heirs in the preservation of the family estate was also completely protected"[2] by the right of preëmption ("Näherrecht"), and at the same time proper regard shown for the interest of the owner, preëmption rights more and more displaced the old right of co-alienation, even aside from the exceptional cases of necessity. Alike in the Territorial, the town, and the manorial law, the principle spread that whoever wished to sell his land must offer it first to his heirs. And, in analogy to the prior rights of heirs, although not here derived from an original right of co-alienation, a corresponding independent right was recognized, already in the Middle Ages, in favor of part-owners ("Geteilen"), fellow-occupants of an estate ("Hofgenossen"), the members of a commune, of a manor, etc. (*supra*, § 56). The right to retract a feudal feoffment ("retractus feudalis"), developed in the Lombard law, was also adopted by modern feudal statutes, as for example in the Prussian "Landrecht" (*supra*, p. 344); it was possessed not only by the original lord but also by the successive holders of the fief.

These rights of preëmption which thus appeared in the course of the Middle Ages were by no means swept away by the Reception. On the contrary they were developed with special preference, both in theory and in legislation, in the period following. The doctrine of retractive rights ("Retraktrecht") was adopted in Germany in the form in which it had been developed by medieval jurisprudence, and with the aid of this the attempt was made to give to the institute as nearly universal authority as possible.

[1] In this manorial law (of 1023–1025) the general retractive right of the heir ("Erbeinspruchsrecht") is referred to in § 6. *Cf. Heusler*, "Institutionen", II, 60.

[2] *Heusler, op. cit.*

Doubtless with some exaggeration, men claimed for it a basis in Holy Writ, in the Canon law, and in the secular law.

Although only the feudal right of retraction actually attained authority as common law, other rights of preëmption received all the more commonly, for that reason, an exhaustive regulation in regional legislation. This added to the traditional forms a series of new ones, such as the retractive right of the imperial knightage and the rural ("landsässiger") nobility, the so-called "Territorial" redemption ("Landlosung"), retraction of conveyances in mortmain and to Jews, etc. Special rights of retractive purchase were later recognized even as to chattels; for example, in favor of co-shipowners ("Mitreeder") in the sale of interests in a vessel ("Schiffsparten").

The reason for the striking favor thus shown to preëmption rights in the legislation of modern times we must doubtless find, with Huber,[1] in the fact "that the solidary character of landed estates first began to weaken, under the influence of new economic ideas, at the end of the Middle Ages, and that statutes thereafter endeavored to maintain intact, or so far as possible defend, that which tradition and custom no longer sufficiently protected." In the end, however, the artificial element involved in such legislation, and its inconsistency with the altered economic ideas of modern times, were bound to make themselves felt. From the 1700 s onward men came to regard such prior rights as harmful fetters upon commerce, and began to combat them in principle, and either wholly abolish or at least considerably restrict them in practice. Especially in the 1800 s most of the old retractive rights ("Retraktrechte") were abandoned, after the legislation of the French Revolution had led the way in their complete suppression. Whereas the Prussian "Landrecht", for example, had still recognized the retractive rights of co-shipowners ("Schiffsreeder"), of feudal lords, of agnates, of co-feoffees, and of tithe payers, as well in certain provinces as the preëmption rights of part-owners ("Gespilderechte") and of neighbors, and the heir's right of redemption by purchase ("Erblosung"), — the Prussian statute of March 2, 1850, abolished without compensation almost all retractive rights whatever. Only the preëmption ("Vorkaufs-") rights of community owners and the recently introduced preëmption right of one dispossessed by expropriation ("Enteignete"; see p. 256) were retained; to these there was later added the similar right of co-heirs in estates subject to the rule of single

[1] "Schw. Privatrecht", IV, 719 *et seq.*

heirship. In other States, as for example Hesse, preëmption rights were abolished without exception. The new Civil Code has adopted toward them the same unfriendly attitude. Under the imperial law there exists, as a statutory preëmption right, solely the preferential purchase right of co-heirs, which is also recognized by the Code Civil; others can be created only within the field reserved to the State law. Among preëmption rights based upon contract must be counted those preëmption rights that are registered in the land-book and thereby acquire real effects.

(III) **Legal Character and Enforcement.** — (1) Whereas the older German jurisprudence, following the Italian theory, conceived of preëmption rights, in general, as obligational rights of a special kind, — a view which has been shared in late days by Gerber, among others, — the view has lately triumphed that they are *real rights;* and this view is certainly correct. In Gierke's phrase, a preëmption right is "a right in expectancy in a thing." [1] In case the owner sells to a third person, then the real right of the person preferentially entitled, which until then constitutes a restriction upon the ownership, becomes fully effective. Such a sale, however, though an indispensable precondition to the enforcement of the retractive right, is not such to its creation. The sale is "not the fact which creates but only the fact which justifies redemption." [2] The retractor does not, as Laband endeavored to show, bring his action for judicial recognition and definition of his right to acquire the ownership of the land by unilateral act, but brings an action "for the recognition of his own ownership, now become clear." [3] The retractor becomes the owner so soon as the preconditions requisite to the effectiveness of his right have been realized.

(2) These *preconditions* are of two kinds: first, a sale must have taken place by the owner, — and only a sale, for a gratuitous gift ("Schenkung"), or exchange, or a so-called sale for affection would not suffice; and secondly, the retractor must perform all obligations which the first seller has assumed or performed. From this it follows that the preferential right of purchase ordinarily takes the form of a right of prior purchase ("Vorkaufsrecht"), and in the absence of specific provision includes such a right; just as it first appeared, historically, in the form of such a right.

[1] "Privatrecht", II, 771.
[2] *H. O. Lehmann* in *Stobbe*, II. 1 (3d ed.), 484.
[3] *Heusler*, "Institutionen", II, 63.

But it is distinguished from an ordinary and purely contractual option of prior purchase by the fact that the latter secures merely a claim for damages against the alienating owner, whereas the true preëmption right (" Näherrecht "), as we have seen, is effective, thanks to its real character, against each acquirer, and requires the delivery of the thing alienated subject to compensation for the purchase price.

(3) The *enforcement* of the preëmption right is ordinarily limited to a definite period, running from the moment that knowledge is acquired of the sale or conveyance of the property. In the Middle Ages it was a year and a day; in the modern law it was commonly two months, as it is under the Civil Code. Renunciation may effect the termination of the preëmption right exactly as does the running of a prescriptive period.

(4) When, as was easily possible, *several persons* were *entitled* to preëmption rights, either as members of a class (as for example several heirs) or as members of different classes (as for example kinsmen and neighbors), complicated relations might result. The medieval sources were unable to solve the difficulties herefrom resulting except in an imperfect manner. Not infrequently decision by lot was resorted to as the final means of judgment. In the law of the present day these questions play hardly any rôle at all, since, as already stated, only the single group of co-heirs is still recognized as possessing preferential rights, and their enforcement is left under the general principles of the inheritance law.

§ 56. **Individual Preëmption Rights.** (I) **Statutory Preëmption Rights.** — (1) *The Heir's Preferential Right of Purchase* (" Erblosung ", " Beschüttungsrecht ", " retractus gentilicius ", " retractus consanguinitatis ", " retrait lignager "). This was the oldest, and formerly by far the most important, statutory preëmption right. Of its creation we have already spoken (*supra*, p. 395). It existed in favor of the nearest statutory heir at the moment of alienation; in this connection the circle of those entitled to the right was drawn narrower or wider under different circumstances. The order of priority was determined by the degree of blood relationship; frequently only the descendants of the first acquirer were entitled. Among several relatives of the same degree, lot or prior claim (" Prävention ") was frequently made decisive, or an equal partition was made. At the present day such preferential rights of purchase in the heir exist only within the field reserved to State law, and in the case of entailed estates (in Württemburg, Bremen) and estates subject to single heirship (in Prussia and in Mecklenburg).

(2) *The Preëmption Right of Mark-associates* ("Marklosung", "retractus ex iure incolonatus"). This existed in case of alienation to a non-member of land lying within the mark. There is already evidence of this in the provision of Title 45 of the "Lex Salica", which permits any markman to prevent the alienation of a curtilage ("Hof") to a non-member (*supra*, p. 120). Since public interests were also involved in these cases, the commune, as such, later had a right of retractive purchase under some legal systems (*e.g.* the town law of Biel in Switzerland) in case no communist should exercise it. Generally speaking, the markmen's retractive right was by far not so common as the heir's right of preëmption.

The *retractive rights of the imperial knightage*, which were later developed, rested upon similar preconditions. The markmen's rights of preëmption developed in rare cases into a so-called right of *"Territorial" retraction*, in favor of the Territories. These forms of retractive right no longer exist in the present law.

(3) *Preëmption Rights based on Vicinage* ("Nachbarlosung", "Fürnossenrecht", "retractus ex iure vicinitatis"). This existed in favor of a next neighbor ("Anrainer") of a rural or of an urban piece of land. Like the markmen's right of preëmption, it was a special development of the heir's preëmption right. It was known only to a few regions, especially in Friesland and in Saxony. It has disappeared from the present law.

Allied to it was the *right of associational retraction* ("Genossenlosung") which existed in favor of the members of a real commune, such for example as an Alp-association, with respect to the shares in its profits.

(4) *Preëmption Rights based on Co-ownership* ("Retrakt aus dem Miteigentun", "retractus ex iure condominii"). — This was particularly important in the form of the right enjoyed by *conventional co-heirs* ("Ganerben"). It entitled them to retraction in case of the alienation of an ideal share of land held in collective or co-ownership. Preserved in the French law in the case of the herital community, and adopted in the Code Civil, it has passed over into the German Civil Code, and in the form of a statutory preëmption right of purchase enjoyed by co-heirs (§§ 2034–2037) has thus become imperial law. With this exception no retractive right based on co-ownership is possible today save in the case of communities subject to the rules of State law.

(5) *The Preëmption Right of Part Owners* ("Gespilderecht", "Teillosung", "retractus ex iure congrui"). This was a right widely prevalent in older times, both in rural and urban localities, which secured a preëmption right to part-owners ("Teilgenossen", "Geteilen"), — that is, to the owners of parts of an original unit of land which was afterwards divided or split ("gespalten") among them, —in order to make possible a reunion of the parts. It was especially favored in so-called "Einzinsereiverhältnisse" (pooled-rent tenancies), since here the connection of the parts was preserved by means of one rent-payer ("Zinsträger") appointed by the co-associates. It has been done away with in the modern law of Germany. The Swiss Civil Code (§ 682), on the contrary, has recognized a statutory preëmption right in each co-owner as against any non-owner who acquires a share.

The right of one whose land is taken by *expropriation* to regain possession in case it has become useless for the purposes for which it was taken, is a modern form of the old "Gespilderecht" which is still recognized in the State law of the present day; for example in Prussia.[1]

(6) *Manorial Preëmption Rights* ("grundherrliche Retraktrechte", "retractus ex iure dominii directi"). Such rights of the lord in the case of peasant holdings, and of the feudal lord as well as of the "agnates" (collateral kin) in the case of fiefs, could originate only after rentalers and feudal tenants had acquired dispositive rights over their tenements. They have almost completely disappeared.

(II) **Preëmption Rights based on Contract (Options).** — These were common in the medieval law. When land was conveyed or leased and an optional right of purchase was given to the alienor or to a third person, there originated a real right effective against anybody whatever, which real effect was based upon a public act of transfer. After the Reception men continued for a while to recognize the possibility of creating "real" rights of option, that is, true rights of "preëmption" ("Näherrechte"); and distinguished them from the statutory form as "retractus conventionales." But later, when public forms of transfer were abandoned, legal theory found itself obliged to deny the real effect of such rights. Thereafter the conception of "preëmption" ("Näher-") rights based upon contract was in many localities wholly abandoned, merely an obligational effect as against the other party to the contract being attributed to option ("Vor-

[1] *Gierke*, "Privatrecht", II, 797.

kaufs-") rights created by agreement. In modern times this viewpoint was represented by Eichhorn, Gerber, Gengler, Beseler, Roth, Stobbe, and H. O. Lehman, among other scholars. However, the introduction of the modern land-book system made possible, here also, a return to the older law. Just as the Prussian "Landrecht" and the Austrian legislation made it possible to give a real character to a purchase-option by entry in the land register, thereby transforming it into a real preëmption right ("Näherrecht"), so the new Civil Code (§§ 1094–1104) has recognized for all Germany, in a purchase-option created by registration (that is, by contract), a consensual "Näherrecht" of imperial law which is a limited real right. This present preëmption right has the effect against third parties of a cautionary notice ("Vormerkung"), in securing the claim to a conveyance of ownership which arises from the exercise of the right (§ 1098). The provisions of the Swiss Civil Code (§ 681) are to the same effect.

CHAPTER VIII

THE LAW OF CHATTELS

Topic 1. Possession of Chattels

§ 57. **Possession of Chattels, in general.** (I) **Seisin of Chattels in the Medieval Law.** — Seisin of chattels was no different, in theory, from seisin of lands. In one case as in the other it signified actual control of the thing. This physical control, however, was required in the case of movables to co-exist under all circumstances with actual custody ("Innehabung", "Gewahrsam"). For, unlike the case of lands, an economic usufruct of chattels without actual possession of them was impossible. Seisin of chattels, therefore, could be created only by physical custody or by the corporeal transfer of the thing; and the loss of the physical possession or a giving away of the thing necessarily destroyed the seisin. In the law of chattels seisin was necessarily and inseparably "bound up with the corporeal element."[1] It followed — an important difference between the law of chattels and of land — that multiple seisin in chattels was impossible; for only one person could ever exercise actual control over a thing in the sense of physical possession. Therefore no ideal seisin was possible in the case of chattels, nor a dormant or expectant seisin; whoever had lost the actual control or had not acquired this was unable to enforce in his own interest the effects of seisin. Although the medieval law did recognize one exception to these rules, as regards the loss of seisin, which will be discussed in the following paragraph, that exception only confirmed the rule. Again, there was originally no place in the law of chattels for the conception of citation seisin; for that originally presupposed a seisin created as the result of a judicial release, and in the case of chattels no judicial release could establish a seisin that could take the place of a corporeal delivery. The exception just mentioned to the general rule that the termination of physical control involved the destruction of seisin and its effects, was capable, however, as will be shown, of producing effects in certain cases in the law of chattels which were equivalent to those of judicial seisin. Finally, the rule that every real right must be manifested in the form of seisin and could be conveyed only under that form, — the so-called "translative" effect of seisin, — held good, also, in the law of chattels. But, as has been already mentioned (*supra*, p. 207), it was more strictly adhered to in the law of chattels than in the law of lands. For whereas in the latter the public and manifest act of release ("Auflassung") and of entry in the land-book were given by force of law the effect of a conveyance, without the necessity, in addition, of any livery of the corporeal seisin, this last remained the essential precondition to the transfer of a right under the law of chattels. Such a transfer could there be perfected only "by a change in the visible corporeal possession."[2] Thus, in the law of chattels, in a still stricter sense than in the law of land, seisin, in the sense of physical possession, was the exclusively necessary and under all circumstances the sufficient dress, of a real right in a thing. It was not legally replaceable and actually displaced, — as it came to be in the law of land as a result of the development

[1] Gierke, "Privatrecht", II, 193. [2] *Ibid.*, 207.

of the land-book system, — by a public and officially attested mode of creation.

(II) **The Modern Development.** — It has already been remarked (*supra*, p. 206) in discussing the law of land, that the distinction between the law of land and the law of chattels which was unknown to the Roman law disappeared after the Reception, at least in the common law. But this view, which was inconsistent with the ideas of the native law, did not attain any general prevalence and authority. On the contrary, that contrast was deepened in a noteworthy respect by the introduction of the land register. True, the Swiss Civil Code has very recently made a novel attempt in one case to assimilate the law of land and of chattels: namely, when a chattel is conveyed subject to a reservation of ownership, such a reservation is only effective when entered in a public register at the then residence of the acquirer (§ 715). The peculiar form of chattel mortgage ("Fahrnisverschreibung") in a pledge of cattle may also be classified under this principle (*infra*, § 66). In other respects, however, the "publicital" effects peculiar to the old seisin, which were attached in the land law to entry in the land-book, were attributed to mere possession in the law of chattels. There resulted from this distinction different consequences in the modern law of land and of chattels as regards a transfer of rights ("Rechtsübertragung") and of legal title ("Legitimation", — *cf.* § 58 *infra*).

The law of seisin recognized the economic usufruct of a thing as the characteristic of actual physical control; and therefore, as already stated (*supra*, p. 186), it recognized the possibility of multiple seisin in the case of lands, though not in the case of chattels. In the case of movables, this view led to the same result as in the Roman law, which ascribed possession ("Besitz"), generally speaking, only to one holding a thing with "animus domini", while speaking merely of "detention" in the case of every other person in physical control of a thing. This view, however, has been abandoned by the law in its latest stage, for according to the new Civil Code a multiple possession is possible in movable things precisely in the same manner as in land. Not only the "immediate" possessor who derives his possession from another person, — the "superior possessor" ("Besitzherr"), — but also such superior possessor, has actual possession: the present law considers the requirements of possession to be satisfied in the general control ("Sachherrschaft") which he also exercises over the thing. There is here involved a consistent further development and perfection of ideas which underlay the old Germanic law; for the repudiation of the naïvely sensuous test of usufruct in the sense of seisin made it possible to bridge the difference between the law of chattels and of land, without doing violence to the theory of the old law.

For the rest, there remains as the most important difference between the possession of movables and immovables the respective forms of actions for the protection of possession, which are at times subject to different conditions; and the consequently different effect of possession upon the substantive rights it covers.

In the following paragraphs we shall speak in the first place of the former difference; the substantive law, particularly the acquisition of the ownership of chattels by persons not entitled to their possession, will be discussed below (§ 63).

§ 58. **Chattel Actions, particularly the Rule "Hand must warrant Hand."** [1] (I) **The Doctrine of the Older Law.** — The legal protection which was associated with seisin in the Middle Ages

[1] *Sohm*, "Der Prozess der Lex Salica" (1867); *Laband*, "Die vermögensrechtlichen Klagen nach den sächsischen Rechtsquellen des Mittelalters" (1869); *Heusler*, "Die Beschränkung der Eigentumsverfolgung an Fahrnis und ihr Motiv im deutschen Recht" (1871); *Herrmann*, "Die Grundelemente der altgermanischen Mobiliarvindikation", no. 20 (1886) of *Gierke's* "Untersuchungen"; *London*, "Die Anfangsklage in ihrer ursprünglichen Bedeutung", ed. by *Pappenheim* (1886); *O. Gierke*, "Die Bedeutung des Fahrnisbesitzes für streitiges Recht nach dem BGB" (1897); *Zycha*, "Zur Auslegung des Titels 37 der Lex Salica, 'De vestigio minando'", in Z². R. G., XXII (1901), 155–180; *Herbert Meyer*, "Entwertung und Eigentum im deutschen Fahrnisrecht" (1902); *Wellspacher*, "Publizitätsgedanke und Fahrnisklage im 'Usus modernus'", in Z. Priv. öff. R., XXXI (1904), 631–694; *Alfred Schultze*, "Gerüfte und Marktkauf in Beziehung zur Fahrnisverfolgung", in "Breslauer Festgabe für F. Dahn", I (1905), 1–63, with which compare *Rehme* in Götting. G. Anz., CLXXI, 1 (1909), 250–258; "Publizität und Gewährschaft im deutschen Fahrnisrecht", in *Ihering's* J. B., XLIV (1905), 159–186; *Rauch*, "Spurfolge und Anefang in ihren Wechselbeziehungen, ein Beitrag zur Geschichte des deutschen Fahrnisprozesses" (1908); with which compare *A. Schultze* in Z². R. G., XXIX (1908), 428–440; *Herbert Meyer*, "Das Publizitätsprinzip im Deutschen Bürgerlichen Recht", in *O. Fischer's* "Abhandlungen", XVIII, 2 (1909); and cf. *A. Schultze*, in Z². R. G., XXXI (1910), 641–651; *Wahle* in Krit. Vj. G. R. W., XLIX (3d ser. XIII, 1911), 313–346; and *J. v. Gierke* in Z. ges. H. R., LXX (1911), 382–398; *Rauch*, "Gewährschaftsverhältnis und Erbgang nach älterem deutschen Recht", in the "Festgabe für K. Zeumer" (1910), 529–555; *A. Schultze*, "Die Bedeutung des Zuges auf den Gewähren im Anefangsverfahren", in "Festschrift für O. Gierke" (1911), 759–792; *Hübner* and *K. Lehmann*, art. "Anefang" in Hoop's "Reallexikon", I (1912), 82–84; *Wahle*, "Die Wadiation im Spurfolgeverfahren", in Inst. öst. G. F., XXXIII (1912), 79–86; *Müller-Erzbach*, "Gefährdungshaftung und Gefahrtragung" (1912), 297 *et seq.*, also in Arch. zivil. Praxis, CVI, 309–476, CIX, 1–142; *J. B. Ames*, "The Disseisin of Chattels" in Select Essays A. A. L. H., III (1909), 541–590; *O. W. Holmes*, "Das gemeine Recht Englands", translated by *Leonhard* (1912), 163–207, on the bailee in Anglo-American common law.

received effect in the law of land (*supra*, p. 195) not only in favor of the holder of a corporeal seisin who was disturbed in his immediate control of the land by the wrongful action of a third party, but also in favor of the holder of an ideal, dormant, or expectant seisin.

Accordingly, when a question was involved of a violent disseisin, or when a rentaler violated the proprietary seisin of the landlord by wrongful acts, the seisin so displaced or violated exercised its "defensive" and "offensive" effects. Thanks to the "publicital" character lent to it by the overt act creating it, it made possible the reacquisition of the land from any third person without regard to the question whether such present holder had acquired through a wrongful disseisin of the owner or his tenant, or through a wrongful act of the tenant.

This was not true in the Germanic law of chattels. From the earliest times this has distinguished the two cases of a voluntary delivery of a thing and an involuntary loss of possession, and has applied the general principles of the law of seisin in the first case alone.

(1) *Voluntary Delivery. Action of a Bailor.* — Whoever gave a movable into the hand of another person thereby deprived himself of its seisin, for he released it from his custody. He did not, however, on that account need to abandon his rights to it entirely. This happened only in case of a conveyance; not when he loaned it to another, or otherwise entrusted it to him. For in this case he gave the thing out of his own hand only upon a condition, an agreement to return it ("Rückfallsgeding"). The obligation of such other person to him varied with the nature of this agreement: if, for example, this was to return the thing loaned at the termination of a certain period, the action was then based upon an allegation that the time had run, and that the defendant was retaining possession beyond the stipulated time ("over bescedene tiet"). Only the other party to the contract, however, had subjected himself by the contract to the legal rights of the owner. The owner could therefore demand the return of the thing, that is a reconveyance of the seisin, from him alone. He could not demand it from a third party to whom possibly the thing had meanwhile passed. So, for example, if the bailee had sold the thing to C, — which of course he had no right to do, since he was only a loan-possessor ("Leihbesitzer"), — or if D had stolen it from the bailee to whom it was entrusted, then the owner had no power or protection as against such third persons. He must always proceed against the bailee only, because the agreement was made

with him alone; he was obliged to rely exclusively upon such bailee; he might possibly obtain damages from him, but he did not reacquire the thing.

This was a limitation upon chattel actions peculiar to the medieval law of things, — not only to the German but also to the French and Anglo-Norman. It was a necessary consequence of the cardinal principles of the law of seisin, which were bound to lead at this point to a fundamental distinction between the law of land and of chattels. If one, for example, let land to a peasant for rent, he nevertheless retained a proprietary seisin which he could enforce even against third persons. But whoever abandoned possession of a movable renounced the right therein which found visible expression in his seisin, without which its "publicital" quality was ineffective; and therefore, also, the power to enforce his right against third persons.[1] Inasmuch as the seisin of the former holder, — in our case that of the owner A, — was extinguished by a voluntary delivery of the thing, it followed that if the bailee was disseised, he alone, and no longer the owner, was entitled to exercise against a third person the action allowed one who was robbed for the return of the object and the fine imposed for the theft. And if the bailee wrongfully alienated or pledged the thing, then the owner could not require it of a purchaser or a pledgee or from their legal successors, but was obliged to satisfy his claim by recourse against the bailee himself. Whether the thing had been taken from the seisin of the bailee, and how it had come into the seisin of the third person, whether it was stolen from or alienated by the former, and whether such third person had acquired possession with or without knowledge of the wrong, and the like questions, were therefore wholly disregarded.

This principle, which there is good reason to regard as a general one of Germanic law, already found clear expression, in part, in the ancient folk-laws.[2] In the sources of the time of the Law-Books it is laid down in many places in form so clear as to be incapable of misunderstanding, and with express mention of both the consequences above stated.[3] Frequently it was expressed in the form of a legal maxim: "hand must warrant hand" ("Hand muss Hand wahren"), — that is, the hand in which one has laid the seisin, and that hand alone, must warrant its return; or, "where you have put your faith there you must seek it" ("wo du deinen Glauben gelassen hast, musst du ihn suchen").

[1] *Schultze*, "Gerüfte und Marktkauf", 3. [2] *Liutprand*, 131.
[3] Ssp., II, 60, § 1, and "Rechtsb. nach Distinctionen", II, 42, 6.

(2) *Involuntary Loss of Possession. Action for Lost Chattels.* — Not only he who voluntarily gave a movable out of his hand, but also he from whose hand it was taken with or without his consent, lost the seisin in it. The chief case of involuntary loss of possession was that of wrongful disseisin through larceny or robbery; in the folk-laws no other case is referred to. But things lost, or which otherwise were taken out of the hand of the owner, were treated from an early day in the same way as those stolen, notwithstanding this was not explicitly declared except in the later sources. In case of involuntary loss of possession no restriction upon chattel actions ever existed in Germanic law. The oldest of its legal records already recognize various distinct chattel actions, of which several made it possible for a person from whom some thing was taken by a thief or robber (the usual case was the theft or robbery of cattle) to regain possession of the thing even from a third person.

(A) Procedure upon detection in the act ("auf handhafter Tat", "hand-having" procedure).[1] This was possible in case the wrongdoer was discovered carrying evidence of his wrong in his hand, and this had been publicly proclaimed by the hue and cry ("Gerüfte" or "Gerüchte"),—that is, by the call of the injured person summoning his neighbors to hurry to his aid. It resulted in the severe punishment of the wrongdoer. The thing was returned to him from whom it had been stolen.

(B) Action of larceny or robbery. — This action was brought in cases where the wrongdoer was not discovered "red-handed" against a person directly accused, and involved "an assumption of the subjective circumstances of the robbery or the theft."[1] The purpose of the action was a condemnation of the thief or the robber to a penalty imposed by statute for larceny or robbery, or a judgment for the return of the things taken or of their value.

(C) Following the trail ("Spurfolge"). — This was resorted to in case no thief or robber was discovered, and also nobody could be directly charged with being such; subject to the observance of strict formalities (hue and cry, "house-searching"), it was allowed to the injured person "who learned early enough of his loss" for the discovery of the thing whose possession was lost. If the search was successful within a certain time, as for example within three nights, then the owner ("Spurfolger") could take

[1] *Brunner*, "Geschichte", II, 481 *et seq.*, 495 *et seq.*
[2] *Ibid.*, 275.

possession of the thing. This, however, did not by any means involve under all circumstances the punishment of the holder of the thing. It was possible that a house-owner, conscious of his bona fide acquisition of the thing, permitted the search of his house and vouched a warrantor (" Gewährsmann ") from whom he had acquired it. In that case the searcher must swear (" gelo-ben ") to bring the thing before the court for the purpose of observing the "third-hand procedure" ("Lex Salica", 37: "per tercia manu agramire"), which will be discussed below under (D). Only after so doing was he permitted to take temporary possession of the thing pending the arrival of the term of court, at which the third-hand procedure then took its regular course. If, on the other hand, the householder prohibited a search of his house, but this resulted nevertheless in a discovery of the missing thing, he was deprived, by his prohibition of the search, of the right to vouch a warrantor of his possession. In this case he was regarded as indubitably a thief, and must therefore not only return the thing but also pay the penalty imposed for larceny. On the other hand, the searcher forfeited a penalty if the search of the house proved fruitless.

(D) THE "ANEFANG" ("hand-laying") PROCEDURE.—This was resorted to when he from whom the thing was stolen found it in the hand of a stranger without search, or after the expiration of the statutory period to which such search was limited. He could then take possession of it subject to the observance of certain formalities which certainly went back into a great antiquity. He was bound to " lay hold of it " (" anfassen ") in a manner which was exactly prescribed. For example, in the case of cattle, he must grasp the right ear of the animal with his left hand and with his right foot step against the animal's fore-leg. The whole procedure received its name from this legally prescribed act, — designated in the Frankish sources as " anafangjan ", " furifangôn "; in the Low German sources of the Middle Ages, " anefang "; in the High German, " furfang ", " verfang." By it the plaintiff identified the thing as one stolen from him. Of course, he did not by such " hand-laying " directly charge the possessor himself with the theft or the robbery. The purpose of the " Anefang-" procedure was, indeed, to reach the thief through the identification of the thing stolen; but though he was not in this way discovered, nevertheless the procedure held the thing for the complainant.[1] If the possessor had not been, then a third per-

[1] *A. Schultze* in Z². R. G., XXIX, 432.

son must have been, the thief or robber. The "Anefang" was "the beginning of the action"; therefore the possessor was obliged to make answer to the act of the plaintiff, and to clear himself of the charge of theft which was objectively implicit in the action. The ordinary reply of the possessor, in case he was not himself the thief, consisted in his naming the third person from whom he had received the thing; that is, he vouched a person to warranty for his possession, he appealed to a third hand: whence the expression "intertiare" or "third-hand procedure" in the sources of the Frankish period. According to the Gothic, Frankish, High German, and later Saxon law, the possessor was bound to bring his warrantors before the court within a certain period, and to make formal oath of his complaint immediately after the "Anefang" had taken place ("agramire", "adramire"). According to the more ancient Lombard and early Saxon law, on the other hand, the possessor led the plaintiff to the warrantor.[1] The warrantor thus appealed to might in turn appeal to a predecessor in title, and he again to another; and in some legal systems, — as *e.g.* the Frankish, and in the Sachsenspiegel,[2] — this could be indefinitely repeated; whereas under other systems, — as *e.g.* the Saxon town laws, — such vouchers to warranty ceased at the third, or at the second, fifth, sixth, or seventh man. There existed also restrictions of locality; for example, in the Sachsenspiegel the appeal could not be made across navigable waters.[2] An obligation was thus imposed upon the warrantor to defend the action in place of the original defendant.[3] The chattel whose title was in dispute was delivered ("zugeschoben") to the warrantor, "he received the 'shove' ('Schub')"; and he thereby acquired, in relation to the original defendant, who was thus eliminated from the suit, the position of a fiduciary ("Treuhänder"): he was bound to redeliver the thing to him in case of a successful defense against the plaintiff. The warrantor might vouch a further warrantor from whom he had acquired the thing. In this case, that is in case of repeated vouching to warranty, "the thing wandered back from hand to hand through which it had formerly passed by successive juristic acts."[4] If the defendant was guilty of a breach of warranty, that is if the warrantor did not appear, or refused to assume the defense "shoved" upon him, or

[1] Ssp., II, 36, § 5. [2] *Ibid.*, § 6.

[3] Note the manner in which the Ssp., II, 36, § 5 continues.

[4] *Brunner*, "Geschichte", II, 504, following *Sohm*, "Prozess der Lex Salica" (1867), 113.

if he was defeated in the suit, then such defendant received back the purchase price from his warrantor who thus broke his warranty; but since he had been defeated in the suit the warrantor was himself obliged to deliver the thing to the plaintiff, and in addition to pay the penalty for theft. He was, of course, released from the latter obligation in case he was able to clear himself of any suspicion of theft; and this he could accomplish by a purgative oath by which he proved an honest acquisition of the thing, particularly a notorious acquisition such as a purchase in market overt.[1] This was also open to him who could not resort to a voucher to warranty, because, for example, he was unable to name the warrantor, or because the warrantor had died or could not be found in the time prescribed, or because the prescribed number of warrantors had already been reached, or because the defendant had lost possession of the thing during the action. If, in a case of limited voucher to warranty, the last warrantor under such limit could prove a lawful acquisition from a predecessor, he must, to be sure, deliver the thing to the plaintiff, but he cleared himself by that proof from the suspicion of theft; the plaintiff thus received back the thing, but he had to go without any penalty for the theft.[2] In addition to voucher to warranty other defenses were open to the defendant. Certainly under the earlier, and probably still under the older, law he could allege original acquisition of the thing; declaring, for example, that he had gained it in rightful feud; that he had raised the animal in his stable; that the linen was spun in his own house; etc.[3] The Frankish sources already mention a plea by the defendant that he had inherited the thing. In this case, he could not vouch a warrantor, because the obligation of warranty was not heritable; consequently, the law let the matter drop upon proof of lawful acquisition, or demanded in addition a proof of rightful acquisition by the decedent.[4] If he proved these allegations, — in the last case he must include proof, under the "Lex Salica", of the right of the decedent,—he thereby succeeded, not only in freeing himself from the suspicion of theft, as in case of a purgative oath, but in completely defeating the complaint. In this case the plaintiff who had thus lost his suit was obliged to pay a penalty for his unjust "Anefang";

[1] Ssp., II, 36, § 1.

[2] *A. Schultze* in "Festschrift für Gierke", 783.

[3] Ssp., II, 36, § 3.

[4] *Rauch* has shown this in his essay in the "Festgabe für Zeumer"; his view has been indorsed by *A. Schultze* in the "Festschrift für Gierke", 768, and by *Heymann*, in Z[2]. R. G., XXXII (1911), 431.

and, if a personal charge of theft had been made, to bear the legal consequences of a false accusation.[1] Instead of throwing the responsibility upon a predecessor in title, every warrantor, equally with the original defendant, might allege original acquisition, such as the breeding of the animal or the making of the thing, thus establishing his claim to it as against the original defendant, and so win it for the plaintiff.[2] The "Anefang" action was based solely upon involuntary loss of seisin, and even in the earliest times it was available when a thing had not been stolen or robbed, but lost, or possession thereof otherwise involuntarily lost. It was "not so much an action by an owner as by the person who had held the thing in his custody before it was taken from his possession by theft or by robbery."[3] It was not based, in and of itself, upon a right to the thing, any more than in case of a wrongful dispossession of lands. Though the plaintiff designated as "his" the thing he laid his hands on, he thereby merely alleged the identity of that thing and the one he had lost. Therefore the "Anefang" action was available not only to the owner but also to a finder and to any other person in whose hand the owner had put it, — for example, a bailee ("Verwahrer"), a borrower, a hirer, or a pledgee; for only these were deprived of the seisin by the theft, and not the owner who had already given to another his seisin by delivery of the thing. The owner, therefore, could not himself bring the "Anefang" action when the thing was stolen from his bailee ("Vertrauensmann", — *supra*, p. 408). On the other hand, when members of his family or of his personal following, — in other words, his household companions, — alienated a thing, the house-lord could reclaim it by "Anefang": this was the case of so-called "abgetragene" things (things "carried off").[4] This apparent exception, however, was quite reconcilable with the general principles, for the owner had not deprived himself of seisin of the things by delivery of them to his wife or children or servants, since these persons, who were his mere instruments, received no dispositive power thereover, and consequently no seisin.

(E) Finally, in addition to the "Anefang" action for cases of involuntary loss of possession there existed in the medieval law a so-called "DIRECT" OR "SIMPLE" ACTION ("schlichte Klage").[5] This was "substantially the same action as the 'Anefang.' It

[1] *Brunner*, "Geschichte", II, 509.
[2] *A. Schultze* in the "Festschrift für Gierke", 780.
[3] *Brunner, op. cit.*
[4] Ssp., III, 6, § 1.
[5] "Richtsteig Landrechts," 11, § 3.

was lacking merely in the particular element with which the 'Anefang' was begun."[1] It was less dangerous to the plaintiff than the "Anefang" action to this extent, that if he was defeated it did not involve a penalty for wrongful laying on of hands, or, as the case might be, a penalty for false accusation. On the other hand it did not offer the same advantages in adducing proof.

(F) Involuntary loss of possession was therefore sufficient basis in the medieval law of chattels for a claim against third persons for the redelivery of the thing, in the form either of an action of "Anefang" or of a direct action; and the rule "hand must warrant hand" was in so far excluded. But this exclusion could not be based upon the rules of the law of seisin. For these rules could not have given the injured person a better claim to things he had lost than to those he had bailed. Indeed, unlike the case of land, where multiple seisin and, particularly, in the case of loss of possession an ideal seisin were recognized, he had lost the seisin equally in the two cases, and thereby lost the protection which it assured him. The right to pursue a thing possession of which he had lost was in fact inconsistent with the "*publicital*" idea which dominated the law of seisin; "yet despite the absence of the publicital element which was lost with the seisin and was not replaced by other means, there was granted, here also, an action against the third party."[2] The cause of this peculiar state of affairs can only be found, as Schultze contends, in the breach of peace that was made by the disseisin, and which was required to be cured not only by a penance under the criminal law but also under the private law. The allowance of a chattel action in case of wrongful disseisin was inconsistent with the theory of the law of seisin, but was permitted out of regard for the preservation of the legal order. "The reaction of the existing legal order against the breach of peace involved in theft was so strong among the primitive Germans that the law not only gave the victim of the theft a delictual action under the private law against the thief and his associates (concealers of stolen goods and persons cognizant of the theft), but also a claim under the private law against every third person, — even one who was entirely innocent and free from any imputation of negligence, — for the redelivery of the thing."[3] And though all cases of voluntary de-

[1] *Herbert Meyer*, *op. cit.*, 81.
[2] *A. Schultze*, "Gerüfte und Marktkauf", 56.
[3] *Ibid.*, 58.

livery were treated alike and brought within the rule "let hand warrant hand", things that were stolen or robbed, or which were taken from the owner's hands otherwise than by theft or robbery, were necessarily treated like these, inasmuch as they, as much as the latter, were distinguished from things bailed to another by the involuntary loss of possession. The fact that the principle was carried no further in the medieval law, and that the "Anefang" action, in particular, was not extended to the case of a wrongful alienation by the bailee, was directly "connected with the fact that Germanic law, unlike the Roman, distinguished concealment of stolen goods from larceny."[1] In this case, therefore, the precondition of theft was no more present than was that of involuntary loss of possession.

(II) **Exceptions to the Theory of the Older Law.** — The clear and simple system of the older law was somewhat confused, even in the course of the Middle Ages, by blurring the difference between goods bailed and goods lost. In the case of the former the limitations upon chattel actions were at first perfectly reconcilable with practical requirements, and the unlimited right of pursuit allowed in the case of the latter accorded with sentiments of justice, but as commerce increased there came about a restriction of the rule "hand must warrant hand" and an increasing protection of the acquirer of stolen things. That rule involved, in fact, a considerable danger for the owner of chattels. For in case a thing was lost from the hand of a bailee, and the latter was not in a position to afford damages, the owner not only lost the thing itself but forfeited also its value. On the other hand, the absolute duty to return to the owner a thing which proved to have been stolen was a great hardship upon third persons; for they also were forced to rely entirely upon their warrantor, and he might well be propertyless. Thus, in time exceptions were established which mitigated the harshness of both rules.

(1) *Exceptions to the Rule "Hand must warrant Hand."* (A) Under the town law of Goslar anyone who had given a thing to a BAILEE FOR CUSTODY was permitted to follow his property against third persons if the bailee ("Verwahrer") alienated it or involuntarily lost it. And according to the law of Augsburg, if a CONSIGNEE sold the goods in payment of his own debt, the consignor could recover them from the third party.

(B) When artisans sold or pledged things entrusted to them as BAILEES FOR ALTERATIONS, the owners of such things had the

[1] *Brunner*, "Grundzüge" (5th ed.), 206.

right in many cities, — *e.g.* in Lübeck, Brunswick, Dortmund, Munich,—to require their return from the third person, subject to payment of the wages owed to the laborer; a power which is to be explained as a consequence of the right possessed by handicraftsmen, under statutory rights of pledge or detention, to pawn their finished work for the amount of their wage (*infra,* § 66).

(C) At times an action was allowed to an original possessor against a present possessor, at least in cases where a FIDUCIARY BAILEE, the person from whom the thing had been stolen, had died or had avoided the suit.[1]

(D) Finally, a few legal systems (particularly that of Lübeck but also those of Schleswig and of Munich) gave an action to the BAILOR AGAINST ANY THIRD PERSON in the case of any bailed property,—and this so early as the end of the Middle Ages,—when the plaintiff was ready to compensate the possessor in full for his outlay for the thing.[2] In this case, therefore, the possessor received a claim for compensation. There was involved in this a total abandonment of the old viewpoint of the law: the rule "hand must warrant hand" was abandoned in favor of the first possessor.

(2) *Exceptions to the Unlimited Right of Pursuing Lost Chattels.* (A) As regards THINGS BOUGHT IN OPEN MARKET, an unrestricted claim for their redelivery was transformed in the later Middle Ages into a mere claim to compensation for their value, although, to be sure, only here and there within the regions of Germanic law, and not so generally as in France. In other words, when the original possessor of a thing, who had been involuntarily deprived of seisin therein, found it in the hand of a third person, he could demand it of the latter only upon compensation for the purchase price in case such third person proved that he had bought it in market overt. Here, therefore, it was not the manner of the loss but the mode of acquisition that was considered, and the proof of a market purchase relieved the holder not merely, as formerly, of the suspicion of theft (*supra,* p. 413), but also of the unconditional obligation of redelivery.[3] The reason for this special treatment of market sales is doubtless to be found in the fact that men saw in a transaction entered into in the market, — as in the public conclusion of any agreement whatever, — an "objective" or "typical" evidence of innocence and honesty, as contrasted with a secret, and therefore suspicious, sale. "For this reason such

[1] Sswp. (W.), 191.
[2] "Lüb. Recht", II, 194 (of 1294).
[3] See for example the "Jülicher Landrecht" (1537), 48.2.

public purchase took the place, in clearing the purchaser of a criminal charge, of warrantors, who in case of a purchase from unknown parties were not available; and on this account it even acquired importance in the field of the common ("zivilistische") law, in the action for compensation ("Lösungsanspruch").[1] The inclination to increase traffic in public markets as much as possible, and so to favor to the utmost sales in open market, may also have contributed to the rule, as Rietschel has remarked.[2] It was desired to protect a person buying in the market against the danger of being compelled, not only to return the goods, but also to forfeit the purchase price. Practical considerations triumphed, here, over the strict principle.

(B) According to the law of the Hansa cities THINGS FROM OVER SEAS could not be claimed at all, AND STOLEN THINGS INTRODUCED FROM OTHER JURISDICTIONS BY LAND could not be claimed, under the chattel action for lost seisin, after a year and a day.[3] This rule is explainable by the idea of municipal freedom and the town peace; it has the appearance of being "a reflection, in a way, in relation to chattels, of the principle 'city air makes free' ('Luft macht frei')."[4]

(C) Finally, the principles of Germanic law found no application whatever in the case of one entire class of the population, which was particularly interested in trade, — namely THE JEWS. On the contrary, thanks to the Jewry privileges they received, their own Jewish law was left in force, as for them, in Germany as in most Christian countries. And that law was much more favorable to them. According to the Jewish law respecting concealment of stolen goods, which was derived from the Talmud, a Jew could always demand the purchase price he had given for a thing either bought or received in pledge, in case it was demanded from him; the amount of the price he established by his oath. Only, he must not have known that the thing was stolen. A mere suspicion, however, or acquisition from a notorious thief, or for a price which would raise suspicion of theft, did not prejudice him. In time, it is true, this privilege, which carried with it certain hateful implications, was restricted under the influence of the law of seisin. A public purchase was required, a purchase from suspicious or unknown persons was forbidden, and a large

[1] *A. Schultze* in Z². R. G., XXXI (1910), 650.
[2] Z². R. G., XXVII (1906), 434.
[3] Hamb. Stat. of 1270, VII. 9, 1.
[4] *J. v. Gierke* in Z. Hnls. R., LXX, 387.

number of things were excluded from the rule on account of the suspicion of theft which their mere possession would create, such as vessels of the Church, wet or bloody garments, agricultural implements, tools, weapons, etc. But in this form the privilege was maintained throughout the Middle Ages and even long thereafter — in isolated cases even into the 1800 s — notwithstanding that it was nominally abolished, first within certain regions and then, in the 1500 s, for the entire Empire. On the other hand, the Jewry privilege was extended to some Christians; for example, to publicans, goldsmiths, frippers, pawnbrokers, and everywhere and especially to Lombards and traders from Cahors in Southern France, — foreign merchants who were everywhere engaged, along with the Jews, in money-changing and pawnbroking on a small scale. The last traces of the application of the Talmud rules to non-Jews is to be found in the privileges of municipal pawnhouses.[1]

(III) **The Development Since the Reception.** — It follows from what has been said above that the medieval chattel action, like the action for land, was neither a purely possessory nor a purely proprietary action. It was an action based upon seisin, and was available to every holder of seisin; but in the course of every suit it became a controversy as to the right that was covered by the seisin. Inasmuch, however, as it was allowed, in theory, only to one who was the subject of a physical seisin (for the exception in the case of stolen chattels represented a break with the principles of the law of seisin), it had a narrower field of application than the action for land, which was also allowed to the holder of an ideal seisin. All this contrasted sharply with the Roman law. For this distinguished between possessory and petitory remedies, but not between movable and immovable things. And yet, as already remarked (*supra*, pp. 205 *et seq.*), the Roman law of possession was nevertheless received into Germany. Despite this, however, the Germanic views were not wholly lost. We have already remarked that the possessory remedies that were borrowed from the Roman law had been given a subsidiary petitory character in medieval Italian jurisprudence, and that this secondary character was even somewhat accentuated in the development of the common law. What has there been said (pp. 214 *et seq.*) holds true in the law of chattels in the same manner as in the law of land: "possessorium ordinarium" and "summariissimum" were by no means confined to land. The Roman pro-

[1] *H. Meyer*, "Entwertung und Eigentum", 268.

prietary action ("rei vindicatio") rested upon the right of the plaintiff, and therefore made possible a vindication of his ownership as against any third person even when the case was one involving movables ("ubi rem meam invenio, ibi vindico"); but though it therefore had nothing in common with the Germanic chattel action in principle, it was nevertheless received in its classical purity into Germany, and later found entry into the common law. However, aside from the fact that there existed side by side with it the common law possessory remedies just mentioned which had marked petitory characteristics, and that the common law actually continued to make frequent use of the old chattel action under the names of the alien "vindicatio" and the alien action of larceny, or "condictio furtiva", the principles of that action were also everywhere maintained in the regional legal systems, albeit with more or less fundamental transformations in their substance, until finally, in recent years, they again became the common law of Germany.

(1) A number of the regional systems clung to the old *distinction between voluntary and involuntary loss of possession.* This was true of many systems of town law (for example those of Lübeck, Hamburg, and Rostock), many Swiss laws, and, among the great modern codes, the Code Civil, the Austrian Code, the German General Commercial Code, and the Zürich Code.

(A) In the case of VOLUNTARY LOSS OF POSSESSION the principle "let hand warrant hand" was maintained in these systems; and along with it the traditional limitations of the chattel action to a claim based exclusively upon a right against a bailee.[1] At the same time, however, there were preserved the exceptions already recognized in the Middle Ages; such as that respecting things alienated or sold by artisans, and also, generally, that as to things stolen from a bailee. The Lübeck law maintained a peculiar view, in that it accorded the owner at least a right to repurchase the thing from a bona fide third person who purchased it.[2] All these systems gave full effect to the rule "hand must warrant hand" "almost always" only when such third person had acquired the thing bona fide. So, in particular, the Code Civil, the Austrian Code, and the General Commercial Code, the latter two of which also require a purchase for value.[3]

[1] "Rev. Lüb. R." (1586), III, 2, 1. [2] *Ibid.*, III, 2, 2.

[3] Austrian Code, § 367: "An action alleging ownership cannot be sustained against the bona fide possessor of a chattel when the latter can prove either that he acquired the same at public auction or from a tradesman authorized to deal in such articles, or acquired it, in exchange for

(B) In the case of INVOLUNTARY LOSS OF POSSESSION the theoretical availability of the action against every third person was of course preserved; but here too the Roman law had agreed with the German in this result. This agreement was qualified, however, by the fact that exceptions to the principle were either newly introduced or were preserved from the older native law. In the law of Hamburg and of Lübeck, for example, it continued to be true that chattels introduced from over seas were absolutely free from pursuit. Other legal systems gave the person who had acquired in a public manner goods of which another person had lost possession a right to have them redeemed. This was true of the French law, and of a considerable number of the Romanistic systems of Switzerland, in case of acquisition at public auction, or in market overt, or from a merchant dealing regularly in similar things.

(2) It is true that many legal systems treated *voluntary and involuntary loss of possession* in exactly the same way, either under all circumstances or as regarded certain classes of chattels. But only a few of the older statutes, such as the Reformations of Nuremberg, Frankfort, and Lüneburg, adopted the pure Roman principle of the vindicatio. For the most part this was subjected to considerable modifications.

(A) Thus, in the first place, the action was wholly denied against a BONA FIDE POSSESSOR, no matter whether the loss of possession had been voluntary or involuntary, whenever the question involved was one of money or of bearer paper, of bills of exchange or other forms of order paper, or of things acquired at public auction. This rule became the common law of Germany through the Bills of Exchange Act [1] and the Commercial Code; [2] according to the

value, from a person to whom the plaintiff had entrusted it for use, for preservation or for any other purpose whatever. In these cases title is acquired from such bona fide possessors, and the former owner has merely a right to compensation against such persons as were responsible to him for the chattel."

AHGB, Art. 306: "When goods ('Waaren') or other chattels have been sold and delivered by a merchant in the course of his business, the bona fide purchaser acquires the title ('Eigentum'), even though the seller was not the owner. The title formerly existing is extinguished. . . . This article is not applicable when the chattels have been stolen or lost."

[1] "Wechselordnung", Art. 74: "The holder of a bill of exchange whose title is legitimate under the rules of Art. 36 can be required to surrender it only when he acquired it in bad faith, or is chargeable with gross negligence in connection with his acquisition thereof."

[2] AHGB, Art. 307: "The provisions of the foregoing article are applicable to bearer paper even when it is transferred . . . otherwise than by a merchant in course of trade, in case such paper is stolen or lost."

Austrian law it also applied in cases of acquisition from a dealer entitled to trade in such articles.[1]

(B) The Prussian "Landrecht" did not consider the manner in which possession was lost, either in the case of particular chattels or under any other circumstances. On the contrary, it attributed decisive importance solely to the MANNER IN WHICH POSSESSION WAS ACQUIRED. If a present possessor had acquired possession in good faith and for value from a person not under suspicion, any claim for the return of the chattel was barred, and ordinarily only a claim for compensation existed, the plaintiff being obliged to make good what was paid by the honest acquirer to the dishonest vendor.[2] In special cases, however, not even this was permitted, so that in such cases a present possessor in good faith was safe against any claim whatever. This rule prevailed in favor of one who had acquired a movable either from the public treasury or at public auction; also in favor of one who had acquired it in the shop of a merchant who was a member of a gild (although the general right to compensation existed even as to purchases at fairs or in open market), and, finally, in favor of one who acquired gold and bearer paper in good faith. The Saxon Code likewise permitted the pursuit of stolen chattels, without distinction between those that were bailed or lost; but in certain cases allowed only a demand for compensation.

(3) Finally, *the Civil Code* has brought the past development to an end in such a way as again to give general authority in the law of chattels to the old idea of the publicital function of seisin. It distinguishes between involuntary and voluntary loss of possession in the manner of the Germanic law. In the case of involuntary loss of possession he who has lost possession can, in theory, demand the redelivery of the thing from any acquirer whatever (§ 935, 1); "the thing whose possession has been lost is immediately subjected to a levy ('Bann') in favor of its owner, and remains under this even in the hands of all later possessors."[3] The mode of acquisition is of no importance. The Civil Code no longer recognizes any claim for compensation. An exception is

[1] See p. 420, n. 2, *supra*.

[2] Allg. L. R., I, 15, § 25: "When things whose possession has been lost by their rightful owner or possessor are bought from a person not himself under suspicion by a contract for value, the buyer must indeed . . . return it," § 26; "But he may, in turn, require compensation for all he has given or done in payment therefor." Many systems of Swiss law (Zürich, Schaffhausen, Zug, Glarus, St. Gallen, Thurgau, Appenzell A.-Rh.) adopted the same rule.

[3] *Cosack*, "Bürgerliches Recht", II (5th ed.), 126.

made only in the case of money, bearer paper, and things acquired at public auction; in these cases the unrestricted assignability of the thing, and the special publicity of the manner in which possession is acquired, are the reasons why the owner cannot follow his property.

On the other hand, in the case of a voluntary renunciation of possession, — that is, in the case of things entrusted to another, — the old rule "hand must warrant hand" is once more generally prevalent to-day; though, to be sure, — and this is a concession to the post-medieval development, — only upon condition that the acquirer acquired possession in good faith; the requisites of good faith being differently defined, in this connection, in the Civil and Commercial Codes (BGB, § 932; HGB, § 366). The rule "let hand warrant hand" has been again accepted for good reasons, and not from any sense of historical piety. For although it does involve the danger, as to owners, that they may lose a chattel and be unable to enforce against their fiduciary the claim for damages to which they are entitled, nevertheless the principle serves the usual interests of parties better than the Roman principle of the vindicatio. Whoever has voluntarily given up possession of a thing has himself chosen a fiduciary, and he must be responsible if the latter prove unworthy of confidence. But it is different in cases of involuntary loss of possession. In these the reaction against injustice once led to the allowance of an unlimited right of pursuit; and even from the viewpoint of the present day it seems just to impose upon a third acquirer of the thing an unqualified obligation of redelivery, for a person can select his vendor, whereas one whose chattel is stolen does not choose the thief.[1]

Finally, the Civil Code has so far followed the old law of seisin that although it classifies the old chattel action along with mere possessory remedies equally applicable to all things, it nevertheless allows it to a mere possessor in accord with the Germanic law, and does not base it as in the Roman law exclusively upon a proprietary right in the claimant. With this change there was again adopted, in the law of chattels above all, the old publicital function of seisin, — whereas in the common law possession neither gave rise to a presumption of right nor sufficed as a basis for a petitory action, only possession in good faith and under color of title ("titulierter gutgläubiger Besitz") having been treated as a real right in the nature of ownership and protected by

[1] *Cosack, op. cit.* (4th ed.), 93.

the actio publiciana. There is here involved, in the first place, the presumption recognized in § 1006 of the Civil Code, which goes back historically to the rules earlier adopted in the Bavarian, Prussian, and French law: in the case of money and of bearer paper there exists an absolute, and in the case of other things of which a predecessor was not dispossessed against his will a rebuttable, presumption in favor of a present holder, that he is the owner; and similar presumptions in favor of an earlier possessor that he was the owner of the thing during the continuance of his possession. An advantage has thus been conceded to a possessor giving evidence in court, similar to that once enjoyed by the holder of seisin; in particular, because he can rely upon this presumption of ownership in a proprietary action brought against him by another person ("defensive" effect of seisin). In the second place, § 1007 of the Code gives the earlier possessor, — whether an owner, usufructuary, pledgee, or other person personally entitled to the possession of a thing, — an action against a present possessor for the redelivery of a thing formerly in the plaintiff's possession. This right exists, in the case of things possession of which was involuntarily lost, against every acquirer; whereas in the case of chattels bailed, and under all circumstances as regards money and bearer paper, such a right exists only when the acquirer did not gain possession in good faith. We meet again in this the old " offensive " effect of seisin in a new form; but this time in the law of chattels, and not as before in the law of land. Moreover, the law has come to consider the manner in which the third person has acquired possession, — a viewpoint unknown to the old law.

The *Swiss Civil Code*, — following the earlier codification of the Swiss law of obligation, which had in turn followed the Zürich Code (*supra*, p. 420), — has likewise adopted the principle " hand warrant hand " (§ 933) in the case of bailed chattels, while permitting an unrestricted right to pursue chattels possession of which has been involuntarily lost. Gold and bearer paper, however, are excepted from the latter rule (§ 935). Moreover, in the case of chattels bought at auction or in open market, or from a merchant dealing in wares of the same kind, there is allowed against a bona fide acquirer (§ 934, 2) merely a claim for compensation. And, finally, the right to demand the redelivery of chattels lost or stolen is lost with the expiration of five years (§ 934); by which provision the Swiss Code protects more adequately than does the German law the interest of strangers who acquire chattels.

TOPIC 2. OWNERSHIP OF CHATTELS

§ 59. **The Origin and Content of Ownership in Chattels.** — (I) **Origin.** — It can be assumed with certainty that private ownership of chattels, like that of land, was only gradually developed from collective ownership. Herds of domestic animals, implements of agricultural and household labor, were subject in the earliest times to the ownership of hordes, of agrarian groups, of sibs, and of families. Private ownership developed earlier, however, in the case of chattels than in that of land. And it was earliest realized in the case of things destined for personal use, such as clothes and weapons; it was even customary to lay these in the grave with their dead owner, which could therefore not be inherited. There was later developed as to all chattels a freely heritable individual ownership which displaced the older collective ("kollektiv-") ownership. It was only within the many forms of joint ("Gesamt-") and co- ("Mit-") ownership that the latter was either continued or newly developed.

(II) **Content.** — Individual ownership of chattels overcame the traces of its collectivistic origin far sooner and more completely than did ownership of land. Even at an early day it came to signify unlimited physical control. Indeed, this idea was developed for the first time in relation to chattels; and it has ever since remained essential in this branch of the law. Since a very early period, and equally to-day, this fact has, in Germanic law, substantially differentiated ownership of chattels from ownership of land, which, as already shown, was characterized in an especial degree by limitations that have remained stamped upon it even in the modern law.

At the same time, at least in the medieval law of chattels, there are still to be recognized a few after-effects, although slight ones, of one-time restrictions due to rights of associational groups and of the family. For whereas, generally speaking, an owner could freely dispose of his chattels, already in the Middle Ages, without being bound by the consent of the heirs[1] as in the case of conveyances of land, this right was conceded to him by the medieval sources only upon condition of his unimpaired physical capacity. For — so it was reasoned — one who disposed of his property when on his sick-bed or death-bed, by provisions that were possibly resolved upon in the absence of full mental clarity, and which at any rate exposed him to no deprivation when actually

[1] The Ssp., I, 52, § 1 expresses this principle clearly.

made shortly before death, thereby harmed his heirs alone; and it should be forbidden him to do that. Hence the various tests of physical strength which were prescribed, in the naïvely realistic fashion of the Middle Ages, as preconditions to dispositive freedom;[1] these have already been referred to in another connection (*supra*, pp. 13, 70).

There belongs here, also, the rule that nobody might make a gift of chattels without an immediate change of possession;[2] because equally in this case the interest of the heirs might be all too easily injured by dispositions that could not be sensible to the alienor himself.

Such provisions as the above, and equally all other restrictions upon dispositive powers over chattels under the private law, are unknown in the modern law.

Topic 3. Acquisition of Title to Chattels

§ 60. **Occupancy. (I) Occupancy of Ownerless Chattels.** — Occupancy ("Aneignung", "Okkupation") is a taking of possession with the intent of acquiring ownership; in the case of ownerless things it is the only possible mode of acquiring title. It was at once the oldest and for a long time the most important means of acquiring ownership, but it lost importance as ownerless chattels became rarer. In the most primitive stages of civilization man gained his sustenance by occupancy of chattels, that is by hunting.[3] But whereas the Roman law clung to the principle that ownerless things might be occupied by anyone at will, Germanic law early restricted this free right of occupancy. It continued to recognize an unrestricted right of occupancy only in the case of certain things, such as wild animals that were not objects of chase (*e.g.* rabbits), birds [4] (particularly doves), products of the sea, berries, and things which were absolutely abandoned by their owner. Aside from this, however, it created numerous special and exclusive rights of occupancy that gave the power of acquiring title by occupancy to certain privileged persons only, — either to landowners or, in the form of regalities, to land-lords and Territorial princes (*supra*, pp. 268 *et seq.*), or even to other persons, such as a first discoverer. This was true particularly of

[1] Note the continuation in the Ssp., I, 52, § 2.

[2] Goslar. Stat., S9, Z8–10. This was expressed by the French law in the rule, "donner et retenir ne vaut" (one cannot both give and retain).

[3] *v. Amira*, "Recht", 125.

[4] Swsp. (G), 198, § 3.

wild animals subject to unrestricted rights of chase, and of river fish; only persons entitled to rights of venery and piscary could acquire property in these (*supra*, pp. 274 *et seq.*, pp. 286 *et seq.*). This idea has been preserved in the modern law. For although the Civil Code subjects ownerless things, generally speaking, to rights of free occupancy, there are excepted from this those things with respect to which the statutes of the individual States shall recognize exclusive rights of occupancy; and among such there are everywhere included to-day rights of hunting and of fishery, and in some localities others also, such as the regalities of amber and of treasure trove. A person without rights of occupancy who hunts or fishes acquires, in any event, no ownership for himself, as is expressly provided in the Civil Code (§ 958, 2), which is here in entire agreement with the rule of the older Germanic law. The question whether wild game killed by a poacher becomes the property of the person entitled to the right of chase, or whether the game so killed remains ownerless, was always a disputed one. The Civil Code has decided it in the sense last mentioned, although the opposite view is perhaps more consistent with Germanic law.[1]

(II) **The Law of Apiculture.** — Special legal rules existed from the earliest times respecting the occupancy of bees. For inasmuch as these cannot be made domestic animals even by apiculture,[2] but, as the Saxon town-law expresses it, are " wild worms ",[3] not only wild swarms but also those which have left a hive were subject to occupancy by any person. This was different from the rule respecting tame domesticated animals, ownership in which, under the German as under the Roman law, is lost only when the animal abandons the habit of resorting to its appointed place (BGB, § 960, 3; similar provision in the Swiss Civil Code, § 719). The Germanic folk-laws already permitted anyone who found a bee swarm in a hollow tree to reduce it to his ownership; namely, by marking the tree in some way. True, there is also found in them the provision that the owner may protect his property by immediate pursuit of the swarm: according to the Bavarian law he might attempt to drive the bees from the tree of the other landholder in the presence of the latter, and only those remaining were lost to him.[4] In later times, also, many legal sources, — for example the Schwabenspiegel, —[5] retained this right of the

[1] *Gierke*, "Privatrecht", II, 529. [2] *Gierke, op. cit.*, 530.
[3] "Sächs. Weichb.", 121. [4] "Lex Baiwariorum", 21, 8.
[5] Swsp. (G.), 305.

owner to pursue his bees; whereas others held, with the Roman law, that the ownership was lost as soon as the swarm had passed beyond the owner's sight. Definite periods were set for pursuit, at the longest two or three days. Moreover bees were often totally excepted from the right of occupancy, perhaps because of the increasing demarcation of lands. First of all a limitation was imposed to the effect that the finder must return a part of the swarm to the landowner or the land-lord. In more modern times the right of occupancy was reserved to the landowner exclusively; this was already true of the Saxon town law (*supra*, p. 427, n. 3), and likewise, at a still later day, of the Prussian and the Austrian law. The Civil Code has reëstablished entire freedom of occupancy, and has regulated the law of apiculture by detailed provisions (§§ 961–964) in complete agreement with Germanic law, starting with the principle that the swarm becomes ownerless upon leaving the hive unless the owner immediately pursues, or if he abandons pursuit. According to the Swiss Civil Code (§§ 700, 725, 2), on the other hand, a swarm that leaves the hive does not become ownerless; on the contrary, the owner can retake the bees at any time, ownership being lost only when the owner renounces his rights or when the swarm flies into a hive occupied by other bees, in which last case the owner of such hive acquires ownership in the bees.

(III) **Things Found (Ordinary Trove).** (1) *The Older Law.* — The problem of regulating the acquisition of title in trove was approached by the medieval law from a viewpoint opposite that of the Roman law; and this it has always consistently retained. For whereas under the Roman law chattels found were not regarded as ownerless, and were therefore incapable of occupancy, according to Germanic law from the earliest times the finder was allowed to acquire property in them. Indeed, in accord with the sensuous character of the old law there was required as essential to becoming a finder a formal act by which possession was taken, — for example, in the Lombard law the raising of the chattel higher than the knees. The acquisition of ownership, however, did not follow without further formalities; for since the finder might easily be exposed to a suspicion of theft, even the oldest law required some special act on the part of the finder calculated to repel any suspicion. He was bound, under penalties, publicly to expose the chattel he had found, or to deliver it to the public authorities that they might issue a citation to claimants. With this citation there early became associated the principle of negative prescription ("Verschweigung"): if the owner did not make himself known within a certain time (usually six weeks) he thereby lost his ownership. In such a case the title of the chattel originally passed to the public authorities, — the king, the lord of the land or of the court, the church, or the commune. So long as this principle was recognized it was permissible to speak of a regality in trove ("Fundregal"). As regards the most usual case of finding, namely that of estrays ("mulaveh", "Maulvieh", "Irrgang"), this rule was still widespread in the sources of the Middle Ages.[1] On the other hand, other legal systems provided for a division between the finder and the government;[2] and some gave the whole to the finder. The finder was bound to keep the chattel he found for some time, in order that the owner might make himself known. This might easily result in costs to the finder, particularly in the case of strayed cattle, and consequently he had a claim for "cost-money"; which either the owner or the government, according as the chattel was delivered to one or the other, was bound to make good to him. The idea of the finder's-reward ("Fundlohn") seems to have developed from this cost-money. Such rewards were first assured to the finder in the later Middle Ages, the Schwabenspiegel, for example, having still left his reward to the discretion of the public authorities.

(2) *In modern times* the traditional legal rules were generally maintained in the regional legal systems; notably the duty of the finder to give immediate notice of the finding, and to preserve the chattel. He could free himself from the latter obligation, however, by delivering the chattel to the police. There were also retained the citation issuable by the government or by the finder himself, and the reward that was given the finder in case the owner appeared and the chattel must be given or returned to him. The reward was adjusted to the value of the chattel found. The new Civil Code has adopted the old law as to these matters. If no owner appeared, then according to the earlier modern statutes the finder himself became entitled to the ownership, but no longer the government or other superior authorities save exceptionally, when a certain fraction of the chattel's value was confiscated for public purposes, — for example under the Prussian "Landrecht", if the value exceeded one hundred Taler, one-half of the excess for local charities. The present Civil Code has done away with such exceptions.

[1] Dortmund arbitral decision ("Schiedsspruch") of 1240, cited by *H. Meyer*, "Entwerung", 161.

[2] Ssp., II, 37, § 1.

Some legal systems — for example the Austrian Code and the Code Civil — gave the finder power to acquire title to the chattel, as a result of the owner's self-preclusion by silence, by using it as a bona fide possessor for the period of negative prescription; a proprietary action against the finder being barred after the expiration of the usual three years. Other legal systems, on the other hand, treated the ownership as passing to the finder immediately upon the expiration of the period within which the owner was permitted by statute to appear and claim it; for example, in the common Saxon law and (following that) the Saxon Code, after one year. These principles were analogous to those of the older German law. The Prussian "Landrecht" required a judicial adjudication ("Zuschlag") for the acquisition of title; but this has disappeared since the imperial Code of Civil Procedure came into effect, the title passing immediately, since its adoption, even under the Prussian law. The present Civil Code has likewise conformed to this rule, permitting the acquisition of title immediately upon the expiration of the statutory period of one year (§ 973). This period, however, no longer runs, as in the older German and in the Prussian law, from the moment a public citation is issued, but is begun in case of valuable trove by notice to the police, and in the case of trove of slight value (namely that of less value than three marks), by the finding itself. The Swiss Civil Code (§ 722) is to the same effect; but it extends the period to five years.

(IV) **Treasure Trove.**[1] — Just as there existed quite commonly in the Middle Ages in the form of a regality an exclusive right of appropriating ordinary chattels found (ordinary trove), so also this existed in the case of treasure trove ("Schatz"); that is, things that had once been objects of ownership but which had lost their owners owing to long concealment. According to an attractive presumption,[2] we must believe that German law indicated by the word "Schatz" treasures buried in graves, the valuable things that were laid therein in heathen times with dead persons; the "mound-silver" ("Hügel-silber") as the Danish legal sources call them. The existence of a regality of treasure

[1] *Zeumer*, "Der begrabene Schatz im Sachsenspiegel", I, 35, Inst. öst. G. F., XXII (1901), 420–442; *Eckstein*, "Das Schatz- und Fundregal und seine Entwicklung in den deutschen Rechten", in same, XXXI (1910), 193–244. See also the dissertation of *E. Schmidt* cited on p. 293, *supra*.

[2] *K. Lehmann*, "Sachsenspiegel, I, 35, und das altnordische Schatzregal", in Z. deut. Phil., XXXIX (1907), 273–281; "Grabhügel und Königshügel in nordischer Heldenzeit", in same, XLII (1910), 1–15, XLIV (1912), 78–79.

trove in Germany, — which is similarly attested in the Scandinavian as well as in the Anglo-Norman and French law of the Middle Ages, — is shown beyond all doubt by certain documents of Henry V and Konrad III, and especially by a much discussed passage of the Sachsenspiegel,[1] the bearing of which upon treasure trove it has been mistakenly attempted to deny. Moreover, the matter is attested also by proofs of a later time. The regality was maintained in full extent only exceptionally (until recent times in Schleswig and Schwarzburg-Rudolstadt, this condition being preserved by the Introductory Act to the present Civil Code). A few of the modern codes gave effect to the old view to the extent of assigning at least a definite part of the trove to the fisc; as did the Austrian Code and the Prussian Landrecht, for example, at least in cases where the trove had been dug up from the ground. Most legal systems, however, — including the Prussian "Landrecht", the Austrian and Saxon Codes, and the Code Civil, — adhered to the Roman principles, which were substantially adopted by the Schwabenspiegel [2] and which also acquired a common law authority. According to those rules, in case the finder had not made intentional search, or employed prohibited devices, or otherwise laid himself open to punishment, the trove belonged half and half to the finder and the landowner; in case the landowner himself discovered the treasure, the whole was assigned to him. At the same time, in the case of ordinary trove a citation procedure was frequently prescribed. The present Civil Code has followed the Roman law in all cases, and therefore always divides the treasure between the finder and the owner of the land or other thing in which it is found (§ 984), treating the ownership of the treasure as passing with the taking of possession upon the ground of the discovery, and without further requirements. The rule of the Swiss Civil Code is entirely different. According to it, the finding of the treasure confers title thereto upon the owner of the thing in which it is found, and this through the mere finding, so that the case becomes one of natural accession ("Anwachsung"); the finder has merely a contractual claim for proper compensation (§ 723). Moreover, the Swiss Code has formulated, for the first time, special provisions concerning the finding of ownerless natural bodies ("Naturkörper"), or antiquities of more than trivial scientific value; they become the property of the canton within whose boundaries they are found (§ 724).

[1] Ssp., I, 35, § 1.

[2] Swsp. (G), 285.

(V) **Acquisition of Ownership in Wreck** ("gestrandete Sachen").[1] — From the one-time "rightlessness" or outlawry of aliens the medieval law deduced the cruel rule that when a ship stranded on the sea coast or in a river (the Rhine was usually involved), that is touched the land, the dwellers on the shore had a so-called "strandage right" ("Strandrecht"), or in the case of rivers a "groundage" ("Grundruhrrecht") right, to the wreckage; that is, they had the right to appropriate the stranded chattels, and this originally involved even an enslavement of the shipwrecked persons (*supra*, p. 77). Rulers attempted at an early date to set limits to these rights of occupancy, which were a disgrace to civilization and which made impossible any close relations of commerce. Thus, for example, Emperor Frederick II in 1220 directed against it an imperial statute that was received into the Corpus Iuris as an authentic "Navigia"; and this example was followed by kings William of Holland, Ludwig of Bavaria, and Karl IV. However, the Territorial rulers themselves later asserted claims to all wreck washed upon the shore, inasmuch as they regarded the sea-shore as their property, so that there was developed, here also, a regality, which in turn was conveyed by the kings to the Territorial princes; and consequently such statutory prohibitions could have but little effect. The right of "groundage", it is true, disappeared at an early date, although not on the Rhine and the Main. There, and on the sea-coast, grants of the regality long remained a source of constant and violent disputes between their privileged holders and the coast or riparian dwellers. The commercial cities, particularly, had an urgent interest in preventing the exercise of the right of wreck by the Territorial rulers, — Rostock, for example, caused a Territorial bailiff to be hung as a robber so late as 1485 because he had seized the goods of a stranded vessel for his lord. Even the prohibition of the Carolina[2] had no deep-reaching effect: the duke of Mecklenburg, for example, declared that the emperor had no power to abolish the regalities of the princes. It was only in the 1700 s that the right of wreck disappeared as respected the sea-coast; the prayers of the church customary "for a blessed wreck" were done away with in Mecklenburg only in 1777. In place of wreck a right to salvage was recognized in favor of salvors, In this manner there was developed the modern "Strandrecht". which has been unified for Germany by the Salvage Ordinance

[1] *K. Lehmann*, art. "Bergung" in *Hoop's* "Reallexikon", I (1912), 259.
[2] Peinliche Gerichtsordnung of Charles V, Art. 218.

("Strandungsordnung") of May 17, 1874. A citation procedure is opened, and if the owner thereupon appears the property is delivered to him upon his satisfying the salvage claim. If no owner appears, then such wreck, — wreck in the technical sense of "Strandgut" or "Seeauswurf", *i.e.* things which are dug out of the strand or thrown upon it by the sea ("strandtriftiges Gut"), — falls to the public treasury after deduction of the salvage money payable to the salvors. Buried chattels that are dug out of the sea-bottom, and goods that are washed ashore, that is dug out by the sea itself, fall in their entirety to the salvor. Here again, therefore, exactly as in the case of trove, ownership results from occupancy.

(VI) **Booty of War.** — In the Middle Ages acquisition of ownership by private capture in feud or war played an important rôle, and it was variously and exhaustively regulated. In modern times this right of capture ("Beuterecht", "booty-right") has been very greatly restricted by international law; in particular, it has been entirely abolished as against enemies not belonging to a hostile army. The right of private capture at sea, also, was totally abolished by the declaration of Paris, of April 15, 1856. In the present Civil Code private rights of capture are not even mentioned.

§ 61. **Accession of Fixtures and Specification.** (I) **Accession of Fixtures** ("Verbindung"). — The Roman law, and likewise the modern law generally, including the present Civil Code (§ 946), start with the principle that a chattel affixed to land becomes an essential part thereof, and consequently passes without further act into the ownership of the landowner; in particular, this principle holds for buildings erected upon the land of another ("superficies solo cedit"). The medieval law took a different position (*supra*, pp. 173 *et seq.*). Though houses were originally movable in fact, they did not become part of the land. Consequently, whoever built upon another's land was bound to remove his house when he had built without right to do so, but he remained the owner if he had built it of his own materials. Only after the Reception was the concept of a special property in the building abandoned and the Roman principle recognized; to which result the increasing use of stone structures must certainly have contributed. Nevertheless the old Germanic conception was still so far recognized in the Prussian "Landrecht" and in the Code Civil that the former allowed a landowner to acquire title to a house erected on his land only after he should have decided to appropriate it, but not by its mere erection; and the Code Civil permitted rebuttal of the presumption that all buildings are erected by the landowner. The present Civil Code has also adopted the Roman principle of accession ("Akzession"), although recognizing (§ 95) as possible objects of special rights buildings erected upon the land of strangers, at least those erected for temporary purposes or upon the strength of a real right. The rule that he who builds upon another's land acquires ownership for himself in the land built upon (the exact opposite of the Roman principle) was unknown to the medieval law, but prevailed in the law of Württemberg, the Prussian "Landrecht", the Austrian Code, and several of the Swiss codes. It has been adopted in a somewhat altered form by the present Civil Code, and the Swiss Civil Code has also retained it (*supra*, p. 267).

(II) **Specification** ("Verarbeitung"). — When a person prepared a new object from material belonging to another, the older Germanic law seems to have ascribed title to the owner of the material. At least this is the rule laid down in the Schwabenspiegel,[1] which passed from that into the law of Kulm. At the same time the Schwabenspiegel (W, 390) gave the owner of the material a claim for damages against the improver ("Verarbeiter") in case he did not desire to take the object made, because useless to him. No other provisions are to be found in the older sources. As a result of the Reception the opposite view of the Roman law attained supremacy, and this has been adopted in the present Civil Code (§ 950) as well as in the Swiss Civil Code. The latter permits the judge to make an exception to the principle of increased value in case the party using the material of another acted in bad faith (§ 726).

§ 62. **Appropriation of Fruits** ("Fruchterwerb"). (I) **The Older Law.** — The medieval law started from the idea that, like houses, meadows, and woodlands, fruit-bearing things were not parts of the soil in which they grew but independent things, which could enjoy independent juristic existence. Nevertheless, as has been already mentioned (*supra*, p. 175), fruits of the field, the product of the seed as distinguished from the soil, were expressly conceived of and designated as movable property.[2] There was no necessity for the older Germanic law to subject such fruits to the right of the landowner under all circumstances. On the contrary it permitted them to become the property of the person who had cultivated them. He who had expended the

[1] Swsp. (L), 373. [2] Erfurt Statute of 1306.

labor necessary for their creation acquired property in them as "earned" ("verdientes") property; the rule was applied, "whoever sows, reaps." As to the moment that was decisive for the acquisition of title, namely that when the labor of cultivation was completed, it differed, of course, in the case of different products of the soil. In the case of grain it was considered necessary that this be harvested and the land again harrowed; whence the maxim, "if the land has been harrowed the grain is harvested." Garden fruits must have been sown and the garden raked; in the case of tree fruits and wine the care of the spring season must have been ended; in the case of ground-rents and tithes the Saint's Day was decisive upon which they were rendered.[1] But it was a precondition that the person whose rights were in question must have cultivated the land in good faith or in the exercise of a usufructuary right to which he was entitled.[2] These contradictions were especially apparent in the following cases: the allodial heir, who was bound to deliver the fief to the lord of the fief or his successor, took the fruits "earned" by his labor. So, also, a husband who lost the usufruct of his wife's lands upon her death, and his heirs if compelled to hand over his lands in dower ("Leibzucht") to his widow. In the same manner the creditor could collect the fruits of land pledged to him in case of redemption after tillage, and the same was true when an earlier possessor was obliged to surrender to the holder of a preëmption right.

In all these cases the underlying idea was that the tiller, by the tillage, acquired a special property before the separation of the soil and its products; it was only later that a real right of expectancy was assumed, from which ownership was developed by the act of taking possession.

(II) **The Modern Law.** — After the Reception the Roman rules concerning appropriation of fruits were recognized alike in the common law and in most of the regional systems. They were absolutely opposed to the rules of the native law. In place of the principle of "production" ("Produktionsprinzip") they substituted the principle of "substance" ("Substantialprinzip");[3] that is, whoever is the owner of the land at the moment its fruits are separated from it is also the owner of the fruits. Only a few exceptions were recognized. Under the common law the emphyteuta and a "bonæ fidei possessor" acquired the fruits instead of the landowner, and from the moment of their separation; and

[1] Ssp., II, 58, §§ 1, 2. [2] *Ibid.*, 46, § 2.
[3] *Gierke*, "Privatrecht", II, 588.

likewise a usufructuary and a usufructuary lessee ("Pächter"), but these only from the moment of collection ("Perzeption"). And in the regional systems, including the Austrian and the Saxon Codes and the Code Civil, title to the fruits was similarly given to these same parties either from the moment of separation or from that of collection. The Prussian "Landrecht" preserved intact the Germanic principle, ascribing to the person entitled to the collection of the fruits a separate property even in the growing products of the soil, in true Germanic fashion.[1]

The present Civil Code has adopted the Roman principle: the rule is the identity of ownership in the fruit and the thing it grows from. But, unlike the common law and with a practical approximation to the principle of the Germanic law, it permits, under some circumstances, the acquisition of ownership in the fruits by other persons from the moment of their separation; especially in favor of usufructuaries. Other persons entitled to the fruits become owners only upon taking possession of them (§§ 953–957). Under the Swiss Civil Code, also, natural fruits belong to the usufructuary if they ripen during the time that he enjoys such rights; and, moreover, he who cultivates the field has a claim for proper compensation against one who receives the fruits when ripe (§ 756).

§ 63. **Alienation of Chattels.** (I) **Alienation by Persons Entitled to Convey.** — (1) The conveyance of chattels was made in the *older Germanic law* differently than a conveyance of land. Publicity and a sensuous formalism were not necessary in the case of the former; for the chattel itself could be given from hand to hand, which was not possible in the case of land. This transfer of physical seisin, which was of course required to be associated with a will to convey the ownership, was necessary under all circumstances. The view that a contract to convey was sufficient,[2] is without support in the sources. Nor did Germanic law recognize a declaration by a proprietary possessor of a will to possess thenceforth for another, to whom the title should be thus conveyed; since here the requirement of a manifest "change of physical control" was unsatisfied. It was probably satisfied, however, when the acquirer, instead of taking the physical seisin of the thing, marked it with some visible and symbolical sign of his

[1] Allg. L. R., I, 9, § 221: "The fruits ('Früchte', — offspring, produce) of a thing are, from the moment of their origin, the property of him who has the right of usufruct in such thing."

[2] *Sohm*, "Das Recht der Eheschliessung" (1875), 80 *et seq.*

control, such *e.g.* as a "house-" mark. Moreover, there was already developed in the early Middle Ages, as a logical result of this idea in connection with the "traditio cartæ" of the Frankish period, the conveyance of certain goods by a delivery of commercial paper that embodied in writing a right to the delivery of the goods therein mentioned; a principle which was later to acquire particularly great importance in commercial law (bill of lading, way bill, warehouse receipt; *supra*, pp. 212 *et seq.*).

(2) *The Modern Law.* — The Roman law likewise required for the conveyance of movables a physical delivery united with an intention on the part of the alienating owner to transfer his title and an intention on the part of the transferee to acquire such; that is, a physical delivery united with a "valid title" ("gültiger Titel"). To this extent, therefore, the alien was in agreement with the native law. But the Roman law, and the common law which followed it, recognized certain exceptions (as already noted *supra*, p. 211) to the rule that possession of immovables could be transferred only by corporeal delivery. And these exceptions, — which were classified along with cases of incorporeal delivery derived from Germanic legal ideas under the name "traditio ficta", — were now generally applied to conveyances of chattels, with the result that corporeal delivery continually lost importance in the conveyance of ownership in movables. To be sure, only the French law abandoned entirely the requirement of physical transfer, attributing to the contract of conveyance, solely and exclusively, the efficacy of the conveyance. The Prussian "Landrecht", and the old Commercial Code which followed it, gave effect to the same principle in the conveyance of ships and interests therein ("Schiffsparten"), but with this exception the requisite of physical delivery was maintained. And so in the present Civil Code, which requires a real agreement to convey ("Willenseinigung", "Übereignungsvertrag") and a visible transfer ("Übergabe") in accord with the pre-existing law, but also recognizes as sufficient for such transfer certain substitutes (*supra*, p. 212) which in part do not require any change whatever of possession. Of course, the real ("dingliche") effects of the bearer paper of commercial law were also preserved unchanged.

(II) **Acquisition of Title from Persons only apparently Entitled to Convey it.** — The rule, already discussed, "hand must warrant hand", which dominated the medieval law of chattels, deprived the owner of the possibility of demanding the return of his chattel in case it had passed in any manner from the bailee's hand to the hand of a third person. In many cases, a stranger acquiring the chattel was thus completely protected against any claim for its redelivery; as, for example, when the bailee had meanwhile died. For practical purposes this was the same to him as if he had acquired the ownership of the chattel. Nevertheless, a transfer of title did not take place. If, for example, a third person had bought the chattel from the bailee and had thereafter returned it to the latter as a loan ("leihweise"), then the instant it returned to the seisin of the bailee the owner was again in a position to demand it from him, and the third person, notwithstanding the sale to him, had no right which he could oppose to such demand. In the same way the third person must yield to the right of the owner if the thing was returned by accident into the seisin of the owner. After the Reception it must have been natural to regard the limitation imposed upon chattel actions by the rule "hand must warrant hand" as one upon proof of absolute title ("Vindikation"), although the two actions were, as we have shown, of totally different character. But men did not rest content at this point; only the French law retained this view. Other modern legal systems regarded this effect of seisin not only negatively, as a limitation upon the ownership of him who transferred the chattel, but also positively, as a basis for the acquisition of the title by a third person. This was true of the Prussian "Landrecht", the Austrian Code, the German Bills of Exchange Act, and (for the first time with any formulation of theory) of the general German Commercial Code (§ 306).[1] The new Civil Code has also adopted the same rule (§ 935), for according to it (*supra*, pp. 423 *et seq.*) a person who acquires in good faith chattels that have not been stolen from their owner, or lost by him, or otherwise removed from his possession, — in other words chattels he has bailed, — acquires the ownership, notwithstanding that the apparent owner ("Eigenbesitzer", possessor with color of title) was in fact not the true owner. The Swiss Civil Code, as already mentioned, has also taken the same position, save that it limits the possibility of acquiring title to a five-year period. With these changes "the relative effect of the rule 'hand warrant hand' has been strengthened into one of absolute character."[2] The title of the person originally owner has disappeared, and ownership has been transferred by the juristic act of one who was merely an apparent

[1] See the citations on pp. 420 *et seq.*, *supra*.
[2] *Gierke*, "Privatrecht", II, 566.

owner. This, too, is a further development of principles of the law of seisin, which have abrogated the Roman rule "nemo plus iuris transferre potest quam ipse habet."

§ 64. **Positive Prescription.** (I) **The Older Law.** — Under the older Germanic law it was impossible to acquire ownership in chattels by mere lapse of time, for the institute of citation seisin was here unavailable, since a release, such as created judicial seisin in lands, did not exist in the transfer of chattels (*supra*, p. 405). A consequence of this was that, as the Sachsenspiegel says, the vendor of chattels was bound to warrant so long as he lived the title of the acquirer.[1] Mere lapse of time has since been recognized, exceptionally, as a basis for the acquisition of ownership. Thus, for example, under the law of Hamburg and Lübeck a person entitled to a chattel action for the recovery of property introduced from abroad was precluded by silence after a year and a day (*supra*, p. 418). At the same time, the rule of the impossibility of judicial seisin applied only to cases of derivative acquisition of title, since it was only in such cases that the absence of a release and of the citation therewith associated need be considered. In the case, however, of original acquisition, as for example in the case of trove, ownership might originate, as already mentioned (*supra*, pp. 428 *et seq.*), in acquiescent preclusion by silence following a citation of claimants.

(II) **The Modern Law.** — But here also the Roman law prevailed; its principle of acquisitive prescription of chattels became the common law of Germany, and the principle was also adopted in the regional legal sysems. Only, in these the prescriptive periods were not always identical with the Roman (three years in the case of ordinary, thirty or forty in the case of extraordinary prescription), but frequently varied from these as a result of the influence of the Germanic law. For example, in the common Saxon law the periods of a year and a day and (for extraordinary prescription) thirty-one years and one day were customary. Again, the Roman law excepted from the rule of ordinary prescription chattels stolen or robbed, and in the common law the question remained a controverted one; but in the regional systems there was applied to such chattels, sometimes the ordinary acquisitive prescription (although often, for example in the Prussian "Landrecht", only when they were in the hand of a third acquirer) and sometimes the extraordinary. Only the French law clung to the Germanic view, refusing to recognize at all a positive prescription. The

[1] Ssp., III, 83, §§ 2, 3.

rule adopted by the present Civil Code is novel. Its acquisitive prescription of movables, including chattels stolen and robbed, is perfected in ten years, but it also requires apparent possession in good faith on the part of the acquirer; a requisite nowhere else recognized, save in the common law in cases of extraordinary positive prescription. In addition to this it recognizes a preclusive prescription of proprietary actions that is perfected in thirty years. The Swiss Civil Code requires apparent proprietary possession, unchallenged and uninterrupted, for five years only.

Topic 4. The Law of Chattel Pledges

§ 65. **The Older Law of Pledge.**[1]— Owing to the earlier development of ownership of chattels, pledge rights in movables are also of greater age than those in land. It is probable, indeed, that the conception of a right of pledge as an independent real right originated in the law of chattels and was only later transferred to the law of land. The two institutes continued to be dominated by the same fundamental ideas (*supra*, p. 377), and consequently the same technical expressions are used in reference to both. It is true, however, that the development in details, and the point to which development was carried, differed in the law of chattel and of real pledges.

(I) **The Possessory or Ordinary Pledge** ("Faustpfand").—The chattel pledge was originally, and for a long time remained, exclusively a possessory pledge: "ohne Faust kein Pfand", "no pledge without detention" ("fist"). The pledge itself, the object of the pledge right, whether a lifeless thing ("chest-" or "cabinet-" pledge) or an animal ("eating-" pledge), was necessarily subject to the physical seisin of the pledgee, since every real right in chattels was associated with actual physical custody of the same (*supra*, p. 404).

(1) *Creation.* — Such a possessory pledge could be created in various ways.

(A) Already in the folk-laws mention is made of a PLEDGE BY WAY OF CONTRACT ("vertragsmässige Pfandbestellung", "Satzung"), by which the debtor transferred some movable to his creditor for security. For this purpose the "letting out of the debtor's seisin" ("lassen ut von sinen geweren",—Ssp. II, 60, § 1) was required, but not the form required in the gage of lands. The technical name of a "given" or contractual pledge ("gesetztes

[1] See the literature cited under § 53 *supra*.

Pfand", "Satzung", "Pfandsatzung") was "Wette", wed (*supra*, p. 375). The contractual pledge was the chief type of chattel pledges.

(B) PRIVATE DISTRESS, in which a right of pledge was created by the independent power of the creditor, was an application of the right of self-help, which owing to the inadequate supply of money long continued to be practiced (although only within definite limits set by the law) even after the state assumed the administration of justice. The name "pledge" ("Pfand": basic meaning = "includere", at first applied to impounded cattle) was commonly used in the Middle Ages solely for this "taken" ("genommenes") pledge. Private distraint occurred in two forms:

As distraint *for the satisfaction of contractual debts*. Although according to the most ancient sources, those of the Lombards, this was still generally permitted when a debtor did not perform an obligation assumed in a duly legal manner, in the other folk-laws it was already permitted only upon the basis of a judicial authorization. In accord with this principle it was repeatedly laid down in later Territorial Peaces that nobody might enforce his rights himself, "sine auctoritate iudicis", by taking a pledge.[1] At the same time, however, it continued to be recognized that the debtor might by means of a clause of distraint subject himself contractually to an extra-judicial distress, — a distress "with or without right" ("mit und ohne Recht"), — in addition to the judicial; and such clauses, which were explicitly safeguarded in the Territorial Peaces,[2] remained in exceedingly common use throughout the Middle Ages. Similarly, it was still common in the Middle Ages to regard a so-called "kundliche" (notorious) or "redliche" (honest) debt, — that is, one which was admitted before the judge, — as enforceable, and to permit private distress in such cases;[3] and this was especially common in agreements between different cities and localities as a mutual concession in favor of their respective residents, adopted in order to lessen the lack of an effective administration of justice. Particularly widespread were the rights of distraint for arrears of ground and capital rents which existed in favor of the owners of such rents as against peasant rentalers and debtors. In many

[1] For example, the "Constitutio Pacis Friderici II", of 1235, c. 14 (M. G., Constitutiones, II, 244).

[2] For example, the "Constitutio pacis generalis Alberti I ad Rhenum superiorem", of 1301, c. 9 (M. G., Constitutiones, III, 102).

[3] For example, King Wenzel's Land-Peace of 1398, § 5.

regional systems this grew into a landlord's right of distress in things which were in the custody of his debtor (the hirer), without being his property, provided the hirer ("Mieter") possessed a claim to them as against the owner. For example, a lessor ("Vermieter"), if a tailor owed him rent, might distrain a suit for which payment was still owing to the tailor. Again, a guest who did not pay his tavern bill must submit to a distraint by the innkeeper; and in this we must doubtless recognize the last remnant of a right of private distraint that once existed against all strangers, since this distraint occurred only in taverns on the highways, and not in the drinking-room of gildsmen.[1]

As distraint *for security against damages other than from breach of contract,* and directed against either human beings or animals. This served originally not only to insure a landholder compensation for damage done by men or by animals, but also to preserve the evidence of damage. The distress of cattle ("Schüttung"), especially, was one of the most widely spread legal institutes in the rural economic life of the Middle Ages; the dooms are full of provisions respecting it, and it is exhaustively treated also in the Law Books.

(C) Finally, a right of pledge might also arise in favor of a creditor through JUDICIAL DISTRESS. True, the folk-laws did not originally recognize any process of judicial execution. However, in a royal Merovingian statute so old as to be included in the "Lex Salica" ("L. Sal.", Tit. 50, 3) there was allowed the creditor, in lieu of private distraint against his debtor, a distraint against him (known in the "Lex Ribuaria" as "strudes legitima"—"Strud" = "Raub", rape, carrying off) exercisable through the royal counts, provided the precondition essential to a private distress was present, namely a promise to pay made in proper legal form. To be sure, this Frankish "Strud", which was developed as a special outlawry limited to the debtor's property,[2] immediately gave the creditor full ownership of the chattels seized. A judicial distress that created a mere pledge right was first recognized in the Lombard and Visigothic law, in imitation of the creditor's extra-judicial distress. In the Middle Ages execution by judicial process against the debtor's movables became the ordinary end of an action for debt. The judicial deprivation of a debtor of custody over chattels in his possession, effected by the bailiffs of the court ("Fronboten"), for the purpose of satisfying his creditor, created

[1] *Huber*, "Schw. Privatrecht", IV, 827.
[2] *Brunner*, "Geschichte", II, 452 *et seq.*

a pledge right in the creditor which enabled him to satisfy himself if the pledge was declared forfeited to him by the court.

(2) *Content of the Pledge Right.* — In conformity with the principles of the Germanic law of liability ("Haftungsrecht", — *supra*, p. 375 and *infra*, § 68) there was created by the pledge of a chattel a strictly real liability of the thing that was taken or given in pledge. The obligee received in the pledge an object of value upon which he could rely, and must exclusively rely, in case the obligation was not satisfied. He possessed in it a real right clothed in the form of a pledge-seisin ("ut de vadio"), which, as in the law of landed gages, was limited by the agreement ("Gedinge") made with the debtor, or in the case of the "taken" pledge by the tacit condition that the thing should be treated as the equivalent of the debt in case of default in paying the latter. Whether the debtor who created the pledge or from whom it was taken was or was not its owner was immaterial, for the effect of the principle "hand must warrant hand" was that the pledgee, even when he acquired his pledge-seisin from another who was not an owner, was protected against a demand for redelivery made by a third party.[1] The debtor retained a right to redeem, notwithstanding that no duty of redemption was imposed upon him. If, however, he offered to redeem the pledge, or if the debt was canceled in some other manner, then the creditor was bound to redeliver the pledge in the same condition in which he had received seisin thereof. There was therefore united with his right of custody a duty to keep and preserve the pledge, which involved in the case of "eating"-pledges their feeding and care, although he was entitled to his outlay therefor. He was therefore bound to give damages to the debtor in case he lessened the value of the pledge by use, except in those cases in which a right of user and of usufruct was expressly granted him. He was likewise liable to pay damages if he alienated the pledge or repledged it; for in consequence of the rule "hand warrant hand", the debtor could not go against a third person but was limited to his claim against the other party to the contract, that is the pledgee. Even when the pledge was destroyed or was lost or lessened in value while in the seisin of the pledgee, without his fault, he was bound to make good the damages thereby caused to a debtor who offered to redeem. For the creditor's duty to redeliver was the counterpart of the debtor's right to redeem. But if the thing was accidentally destroyed or if it deteriorated

[1] Ssp., II, 60, § 1. See p. 409 *supra*.

in quality while in the possession of the pledgee, the latter could not in turn demand compensation from the debtor for such loss of value; for by accepting the pledge he had declared that it should answer for his claim, and that liability should be limited to its value.

Thus, as a necessary consequence of the principles of the older law, the pledgee, as the holder of the seisin, bore the entire risk of deterioration in or destruction of the pledge, even though by accident. The Sachsenspiegel lays this down as still the general theory.[1] This strict view was first departed from in the case of "eating-" pledges, the pledgee being released from his obligation to pay damages in case of their destruction without his fault. The Sachsenspiegel already states this exception to the rule.[2] Later legal systems (first in South Germany, but later *e.g.* that of Lübeck also) released the pledgee in all cases from liability for accident, making him responsible solely for damages due to his own fault. This became the general rule also for the "taken" pledge; the pledgee had to bear the risk so long as he was bound to keep the thing, that is so long as the debtor was not in default in redemption.[3] With this new rule, there was therefore secured a division of the risk between creditor and debtor: "in the case of accidental destruction the creditor lost his money, but the owner lost the value of the thing."[4]

A further weakening of the old principles is seen in the fact that it became customary from the 1200 s onward to unite a so-called "Geloben zum Pfande" ("promise in pledge", covenant accessory to a pledge) with the contract pledge ("Satzung") of specific chattels, as is shown by a later supplement to the Sachsenspiegel.[5] By this the debtor assumed an additional liability in that he subjected his other property to attack by the creditor. In time such general real liability commonly became a statutory part of the law of chattel pledges. Where the law was thus extended there no longer existed any danger for the pledgee, since he could reimburse himself from the debtor's other property for any loss suffered by the destruction or deterioration of the pledge. That is, he could distrain, by authority of the covenant ("Gelübde") or by authority of a

[1] Ssp., III, 5, § 4. [2] *Ibid.*, § 5.

[3] *Heusler*, "Institutionen", II, 209.

[4] *Gierke*, "Privatrecht", II, 959. *Cf.* the "Magdeburger Fragen", I, 6 d, 6.

[5] It adds to III, 5, § 5, at the end, the words: "ire gelovede ne stünde den anderes."

statutory liability of other property, upon other pieces of the debtor's property to the extent of the excess of his claim above the value of the original pledge; by which means he secured a pledge right in them also. Conversely, however, he was bound to return to the debtor, when the latter redeemed, any amount by which the value of the pledge should have exceeded the amount of his claim. At this stage of its development the right of pledge had completely lost its original character of a strictly real liability, and had become "a purely secondary security instead of being an optional means of satisfaction in place of payment." [1]

(3) *Satisfaction.* — It followed from the original character of the pledge as a provisional "spot" payment ("Barzahlung") that the chattel pledge was by nature a forfeiture-pledge. If it was not redeemed in due time, it was definitively forfeited to the creditor in place of the payment of the debt, without regard to the relative value of the pledge and the claim. The rule was that the title of the chattel of which the creditor held a pledge seisin was conveyed to him by decree ("Erklärung") of court, after demand thrice repeated upon the debtor; however, an immediate forfeiture could be agreed upon by contract between the parties. As the result, however, of the appearance of the covenant accessory to a pledge ("Sichgelobens zum Pfande"), the forfeiture-pledge was necessarily transformed into a sale-pledge. For since the creditor, in case the pledge was of insufficient value, could thenceforth bring further claims against the debtor, while the debtor in case of the excess value of the pledge could in turn demand the delivery of such surplus, it became necessary to determine the value before the creditor was satisfied. This necessitated a sale of the pledge. If a private right of sale was not expressly reserved to the creditor, the sale was made judicially, and ordinarily only after a thrice repeated citation of the debtor. Moreover, the creditor was bound to seek satisfaction, in the first place, by a repledge. If neither this nor a sale proved successful, the pledge was conveyed to the creditor at an appraised value.

(II) **The Modern Contract Pledge** ("Satzung") **of Chattels.**[2] — In the last centuries of the Middle Ages there became usual in Germany, — if not everywhere, at least within the territory of some of its legal systems, — a pledge of movables effected

[1] *Heusler*, "Institutionen", II, 205.
[2] *Herbert Meyer*, "Neuere Satzung von Fahrnis und Schiffen" (1903).

without livery of seisin; in other words, a form of pledge that corresponded to the execution-gage in the law of land pledges. This Germanic hypothec of chattels, the earliest bases of which are to be found in Scandinavian law (Iceland), was utilized especially in Lübeck and the region in which its law prevailed, and as respects chattels of the most varied kind. Of course, it recommended itself especially in the case of things which because of their nature could not easily be removed from the place of their origin or usual location in order to put them in the custody of the creditor; for example, wine in vats, heaps of grain, stocks of goods, agricultural products, agricultural implements, chests of unknown content, etc. But this was a necessary precondition only in Hamburg and in Wisby. In Lübeck the transfer of seisin was also waived in the case of other objects. For example, it happened there in the 1400 s that a painter pledged an altar painting upon which he was working to two burghers of the town because they had been sureties for his repayment, by completion of the picture, of an advance made to him by those who ordered the painting. The picture was not delivered to the pledgees, although it might easily have been transported; the painter could not remove it from his workshop if he were to complete it, and the two burghers trusted him not to deceive them by a secret alienation of the painting to other persons. Above all, ships of every kind were pledged, without transfer of possession, in the sea towns of the Lübeck law (namely, in addition to Lübeck itself, in Wismar, Rostock, Stralsund, Greifswald, Danzig, Riga, Reval), and likewise in Hamburg and in Kiel. But for such contractual pledges a public and formal act was always necessary in place of a livery of seisin. According to the oldest law, as it has been preserved in the town law of Wisby, in Gotland, the giving ("Setzen") of the pledge was a solemn act that took place before witnesses expressly called for the purpose; only later (from the 1300 s onward) was an entry also made in the town register, and this entry had at first merely the significance of a memorandum to identify the witnesses. Finally, in accord with the general development of the law of land registry (*supra*, pp. 218 *et seq.*), the entry became, in this case as in others, the formal act that consummated the creation of the pledge.

The chattel hypothec made the pledge liable to the creditor in the same way as in the case of a possessory pledge. It is true that the pledge right lost its real ("dingliche") effect in favor of the creditor if the chattel was removed from the debtor's possession; but this restriction upon pursuit of the chattel against third parties was here again the simple and necessary consequence of the principle "hand must warrant hand."

Outside the region of the Lübeck law the chattel hypothec was adopted in a few other Territories and cities. Its most important forms were the mortgages ("Verschreibungen", "Insätze") of movables in Frankfort o. M. But above all it prevailed in the South throughout an area that equaled in importance that in which it prevailed among the North Germans: it conquered for itself the whole of Switzerland, — to be sure somewhat later than the cities of the sea-coast, — and has maintained its authority there from the 1400 s down to the present day.

§ 66. **The Modern Development of the Law of Chattel Pledges.** — (I) **In general.** — In the law of chattel as in that of land pledges the rules of the native law were at first displaced in large measure by those of the Roman law. Some of them, however, maintained themselves in the regional systems, and in time a return was made to the old law, so that here too there resulted "a more or less clumsy union of Roman and Germanic rules."[1] Modern legislation, first in the great codifications and then in numerous special statutes of the 1800 s, explicitly recognized the concepts of the Germanic law. In the end these were once more raised, in their most important points, to the rank of a common German law by the present Civil Code, which was preceded, in this respect, by the General Commercial Code as well as by the imperial judicature acts.

(1) *Creation.* (A) CONTRACT or "given" PLEDGE. — As a result of the Reception the Roman chattel hypothec acquired the prevalence of common law. At least in Germany the modern form of contract pledges of chattels that grew up on a basis of Germanic law sooner or later gave way before it, with the exception of the law of ship mortgages (*infra,* under (II)). In Lübeck it was done away with already in the 1500 s; most of the derivative systems of Lübeck law soon followed this example. In Hamburg it was maintained until the 1800 s, and the "Insätze" of Frankfort likewise fell into desuetude only in the 1800 s. It has already been mentioned that it remained actual law in Switzerland down to very recent times.

To be sure, the chattel hypothec suffered modifications under the influence of the Germanic law. It gave the creditor a real right which was effective only to a limited extent, and which could

[1] *Cosack* in *Gerber's* "System" (17th ed.), 300.

not be enforced against a bona fide third possessor: an after effect of the rule "hand must warrant hand." It was postponed to a later right of possessory pledge. Though a general hypothec in chattels was, as such, recognized, this did not restrict the debtor in his power of disposing of individual chattels. Above all, certain formal requirements for the creation of a pledge were maintained; in particular, a document was required to be executed containing an acknowledgment of the debt and an assumption of the obligation to pay it.

From the 1700 s onward the chattel hypothec was again repudiated. It was already rejected in the Prussian hypothec and bankruptcy ordinance of 1722. In the 1800 s it once more became a general principle that a contractual pledge right in a chattel could be created only by means of a possessory pledge; that is, by an outwardly manifest act of delivery, or in such manner as otherwise to secure to the creditor actual control of the thing. For this reason its creation by "constitutum possessorium" was excluded. On the other hand, in the commercial law pledges were allowed to be created by delivery of "real" documents of title ("dingliche Traditionspapiere"), — bills of lading, way-bills, and warehouse receipts.

Although a few regional legal systems, for example the Code Civil, required the execution of a document in addition to delivery of the chattel, the General Commercial Code abrogated such formalities in the case of merchants (§ 309), and in harmony with this tendency of development the present Civil Code requires for the creation of a chattel pledge by juristic act both a real contract and either delivery of the chattel or a proper substitute for such delivery. An agreement to hold possession for the pledgee ("Konstitut") is therefore no longer sufficient (§ 1205). The Swiss Civil Code is to the same effect. But, in addition to the possessory pledge, the Swiss Code recognizes in pledges of cattle, and in the interest of banks loaning on the security of cattle ("Viehleihanstalten"), a mortgage whose publicital effect is derived, not from possession, but, as in the case of a mortgage of land, from an entry in a public register (§ 885).

Moreover, in those legal systems that retained the Germanic principle "hand must warrant hand" either in its pure or in a modified form, it was not necessary in all cases that the debtor should himself be the owner of the pledge. For under the same preconditions that sufficed for creation of title by a person not an owner, a pledge right could be created by a pledge made by one who was not an owner. The General Commercial Code established for all Germany the rule that when a merchant pledges to another articles included in his stock that have neither been stolen nor lost, a bona fide pledgee acquires a right against which an earlier title, or pledge right or other real right, cannot be enforced to his prejudice (§ 306). In the same way, under the present Civil Code a pledge by any person not an owner creates a right of pledge to the same extent that a putative transfer of ownership by one not an owner creates ownership (§§ 1207–08). The same is true of the Swiss Civil Code.

(B) STATUTORY PLEDGE RIGHTS. — Whereas the medieval law did not recognize statutory rights of pledge, but conceded to certain persons only (for example to a landlord; *supra*, p. 441) an extraordinary right of distress, there existed in the Roman law a considerable number of special statutory pledge rights, notably that of a landlord ("Vermieter") in the farm stock of the hirer, and that of a usufructuary lessor ("Verpächter") in the produce of the land leased. The native right of distress had prepared the way for the reception of Roman statutory rights, and these everywhere secured recognition in Germany. In details they were regulated very differently in regional legislation. They also found important practical supplement in the right of retention of the mercantile law (*infra*, under (V)). But, in contrast to the Roman law, their admissibility was limited to cases in which the creditor held the pledge; or at least exercised over it a control similar to possession, as in the cases, for example, of an ordinary or a usufructuary lessor ("Vermieter", "Verpächter"), who had no possession under the common law. The diversity of norms recognized in the regional systems was first lessened by the General Commercial Code, which regulated uniformly for all Germany the statutory right of pledge of commission merchants, forwarders, carriers, and shippers in goods sold on commissions, forwarded, carried, or freighted. Moreover, in its sections upon maritime law it created a uniform law for a whole series of statutory pledge rights, including those of a freighter and a salvor and particularly the peculiar pledge right of creditors of ships, which last is independent of any requirement of possession. A further simplification of the private law was accomplished by the Bankruptcy Code, which (§ 41) assimilated the creditors of a bankrupt to possessory pledgees, conceding them the most important right of the latter, namely the right to require separate satisfaction of their claims from the property. The differences that still remained unaffected by this provision were in turn completely done away with by the present Civil Code, which, in addition to the right of detention recognized in the commercial and the admiralty law, and also as to merchants in the private law, gave similar rights to ordinary (§ 559) and to usufructuary lessors (§ 581), and also to persons with whom money or commercial paper is deposited (§ 233).

(C) The "taken" Pledge. — As a security against tort damages the right of private distraint was preserved throughout Germany, even after the Reception, in the institute of cattle-distraint ("Viehpfändung"). This has been regulated in detail by many modern statutes, — *e.g.* in the Prussian statute concerning agricultural and forest police of April 1, 1880. Distraint of cattle was permitted, generally speaking, only as to lands used for agriculture or for forestry; but in many cases no actual damage was required, a mere trespass after prohibition being regarded as a sufficient ground.

Whereas there ordinarily resulted from the taking of possession, in favor of persons entitled to distrain, merely a lien, a right of detention, with some effects analogous to those of pledge rights (and comparable to the detention rights of the commercial law), there was created by the distress under some legal systems (for example the Prussian) an actual pledge right for the claim to damages. The right of distraint against the body ("Personalpfändung") was more rarely preserved; for example, in Saxony. The Civil Code has reserved to the law of the States the entire institute of private distress (EG, § 89). In the case of distraint against the body ("Personalpfändung") the general principles relative to self-help (§§ 229–230) of course apply.

Distraint by judicial process has been uniformly regulated by the provisions of the Code of Civil Procedure concerning execution. The creditor acquires, as a result of distraint in this form, a pledge right in the thing. The distraint by the bailiff of the court need not be an actual taking of possession, but may be made visible by attachment of seals or otherwise.

(2) *Content.* The idea of an exclusive real liability, which was already clouded in the Middle Ages by the covenant accessory to a pledge ("Geloben zum Pfande"), disappeared finally and completely after the Reception. According to the modern law not only the pledge was liable, but also, secondarily, the remaining property of the debtor. Thus, precisely as in Roman law, a strictly secondary character, a dependence upon the personal claim, became an

essential quality of the chattel pledge. The Civil Code has preserved this principle; and the same is true of the Swiss Code. But although on this point the alien law triumphed, most legal systems ultimately abolished the Roman rights of "general"-pledge which they had originally received, thereby reëstablishing in the law of chattels, as in that of land, the Germanic principle of "speciality." General-pledges are unknown alike to the German and the Swiss Codes. But this does not exclude rights of pledge in an aggregate ("Inbegriff") of things. The principles of the native law retain authority, in essentials, as respects the rights and duties of the pledgee. Although the burden of risk was everywhere removed from the creditor, this was in conformity with the view adopted as early as the late Middle Ages. A usufructuary right was given to the pledgee in the modern legal systems only when such was expressly conceded to him by contract. The present Civil Code has also adopted this view, although, to be sure, assuming (§§ 1213–1214) that when the pledgee receives exclusive possession of a thing that is by nature productive, he is entitled to the profits ("Fruchtbezug") in the absence of specific agreement to the contrary. Such a presumption is not recognized in the Swiss Code (§ 892, 2).

(3) *Termination.* — Most legal systems (including the Prussian "Landrecht", the Code Civil, and the Saxon Code) treated rights of chattel pledge as destroyed by voluntary redelivery of the pledge to the debtor. This rule was consistent with the possessory nature of the pledge, and is that declared by the present Civil Code (§ 1253). On the other hand a delivery of the pledge to a third person did not originally result in the destruction of the pledge right; but this was the result, — in those legal systems which recognized the principle "hand must warrant hand", — once a stranger had acquired the thing bona fide from such third person, either in ownership or as a pledge. For the pledge right of the original pledgee was thereby necessarily either destroyed or at least subordinated in its effect to the newly acquired pledge right of such third person, which was united with possession. This rule was made general in commercial law by the General Commercial Code (§ 306). Under modern statutes it also prevailed in some States in the civil law. It has now been given general authority in the private law by the Civil Code (§ 1208). On the other hand, involuntary loss of possession always remained without effect upon the pledgee's right unless the pledge was money or bearer paper. The statutory pledge rights of the com-

mercial law are subject for the most part to the continuance of possession; the contrary is true only of carriers and shippers of freight. The statutory pledge rights of an ordinary or usufructuary lessor, or of an innkeeper, are extinguished when the chattel is removed from the land and a month is allowed by the creditor to pass (whether the chattels were removed without his knowledge or despite his prohibition) without the bringing of a legal action to enforce his claim for their return.

(4) *Satisfaction.* — A sale came to be the only permissible manner of satisfying a claim out of the pledge. The complete displacement of the forfeiture-pledge, which by the end of the Middle Ages was steadily becoming less prominent, was furthered by the adoption of the Roman prohibition of the "Lex commissoria", inasmuch as that statute made impossible a forfeiture provision in the contract. But whereas the Roman law always gave the creditor the right to sell the pledge privately, most of the regional systems, in harmony with the views of the native law, required, in theory, a judicial execution (as in the Prussian "Landrecht") or at least a judicially declared right of sale (as in the Code Civil and the Bavarian "Landrecht"). At the same time, the regional systems commonly left open to the parties the possibility of agreeing to a private sale in their contract. This was true, for example, of the Prussian "Landrecht"; and the rule was made general as to the pledge rights of merchants by the General Commercial Code. In very recent years, however, the legislation of some of the States (Saxony, Hannover, Oldenburg, and Brunswick) has again departed from these principles in according the creditor a right of private sale like that of the Roman law, although indeed subjecting this to definite requisites as to form; in particular, a sale at public auction is ordinarily required. The Civil Code has followed this Romanistic tendency, thereby creating new law for the greatest part of Germany. It gives a pledgee the right of private sale; but the exercise of this must conform to definite statutory forms (§§ 1228–1248) in the interest of the debtor.

(II) **Contractual Pledges of Maritime Law.** — (1) The fact has already been mentioned that in the cities of the Lübeck law the Germanic law had already developed independently a *pledge of ships* without transfer of possession. This was preserved even after the Reception, and many of the regional systems constructed from ideas of Germanic law a law of bottomry in which no transfer of corporeal possessions was required, documentary authentication ("Beurkundung") being employed as the act by which the pledge was created. The transfer of certain documents referring to the ship was at first chiefly used for this purpose, — so, for example, in the Prussian Landrecht. In the 1800 s, however, following the example of England, an entry in a register was introduced as the most common form of admiralty pledge (" Schiffsverpfändung ") ; and this completely displaced the ship-hypothec of the common law. To be sure, the General Commercial Code did not succeed in establishing a uniform system, for all Germany, of registry pledges ; and therefore the maritime States of Germany proceeded for a time by way of independent legislation. After the Inland Navigation Act of June 15, 1895, had provided a provisional regulation for ships engaged in inland commerce, the Civil Code finally created a uniform law for ocean and inland vessels (§§ 1259–1272). Only the law of registry pledges of vessels under construction was left to State legislation (EG, § 20). Registry pledge rights under the imperial law, — which are available only in the case of vessels entered in the maritime register, but constitute for these the sole permissible form of contractual pledge, — are subject, in many respects, to the principles of the law of land pledges. In particular, their creation is accomplished by a real agreement (" Einigung ") and entry in the registry. And this shows that such pledge rights are, historically considered, essentially a variant and subordinate form of the modern contractual pledge (" neuere Satzung ") of Germanic law.

(2) A special form of pledge in the maritime law, in which Germanic ideas have probably been of decisive influence, was developed in rights of *bottomry* (" Bodmerei ", " Boden ", bottom).[1] Evidences of this exist from the 1100 s onward in Southern France and Italy. It was characterized from the beginning by the principle of pure real liability, which was strictly enforced in it, unlike the " foenus nauticum " of the law of antiquity. In return for loans taken in cases of maritime necessity, the ship, freight, and cargo, or one of these, was pledged ; that is, it was made exclusively liable for the satisfaction of the creditor's claim. This was later adopted in Scandinavian and in German commerce, whither it seems to have been brought from Mediterranean lands. It was exhaustively regulated by the General Commercial Code, and belong seven to-day to the existing maritime law (HGB,

[1] *Matthias*, "Das foenus nauticum und die geschichtliche Entwicklung der Bodmerei" (1881); *Pappenheim*, "Zur Entstehungsgeschichte der Bodmerei", in Z. Hand. R., XL (new ser. XXV, 1892), 379–393; also in his "Handbuch des Seerechts", II (1906), 136, 225 *et seq.*; *K. Lehmann*, "Lehrbuch des Handelsrechts" (2d ed., 1912), 560 *et seq.*

§§ 679–699), but is actually regarded as "a moribund institute",[1] inasmuch as it has become superfluous under modern conditions of commerce. Bottomry pledges are cases of a pure real liability for a real debt. There results from the giving of the pledge ("Verbodmung") a debt, but not a personal claim against the bottomry pledgor which would entitle the creditor to bring an action against the debtor for payment. "The bottomry debt must, indeed, be paid when it is due, but in case it be not paid the creditor can seek satisfaction solely from the vessel pledged (HGB, § 696). The action in which he demands this satisfaction is brought merely to secure permission so to satisfy himself, and not for the payment of the debt; but it may be avoided by such payment."[2]

(III) **Rights of Pledge in Rights.** — Under the medieval law a pledge right could already be created in rights, these being conceived of as incorporeal things and treated in analogy to corporeal things (*supra*, p. 161). If a document was executed embodying such a legal relation, then such right could be pledged by manual delivery of the document (*e.g.* a "Rentenbrief"). The conception of a contractual claim as the object of a right was foreign to the Roman law, and therefore also equally the pledge of rights, but such pledges nevertheless persisted as a recognized legal institute under modern statutes, by which they were variously regulated. The General Commercial Code created a uniform law to the extent that it (§ 309) did away with the formalities of the private law as respected the pledge of order and bearer paper when the pledge was given between merchants for a claim resulting from mutual trade transactions. It recognized as sufficient the delivery of possession in the case of bearer paper, or the delivery of the indorsed paper in the case of order paper. The institute has again received detailed regulation in the Civil Code (§§ 1273–1296). This subjects pledge rights in rights, generally speaking, to the rules of chattel pledges; it is only in the case of rights in alieno solo ("liegenschaftliche Gerechtigkeiten"), which are treated as land, that it has given effect to the rules of land-pledges. The earlier special provisions of the General Commercial Code for the pledging of order and bearer paper among merchants have been replaced by general provisions regulating the pledge of commercial paper generally (§§ 1292–1296). The creation of a pledge right is effected in different ways

[1] *Lehmann, op. cit.*, 562.
[2] *Pappenheim* in Z. Hand. R., XLVII (new ser. XXXII, 1898), 145.

according to the nature of the right pledged: in the case of rights in lands, by entry in the land-book; in the case of rights embodied in commercial paper, by a change of possession of the document; in the case of mere contract claims, by notice to the original debtor. The Swiss Civil Code has regulated rights of pledge in rights similarly in essentials, but with deviations as to details (§§ 899–906).

(IV) **Pawnbroking.** — Special rules, differing from the general rules of the law, have been developed for the regulation of pawnbroking. Already in the Middle Ages, earliest in Italy, public pawn shops ("montes pietatis") were established which, as "pia corpora", enjoyed many privileges, notably exemption from the Canonic prohibition of interest (*infra,* § 86). Even at the present day there exist loan-offices which are public foundations ("Anstalten") of the State and of the communes; their legal status is regulated by State legislation. In the 1800 s there was developed beside them the private business of pawnbroking. Under the older State legislation private pawnbrokers needed licenses from the government. The Industrial Code established the theoretical freedom of the business, but in consequence of the evil experiences resulting therefrom the industry was again subjected to the license system in 1879 by an amendment to the Code; and this was extended in 1900 to agents ("Pfandvermittler"). Among the many important special provisions of State legislation those are most important, in the law of things, which prescribe the registration of all pledges in a register kept according to prescribed forms, and which require the delivery of a pawn ticket for every pawn. Under many statutes (*e.g.* the Prussian Act of March 17, 1881) an entry in the pledge register, in addition to a real agreement and manual delivery, is essential to the creation of the pledge right. Special rules also exist concerning the sale of pawns, and the broker's obligation to preserve them. Further, some statutes have adopted the principle of pure real liability; and many even impose upon the pledgee the entire risk of destruction. A right to have the pledge redeemed may be given to the public loan-offices by State legislation. The Swiss Civil Code has provided a number of general rules (§§ 907–911) applicable even to the "security-pawn" ("Versatzpfand"),—that is, to this form of chattel pledge which is given to public or private loan-offices to secure the payment of money loans; but it has left to the cantons (§ 915) the regulation of pawnbroking as an industry under the public law.

(V) **Merchants' Rights of Detention.** — Statutory rights of pledge were, as has been remarked, unknown to the medieval law. On the other hand, in certain cases, and subject to the precondition of what was called "Konnexität" ("lien nexus") it gave in place of these a right of detention. So, for example, to the artisan who had a claim for labor, a right to detain the chattels delivered to him for alteration; to the shepherd, a right to detain for his wages the animals intrusted to his care; to the householder, a right to retain possession for the improvements which he had made on the premises; and so on. At the same time it was a rule that a pledgee entitled to a counter claim might not only refuse to deliver the chattel pending his satisfaction, but might also, under some circumstances, himself repledge the chattel for the amount of his claim, in order to cover himself from damages due to the conduct of his debtor. With this step the right of detention came to approach an actual pledge right. Nevertheless, the native law was abandoned after the Reception in favor of the corresponding Roman institute, which was relatively far less developed and which never entitled one to more than a right of detention. On the other hand, there persisted among merchants, as to transactions between themselves, customs which had wider effects. These customs led to the development of a special mercantile right of detention, evidences of which exist from the 1500 s onward. This conquered an independent field in Germany beside the detention rights of ordinary citizens, and was regulated (variantly, to be sure) in State statutes. Sometimes it was regulated as an express statutory right of pledge; sometimes it was given effects analogous to those of pledge rights, at least in case of the bankruptcy of the debtor. The requirement of "Konnexität" was everywhere abandoned. These legal differences were done away with by the General Commercial Code; though it is true that this, while attributing to such mercantile rights of detention effects analogous to those of pledge rights, did not declare them outright to be pledge rights (as was originally the intention of the legislators), — thereby putting in doubt the actual legal nature of the institute. The new Commercial Code has taken the same position (§§ 369–372).[1] The detention right of the Civil Code (§ 273) has no kinship with a pledge right; it is neither a personal nor a real right, but a mere defense ("Einrede", plea) against a personal or real claim.[2] On the

[1] *Lehmann, op. cit.*, 576.
[2] *Crome*, "System", I, 546.

other hand, the detention right of the Swiss Civil Code (§§ 895–898) corresponds to that of the German Commercial Code: the creditor, in case the debtor does not fulfill his obligation, may sell the chattel detained as though it were a possessory pawn.

BOOK III. THE LAW OF OBLIGATIONS

Chapter IX

GENERAL PRINCIPLES

§ 67. **Introductory Sketch of the General Development of the Law of Obligations.** (I) **The Older Law.** — It may be safely assumed that the primitive Germans ("Germanen"), like other peoples in a primitive stage of civilization, lived under conditions in which non-credit transactions alone were known. The scanty trade of the time was accomplished, for the most part, under the forms of barter. Even sale was a simultaneous exchange of performance and counter performance. Contract and non-credit or "spot" transactions were not as yet notionally distinguished. A postponement of performance to a future time was unknown; indeed, it was inherently impossible in the absence of a public power that protected property interests. Nevertheless, from the earliest times obligational effects might be associated with such spot transactions; particularly if it eventually appeared that the thing sold was claimed by a third person as belonging to him. But "in such case the person damaged (the purchaser) regarded the damage done to his property in the same way as he regarded any damage, as for example, that of theft or robbery."[1] He therefore resorted, here also, to the sole means that was always open to him in such cases, — namely, self-help. By means of feud and blood-revenge he secured for himself satisfaction and damages.

The oldest obligations were therefore the outcome of misdeeds. Whoever violated the law was forced by the instrumentality of the criminal law to do penance for his misdeed; an action was brought against him, judgment was passed upon him, and if he disregarded the complaint or the judgment he was, as a last resort, declared to be outside the peace. Thus, as a matter of fact, "the whole law of obligations entered legal life from the side of delicts."[2]

Beside this oldest obligation ("Schuld-") law, however, which was a penal ("Straf-") law, there gradually appeared a private law of obligations, in which tortious acts were, as such, no longer the exclusive origin of legal obligations, a free will entering also into their basis. Partly as a further development of spot transactions, and partly from a form of agreement ("Willenserklärung") that was perhaps first employed in judicial procedure and later extra-judicially, there was developed a peculiar system of debt ("Schuld-") contracts which was adapted to the needs of trade (*infra*, § 71).

The law of contract remained scanty, to be sure, for centuries as compared with the law of things. In the sources of the Frankish period only very few contracts are mentioned, and these few are in large part either institutes of the law of things (as, for example, leases of land) or else manifestly of Roman origin (like the "cautiones", "mandata", "cessiones" of the formularies). This meagerness of forms did not indicate a general weakness of the private law in the early Middle Ages; it necessarily resulted from the paucity of problems that fell to the law of contract during the dominance of the economic and social system of that time. It was "the necessary consequence and counterpart of a legal order in which an unusually rich and subtly developed private law confronts us in other legal fields."[3]

Two points demand attention here. The first is the fact that there existed even at that time the same problems that had to be

[1] *Heusler*, "Institutionen", II, 230. [2] *Ibid.*, 231.
[3] *Huber*, "Schw. Privatrecht", IV, 901.

solved in the classic Roman and in the modern law of obligations, namely the regulation of the purely economic relations of individuals, as subjects of rights, with one another, and the distribution of values in the form of credits and debts among all persons participating in legal life.[1] These problems were not solved in the early Middle Ages by a system of contracts, — by regulating purely individual legal relations between mutual and equal parties to agreements; but, primarily, through a multitude of complicated real and personal rights of land-lordship that had grown out of and were accordant with an agricultural economy. Many legal relations which in periods of a predominant money economy and generally "mobilized" property values appear solely in the form of debts and credits, assumed at that time the form of real rights in the soil, or of personal privileges against dependent fellow-members of society. The procurement of nourishment and clothing, for example, which in times of greater economic development is the source of countless obligations of daily life, was mainly realized, among the rural classes of the population, — in so far as it was not effected by independent production, — by means of tributes ("Leistungen") rendered by the occupants of dependent lands (slaves, serfs, and villein rentalers) to landowners entitled to feudal tributes and services. And these tributes satisfied, almost perfectly, the ends which are realized in a money economy through free contracts for labor and service. The fact that even in the prosperous economic system of the towns the demands of capital for credit were long satisfied in the form of real rights, — capital rents ("Renten"), — is particularly significant in this connection. How this tendency of the medieval law toward the "materialization" ("Verdinglichung") of rights led men to treat as incorporeal things rights that secured a permanent usufruct in things, and how rights in rights and the so-called "ius ad rem" were developed into peculiar institutes lying between real and contract rights, has already been discussed (*supra*, pp. 168, 162 *et seq.*).

To this was added the fact that a free exercise of individual will, without which no considerable development of the law of contract is conceivable, was in those times possible only within narrow limits. Business transactions ("Geschäfte") were not only rare, but conformed strictly in both form and content to traditional lines. There was rarely any opportunity to adopt special rules for a particular case, or for new circumstances of fact; the old

[1] *Huber*, "Schw. Privatrecht", IV, 901.

forms handed down by the customary law amply sufficed for needs that did not vary. Moreover, the transactions involved were in great part not concluded by individuals, but transactions to which groups, — such as the members of a family, the associates of a mark, the brothers of a craft, etc., — were necessary parties; and this coöperation of many persons was another strong surety for the preservation of the traditional law.

(II). **The Town Law.** — Owing to the increasing prosperity of city life, however, a fundamental change had already set in at the meridian of the Middle Ages, and long before the reception of the Roman law. It was, primarily, the commerce among merchants ("Handel") that was becoming established in the cities which everywhere produced an active general traffic ("Verkehr"), and with this necessarily a trade law ("Verkehrsrecht") that gave heed to the new economic conditions. Town law and merchants' ("Kaufmanns-") law became, in large part, identical conceptions, and thenceforth, in Germany as elsewhere, the mercantile ("Handels-") law played within the fields of contract and partnership law the rôle of a forerunner of the general private law, although this followed only slowly and with hesitancy; until finally, in our day, the principles of the commercial law have become authoritative in the general private law. In the eastern parts of Germany, especially in the districts on the East Sea whose culture was determined by their relations with the Hanseatic cities, legal development was based upon old native ideas and was in many respects independent. But the West and the South of Germany soon fell under the dominant control of a general European commercial ("Verkehrs-") law which was first developed in Italy, the country of the richest trade by land and sea and the leader in the development of legal practice and theory. It originated in a union of Germanic ideas acclimated among the Lombards with elements of Roman law, and was carried thence into international commerce ("Handelsverkehr") through the international fairs of Champagne, the Netherlands, and France, creating thus an international uniformity of commercial law which has not again been realized down to the present day. The largest and most important part of this law lived on both in Germany and elsewhere; not, however, without modification and further development, which was effected in modern times under the emancipating influence of Holland, France, and England. In this way the whole of the modern maritime and commercial law, the law of commercial paper, the law of copyright, and above all the law of bills of exchange, insurance, and commercial partnerships, which is still fundamentally Germanic in basis and Roman to but a very slight extent has kept a strikingly modern character.

(III) **The Roman Law.** — Even greater, however, was the victory gained by the Roman law, through the Reception, where the problem was not the detailed regulation of modern conditions unknown to the ancient world, but general and fundamental rules of the law of obligation, and, in particular, the theoretical development of the typical forms of contract. The Reception was therefore more complete, and more pregnant with consequences, in these fields than in any other part of the private law; it accomplished here its "most striking and most universal"[1] feat, — one which was not limited to that time or place. True, the reception of the Roman law, here again, merely completed and carried to ultimate victory changes that at many points had already begun within the native law. And although the contract law of modern times and of the present day is Roman in its essential outline, and will remain so, nevertheless many Germanic ideas have maintained themselves therein, not alone within the special fields of commercial law above mentioned, and in some others of the civil law, but also even in fundamental legal theory.

TOPIC 1. FUNDAMENTAL CONCEPTIONS OF THE LAW OF OBLIGATIONS[2]

§ 68. **Legal Duty and Liability Generally.** (I) **Perception of the Distinction between Legal Duty and Liability.** — In the theory of the Romanistic common law that prevailed until recent times

[1] *Gierke* in *Holtzendorff-Kohler*, 152.

[2] *Val de Lièvre*, "Launegild und Wadia, eine Studie aus dem Langobardischen Rechte" (1877); *Franken*, "Geschichte des französischen Pfandrechts, I: Das französische Pfandrecht im Mittelalter" (1879, only vol. published); *v. Amira*, "Nordgermanisches Obligationenrecht", Vol. 1: "Altschwedisches Obligationenrecht" (1882), Vol. 2: "Westnordisches Obligationenrecht" (1895); *Puntschart*, "Schuldvertrag und Treugelöbnis des sächsichen Rechts im Mittelalter, ein Beitrag zur Grundauffassung der altdeutschen Obligation" (1896); *v. Schwind*, "Wesen und Inhalt des Pfandrechts" (1899); *Egger*, "Vermögenshaftung und Hypothek nach fränkischem Recht", no. 69 (1903) of *Gierke's* "Untersuchungen"; *Frhr. v. Schwerin*, "Die Treuklausel im Treugelöbnis", in Z². R. G., XXV (1904), 323–344; *Puntschart*, "Treuklausel und Handtreue im deutschen Gelöbnisrecht", in same, XXVI (1905), 165–194; *Rintelen*, "Schuldhaft und Einlager im Vollstreckungsverfahren des altniederländischen und sächsischen Rechts" (1908), with which compare *Frhr. v. Schwerin* in Z². R. G., XXIX (1908), 464–468, and *Korsch* in Krit. Vj. G. R. W. (L, 3d ser. XIV, 1912), 128–142; *Puntschart*, "'Pfandrechte an eigener Sache' nach deutschem Reichsrecht", in "Festschrift für *K. v. Amira* zu seinem 60. Geburtstage" (1908), 103–

obligations were explained as "legal relations which consist in the duty of an obligor ('Schuldner', debtor) to perform (pay) something of value to an obligee (creditor)."[1] That theory imagined this to be a definition of the concept which was accurate under all circumstances, independently of time and locality. It has since become clear, however, that the theory was here in error; it was too much influenced by the form of the classic Roman and the common law. Even some Romanists raised doubts. Brinz, especially, attacked the prevailing view; he found the essence of an obligation to be the subjection of the obligor to judicial execution; in other words, the liability of the person and the property of the debtor in case of non-payment of the debt. A decisive advance was first made, however, when Karl von Amira adduced indisputable proof from the old Swedish and old Norwegian sources that in them the law of obligations was based upon the distinction between the two conceptions of legal duty ("Schuld") and liability ("Haftung"). An understanding of the Germanic law of obligations was first made possible by this discovery. For the same principles which Amira discovered in the old Scandinavian law were later established, by him and by other scholars (Puntschart, von Schwind, Egger, Gierke, and others), in the case of South Germanic legal systems, and notably in large groups of medieval Germanic legal systems. Nor was the significance of the new theory limited to this. It was able to show that the difference

175; *v. Amira*, "Der Stab in der germanischen Rechtssymbolik" (*supra*, p. 11), 151–157; *Gierke*, "Schuld und Haftung im älteren deutschen Recht, insbesondere die Form der Schuld- und Haftungsgeschäfte", no. 100 (1910) of *Gierke's* "Untersuchungen"; with which compare *v. Amira* in Z². R. G., XXXI (1910), 485–500; *Strohal*, "Schuldübernahme" (1910), also in *Ihering's* J. B., LVII (2d ser. XXI, 1910), 231–494; *Lenz*, "Zur Geschichte der germanischen Schuldknechtschaft", in Inst. öst. G. F., XXXI (1910), 521–537; *v. Amira*, "Wadiation", in K. Bayer. Akad. Wiss., Sitz. Ber., 1911, 2d Abhandlung; *Herbert Meyer*, "Zum Ursprung der Vermögenshaftung", in "Festschrift für O. Gierke" (1911), 973–1005; *Frhr. v. Schwerin*, "Schuld und Haftung im geltenden Recht" (1911), with which compare *Puntschart* in Z. ges. H. R., LXXI (3d ser. XII, 1912), 297–326; *v. Gierke*, "Schuldnachfolge und Haftung insbesondere kraft Vermögensübernahme", in the "Festschrift der Berliner juristischen Fakultät für F. v. Martitz" (1911), 33–80; *Peterka*, "Das offene zum Scheine Handeln" (*cf.* p. 244 *supra*), 13–17; *Planitz*, "Die Vermögensvollstreckung im deutschen mittelalterlichen Recht, 1er Band: Die Pfändung" (1912); *Puntschart*, art. "Bürgschaft" in *Hoop's* "Reallexikon", I (1912), 356–357; *Buch*, "Die Übertragbarkeit von Forderungen im deutschen mittelalterlichen Recht", no. 113 (1912) of *Gierke's* "Untersuchungen", 60 *et seq.*; *Partsch*, "Griechisches Bürgschaftsrecht, 1er Band: Das Recht des altgriechischen Gemeindestaates" (1909); *Koschaker*, "Babylonisch-assyrisches Bürgschaftsrecht, ein Beitrag zur Lehre von Schuld und Haftung", (Festschrift) (1911).

[1] This is *Dernburg's* definition, "Pandekten", II (1886), 1.

between duty and liability was not something specifically national or "historical", but that there was here involved "a logical distinction" that was "indispensable to every law of obligations", although it might be more consistently developed in the law of one country than in another.[1] This view found surprising confirmation when exhaustive investigations, based upon the foundation laid by the Germanist school, made clear the existence of this distinction between legal duty and liability in the old Greek and Babylonian law. That it is not absent in the law of the present day has recently received significant recognition, and from the side of the Romanistic school. Of course, many objections have been raised against all this. And even as regards the older Germanic law, and among the supporters of the new theory, there are very important differences of opinion. These appeared with extreme clearness when Otto von Gierke undertook to give the first detailed and comprehensive statement of the Germanic system of "Schuld" and "Haftung", — not without expressly explaining that there cannot yet be talk of a complete solution of the problem. What is said in the following pages is only intended to give a summary, as judicious as possible, of the present results of investigation, seeking to choose what appears best established. It is to be hoped that the continuation of Gierke's "Germanic Private Law", as well as the work contemplated by von Puntschart on the law of "Schuld" and "Haftung" in the oldest South Germanic legal records, — and other investigations which certainly will not be lacking, — may clear up the many obscurities still remaining. It is also to be hoped that we shall soon receive from Amira's hand the conclusion of his work on the North Germanic law of obligations.

(II) **Legal Duty.** — "Schuld", in the broadest sense of the word, signifies "a legal duty" ("rechtliches Sollen"). And therefore Germanic tongues used the word "Schuld" (from the verb "skulan"), in this quite general sense, to indicate the existence of any legal duty. A legal "duty" ("Sollen") however, means — as the German legal terminology of the Middle Ages shows — a duty legally defined or certain ("rechtliches Bestimmtsein"). "In the very word 'Schuld', in the sense of 'sollen', there is etymologically implied the idea of something legally determined; the relationship appears as one strictly of legal definition ('Bestimmungsverhältnis')."

[1] *v. Amira*, in Z². R. G., XXXI (1910), 486.
[2] *Puntschart* in Z. Hand. R., LXXI (3d ser. XII, 1912), 303.

(1) *The legal duty of the obligor* (" Schuldnerschuld "). Such a definite legal duty (" rechtliches Sollen " = " rechtliches Bestimmtsein " = " Schuld ") exists, above all, on the part of that person whom we designate in our present legal terminology the obligor (" Schuldner "), and with whom we contrast the obligee (" Gläubiger "). Indeed, when we speak of a legal obligation we think almost exclusively, in the first place, of the obligor. The obligation on the part of the obligor consists in a legal duty to perform (" Leistensollen "). This duty to perform is the legal order (" Bestimmung ") to undertake a certain performance (" Leistung "), as a result of which undertaking there is created a relation imposed by, consistent with, and protected by the law. If an obligation is involved that was created by contract (a " Schuldvertrag "), then the end of such contract is found in the duty to perform; for that reason the contract is concluded. Performance is the positive content of the debtor's contract. In case of such contract there exists, further, as a negative command, an obligation of " abstention " (" Haltensollen "); that is, an obligation to do nothing that could in any way make impossible performance of the contract. In particular, the obligor may not in any way either evade the contract or undo the condition created by its performance. These two obligations of abstention and of performance frequently coincide, but not necessarily. This appears in the case of an obligation subject to a condition precedent. Here there exists a duty of abstention from the moment a contract is concluded; on the other hand the duty to perform arises only upon the taking effect of the condition precedent, and therefore under some circumstances (namely, when such condition is not satisfied) never.

(2) *The legal duty of the obligee* (" Gläubigerschuld "). Just as the word " Schuld " raises in our minds, in the first place, the conception of the obligor's legal duty, so in the original meaning of the word, as a matter of usage, a " Schuld " was first conceived of as a duty to perform.[1] But modern Germanistic legal theory has established the important and pregnant fact that in both the law and the speech of the primitive Germans, and even of the later Germans, the obligee (" Gläubiger ") was also thought of as a " Schuldner ", and was so designated. This was possible because the conception of " Schuld " was based upon the wholly general idea of a duty legally prescribed. Even in our sense of the word there is a duty, legally determined, on the part of the creditor:

[1] *Puntschart* in Z. Hand. R., LXXI (3d ser. XII, 1912), 304.

equally as respects him there results from the obligational relation a legal command, namely to accept the performance to which the other party is obligated. He too "shall" do something; it is his duty to receive what is owing to him. To the obligation of the obligor, namely a legal duty to perform (and to "abstain"), there corresponds an obligation of the obligee, namely a legal duty to accept performance. And therefore in the sources we find the obligee and obligor designated by exactly the same terms; a fact which cannot be disregarded, else many a statement of the medieval legal sources will remain unintelligible. In the Latin records of the folk-laws, — for example in the "Lex Burgundionum" (19, § 10), — in the extravagants of the "Lex Salica", and in documents down into the 1300 s, the word "debitor" is used in the sense of "creditor"; the duty of the obligee to receive is called his "debitum." Down into the 1500 s the German sources occasionally designate the "Gläubiger" (obligee) as "Schuldner", "Schuldiger."

(3) *The relation of the obligor's and the obligee's duties.* — In an ordinary obligation the legal duties of the obligor and of the obligee are united: an obligor is bound to perform to his obligee, an obligee is bound to receive from his obligor. It has recently, however, been asserted that the legal duty of the obligee is conceivable without a corresponding legal duty of an obligor, — in other words, a mere duty to accept something without a corresponding duty of the obligor to render it; that the duty to receive is, but the duty to perform or pay is not, essential to the concept of an obligation; that the obligation is primarily a duty of the obligee; the obligor may be lacking (so von Amira, Strohal, von Schwerin, Puntschart). It has been supposed that this obligation without an obligor could be applied to explain institutions such as the real-charge ("Reallast") and the land-debt ("Grundschuld"), whose derivation from the conception of a "real obligation" (*supra*, pp. 362, 391) must (it is said) be rejected; that there are involved here simply unilateral obligations of an obligee. But this theory of an obligee's legal duty without an obligor's legal duty, of an obligation without an obligor, is in my opinion unsound. Not, to be sure, because it might "unduly shock the nerves of a pedantic theorist",[1] but because it breaks a logically necessary relation. As Gierke rightly says,[2] inasmuch as all legal relations are in last analysis relations of power between persons considered as subjects of will, no duty to accept performance

[1] *Puntschart's* words, Z. Hand. R., LXXXI (3d ser. XII, 1912), 305.
[2] In the "Festschrift für Martitz", cited *supra*, 41.

can be conceived of without a corresponding duty to perform. The origin of this theory of an 'obligor-less' obligation may perhaps have been an exaggerated equalization of the respective legal duties of obligor and obligee, which itself may have been derived from the use of the word "Schuld", in the older sources, for both sides of the obligation. In my opinion, however, it must not be overlooked that the legal duty of the obligee, — despite such identity of expression, and despite also the fact that it does signify a legal duty, something legally determined, — is of quite different content from the legal duty of the obligor, and without this would be a concept without basis. True, the obligee "shall" do something, but this duty is passive; not, like the duty of the obligor, active. The purely passive duty of the obligee, the duty to receive, cannot be conceived of apart from the active duty of the obligor; for the sentence "the obligee shall receive" is logically no less imperfect than the other, "the obligor shall perform." In the first we must add, from whom; in the latter, to whom. To be sure, this does not mean it is impossible that it should be temporarily, or for a certain time, undetermined who shall make performance to the obligee; nor is it inconsistent with the fact that even most legal systems treat as immaterial the question from whom the obligee receives the performance that is due to him. But there must always be some person who performs; for only a person, not a thing, can perform, and acceptance of performance without performance is impossible. This same uncertainty that prevails in many cases with respect to the identity of the obligor may also exist as respects the obligee. To whom performance shall be made may for the time be uncertain; for example, who will be the last holder of commercial paper, to whom payment is made. But it could not be concluded, because of the existence of such possibilities, that there is here only an obligation of a debtor and no obligation of a creditor; and, conversely, there can just as little be assumed a creditor's obligation existing independently, without the obligation of a debtor. Performance by the obligor and acceptance by the obligee depend mutually upon each other.

(III) **Liability** ("Haftung"). — In the concept of "Schuld" there is always involved a legal duty only; never a legal "must." If the legal duty is performed, a certain legal condition results in accordance with the law; but nothing is involved in the concept of "Schuld" which of itself could bring about such condition. The concept of legal duty is free from any element of compulsion. The recognition of this fact that the content of the "Schuld" is solely a "shall" and not a "must", was derived directly from the study of primitive legal systems. The necessity of a concept complementary to that of legal duty appears more plainly in them than in a mature legal system. This is true of the Germanic and the old German law. Whoever failed to fulfill his legal obligation was guilty of a breach of law. But whether or not he would fulfill it was a question for himself; no compulsion to perform resulted from the obligation, in itself. An obligor who acted contrary to the law might well be expelled from the legal community, but he could not be forced to perform his obligation.

Hence the concept of liability ("Haftung") was added to that of legal duty. It first afforded the legal compulsion that was indispensable to a secure and developed legal intercourse. Through it there was first realized a legal guaranty for the performance of the legal duty.

The nature of "Haftung" is clearly reflected in the expressions used for it in Germanic legal terminology. Their near kinship with the corresponding Roman terms justifies the conclusion that there are here involved very ancient ideas of the Indo-Germanic races; but they were current also in the ancient Orient. Just as the Romans employed the technical expressions "obligare", "obligatio", so in medieval Germany words such as "Gebundenheit", "Bindung", "Verbindlichkeit", "Verstrickung", and "Haftung" were similarly used, as technical terms perfectly understood; and other languages, as for example the Scandinavian, employed a terminology that exactly corresponded to these. As appears from the language, the problem involved was the creation of a legal bond. An object is "bound" ("gebunden"), "entangled" ("verstrickt"), "liable" ("verhaftet"); and this for the purpose of constituting a guaranty for the performance of an obligation: it is to warrant ("Gewähr", "ware", "werescap") such performance. For this reason a control over the thing so liable is given to the obligee. If the legal duty is not performed then the obligee can rely upon the object so made liable, and from it procure satisfaction of his claim and compensation for the non-performance of the duty owing him. He receives a power to go against the object liable to him. The thing thus liable to his attack is therefore, by such subjection, constituted a security ("Unterpfand", hypothec, — Germanic "vadi", "wadium", "Wette", *supra*, p. 375; corresponding to the Roman "vas", "vadimonium"); it becomes bound by a legal duty ("verpflichtet" "plegium") to answer for the obligation; the pledge "stands for" ("vorstân";

cf. Lat. "prae-stare") the duty. And so, in an important passage of the Sachsenspiegel (III. 5, § 5), we read: "Stirft aver en perd oder ve binnen sattunge ane jenes scult, de it under ime hevet, bewiset he dat unde darn he (getraut er sich) dar sin recht to dun, he ne gilt is nicht; he hevet aver verloren sin gelt, dar it ime vore stunt." ("But if a horse or ox dies while in pledge without the fault of him who has it in possession, if he proves this and if he offers legally to support his statement, then he is not liable for it. However, he has lost his money because that stood in its place"). Whatever must answer for the performance of an obligation warrants ("bürgt") it; the conception of warranty ("Bürgschaft") in the broader sense "(Old High G. 'borgēn', 'purigo'; A. Saxon 'borg', Old Norse 'borghan', 'borgha', 'abyrgjask', 'abyrgd') originally coincided, notionally, with liability ('Haftung')."[1] The property which is "entangled" or made liable (the "pledge" in the broad sense) is therefore an object that serves to satisfy and compensate the obligee in case the legal duty is not performed, or not properly performed "Haftung" is a "standing in place of" something else; to "be liable" is to be substituted for the legal duty; and, as already remarked (*supra*, p. 375), this "subjection" ("Bindung") continues so long as the legal duty exists. Only through the performance of the legal duty is the object bound by the "Haftung", as by a fetter, freed ("lösen", *cf.* Lat. "solvere").

Only a human being can owe a legal duty. "For the duty to perform (and to abstain) presupposes the operation of an ethical factor, which always presupposes a person."[2] In the case also of a "real obligation" (*supra*, p. 391) the subject of the legal duty (obligor's duty) is always a human being, namely the owner of the land charged. It is equally true that a legal duty in the sense of an obligation to receive can be postulated only of a subject of rights. Therefore things cannot be under obligations ("Schulden"). But men and things can both be liable ("haften"); for both can be subjected to the power of the obligee, that is can be exposed to his attack. If a human being is made liable, then according to the terminology of the Germanic sources of the Middle Ages, unlike that of to-day, the obligee held a "Forderung." For in the sense of Germanic law a "Forderung" (to-day = contractual claim) was "the exercise of power against the person who was liable", and a "Forderungsrecht" was "a right to exert

[1] *Puntschart* in *Hoop's* "Reallexikon", I, 356.
[2] *Puntschart*, "Schuldvertrag", 107.

one's own power, under certain preconditions, against the person liable."[1]

The choice of the object liable, whether a thing or a person, depended upon the circumstances of the particular case. In and of itself the liability of a thing, like that of a person, offered quite sufficient guaranty that the obligor would perform. It was in nowise necessary that the obligor should also be personally liable, notwithstanding that such a conjunction of the liability of a thing or of a third person with the liability of the debtor's own person was quite possible. Whoever made a thing or another person liable for his obligation (" verpfänden ", to pledge; " vergeiseln ", to give hostages; " verbürgen ", to give a person as a pledge) was, indeed, an obligor, but he was not himself liable. On the contrary, the pledge, whether a thing or a person, was exclusively liable. And just as a thing pledged was liable but not obligated, so the person who was made a pledge for another's debt was not himself obligated. The legal duty remained exclusively that of the obligor who was bound to perform that which was the object of the duty.

" Schuld " and " Haftung " therefore became distinct in all those cases where the obligor was not himself made personally liable. According to the view of the Germanic law there was " always merely a personal union when a person liable was also obligated, or an obligor was at the same time liable (a pledge)."[2] But whereas a legal duty could exist — and especially in early times, as we have seen, actually did frequently exist — without liability, every liability notionally presupposed a "legal duty" in all cases. "There [was and] is no liability without a 'where-for', which is directly or indirectly the obligation; it always exists with reference to an obligation."[3]

The early Germanic and old German law show with exceeding clearness the difference between legal duty and liability. They open a view into conditions when obligation was clearly distinguished from liability.

It is true that in the oldest recognizable stage in the development of the Germanic law there existed a usual, even though only an outward, union of duty and liability. This resulted from the fact that every legal duty was originally the consequence of a misdeed that was subject to a penalty (*supra*, p. 460). If the wrongdoer

[1] *Puntschart, op. cit.*, 231.
[2] *v. Amira*, "Obligationenrecht", II, 77–78.
[3] *Puntschart* in Krit. Vj. G. R. W., XLVII (3d ser. XI, 1907), 63 *et seq.*

did not pay the penalty which he owed, — *e.g.* the bót imposed upon him by a judgment, — there was no possibility under the oldest criminal and procedural law of directly compelling him to perform his obligation. If he failed to do this, of course he violated the law; but neither the creditor nor the court had the power to compel him to do his legal duty, and nothing else was possible than to expel from the legal community the member who thus disregarded the law; in other words, to declare him outside the peace. Outlawry was the sole weapon wherewith the oldest law could both enforce atonement for misdeeds and punish the wrongdoer. For outlawry affected not only the person but also the property of the outlaw. This could be confiscated and given as damages to the injured person to the amount of the bót to which he was entitled. The body, too, of the outlaw might be delivered to him, that he might satisfy his claim from it. To this extent, therefore, one who was guilty of a misdeed was "liable" to the injured person as well with his person as with his property; but the material satisfaction of the injured party was in such cases only an indirect result of the judicial outlawry ("Acht") imposed upon the debtor, and the confiscation of his property; and it resulted only when the debtor allowed matters to go to that extreme. This liability of the oldest law "within the bounds of outlawry"[1] was strictly limited to the criminal law; it was the consequence of a misdeed that was subject to a money penalty or bót ("bussfällig"), which misdeed the debtor failed to expiate by payment of the penalty imposed. It might exist wherever the law imposed bóts; and, consequently, even where the non-performance of a legal duty voluntarily assumed was penalized with a bót (*infra*, § 76). Here also there was involved, from the viewpoint of the old law, a misdeed; for it invariably treated such non-performance as a punishable violation of law, without regard to the manner in which the obligation was created.

This liability, which was imposed by law as the consequence of outlawry, gave way in the course of the development of the private law to liabilities created by contract. And it is precisely the liability created by contract and superimposed upon an existing obligation which shows that no liability arose from the legal duty as such. Nor was this less true when, — as was certainly true at an early day, — the transaction creating the duty came to be ordinarily united with that which created the liability; nor when, as a result of further development, a liability was directly attached

[1] *Brunner*, "Grundzüge" (5th ed.), 214.

to the duty, as a consequence of the contract by which the latter was created. This actual or legal union of the creation of legal duty and the giving of security became the more necessary the more the law of obligations was developed; for who would content himself with a legal duty that was unguaranteed? For this very reason the notional distinction between duty and liability continued to exist in its old sharpness. Henceforth they ordinarily originated simultaneously, in one transaction which was equally a transaction of "Schuld" and of "Haftung"; but though this might make the distinction between them more difficult it did not in the least alter the concepts themselves. Afterward as before it remained possible that "pure" obligational-transactions might be entered into that did not create a liability; and, conversely, that "pure" liability-transactions might occur that were limited in content to the creation of a liability, and were intended merely to secure the performance of an obligation already existing. In particular, the frequent occurrence in practice of such "pure" liability-transactions, — including particularly the assumption of a guaranty ("Bürgschaft") for the obligation of another person, — is of the utmost importance for the understanding of the conceptional distinction between legal duty and liability. Von Amira is therefore right in saying of such instances, that their importance cannot be over-estimated, whether in the old or in the modern law.[1]

§ 69. **Varieties of Liability.** (I) **Real and Personal Liability.** — According to the object which is liable, and therefore subject to attack by the creditor, there may be distinguished various kinds of liability. As already remarked (*supra*, p. 471), persons as well as things may be liable; consequently, all relations of liability are either personal ("Personen-") or real ("Sachhaftungen"). "Liability of persons and liability of things are the primary principles that have dominated from the beginning the entire law of obligations."[2] By means of this twofold division it is possible to classify in a logically satisfactory manner all known forms of liability. A divergent view, represented particularly by Gierke, assumes on the other hand a threefold classification of liabilities. It places beside the liability of persons and of things, as a third independent class, the liability of property ("Vermögenshaftung"). But, as will be shown below under (III), "so-called 'property' liability is only one form of personal liability",[3] which was origi-

[1] In Z². R. G., XXXI (1910), 497.
[2] *v. Amira* in *ibid.*, 494.
[3] *Ibid.*, and also in his "Wadiation", 33.

nally always united with the other form of personal liability, namely corporal ("leibliche") liability, but which later became independent, and eventually completely displaced corporal liability in legal life. In the case of corporal liability a person is liable with his body; in the case of a property liability he is liable with his property. In both cases the person is liable; only the incidence and measure of the liability, in one and the other case, is different. Either the liability affects his "personality" in the full extent of his physical and legal existence, or it affects exclusively either his body and physical powers of labor (corporal liability) or his economic position as defined in legal relations ("property" liability). But it is quite different in the case of real-liability. This attaches to the things or objects as such, without regard to the person who would otherwise be entitled to dispose of them. In this case the thing, strictly, is liable, and not a person through or with a thing. But in the case of "property liability", the latter is true; and the creditor is accorded a liability of the debtor's property through the person of the debtor.[1] Even Gierke admits[2] that "property"-liability is "in essence a liability under the law of persons." He contrasts it, nevertheless, with personal liability as an independent type of liability. This may be explained by the fact that he makes the concept of personal liability coincident with that of corporal liability; but to do so is neither acceptable in theory nor reconcilable with the historical development of the Germanic law of liability.

(II) **Real Liability.** — A thing is made liable by giving it to the creditor in pledge. Hence the development of real liability coincides with the development of the law of pledge; a pledge right is a right to a real liability.

(1) *Chattel pledges* ("Fahrnispfand").[3] The chattel pledge belongs already to the oldest law. The thing that was made liable passed into the physical seisin of the pledgee (possessory pledge), who thereby acquired a real right therein. This right, however, amounted only to a power to retain the thing in his custody; it did not include a power to destroy the thing, or to sell it, or take its profits. For the debtor had the right to release the thing from its "bondage" by performance of the obligation.

[1] *Strohal* (*supra*, p. 409), 36. He refers to § 2092 of the Code Civil in which this idea is expressed with especial clearness. "Whoever has personally bound himself is liable with all his property, movable and immovable, present and future, to fulfill his undertaking."
[2] "Schuld und Haftung", 77.
[3] *Cf.* pp. 440 *et seq.*, *supra*.

If on the other hand he failed to perform his legal duty, then the pledge right of the pledgee was transformed into full ownership, — in earliest times immediately (forfeiture-pledge), and later as a result of a sale effected by the creditor (sale-pledge). The creditor could rely upon the thing so liable, only; but upon this under all circumstances, no matter in whose possession it might be. If it afforded him no, or only an incomplete, satisfaction, or if it was destroyed, he had no further claims. For he had been given and had accepted the pledge, and it exclusively, as security. It served him as a full guaranty for any damage he might suffer from the non-performance of the duty. And since the obligor originally had only a right, — but was under no duty, — to redeem the pledge by performance of his obligation, the possessory pledge constituted provisionally such counter-performance, assuring the creditor, in case it was not redeemed, complete compensation for non-performance.

(2) *Pledge of lands.*[1] — The pledge of lands was of later origin than the pledge of chattels, but in consequence of the greater importance in the Middle Ages of transactions in land, it was more widely disseminated and more richly developed. Whereas the creditor originally received a "qualified ownership" ("bedingtes Eigentum", "Eigentumspfand" = proprietary pledge) in the land gaged, and later received a right of pledge that was manifested in a seisin "ut de vadio" and a right of usufruct ("ältere Satzung", usufructuary gage,—the "older" form of gage), the gage of lands without possession ("jüngere Satzung", execution gage,—the "younger" form of gage) gave the creditor in case of non-payment a right to satisfy himself from the land by a judicial execution. But in the case, also, of the execution-gage the creditor received directly a real right in the land pledged; and in case of a pledge land, such pledge,—which in case of non-payment of the debt likewise passed in full ownership to the creditor, either by forfeiture or by sale, — was a substitute for the defaulted payment to the full amount of the latter. The pledge of lands, in all its forms, created a pure real-liability. The creditor could rely only on the land pledged, but he could enforce his "liability-right" ("Haftungsrecht") against any third person who acquired the land.

(III) **Personal Liability.** — The development of personal liability was more complicated and is as yet more obscure than that of real liability. The stages of its development certainly

[1] *Cf.* pp. 374 *et seq.*, *supra.*

corresponded to the contemporary development of personal credit.[1]

(1) We are justified in assuming that in the *earliest period* personal liability signified a pawn ("Einsatz") of the entire "personality" ("Persönlichkeit") of the person liable, which was exposed in all respects to the attack of the creditor. This liability of the person might, however, be created in two different forms, which corresponded to the two forms occurring in real liability: it secured to the creditor either a power in the nature of a possessory pledge or merely a hypothecary right.

(A) Liability in the nature of a POSSESSORY PLEDGE OF THE BODY of the debtor ("Geiselschaft").[2] This was the oldest of all modes in which free persons could be subjected to liability by juristic act. "The hostage remained a prisoner of the creditor exactly as a possessory pledge was held in his possession."[3] The giving of hostages was the counterpart of the possessory pledge of things; the hostage was "a human pledge."[4] The hostage gave his person into the power of the creditor, and this immediately; so that he was thenceforth "literally 'bound' or 'entangled' for the debt."[5] If the debt was canceled the hostage was thereby released from his liability, and again became free. On the other hand, in case of a breach of legal duty or delay in its performance he was forfeited "ipso facto to the creditor, with his person and with all that he wore, with his freedom and with his honor; but things that he had left at home were free from the creditor's attack."[6] Under the primitive law the creditor had the right to kill him, or mutilate him, to keep him as a slave, or to sell him. Since the debtor, when he gave himself as a hostage, could no longer be active in the performance of this legal duty, because a prisoner of the creditor,

[1] This is emphasized by *v. Amira*, "Wadiation", 42; the weighty suggestions made by him in this work, 42–47, and in the Z². R. G., XXXI (1910), 490—unfortunately all too concise—are the basis of the treatment in the text. See also, in addition to the sections of *Gierke's* "Schuld und Haftung" that are in question, *v. Schwerin's* "Schuld und Haftung", 10.

[2] As *Herbert Meyer* remarks in the "Festschrift für Gierke", 982, recent etymological interpretations (*Edward Schröder, Much*) connect the word "Geisel" (hostage) with "Geissel" (Lombard "gīsil" = arrow-shaft, Icelandic "geisl", old Norse "gisli" = staff); so that it seems one may justifiably interpret "Geisel" as a staff or a staff-bearer. This would fit in well with the importance which the staff acquired, as will appear below, in the creation of liability.

[3] *v. Amira*, "Wadiation", 42 *et seq.*

[4] The Sachsenspiegel (III, 39, § 2) says of the debtor held for debt: "so long as he has not paid him (the creditor), and is unable to do this, he remains himself his pledge for the money."

[5] *Gierke*, "Schuld und Haftung," 31.

[6] *V. Amira*, "Wadiation", 42 *et seq.*

such a form of self-hostageship, although it was possible and did occur, must doubtless have been rarer than hostages for the debt of another. The sources, moreover, assume the latter form as the normal case. "The giving of hostages or a contract for their delivery was a transaction of pure liability; it was the typical form of transactions creating personal liability."[1]

(B) A person could make himself liable without immediately making himself the prisoner of the creditor. Like the thing in the case of an execution-pledge his body might at first be free. Von Amira therefore speaks in this case of "FREE" PERSONAL PLEDGES ("freie Bürgschaft"). This pawning ("Einsetzung") of a person for a debt without a delivery of his body to the creditor first arose as a "variation of hostageship." But how could it be possible, in this case, for the creditor to secure himself by the body of the person liable, — the pledge ("Bürge"), — for the non-performance of the latter's legal duty? From the viewpoint of the oldest law the creditor possessed a right to go against the person liable only when the latter had been deprived of the law's protection; that is, when he had been declared outside the peace. If, therefore, it happened that the creditor was obliged to rely upon the pledge for his security, — let us suppose because another person, the debtor, for whom such pledge had assumed liability, had not performed his legal duty, — then, originally, an outlawry of the person liable was proclaimed at the instance of the creditor. He could then, as a result of the outlawry, levy distress upon the property of the person liable; that is, could take pieces of his property into possession as "taken" pledges, which compensated him for the unperformed obligation. This declaring one outside the peace ("Friedloslegung"), this process of judicial outlawry ("Achtverfahren"), originally had the effect of abandoning the outlaw to every person, and this not only with his body and whatever he wore but with all his belongings, the things over which he could dispose. In this case, therefore, his person as well as his property "through his person" were exposed to attack by the creditor. But such liability resulted solely from an outlawry actually declared. In time, an amelioration was introduced: the prior process of outlawry ceased to be a precondition of distraint. On the contrary the law eventually gave the creditor the right to take his debtor as a pledge without the latter having forfeited his sacred rights as a man, that is without his having been declared an outlaw; and he might do this either by way of private distress,

[1] *V. Amira*, "Wadiation", 43.

— either as self-help or by judicial authority, — or, after the introduction of judicial execution, through official action. But this was allowable, of course, only when the same preconditions were satisfied that were required in outlawry as a judicial process; there must be an indisputable legal duty, that is a legal duty created in observance of definite formalities. (As to this see § 71 ,*infra.*) It has already been mentioned (*supra*, p. 442) that in the Salic Law the introduction of official distress can be traced back to a royal statute ("L. Sal.", Tit. 50, 3) interpolated in the text of a folk-law, which accorded the creditor, in addition to the private distress that was alone customary theretofore, "a distress upon the debtor, subject to certain conditions, by the hand of the royal counts."[1] This official distress, effected with definite formalities, — so-called "Strud" or "Raub", — has the appearance of a weakened outlawry that is limited to the debtor's property.[2] It secured to the creditor an immediate ownership in the things taken; whereas a private distress originally created in favor of the creditor merely a pledge right in the debtor's things which he distrained. Later, this became the law in case of official distress, also. In this case, of course, the debtor's personal liability, which continued so long as the right of distress was not exercised, was transformed by the distress into a real liability of the object taken as a pledge. It is clear from this course of development that distress, inasmuch as it remained subject to the same preconditions as outlawry, was a consequence of the personal liability of the debtor; the only difference being that it no longer involved, like the old and strict process of judicial outlawry, a pawning ("Einsatz") of the entire personality, but merely a liability of the debtor's property. The creditor distrained upon certain objects of the debtor's property which he thought might compensate him for the defaulted debt. Title passed to him either immediately or after a forfeiture or sale. Originally, however, a debtor's assumption of liability in itself created for the creditor merely a right of distraint; and not, as was true in the case of real liability, an immediate pledge right. Moreover, no definite thing was made liable for the debt by the transaction that created a right of distraint; the debtor made his property liable in the sense that he gave the creditor a right to distrain any objects whatever- therein included, as the creditor might choose. Hence, this subjection of the entire property of the debtor was known as a "property" liability. But one must not be misled by this expression into regarding such a "property"

[1] *Brunner*, "Geschichte", II, 454. [2] *Ibid.*

liability as a form of liability to be classed with "real" obligations. The debtor's property was not " liable " from the viewpoint of the old law, inasmuch as a thing could be made an obligor, according to it, only through a pledge right. But here no more was given than a right of distraint. It was therefore rather the person of the debtor that was liable; only this liability was not, as in the case of the old and strict judicial outlawry, one which attached to his entire personality, nor was it such a liability as attached, as in the case of hostages, to his body, but on the contrary it was enforced solely by an attack upon his property. No real right was here given to the creditor, such as existed even in the case of the execution-gage, — which *did* involve a " real " liability. The right of distraint, moreover, extended only to the debtor's chattels, which included for this purpose all objects that were in the debtor's seisin, thus constituting an entity of movables. That is, it extended to a unitary mass of objects, the debtor's property, which were affected by the formal act by which the liability was created, but only so long as they remained within the circle marked by the seisin of the debtor.[1] All these circumstances make it a reasonable assumption that what is called " property " liability " is derived from personal liability "; that is, from that liability which had originally involved the debtor with his body and his goods, and which was subject to the precondition either of actual or at least of possible outlawry.[2]

(2) *In the second stage of development* of the law of liability the consciousness of this earlier precondition became completely lost. The result was that in all cases where it was desired to guarantee performance by an obligor, it became possible to create a personal liability by contract without his becoming a hostage in the nature of a possessory pledge. And since the person who was liable remained for the time being free, the result of such a contract was, — in the sense of Amira's terminology, — a " free suretyship." This contract may be designated the *contract of suretyship in the narrow sense.*[3] So long as the right of distraint was subject to the precondition of an actual or a possible judicial outlawry the debtor himself must ordinarily have been liable, since that precondition was satisfied precisely in his person. Afterward, when " free " suretyship could be created in all cases by contract, it became the rule for a third person to assume suretyship for the

[1] *Egger*, "Vermögenshaftung", 401.

[2] *v. Amira*, in Z². R. G., XXXI (1910), 491. A different derivation of "Vermögenshaftung" is suggested by *Herbert Meyer* in the "Festschrift für Gierke," 978 *et seq.*

[3] *v. Amira*, "Wadiation", 44.

debt of another, as in hostageship. Suretyship in the narrow sense was thus, at first, ordinarily suretyship by a third person ("Fremdbürgschaft", "outside" suretyship). It was a transaction of "pure" liability. That is, its sole content was the establishment of a liability ("Haftung"); it did not, in itself, refer at all to the creation of a legal duty ("Schuld"). This contract of suretyship, as a "pure" liability transaction, was adapted "to the security of any obligation ('Schuld') whatever, without regard to its basis or to its nature, and without regard to the person of the debtor." [1] Precisely for this reason there was nothing to prevent the debtor himself from undertaking to guarantee his own obligation. The self-suretyship that appeared among the Franks, Lombards, Bavarians, and Alamanians, and whose form, at least among the Franks, appears as an imitation of the form of "outside" suretyship (*infra*, § 71), may possibly be best explained as a further development of the latter form, which alone was originally usual.[2] Self-suretyship played a great rôle in the older law; naturally enough, since originally there did not simultaneously result from the obligational contract ("Schuldvertrag"), as such, a liability. Only when this union of legal duty and liability became the rule was it again possible to dispense with the institute of self-suretyship; thereafter the word acquired definitely the meaning in which it is current today, namely an assumption of liability for the obligation of another.

The contract of suretyship had as its end the assumption of a personal liability. The surety ("Bürge") pledged his person for the performance of another's obligation; he subjected himself to an attack by the obligee in case of non-performance by the obligor. The extent of this liability might vary. The surety might, in accord with the original measure of personal liability, pledge ("verstricken") his entire personality without restriction. This "se et bona obligare" of the surety certainly offered to the creditor the greatest security, but in time it became exceptional. The surety either pledged his body or his property only; the contract of guaranty ordinarily created either corporal or property liability on the part of the surety.

(A) Corporal liability of the surety goes back to the old practice of giving hostages, save that, as already mentioned, it left the surety for the time being free; the creditor received, as a result of the contract of guaranty, merely a right to take possession of the

[1] *v. Amira*, "Wadiation", 44.
[2] *Gierke* is of another opinion, "Schuld und Haftung", 60.

person of the surety, acting either alone or through the court. Whereas a judicial execution against the person of the surety originally effected a complete abandonment of the latter to the creditor, it later resulted merely in a "debtor-bondage" ("Schuldknechtschaft") that restrained the creditor within certain narrow limits. The surety, also, might obligate himself to place himself, by way of "self-surrender", at the disposition of the creditor as a debtor-bondsman. This always signified, in the oldest period, and equally whether the surety was reduced to debtor-bondage by the court or by his own act, a definitive reduction to the status of a slave; it was a conveyance in place of payment, by means of which the creditor was finally and irrevocably compensated for non-payment of the debt. But already in the Frankish period it became possible to free the debtor-bondsman from his bondage, even after he was in default, by a subsequent satisfaction of the debt; so that, exactly as in the case of the oldest proprietary pledge, the establishment of the bondage was regarded as resulting from a condition subsequent. A further amelioration was quite commonly realized in the Middle Ages in that the person liable, who gave himself into the creditor's power, could thenceforth be required to render services as a household follower ("Schulddienstbarkeit", "Gesindediensten") only. And, finally, the subjection ("Bindung") of the person liable was transformed into a mere restriction upon his freedom (private and public imprisonment for debt): the person liable could be held a prisoner until the satisfaction of the debt, but could not be compelled to do any kind of work. To be sure, agreements of a harsher nature were not excluded.

Wherever a contract of guaranty created a corporal liability on the part of the surety there resulted in favor of the creditor a right which, as distinguished from the old institution of hostageship, was merely a temporary hypothecary right against the person of the surety; a right which could be enforced only when the condition happened that made the surety liable. This right of the creditor to attack the surety's person corresponded to the creditor's right, already mentioned (*supra*, p. 478), to distrain upon the property of one who was liable to him. It made no difference whether the debtor himself or a third person was the surety. Just as the debtor paid with his own person when he made himself liable with his own body, so he paid, if he offered another as a surety, with the person of the latter; the creditor must rely solely upon the person of the guarantor in case of non-performance by the debtor. The guarantor alone was exposed to attack by the creditor. If he died, the right of the creditor was ipso facto extinguished; no liability passed to the guarantor's heirs.

The close historical connection between the giving of hostages and the corporal liability of the surety is evidenced by the circumstance that the typical form which was created by the Frankish law for the enforcement of the surety's corporal liability, and which was later long and commonly employed in other legal systems, — the so-called "Einlager" ("quartering"), — was derived directly from hostageship; and developed in a peculiar manner[1] the latter's external characteristic, namely the restriction of the right of the person pledged to move about. "Quartering", — whose other names ("Giselschaft"; "obstagium", from "obses"; "ôtage") show in their terminology the connection of the two institutes in legal history, — consisted in this, that a person who was liable (usually a surety, but it might be the debtor himself or the debtor and a surety) was obligated, in case of the debtor's failure to perform and upon notice of the creditor, to go to a place agreed upon, and there remain until payment of the debt. As Rintelen has shown, this "quartering" of the surety developed in some legal systems, especially in the Netherlands but also in some localities in Saxony, into a form of corporal pledge ("Bürgschaft"), created by law as a statutory form of execution; so that, there, the creditor had the right to demand of the debtor an extra-procedural "quartering", although of course usually only in case of claims particularly favored. Ordinarily, however, the duty to

[1] *E. Friedländer*, "Das Einlager, Ein Beitrag zur deutschen Rechtsgeschichte" (1868); *Lechner*, "Das Obstagium oder die Giselschaft nach schweizerischen Quellen" (1906); *Rintelen*, "Schuldhaft und Einlager im Vollstreckungsverfahren des altniederländischen und sächsischen Rechts" (1908), and *cf. Korsch* in Krit. Vj. G. R. W., L (3d ser. XIV, 1912), 128–142; *Kisch*, "Das Einlager im ältesten Schuldrechte Mährens, I: Historischer Teil", in Zeitschrift des deutschen Vereins für die Geschichte Mährens und Schlesiens, XXV (1912), 4; also, "Über das Einlager im älteren böhmischen Stadtrechte", in "Mitteilungen des Vereins für die Geschichte der Deutschen in Böhmen", L (1912), 2. — See also *Gierke*, "Schuld und Haftung", 52 *et seq.*, 251 *et seq.* *Von Amira*, Z². R. G., XXXI (1910), 498, contends that it is impossible to connect the "Einlager"-contract with hostageship because the *promise* to give one's self up as a prisoner is not a *pledge* of one's freedom, any more than a promise to give an ordinary pledge is itself a pledge. But why should it not be possible to regard the development from hostageship to corporal liability of the surety ("Bürge", pledge) and to "Einlager" as a phenomenon similar to that from the "older" (usufructuary) to the "younger" (execution) pledge? The contract of suretyship in the narrow sense certainly produces a liability of the surety, because the creditor is given immediately a right to go against the person and property of the surety, notwithstanding that the enforcement of this right is made dependent upon the happening of the condition with respect to which the liability was created. And it seems to me that this is similarly true in the "Einlager-" contract.

submit to "quartering" in case of demand must have been assumed by special contract. Such contracts were often made in Germany from the time of the Crusades onward, after the model of those in France. This was most frequent among the knightage, but in Switzerland equally among burghers and peasants. The original idea of hostageship, that the hostage must put himself in the power of the creditor, was very considerably relaxed. This appeared above all in the fact that the creditor frequently had the power to determine the place of performance; although this need no longer necessarily be at his residence or within a district he controlled, his assent was necessary to another place. Usually it was a tavern or a hospitage, to which the surety rode, frequently with a great following, and where he maintained himself with his servants and horses until the time for performance of the obligation or the expiration of a given period. All this was at the debtor's expense, and was designed to exert pressure upon him for the performance of his obligations. Wherever statutory "quartering" existed it was customary to prescribe by a special tariff a minimum and maximum expenditure; but in the case of "quartering" under contract no statutory limitation of the quartered surety's expenses was possible. Accordingly, the contractual form, especially when employed by knights fond of good living, was gladly utilized as a welcome means of leading an exceedingly prodigal life, as we are reminded by the proverb, "Geiselmahl köstliches Mahl" (a hostage's meal is a delicious meal). In the 1500 s quartering was abolished by imperial statutes. Despite this, however, it did not wholly disappear. In some regions it has persisted down to the present time, as in Holstein, — where indeed it was later expressly authorized by the Peace of Westphalia (VII, § 5) and by the recess of the imperial Diet of 1654 (§ 170), — and in Switzerland.

(B) Property-liability of the surety. — With the increase in value of the rights enjoyed by individuals under the property law, the corporal liability of the surety became less important and his property liability became the usual and dominant form of suretyship. Here the surety was not liable with his body or physical labor, but with his property. He was liable to the creditor in the sense that in case of the non-performance of an obligation, whether that of a third person or of the surety himself, he gave the creditor a right to go against his movable property. The creditor received, therefore, through the contract of suretyship, no pledge right in objects already determined, but a right of distraint, by the exercise of which certain objects, when taken by him, passed to him in ownership or as pledges; all of which has already been referred to (*supra*, p. 478) as essential to so-called "property" liability, — that is, to the liability of a person through his property. If there was involved a suretyship for the debt of another person ("Fremdbürgschaft") there resulted in the old law of suretyship, as is clearly shown (*infra*, § 71) by the formalism of the contract of guaranty, a double relation of liability: the surety was liable with his property to the creditor, and the debtor was liable with his property to the surety; a right was given to the creditor to distrain upon the chattels of the surety, and to the latter a right was given, in turn, in case he was compelled to satisfy the creditor from his own property, to recoup himself from the debtor's property. Moreover, the creditor must rely exclusively upon the property of the surety, since this alone had been made liable to him. The property liability of the surety, consequently, like all other forms of liability by a surety, was according to the Germanic law of suretyship a primary, and not a secondary or accessory, liability. Further, since the surety alone, under the contract of guaranty, entered into a relationship of liability to the creditor, and since he subjected to that liability only such property as was in his seisin, and which was held together by his seisin as an entity (*supra*, p. 478), no inheritance of the surety's liability was possible. A debtor might himself be liable as his own surety, as with his body so also with his property. Indeed, as already mentioned, it may well be assumed that, even at an early day, an obligational contract ("Schuldvertrag") ordinarily came to include a simultaneous assumption of liability by the debtor. And when corporal liability had become less prominent this assumption of liability signified a liability of the debtor's property. Of course this did not make it impossible for a third person, in addition to the debtor, to be a surety through his property. In such cases several sureties might be liable at the same time. In such cases, also, originally, the property of each surety was directly and primarily bound in case of non-performance of the obligation. True, the surety was no longer substituted for the debtor, in such cases, as the sole person liable, but was liable with the debtor. But here also there was no question (*infra*, § 81) of a preliminary action against the debtor, *i.e.*, of a "beneficium excussionis." In the course of the Middle Ages, it is true, many legal systems departed still further from the old standpoint, and introduced, either alone or in connection with the old form, a new variety of warranty ("Bürgschaft", guaranty and suretyship) in which the liability of the guarantor could be enforced only secondarily, after that of the debtor. In this case an action against the guarantor was permitted only when the debtor had been sued without results. With this change a regulation of warranty was attained identical with that of the Roman law; and doubtless an acquaintance with the Roman system was influential in this development. In the same way, the other native principle of the non-heritable character of warranty was abandoned in many legal systems under the incipient influence of the Roman law; the Schwabenspiegel, for example, recognized an inheritance by heirs of an obligation of suretyship.[1] Moreover, not least in importance among the facts to which these transformations were due was the fact that warranty by third-persons ("Fremdbürgschaft") lost in many places that character of a pure liability transaction which was originally essential to it. The surety no longer assumed, by the contract of warranty, a mere liability for the debt of another, but constituted himself at the same time a debtor of the person to whom the security was given. "The idea was developed that the surety is obligated ('schuldig') either to perform the obligation that he has guaranteed or to give compensation."[2] This view was especially natural in cases where a surety pledged himself for a personal act that was performable by another; but it also became established in the case of money debts: the surety was regarded as legally bound to compel performance of his obligation by the primary debtor or else himself to perform, as a primary debtor ("Selbstschuldner", "Selbstzahler"), the obligation so guaranteed.

§ 70. **Legal Duty and Liability in the Modern Law.**[3] **(I) The Common Law Theory of Legal Duty.**—Inasmuch as the theoretical distinction between legal duty and liability is required, as already remarked (*supra*, p. 464), by logic, and is therefore present in every law of obligations, it cannot have disappeared in Germany because of the fact that the old native rules and views were everywhere influenced and in many points displaced by the Roman law received into Germany. The consciousness and recognition of the distinction merely became less evident, or failed to develop,

[1] Ssp. (G.), 9 S, 1.

[2] *Gierke*, "Schuld und Haftung", 105.

[3] Of the literature cited under § 68 *supra* see in particular *Strohal*, "Schuldübernahme"; *v. Schwerin*, "Schuld und Haftung", and the works therein cited, p. 5, upon the present law, to which should be added *Puntschart's* essay in the Z. Hand. R., LXXI (3d ser. XII, 1912), 297–326 and *Binder*, "Rechtsnorm und Rechtspflicht" (address, 1912), 3–15. See also *Ehrenberg*, "Die beschränkte Haftung des Schuldners nach See- und Handelsrecht" (1880).

because the Romanistic theory, in consequence of the dogmatic form of the classical Roman law, overlooked the notional distinction between duty and liability. Roman law regarded every "obligatio" as directly involving a liability, a "must-perform" ("Leistenmüssen"), an action of the debtor performance of which could be compelled by judicial action and judgment. "Natural" obligations constituted a sole exception, little reconcilable with the prevailing theory. The distinction, too, between real liability and personal liability was either unknown to, or is no longer discernible in, the Roman law in its final form. On the contrary, after personal or real execution had been had the Roman obligation attached to the entire property of the debtor without exception.

Now, in the Germanic law also, from the earliest period, it was an ordinary consequence of an obligational contract that it involved a liability, whether one created simultaneously with the legal duty or one based upon a distinct ("pure") liability-transaction designed to supplement the obligation with a warranty. This was true except when an independent obligation was created, without any actual or any possible liability. That legal duty and liability were in most cases united — for an unguaranteed debt can never have been common — was therefore hardly less an actual fact in the medieval law than in the later Romanistic common law. It was not yet possible, however, to appreciate the significance, for an understanding of the fundamental concepts of the law of obligations, of such obligations as still continued to occur without any liability, and of the various special forms of real liability. They were regarded merely from the standpoint of the common law theory — and consequently the latter attained an unlimited and unchallenged supremacy. Legal enforceability was held to be an essential quality of every obligation; "natural" obligations continued to be regarded as exceptions to general principles, and therefore only "imperfect" obligations. This view still finds clear expression in the definition of the present Civil Code: "by virtue of an obligation the obligee is entitled to demand performance by the obligor" (§ 241).

Like the theoretical concept of obligations, the theory of suretyship came to be extremely dependent upon the doctrine of the alien law. Here again this result was facilitated by the form assumed by suretyship in the last stages of the development of the medieval law. For as already mentioned (p. 484), there was realized even before the Reception a transformation of the older principles into something similar to the Roman law; and this change was carried much further after the Reception. The liability of the surety became quite generally a purely secondary liability (a guaranty), as in the Roman law: only when demand had been made upon the debtor, — or according to other legal systems when an action had been brought against him, — without satisfaction, could the creditor have recourse against the guarantor, to whom was conceded in principle the "beneficium excussionis." It was only in the commercial law that the plea of an earlier action, and therewith the purely secondary character of the guaranty, found no recognition. This exception passed into the General Commercial Code (§ 281), which provided that such a plea should be rejected "when the debt results from a commercial transaction on the part of the primary debtor, or when the contract of guaranty is itself a commercial transaction." The same rule is recognized in the present Commercial Code (§§ 349, 351); constituting, therefore, an exception to the rule of suretyship which was formerly the common law and which is adopted in the Civil Code (§ 771). Similarly, the original non-heritability of suretyship was preserved in but few legal systems. Most of them made it heritable, and this rule was adopted by the Civil Code.

(II) **Present Existence of the Distinction between Legal Duty and Liability.** — Notwithstanding that the modern law of obligations has thus departed from the old views in many fundamental respects, and that modern statutes (all of them drafted under the influence of the Romanistic theory of the common law) have never, of course, employed in their terminology the concepts "Schuld" and "Haftung" in the sense given those words in the theory of the Germanist School, the modern law exhibits not a few phenomena that can be satisfactorily explained only by attending to the distinction between them. We must content ourselves here with a brief reference to a few of the most important points where the concepts of duty and of liability appear in the existing law in the sense first discovered in the old Germanic and medieval German law.

The present law, also, knows legal duties without liability, recognizes "pure" liability relations that involve no legal duty, and recognizes various sorts of liability.

Natural obligations find in it a satisfactory explanation as cases of legal duties (legal duties in the sense equally of a duty to perform or to receive) without liability; especially, natural obligations arising from gaming or betting. They ought to be performed, but no liability exists. Therefore they cannot be enforced by a legal action; but, on the other hand, when performed they cannot be undone on the ground that no obligation existed. Perhaps we may, with Strohal,[1] include here those cases where a person makes a loan to another with the statement that though he will accept repayment at any time he will never demand it.

As regards liabilities without legal duties, it is true even in the present law that, on principle, whoever is liable also owes a legal duty. The suretyship of the present law can therefore no longer be conceived of as a pure relationship of liability.[2] At the same time examples can be given to show the possibility even to-day of liabilities existing independently of legal duties.[3] Thus, for example, a personal liability arises, without incurrence of a legal duty, "when the usufructuary lessee ('Pächter'), or other person entitled to the profits of a mercantile establishment, assumes a liability for business obligations of the earlier owner of the business by continuing the firm name."

Of the different varieties of liability, personal liability in the sense of corporal liability has disappeared from the present law since imprisonment for debt ("Schuldhaft"), — which was last applied against debtors upon bills of exchange ("Wechselhaft"), — was abolished for all Germany by an imperial statute of May 24, 1868; thus doing away with every consequence of non-performance of an obligation of private law which affected the person of the debtor. Although a "personal" liability is spoken of in the modern and even in the present law, the expression signifies something different than the pledging of one's physical person. It means liability with one's "personality under the law of property", or "property-liability" in the sense already several times referred to (*supra*, p. 478). This "personal" liability ordinarily signifies a liability with all one's property, as distinguished from a liability on one hand with a special estate ("Sondervermögen") and on the other hand with a particular thing. This last sort of liability, — real liability, — is still of the utmost importance in the law. Exactly as in the real liability of the medieval law, only perfectly definite things or objects are pledged for the debt, so that its satisfaction is guaranteed by them exclusively, and the creditor is given a right of attack against them alone. "Pure" real liability for real obligations occurs in perpetual land charges ("Reallasten"), and

[1] *Op. cit.*, 61.

[2] *Gierke*, "Schuld und Haftung", 106, and the contrary view maintained by *Isay* in *Ihering's* J. B., XLVIII (2d ser. XII, 1904), 193 *et seq.*

[3] *Gierke, op. cit.*, cites the example given in the text and a long list of others.

in the law of pledge in the case of real rights granted as security ("Grundpfandrecht"). The purest form of the latter is the non-accessory land debt ("Grundschuld"), since this is created independently of any legal connection with a contractual claim, and even though a personal obligation continues to exist or is newly created beside it such claim is of no consequence under the law of things.[1] A counterpart of this in maritime law is bottomry (*supra*, p. 453), which, along with a purely real obligation that creates merely a legal duty of the debtor to pay ("Leistensollen"), includes, as a guaranty of performance, a pledge of the ship that is enforceable by a real action. Here belong, also, the ship's-debts and lading-debts of the maritime law and law of inland navigation, in which there may be added by contract, — along with a pure real liability (namely, of the ship and the freight), which always exists by force of statute, — a personal liability; that is, a liability of the entire remaining property of the shipowner ("Reeder"). This is analogous to the medieval covenant accessory to a pledge ("Geloben zum Pfande"; *supra*, pp. 444, 450).

Such liabilities restricted to particular things may also have as their object a heritage, or the community property of husband and wife; or may be constituted in other ways by contract of the parties.

In addition to these there also occur liabilities that are quantitatively limited; that is, liabilities that expose the property of the debtor to attack by his creditor only to a limited extent, defined by a fixed sum of money, such *e.g.* as the liabilities of limited partners, of shareholders, of the members of a partnership of fixed liability, and of sureties who are liable only for a maximum amount.

The explanation, by reference to the distinction between legal duty and liability, of these and of many other institutions of the modern law was first made possible by the theory of the Germanist School. Strohal justly ascribes to this an extraordinary "creative" value in the theory of the present law: "it has led us from the field of imagination to the firm ground of historical evolution, from an ethereal ideology into the world of actual phenomena, from abstract dialectic to an unfettered observation and appreciation of actual legal processes."[2]

[1] *Gierke*, "Privatrecht", II, 910 *et seq.*
[2] *Strohal, op. cit.*, 77.

Topic 2. The Historical Origins of Obligations

§ 71. **Obligational Contracts: Forms of Obligational and Liability Transactions in the old Law.**[1] (I) **Formalism of Transactions creating Legal Duties and Liabilities in general.** — Until a recent day the view prevailed that it was an original principle of Germanic law that a contractual creation of obligations resulted from an informal declaration of will, to which was attributed a power of creating legal and binding rights. This assumption was definitively disposed of by the brilliant investigations of Sohm. They showed that this older theory of the Germanic law of obligations involved an error similar to that in the Romanistic theory of the original political organization of the ancient Germans, which thought to find in the primeval forests of Germany the ideal of political freedom. We know now that the law of primitive peoples everywhere is filled with compulsory formalism (*supra*, pp. 12 *et seq.*); that primitive man can no more conceive of a right apart from forms than of a religion without a cult.[2] And so too among the ancient Germans the law of obligations, like all the rest of the law, was governed by strictly prescribed forms. Sohm (whose theory was immediately accepted) showed that according to the old law a contract could be concluded only as a "real" or as a "formal" contract. In the real contract the binding force lay in earlier performance by one of the contracting parties; in the formal contract, in the observance of some formality, whether the doing of certain acts or the speaking of certain words. At the time of Sohm's investigations it was still impossible properly to appreciate the distinction between legal duty and liability. It proved necessary to combine this with his views. The synthesis was undertaken, particularly, by Gierke; but in the end he found it necessary to reject Sohm's theory in one important point. Adopting ideas which had ready been expressed by Puntschart,[3] he developed in the broadest manner, in his work on "Schuld und Haftung", the view that a distinction between these two concepts in the law of obligations must be the basis and point of departure of legal theory even as respects the formal aspect of juristic acts; that

[1] *Sohm*, "Das Recht der Eheschliessung" (1875), 24 *et seq.*, 34 *et seq.*, 78 *et seq.*; *R. Löning*, "Der Vertragsbruch im deutschen Recht" (1876); *Siegel*, "Der Handschlag und Eid nebst den verwandten Sicherheiten für ein Versprechen im deutschen Rechtsleben", Sitzungsberichte der Wiener Akademie, CXXX (1894). Also the literature cited under § 68 *supra*.

[2] *Brissaud*, "Manuel", 1358.

[3] "Schuldvertrag", 404 *et seq.*

the old Germanic and medieval German obligational (" Schuld ") contract was always an informal one, and that only transactions creating liability were dominated by formalism. This new view has found adherents, notably Herbert Meyer,[1] but it did not fail also to meet with opposition, and most especially that of Amira.[2] This opposition, it seems to me, is justified. The theory of Gierke and Puntschart seems to rest " upon an exaggeration of the difference between legal duty and obligation." No proof, drawn from the sources, is offered for the conclusion that no special form was necessary in the obligational contract of the old German law. According to Gierke's view every form that occurs is due to the presence of a liability transaction. But in reasoning thus the fact is forgotten that such an absolute separation of obligational and liability transactions is impossible. As has already been remarked (*supra*, p. 473), legal duty and liability must, indeed, always be distinguished as regards their nature, but it is not necessary to distinguish them as respects their basis.[3] The fact that is the basis of the obligation may at the same time include the basis of the liability. Consequently, " pure " obligational contracts were rare even in the old German law. But that they were concluded informally where they occurred, and that where contracts created both a liability and a legal duty their form was associated with the creation of the liability only, and not with the creation of the duty, would contradict everything otherwise known of the nature of formalism in early law. Von Amira points convincingly[4] to the fact that the " necessity of a form exists not only in transactions creating liability, in transactions of the law of things and of kinship, and in transactions under the public law ", " but also in all unilateral offers, notifications (' Ansagen '), notices of rescission, demands, protestations, and all procedural acts." If no declaration could be made between the parties in judicial proceedings without the observance of strict formal requirements, this must have been all the truer of transactions out of court if it was hoped to produce thereby any legal effects. In this respect it could have made no difference whether such effects were limited to the parties themselves or affected third persons, — whether they were directed " inward " or " outward ", as the phrase goes. Every probability is against the assumption " that obligational contracts alone required no special form."

[1] In the "Festschrift für Gierke", 974.
[2] Z^2. R. G., XXXI (1910), 494 *et seq.*, and "Wadiation", 20 *et seq.*
[3] *v. Amira*, "Wadiation", 20.
[4] Z^2. R. G., XXXI (1910), 495.

But because, as a matter of fact, transactions creating legal duties and liabilities ordinarily coincided, the form of the liability-transaction served at the same time, in normal cases, as the form of the obligational contract; in other words, such form made the transaction effective at once as respects the liability and the legal duty.

Disregarding for the moment real contracts (as to which see (III) *infra*) one is justified, therefore, in holding to Sohm's theory that a contract directed solely to the creation of performance of a legal duty required, like every other juristic act, a particular form, and produced legal effects only as a formal contract. The old law required for an obligational contract, exactly as for every other contract, a " visibility and notoriety in its creation "; it " must be audible and visible."[1] The requirement of audibility could be satisfied only by the use of particular words, often prescribed by statute. This is the meaning of Lower Saxon documents when they allow the making of a simple obligational promise " redend " (orally).[2] This formalism in the content of the promise, often painfully strict and frequently permanently prescribed in formulas and formularies, would have been meaningless if the promise creating the duty had not, as such, been regarded as requiring a form quite aside from the legal consequence of liability. Especial importance was attributed to the visibility of the contract; for it seemed from the sensuous viewpoint of the older law far more important to have seen an act than to have heard certain words, as many legal maxims show, — " seeing counts more than hearing " (" sehen geht über Hören") " one trusts his eyes farther than his ears " (" man glaubt den Augen weiter als den Ohren "), and the like. Visibility could be secured directly in contracts under the law of things for the transfer of possession, but it was necessary to resort to symbols for this purpose in the law of obligations. Particular gestures were required, or in addition to such the use of certain instruments for objects. It was an application of the same idea when the delivery of a deed, which was borrowed from the later Roman law, was transformed into a formal act capable of creating not only liability but also a bare legal duty (as to this see details under II, below). That the transaction had not merely been audible and visible, but had actually been heard or seen, must be proved by witnesses.[3]

[1] *v. Amira*, "Recht", 136.
[2] *v. Amira* in Z². R. G., XXXI (1910), 496.
[3] *v. Amira*, "Recht", 138.

(II) **Special Forms of Liability Transactions.** — The purpose peculiar and essential to transactions creating liability, namely the "binding" of a thing or a person, induced an exaggerated formalism. Since the types of real liability — that is, the modes of creating pledges, — have already been discussed (*supra*, pp. 374 *et seq.*, 440 *et seq.*), we have to deal here merely with the forms of personal liability, in which a person pawned either his entire personality, or his body or his property alone.

(1) *The pledge of faith* ("Treugelübde", "fides facta"). The pledge of faith of the Germanic law was "the formal transaction by which a person subjects his person, in case of non-performance of his own or another's obligation, to attack by the creditor."[1] It may be assumed that the pledge of faith "originated as an ideal hostageship, in imitation of actual hostageship", a mere legal restriction being substituted for physical restraint; although if the pledge became liable the creditor was given the same rights that he possessed from the beginning against the hostage.[2] Not only may we assume that the pledge of faith was everywhere common, even in early Germanic times, as a means of subjecting a person to liability for a legal duty, but the special name for such a liability-transaction already appears in Tacitus. In the celebrated passage of the "Germania" concerning gambling among the primitive Germans (Chap. 24) it is reported that they sometimes gambled with dice for stakes so high that when everything else was lost they wagered on the last and supreme throw their freedom and body; and in such a case the one who lost abandoned himself to voluntary slavery. To the Roman writer this extreme obstinacy in an unworthy matter appeared astounding; they themselves, he adds, called this "faith" ("ipsi fidem vocant"). The act itself, evidently correctly observed, becomes intelligible only "when we assume that a pledge of faith preceded the final cast of the dice."[3] The expression "fides" was later employed technically in the Latin sources of the Frankish period; they call the transaction "fides facta." So especially the "Lex Salica", whose 50th Title, obscure and much debated, relates to such "fides facta." The expression "fidem facere", which survived even in the Middle Ages in various forms ("fidantiam facere", "faire foy", "donner fiance", etc.), shows clearly what was here involved. The faith is pawned or pledged. Inasmuch, however, as "the moral worth

[1] *Gierke*, "Schuld und Haftung", 132.
[2] *Ibid.*, 141.
[3] *Ibid.*

of individuality is manifested, according to the Germanic view, in one's faith, his whole personality is bound by the pledge of his faith, and his personal rights are absolutely forfeited by failure to redeem the pledge."[1] In accordance with the original measure of personal liability (*supra*, p. 475), a pledge of faith originally involved liability of the entire personality, without any qualification whatever; and therefore in primitive social conditions almost exclusively a surrender of the body, as a pledge of body and freedom. Later, there was also added a pledge of the person through his property. In the medieval sources, also, there was still quite commonly understood by a pledge of faith a corporal liability, notwithstanding that such liability never constituted its exclusive content. The pledge of one's personality was made audible and visible in the form of the pledge of faith. The first end was secured, in this case as in others, by certain formal words by which the pledge of the faith ("Treuverpflichtung") was assumed; they frequently served at the same time, however, for the creation of the legal duty. The medieval sources refer countless times to this "geloben" (promising) "in" or "with" faith ("in", "bei", "mit Treue geloben"); but also frequently to a mere "geloben" It is doubtful whether we are to understand by this simple "Geloben" the technical pledge of faith. If this question be answered with Puntschart in the affirmative, it would also be permissible to regard the simple "loven" of the Sachsenspiegel, — which is referred to in certain much disputed passages of that Law Book, — as the formal pledge of faith.[2] In addition to the words prescribed there was always essential to the formalism of the pledge of faith a certain ritual of gestures ("Handritus") which very likely had always consisted in the pledgor's extending his right hand to the creditor. We may assume that every suretyship ("Verbürgung") in the broad sense, and so every assumption of personal liabilities, was effected, even under primitive Germanic law, by offering one's hand.[3] The hand symbolized the pledge of the person; since faith was pledged with the hand the hand was regarded as the pledge. According to primitive Arian notions the hand stood for the person because the power of the person was

[1] *Gierke*, "Schuld und Haftung", 132.

[2] *Cf.* especially Ssp., I, 7. Puntschart's views are attacked by *von Schwerin* in Z². R. G., XXV (1904), 323 *et seq.*, and very strongly by *Gierke*, *op. cit.*, 197, 208 *et seq.*, 233. The latter sees in the "loven" of the Sachsenspiegel nothing more than a colorless expression for "promise", and in an elaborate exposition interprets the statements of Eike in harmony with the theory of informal obligational contracts.

[3] *v. Amira*, "Wadiation", 23.

embodied in the hand "as the tool of tools." Because it was given by hand-clasp (in French law "palmata", "paumée") the corporal pledge of faith ("körperliche Treue", "foi de corps") was also called simply hand-pledge ("hand-faith", "Handtreue"). In addition to the hand-clasp, in which the promisee clasped in his right hand the right hand of the promisor, the illuminations of the Sachsensipegel show us a form of manual ritual in which the parties to the contract simply laid the palms of their hands together, holding them above their heads; in other words, the gesture consisted merely in touching and not in clasping hands.[1] It was also a Saxon custom for the promisor to raise above his head the four fingers, and later two fingers, of his right hand, so that the hand was merely offered but not taken. But the prevalence of the expression "manum (or 'fidem') levare", proves that such an elevation of the hand served for the symbolization of the pledge outside of Saxony also, and that in general this raising of the hand, and not the special gesture with the fingers, was the principal thing in such a form of pledge.[2] Moreover, the formalism of personal pledges was not confined to an offer of the hand. Among the Franks, particularly, it was also customary to employ in the transaction a proffer of a staff; to pledge one's faith by transfer of a staff ("fidem facere per festucam"). This may have been associated with the appearance of self-pledge, which was effected in the form of a wed-giving (*infra*, under (2)).

In all these forms, however, change as they might in different times and in the law of different racial branches, the content and effect of the transaction remained the same. Even in the medieval sources the end sought was the creation of a personal liability for the obligation either of one's self or another, a pledge of faith that involved the entire personality of the pledgor. Even in the Middle Ages the pledge of faith might still lead to a complete corporal liability, with the consequences of debtor-bondage or imprisonment for debt, and the effect of a breach of faith was that the party might be declared by judgment of a court "honorless" and "rightless." Frequently, the pledgor expressly gave the creditor a right to take control of his honor, so pledged, by means of symbolical acts, such as by the exhibition of an infamous picture. "The honor of the debtor was forfeited to the creditor by his inability to pay, and could be publicly offered for sale and thrown away."[3]

[1] *v. Amira*, "Handgebärden" (*cf.* p. 11, *supra*), 239.
[2] *Puntschart* in Inst. öst. G. F., XXVIII (1907), 367.
[3] *Heusler*, "Institutionen", II, 248.

"By means of the pledge of faith there was doubtless also created in the Middle Ages a liability through one's property. In case the obligation secured by the pledge was not performed, the creditor could proceed to distrain chattels, either by way of self-help permitted for particular reason or by resort to a judicial distraint."[1] In this fact there appears in especially tangible form the unitary character of personal liability, which is merely realized in a different manner according as it extends to the entire personality of the debtor or only to his physical person or to the property rights included in his legal personality. And it is instructive that the liability of a person through his property became in time the primary matter, to which recourse against the debtor's body was subordinated, being resorted to only when attack upon the property was fruitless. In this sense, however, "corporal liability appears in the medieval German sources as the normal accompaniment of property liability."[2]

As regards the relation between the pledge of faith and obligational contracts, it is agreed that the former was, in and of itself, a means of guaranteeing an obligation, and consequently presupposed an obligation which it was intended to secure. This purpose was effected particularly well by the promise to satisfy judgment ("Urteilserfüllungsgelöbnis"), in which we have, possibly, the oldest way in which a liability was contractually assumed. As already stated, obligation ("Schuld") was in the earliest times a delictual concept. It resulted directly from a misdeed, when action was brought by the injured person and the defendant condemned. If now the party who lost in the action took oath, in the form of a "fides facta", to fulfill the judgment and render to the plaintiff the satisfaction so awarded, he necessarily added to the legal duty, — which was not created by a juristic act between the parties but by law ("gesetzlich"), the liability that was necessary to secure it and necessary for judicial execution; and this addition was effected by contract. In the course of the law's further development it also became possible to create an obligation voluntarily, by way of contract. And this was the point where, as already remarked (*supra*, pp. 473 *et seq.*), the creation of legal duty and of liability came to be united, though not at all in theory at least in fact, in normal cases. To be sure, in the case of an obligation created by a promise ("Versprechensschuld") the promise of performance, and not the pledge of faith, was the basis of the legal duty. However, "the obligational promise

[1] *Gierke*, "Schuld und Haftung", 202. [2] *Ibid.*, 209.

might also be embodied in the pledge of faith"; [1] not because it was free from any requirement of form (Puntschart, Gierke), but because it also could be covered by the form of the pledge of faith.

As a formal act, the pledge of faith had a certain similarity to the stipulation of the classic Roman law, notwithstanding that the Germanic law, unlike the Roman, made the promise of the obligor the essential element in the conclusion of the contract, and not the declaration of the obligee's will, that is the stipulation. This outward resemblance, however, frequently led the copyists to use the Roman expression "stipulatio" in their documents and formulas, although very often in a wrong sense. The designation of the transaction as "fidem facere" also had its prototype in Roman terminology.

Already in the Middle Ages changes took place in the pledge of faith and its formalistic elements. The personal liability of the debtor with his entire property, and in case of necessity with his body, came to be regarded as a consequence of the legal duty, independently of the pledge of faith. Where this happened the pledge of faith, although it continued "in most common use", was transformed from a means of creating liability into a mere means of increasing liability; and under some circumstances, in consequence of the special restrictive agreements which it was possible to make use of, into a means of lessening liability. For the former purpose resort was had especially to pledges of one's honor, — particularly one's status, — by means of special "honor-clauses." This accounts, in part, for the fact that the hand-clasp had come to represent merely an "old traditional formal element, which was no longer essential." [2] On the other hand, pledge of faith was frequently united with or replaced by an oath. Indeed, this was originally itself a formal pledge of faith that served as security for a legal duty and was sanctified by religion, and which, because of its binding effect upon the conscience and its sanction by the Church, was regarded as the stronger means of creating obligations.[3] In place of the oath there also appeared, later, a declaration made before a court or city council, or in a sealed instrument, and finally (at least in France) in a notarial document.

(2) *The staff-formula* ("wadiatio"). *The formal or wed-contract* ("Wettvertrag").[4] — The "wadiatio" was another formal

[1] *Gierke, op. cit.*, 206, referring to *Puntschart*, "Schuldvertrag", 290–292, etc. [2] *Ibid.*, 257. [3] *Ibid.*, 240 *et seq.*

[4] As regards the "wadiatio" the views of *v. Amira*, "Stab" (*supra*, p. 11), 151 *et seq.*, and "Wadiation", and of *Gierke*, "Schuld und Haftung", 259 *et seq.*, are sharply opposed. Von Amira regards the "wadiatio" as a trans-

transaction for the creation of personal liability, and was notionally distinguishable from the pledge of faith. In the form in which it appears in the folk-laws we find it most clearly revealed in the sources of the Lombard law. It was applied in the same manner in the Frankish and Bavarian, and also in the Frisian and Anglo-Saxon and old Swedish law. The medieval law developed from it the so-called wed-contract. The transaction derived its name from its essential ceremonial act of delivering a staff. The staff or rod was called in the Lombard sources " wadia " (" guadia "), " vadimonium "; the transaction was designated as " wadiam dare ", " wadiare ", " wadiatio." The word " wadia " (" wadium ") was the Latinized form of the Lombard " wadi" (Gothic " vadi ", Old Norse " ved ", A. Saxon " wed ", Old High G. " wetti "), and was usually used as the equivalent of the word " vidan " = to bind (*cf. supra*, p. 375).[1] The Lombard " wadia " was in theory always a rod, exactly as was the Frankish " festuca." Now this " wadiatio " or staff-formula, wherever it was employed in the Lombard law, served as the first step in the creation of a suretyship.[2] It was the same in the Bavarian [3] and old Frankish laws, as well as in other legal systems to which the " wadiatio " was known. This form was, then, a transaction resorted to by a person who wished to give another a surety, and thereby afford him security for the performance of an obligation. It was a formal act performed by the pledgor, not by the surety, and was thus distinguished from the " fides facta ", which was performed by the surety in accepting the suretyship. As the Lombard sources clearly show, the " wadiatio " was effected by the pledgor's, — that is by the debtor's, — handing to his creditor a staff (" wadiam dare "). The person given as pledge accepted the staff from the creditor, in order to give it back to the debtor after satisfaction of his obligation of suretyship. The staff therefore passed from the debtor (pledgor) to the creditor, from the creditor to the surety, and finally from the surety back to the debtor. What was the significance of this procedure? What legal conception underlay it? This question can be completely and satisfactorily answered only by Amira's hypothesis of the messenger-staff (" Botschaftsstab").

action serving merely to create a suretyship. Gierke sees in it a generic transaction for the creation of "property-" liability (in his sense), as contrasted with the pledge of faith, which creates a mere "corporal" liability. The text follows the view of v. Amira.

[1] Exceptions to this derivation are suggested by *v. Amira*, "Stab", 152.

[2] "Edictum Ratchis", c. 8 (746 A.D.). *Cf.* with this *v. Amira*, "Wadiation", 6.

[3] " Lex Baiwariorum ", appx. IV.

The "wadia" which thus passed from the debtor to the creditor, from the creditor to the surety, and returned from the surety to the debtor, was a messenger-staff. The debtor gave it to his creditor in order, through the creditor, to send him whose suretyship he wished to bespeak a request that he appear as surety. It was, consequently, a commission that was to be carried from the debtor to the surety, and which the creditor was empowered to perform by the staff he had received. He fulfilled his mandate by delivering to the surety the staff, which at the same time evidenced his power. "The creditor is the debtor's messenger to the surety."[1] In reality the creditor doubtless sought out the surety only rarely, in order to deliver to him the message and perform the mandate; in most cases, probably, the debtor brought with him a surety whom he knew, or caused him to seek out the creditor. Legally, however, the surety might be treated in all cases, including those just mentioned, as one who was acquainted with the mandate of the debtor through the creditor, by delivery of the staff. If the surety accepted the staff he thereby declared his acceptance of the charge and assumption of the suretyship; for which purpose the Frankish law, at all events, required a pledge of faith with handclasp ("fidem facere"). The debtor, who was not necessarily present at this transaction between the creditor and the surety, acquired knowledge of the acceptance of the suretyship through the delivery to him by the surety, in his turn, of the messenger-staff; so that this thus completed its circle. If, as was possible, the surety declined acceptance of the staff, then of course he entered into no legal relations with the creditor and debtor. Whether in such a case the debtor became liable to the creditor as a result of the delivery of the wed, notwithstanding that it had not resulted in the end contemplated (the creation of a suretyship), is a question that must apparently be answered, as respects the oldest law, in the negative. In such a case he might, however, be liable to the creditor upon some other ground, though not through the delivery of the rod; for example, because his obligational promise of itself created a liability. Since, as we have remarked, the surety might refuse to accept the staff and the charge, it clearly follows that the wed-contract, notwithstanding that it always contemplated a suretyship, need not under all circumstances necessarily lead to such. The inexplicable point, under any other theory, is the striking fact that the surety, both in the Lombard and the Frankish law, became liable to the creditor by *acceptance* of the

[1] *v. Amira*, "Stab", 154.

staff, whereas otherwise a symbol of liability was *given* to the creditor by him who wished to bind himself. This makes it clear that the "wadia" can have been no symbol of pledge, no simulated pledge or token of pledge. It was not designed to symbolize the property or the chattels of the debtor. And from this it also follows that it is impossible to accept the theory — unacceptable for other reasons (*supra*, p. 495) — which contrasts the wed-contract, as a transaction creating property liability, with the pledge of faith as a transaction creating corporal liability. The "wadiatio" is the transaction by which a suretyship is *created* by the delivery of a messenger's-staff; the pledge of faith is the transaction by which suretyship is *accepted* by a proffer of the hand. The "wadiatio", exactly as the pledge of faith, signified personal liability generally. In what manner the suretyship created by the "wadiatio" should be realized and enforced, whether as a pledge of the entire personality of the surety or only as a limited pledge either of his property or of his body, was a question which had nothing to do with the "wadiatio", as such, in its origin. Again, in the last analysis, it was the debtor's mandate that secured to the surety, in case he saved the creditor harmless by performance of the suretyship he assumed, a right of distraint against the debtor. This right of indemnity resulted directly from the mandate; from which it follows that the mandate was one of those obligational contracts which, even in the theory of the old Germanic law,[1] created simultaneously a liability.

The strictness with which the formalism of the "wadiatio" was observed is shown in the fact that although its steps were adapted to the participation of three persons (pledgor or debtor, creditor, surety), they were also required to be observed when the debtor wished to pledge himself to the creditor as his own surety; that is, in so-called self-suretyship. In this case the staff could not pass indirectly to the debtor through a third person, the surety, but must return to him directly from the creditor's hand. But, in order to preserve intact the idea of the threefold formality, the debtor was nevertheless bound to use both hands in a manner prescribed by law. As the act is described for us in the edict of the Frankish king Chilperich, he must pass the staff to the creditor with his left hand and take or receive it back ("auferre") with the right hand.[2] Thus he actually sent the creditor as a messenger to himself, he received and accepted with the staff the commission that had proceeded from himself, and, finally, he reported to himself

[1] *v. Amira*, "Wadiation", 24.
[2] "Ed. Chilp.", 6.

the result, "not unlike the manner in which, in the modern law of bills of exchange, the drawer of a draft on himself transmits to himself through the payee his own order to pay, and then accepts it."[1] The fact that a self-surety was obliged to proceed, under the old Frankish law, with this strict observance of form, because it was desired to preserve under all circumstances the ceremonialism of suretyship by third persons, shows that self-suretyship was first recognized in jural life merely as a special case of "dual-" suretyship and as a substitute therefor (*cf. supra*, p. 480). Later, self-suretyship was again dispensed with, because it came to be regarded as an ordinary consequence of a contract that the debtor should himself assume liability for the performance he promised, even though without expressly binding himself as surety; but the Lombard law still required that the debtor should give himself as surety ("de guadia", "quam dedit", "mediatorem ponere se ipsum").[2]

The wed-contract was in origin a transaction creating liability. But it might also serve as a form of obligational contract. The self-suretyship assumed through a "wadiatio" was calculated to suggest such a use; for when it came to be regarded as a legal requisite that the debtor, in concluding an obligational contract, should personally pledge himself to his creditor by delivery of a wed, it was natural to see in the delivery of the wed the formal act that concluded the contract. In this manner there was developed from the "wadiatio" of the folk-laws the formal contract of medieval law as we find it in the lands of many Germanic racial branches. So, for example, the formal contract of the Frisians evidently included the concept of an obligational promise;[3] and in the Saxon law the "wadiatio" seems likewise to have been early transformed into a pledge of faith, whereas "Wette" (wed) and "wetten" (to give a wed) had therein the meaning of "penalty" and "payment of a penalty."[4] On the other hand, in South Germany and in Friesland the expression "wed" acquired for a time the general meaning of a legally formal oath ("Gelöbniss").[5] This terminology, however, in turn died out, and where the meaning of a penalty did not survive, — that is, in other regions than those of the Saxon law, — the word "Wette" (wed) acquired its restricted meaning of the present day, a bet or wager. The old,

[1] *v. Amira*, "Wadiation", 29.
[2] *Brunner*, "Forschungen", 593.
[3] *Gierke*, "Schuld und Haftung", 320.
[4] *Ibid.*, 322. [5] *Ibid.*, 326.

strict formalism of the "wadiatio" was also lost in the medieval formal ("Wett-", wed, or wager) contract. The first result was a certain confusion, when various other objects (ring, glove, sickle, knife, kreutzer) came to be employed as symbols in addition to the staff; but later the giving and taking of a symbol in concluding a contract completely disappeared from the law, giving way to such colorless practices as the hand-clasp.

The "wadiatio" acquired a particular importance in the jural life of the early Middle Ages (as Brunner's researches [1] first showed) through the fact that the primitive Germans, — first the Lombards, and then also the Franks, Bavarians, and Alamanians, — borrowed from the late Roman law the act of delivering a deed as a formal means for the conclusion of contracts. In that law there had appeared, in place of the exchange of formal question and answer essential to the classical stipulation, the delivery of a dispositive document (*infra,* § 88) embodying the desired juristic act; the act of tradition being treated as a formalistic act. Now just as here "the direct delivery of the dispositive document displaced the verbal stipulation, so according to Germanic law the document was regarded as a contractual symbol that might represent the 'wadia'." [2] True, delivery of a document was applied primarily in the law of things, — as "investitura per cartam", — for the purpose of conveying ownership in lands (*supra,* pp. 244 *et seq.*); but it was also utilized for the conclusion of obligational contracts. Like the "wadiatio", the delivery of a document might signify merely the creation of a liability in the form of self-suretyship. This was the case when one who received a money loan delivered to his creditor a so-called "cautio", in which he promised to pay the debt upon condition of receiving back the "cautio." In this case there was superimposed upon the obligation that arose from the delivery of the loan, — or in other words by real contract — *infra,* under (III), — a liability created by the tradition of the document; just as it was common, in such transactions, to give the creditor simultaneously a pledge, by means of the "cautio." However, a document might be used, as well as a "wadia", to create the legal duty itself; either a unilateral obligation being established by the delivery and acceptance of the docu-

[1] "Die fränkische-romanische Urkunde als Wertpapier", in Z. Hand. R., XXII (1877), 64 *et seq.*, 505 *et seq.*, reprinted in his "Forschungen" (1894), 524 *et seq.*; "Zur Rechtsgeschichte der römischen und germanischen Urkunde" (Vol. 1, the only one published, 1880). And today see also *Gierke,* "Schuld und Haftung", 330 *et seq.*

[2] *Brunner,* "Rechtsgeschichte der Urkunde", 66.

ment (for example, the duty to pay liquidated damages,—"Vertragsstrafe"), or a transaction concluded (for example a contract of sale) that bound both contracting parties to mutual performances. In this case the delivery of the document served, like the delivery of the "wadia", as a formalistic mode of concluding the contract. The document became, "like the hand-clasp, a substitute for the 'wadia'"; "the act of delivering the document perfected the contract exactly as did the Germanic act of delivering the staff." [1]

(III) **The Real Contract.** — As already mentioned (*supra*, p. 459), the oldest transactions of trade were non-credit transactions. The performances of the two contracting parties took place act for act. When one party performed the other was ipso facto obligated to follow with a counter performance, and this immediately. From the precedent performance there arose the legal duty ("Verpflichtung", "Schuld") of immediate counter performance. That is, the transaction was a real contract, provided there be understood by this term, which is derived from the Roman law, every contract in which the giving of a thing ("res") creates the legal duty of counter performance. Now in spot transactions the duty of immediate counter performance was essential: after the goods were delivered or the price was paid there immediately followed the delivery of the object that was to be bartered or purchased. A duty of immediate counter performance, however, must have conflicted intolerably with the necessities of trade. In many cases an immediate counter performance was impossible; still oftener it was not at all desirable. The need of credit was bound to result in permitting the second party to postpone counter performance; was bound to make possible a contract under which the party to whom performance was first made was not himself required immediately to perform. The other party's prior performance merely imposed upon him a legal duty to perform in future, thereby making him a debtor of the party first performing. Thus the Germanic law, also, developed a real contract corresponding to the Roman. In it, as well, there arose, not exactly by mere agreement of the parties but by the precedent performance by one party (the "res"), the legal duty of the other to perform. It is clear that only those obligations could be thus created in which performances were due from both parties. Here belonged, according to the theory of the Germanic law, — herein differing from the classic, though doubtless agreeing with the older, Roman law, — the contract of sale. Through the delivery to the pur-

[1] *Brunner*, "Forschungen", 630.

chaser of the object sold there arose on the purchaser's part a legal duty to pay the purchase price later, according to the agreement of the parties; through a pre-payment of the purchase price to the seller there arose on the latter's part a legal duty to deliver the object sold later, according to agreement. In the former case the purchase price was credited and the purchaser was a debtor; in the latter the payment was credited and the seller was the debtor. It is true that a liability of the other party did not yet exist as a result of such precedent performance; as we know, this could be created only by giving a legal right of action, either through creating a real right of pledge or through the assumption of a personal liability. The acceptance of the precedent performance originally obligated the receiver merely to a return of the object received, and to nothing more. "The liability of the receiver for the debt that was promised, or in other words the claim of the creditor for the performance of this obligation, is the result, in Germanic as in the Roman law, only of modern development."[1] There may therefore have been associated with precedent performance by the seller, in delivering the object of sale, a pledge of faith by the purchaser by which he gave the seller security for the future payment of the purchase price; and with payment in advance by the purchaser of the purchase price, a pledge of faith on the seller's part by which he guaranteed to the purchaser the future delivery of the object sold. In the Lombard law the "wadiatio" was required to be performed as in the institution of self-pledge (*supra*, p. 501). But this signified here, exactly as did a pledge of faith accompanying a real contract, merely the creation of liability, not the creation of legal duty; for this already existed as the result of precedent performance (the "res"); the "wadiatio" merely accompanied the obligation (legal duty).[2]

Precedent performance, as a fact creating liability, may therefore also be designated as a "gift with a charge" ("Gabe mit Auflage"). It was made, not merely in order to satisfy the person in whose favor performance was given, but equally in order to obligate him to counter performance. And in the "wadiatio", — that is, in

[1] *v. Amira*, in Z². R. G., XXXI (1910), 499. In my opinion v. Amira here raises conclusive objections to the concept of "Empfangshaftung" that is suggested by Gierke.

[2] *Franken*, "Französisches Pfandrecht", 218. On the contrary *Gierke*, "Schuld und Haftung", 337 *et seq.*, sees in the real contract, not a formalistic transaction that creates an obligation but one serving exclusively for the creation of liability, whereas he regards the obligational relation as originating even here in the mutual promises of the parties.

[3] *v. Amira*, "Recht", 135.

the delivery of a staff to the party first performing, upon acceptance of such precedent performance,—in so far as it created a liability in the nature of a self-pledge for a legal duty already existing, there was involved at the same time an acknowledgment by the debtor of its receipt.

In time changes took place which relaxed the requirements relative to precedent performance. Although it was originally required that the party so performing must immediately perfect the full performance to which he was obligated, in order to create an obligation on the part of the other party, it gradually came to be held sufficient if merely partial performance was made. In particular, the immediate payment of the whole purchase price by the purchaser was no longer required; a payment on the price was held sufficient. Thus there came into use the "Arrha" ("Dran-", "Drauf-", "Haft-", or "Handgeld"; money paid "on" the price, "liability" or "hand" money), — the earnest; usually consisting of a small sum of money, a small coin. The Germanic earnest, as is particularly clearly described, for example, in the folk-law of the Visigoths,[1] obligated only the party receiving it, who in the great majority of cases was the seller; and not the purchaser who paid it. By the acceptance of the earnest, — that is, of a merely symbolical precedent performance, — the vendor, the lessor, and so on, was obligated to perform in turn. The earnest, therefore, also had the effect of a "renunciatory penny"; the receiver, by his acceptance, renounced his right thereafter to dispose of the object of the contract to the prejudice of the creditor (for example, to alienate a thing to a third party before the end of a stipulated period). If he nevertheless did this, he committed an unlawful act; the purchaser could bring an action in the form of a "dare debes" for the delivery of the thing, upon the basis of the contract. On the other hand it is presumable that the receipt of the earnest could not originally create a liability on the seller's part, because the real contract, in itself, always created an obligation only, and not a liability. If, therefore, a liability of the seller must be added to his legal duty, it remained equally necessary after full precedent performance had been replaced by an earnest that he should enter into a liability transaction, — for example a "wadiatio" in the sense of a self-pledge. However, just as the vendor did not become liable, by the receipt of the earnest, to

[1] "Cod. Euriciani", fr. 297 (M. G., Legum sectio I, tom. 1, 14). "Lex Wisigothorum", 5. 4, 4. *Cf.* with this *Zeumer* in N. Arch. Gesel. ä. deut. G. K., XXIV (1899), 580 *et seq.*

deliver the thing, so the purchaser was as little made liable by the payment of the earnest, the only result of which was the conclusion of a contract for a later payment of the full purchase price. A liability of the purchaser, moreover, could only be created by a special and independent creation of liability; that is, ordinarily, by a "wadiatio" performed by himself.[1]

But this distinction between the delivery of the earnest-money (which concluded the contract) and the "wadiatio" (which established the liability), though one that accorded with the law's original view, was not maintained. On the contrary, here again a confusion resulted between the transactions thus created, respectively obligations and liabilities, and this resulted in a simplification of the law. But it was not here, as in the "wadiatio", the "wadia" that was retained and created the legal duty, but the earnest-money, which came to perform the services of the "wadia." In this connection the circumstance was especially important that the contract of sale was transformed, through the use of documents as "wadia", into a formal contract (as above mentioned, p. 502), so that in its case both the function of creating the liability and that of creating the legal duty were assigned to the transfer of the "wadia." In time it came to be regarded as superfluous "that the purchaser, who already gave earnest-money, should also give a wadia."[2] The earnest assumed the functions of the "wadia", so that its delivery created not only a legal duty and a liability on the seller's part, but also a legal duty and a liability on the buyer's part. The Bavarian folk-law already attributed to the giving and taking of hand-money this effect of creating mutual liability;[3] which fact can only be explained by the fact "that the hand-money had absorbed the functions of the 'wadia'."[4] The earnest-contract thus became in fact a compound of a real and formal contract. In so far as the coin that was given was regarded as a "wadia", it was a formal contract; on the other hand in so

[1] *Gierke*, "Schuld und Haftung", 344, alleges against this assumption that it is devoid of any support in the sources. Nevertheless it seems to me a hypothesis necessary to the explanation of the transformation of the real contract, in which one party gives full precedent performance, into an earnest-contract. If even in the perfect real contract the liability of the party receiving performance is effected not by the acceptance, as such, of such performance, — for the contrary theory of Gierke is in my opinion incapable of support (see p. 504, note 1, *supra*), — but in the declarations of the parties, the same must necessarily have been true originally in the earnest-contract.

[2] *Heusler*, "Institutionen", II, 256.

[3] "Lex Baiwariorum", XVI, 10. *Cf. Gierke*, "Schuld und Haftung", 348 *et seq.*

[4] *Gierke*, *op. cit.*, 350.

far as the earnest still symbolized a perfected precedent performance on the part of the purchaser that created an obligation on the part of the seller, it retained the character of a real contract. As a special type of contract, the earnest everywhere came to signify "Haft-" money that imposed a liability on both parties. It was employed throughout the Middle Ages as a payment binding the vendor or lessor equally with the purchaser or lessee. It preserved the *appearance* of a real contract.[1] The fact that the earnest was always merely a simulated ("Schein-") performance, explains the widespread custom in the Middle Ages that the receiver, instead of retaining it, consumed it in drink (hence "Weinkauf", "Leitkauf", "ervekop", "bodewîn", "mercipotus"; earnest-wine) with the aid of the purchaser and the witnesses, — "winkopesluden", the "wine-cup-people"; or gave it to the church or the poor ("God's-penny", and "Holy Ghost penny"). By this was meant "that the payment received was in fact *no* performance as regarded the party receiving it; that it was no satisfaction, that the transaction was merely a fictitious performance for the purpose of a formal perfection of the juristic act."[2] How deeply rooted the view was that the transaction was completed with the delivery of the hand-money, the God's-penny, the earnest-wine, is clearly shown, however, by the use occasionally made of the custom in poetry, in order to express the idea of the inevitableness of death.[3]

(IV) Even the older German law recognized **formal acts which**, though indeed they might equally well be used in the conclusion of a contract, did not like those above discussed (under (II)) constitute an essential requisite to the creation of a relationship of legal duty or of liability, but on the other hand **contributed to the contract some special effect**, particularly as regarded its proof. Here belonged, above all, the conclusion of the contract in court ("Gerichtlichkeit"), the occurrence and prevalence of which, especially in transactions involving land, has already been discussed (p. 246). In the Sachsenspiegel's system of proof, notably, such judicial conclusion of the contract in court alone made it provable in law; and in defect thereof the defendant might, save in certain exceptional cases, repudiate his legal duty. In the cities

[1] *Sohm*, "Eheschliessung", 30. [2] *Ibid.*

[3] Thus for example we read in *Sebastian Brandt's* "Narrenschiff":

"Der winkouff ist gedrunken schon
Wir mögen nit dem kouff abston,
Die erste stund die lest ouch bracht."

Cf. Siegel, "Das Versprechen als Verpflichtungsgrund" (1873), 31.

it later became usual — as has likewise been mentioned (*supra*, pp. 219 *et seq.*) — to execute an official document embodying the obligational promise, which document was made or acknowledged before the town council or the skevins; or else to make an entry in the town register; formalities which not only made the transaction incontestable but also made it possible to take out execution immediately upon default in performance.

Even where the German law, to insure publicity in the conclusion of the contract, required the presence of witnesses, this was a formal requirement which (unlike certain analogous institutes of Scandinavian law) was important solely in relation to the contract's provability, and not essential to its validity.

§ 72. **The Conclusion of a Contract in Modern Law.**[1] (I) **The Principle of Informality** (" Formfreiheit "). — The Germanic system of real and formal contracts was more and more broken down, and finally wholly destroyed, in the last part of the medieval period; and was replaced, under the decisive influence of the Roman-Canon law, by the principle of informality of contract. To be sure, the contractual system of the classic Roman law was based upon a view fundamentally related to that of the Germanic; for alongside real contracts (" mutuum ", "depositum ", " commodatum ", " pignus "), the verbal contract (stipulation), and the literal contract, only four agreements of typical and exactly defined content were recognized as pure consensual contracts, — namely sale, hire, mandate, and partnership. These constituted, as such, an exception to the principle that informal contracts, " nuda pacta ", were generally unenforceable by action. It was the theory of the medieval canonists that broke for the first time with this principle, which had been still defended by the Glossators. Modern theory misconceived the formal contract that was developed in the later Roman law from the stipulation and was concluded by the delivery of a document (*supra*, p. 502). It regarded the document as invariably mere evidence, and " in consequence of this error derived from actual legal practices the rule that the contract could be perfected by an informal declaration of the parties' agreement." [2] In time this view attained complete supremacy, in Germany as in France, although it might still occasionally happen, at first, that the same source which laid down the principle " pacta sunt servanda " also prescribed the old formality.[3] Finally,

[1] *L. Seuffert*, "Zur Geschichte der obligatorischen Verträge" (1881).
[2] *Brunner*, "Rechtsgeschichte der Urkunde", 66.
[3] *Pollock* and *Maitland*, II, 194.

when the Law of Nature also took a firm stand in favor of informality, the common law went so far as to reject even a theoretical requirement of form.[1] In fact informality was also far better adapted than the strict view of the earlier law to the greater necessities of trade in modern times, notwithstanding the danger it undoubtedly involved of an easier overreaching of one party by the other. This principle has also been retained in the law of the present day. From immemorial times commerce among merchants (" Handelsverkehr ") had been less fettered than non-mercantile transactions. This fact was expressly recognized in many places in modern legislation. So, for example, the Prussian " Allgemeines Landrecht " (I, 5, § 149) released certain transactions between merchants (" Kaufhandlungen ") from the requirement of a written form. The General Commercial Code, going further than this, gave to all commerce between merchants (" Handelsverkehr ") almost complete freedom from prescribed forms. The advanced position earlier attained by the law merchant has been adopted by the new Civil Code with respect, also, to legal transactions in general. In accordance with the principles of the common law it permits the creation of obligatory juristic acts (as does the Swiss Law of Obligations also, § 11) by a mere agreement of the parties. Even contracts "for return " (" auf Rückgabe "),[2] — loans, leases, bailments, creation of proprietary pledges, — which correspond to the real contracts of the Roman law, no longer have their formal legal basis in the present law in a performance by the creditor (the giving of a " res "); it is merely the special nature of the obligation assumed in these contracts that involves the necessity of delivering a thing in addition to an agreement of the parties.

It is true that the principle of informality has nowhere been realized without exceptions. The regional legal systems, in particular, maintained the native forms in the case of particular obligational contracts, or introduced new formal requirements as a counterweight against the modern principle that was attaining supremacy. The Prussian " Landrecht " went farthest in this direction. The new Civil Code, also, recognizes a series of exceptions that " are more numerous and practically more important than those recognized in the common law, and also than

[1] From his standpoint *Gierke* regards the establishment of informality in obligational contracts as a triumph of what he assumes to have been an old principle of German law over the Roman principle of formality. "Schuld und Haftung", 384 *et seq.*

[2] *Crome*, "System", II, 168.

those of the earlier Territorial systems with the exception of the Prussian."[1] On the other hand the commercial law has only to a slight extent broken the principle of informality by exceptions.

(II) **Exceptions to the Principle of Informality.** (1) *Written form.* — The most important formality with which the validity or the legal enforceability of a contract was formerly associated, and is associated in certain cases in the modern law, is writing. In the second half of the Middle Ages, and in connection with the renewed vitality of dispositive documents (*infra,* § 88), the obligational effect which had been associated in the older law with the delivery of the document was transferred to the perfected execution of the instrument by subscription; although in certain cases the delivery continued to retain its old character as the act by which the obligation was created. Either the nature of the contract or the value of the object that was its subject matter was decisive of the necessity or non-necessity of a written form, in one or another sense. So, in particular, the Prussian "Landrecht" required a written form for all contracts the subject of which had a value of fifty talers or more (I, 5, § 131). If a contract for which a written form was necessary under this rule was concluded orally, no legal action could be based upon it; but of course a party who despite the imperfect form in which the contract was concluded had accepted from the other party partial or complete performance, was also bound, on his side, either to perform or to return what he had received, or to compensate the other party therefor (I, 5, §§ 155–56). The Code Civil (§ 1341) required a written form for all contracts concerning things of a value exceeding 150 francs, but only in so far as such contracts could be proved only by documents, and not by witnesses. Contracts that were required to be concluded in writing without regard to the value involved, included under the Prussian "Allgemeines Landrecht" contracts affecting the title to lands, or rights "in alieno solo", or permanent personal charges and duties, etc.; according to the Austrian Code, promises of gifts, herital contracts between husband and wife, etc.

Aside from the written form prescribed by statute, this could also be required by agreement of the parties. In this case it was ordinarily presumed that the writing should serve only as evidence, and not to determine the substantive content of the contract.

In the private law of the present day a writing is required in the following cases:

[1] *Cosack,* "Bürgerliches Recht", I (3d ed.), 291.

For the validity of a contract by which a life annuity ("Leibrente") is promised, the promise must at least be in writing (§ 761); that is, in so far as a judicial or notarial authentication is not prescribed. It is equally necessary to the validity of a declaration of a surety's promise (§ 766), of a bare ("abstrakt") obligational promise (§ 780), and of an acknowledgment of an existing obligation (§ 781). Further, the written form is necessary in contracts for the hire ("Miete") or lease ("Pacht") of land that are concluded for longer than one year (§§ 566, 581, 2). An order to pay or deliver ("Anweisung") is also required to be in written form (§ 783); and of course the same is true of all contracts concerning rights embodied in commercial paper, especially in so-called "Skriptur"-obligations (*infra*, § 88, — negotiable choses in action protected by the principle of "public faith").

In contrast to these requirements of the Civil Code, the Commercial Code has abandoned the requisite of the written form as regards a promise of suretyship, a bare obligational promise, and an acknowledgment of existing obligations, subject to the condition that such suretyship be a commercial transaction on the part of the surety, and that such promise creating or acknowledging an existing obligation be such on the part of the debtor, and that the surety of the debtor be a regular ("Voll-") merchant (§§ 350–351).

In the present Swiss law a written form is required, in addition to suretyship (Swiss Code of the Law of Obligations of March 30, 1911, Art. 493), for the assignment of choses in action (§ 165), for contracts of warranty in cattle sales (§ 198), for the taking of stock under leases (§ 276), for the creation of life annuities (§ 517), and for the transfer of one's property in exchange for a life annuity ("Verpfründungsvertrag", § 522). To these must be added, of course, the cases of rights embodied in written instruments.

(2) *Reduction to writing, in court or before a notary.* — The requirement that contracts should in many cases be concluded before public authorities, which originally existed in the older law in the interest of judicial proof (*supra*, p. 508), was not only preserved in the regional legal systems but in many cases was made by them an absolute formal requisite. Thus, for example, from the 1500 s onward many state statutes required certain transactions to be concluded in court, especially when between peasants, imposing upon the court in this connection, in the interest of the persons concerned, the duty of making a formal and substantive test of the transaction in the exercise of a sort of superior guardian-

ship; so that the judge's approval alone gave legal validity to the contract. This requirement of a "judicial" contract was most common in case of transactions in lands (*supra*, pp. 221, 247 *et seq.*). In other cases, also, the judicial form was frequently required, but merely to facilitate proof of the transaction, or for the sake of other advantages which it involved. And besides this judicial character prescribed by statute such might be voluntarily agreed on by the parties. Where this was required merely to facilitate proof there was often recognized, in connection with it, the acknowledgment of the document before a notary and two witnesses; and the notarial form was eventually made equivalent, in most cases, to the judicial form.

The present Civil Code requires judicial or notarial authentication of a declaration promising a future and gratuitous act of performance (§ 518); as well as of a contract by which a person obligates himself to convey land (§ 313), or alienates, or charges with a right of usufruct, a part or all of his property (§ 311), or by which expectant heirs regulate their statutory or compulsory shares of the inheritance (§ 312, 2); and of contracts for the purchase of an inheritance (§ 2371). The Commercial Code recognizes no peculiarities in contracts of such character. In addition to the above there are special formal requirements in the law of family and the law of inheritance. The Swiss Law of Obligations requires a public authentication only for contracts of sale whose subject is land; for contracts, whether preliminary or final, that create rights of purchase or repurchase in land (§ 216); and for gifts of land or real rights, as such (§ 243).

(3) *Confirmation of the contract.* — Despite the disappearance of the old formal contracts a few of the forms that were developed in them were retained in the modern law, although they were necessarily completely altered in their legal character.

This is particularly evident in the case of earnest-money.[1] Like the earnest of the Roman law, this served, during the dominance of the principle of informality of contract, merely for the confirmation of a contract that had already come into existence by agreement of the parties. It was only in the case of contracts for the hire of servants that it preserved for a time its old character; and even to-day such contracts can only be concluded, in many systems of State law, by the delivery of a handsel-dollar, — for example under the Prussian Servants' Code of November 8, 1811. Already in the Middle Ages the handsel had been transformed, here

[1] See *Gierke*, "Schuld und Haftung", 371 *et seq.*

and there, into smart-money ("Wandelpön", "arrha pœnitentialis"); the giver having the right for a certain time, because of such payment, and the receiver upon repayment of twice the same, to withdraw from the contract. In some statutes it has retained this character; and in other cases it is always free to the parties to agree upon smart-money in their contract. According to the Civil Code, on the other hand, earnest-money ("Draufgabe") is always mere corroborative proof of the contract, — in the sense that it is unequivocal proof of the fact of its existence; it has lost its character as smart-money (§§ 336–338); which it still retains in the French law. In the Swiss law, also, the earnest ("An-", "Draufgeld") is given only for the purpose of creating the liability, and not as smart-money (Oblig. R., § 158).

§ 73. **Unilateral Promises.**[1] (I) **The Older Law.** — According to the principles of Germanic law already discussed, the creation of an obligation by means of a juristic act could only be realized through contract; that is, only by the participation of both the parties interested, — of the one, in that he performed in advance, fully or symbolically, the obligation resting upon him (real contract), or delivered in advance a symbol of contract (formal contract); of the other, in that he accepted such performance or such symbol. There were variations of this principle, but they must be considered as of merely superficial character, and not as violations of the underlying idea. Under some circumstances an obligational relation might be created by a unilateral promise or other juristic act.

(1) Although the legal sources contain nothing on this point, other notices which we possess put the matter beyond doubt. As in the Scandinavian sagas,[2] so also in German poetry, epics, fairy tales, and ballads, it is frequently related how a king promises his daughter as wife to whomsoever shall kill a dragon,[3] or promises a part of his kingdom to whomsoever shall find a daughter of the king who has been kidnapped. Kriemhilde obligates herself, as the poem of the Rosengarten informs us, to give to every hero who shall conquer one of the defenders of her rose garden, roses for a crown, and also "an embrace and kisses", and this she exactly performs in favor of each of the victors. In such case there is

[1] *Siegel*, "Das Versprechen als Verpflichtungsgrund" (1873); *v. Lüdinghausen-Wolff*, "Die bindende Kraft des einseitigen Versprechens im heutigen gemeinen Privatrecht" (1889).

[2] See *v. Amira*, "Obligationenrecht", II, 382 *et seq.*

[3] Compare the fairy-tale of the two brothers in the collection of the brothers Grimm, No. 60.

involved a so-called "Auslobung" (public offer). Whoever fulfilled the conditions set by the offeror became ipso facto his creditor, and acquired at the same time a legal claim to the performance promised; this could not be denied him, for the offeror had irrevocably bound himself by his unilateral promise. The conception of the Germanic law was, clearly, that the acceptance of the symbol, of the hand-clasp, or of the oath ("Gelöbniss"), which in the case of a formal contract followed act for act, was here replaced by the performance of the act required. The unilateral promise "bound the offeror to his word" ("Gebundenheit ans Wort"); created an obligation in the sense of a legal duty to keep one's promise ("Haltensollen", *supra*, p. 466). Upon performance of the condition there arose the legal duty to give the promised reward, and therewith an enforceable obligational relation between the offeror ("Auslober") and the acceptor ("Vollbringer", performer).

(2) *The binding force of the offer* ("Antrag"), which was always recognized in Germanic law, rested in the same idea. If no possibility existed that the bilateral formal act could be performed "uno actu", as was necessarily the case in a contract concluded between absent parties, permission to the other party to perform at a later time the act necessary for the perfection of the contract was bound to appear a dictate of good faith. The party from whom the offer proceeded was bound by his unilateral word, that is by his offer, until he received a declaration by the other party. Only after the running of the time expressly set for acceptance of the offer, or only when according to usages of trade he need not longer await the receipt of an acceptance, was he free, and able to recall his offer or treat it as if not made.

(II) **The Modern Law.** — As a result of the Reception, it is true, the principle of the Roman law was accepted, according to which a unilateral promise of the debtor had, as such, no obligatory force except in testamentary dispositions, but became legally binding only by an acceptance on the part of the creditor. Some of the modern codes, also, expressly laid down this rule; for example, the Prussian "Allgemeines Landrecht"[1] and the Saxon Code.[2] The Roman law, however, had also recognized a few, although unimportant, exceptions to its principle; namely the legal obligation

[1] I, 5, § 5: "Nude covenants ('Gelübde'), like nude unilateral promises generally, have no binding force under the private law."

[2] § 771: "An unilateral promise to perform something, made inter vivos, is not binding."

of a "votum" and of a "pollicitatio" (*i.e.* a promise given to a municipality). These Roman exceptions, however, scarcely became practical matters in Germany; and in many cases they were abrogated simply through desuetude. On the other hand, the exceptions of the Germanic law above referred to, the binding force of a public offer and of other offers, remained almost everywhere in force. They were recognized in many statutes, notably in the Prussian "Allgemeines Landrecht" (I, 5, § 988, 96 *et seq.*); and the binding force of the offer between absent parties, which was indispensable for the security of trade, was made a general rule in commerce by the old (General) Commercial Code (§§ 338 *et seq.*). Both rules have been adopted, in turn, by the present Civil Code (§§ 657, 145 *et seq.*). The Swiss Code of Obligation Law (§§ 8, 3, 5) also expressly adopts them. In this connection special provisions were adopted in modern statutes regarding the circumstances under which, and the moment at which, a contract between absent parties should be regarded as concluded. Until recently a diversity of legal rules prevailed upon this matter. The theory requiring a receipt of the acceptance ("Empfangstheorie") had, indeed, been generally adopted by the Codes (for example, by the Prussian "Allgemeines Landrecht", the Austrian and Saxon Codes, and the old Commercial Code; on the other hand, in legal theory and practice the "outward expression" ("Äusserungs-") theory (Thöl), the "mailing" ("Absendungs-") theory, and the "hearsay" ("Vernehmungs-") theory were also represented. The present Civil Code has created uniformity in the law, following the example of the Prussian and the Commercial law, by adopting the "receipt" theory. The same is true of the Swiss law.

TOPIC 3. THE CONTENT OF OBLIGATIONS

§ 74. **Nude Obligational Promises. (I) The Older Law.** — Every obligational contract is of course concluded for a particular reason and for a definite purpose. These motives ("Beweggründe") give to the contract its distinctive character, and contracts based upon identical motives may be classified, as regards their nature, in typical groups. These motives, however, need not necessarily always appear when the contract is concluded. If they do not appear, if the basis of the legal duty ("Schuldgrund") is not named when the obligational promise is made, then the contract is one that cannot be classified among the special contract types which are so distinguishable in their content.

As in the older Roman law, in which a motive was not stated in the " stipulation ", so in the old Germanic law such " abstract " or nude obligational promises were known from the earliest times. This was a natural consequence of the formal manner in which the contract was concluded. In the case of the Roman stipulation, as in the Germanic formal contract, the force that created the obligation lay solely in the form, in the giving and accepting of mutual promises in formalistic words; which, moreover, in the Germanic law were given audible and visible expression by the delivery of a symbol of contract. Any act of performance (" Leistung ") whatever could in this way be promised and made legally effective without mention of the reason or basis of the legal duty. Whoever undertook in a wed-contract or by a solemn promise in due legal form ("rechtsförmliches Gelöbniss"), to pay a sum of money, to deliver an object, to render a service, or pay a penalty, or the like, thereby became a debtor of the promisee; and this simply because he had concluded a legally valid formal contract, without regard to the motive (" Beweggrund ") that might underlie the promise or the legality of the " causa " (" Versprechensgrund "). Therefore, it was also unnecessary to mention the " Schuldgrund " in instruments creating obligations; so-called " indiscreet " documents, that is, documents, that did not express the " Schuldgrund ", could be the basis of a judgment against the debtor. For it followed, for purposes of a lawsuit, from the obligatory force of the nude obligational promise that the obligor who sued to enforce the obligation need not specify a " Schuldgrund ", and that the judge could not reject such an " unsubstantiated " action. On the contrary, it was sufficient if the plaintiff satisfied procedural requirements by a mere allegation that he brought the action " von gelobdes wegen "; that is, upon the basis of a formal contract.

(II) **The Modern Law.** — Notwithstanding that the recognition of nude obligational promises furthered in the happiest manner the increase of money transactions, they were abandoned after the disappearance of the formal contract, and there was adopted in the common law in their place the Italian theory that a promise without the support of some substantial " causa " was not enforceable; so that a document containing merely a promise of performance without the material motive (" Grund ") therefor could not establish a claim. In particular, there prevailed almost universally in the literature of the common law the view,—represented also by Germanists of note (*e.g.* Thöl, Gerber), — that a "cautio indiscreta" could be used only in certain exceptional cases as evidence, and that ordinarily a person giving such might refuse performance pending proof by the plaintiff of the "causa debendi." The practice of the common law was also adapted, in general, to this theory, which was likewise adopted in many statutes, for example in the Territorial Law of Württemberg. It was read by implication into the Prussian "Allgemeines Landrecht" in the older Prussian practice and theory, although in Dernburg's opinion[1] unjustifiably. At the same time, however, various of the regional systems maintained the validity of the "cautio indiscreta" (for example, the Hamburg Statutes, I, 20, Art. 2). Moreover, the old view was never abandoned in commerce, the nude form being retained, in particular, in bills of exchange. This rule was made the general law of Germany by the Bills of Exchange Act (Art. 4); and the General Commercial Code (§ 301) provided that it should not be requisite to the validity of "orders to pay or deliver ('Anweisungen') and written acknowledgements of obligations ('Verpflichtungsscheine') made out by merchants for the delivery of money or a quantity of fungible things, or of commercial paper", that they include a statement of the basis of the obligation. More recently the same principle was recognized in the case of bearer paper. In several codes the hypothecary charge ("Hypothekenschuld") was also developed as an abstract obligation, or a non-accessory land-debt ("Grundschuld") introduced beside it (*supra*, p. 394).

In view of these increasingly prevalent forms of the nude promise in positive law, and because of the slight justification in the sources for the theory of the common law, a return to the old principles became more and more imperatively necessary. In this connection Bähr,[2] the leading champion of the movement, developed the theory of the obligatory force of a nude acknowledgment of liability ("Anerkennungsvertrag") with convincing arguments which immediately found acceptance, notwithstanding the opposition of some scholars, in literature, practice, and legislation, — for example, in the Saxon Civil Code (§§ 1397 *et seq.*).

The present Civil Code has followed this tendency. It has established the validity of a nude or "unmotived" ("abstrakte", "selbständige", § 780) obligational promise; and equally that of the nude acknowledgment of a legal duty ("Schuldanerkenntnis", § 781), though indeed with the restriction, unknown to

[1] "Lehrbuch des preussischen Privatrechts", II (5th ed., 1897), 36.
[2] "Die Anerkennung als Verpflichtungsgrund" (1855, 2d ed., 1867).

the earlier law, that such contracts must be at least concluded in writing. The Swiss Code of Obligation Law (§ 17) recognizes the validity of a nude obligational acknowledgment without such restriction.

§ 75. **Contracts for the Benefit of Third Persons.**[1] (I) **The Older Law.** — Germanic law, which allowed the formation of a formal obligational contract by the giving and acceptance of a formal promise ("Gelöbniss") that was consummated by tradition of a staff, was in a position to recognize, also, without question, those contracts in which the person to whom performance was rendered was another person than the promisee. For upon the acceptance of the promise this immediately passed "beyond the power of the one who gave it", and he might "be held to it, no matter whether he had promised performance to the promisee or to a third person."[2] In such contracts for performances to or for the benefit of third persons the creditor promised either that he would perform directly to a third person, or that he would perform to the promisee or to a third person. If performance was to be made for the benefit of a third person, which was doubtless ordinarily although by no means necessarily the case, — it was not, for example, the case when the third party was to receive performance merely as an agent ("Beauftragter") of the promisee, — then the contract was one for the benefit of the third person. A third person to whom performance was to be given, either certainly or possibly, might be named by the parties when the contract was concluded. But it was also possible to leave his appointment to the future; in this case the creditor had the power to determine who should receive performance.

Such contracts satisfied a crying need, since in litigation the older law recognized powers of attorney either not at all or only to a very limited extent, and moreover did not recognize the free assignability of contractual claims (*infra*, § 78). Consequently, such contracts were widely known in all Germanic countries, and were utilized for the most varied purposes; as an example of which we may refer to the fact that in Iceland "it was customary to give to religious vows ('Gelübde') the forms of a contract for the benefit of God or of a saint."[3] Especially in Italy, France,

[1] *Brunner* in Z. Hand. R., XXII (1877), 90 *et seq.*, reprinted in his "Forschungen", 546 *et seq.*; *Unger*, "Die Verträge zu Gunsten Dritter", in *Ihering's* J. B., X (1871), 1–109; *Gareis*, "Die Verträge zu Gunsten Dritter" (1873).

[2] *v. Amira*, "Recht", 35.

[3] *v. Amira*, "Obligationrecht", II, 378.

and Germany, contracts for the benefit of third persons were in most common use from the Frankish period onward. Lessors, for example, provided in their leases that the rent should be paid to the "missus." Very often donors who in conveying land to a Church in fee reserved the usufruct, reserved not to themselves but to third persons; as for example to their wives or to living or expected children, or to their descendants; or else they perfected a "donatio post obitum" by providing that the gift should pass to the Church only after the death of some third person surviving the donor, and should remain the property of such person until that time. And if a Salmann was entrusted with the commission of conveying a testamentary gift to such an institution after the owner's death, the contract was concluded between the donor and the Salmann for its benefit. In such cases a clause was embodied in the deed of conveyance ("Traditionsurkunde") expressing such dispositions made in favor of third persons, — for example, the reserve clause in the cases just mentioned. Similar clauses occurred, as may be proved in Italy from the 1100 s onward, in pure obligation instruments, though of these, for evident reasons, a much smaller number have been preserved. That obligational contracts of this kind were customary also in Germany is shown, for example, by a town register of Stralsund of the 1200 s: according to the register, a burgher promised a notary that in case the latter should not return from his student tour he would pay the sum owed to the notary to such person as the latter might indicate in his testament. Similarly, it might be that a person paid a sum of money to another and the latter obligated himself to assure to a third person, in return therefor, an annuity for life.

The most important application of promises for the benefit of third persons in the medieval law was in the treatment of bearer commercial paper payable to order or bearer, which developed from a concept of Germanic law into one of the most important institutes of modern business (*infra*, § 88).

In all the applications of the principle, including those last named of order and bearer paper, the obligation originated in the usual manner, in a formal contract; that is in a bilateral act, usually perfected by the delivery of a document, and not in a unilateral promise of the obligor. The right of the third person, for whose benefit the contract was concluded between the promisor and the promisee or transferee of the instrument, doubtless sprang, according to the view of the older law, directly from the conclusion of the contract. Joinder of the third person in the contract, or assent by him thereto, was not at all necessary for the creation in his favor of the promisor's obligation. This was created, even as regarded third persons, by the contract itself; and a promise once given could therefore not thereafter be revoked.

(II). **The Modern Law.** — The classic Roman law, which proceeded from the principle "alteri stipulari nemo potest", never attained to any general recognition of contracts for the benefit of strangers. With few exceptions it gave a right of action against the promisor neither to the promisee nor to the third person. The theory of the native law was wholly displaced by this conflicting principle of the Roman law. The prevailing opinion in literature and practice no longer held it correct to concede the third person a right arising directly from the contract, but regarded the right as arising only from his joinder or acceptance; until then the promisee might release the promisor, or the contract might be revoked by "mutuus dissensus" of the contracting parties. This view, also, passed over into the modern codes. So far as they recognized such contracts at all, they all required, as preconditions to the acquisition of rights by third persons, either ratification and acceptance (as in the case of the Bavarian Territorial Law), or joinder in the contract with the consent of the contracting parties (as in the Prussian "Allgemeines Landrecht", I. 5, §§ 74–77), or acceptance of the performance (Saxon Code, § 854).

In time, however, these restrictions, which were unknown to the older law, were one by one abrogated. In the first place, in a few cases which evidently constituted exceptions, an immediate acquisition of rights by the third person, even without a declaration of accession, was either preserved or newly introduced. So, for example (without reference for the moment to order and bearer paper, which followed a peculiar course of development, — *infra*, § 88), in contracts of freight, as to which the General Commercial Code (§ 405 = HGB, § 435) provided that after the carrier's arrival at the place for delivery the consignee named in the bill of lading should be entitled to enforce against the carrier, in his own name, those rights which had been created by the contract between shipper and carrier, and especially to require the latter to deliver the bill of lading and hand over the goods. So also in the case of the purchase of a mercantile business, the result of which under the general customary law was that the creditors of the business immediately acquired independent rights against the new owner thereof. So also in the case of life insurance policies, the person for whose benefit the insurance was taken becoming entitled upon the death of the insured, eo ipso, to an independent right against the insurer. So also, according to invariable customary law, in the case of contracts by which one son took over a peasant holding from his father. Here, the son who so took over the estate was obligated to render to his mother and brothers and sisters certain economic compensation, and the obligees acquired directly from the contract a corresponding right without joining in the contract and without having declared a will to acquire; they could demand performance exactly as if the father were dead and had so provided for their indemnity in his testament.

There was a tendency in legal theory, which became increasingly strong with time, to go beyond these exceptions and abandon in all cases the requirement of joinder. Although it might be doubted whether this became established in the common law, the new Civil Code has adopted this view without qualification, and has thereby given the law's development a conclusion in accord with Germanic principles. It recognizes the validity, on principle, of contracts by which performance is promised to a third person, and attributes to them the result that the third person immediately acquires a right to compel performance (§ 328). It has expressly recognized the same principle in contracts of life insurance, annuity contracts, and contracts for the taking over of another's entire property ("Vermögens-") or lands ("Gutsübernahmeverträge), — that is, including debts owed to third persons (§ 330). The Swiss law has taken the same attitude (OR, § 112).

TOPIC 4. PERFORMANCE AND NON-PERFORMANCE OF OBLIGATIONS

§ 76. **Contractual Penalties and Damages.**[1] (I) **The Older Law.** (1) *Penalties for default in the earliest law.* — The oldest obligations were, as has been seen (*supra*, p. 460), those that resulted from misdeeds. These made the wrongdoer the debtor of the person wronged; the latter had a creditor's claim for the

[1] *Stobbe,* "Zur Geschichte des deutschen Vertragsrechts" (1855), 31 *et seq.*; *R. Löning,* "Der Vertragsbruch im deutschen Recht" (1876); *W. Sickel,* "Die Bestrafung des Vertragsbruchs und analoger Rechtsverletzungen in Deutschland" (1876); *Hammer,* "Die Lehre vom Schadensersatz nach dem Sachsenspiegel und den verwandten Rechtsquellen", no. 19 (1885) of *Gierke's* "Untersuchungen"; *Sjögren,* "Über die römische Conventionalstrafe und die Strafklauseln der fränkischen Urkunden" (1896); *A. B. Schmidt,* "Die Grundsätze über den Schadensersatz in den Volksrechten", no. 18 (1885) of *Gierke's* "Untersuchungen"; *Heuer,* "Der Annahmeverzug im älteren deutschen Privatrecht", in *Beyerle's* "Beiträge", VI. 1 (1911).

payment of the statutory bót. In so far as the bót fell to the creditor, — a fraction of it was delivered to the public authorities as a wite ("fredus"), — it signified, from his viewpoint, compensation for the injury he had suffered. As an aspect of the process of outlawry the entire property of the wrongdoer was indirectly liable to the person wronged; by virtue of the promise given to perform the judgment rendered, the debtor who so pledged his faith was liable with his property for the payment of the compensation awarded. When obligations of private law came to be created by voluntary contracts concluded out of court, the idea remained at first predominant that non-payment, even of a debt voluntarily assumed, was a punishable wrong. Penance, by payment of a statutory bót, was therefore required for it also, the amount of the debt being correspondingly increased. The debtor, however, did not in this case incur a penalty by mere default, as was the case with other misdeeds. The debtor must "be *put* in a punishable wrong that made him liable for a bót"; [1] the obligation of the private law was "strengthened" into one of the criminal law. This was accomplished by a monition ("Mahnung") in which the creditor, in legally prescribed manner, called upon the debtor to fulfill his obligation, to pay his debt, or to deliver the thing which was the subject of the obligation. The "Lex Salica" describes clearly this monitory procedure in both the forms known to it under the law of private obligations. In the case of the "fides facta", the pledge of faith (*supra*, p. 493), the creditor was bound, when the time of payment arrived, to demand payment of the debtor extra-judicially at his home, and before witnesses. If the debtor thereafter failed to pay the monition made him guilty of default, for which he forfeited a bót of fifteen shillings; which in case of continued refusal to pay could be collected by the creditor along with the contractual debt by suit. If after judgment was given the debtor still did not pay, three further demands were made from week to week, each of which increased the debt by three shillings; as a last resort the creditor resorted to the extra-judicial right of distraint which he possessed, as regards the contractual debt by virtue of the pledge of faith, and as regards the penalties incurred by virtue of the judgment ("L. Sal.", Tit. 50). In case of a loan ("res præstita") [2] the debtor must have been

[1] *Brunner*, "Geschichte", II, 520.

[2] *Eliason*, "Die Klage der 'res præstita' in der Lex Salica und ihre Entwicklung zum Mahnverfahren" (Breslau dissertation, 1910); *Gierke*, "Schuld und Haftung", 165 *et seq.*

thrice admonished by the creditor to return the chattel, the debt being increased, here also, by three shillings for each demand. If he still did not perform his obligation he incurred a bót of fifteen shillings, which could be recovered by legal action along with the nine shillings ("L. Sal.", Tit. 52). Here again the payment of the bót, or the distraint permitted for its recovery, was a penalty for the breach of contract and compensation for the damage, and they inured to the creditor from the failure to perform or duly to perform the obligation. Similar provisions occur in the other folk-laws. Indeed, enforcement of contracts by remedies of the criminal law was characteristic of Germanic law. How long it continued to express the popular legal sentiment is clearly shown in the wide-spread custom, connected with the Roman documentary system and the "stipulatio duplæ", of embodying in contracts express provisions penalizing the breach of the agreement stated in the instrument. It may appear singular that the parties should prescribe by private agreement what existed independently by force of law, namely the penal character ("Strafbarkeit") of a breach of contract. The explanation of the use of such penal clauses, so extremely common precisely in the Frankish period, may perhaps lie in the fact (among others) that with the disappearance of the bót system the statutory penal law of contracts was becoming increasingly weak, so that the parties found themselves compelled, in individual cases, to provide by special declaration the security afforded by the threatened penalty. Such penal clauses also increased the probative value of the documents.

Where the criminality of the delinquent debtor depended upon monition by the creditor, — in other words, when the debtor became in default only after monition, — the debts were known as "fetch" ("Hol-") debts; because, monition being necessary, the creditor must seek his money at the debtor's home.

(2) *The medieval law.* — In the Middle Ages a default of the debtor was likewise regarded as an unlawful act; so that in Scandinavian law, for example, default in performance was always regarded, in theory, as a delict ("Übeltat"). The statutory penalties for default, however, which became less prominent already in the Frankish period, now completely disappeared. In fact they ceased to be indispensable, inasmuch as the creditor's power of distraint under the contract also secured him, in case of default, — from the instant that delayed performance could be regarded as non-performance, — a recourse against the chattels of the debtor

that were liable for his debt. The idea of a penalty arising directly from mere delay was preserved only in the primitive custom, — widespread in the Middle Ages and even later, — of the "Rutscherzins." This rent-for-delay ("Zweigilt", "census promobilis") was a sum paid by a rentaler ("Zinsmann") as a penalty for delay, in strict accordance with the above mentioned provisions of the Salic folk-law. It progressively increased the amount of the debt, usually doubling it. Indeed, the "Rutscherzins" proper, as we find it in the Sachsenspiegel and in many dooms, was not increased by years, as was at times provided in older documents, but by days and hours.[1]

With these exceptions it was left exclusively to the parties, in medieval times, to agree upon liquidated damages in case of delayed performance, the debtor promising either to pay such damages as interest-for-delay or to make good the damages otherwise.[2] In this connection the creditor, who had the burden of proving the damages, was very often empowered by the debtor to fix their amount without oath and without witnesses, by his bare word; a clause which bore the name in Steiermark of "Schadenbund" ("damage-contract", "Bund" = "Gedinge"). It was also a favored practice, especially in South Germany, to permit the creditor to raise the money owing him at a Jew's, to whom the debtor must then pay the defaulted sum with interest (so-called "raising money on damages", "Geld auf Schaden nehmen"). Indeed, the parties might go even further and agree that the creditor should have a right, in case of default by the debtor, to withdraw from the contract; in which case he was occasionally also given an express power of sale by way of self-help.

The medieval law had thus attained a rule of compensation, — at least when we assume a precedent agreement of the parties, — that was adjusted to actual damages, and which corrected the rigidity of the old contractual penalty. Of course a claim for such compensation existing by general rule of law was not yet recognized. At the same time, in some legal systems of the later Middle Ages, notably in those of the Hanseatic cities, effect was already given to this principle, at least in certain cases. Under these systems, in contracts that provided for the delivery of things or performance of services, the party not performing the contract

[1] Ssp., I, 54, § 2. See this and other extracts in *Grimm*, "Rechtsaltertümer", I, 534 *et seq.* Compare also, for example, the Aspel manorial law.

[2] System. Schöffenrecht, III, 2 c, 23.

was obligated to pay a sum proportioned to the other's interest under the contract. Under a contract of hire ("Miete"), in particular, the party who wrongfully withdrew therefrom was bound to pay either an entire or a half year's rent, according to circumstances. Under similar circumstances, in contracts for labor and for freightage all or half the wages and the whole or half of the freight charges were forfeited. Such obligations, incurred in lieu of performance of the original contract, really involved a payment of damages fixed by statute and quite independent of the parties' agreement. Moreover, the vendor's power to withdraw from his contract in case of the vendee's default was likewise expressly granted by statute in many town laws.[1]

With the disappearance of statutory contractual penalties and the alteration of execution procedure, the extra-judicial monition also fell into disuse. A monition was no longer a precondition either to private or public distraint based upon a formal ("Wett-") contract, or to judicial enforcement of contractual penalties fixed by agreement. With this change, at least those money debts for whose payment a definite time was agreed upon ceased to be "fetch" ("Hol-") debts; they became "bring-" ("Bring-") debts. In Germany, though not in France, the rule was established and retained authority even down to present days that the debtor who had promised to make a payment on a certain day must at that time tender payment to the creditor; in this case default did not result from a fruitless monition, but from omission at the time agreed upon ("dies interpellat pro homine").[2] To this rule those cases were an exception in which a vain monition was required, in the old manner, as a precondition to collection of the debt by legal action. This was the rule for debts based upon so-called "presentation" commercial paper (*infra*, § 88).

(II) **The Modern Development.**[3] — The modern law recognized the unqualified statutory duty of a delinquent debtor to make good the damages resulting from his default. In particular, after hesitation at the outset, statutory interest for default was everywhere introduced. The Recess of the deputation of the imperial estates of 1600 provided that in case of a money loan ("Darlehn")

[1] "Münchener Stadtrecht", Art. 39. To the same effect today in the Austrian Code, § 1062: "The vendee is bound to accept delivery of the chattel, either immediately or at the time agreed upon; if he does not, the vendor becomes entitled to refuse delivery to him."

[2] Ssp., I, 65, § 4.

[3] *Hedemann*, "Fortschritte des Zivilrechts", 1, 81 *et seq.*, 135 *et seq.*

the creditor should receive five per cent. interest after default, and if his damages should be greater he might recover the excess. Thus he was given a choice between special interest after default, and damages. This rule was later extended to all money debts, and with variations in detail was adopted in the regional systems. Other codes or statutes continued, it is true, to allow interest for default in the case of money loans only, and did not allow a claim for greater damages. This was true of the Prussian "Allgemeines Landrecht" (save in cases of gross negligence) and of the Code Civil. The interest rate after default was fixed without regard to the rate fixed in the contract, however low; usually at five per centum (in some legal systems, — for example the Austrian Code, — at four, in the General Commercial Code at six) for commercial transactions. If the contract interest rate was higher than five per centum a correspondingly higher rate was authorized as the statutory interest after default. The final result of the development was that the Civil Code, following the rule last mentioned but with the addition that additional damages might be collected, has fixed the interest on defaulted money debts at four per centum (§ 288), and that the Commercial Code (§ 352) has fixed the rate for commercial debts at five per centum. The Swiss Code of Obligation Law fixes the statutory interest rate in all cases at five per centum (§ 563).

In such statutory interest for default we may see an after-effect of the invariable contractual penalties of the earliest law, since they can be demanded without regard to the damage actually suffered, and therefore even although this be less.

In accord with the principle of free contract recognized in modern times, contractual penalties might be fixed by agreement of the parties under the earlier modern statutes as under the present law; that is, either in addition to performance or in place of performance, — in the latter case as a minimum interest. In such cases, and in the absence of specific provision, the creditor has a choice between the two claims; if the choice is left to the debtor, such penal interest assumes the character of smart-money ("Reugeld", "Wandelpön"). In place of the statutory restrictions upon contractual penalties that were formerly common, the present Civil Code has introduced a right of judicial reduction (§ 343); and a similar right is recognized also in the Swiss law (OR, § 163, 3).

In certain contracts, particularly in sales, a right was even given to the creditor in the Middle Ages to refuse performance by a debtor who had defaulted, and not only to demand damages for non-performance but to withdraw, himself, from the contract. This right has been adopted and generalized by the Code Civil, the Swiss Code of Obligation Law (§ 107), the German Commercial Code, and the present Civil Code; not, however, without subjecting it to definite conditions, which are differently regulated in the case of the private and the commercial law (BGB, § 326; HGB, § 376).

Finally, even after the Reception the authority of the medieval rule "dies interpellat pro homine" was for a time maintained by the customary law; and later this was adopted in many codes, including the Prussian and the Saxon, and the Swiss Code of Obligation Law (§ 102). It is the rule today of the present Civil Code (§ 284); save that debts represented by "presentation" paper have of course continued to be "fetch" ("Hol-") debts.

§ 77. **Fault ("Verschulden") and Accident ("Zufall") in the Law of Contract.**[1] (I) **The older Law.** — (1) *General principle.* — In deciding the question whether and to what extent a wrongdoer shall answer for his illegal conduct, the law, as finally developed, examines the will of the guilty person, and adjusts his liability to the degree of his mental fault. It distinguishes, upon the ground of certain general principles, — intent, negligence, and accident, — whether the question involved be one of tort unassociated with contract or a simple breach of contract.

The older law, which originally attributed importance only to what was physically sensible, did not recognize such distinctions. The criminal law, therefore, did not inquire whether in a specific case the act causing damage involved "dolus", "culpa", or "casus."[2] At the same time it did not entirely disregard the distinction between voluntary and involuntary actions. For even in early times heed was so far given to the quality of the wrongdoer's will, in measuring penalties, that one who was guilty neither of negligence nor premeditation was more leniently treated than when he had acted with malevolence. As regards the question, however, of compensation for damage done by tort or by breach of contract, no corresponding distinction was recognized between a voluntary act and an involuntary act ("Ungefähr"). On the contrary, as the bót imposed for the act in the case of damages by tort ("ausservertragliche Schädigung") must be

[1] *Müller-Erzbach*, "Gefährdungshaftung und Gefahrtragung" (1912), particularly 225 *et seq.;* also in Arch. zivil. Praxis, CVI (1910), 309–476, CIX (1913), 1–143.

[2] *Brunner*, "Geschichte", II, 544.

paid under all circumstances, in so far as it represented compensation, so in contracts the promise must be performed under all circumstances, or else the damages be paid that were prescribed by the law or fixed by the contract for non-performance. The objective result of the act or the non-performance, — the damage, the loss of property, — was alone considered, and imposed upon the debtor. His state of mind was wholly disregarded. Under the sensuous and formal view of the old law, even one through whose negligence damages resulted was bound to give compensation, despite the absence of intent; for his conduct was responsible for the doing of the act, or for the non-performance of the legal duty. To this extent he was therefore legally in fault; namely, the fault of inattentiveness. Indeed, the very concept of accident was quite unknown, or at least was scarcely recognized, in the old law. That always sought a responsible person, and whenever it could find such it attributed to him some fault ("Schuld"), and therewith the duty to give damages. It did this wherever the cause of an unintended effect was linked in any way with the immediate sphere of an individual's action ("Lebenssphäre"),[1] or sprang from such sphere. It is quite possible, in this connection, to speak of an "intrinsic" ("innerer") accident.[2] But it must be borne in mind, in so doing, that in the view of the old law there was in such cases no accident at all, but an act for which a particular man was accountable; an act, moreover, which could be attributed to him with good reason, — for a man takes all his happiness from the environment of his individual life ("Lebenskreis"), whether or not he may have deserved it, and should therefore accept misfortune that arises within that environment even though it also be undeserved by him.[3] Only those events were regarded as properly accidents ("extrinsic accident", "äusserer Zufall"),[4] as misfortunes ("Unglück"), which could not be associated with an individual's life even in this loose way. And these accidents were not taken account of by the law. The person declared responsible could avoid the responsibility thus imposed upon him only when he could prove that he had found himself in circumstances of positive ("echte") necessity. As cases of positive necessity, the town-law of Görlitz, in agreement with the sources of the Frankish period, designated, for example, sickness, imprisonment, and service

[1] *Brunner*, "Geschichte", II, 549.
[2] *Cosack*, "Bürgerliches Recht", I (6th ed.), 291 *et seq.*
[3] *Ibid.*, 292. [4] *Ibid.*

under the king ("sûche", "unde gevengnisse", "unde des riches dienst").[1]

The result in the older law was therefore a very strict responsibility of an obligor. It was illustrated, notably, in the following applications.

(2) *Following property* ("Folgerungen"). (A) LIABILITY OF BAILEES. — Whoever has received a thing belonging to another, — for example a borrower or pledgee, — was theoretically bound to return it in due time, under all circumstances (*supra*, p. 443). This rule followed with absolute necessity from the rule "hand must warrant hand" (*supra*, p. 408 *et seq.*). The owner of a thing entrusted to another must rely solely on the faith of the bailee ("die getreue Hand"), not on a third person; but he could do this under all circumstances, and, notably, even when the thing had been stolen from the bailee by a third person. The bailee's loss of possession by larceny, in the sense of the medieval law, may therefore be designated "the legal type of 'culpa'."[2]

But it was precisely in certain cases of things received in bailment that the principle of unlimited liability broke down, even in early times; namely, whenever an "external" accident occurred, a misfortune in the sense above indicated. Such exceptions were treated at first in the formalistic manner then favored: regardless of the circumstances of the particular case, certain external facts, — at first a few, then an increasing number, — were treated as typical cases of misfortune, and their existence deprived the owner of all claims for damages against the bailee.

One of the oldest typical exceptions was the death of animals; that is a natural death, of which a person was wholly innocent, a so-called "common" ("gemeine") death.[3] Other similar cases of misfortune were fire, storm, flood, avalanches, the collapse of houses, bad harvests, Sticken der Frucht, depredations by wolves, plundering by pirates, etc. In the law of transportation it was usual to employ the suggestive phrase "acts of God and the King's enemies" ("Gottesgewalt und Herrennot"); if such things caused damage to a shipment of goods there could be no question of obligation.

Despite the recognition of these exceptions, however, no such clear and fundamental principle was developed, for example, as

[1] Art. 138, in *Gaupp*, "Das alte Magdeburgische Recht" (1826), 318.
[2] *Franken*, "Französisches Pfandrecht", 326.
[3] Swsp. (G), 185.

that liability always existed solely for legal duty ("Schuld") and never for misfortune. On the contrary it depended upon the legal relations of the specific case whether the liability of the possessor of a thing was for legal duty only or for legal duty and misfortune. The Sachsenspiegel, also, did not get beyond such a casuistic mode of treatment.[1]

At the same time importance was attributed, even at an early date, to certain collateral circumstances that might accompany such cases of misfortune. Some of the folk-laws already made a distinction according as the bailee had taken animals for pay or gratuitously, excluding liability in the latter case only. Here, and in later sources which further developed these ideas, the consideration involved was that whoever derives advantage from receiving something is to be treated more severely than one who has accepted it merely for another's accommodation.

Another idea, which likewise appeared as early as in the folk-laws and was later frequently applied, emphasized the question whether in such a case of misfortune a thing of another person (the bailor) was alone destroyed or injured, or with it something of the custodian. And under the assumption that the custodian had given proper care only in the latter case, he was relieved from liability for damages in that case only. This rule reminds one of the Roman "diligentia quam in suis rebus adhibere solet"; although in its pure and typical form it was very much less perfect. Here again it was an adherence to typical forms that prevented a satisfactory distinction in theory; there was lacking the necessary power of abstract thought.

(B) Liability of some persons for others. — From the principle that only "external" accident could be regarded as innocent, there resulted a far-reaching liability of some persons for others. According to Germanic law the sib was responsible for the conduct of its members, the house-lord for the conduct of the members of the household, the land-lord for that of his villeins ("Hintersassen"). In the same way the owner was answerable for the damage which his slaves might do, and the owner of a business or master of dependent servitors for the damage which his dependents might do; and similarly he was liable in damages to them, in turn, for misfortunes they suffered. When an act was in such cases attributed to another than the actual actor, — to the house-father, the master, etc., — the reason for this was simply that such harmful event originated in the personal environment

[1] Ssp., III, 5, §§ 3–5. (*Supra*, p. 470.)

(" Lebenssphäre ") of such other person. To be sure, it was from his viewpoint an accident, but it was a " personal " (" innere ") accident. The old law considered it juster in such cases to impose the duty upon the house-lord, the owner of the business, etc., than to let the injured person bear it.

(II) **The Modern Development.** — The principles of the native law were displaced, for the most part, by those of the alien law. The latter's theory of " culpa ", with its degrees of " culpa lata " and " culpa levis ", — to which there was frequently added, following the theory of the medieval Canon Law, the additional degree of " culpa levissima ", — became the rule of the common law; and this threefold division passed thence into the modern codes, — for example, into the Prussian "Allgemeines Landrecht." The Roman concept of " diligentia quam in suis ", — also known as " culpa in concreto ", — was capable of merger with views already prevailing in native practice (*supra*, p. 529). The conception of " culpa levissima " has been abandoned by the law in its latest stage; aside from the " care " exercised in one's own affairs, the Civil Code recognizes only gross and ordinary negligence. In the absence of premeditation liability is generally imposed whenever the latter is present, — that is, for disregard of the care properly requisite to human intercourse (§ 276); whereas when only the care exercised in one's private affairs is required, liability exists for gross negligence at least. This relaxation of the requisite of care is made in favor of a gratuitous bailee, of a partner, of spouses, of parents in the exercise of parental authority, and of an initial heir (" Vorerbe ", — other heirs taking in remainder).

The Roman rule also became controlling in the distinction between legal fault (" Schuld ") and accident. The old materialistic (" sinnvolle ") distinction between " external " and " internal " accident was abandoned,[1] and, in general, the principle was recognized that nobody is responsible for accident.

Nevertheless, the strict rules of the Germanic law regulating liability for accident were in some cases preserved; indeed, in very recent years their scope of application has even been somewhat widened. The cases thus treated are those where liability is imposed for accident except when due to constraining power ("bis zu höherer Gewalt", "vis maior"). The modern conception of constraining power was by no means exclusively derived from the Roman law and its rules concerning liability of " nautæ ", " caupones ", and " stabularii " — who upon proof of a " vis maior "

[1] *Cosack*, "Bürgerliches Recht", I (3d ed.), 246.

could free themselves from the unlimited liability otherwise resting upon them. On the contrary there is also vital in it the native law, with its distinction of "internal" and "external" accidents. The conception of "vis maior" is applied especially in modern commercial law, particularly in the law of railway carriers. A railroad, unlike an ordinary carrier of freight by land or sea or river, is liable by virtue of positive provision in the Commercial Code (§ 456) for misfortunes ("Unfälle") to the freight it has accepted; and also for misfortunes to travelers or other persons incidentally to their operation, by virtue of an imperial statute of June 7, 1871 (§ 1), regulating carriers' liabilities. In the same way the post-office is liable for misfortunes to postal matter or to travelers in mail conveyances, by force of the Imperial Postal Act of October 28, 1871 (§§ 6, 11). And finally, innkeepers are liable for the baggage of travelers by force of the Civil Code (§ 701), which has followed in this matter the Prussian and the Saxon law. In all these cases the liability is for every "internal" but not always (assuming, of course, the absence of legal fault) for "external" accident; *i.e.* not for those involving "vis maior." The conception of "vis maior", however, which moreover is a much debated one, includes only "external" cases of misfortunes; that is those not caused by the ordinary conduct of an industry, but due to an outside inevitable and irresistible cause. But we must remember in this connection that no absolute test can be laid down by means of which to differentiate cases of this nature from "ordinary" accidents for which liability exists.[1]

What is more, the old liability for faults of third persons, — notwithstanding that it was decidedly subordinated in the common law and regional systems to the much milder Roman rules of "culpa in eligendo", and was retained in general form only in the French law, — is still applied in the present law, at least under some circumstances. In particular, when a person undertakes a juristic act under a power of attorney held by virtue of statute or prior juristic act, any fault of which he is guilty in such transaction is attributed to him either not at all or not alone, but to his principal. And the same is true when a person, by virtue of a power of attorney held by him under a statute or juristic act, or of a commission ("Auftrag") imposed upon him, coöperates with the person at fault as his agent or assistant ("Gehilfe"); and equally when a person, by virtue of a power of attorney under the by-laws of a corporation,

[1] See *Cosack*, "Lehrbuch des Handelsrechts" (7th ed., 1912), 456 *et seq.*

performs acts within the private law for such juristic person (§ 278).[1]

As respects liability for torts in non-contractual relations, the reader is referred to the remarks in § 89, below.

Topic 5. Assignments of Obligations by Obligee and Obligor

§ 78. **Assignments of Claims by the Obligee.**[2] (I) **The Older Law.** (1) *Transfer by juristic act.* — In the older law the principle prevailed that a creditor could not freely assign to third persons (*i.e.* without the debtor's consent) contract claims ("Forderungen") existing under an obligational contract; a principle which equally with the impossibility of personal representation ("Stellvertretung") reflected the formalistic character of the law. The effects of an obligational contract were determined by the precise and literal words of the agreement, and the obligor promised performance to the other contracting party only, and not to any third person; consequently a third person could have had no legal right of action against the obligor. To this was added the fact that in many cases, particularly when a personal liability was assumed, the obligor could by no means be indifferent whether one or another creditor was the other contracting party. Thus the rule long prevailed that a contract claim, — unless it was associated with possession of a piece of land, so that its holder could change with the land, — was not assignable without the obligor's consent. This rule was characteristic of the older Scandinavian law, and prevailed in Germany as late as the time of the Law Books.[3] In the Netherlands it was generally abandoned only in the 1400 s. The French customary law recognized it in the form given it, for example, by the Custom of Paris (1510, 1580): " simple transport ne saisit point ", — that is, until the conveyance had been notified to the obligor or accepted by him he might release himself by payment to the assignor. According to the English common law, until 1873 (statute of August 5), the king alone had the right, in theory, to assign contractual claims and to receive them as assignee; whereas in other cases an actual transfer could be effected only indirectly, through a power of attorney.

[1] *Cosack*, "Bürgerliches Recht", I (4th ed.), 254.

[2] *Buch*, "Die Übertragbarkeit der Forderungen im deutschen mittelalterlichen Recht", No. 113 (1912) of *Gierke's* "Untersuchungen." In my opinion the attack made in this essay upon the prevailing theory is not convincing.

[3] "Kleines Kaiserrecht", II, 38.

As was natural, with the increasing development of trade means were sought for effecting directly what the strict principle in question expressly forbade. And the power of attorney proved available for the purpose: one could convey to a third party the right to enforce the contract claim at law, at the same time, for greater security, frequently expressly renouncing one's own power to enforce it. The third person thus acquired a position comparable to that of the Roman "procurator in rem suam." But aside from the fact that this means was very imperfect, — since the right of action always existed in favor of the attorney only, not his heir, — it presupposed in all cases the possibility of representation by attorney in litigation. The impossibility of this, however, was a legal principle so deeply rooted in Germanic law "that it survived in some regions of Germanic law the whole Middle Ages." [1] Accordingly, where the grant of such power was either never or not yet permitted, the only feasible (at first the only possible) way of attaining the same end was for the debtor originally to promise performance either to the creditor or to a third person; and the wide and early prevalence in the Middle Ages of such promises of performance to third persons, and their development in clauses of order and bearer commercial paper, is explainable precisely by the inhibition of assignments of contract claims, and of powers of attorney (*infra*, § 88).

It was only at the end of the Middle Ages, from about the 1400 s onward, that the principle of the assignability of choses in action was recognized in a few legal systems, notably in town-laws (Magdeburg, Breslau), of Germany; empowerment in the presence and registration in the records of the court being generally required in such cases.

(2) *Statutory transfers.* — In a few cases it was possible already in the Middle Ages to speak of a statutory transfer of contract claims. Such a transfer occurred, for example, when a house-owner was permitted to distrain for unpaid rent upon chattels made by an artisan who was his tenant, and to collect from persons who had ordered them any sums still owing for the labor (*supra*, p. 442); or when the creditor of a city was secured by its tax claims against the citizens (*supra*, p. 149). Whenever, in these and in similar cases, a creditor (A) was permitted to proceed against the goods of a debtor (C) of his own debtor (B), and in a proper case distrain upon them, — that is to the amount of his credit, — this

[1] *Brunner*, "Forschungen", 599. *Cf.* his essay, "Das französische Inhaberpapier des Mittelalters" (1879), 13 *et seq.*

actually treated the claim of his own debtor (B) against the latter's debtor (C) as transferred to the former's creditor, the plaintiff (A).

(II) **The Modern Development.** — With the Reception general supremacy was attained by the rule, — which was inconsistent with the old Germanic law, — that contract claims might be assigned from the creditor to a third person even without the debtor's assent. This rule was adopted by all the earlier modern codes, and has been also adopted by the present Civil Code (§ 398). However, though the possibility of assignment has been recognized, the theory of the Roman law regarding its essential character has not been accepted. For in contrast to the Roman view, according to which the obligee was only a "procurator in rem suam", the assignor remaining the obligee, the rule was generally maintained in Germany that the identity of the claim was unaffected by transfer.[1] This view was adopted in all modern legislation, including the present Civil Code (§ 398), which permits a transfer of the claim by a nude ("abstrakt") contract of assignment. As respects the form of the transfer, no requirements were laid down, generally speaking, in the earlier law; the Prussian Allgemeines Landrecht required writing. The obligor was not required to be a party, but in order that the contract should have full effect against him notice to him was required, as in the Roman law. The effect of such notice was regulated by precise rules, such as the present Civil Code also contains (§§ 407 *et seq.*).

From the earliest times there were some contract claims that were non-transferable. Among these belonged, notably, those that were in a high degree personal, those which were not subject to distraint, and those that were declared non-assignable by agreement. All this has also been recognized by the Civil Code.

Where transfers of claims were permitted in the later Middle Ages, Jewish creditors were frequently forbidden to convey claims against a Christian to another Christian, in order to prevent a worsening of the debtor's position; and similarly the Roman Lex Anastasiana, which served in principle a like purpose, was adopted in many places, and even further extended. But it proved impossible to maintain this rule. It obtained no footing whatever in mercantile transactions. Many of the modern codes, for example the Prussian "Allgemeines Landrecht" and the Austrian Code, totally abolished it. It was not done away with throughout Germany until the General Commercial Code (Art.

[1] *Cosack*, "Bürgerliches Recht", I (4th ed.), 389.

299) was adopted. On the other hand, the present Civil Code permits its use, since it contains no similar prohibition.

The rule by which certain choses in action pass directly to another creditor by force of statutory provision has found far wider dissemination in modern times than in the medieval period. The Prussian "Allgemeines Landrecht" provided (I, 16, § 46) that a person paying another's debt should ordinarily be subrogated, without any express assignment, to the rights of the creditor so paid against the debtor; and similarly under the present Civil Code (§ 268, 3) the rule holds that a third person who has, of his own motion, satisfied another person's creditor, — whether canceling it by performance, or by payment in place of performance, or by depositing security, or by a mutual accounting, — acquires by force of law the claim of the creditor so satisfied. But the claim may not be enforced to the detriment of the original creditor. Special cases in which this principle is applied exist in insurance law and in commercial law (HBG, §§ 25, 28, 435, 804).

§ 79. **Assignment of Obligations by Obligor. (I) The Older Law.** — In view of the original non-assignability of claims, legal transactions for the purchase and assumption of the obligations owed ("Schulden") must equally have been unknown to the German law, as they certainly were, for example, to the Scandinavian. For the debts were associated with the person of him who had assumed them, and could not be transferred inter vivos to another person. Similarly, personal and property liabilities, such as the liability assumed under a contract of suretyship (*supra*, pp. 480 *et seq.*), bound solely the creator of the liability. On the other hand, even under old Germanic law a change in the possession of a thing involved a change of the person obligated in those cases where the purpose of the obligation was a transfer of such object;[1] and in the Middle Ages the same thing was true of the exceedingly numerous land-charges required to be rendered by the temporary holder of the seisin. Moreover, a change in the person of the debtor also took place when an entire estate passed by inheritance ("Vererbung") to a new possessor, which might happen not only "mortis causa" but also "inter vivos"; notably, when one person transferred his entire estate to another in return for lifelong maintenance and the assumption of all the transferror's liabilities ("Vitalizienvertrag"), or when a peasant surrendered his holding to his next heir and the latter promised to pay the debts. Whenever a new debtor took the place of the old, as a result either of

[1] *v. Amira*, "Recht", 134.

such contracts involving the entire estate, or, — as later became possible with the increasing use of money, — of special agreements between the two directed to the transfer of particular debts, the old debt passed to the new debtor unchanged in nature.

(II) **Modern Development.** —This rule was maintained in Germany even in the modern period. The Roman rule, according to which a debt could be assumed only by creating a new debt that was assumed by the new debtor, and which in content was identical with the old, found no acceptance in Germany. Moreover, contracts for the assumption of debts came to be generally recognized and commonly employed, in the form both of a contract between the new debtor and the creditor and of a contract between the old and the new debtors. In the latter case, to be sure, it was not ipso facto effective against the creditor. Exhaustive rules concerning this, as well as the question when the old debtor was finally eliminated from the relation, were adopted by the common law and the regional systems; to these the rules of the present Civil Code essentially conform. In addition to such assignments, the transfer of debts to the acquirer of an entire estate, as a part thereof, also remained of great practical importance in the modern law; both in "maintenance" contracts ("Vitalizienverträge") and in the taking over of peasant estates by an expectant heir, which were already represented in the Middle Ages, and, especially, in the commercial law (HGB, §§ 25, 27, 30). The acquisition of the estate now implies such a transfer by positive provision of the Civil Code, but does not affect the continuing liability of the first debtor (§ 419); and though the liability imposed upon the party assuming the debt can neither be avoided nor limited, it is limited to the value of the property taken over. A corresponding provision has been adopted in the new Swiss Code of Obligation Law (§ 181); only, here, the continuing liability of the first debtor is limited to two years.

TOPIC 6. CASES OF SEVERAL DEBTORS AND CREDITORS

§ 80. **Plurality of Creditors.** — Several persons may be interested on either the active or on the passive side of an obligation. At the same time the relations inter sese of such creditors and debtors, and their shares in the claim or the obligation, may assume various forms. These correspond for the most part to the different forms of control which several interested persons can exercise over one thing (*supra*, pp. 234 *et seq.*), and they are consequences, equally with these, of the principles of the law of persons respecting communities (*supra*, pp. 146 *et seq.*), wherever creditors or debtors are united in one community.

(I) **Severable Credits, — Claims severable pro rata** ("Teilgläubigerschaft"). — In this case an act of performance is due to several creditors, and each creditor is entitled to receive, and can bring action for, only a quotal part thereof. Since ancient times this has been the rule adopted by the German law, in the absence of specific provision, in the case of partible obligations, and consequently in the case of money debts in particular, whether arising from contract or, like the wergilds and bóts of near kindred, from delicts. To be sure, this rule, which passed over into modern codes, including the present Civil Code (§ 420), has been much impaired by very numerous exceptions. This is true of the present law, in which the exceptions are more important than the rule. Otherwise this relation is a simple one, and has always been treated as one in which the partial claims are, aside from certain common effects, completely independent of each other, being simply shares in the debt, which shares, in the absence of special provisions, are treated as equal.

(II) **Inseverable Co-credits** ("ungeteilte Mitberechtigungen"). — More complicated were the relations, always richly developed in Germanic law, where one and the same claim, instead of being divided among several creditors, belonged to them as a whole. This may appear under three forms:

(1) *Co-credits held in solidum* ("Gesamtgläubigerschaft"). — This corresponds to the community of full co-rights (*supra*, p. 239). The relation was imported into Germany with the Reception, but hardly possessed any noteworthy importance in the older German law. It is regulated to-day in the present Civil Code much as it was in the Roman law (§§ 428–430). Here, where the common law theory spoke of "active correal obligations", each creditor was entitled to demand full performance without regard to his co-creditors, and a payment to one creditor satisfied the entire debt as against all the others. There was here involved, therefore, a right of each co-creditor which was wholly independent; although, unlike the case of several creditors of a common debtor, it was dependent in a high degree upon the like rights of the other joint creditors, inasmuch as it was extinguished if one of those was satisfied. On the whole, this relationship is very rare. In statutory form also, it occurs only in a few cases under the present Civil Code.

(2) *Co-credits for undivided shares* ("Mitgläubigerschaft nach Bruchteilen").—This corresponded to co-ownership in undivided shares (*supra*, p. 238) and to the communities in undivided shares of the law of persons (*supra*, p. 152). This relation applied, particularly, to all claims to an impartible performance, and according to the present Civil Code (§ 432) it is the rule assumed, in such cases, in the absence of specific provision to the contrary. Each co-creditor is here entitled to enforce the entire performance, "but without prejudice to the similar right of the other creditors."[1] That is, above all, he cannot demand that the debtor shall perform to him alone, but only that he shall pay to all the co-creditors together, since the debtor is entitled to make such performance only to all.

(3) *Co-credits held in collective hand.*—This corresponds to ownership in collective hand (*supra*, pp. 234 *et seq.*) and to communities of collective hand (*supra*, p. 150). The older German law ordinarily applied the principles of collective hand to claims held by a number of creditors (true, the medieval sources contain only scanty references to the subject). Where the principle of collective hand prevails the credit belongs to all the creditors, and is therefore undivided and undivisible.[2] None of the creditors may enforce the entire claim alone in his own name nor any part of it, since here the debt is simple, and not divisible into independent parts. Only all the creditors together, acting in collective hand, can claim performance. To an action by but one of them, for himself, the debtor would not be bound to answer; although according to medieval legal systems it was quite possible to appoint one of the creditors attorney for all, exactly as when one rentaler paid for himself and other tenants of a severed rental holding ("Einzinsereiverhältnis"); and this might even be done by lot. In the same way the debt cannot be partially satisfied by payment of a quota to one creditor, as such, nor wholly by payment of the whole to one creditor. It is satisfied only by full performance of the entire obligation to all the obligees jointly.

This form of community credit naturally resulted in all cases where the creditors stood in a personal relation of collective hand, and in such cases it was preserved even after the Reception. Similarly according to the present Civil Code it exists by force of law "in the case of all claims acquired against third persons by

[1] *Cosack*, "Bürgerliches Recht", I (3d ed.), 391.
[2] *v. Amira*, "Obligationenrecht", II, 104.

members of a contractual partnership"[1] (§§ 709, 718); and further in the marital community of goods, after its dissolution and pending distribution (§ 1472). Moreover, it can always be adopted by the parties' agreement.

§ 81. **Plurality of Debtors.** — All those cases where there are several obligors and only one obligation ("Schuld") are explainable, from the standpoint of Germanic law, by the distinction between legal duty, or obligation ("Schuld"), and liability ("Haftung", *supra*, pp. 463 *et seq.*). So many obligors, so many liabilities; but these liabilities are for one and the same obligation. For the rest, there are here exactly the same possibilities as in the case of a plurality of creditors.

(I) **Several Obligations** ("Teilverpflichtung"). — When several persons are liable for the same obligation ("Schuld"), but the obligation is divisible, the liability can also be apportioned among them. No one of them may then be held for the entire obligation but each is responsible for a certain share thereof, — known in the sources of the time of the Law-Books as "anzahl" ("number"); and if he satisfies that he thereby drops out of the group of those liable.[2] Such several obligations are therefore, in respect of their legal existence, wholly independent, and do not substantially affect one another. In case of apportionable performances it was assumed in the Middle Ages, in default of specific provisions,[3] that this was the kind of obligation intended; an agreement to the same effect was known as "schlicht geloben."[4] In modern times the principle was preserved in some codes, — for example, in the Austrian and the Saxon codes, the Code Civil, and the Swiss Code of Obligation Law (§ 148); but like the corresponding principle of several claims it was subject to numerous exceptions. Thus the Civil Code provides that when several persons are obligated to an apportionable performance, at least when so obligated by force of law, each of them shall, in the absence of express provision, be obligated only to a partial performance, namely an equal performance (§ 420). But in very many cases such division is excluded, — for example in the liability of co-sureties, of several obligors of an active land-charge ("Reallast"), in torts, and particularly in the law of family relations and inheritance.

(II) **Inseverable Co-obligations** ("ungeteilte Mitverpflichtung").

[1] *Cosack, op. cit.*, 393.
[2] *v. Amira*, "Obligationenrecht", I, 171, II, 193.
[3] *Heusler*, "Institutionen", II, 258.
[4] *Cf.* the variant readings of the Ssp., III, 9, § 2.

— If several persons are liable for the same obligation the liability for the whole may be imposed upon each. Here again, as in the case of several obligations, there exist as many liabilities as there are persons liable, and all these liabilities refer to one and the same obligation. But in this case each of the persons liable can be charged with the entire obligation. On the other hand, an obligor who satisfies the entire obligation in satisfaction of his own liability releases not only himself but also all co-obligors from liability.[1]

Such an undivided co-obligation may appear in two forms: the individual is either liable for the whole independently of the other co-obligors (severally), or only jointly with these.

(1) We may call a *collective* (" Gesamt "; loosely = 'joint and several') obligation [2] that form in which each co-debtor is bound to perform the entire obligation, but subject to this, that all the debtors shall be bound to satisfy the obligation only once. The creditor may select from among the co-obligors any one at his pleasure and compel him to perform, or in case of non-performance hold him liable therefor.[3]

This form of co-obligation was common in the older law: it sometimes occurred in obligations for torts, sometimes in obligations under juristic act, as for example in the liability of a surety and the surety-giver. If the one against whom action was brought satisfied the obligation, it was left to him to effect an arrangement with his co-obligors. In the later Middle Ages, to be sure, it was frequently provided, in contradiction of the fundamental idea of the institute, that the creditor might hold each of the joint and several debtors liable for a quota only; but in case the quota due from one or several co-obligors was not obtainable, they all remained liable pending complete satisfaction of the obligation, so that the others were obliged to assume the quotas of those not paying. This view corresponded to the " exceptio divisionis " of the later Roman law, which was adopted in many statutes of the period of the Reception. But with this exception the attitude adopted towards the Roman rules of multiple obligation was rather unreceptive, mainly because the concept therein developed of an opposition between solidary (" Solidar ") and correal (" Korreal- ") obligations was then, and remained, a much debated one. The modern codes, on the other hand, in regulating collective

[1] *v. Amira*, "Obligationenrecht", I, 177.
[2] *Cosack*, "Bürgerliches Recht", I (6th ed.), 465.
[3] *v. Amira*, "Obligationenrecht."

obligations, conformed far more nearly in important matters to the older native views. They recognized the creation of collective obligation both by force of law, and by virtue of the parties' will. In the latter case certain formal expressions remained customary; as for example "one for all and all for one", "all and sundry", "solidarily", etc. Whereas some codes have established a presumption in favor of several liabilities ("Teilverpflichtung"; above, under I), the Prussian "Landrecht" and the General Commercial Code (§ 280) prescribed joint and several obligation in the absence of specific provisions. Among obligors treated as joint and several debtors by force of law were persons liable in damages for some legal fault (and so, for example, "concubentes" as regarded obligations of maintenance), — various sureties, various guardians, and various signers of a bill of exchange (WO, § 81). At the same time the creditor is left a choice "whether he", as it is expressed in the Austrian Code (§ 891), "will claim the whole from all or from some of the co-debtors, or from a single one. . . . If he is satisfied only in part by one or by another of the co-debtors, he can claim the balance from the others."

In contrast to the clouding of the institute's basic idea that was introduced in the Middle Ages when a joint and several debtor was made primarily liable only for a quota, and in contrast to the "beneficium divisionis" consequently recognized in the common law, the older Saxon practice, as well as all the modern codes with the sole exception of the Zürich Code, charged each debtor with the whole in accord with good Germanic law, but gave the debtor who paid the whole a claim for indemnity against his co-debtors whom he so released, without any assignment to him of the creditor's claim.

The present Civil Code has conformed in essentials to these statutes; particularly to the Prussian "Allgemeines Landrecht." Like that it recognizes a presumption of joint and several obligation (§ 427), even in the case of apportionable obligations, when the obligation is created by contract; and in accord with the pure Germanic law it makes each of the joint and several debtors liable for the whole. According to it, also, the creditor has a choice whether he will go against a single debtor for the whole or for a part, or against all for the whole or for shares. These different liabilities are dependent upon one another, inasmuch as various legal facts exercise their effects upon all collectively, — for example performance, accord and satisfaction, judicial or public deposit, set-off and counter claim, impossibility of performance, failure of the creditor to accept performance; not, on the other hand, ordinarily, demand of payment, mere delay in performance, negative prescription, etc. In their relation with one another the debtors are obligated for equal parts (§ 426); they therefore constitute in theory a legal community, and this imposes upon them a mutual duty of indemnity.

(2) *Obligations in collective hand* ("zu gesamter Hand"; loosely = 'joint'). — Here again each co-debtor is (theoretically) bound fully to satisfy the performance that is due; but this performance can be demanded only of all together. The obligee cannot, in this case, demand of any one of the co-obligors at his pleasure that he alone perform or be liable for non-performance. On the contrary he must bring his action against all of them jointly; for though they are liable for the whole they are liable only with one another. This relation was common in the older German law, along with the widespread prevalence of communities of collective hand. Where it was created otherwise than by force of law it was created by the formality peculiar to the principle of collective hand; that is, by common act in concluding the contract "coniuncta manu." Nevertheless it was and is less important than the joint and several obligation. Whereas the Prussian "Allgemeines Landrecht" recognized obligations of collective hand in the case of all unapportionable obligations created otherwise than by act of the parties, the present Civil Code recognizes them only where the co-debtors are liable with a definite special estate; that is, particularly, in the case of partners so far as they are liable with the partnership estate, and in the case of co-heirs so far as they are liable with the inheritance and this is still undistributed (§ 2059).[1]

[1] *Cosack*, "Bürgerliches Recht."

Chapter X

SPECIAL FORMS OF OBLIGATIONS

Topic 1. Obligations ex Contractu

§ 82. **Obligations ex contractu, generally.** — The development of distinct types of contract, distinguished by legal characteristics, is always the result solely of increased trade and advanced juristic technic. In the development of the medieval law one can trace the gradually appearing differentiation of the various forms of contract. Like the law of things, the law of obligations started with a single legal form, which it at first adjusted to all the needs of life. This oldest contract was that of sale, "the typical contract of Germanic law."[1] Hence we find the word "chouf" in the old High German glosses, for example, employed in the general sense of "negotium", "merces", "business transaction" ("Geschäft"); and the Scandinavian languages designated with the words "kaupa" and "kaup" every contract "that can be called in any sense a trading transaction ('Handelschaft')."[2] A sale ("Kauf") in this oldest sense, however, was nothing else than a gift ("Gabe") that obligated the person receiving it to some counter performance. Consequently, all transactions that could in any way arise could be regarded as varieties of this all-inclusive concept, for the transactions of primitive legal traffic, — which could be concluded only as non-credit transactions (*supra*, p. 459), — invariably consisted in a mutual delivery of goods for goods (barter) or of goods for a money price (sale in the narrow sense). And this was not affected by the fact that the spot transaction could be replaced by a real contract, for here also the delivery of the thing created the obligation of the other party. This delivery was a "gift with a charge" ("Gabe mit Auflage"); a type of contract whose characteristics resembled not only those of a sale on credit but also those of a loan and a bailment for custody.

The gratuitous gift or donation ("Schenkung"), also fell within this category. For although the essential characteristic of the donation as the law was finally developed lay in the gratuitous nature of the payment ("Zuwendung"), this characteristic was originally alien to Germanic law. Like all other primitive legal systems it recognized solely transactions for value. Every performance ("Leistung"), if it was to produce legal effects and enjoy legal protection, required a counter performance. Therefore the "Schenkung" also required a counter gift. This principle, however, which necessarily followed from the exclusive recognition of non-credit contracts, was felt to be at the same time a moral obligation; since the present required the thanks of the recipient, the latter, it was said, should repay gift with gift. The legal aspect of this

[1] *Schröder*, "Lehrbuch", 64.
[2] *v. Amira*, "Obligationenrecht", II, 287.

idea was developed most logically by the Lombards. Their law required for the legal validity of the donation that something pass in turn from the donee to the donor, — which, however, in order that it might not disappoint the good will expressed in the donation, was a mere nominal gift, a so-called "launegild" ("Lohngeld").[1] It was only the "launegild" which made the donation irrevocable; through it this acquired the character of a spot contract.[2]

To be sure, already in the Middle Ages the various transactions that were needed in commerce were developed with increasing distinctness from the single, originally all-inclusive, normal type of contract; a distinction between the purposes of trading transactions being followed by a distinction between the corresponding institutes of the law. Sale, hire ("Miete"), lease ("Pacht"), pledge, and other contracts were thus legally differentiated from one another. The German law, however, did not attain to any perfection of theory in its law of contracts. As already mentioned (*supra*, p. 463), that was first realized under the influence of the Roman law. It is significant that the legal sources of German Switzerland, where the influence won by Roman law was very much weaker, maintained down into the 1700s an almost absolute silence concerning different forms of contract.[3]

In view of these facts we need only emphasize in the following pages a few matters in which the Germanic law either attained a noteworthy independent development, or preserved old rules as part of the modern law of trade that has been developed upon the basis of the Roman law.

§ 83. **Contracts of Sale.**[4] — (I) **Prohibitions** ("Verbote"). — The fact, above mentioned, that every sale was originally concluded as a non-credit transaction explains the other fact that there still existed in the Middle Ages such a preference for spot sales that sales for future delivery, — also known as "Vorkauf" ("forestalling" a sale before the goods are available), — although common in practice, were repeatedly forbidden by statute. This was still the case in the 1400 s at Hansa fairs, and

[1] *Liutprand*, 73.

[2] *Val de Lièvre*, "Launegild und Wadia" (1877), and "Revision der Launegildstheorie", Z². R. G., IV (1883), 15–54; *Pappenheim*, "Launegild und Garethinx", no. 14 (1882) of *Gierke's* "Untersuchungen."

[3] *Huber*, "Schw. Privatrecht", IV, 849.

[4] *Conze*, "Kauf nach hanseatischen Quellen" (dissertation, Bonn, 1889); *Rabel*, "Die Haftung des Verkäufers wegen Mangels im Rechte, Erster Teil: Geschichtliche Studien über den Haftungserfolg" (1902).

likewise in many of the Hanseatic systems of town law (Breslau, Lübeck, Riga) and in Swiss legal systems.

Other prohibitions and restrictions originated in considerations of a lego-political nature. In order to discourage usurious over-reaching (*infra,* § 86), the sale of uncut grain was frequently prohibited, and in general all sales whatever in which measures were resorted to by which the just relation between price and goods was falsified or the recognition of the relation made impossible. In order to suppress middlemen, and to insure the conclusion of all sales under the eyes of public authorities, it was forbidden to sell goods that had not yet reached their final (" eigentlichen ") market; particularly, sales outside the gates of the city (likewise known as " Vorkauf ", forestalling), and the like.

(II) **Obligation of General Warranty and of Warranty of Title.** — Germanic law imposed upon the seller a duty of warranty corresponding to the old Roman " auctoritas."[1] That is, when a third person, by legal action, demanded of a purchaser the delivery of the thing purchased, the seller was bound, upon formal citation by the impleaded buyer, to appear in court, give warranty, take the place of the buyer as defendant in the action, and by a favorable prosecution of the suit preserve the seisin of the thing to his buyer (*supra,* p. 411); for, as it is expressed in the French coûtumes, " tous vendères doit varandir." To be sure, there was no procedural compulsion thus to assume the defense (" defensio ", " Schirmung "). But a warrantor who did not appear was regarded as a thief, and was obliged to pay to the complaining third party the bőt for larceny and to repay the purchase price to the purchaser, since the buyer whose warrantor made default was obliged to deliver the thing to the third person. In the same way the seller was liable in damages if defeated in the action he undertook to defend. Although this duty of warranty existed by force of law it was nevertheless customary, when a contract of sale was concluded, to promise it in penalty clauses in the instrument; in these the seller not only promised for himself and his successors in title not to disturb in future the possession of the vendee, but also expressly assumed the duty of warranty against legal attacks by third parties.

This law of warranty, which was closely associated with the medieval system of procedure as well as with the principles of seisin, was maintained in essentially undiminished authority so long as

[1] This view is attacked by *Herbert Meyer* in the "Festschrift für Gierke", 995 *et seq.*

the body of the Germanic law remained intact. As late as the beginning of the 1600 s it was possible to say in Austria: "every sale carries warranty and protection 'on its back' ('auf dem ruckhen')." [1] Indeed, the old system of warranty remained in force in many places after the Reception, although only in a weakened form. In France voucher to warranty was transformed into a "guaranty-action", by which the naming of a warrantor became merely a defense available to the defendant at his option; it was at his disposal in case he did not wish to make use of the right of independent defense that was now permitted to him in all cases.[2] In Germany, the reception of the alien law gradually sapped of vitality the traditional native principles. In consequence, acceptance was generally accorded to a theory which, under the controlling influence of the Germanic idea of voucher to warranty, had developed in medieval Italy out of the purely substantive liability of the vendor in Roman law for the "habere licere" a procedural duty of "defence" or warranty ("Defensionspflicht") that was exercisable through a "litis denuntiatio," and also an action to compel such defense. Native and alien ideas, principles of substantive and procedural law, rules of positive law and theories of natural law, were combined in this theory, which created in the law an exceeding confusion that is here and there reflected in the great modern codes. Clarification was introduced for the first time when the Historical School of the 1800 s rediscovered the pure Roman law and its liability for "habere licere", — the so-called warranty of title (warranty against eviction, "Eviktionsklage"), — and taught students that under the Roman law the vendor, as such, was obligated merely to perform the act of conveyance and was not responsible for the result of such conveyance; and that consequently he must assume a supplementary warranty of possession, — that is, of the "habere licere." The Civil Code, finally, has done away with all earlier differences and doubts by establishing the principle, which is substantively in agreement with the early Germanic law, that the vendor is obligated to secure to the vendee an unimpeachable ("lastenfreie") title to the thing purchased (§§ 433–434): a rule that was unknown to the Roman law, and which could not have been laid down in that form even by the medieval law, because this did not proceed from ownership but from seisin. The vendee is entitled to-day (as he was earlier under

[1] *Rabel, op. cit.*, 204.
[2] *Wach*, "Handbuch des deutschen Civilprozessrechts", I (1885), 657.

the Prussian "Landrecht") not only, as formerly, to an action against his vendor in case of eviction (disseisin), but whenever the better right of a third person can be established. A notification of a claim by a third party is accordingly no longer requisite. On the other hand, in all those cases in which the vendee, despite the defective title of his vendor, acquires ownership without further steps through the rule "hand warrant hand" or as a result of the public faith of the land register (*supra*, pp. 223, 438), it is no longer necessary to sue the vendor.

(III) **Defects in the Thing Sold.** — Although the old Germanic duty of warranty already imposed upon a seller, in modern phraseology, liability for defects of title ("Mangel im Recht", defects "in law"), there did not exist, generally speaking, a liability for physical defects in the thing sold. To be sure, good faith required that the thing sold should possess the qualities positively agreed upon, and should be without any considerable faults ("Fehler"). But if the buyer had once seen and accepted the thing he could not thereafter bring an action for defects that became apparent later. His acceptance was regarded as an approval which deprived him of the right of later objection ("Rüge"). Hence the maxims, "he who does not open his eyes opens his purse", "he who buys like a fool must pay like a wise man." It was only when the seller concealed defects with intent to deceive ("arglistig"), or when there were involved certain especially serious defects (which were typically defined for different sorts of goods), or defects of qualities expressly averred to be present, that the seller was liable for these. In such cases the seller might within a certain short period "wandeln" the transaction, that is rescind it, and then demand the repayment of the purchase price upon redelivery of the goods. In case of concealment with intent to deceive, the purchaser also had a claim for damages. This treatment of the seller, in general mild, was made decidedly harsher by the adoption of the Roman rules. For from that time onward a liability was imposed upon the seller, in accordance with the Roman law, for all so-called "latent" ("heimlich", secret) defects, — that is, defects not perceptible at the time the sale was concluded; and this was not excluded even by an acceptance of the goods without reservation of rights. More than this, the buyer was accorded at his will the so-called ædilian actions of Roman law, — namely the "actio redhibitoria", which corresponded to the action for rescission ("Wandelungsklage") of Germanic law, and the "actio quanti minoris " (" Minderungsklage ", action for abatement of price), — and in addition to these, in case of special warranty (" Zusagen ") or culpable conduct on the part of the seller, an action upon the contract for damages (" actio emti "). The system of actions which was thus established by the common law passed over into the modern codes. At the same time after-effects of the old native law continued, — so, especially, in many legal systems the rule that the buyer forfeited his right by an acceptance without reservation thereof. This continued to be recognized in the Hamburg law in its original strictness, and in case of all (even latent) defects. The Prussian " Landrecht " adopted it, at least in the weakened form that the buyer must immediately object to such defects as he noticed at the time of acceptance, or ought to have noticed. The General Commercial Code also adopted the view of the Germanic law, requiring in sales between absent parties that the buyer, immediately after the delivery of the goods sent to him, should examine them with due care, and must then without delay give notice to the seller of defects known to or knowable by him; defects which became perceptible only later must be reported immediately upon their discovery (§ 347). The present Civil Code has rejected, in favor of the opposite Roman rule, the view of Germanic law that the buyer lost his rights, in case of possible defects in the thing, by an acceptance without reservation; it is only as to those defects which the buyer has demonstrably known at the time of acceptance that it requires a special reservation of his rights (§ 464). But the new Commercial Code has in turn preserved the duty of examination and objection in all sales between merchants; in other words, it has preserved the stricter treatment of the buyer under Germanic law (§ 377).

Finally, in the case of cattle transactions, the rule of the old law was preserved throughout a great part of Germany, and most especially in the entire South and in Saxony; the seller being made liable only for certain particularly important defects known as " chief " (" Haupt- ") defects, which are exactly defined by statute. There was not at all involved in this, originally, a preference of those selling cattle as compared with other vendors; for under the old law, as already stated, every seller had enjoyed the same favorable treatment. After the reception of the stricter Roman rules, however, which made the seller liable for all latent defects, the preservation of the old rule in such cases actually became a privilege of those who sold cattle. The "ludicrous Mosaic of legal diversities"[1] presented by the theretofore existing law of the cattle trade was done away with by the detailed provisions of the present Civil Code (§§ 482–492). It has adopted in this matter the traditional native rules. Liability exists only for certain "chief" defects which are listed in a catalogue prepared by imperial order; and this only when they appear and are duly objected to within a definite and unusually short period (3, 10, 14, or 28 days). Moreover, the buyer has no action under the Code for abatement, but ordinarily only a right of rescission, — and in the case of animals purchased for breeding the right to a later delivery of an undefective in place of the defective animal. In the new Swiss Code of Obligation Law the rule has been adopted, in the case of a sale of cattle (§ 202), that if the written warranty contains no provision as to time, and there is no question of a warranty of gravidity, the seller is liable to the buyer only when the defect is discovered and notice given thereof within nine days, or when an examination of the animal by experts is demanded of the authorities within a like period.

(IV) **Transfer of Risk.** — The treatment of the question from what moment an accidental destruction of or damage to the thing sold shall be borne by the buyer, and no longer by the seller, was determined in the old Germanic law by the rule that the risk, like the usufruct, should pass to the buyer with the transfer of the seisin. Consequently, the transfer of risk took place in the case of chattels at the moment of acquiring the corporeal seisin, and in the case of lands at the moment of investiture, — originally corporeal investiture, but later, when symbolical investiture was introduced, equally at the moment this was realized, and so, notably, under the medieval law at the moment of release ("Auflassung"). In this case, therefore, the usufruct and the risk might be separated (*supra*, p. 189). These rules of Germanic law, — as contrasted with the opposing Roman rules according to which the "periculum" passed at the conclusion of the agreement to sell, — were preserved in some of the regional legal systems. They were adopted by the Prussian "Landrecht" and by the Austrian Code, and in the case of chattels have finally been recognized by the Civil Code (§§ 446–447). When goods were sent to a buyer from another place the risk passed, according to the older Germanic law, at the moment of dispatch. This rule, also, has been adopted by the Civil Code, following the example of the Prussian "Allgemeines Landrecht",

[1] *Cosack*, "Bürgerliches Recht", I (3d ed.), 429.

but with the difference that such dispatch is no longer treated by the former as a delivery, as it was in the Prussian law.

§ 84. **Hire and Lease.**[1] — (I) Unlike the unitary concept of the Roman "locatio conductio", **hire and lease** were developed by the medieval law as two different although nearly related contracts. The distinguishing characteristic lay in the fact that in the case of the hire ("Miete"), — which, to be sure, occurred only rarely in the Middle Ages, — the user consisted exclusively in the bare use ("Gebrauch") of the dwelling, whereas in the lease ("Pacht") it included also the enjoyment of the fruits and profits of the land. However, inasmuch as in both contracts the hirer or the lessee (the bare or the usufructuary lessee) derived an economic benefit from the thing, he enjoyed, in the theory of Germanic law, the seisin of the object of the contract of hire or lease. Consequently, in the medieval law hire as well as lease secured to the person entitled thereunder a real right, which like all other real rights was effective not only against the other party to the contract but also against all third persons (*supra*, p. 162).

(II) **The Chief Consequence** of the real nature of the right that inhered in the hirer and the lessee by virtue of his seisin, was the rule laid down in numerous legal sources[2] that "a sale does not revoke a hire", "hire precedes title", "hire 'breaks' a sale" ("hur brickt koep"). This meant, in particular, that a buyer or other acquirer of a thing let to hire was bound to recognize the validity of the contract of hire as against himself, and could not evict the hirer before the expiration of the contract term. He was a party by force of law to all contracts of hire affecting the land; such contracts were "concluded by the original lessor ('Vermieter') not only for himself but at the same time in favor of and as a charge upon all future owners of the land hired."[3] To be sure, many legal systems, notably those of the Frisian-Saxon law, had recognized the opposite rule before any contact with alien influences, — "sale 'breaks' hire" ("koep de drift hure ap"), — and this rule (which also prevailed in the old French law) likewise passed, later, into many of the regional systems. Some of the modern codes, such as the Austrian and the Saxon, in turn adopted it; and since it prevailed also in the Roman law it acquired in Germany, in consequence of the Re-

[1] *v. Brünneck*, "Zur Geschichte der Miethe und Pacht in den deutschen und germanischen Rechten des Mittelalters" in Z^2. R. G., I (1880), 138–190.

[2] For example "Rechtsbuch nach Distinctionen", II, 4 d, 5.

[3] *Cosack*, in *Gerber's* "System" (17th ed.), 355.

ception, general validity in the common law. The contract of hire was thus reduced to a mere obligational relation. Other codes, on the contrary, clung to the other view. So, particularly, the Hamburg law, the Prussian "Allgemeines Landrecht" (I, 21, § 358), and the Code Civil (§ 1743).[1] Finally, the rule "sale yields to hire" has been embodied, after violent opposition, in the present Civil Code (§ 571). Whether the real nature of hire and lease essential to the old law of seisin has thus again become positive law is a disputed question, but the affirmative opinion is accepted only in very rare instances.[2]

(III) **Agistment** ("Viehverstellung") was a peculiar contract, regulated in the Germanic law with especial care, by which a bailor delivered domestic beasts of pasture to another, the agistor, for feed and care. The contract was concluded in various ways. In some cases it took the form of a simple contract of lease, in which the agistor took over the cattle, collected the profits thereof, and paid in return a certain rent in money or in kind; if the cattle were lost by "vis maior", the owner ordinarily bore the loss, in accordance with the general principles of Germanic law (*supra*, p. 529), whereas the agistor must bear all other damages. In other cases a "half" ("Halb-") lease was agreed upon,—either the ownership of the cattle remaining with the bailor but he and the agistor dividing the offspring, or the cattle themselves being apportioned; so that the two parties constituted a community or partnership. Again, a so-called "Eisernviehvertrag" ("iron" contract) was frequently concluded: in this the lessee or agistor assumed outright liability for the cattle then upon the land, as regularly taxed; at the expiration of the lease he was obliged to leave behind upon the estate cattle of equal number and of like qualities. The cattle, therefore, could not be lost to the owner; whence the name of "iron" or "everlasting" cattle. The earlier modern codes laid down numerous provisions with respect to these contracts, which were very differently regulated in details (so, too, the new Swiss Code of Obligation Law (§§ 302–304)), but the present Civil Code contains no special provisions concerning them.

[1] *Cf. v. Schwind*, "Kauf bricht Miete", in "Festschrift zur Jahrhundertfeier des (österreichischen) allgemeinen bürgerlichen Gesetzbuchs" (1911), II, 931 *et seq.*

[2] See *Cosack's* decided opinion to this effect in his "Bürgerliches Recht", II (6th ed.), 289 *et seq.*, and *Crome's* equally decided opinion, agreeing with the prevailing view, in his "System", II, 580, and in *Ihering's* J. B., XXXVII (1896), 1 *et seq.*

§ 85. **Contracts for Labor and for Services. (I) Contracts for Labor.**[1] — (1) *The medieval law.* — Although the legal sources of the Middle Ages did not formulate the theoretical concept of a labor contract, and although not even a common name for such contracts was known in the older law, nevertheless there was developed in Germany even early in the Middle Ages an abundant law regulating them. From the time of the folk-laws there existed free laborers with whom independent contracts for labor were concluded; and although these were naturally of no great importance in rural districts they were more important in the cities. For in these there was developed from the 900 s onward an active industry, in the form both of handicraft ("Handwerk"), — that is, labor upon an object made for sale, — and of job work ("Lohnarbeit", "Kundenarbeit"), — labor for customers. In various industries job-labor predominated, as household labor at the home either of the workman ("Heimarbeit") or the customer ("Störarbeit"). In many industries production for future sale ("Handwerk") was even prohibited. In job-work the material was given to the contractor ("Fürgedinger") to be worked up on his own responsibility, whether in his own home or in that of the employer. The labor was always remunerated in goods or money, for wages were of the essence of a contract for labor. The wage was either freely agreed upon, or as was very commonly the case, it was fixed in wage-tariffs established by local governmental authorities or by the craft. In this connection it did not matter, according to the medieval view, whether the producer was remunerated in the form of a task price ("Akkordlohn") for undertaking the work as a whole (in which case men spoke of "ein Werk bestên", or "annemen", "aufnemen"), or in that of a wage by time ("Zeitlohn"). In one as in the other case the contract was treated as a contract or hire of labor ("Werkvertrag", "Werkmiete"), and was distinguished from a contract or hire of services ("Dienstvertrag", "Dienstmiete"),—in which latter, not the laborer himself but the lord entitled to his services "directed the labor of another to the purpose he desired."[2] The job-contract ("verding", "fürgriff") controlled the fabrication of most objects necessary in daily life, but in the case of more considerable tasks the reward was customarily given periodically, particularly in the erection of

[1] *Rothenbücher*, "Geschichte des Werkvertrags nach deutschem Rechte", No. 87 (1906) of *Gierke's* "Untersuchungen."

[2] *Rothenbücher*, *op. cit.*, 24.

larger buildings, cathedrals, city halls, and bridges, and also, later, the castles of princes and moneyed magnates. The lay builders who displaced, after the rise of the Gothic style, the builders and artisans of the church, were customarily appointed for a definite time, not infrequently for life, by a city, a cathedral chapter, or a local ruler, in order to oversee a construction in return for a periodical wage. They in turn employed the artisans under contracts for services, under which pay was usually given similarly in the form of a periodical wage, and only rarely by the task. Inasmuch as the material was ordinarily furnished, under medieval labor contracts, by the employer, and not by the contractor, — although artists, even in later times, almost always furnished the canvas and the paints, especially the gold for their pictures, — the distinction between a labor contract and a sale was easier than in the modern law. Whether an artist's contract should be treated as one of sale or for labor in those cases, which became more common from the middle 1400 s onward, where artists themselves furnished paints and gold, stone and wood, thereby undertaking to deliver non-fungible things that were still to be created, does not appear from the sources. The labor was required to be performed almost entirely by the contractor personally, subcontracting being for the most part prohibited. As a matter of course this was true in especial degree of contracts by artists, notwithstanding which, however, this duty was often expressly imposed. For example, Albrecht Dürer, in his contract for the painting of the Heller altarpiece, expressly bound himself to make the middle piece himself, "and no other human being than myself shall paint one stroke of it." [1] Relatively little importance was attributed to delivery at an appointed date; provisions concerning this are rare, and delays beyond the time appointed ordinarily resulted in no legal prejudice; time was not yet expensive. All the greater insistence was laid, however, upon the excellence and utility of the product. Not only the person ordering the thing, but also the crafts, in the interest of the good repute of their labor, strictly enforced this. The contractor was liable for defects in the product until acceptance by the employer, who was bound to make an examination of the article. By so doing he deprived himself of the right of later objection. If the contract was defectively performed through the fault of the contractor, the employer had an action to enforce its repair ("Chör und Wandel") and for damages. Various

[1] *Rothenbücher, op. cit.*, 49.

beginnings are already found of a right in the employer to abate the price, and in the same way he often reserved to himself in the contract a right of rescission. Conversely, in case the employer defaulted in an act to which he was contractually obligated he must give the contractor damages; and so, for example, Tilmann Riemenschneider received damages because he was obliged to wait ten days for scaffolding that was to be furnished him, and which he needed, for the erection of the tabernacle in the Würzburg Cathedral.[1] The point regulated in greatest detail in such contracts was the duty of every contractor to redeliver the material delivered to him, but which remained in the ownership of the employer; for the loss of this was the greatest danger to which the employer was exposed.

(2) *The development in the modern period.* — The Germanic law of labor contracts was maintained substantially intact, in a few legal systems, down into the 1700 s; notably in those of Bavaria, Lübeck and Riga, and in part in the regions of the Kulm and Hamburg law as well. But as respects some of its rules it retained authority far beyond these isolated districts. For it had been developed already in the Middle Ages as a customary law based upon constant contractual practice, and this basis of customary law retained authority, and made impossible the application of the Roman law. The codes of the modern period, under the influence of the common law, passed over the labor contract, in great part, in silence; others mentioned it merely in connection with contracts of hire ("Miete"); and only a few, as for example the town law of Freiburg, regulated its cardinal principles in agreement with those of the Roman "locatio conductio operis." The treatment of the labor contract that became established in legal theory after the Reception was based substantially upon the Roman law. The consequence of this was that the peculiar character of such contracts was overlooked, and the doctrinal union of labor contracts with the hire of things ("Sachmiete") in the Roman law, which was there due to peculiar historical reasons, was treated as a logical necessity. The Prussian "Allgemeines Landrecht" was the first code to free itself, under the influence of ideas of natural law, from this dependence; it treated the labor contract, as was fitting, under contracts requiring positive acts ("Handlungen"). It was followed by the Austrian Code, which grouped labor contracts with contracts for services under the concept of the wage contract ("Lohnvertrag"); by the Swiss

[1] *Rothenbücher, op. cit.*, 69.

Code of Obligation Law (§§ 363–379), by the Saxon Code, and finally by the present Civil Code (§§ 631–651). This has adopted, as regards assumption of risk and liability for defects, a whole series of rules derived from Germanic law. An important distinction, as compared with the contract of sale, is found in the fact that in case of imperfect delivery the employer has the right and the duty to demand, in the first place, repairs in the work in order to remove the defect. Moreover, in case of delay in performance he has a freer right of rescission than was formerly recognized. If the material is furnished by the contractor and the article to be made is a fungible thing, the Civil Code treats the contract as a pure contract of sale; and in case the thing is not fungible, as a contract intermediate between a sale and a contract for labor.

For the rest, the modern development of the law has led to an extreme specialization of the labor contract. The commercial law has developed the contracts of commission agents, forwarding agents, and of freight; the private law has created special rules for publishers' contracts, broker's contracts, and contracts of building contractors.

(II) **The contract for services.**[1] — The medieval law of Germany, as already mentioned, proved its ability to distinguish perfectly between the hire of labor ("Werkmiete") and of services ("Dienstmiete"). In the latter the worker himself was not regarded as responsible for the result; the owner was bound to direct the work. Moreover, the hire of services, which was at least as widely prevalent under rural conditions as in cities, was outwardly distinguished from the hire of labor; especially by the relation of dependence that ordinarily existed between the parties. The most numerous of all contractual services were those of servants, relatively to which voluntary contracts for services with wage-earners, bakers, etc., were of decidedly minor importance.

(1) *Contracts for household service* ("Gesindemiete"). — The contract for household service played no part in the law so long as the necessary economic needs of the household were partly

[1] *Hertz*, "Die Rechtsverhältnisse des freien Gesindes nach den deutschen Rechtsquellen des Mittelalters", No. 6 (1879) of *Gierke's* "Untersuchungen"; *Hedemann*, "Die Fürsorge des Gutsherrn für sein Gesinde (Brandenburgisch preussische Geschichte)", in the "Breslauer Festgabe für Dahn", I (1905), 165–220; *Lennhoff*, "Das ländliche Gesindewesen in der Kurmark Brandenburg vom 16. bis 19. Jahrhundert", No. 79 (1906) of *Gierke's* "Untersuchungen"; *Könnecke*, "Rechtsgeschichte des Gesindes in West- und Süddeutschland", in *Heymann's* "Arbeiten", XII (1912).

attended to by the householder and the members of his family as an independent economic unit, and partly by unfree, half-free, or even free, persons who were either subjected to his " mundium " as lord, and so subject to a relation of personal power, or entered into a real dependence by accepting a tenancy. In time, however, there appeared, beside these—first of all in the cities and then in the rural districts of the country, although owing to different needs,—a class of free servants. In the cities household servants and industrial apprentices became indispensable; in the rural regions the children of dependents ("Untertanenkinder"), especially, were employed as farm laborers and maids for a modest wage. This servant class entered into relations with the lord employing them by means of contracts for services, which not only possessed a contractual character but also constituted a sort of bond under the family law. The relation was therefore not limited to the performance of the services contracted for and payment of a wage therefor, but also, and in particular, made it the duty of the employer to give the laborers a certain amount of care. However, from the end of the Middle Ages onward, especially in rural regions, the originally favorable condition of the servant class suffered a progressive deterioration. This was associated with the increasing repression of the peasant estate. Especially on the seigniorial estates of the East there was developed a system of compulsory services; the lord's obligation of care wholly disappeared, and it is only since the age of rationalism and reform (" Aufklärungszeit ") that a change has resulted for the better. In Prussia the "Allgemeines Landrecht", and the Servants' Code of November 8, 1810, based upon that which was issued for the rural regions, regulated the legal relations of the servant class, urban and rural: compulsory service was abolished, a certain social duty of solicitude was again recognized, but on the other hand the patriarchial view was still maintained in many respects. The Prussian Servants' Code is still enforced today in such portions of that country as were formerly subject to the Landrecht. In all other parts of Germany relations of household service were similarly regulated anew by statute; in part by the great modern codes themselves, and in part and most frequently by a great quantity of local regulations. Because of the element of social police which the whole matter involves, the Introductory Act to the present Civil Code has left it to State law; but at the same time it has expressly abolished (§ 95) the right of physical punishment formerly enjoyed by persons entitled of legal right to the service of others. In addition to this the provisions of State law are supplemented by the Civil Code itself, and by other imperial statutes.

(2) *Other contracts for services.* — Other contracts for services are distinguished from the hire of household services, at least under the law as it exists to-day, by the fact that in them the person obligated to the service does not live with his employer. They may be of various kinds as respects their content. Their restriction in the Roman law, — which passed over into the common law, — to purely "personal" services, was abandoned by the Saxon Code, and is also lacking in the present German Civil Code. A special importance attaches to contracts for industrial services. The industrial apprenticeship contract, which is distinguished from a simple contract for services by the fact that it imposes upon the employer or master ("Dienstherr") the chief obligation under the contract, namely the education of the apprentice, was already richly developed in the medieval law of the craft-gilds. More recently it has been specially regulated by the Industrial Code and as respects commercial apprentices by the Commercial Code. These statutes, as well as the Civil Code in its most important provisions, have imposed upon the master a certain care for the physical and spiritual well-being of the apprentice that extends beyond the field of pure contract, thus returning to some extent to the more paternalistic viewpoint of the medieval law.

§ 86. **Loans at Interest.**[1] — During the supremacy of an agricultural economy money loans ("Darlehnsgeschäfte") occurred, on the whole, only rarely; for the lack of personal credit and the absence of any generally current representative of value ("Werte") excluded the possibility of interest.[2] Barter and pledge dominated economic life. These actual conditions, which became established everywhere in the Occident after the disintegration of the Roman Empire and the decay of the money economy fully developed in its cities, were favorable to the theories that were advocated by the church, and enforced by it with increasingly severe prohibitions. For whereas Roman imperial legislation

[1] *Puntschart,* art. "Borg", in *Hoop's* "Reallexikon", I, 304, art. "Darlehn", in the same, 389 *et seq.*; *Hedemann,* "Fortschritte des Zivilrechts", I, 9 *et seq.*, 132 *et seq.* The abundant literature, particularly that of economic history, is indicated by *v. Below,* art. "Wucher", in the W. B. der Volksw., II (3d ed., 1911), 1422–1430. Also *Isopescul-Grecul,* "Das Wucherstrafrecht", I (1906).

[2] *Huber,* "Schw. Privatrecht", IV. 866.

actually permitted unlimited interest, and even Justinian's reduction of the interest rate to 6 per cent and 8 per cent had only slight result, the Church, in view of certain passages in the Old and New Testament (especially the saying in Luke, vi, 35: "mutuum date nihil inde sperantes") repudiated the loan for interest as inconsistent with the law of God. The acceptance of interest was first prohibited to ecclesiastics and then in turn to laymen. Carolingian legislation adopted this prohibition, although it attained no great practical importance for the good reason that the transactions so prohibited were as good as unknown in Germanic lands. It was only when a money economy began again to develop with the increasing prosperity of cities, and the allowance of credit began to play an increasingly important rôle, that the church opened a new and energetic opposition, — but one that was henceforth opposed to the necessities of commerce. Alexander III, at the Lateran Council of 1179, threatened the "usurarii manifesti" with excommunication and denial of a churchly burial.[1] Gregory X, in 1274, ordered their expulsion from communes, corporations, and cities, as well as the repayment of all interest collected, under penalty of a denial of absolution and of churchly burial; at the same time he declared them incapable of testamentary dispositions, and their testaments void.[2] Finally, Clement V, in 1311 at the council of Vienna, declared null and void every secular statute opposed to these commands of the Church.[3] In this ecclesiastical legislation, which was defended by the Schoolmen with philosophical arguments, interest was classified under the concept of usury, and the latter was understood in its broadest and most comprehensive sense, including usury alike from credit and from things ("Kredit-", "Sachwucher"). In particular, it was applied to the contract of sale, the principle that only a "pretium iustum" might be demanded leading in this connection to numerous restrictions and to demands for governmental price tariffs. At this point, however, the usury theory of the Church came into conflict with the industrial policy observed by the secular authorities and the craft-gilds in the regulation of handicrafts (*supra*, p. 131). The greater the increase of commerce and the necessities of trade, the less observed was the Canonic prohibition of usury. They created abundant means of evading it, which, though denounced by the

[1] C. 3, X: de usuris, 5, 19.
[2] C. 1, 2, VI: de usuris, 5, 5.
[3] C. un. in Clem., de usuris, 5, 5.

Canonists, were commonly practiced, and were the source of many new and peculiar institutes of law. Such were, for example, the institute of contractual pledge with seisin "ut de vadio", already discussed, as well as the contractual pledge of a lessee (*supra*, pp. 260, 379); the purchase-rent (*supra*, p. 371); the so-called "contractus trinus", in which a loan was concealed under the form of a partnership contract between lender and borrower; and the "montes" that were developed in Italy, — aggregations of capital which were accumulated by a number of capitalists and turned over to state or city as a loan in exchange for an annuity. Inasmuch, moreover, as the Church permitted interest in case of default in payment, and equally in all cases where the interest ("Zins") represented compensation for actual loss or performance of special services, there resulted from these other opportunities for evasion, particularly the possibility of interest on debts evidenced by bills or promissory notes ("Wechselschuld"). Again, although Jews, as such, were by no means excepted from the Church's prohibition of usury, the penalties at the disposal of the Church had of course no efficacy against them. The popes were therefore compelled to be satisfied with inciting the secular authorities to measures against Jewish usurers. But these rulers, on the contrary, very generally granted to the Jews an express privilege to take interest in violation of the Canonic prohibition, since they themselves profited by taxing the Jews upon their usurious earnings. In the course of time the prohibition was more and more frequently violated even by the Christian population, and the rate of interest rose, on account of the difficulty of securing money loans on interest, to an enormous height. Like the rich Italian bankers, especially those of Florence, who were the first international money-changers on a big scale, and who attended in particular to the extensive banking business of the Roman curia; like the lesser Christian money-changers of Asti in Lombardy and Cahors in Provence (so-called "Lombards" and "Kawerschen") who settled in all the lands of the Occident and proved their ability to secure from rulers equal privileges with the Jews—so all other classes of the native population, nobles and burghers, bishops and simple clericals, gave and collected interest on money. At the same time legal theory and legislation clung to the Canonic doctrine. The Humanists and Reformers, with the exception of Calvin, also adhered to it. The Imperial Police Ordinance of 1530 set forth a catalogue of prohibited usurious transactions, and permitted only those contracts for land-credit which were known as "Wiederverkäufe" ("resales"), such as the purchase-rent and the contractual pledge ("Satzung").

Many local legal systems conceded the justice of interest as early as the 1500 s, — for example the Nuremberg Reformation of 1564 and the Saxon Constitutions of 1572; and these were finally followed by imperial legislation. The last Recess of the Imperial Diet of 1654 expressly permitted, in entirely general terms and for the entire Empire, the collection of interest, just as this had already been permitted to the Jews by the Imperial Police Ordinance of 1577. To be sure, complete freedom of interest was by no means thereby introduced. On the contrary a statutory rate of interest was established. The imperial statutes fixed this at 5 per centum; many of the regional systems also adopted this, whereas others introduced the Roman rate of 6 per centum. Still other systems recognized different rates: thus, the Prussian "Landrecht" prescribed 5 per cent. for transactions between ordinary citizens, 6 per cent. for merchants, and 8 per cent. for Jews. Licensed loan-houses were quite commonly granted privileges with respect to the rate of interest. In the meantime, also, the Canonic theory had been overturned by the law of nature, and the Church itself, notwithstanding that it never formally repealed the prohibition, adopted a milder practice. From the end of the 1700 s onward the tendency of the times turned against any restriction whatever upon interest agreements, and in particular against maximum rates established by statute. In 1787 Joseph II introduced for the first time by statute, though but temporarily, the principle of complete freedom in interest agreements, — subject, to be sure, to the observance of the rule that made claims for usurious interest uncollectable by suit. The Code Civil also went over to the principle of unregulated interest; but in this case there followed a restrictive statute (of September 3, 1807) which limited interest upon ordinary loans to 5 per cent and for mercantile loans to 6 per cent. The efforts directed toward the removal of all restrictions were crowned with success in Germany by the General Commercial Code (§ 292) as regarded mercantile transactions, and by the Act of the North German Confederation of November 14, 1867 (which was later extended throughout the Empire with the exception of Bavaria) as regarded trade among other citizens than merchants. In Bavaria a statute of December 5, 1867, similar to the Federal statute, likewise abolished restrictions upon contractual interest. This legislation recognized only two limitations upon the free regulation of interest: if more than 6 per cent was agreed upon, the debtor received a right to give notice every six months, after the expiration of the first half year, of intended payment; and further, interest upon interest could not be agreed upon in advance.

Inasmuch, however, as the complete abolition of usury thus introduced led to great evils, the statute of 1867 was subjected to thorough revision. An imperial statute of May 24, 1880, without again introducing a maximum interest rate, designated certain rates of interest as usurious, namely such as set a rate which is objectively unusually high, and those which rest subjectively upon an exploitation of the necessities, or levity, or inexperience of the debtor. Such usurious agreements, according to the provision of the statute of 1880, were not only void in themselves, but also voided the entire transaction of which they were a part. Further, the concept of usury has been given a comprehensive meaning similar to that which it possessed in the Canonistic theory, first by the Prussian "Landrecht" and by many statutes following that, and now also by imperial legislation. An imperial statute of June 19, 1893, declared void all transactions in which pecuniary advantages in any way excessive should be stipulated in favor of one party as a result of his exploitation of the necessity, inexperience, or levity of the other party to the contract, no matter whether such advantage should or should not be compensation for an advance of credit, — all this, to be sure, only when done in the ordinary course of trade or practice. The present Civil Code has rounded out the regulation of the subject by applying generally the preceding ideas. The general rule is freedom in interest rates; in the absence of special agreement statutory rates apply: ordinarily 4 per centum, in mercantile transactions 5 per centum. But every juristic act is void, as usurious, by which "one person, by exploiting the necessity, the levity, or the inexperience of another, and in exchange for some act or performance on his part, causes to be promised or granted to himself or to another person pecuniary advantages which so greatly exceed the value of his act of performance that such advantages, under all the circumstances, are strikingly out of proportion thereto". (§ 138, 2).

§ 87. **Wagering and Gambling.**[1] — (I) **A wager** is a contract in which "each party promises to the other a pecuniary payment

[1] *Wilda*, "Die Lehre von dem Spiel aus dem deutschen Rechte neu begründet", in Z. deut. R., II (1839), 133–193, and "Die Wetten", in the

('Vermögensleistung') in case such party be wrong and the other party right in their respective assertions."[1] That the expression "Wette" (*supra*, pp. 375, 497), which was originally far more comprehensive, should have thus become restricted for this particular contract is explainable by the fact that the pledge of some object, in the old sense of the law of liability, has always remained essential to it. The stake, — some thing, in ancient times also the human body or a piece of it, — is deposited as is a pledge for an obligation. The obligation in the case of the wager consists in this, that the bettor commits himself to an assertion whose truth is to be later determined.[2] It seems to follow from the scanty evidences of the older sources that according to the legal view prevailing in the Middle Ages wagers that were made "thoughtfully and earnestly", especially if in the presence of witnesses and accompanied by the drinking of earnest-wine (*supra*, p. 507), or were secured by the deposit of a stake, were enforceable by suit, provided they involved no dishonorable or ridiculous object; and that only excessively high wagers could not be enforced. This view was in agreement with the Roman law. It persisted, therefore, in the common law even after the Reception. On the other hand the regional legal systems adopted another view. The Prussian "Landrecht" recognized a right of action at least "when the wager had been made on the spot in cash, and deposited either in court or in the hands of a third person" (I. 11, § 579). Other modern codes, however, — the Code Civil, the Austrian and Saxon Codes, the Swiss Code of Obligation Law (§ 513), — have refused legal enforceability to wagers, though barring a demand for repayment after settlement. This rule has been followed by the present Civil Code (§ 672).

(II) **Gaming** is identical with the wager to the extent that it is a transaction based upon chance. In this case, however, the chance lies, not in an uncertainty concerning the correctness or incorrectness of an assertion, but in an uncertainty of the happening of any other form of future event; this happening is for the one party favorable and for the other party unfavorable. That the parties themselves should contribute by their acts to the happening or the non-happening of the event is not necessary. Again, in the case of gaming a corporeal object may be the thing

same, VIII (1843), 200–239; *Schuster*, "Das Spiel, seine Entwicklung und Bedeutung im deutschen Recht" (1878).

[1] *Cosack*, "Bürgerliches Recht", I (4th ed.), 580.

[2] *v. Amira*, "Obligationenrecht", II, 250. *Puntschart*, in Krit. Vj. S., XLVII (3d ser. XI, 1907), 69 *et seq.*, expresses a contrary opinion.

sought to be won, for Tacitus informs us, as is well known, that the primitive Germans, in gambling, staked their freedom and their body (Germ. 24). But in gambling the stake is not, as in the wager, legally liable under the law of obligations; for there is here lacking any legal duty ("Schuld") for which it could be liable; "it is merely the object of a conveyance of title that is subject to a condition precedent dependent upon the result of the gamble."[1] Gambling contracts were permitted under the medieval law, and they were enforceable; but the action by the winner did not lie against the heirs of the loser.[2] The winner also possessed a right of distraint against the loser. From the 1200 s onward, however, restrictions were introduced directed against the excessive rage for gambling. Gambling debts were quite commonly declared unenforceable at law, and gambling in general, or at least certain kinds of gambling or high gambling or gambling at forbidden places, was prohibited under penalties. It always remained true, however, despite such prohibitions, that the loser could not demand the return of a gambling debt that he had paid. As a result of an acquaintance with the principles of the Roman law, which proceeded from other viewpoints, many uncertainties resulted. The Roman distinction between licensed games, in which the winner was given an action to compel the payment of the debt, and prohibited games, in which the loser could bring an action to compel the return of a debt he had paid, passed over into the common law in the form that games in which there was a money stake were enforceable, whereas those that rested upon credit were treated as unenforceable. But most of the regional systems maintained, in contrast to this rule of the common law, — which, moreover, was a controverted one, — the unenforceability of all gambling claims. This was true of the Prussian "Landrecht", the Austrian and Saxon Codes, and the Swiss Code of Obligation Law (§ 513). The present Civil Code, also, has taken this position; without distinguishing between gaming and wagers, it provides that a legal obligation can be created by none of these transactions, and that nothing performed upon the basis of the game or the wager can be redemanded (§ 762).

§ 88. **Claims based upon Commercial Paper.**[3] — (I) **The Conception and Varieties of Commercial Paper.** — Claims embodied

[1] *v. Amira, op. cit.*, II, 255.

[2] Ssp., I. 6, § 2.

[3] For an understanding of the history as well as of the theory of the law of commercial paper the most important of all works, from the general Germanistic viewpoint, are those of *Brunner*: "Die fränkisch-romanische Urkunde", in Z. Hand. R., XXII (1877), 64–124, 505–554 (reprinted in his

in commercial paper ("Wertpapier") do not involve a group of obligations which belong together because of similar content; the characteristic which unites them is rather one of a formal nature. For the exercise of certain rights it is necessary to have possession of a paper, namely of commercial paper. This paper indicates the person who is entitled to the right, or at least it authorizes him to exercise the same. "A commercial paper is an instrument embodying a private right the exercise of which is restricted, under the private law, by the possession of the instrument."[1]

Very different rights may in this manner be united with a paper.

Many commercial papers are of a "personal" nature, — so-called "corporate" paper; they embody a right of membership in a capitalistic association. Such are shares of corporate stock, provisional shares ("Interimsschein"), mining shares, and shares in the Imperial Bank.

Another group is constituted of commercial papers under the law of things. These are either associated because of their content with the law of land, as in the case of the rent-deeds ("Rentenbriefe" and "Gültbriefe") of the older law, and the hypothecs, land-debts ("Grundschuldbriefe") and land-annuities ("Rentenschuldbriefe") of the modern law; or they are

"Forschungen" (1894), 524–631); "Carta und Notitia, ein Beitrag zur Rechtsgeschichte der germanischen Urkunde. Commentationes philologicae in honorem Th. Mommseni" (1877), 570–589; "Zur Geschichte des Inhaberpapiers in Deutschland", in Z. Hand. R., XXIII (1878), 225–262, also in "Forschungen", 631–661; "Das französische Inhaberpapier des Mittelalters und sein Verhältnis zur Anwaltschaft, zur Zession und zum Orderpapier", in the "Berliner Festschrift für Thol" (1879); "Zur Rechtsgeschichte der römischen und germanischen Urkunde", I (1880, the only volume); "Die Werthpapiere", in "Handbuch des deutschen Handels, — See- und Wechselrechts" edited by Endemann, II (1882), 140–235. On the exceptions recently taken to the historical researches of Brunner by *Brandileone*, "Le così dette clausole al portatore nei documenti medievali italiani", in the "Rivista di diritto commerciale", II (1904), 373–415, *cf. Schupfer*, "I titoli al portatore nei documenti italiani del medio evo", in the "Rivista italiana per le scienze giuridiche", XLII (1907), 175–238. A still more general attack upon Brunner has been recently made by *Freundt:* "Wertpapiere im antiken und frühmittelalterlichen Rechte" (2 vols., 1910). See also *Partsch* in Z. Hand. R., LXX (3d ser. XI, 1912), 437–489; *Philippi* in "Göttingische gelehrte Anzeigen", CLXXIV (1912), 136–143. The contraverted points are still unsettled; *Brunner's* theory is adopted in the text as well as at p. 502 *supra*. See also, in addition to the rich literature of the commercial law which cannot here be cited, *Jacobi:* "Die Wertpapiere im bürgerlichen Recht des deutschen Reiches" (1901); *Langen:* "Die Kreationstheorie im heutigen Reichsrecht" (1906); *Jacobi:* "Das Wertpapier als Legitimationsmittel" (1906).

[1] *Brunner* in *Endemann*, 147.

associated with the law of chattels, as *e.g.* all so-called "delivery-" paper (bills of lading, waybills, warehouse receipts), which not only serves for the enforcement of a claim but also fulfills functions under the law of things, inasmuch as the delivery of the paper has the same real effect as the delivery of the goods themselves.[1]

The greatest legal and economic importance, however, attaches to commercial paper embodying contract claims; that is, documents whose possession determines the right to enforce the obligation that is therein embodied.[2] For this reason, although it is evident that the importance of commercial paper extends far beyond the law of contractual claims, they may properly be discussed in this place. Again, they are very different in their form and content. Thus, some of them are based upon a nude ("abstract") obligational promise, — for example the bill of exchange; whereas others, as for example the interest coupon, express the "causa promittendi" and therefore contain a "specific" obligational promise. Further, as regards the great majority of such papers the debtor's obligation to pay is dependent upon a presentation of the paper ("Präsentationspapier"); although this may in the case of some be dispensed with.

In the case of all commercial paper, — including paper that embodies contractual claims ("Forderungspapier"), — the question is important whether they are necessary only for the enforcement or also for the transfer, or for the enforcement, transfer, and creation of the documentary right. Instruments that are essential to the creation of a documentary right are called "constitutive" instruments. The most "perfect" commercial papers are those in which all three elements mentioned are united.

Of particular importance in the classification of commercial paper is the circumstance that some of them "secure to the holder the documentary right exactly as it is expressed in the instrument"[3] (*infra,* under (III) 2). Brunner calls such instruments "commercial paper supported by public faith" (literal obligations); if they are papers embodying contractual claims they are designated "Skriptur-" obligations.

A very important distinction as concerns the negotiability of commercial papers is found in the fact that in the case of some the

[1] See for a more detailed treatment *Heymann*, "Die dingliche Wirkung der handelsrechtlichen Traditionspapiere", in the "Breslauer Festgabe für Dahn", III (1905), 133–241.
[2] *Brunner, op cit.*, 151.
[3] *Gierke*, "Privatrecht", II, 125.

power to enforce the documentary right exists in favor only of the person expressly named in the paper ("Namen-", "Rektapapier"; "nominal" paper); while in the case of others such right exists in favor of the person designated or whomsoever he shall designate (order-paper); and finally, in a third group, such right exists in favor of the holder as such (bearer-paper). The development of these three different types is the result of a long historical process.

(II) **The Historical Development.** — The use of documents in legal transactions comes down from primitive times. The Germanic system of legal instruments was developed in close dependence upon the Roman notarial instrument of Byzantine practice.[1]

The attitude of the Germanic law, however, in this connection was by no means merely receptive; it added its own valuable ideas, and it was from the union of these with the non-Germanic elements derived from the antique world that there originated the commercial paper of medieval and modern times. Its development constitutes a distinct branch of European legal history. A notably leading part was played in this process, in the early Middle Ages, by Italy, "the home of the European forms of obligational instruments."[2]

(1) "*Carta and Notitia.*" — In the earliest period of the use of legal instruments there already existed the fundamental division of documents used in private legal transactions into "business" ("Geschäfts-") instruments and mere evidential ("Beweis-") documents; a distinction then most sharply developed in the Italian law, and which later became, and is at the present day, fundamental.[3] The "business" instrument of the Frankish period, — "carta", "epistola", "testamentum"; also called, according to the particular transaction involved, "cessio", "venditio", etc., — at once evidenced and was the means of consummating the legal transaction. It was a "dispositive" instrument because its maker effected by means of it a legal disposition; and it was also a "constitutive" instrument, inasmuch as he created by means of it a legal relation. It was ordinarily drawn, as earlier in the late Roman law, in a "subjective" form; the maker, that is the party disposing, expressed his will

[1] *Partsch, op. cit.*, 476. See also *Rabel*, "Haftung des Verkäufers" (*supra*, 546), 34 *et seq.*

[2] *Brunner*, "Forschungen", 647.

[3] *Cf. Redlich*, "Privaturkunden" (*supra*, 219), 4 *et seq.*

in the first person. In case he did not write it himself, but as was then the rule caused it to be written, he at least performed the so-called "firmatio"; that is he subscribed it, or put upon it some manual mark ("signum"), or touched it by laying his hand upon it. Such a "carta", after execution, was delivered by the maker to the other party to the contract, the "destinatary" ("Destinatär"). This delivery of a document, this "traditio cartæ" in a legally formal manner, was, as above explained (p. 502), the formal act that was essential to the consummation of the juristic act, to the creation of the documentary right. In this act the document served as a "wadia." Different from this was the simple evidential document, the "notitia", "breve", "memoratorium"; a statement concerning a legal transaction which was written in the third person by the destinatary or by the other party to the contract, or by a third person at their instance, merely for the purpose of supplying written evidence of a legal act consummated without the execution of a document.

In the post-Frankish period the "carta" disappeared in Germany even among those racial branches that had theretofore commonly employed it, — the Franks, the Alamanians, and the Bavarians. In Italy, also, it lost ground to the "notitia" from the 1100s onward. It was only in the form of the sealed instrument, as "letter ('Brief') and seal", that the "carta" again became prominent in the later Middle Ages. In the end the unsealed notarial instrument attained wide prevalence in Germany, as earlier in Italy; especially after the imperial notarial ordinance of 1512 conferred upon it probative qualities.

(2) *Special clauses of commercial paper, and particularly of order and bearer-paper.* — As has already been mentioned in various places (*supra*, pp. 519, 534), the great practical importance of documents in the early Middle Ages, — and above all, of the dispositive instruments, the "cartæ", — lay in the fact that they afforded a means of avoiding the inconveniences that resulted to increasing commerce from the lack of general powers of attorney in litigation, and from the imperfect assignability of contractual rights. This means was found in the possibility, which was peculiar to the Germanic law (*supra*, pp. 518 *et seq.*), of contracts for the benefit of third persons. This led to the device of various clauses whose introduction resulted in the first great development of the law of commercial paper. These clauses may be grouped, in accord with Brunner's theory, into four groups.

(A) Demand and transfer clauses. — To the first group belong what he calls "Exaktions-" (demand) clauses, and the "Begebungs-" (transfer) clauses derived therefrom. In the Frankish period such clauses were to the effect that the drawer, addressing the destinatary, promised to perform "tibi aut cui dederis ad exigendum" (demand-clause), or "tibi aut cui cautum (= 'cautionem', document) in manum emiseris, cui cartam dederis." In Italy these clauses can be identified from the 500 s onward. In Germany, where the clause "aut cui cartam dederis" was used from the first half of the 800 s onward in gifts of land with reservation of usufruct to secure the same to a third person, it was usual after the 1200 s to employ the phrase: "to you or to whomsoever holds this letter with your will (or, good will)", "to you or to the honest — or, the rightful — holder." In Italy, from the 1100 s onward, there appeared at times in place of the older Frankish transfer clauses the words: "vel cui ordinaveris", "vel cui præceperis." These were later displaced by the national forms "o chi ordinerà", "all' ordine." In France it was customary at first to say "vel cui mandaveris", "à NN ou à son commandement ('command', 'commis')"; and, since the 1600 s quite generally, "ou à son ordre." In Germany also the old forms were displaced, under the influence of the French law, by clauses "an Ordre."

(B) Clauses of attorney. — Frankish: "tibi aut cui hoc scriptum vice tua", or "pro parte tua in manu paruerit." Similarly, the German: "to you, or to whoever shall hold this letter with your good will (or, on your account)."

(C) Alternative bearer clauses. — Frankish: "tibi aut cui hoc scriptum in manu paruerit." German: "to you or to whoever shall hold this letter"; or, "to the holder ('Behälter', 'Inhaber') of this letter."

(D) Pure bearer clauses. — Frankish: the drawer promises to perform "ad hominem, apud quem hoc scriptum in manu paruerit." German: "to the holder (or, presentor) of this letter."

Of these bearer clauses, which were used particularly in the early period in imposing contractual penalties (*supra*, pp. 521 *et seq.*), the alternative form appeared in Italy in the 800 s and the pure form in the 900 s. In Germany countless instruments with bearer clauses of the most various forms are found from the 1200 s onward.

In all these clauses one characteristic was evidently common; namely that the maker of the instrument promised performance under certain circumstances to some third person, still unknown, who should be the holder of the letter, and who was not a party to the contract. But they showed considerable differences in detail. In the case of the demand, the transfer, and the attorney clauses, the third person was not to be determined by the mere fact of holding the instrument but by the future voluntary act of a known and designated person.[1] Brunner therefore groups these clauses together as restricted or qualified clauses to bearers. The demand and transfer clauses were limited by an order of the obligor therein named; the attorney clause, by a representative relation. As contrasted with these, the alternative and pure clauses to bearer were unqualified; only, in the former the bearer was named, alternatively, in addition to the designated obligor, and in the latter he was named alone. The demand and transfer clauses required that the third person presenting the instrument should prove that this had been given to him by the first taker, designated therein; that he had been designated ("ordiniert") by the latter. The proof of the transfer was commonly effected by means of special instruments that were executed to the third person by the designated payee; in Germany they were known as "Willebriefe" ("will-letters"). In France, however, the usage became common in the 1600s to write upon the back of the obligational instruments ("in dorso", "en dos") a notice so empowering the third person, the "order." This was the "endorsement", which finally spread from France to all countries as the sole form for legitimation and transfer of "indorsable" commercial paper.

Just as proof of transfer was necessary in the case of transfer and order clauses, so in the case of the representation clause proof was required of the delivery of a power of attorney. Papers containing such qualified clauses to bearer were therefore "limited by the shortness of the course they could follow from the hand of the person therein named to the hand of the 'order' or representative."[2] In contrast to these, instruments with bearer clauses, whether alternative or pure, "could pass through several hands."[3] For in their case presentation of the paper sufficed, without it being necessary that the holder should prove either a transfer of the right or a grant of a power of attorney. This gave an extraordinarily easy circulation to bearer paper.

[1] *Brunner*, "Das französische Inhaberpapier", 29.
[2] *Brunner*, "Forschungen", 585.
[3] *Brunner*, *op. cit.*

They represented a mode of identifying the subject to a right which was peculiar to Germanic law, and which possesses similarity to real rights.[1] As in the case of the latter a right was so associated with the soil that it inhered in each successive owner of the land (*supra*, p. 178), so here any temporary owner of the instrument appeared as the subject of the right therein embodied.

The institute of bearer paper was more and more shaken in the second half of the Middle Ages by the increasing influence of the Roman law, to which the ideas which it represented were unknown, until finally "the strong Romanistic movement" that made itself felt in France in the 1500 s, and which also decisively influenced other countries, "robbed it of its vital principle and degraded it to the rank of mere 'nominal' ('Namens-') paper"[2] by requiring from the bearer proof that the right in question had been transferred to him, or that a power of attorney had been given him to enforce it. This confusion was due in part to the fact that unrestricted representation in litigation and the assignability of contractual choses in action had been meanwhile established.

However, this crisis was "overcome, first in the Netherlands, and then in France and Germany, in the case of paper with a pure order clause."[3] As respects such paper the dispensability of proof of the right or of the power of attorney became nothing less than international law. Commercial paper with alternative clauses to bearer disappeared from commercial usage, their functions being assumed by order paper, since this was closely assimilated as respects negotiability to bearer paper,—namely, in that whereas the order clause originally permitted only a subsequent transfer of the paper, in accord with its literal expression, an unrestricted negotiability was developed in the 1600 s, first of all in France, whence it found entry into other countries. In the case of bills of exchange, unrestricted negotiability, even in the absence of an order clause, became a statutory presumption, which could be repelled only by a negative clause ("nicht an Order").

With this step, the concepts of the Germanic law were firmly established, in the case of bearer as well as of order paper; and both these legal institutes were transformed into most welcome instruments of commerce, especially in banking. Order papers

[1] *Brunner*, *op cit.*, 545.
[2] *Brunner*, "Das französische Inhaberpapier", 68 *et seq.*
[3] *Brunner*, in *Endemann*, 197.

were legally developed mainly in the commercial law. Most elaborate was the development, in many respects international, of the bill of exchange. The General Bills of Exchange Act, perfected December 9, 1847, one of the most excellent of modern statutes, created for this instrument a uniform law for all Germany, at first merely in fact, but since the adoption of that Act as a statute of the present Empire also de jure. As regards the "perfect" or technical forms of order-paper, which are used almost exclusively in business, the General Commercial Code laid down certain general norms. It declared to be such (Arts. 301–302): merchants' orders to pay or deliver ("Anweisungen"), merchants' promissory notes, bills of lading, way-bills, warehouse receipts, bottomry bonds, and marine insurance policies; an enumeration which was substantially adopted, along with the legal rules respecting them, by the new Commercial Code (§ 363). As respects bearer paper, the present Civil Code has established for the first time uniform rules of law in its section upon "obligations to bearer" (§§ 793–808).

(III) **Chief Germanic Elements in the Present Law of Commercial Paper.** — The Germanic legal ideas which were fused in the early Middle Ages with the late Roman system of legal documents in the creation of commercial paper, still dominate its modern form, however much this has been perfected as compared with its medieval form. Without any attempt to give a systematically complete review of the present law of commercial paper, we will here refer briefly to those points in which its Germanic character is still particularly influential.

(1) *The creation of the debtor's duty to perform.* — The question how there arises in the cases of order and bearer paper (in the case of nominal paper the question cannot arise), the right of a third person, upon presentation of the paper as special indorsee or bearer, to demand from the debtor the performance therein promised, is one of the most debated problems of the modern private law. But if one considers the history of their development, and bears in mind certain controlling Germanic principles, its solution cannot be doubtful. As already stated, the researches of Brunner have shown us that both in the late Roman and in the early medieval law the "Urkundungsakt", that is the act "by which a juristic act is consummated by use of a dispositive instrument",[1] was never the *writing*, the physical preparation ("Kreation"), but always the *delivery* or tradition of the document, — at first

[1] *Brunner*, in *Endemann*, 165.

with legal formalities but later informally, — from the maker to the destinatary. Already in the Frankish period the rule prevailed which was formulated in the 1600 s by the celebrated English jurist Coke for the contemporary law of his country: "traditio facit loqui cartam."[1] The Germanic law did, indeed, under some circumstances, attribute legal force to a unilateral promise (*supra*, pp. 513 *et seq.*); but the element which here produced legal consequences was not a unilateral act of the maker of the instrument, but the bilateral act of delivering the instrument; that is, the contract concluded between the maker and the transferee of the instrument in the form of a "traditio cartae." And therefore it is not the "writing-theory" ("Kreationstheorie"), — which in its various forms (writing-theory proper; "title-theory" "Eigentumsverschaffungstheorie") explains the documentary right as originating in a unilateral act of the drawer, — that is historically justified, but the opposing "contract" ("Vertrags-") theory. True, this would not alone be sufficient to justify one in postulating that as the basis also of the modern law. But what is more, when rightly understood it affords an entirely satisfactory explanation for the modern rules, which were once deemed explainable only through the "writing" theory.

(2) *The "legitimizing" quality of commercial paper.* — As already remarked, the essential nature of commercial paper is found in its purest form in "commercial paper based upon public faith" (Brunner), or as they are also called "literal" obligation papers (Gierke). Among these belong, according to the present law of credit instruments ("Forderungspapiere"), the so-called "perfect" order papers, that is those forms of order paper in which the paper is essential to the creation, the transfer, and the enforcement of the right therein embodied; namely, the bill of exchange, the seven forms of paper recognized by the commercial law which are enumerated in § 363 of the Commercial Code (*supra*, p. 573), and all forms of bearer paper. In these forms of commercial paper the third person, who is in a position to establish his claim under the literal reading of the promise as the person to whom performance is promised, — that is to say, either as the immediate or mediate indorsee ("Order") of the first holder therein named, or as bearer, — can rely absolutely upon the paper. Defenses that do not result from the paper itself but from the defective rights of his predecessors in title, can-

[1] *Brunner*, "Carta und Notitia", 576.

not be set up against him; the paper authorizes him to enforce against the maker, under all circumstances and according to its literal reading, the right therein embodied.

This legitimizing force of commercial paper based upon public faith is so strong that it is effective even where the substantive right and the ostensible right do not coincide. Such a separation occurs, for example, when an unqualified indorsement is made by one who is entitled to such right to a third person merely for the purpose of collection (for which purpose a qualified indorsement is also available under the law of bills and notes, although this form is almost unknown in practice). The third person here appears to others as the owner of the paper, and therefore as the subject of the right; whereas in the intention of the parties he has no independent rights, but is entitled merely to collect the sum as the attorney of the person thereto entitled. This confusion, however, agrees precisely with the intention of the parties. Such a "legitimated" holder of bearer or order paper ought to be entitled to present his claim against the debtor, either in or out of court, "without being obliged to disclose whether he is enforcing his own right as a legal successor to another's title, or is only enforcing, in effect, the right of another, as an agent."[1] To use Jacobi's apt expression, the question here is quite the same as in the transfer of medieval seisin, which likewise always carried the right of representation in a law suit; and this, even when the question was one of the transfer of a mere derivative seisin, dependent upon a higher one.

Such a separation of substantive and formal rights, however, may also take place in such manner that even an unauthorized possessor, who *should* not enforce the right embodied in the paper, nevertheless *can* effectually enforce it. In the case of "perfect" order paper, a bona fide indorsee himself acquires title to the paper, and so to the right therein embodied, by any formally correct indorsement, even when the paper was earlier stolen or lost; as may be the case, for example, if the rightful holder has made an indorsement in blank and the thief thereafter fills in such blank indorsement with his own name, and then reindorses the paper to another party. In the case of bearer paper, however, it is entirely immaterial how the paper has reached the hands of the holder; even when he himself has stolen it, he appears to be the rightful holder as against bona fide third persons. In these cases also the medieval Germanic idea of "legitimation"

[1] *Jacobi*, "Wertpapier als Legitimationsmittel", 58.

has the same effect as in the law of seisin, and in the modern law of the public faith of the land-book. Even the mere writing out of a commercial paper is a "dangerous action,"[1] for a "worthless piece of paper is transformed by it into an instrument adapted to transfer for value."[2] If the drawer of this instrument gives it out of his own hands, and a perfect order paper or a bearer paper is involved, he thereby assumes a contractual obligation to make the promised payment to such third person as may establish his claim by presentation of the paper, as bearer or as indorsee of the original payee. The intention of the contracting parties, therefore, as in the case of every contract for the benefit of a third person, is to the effect that such third person shall be authorized to enforce the right. The third person presenting the paper and legitimizing himself in the manner required by law, has in his favor the presumption of fact ("Rechtsschein") that he too has acquired the paper by contract, that is by transfer; a prima facie right which protects him until proof of the contrary. Nor is it different even in the rare "pathological" case where the paper has gotten out of the hands of the drawer before delivery, and has then been put by a third person into commercial circulation. For here also the drawer has created by his subscription the "dangerous" condition; he has created a thing which is bound to suggest that it has been put into circulation by him intentionally, that is that it has been delivered to the payee under an ordinary contract. For this reason the right of the holder presenting the instrument rests upon a contract whose existence is presumed in his favor. This case also, therefore, by no means requires one to abandon the "contract" in favor of the "writing" theory.

The counterpart of this far-reaching duty that rests upon the maker of the paper is the "emancipatory effect" of payment by him to a person ostensibly entitled thereto. Such payment involves the destruction of the right of the person justly ("materiell") entitled thereto whenever the substantive becomes thus separated from the apparent right.

Topic 2. Obligations based upon Torts

§ 89. **Obligations based upon Torts. (I) Tort Obligations in General.** — (1) *The older law.* — The earliest law saw in every violation of an obligation a misdeed that was subject to penalty. From this viewpoint of penal law, there was no

[1] *Jacobi, op. cit.*, 50.

[2] *Gierke*, "Privatrecht", II, 111.

difference between the consequences of a breach of contract and those of violating a person's non-contractual rights. The violation resulted, in the latter as in the former case, in a liability of the debtor for a bót; and in the one as in the other case the bót served, at first, the two ends of punishment and damages. A public penalty (a wíte), in addition to the bót, was required only in the case of certain acts of a criminal ("verbrecherisch") character.

This viewpoint was abandoned in the Middle Ages; the consequences, under the criminal and the private law respectively, of a violation of another's rights, were separated, and only the latter left to the regulation of the private law. But the influence of the old viewpoint of the criminal law continued to be so far felt that the same strict principles continued to prevail, as respected the obligor's duty of penance, in case of violation of non-contractual rights, as were controlling in obligations originating in a breach of contract (*supra*, pp. 527 *et seq.*). The obligor was bound to make good all damage whatever caused by his unlawful conduct, and no distinction was made between legal fault and an involuntary act ("Ungefähr") so far as regarded this question of compensation. In accord with the principle, "he who has unwillingly done must willingly pay", the damage done by persons not responsible for their actions (children, insane people) was therefore made good from their property; moreover, a child doing such damage might be delivered to the injured person, in order that the latter might cancel the obligation by its labor. But no penalty was imposed upon irresponsible persons.[1] Here too, it was immaterial whether the damage had been done by a positive act or by a failure to act.[2] As in the case of breaches of contract, so here only "external" accident could free one from an obligation to give damages. Aside from that, only self-defense ("Notwehr") was regarded as sufficient to preclude legal responsibility, and therewith the duty to give damages.

(2) *The modern law.* — As a result of the Reception, the Roman principles attained the authority of common law. Inasmuch as the Roman law contained no general principle similar to the Germanic, but recognized an obligation of giving damages (aside from cases of fraud) only in cases under the Aquilian action, — that is, only in case of damage done to things by positive act, — and in certain other special cases, the Reception involved a considerable relaxation of the native rules. The regional legal sys-

[1] Ssp., II, 65, § 1. [2] Ssp., II, 38.

tems, however, continued quite commonly to recognize the authority of the latter. The great modern codes, in particular, again introduced an extension of damages as compared with the Roman law, in that they allowed such for every act that violated another's right, whether by misfeasance or by non-feasance.[1] However, in Germany as in Rome some fault ("Verschulden") was quite generally required. The present Civil Code, also, has laid the element of fault ("Verschuldungsprinzip") at the basis of its regulation of tort damages. But in so doing it has attempted to make a graded classification according to the nature of the wrongful act. If there is involved an injury to life, body, health, freedom, property, or to any other right of another, then mere negligence suffices to constitute fault (§ 823, 1); if a statute designed for the protection of the other person is violated by the wrongful act, it may be that according to the provisions of the statute fault is assumed under some circumstances, only in case of gross negligence or premeditation (§ 823, 2); if, finally, the damage to the other person constitutes a violation of public morals ("gute Sitten"), actual intent is necessary (§ 826).

But the influence of the viewpoint of the older German law, which disregarded personal fault, was felt even in the modern period to the extent that some modern codes retained in some cases a liability for damages against mentally irresponsible persons. The present Civil Code has also adopted this rule, subject to the qualification that such liability arises only when it accords with equity, and when it will not deprive such irresponsible person of the means necessary for his maintenance in a manner befitting his social rank (§§ 827–829). Above all, however, modern legislation — first in various State laws and later in the imperial statute of June 7, 1871 — relating to the liability of railroads and other similar public works has imposed upon persons operating these an absolute liability for deaths and bodily injuries, subject only to the exceptions of vis maior and contributory negligence; and has even placed upon the operator the burden of proving those circumstances which relieve him from his liability, — a reversal of the burden of proof otherwise prevailing in the present law.

Particular provision is made in modern statutes concerning the extent of one's liability for damages in case of the killing or bodily

[1] For example, Code Civil, § 1382: "Any act whatever of one person, which does damage to another, obliges him to whose fault it is due to make reparation therefor."

injury of another person. In case of death they include the cost of any attempted cure, the burial, and the expenses of mourning, and also the claims of relatives to maintenance which are defeated by the death of the one maintaining them; and in case of injuries to the body, to expenses for care and cure, and the claims of the person injured for lost or lessened earning capacity. General principles are now laid down in the Civil Code (§§ 843–844).

As regards bodily injuries there were allowed from the 1400 s onward, in addition to compensation for pecuniary damage, certain punitive damages — so-called "smart-money" ("Schmerzensgeld") — that were unknown to the older law. Somewhat similar to these was the so-called Saxonbót ("Sachsenbusse"), which was retained in the Saxon law even after the Reception, and which, in case the injured person was confined by the injury, was payable to him in the manner of the fixed bóts of the old law. To this group of claims for damages belongs also the claim of a woman, variously developed in the older legal systems, whose virtue has been violated by force or by seduction. In agreement with these old laws, the Civil Code, while generally allowing in case of torts compensation for pecuniary damage only, also allows compensation for non-pecuniary damage in the case of physical injuries, deprivation of liberty, and sexual offenses.

(II) **Liability for Damage done by Other Persons, Animals, and Things.**[1] — (1) *Liability for other persons.* — The idea that every person must be answerable for damages proceeding from his immediate environment ("Lebenskreise") led in the old Germanic law, exactly as in the laws of allied peoples, to peculiar consequences. The lord was originally answerable for harm done by slaves of which he was the owner, since they themselves, as things, were irresponsible under the criminal law. Only in time was an amelioration of this theory realized, notably in the form that the slave's act was attributed to his master as one resulting merely from misfortune, provided the latter delivered him to the injured person; and finally there was recognized an independent responsibility of the slave under the criminal law, the liability

[1] *Brunner*, "Über absichtslose Missetat im altdeutschen Strafrechte", in the "Sitz. Ber. Berliner Acad.", 1890, 815–842; also in his "Forschungen", 487–523; *v. Amira*, "Thierstrafen und Thierprozesse", in Inst. öst. G. F., XII (1891), 545–601; *Isay*, "Die Verantwortlichkeit des Eigentümers für seine Tiere", in *Ihering*'s J. B., XXXIX (1898), 209–322.

of his master being restricted to a mere real ("Sach-") liability.[1] For the same reason the employer ("Dienstherr") was liable in the medieval law for the torts of his employees; both his household servants, obligated to him by contract, and those persons whose services he utilized in the performance of works undertaken by contract, such as artisans, carters, etc. Similarly, the liability of the master of a household continued to be recognized for the members of the family and for other persons resident in his house.

In sharp contrast to these principles, the Roman law (as received in Germany) held the master responsible, in theory, only when he himself had been in some manner at fault. But at the same time it recognized a few exceptions: in addition to the liability of the pater familias for the delicts of persons subject to his household authority, the liability of innkeepers, stablekeepers, and shippers for damages done by their employees. The modern law in Germany followed in general the Roman rule, and accordingly did not, in theory, recognize any liability for faults ("Verschulden") of other persons; which rule involved, particularly, a lessening of such liability for household servants. However, legal practice clung to a considerable extent, despite the statutes, to the stricter native view, as regarded members of the family and household servants; and even the codes, — among which the Code Civil (§ 1384) alone adopted the express principle of the Germanic law, — recognized a greatly increased number of exceptions as compared with the Roman law. Of particular importance was the liability of the ship-owner under the commercial law for damages done by the crew, and that of freight carriers for faults of their employees and agents. Both of these were raised to the rank of general law by the General Commercial Code, and exist as such to-day. In the same way, under the imperial statute regulating the liabilities of railroads, the operator is liable for non-contractual obligations of the employees in cases of death or physical injury, and the operator of other similar enterprises is liable for the employees and for the laborers if death or bodily injury to a human being has resulted from their fault in performing the services required of them. The Civil Code has likewise recognized, in entirely general terms, a liability of the owner of a business for damage wrongfully done by his employees. At the same time, however, it adopts in this connection the view of the Roman law in so far that it treats this liability as arising only

[1] *Brunner*, "Geschichte", II, 552.

in case of some fault on the part of the owner of the business; on the other hand, it deviates here from the Roman law and approaches the Germanic in imposing upon the owner the burden of proving his blamelessness (§ 831).

(2) *Liability for animals.* — Like other Indo-Germanic peoples in their early period the primitive Germans once personified the animal. They assumed that it, although "a dumb thing", "a speechless wight", could commit misdeeds. Therefore they punished the master if he retained an animal that had done damage; for he thereby made himself responsible for the punishable deed ("Verbrechen", crime) of aiding a wrong-doer, possibly an outlaw, by giving it food and shelter. According to the Germanic view, — which agreed with the old Roman "noxæ datio", — he could free himself from criminal responsibility by delivering or abandoning the animal to the injured person. In that case the latter could revenge himself upon the animal. Out of the institute of private revenge, which was often clothed in ritualistic form, there were developed in the Middle Ages under the influence of Biblical passages, especially in France, public punishments of animals ("Tierstrafen") that can be traced down into the 1800 s. Misdeeds of animals came to be treated as results of pure misfortune earlier than were those of slaves. In the case of the former such misdeeds had no further consequence against the owner, even when they were not abandoned, than an obligation to pay a wergeld and bót, or a fractional part of the bót. It was merely required, in addition, that the master should support with a "danger-oath" an allegation that he had not known the dangerous nature of the anmal. This became an absolute liability when wild animals were kept. Abandonment was required only in the case of the worst misdeeds, such as homicide; because these might result in feud. On the other hand, the master, by abandoning the animal, could still free himself even from his duty to give damages.[1]

This possibility of freeing one's self from responsibility by abandonment of the animal, which was recognized also in the Roman law, persisted in many regions even after the Reception, particularly in the Saxon law. Of the codes, the Baden Territorial Law retained it in quite general terms, and the Saxon Code in case no fault had rested upon the owner. For in such case the Saxon Code and the Code Civil made the owner of the animal liable even when he had been guilty of no fault in his oversight

[1] Ssp., II, 40, §§ 1–2.

of the animal. On the other hand, the Prussian "Landrecht" and the Austrian Code abandoned the standpoint of the Roman law in favor of the Germanic principle of fault: they attributed to the owner a liability only in case of his own fault. Here again the present Civil Code has brought the native legal view into honor, and has applied it more logically than did any earlier legal system. The keeper of the animal is made liable for all damages, whether homicide, bodily injuries to persons, or injuries to things (§§ 833–834). For, — this is the idea which characterizes the modern law as distinguished from the conception of antiquity, — whoever enjoys the benefits of property shall also answer for all dangers resulting from it.[1]

Special rules have been developed as regards damage done by wild game (*supra*, p. 278). The Civil Code also contains a few general rules on this subject (§ 835).

(3) *Damage done by things.* — The same primitive ideas that made a master liable in damages for acts done by his slaves and animals as for his own deeds, also made him answerable for misfortune caused by lifeless things, such as weapons, that belonged to him; even when he had not been guilty of the slightest fault. These injuries, also, were regarded as involuntary acts ("Ungefährwerke") for which the owner was liable; and in their case, too, release from the obligation to give damages could be secured by delivery of the thing to the injured person. In the course of the Middle Ages this liability for things ceased to be important in actual legal life. The heathen religious ideas that underlay it, — especially the idea that an object by which, for example, a human being had been killed might no longer be used, — have persisted as superstitions down to the present day.[2]

[1] Unfortunately this provision of the Civil Code, despite its native origin and its intrinsic justice, has been sacrificed to the opposition directed against it. The first amendment to the text of the Code, of May 30th, 1908, adds to § 833 the following: "There is no obligation to give damages when the injury is caused by a domestic animal, which is kept for use in the profession or trade or for the support of its keeper, provided either the latter has observed the precautions required in the public interest in his oversight of the animal or the injury would have resulted notwithstanding the exercise of such care." The same rule was even earlier adopted in the Swiss Code of Obligation Law (§ 56).

[2] *Brunner*, "Geschichte", I (2d ed.), 219.

BOOK IV. FAMILY LAW

CHAPTER XI

MARRIAGE

§ 90. **Introductory: the Beginnings of the Germanic Law of the Family.**[1] **(I) The Patriarchal Family. The Household Authority.** — In view of the present results of historical research it may be asserted with good reason that the primitive Indo-

[1] Of the extraordinarily abundant general literature on the origins of the family and of marriage we may cite: *Dargun*, "Mutterrecht und Raubehe", No. 16 (1883) of *Gierke's* "Untersuchungen", "Mutterrecht und Vaterrecht" (1892); *Bernhöft*, "Frauenleben in der Vorzeit", (1893); *Grosse*, "Die Formen der Familie und die Formen der Wirtschaft", (1893); *Kohler*, "Zur Urgeschichte der Ehe", in Z. vergl. R. W., XII (1897), 197 *et seq.*, and numerous other essays by the same author in the same periodical;

Germanic folk already lived under patriarchal conditions; and at any rate as regards the general Germanic and the German family law, there can scarcely remain any doubt that their historical point of departure was the patriarchal family organization. It prevailed among the primitive Germans (" Germanen ") in a pure and absolute form, so far as their conditions can be traced in the obscure origins of history.

During the dominance of the patriarchal system the family constituted a circle of persons all of whom were absolutely subjected to the power of the house-lord, the patriarch, and were united by this common bond of subjection into a social group. They participated in legal life solely through the mediacy of the " house-father "; he was their representative outside the group. The Germanic languages and the Latin both took the name for this power of the house-lord from the most striking symbol of power, the hand, and named it therefore " Munt " (Old High G. " munt "; North Germanic and Old Norse " mund ", Latinized " mundium "). For the primary meaning of this word is " Hand ";

Wilutzky, "Vorgeschichte des Rechts", part I (husband and wife) and II (parents and children, etc.), 1903; *G. E. Howard*, "A History of Matrimonial Institutions, chiefly in England and the United States, with an introductory Analysis of the Literature and the Theories of Primitive Marriage and the Family" (3 vols., 1904), with elaborate references; *Wundt*, "Die Entstehung der Exogamie", in Arch. R. W. Philos., V (1912), 247–261, 400–414, 537–547; *Marianne Weber*, *op. cit.* in § 9, *supra* (p. 61). On the family organizations of the Indogermanic races see among other works: *Bernhöft*, "Über die Grundlagen der Rechtsentwicklung bei den indogermanischen Völkern", in Z. vergl. R. W., II (1880), 253 *et seq.*, "Zur Geschichte des europäischen Familienrechts" in the same, VIII (1889), 1 *et seq.*, 161 *et seq.*, "Die Prinzipien des europäischen Familienrechts", in the same, IX (1891), 392 *et seq.*; *Leist*, "Graeco-italische Rechtsgeschichte" (1884), "Altarisches Jus Gentium" (1889), "Altarisches Jus civile" (2 vols., 1892, 1896); *Delbrück*, "Das Mutterrecht bei den Indogermanen", in Preuss. J. B., LXXIX (1895), 14 *et seq.*; *Schrader*, "Reallexikon, Grundzüge einer Kultur- und Völkergeschichte Alteuropas" (1901); *Hirt*, "Die Indogermanen" (2 vols., 1905, 1907); *Schrader*, "Sprachvergleichung und Urgeschichte, linguistisch-historische Beiträge zur Erforschung des indogermanischen Altertums" (3d ed., 1907). In addition to the work of *Weinhold*, cited on p. 61 *supra*, there should be examined, for the primitive Germans: *Wackernagel*, "Familienrecht und Familienleben der Germanen", in *Schreiber's* Taschenbuch, V (1846), 259 *et seq.*, reprinted in his "Kleinere Schriften", I (1872), 1–34; *Waitz*, "Über die Bedeutung des Mundium im deutschen Recht", in K. Preuss. Akad. Wiss., Sitz. Ber. 1886, 375 *et seq.*, reprinted in his "Abhandlungen zur deutschen Verfassungs- und Rechtsgeschichte" (1896), 369 *et seq.*; *Roeder*, "Die Familie bei den Angelsachsen" (1899); *Bartsch*, "Die Rechtsstellung der Frau als Gattin und Mutter. Geschichtliche Entwicklung ihrer persönlichen Stellung im Privatrecht bis ins 18. Jahrhundert" (1903); *Boden*, "Mutterrecht und Ehe im altnordischen Recht" (1904); *K. Maurer*, "Zum altnordischen Eherecht", in his "Vorlesungen", II (1908), 471 *et seq.*; *E. Mayer*, "Der germanische Uradel", in Z[2]. R. G., XXXII (1911), 40–228, 172 *et seq.*

the Germanic "Munt" corresponds, etymologically and in meaning, to the "manūs" of Roman family law. "Mundium" was originally a very broad conception, under which there seem to have been classed, in accord with the one-time actual extent of house-hold authority, all possible relations of personal dependence; and which points backward to conditions when no public authority was recognized alongside of or superior to the authority of the family head. Even in medieval law, the meaning of the concept still extended far beyond the law of the family, embracing, — in addition to the house-lord's authority over the family members dwelling in the house, and the servants, — the relation of "a lord ('Schutzherr') to his liegeman ('Mundmann') and to his serf, of jurisdiction ('Vogtei') over strangers, and over churches, and the representation of minors in law suits in so far as this was exceptionally permitted." [1] However, this conception, originally unitary, assumed in time a varying character in the individual cases in which it was applied. For example, the mundium of husband, parents, and guardians, which rested upon relations of kinship, was differentiated as an independent legal institute. And within this mundium of the family law a further division took place: the power of the husband over his wife, of the father over his children, of the guardian over his ward, were each subjected to independent legal rules, differing unequally from their one-time common prototype. The original character of the institute was preserved in its purest form in the relation of a father to his children; the name was preserved, in the end, almost solely in the law of guardianship ("Vormund" = guardian; "Mündel" = ward; "mundtodt" = entmündigt = subject to guardianship). Its original character was that of an unlimited authority of the mundium-holder ("Muntherr") over the persons subjected to his power. At an early day, and thereafter with ever increasing clearness, there were grafted upon this original concept of almost unlimited authority, first moral and then legal restrictions, which recognized a duty, in addition to the right, of the master. And thus "there already appears in our earliest sources of information, the meaning of 'protection', of 'peace.'" [2] The house-lord became a lord-protector, a "mundporo", "foramundo", "mundoaldus," "Muntwalt," of the person subject to his authority; he was bound to exercise such authority, not as formerly in his own interest alone, but equally

[1] *Brunner*, "Grundzüge" (5th ed.), 221.
[2] *Brunner*, "Geschichte", I (2d ed.), 93.

in their interest. With this step, wife and children ceased to be mere things subject to his control. Nevertheless, the mundium of the house-lord, even in this mixed form of right and duty that was characteristic of the Middle Ages, long continued to signify "a power which we, according to our present views, would call one of public law;"[1] it continued to embrace a field into which no public authority penetrated. For the state only the house-lord existed, to him alone its commands were directed; he alone long continued responsible under the criminal and the private law for everything that happened within his house and through the members thereof (*supra*, pp. 579 *et seq.*

(II) **Membership of the Family. "Greater-" Family and "Lesser-" Family.** — The Indo-Germanic family was probably a so-called "greater-" ("Gross-") family; a man's descendants remained together so long as their common "truncal" ("Stamm-") father, or common male ancestor lived, or was capable of exercising physically and mentally his household authority.[2] This Indo-Germanic hearth-community united "in one community not only parents and children, but also the wives of sons, with their sons, and the wives and descendants of the latter."[3] In the greater-family of Old Russia and in the Servian "Zadruga" this primitive family organization has been preserved down to the present day. Among most of the Indo-Germanic peoples, however, the greater-family developed into the looser form of the sib (*supra*, pp. 114 *et seq.*, and *infra*, § 106); that is, into a group of persons who, though conscious of union through common descent were no longer bound together by the authority of their truncal father, but constituted an association ("Genossenschaft") of equal family heads and the members of their households that far exceeded in membership the "greater-" family. But the son, when he married, henceforth ordinarily lighted his own hearth fire. And thus there existed within the sib, as the narrowest independent social group, a separate ("Sonder-") or "lesser-" family that was limited to two generations: parents and children. Among the primitive and the later Germans we meet, in general, with this lesser-family only; though examples in which married children and grandchildren remained living in the parental household are not lacking, they are relatively rare. Nevertheless, in the peasant communities of collective hand common in the Middle

[1] *Huber*, "Schw. Privatrecht", IV, 282.
[2] *Schrader*, "Sprachvergleichung und Urgeschichte" (3d ed.), 359.
[3] *Grosse*, *op. cit.*, 10.

Ages, which have persisted in some localities down to the present day, reminiscences were preserved of the original greater-family. In these communities, after the death of the house-father, the sons and their issue often remained united through many generations as an association (*supra*, pp. 139 *et seq.*). As contrasted with the associational sib and the community of collective hand, the lesser-family preserved the element of authority that was essential to the primitive greater-family. It was the circle within which the household mundium of the house-lord was exercised, over his wife and children as well as over the servants.

(III) **Marriage.** — The primitive patriarchal system did not necessarily involve the institution of marriage. But the family of the primitive Germans, like the supposititious family organization of the primitive Indo-Germans, rested upon marriage from the beginning. Marriage, however, was by no means synonymous with monogamy. On the contrary marriage acquired a special quality distinguishing it from other sexual unions merely from the fact that wife and children, notwithstanding their subjection to the unlimited mundium of husband and father, enjoyed in relation to him a position legally more secure than that of other women with whom he cohabited, and his offspring by such. Marriage was regarded as the legitimate sexual union. The "married" wife ("Ehefrau") was distinguished from other wives ("Nebenfrauen"), concubines, and slaves by the fact that only she could bear him children of "full birth"; that is, above all, give her husband male issue who continued his line and family, performed the obligations of the blood-feud and, especially, were able to offer sacrifices for him when dead and thereby care for the peace of his soul. It was perfectly reconcilable with this religio-political purpose of marriage, however, that the husband might, in case his first wife remained childless, or for other reasons, acquire a second wife, or a third, or as many wives as his social, economic, and political associations made desirable and possible for him. Thus, among the primitive Germans, although according to the report of Tacitus (which was certainly in this respect accurate) they ordinarily contented themselves with one wife,[1] a plurality of wives was by no means legally impossible. Among the northern Germanic races ("Nordgermanen") the prevalence of polygamy long continued to be noteworthy; among their western branches it was still practiced even in Christian times, although only by the richest and greatest men, especially

[1] "Germania", c. 18.

in royal houses, — for example in those of Merovingians and Carolingians. Moreover, in addition to unions with several wives of equal rights there also existed among the primitive Germans a system of legal concubinage (*infra*, §§ 91, 99).

It was essential to the patriarchal marriage that the wife who lived with a man, either voluntarily or because compelled to do so, left her own household community forever, and abandoned all relation of kinship with its members; and also that the children she bore her husband thereby entered into relations of kinship with the father and the father's family only, and not with the house of the mother. Already in the Indo-Germanic period the family was therefore completely agnatic, as is particularly evidenced in the terminology of kinship. The same must be assumed to be true of the primitive Germans. The assumption that they lived originally in a condition of mother-law must be rejected. The expression "mother-right" ("Mutterrecht") has been used since the epoch-making work of Bachofen [1] to indicate conditions of very different character, as reported both in the accounts of ancient writers and in accounts of primitive peoples of the present time. Even if one understand by mother-law simply a form of family organization actually prevailing among a number of peoples, — notably those of a low stage of culture, —in which children are not counted with the father and the paternal kindred, but with the mother and the maternal kindred, and therefore possess rights of inheritance only in relation to the latter, such a condition would by no means constitute, as some were for a time inclined to believe, a necessary transitional stage in the social development of every people. Neither does it enjoy an exclusive authority, under all circumstances, where it exists. Still less does it involve, in itself, any peculiar legal position of the mother, or even a supremacy of mothers or of women ("Mutter-", "Frauenherrschaft"); mother-right is therefore not the equivalent of matriarchy. At all events, in the present light of historical research we must start with the assumption that the Indo-Germanic peoples, from the beginning, never knew conditions of mother-right; nor the primitive Germans, either. It is true that several scholars (von Amira, Dargun, Ficker, Heusler, Opet, E. Mayer) have believed they had discovered traces of original mother-right in the primary monuments of Germanic law; and upon this basis it has been contended that primitive Germanic

[1] "Das Mutterrecht, eine Untersuchung über die Gynaikratie der alten Welt nach ihrer religiösen und rechtlichen Natur" (1861).

law was one of mother-right. Inasmuch as the arguments for this view (championed with most assurance by Ficker) that were derived from the law of inheritance, from the law of the marital community of goods, and from the legal status of illegitimate children have been convincingly disposed of, it now rests, at best, upon interpretations of the institute known as the "avunculate." Tacitus reports in a celebrated passage that the relation between nephews and uncles on the mother's side was quite as close as that between son and father, and that some persons, in giving hostages, treated the former relationship as the stronger security.[1] Now, it is true that this powerful position of the maternal uncle is a characteristic feature of a society under mother-right. In order, therefore, to reconcile the unlikeness between the Germanic avunculate and the patriarchy which elsewhere prevailed among Indo-Germans, the hypothesis has been advanced that we have here a survival of pre-Indo-Germanic society, — which lived under mother-right, as is provable from reports of the Lycians, Locrians, Etruscans, Cantabrians, the Balearians, and Picts.[2] But it is not necessary to resort to this explanation. For the special honor of the maternal uncle may have been merely a consequence of the fact that the maternal kindred came, in time, to be considered along with the paternal, who were at first exclusively regarded; in other words, a consequence of the fact that the family's purely agnatic structure was replaced by a cognatic organization. In this appearance of the idea of cognatic relationship, which transformed in the same manner the family and the sib (*infra*, §§ 106–107), the maternal uncle naturally played the most important rôle: he was the link between the families of the father and the mother,[2] and he was primarily the person upon whom was incumbent, as the representative of the maternal sib,[3] the protection of the wife as against her husband.

(IV) **The Later Development.** — The beginnings of the Germanic and of the German family-law agree exactly with those we find among other Indo-Germanic peoples, and like the latter they can be derived and explained with a great degree of probability from the manners and law of an inferential primitive Indo-

[1] "Germania", c. 20. See also *Rietschel*, art. "Avunculat" in *Hoop's* "Reallexikon", I (1911), 510; *E. Mayer*, *op. cit. supra*, p. 585.

[2] *Bernhöft*, "Staat und Recht der römischen Königszeit" (1882), 191 *et seq.*; *Schrader*, "Reallexikon", 228, 566; "Sprachvergleichung und Urgeschichte" (3d ed.), 368.

[3] *Schrader*, "Reallexikon", 228; also *cf. Brunner*, "Geschichte", I (2d ed.), 128.

Germanic race. In its further development, also, from the earliest times down to the present day, German family-law has similarly followed the broad line marked by the general development of European civilization. True, it must not be forgotten that the family-law of a race is related with especial closeness to its particular mental genius; indeed it is precisely in this field that the law always finds its most important complement in manners and customs, and cannot be understood without attention to these. Despite this fact, however, the influence that has been exercised by the general development of economic and intellectual culture has been far stronger, in the long run, than the influence of national peculiarities. The former influence was greatly strengthened in the family-law by the fact that the most important part of this, the law of marriage, was withheld by the Church for many centuries from national legal development. The result was that an international ecclesiastical law took the place of a national secular law. In this medieval ecclesiastical law of marriage and also in the modern secular law that in turn displaced it, as well as in certain other portions of the family-law that remained more or less completely unaffected by the Church's influence, — for example the law of the marital community of goods and the law of guardianship, — certain general tendencies have prevailed among all nations of the Germanic-Romanistic circle of civilization, and have set identical ends to their legal development, however variant in detail the ways in which those ends were pursued and realized. At the same time, consciously or unconsciously, the development of all institutions of the family-law has undoubtedly been constantly directed toward a curtailment of the original patriarchal power of the husband, an equalization of husband and wife before the law, the legal security of children and other persons under mundium, and a reincorporation of the family-law in the secular law of the state.

§ 91. **The Contracting of Marriage.**[1] — Although different varieties of sexual union were once not only actually practiced

[1] *Friedberg*, "Das Recht der Eheschliessung in seiner geschichtlichen Entwicklung" (1865); *Sohm*, "Das Recht der Eheschliessung aus dem deutschen und kanonischen Recht geschichtlich entwickelt" (1875); *Friedberg*, "Verlobung und Trauung" (1876); *Sohm*, "Trauung und Verlobung" (1876). Also *Brunner*, in the Jenaer Lit. Z. (1876), art. 439; *v. Wyss*, "Die Eheschliessung in ihrer geschichtlichen Entwicklung nach den Rechten der Schweiz", in Z. schweiz. R., XX (1877), 65–186; *Habicht*, "Die altdeutsche Verlobung in ihrem Verhältnis zu dem Mundium und der Eheschliessung" (1879); *K. Lehmann*, "Verlobung und Hochzeit nach den nordgermanischen Rechten des früheren Mittelalters" (1882); *Brunner*, "Zu Lex Salica, tit. 44, 'De reipus'", in K. Preuss. Akad. Wiss.,

but also recognized by law, nevertheless marriage, as that form of sexual community which involved the most far-reaching legal consequences, was always distinguished by a special form observed in its creation, on the strength of which alone it was conceded its privileged rank of full legitimacy. The Germanic law, like the legal systems of other Indo-Germanic peoples, developed special forms for the creation of marriage; forms which were, of course, adjusted to the general principles regulating the conclusion of juristic acts. For even among the primitive Germans the contraction of marriage was regarded as a juristic act, although one that was consummated from the earliest times in an especially formal and solemn manner, because of its far-reaching consequences and its importance in religious and political life. This primitive and purely secular law of marriage contract, however, was later displaced by an ecclesiastical law of marriage, which as a part of the Canon law in the form finally given that by papal codification attained universal authority over the entire Christian population of Europe, until it was divided after the Reformation

Sitz. Ber. 1894, 1289–1297; *Martin Wolff*, "Zur Geschichte der Witwenehe im altdeutschen Recht", in Inst. öst. G. F., XVII (1896), 369–388; *Gothein*, "Beiträge zur Geschichte der Familie im Gebiet des alamannischen und fränkischen Rechts" (1897); *Hermann*, "Zur Geschichte des Brautkaufs bei den indogermanischen Völkern", in the scientific supplement to the 31st "Programm" of the Hansa Schule at Bergedorf (1904); *Hazeltine*, "Zur Geschichte der Eheschliessung nach angelsächsischem Recht", in "Festgabe für Hübler" (1905), 1–38; *Brandileone*, "Saggi sulla storia della celebrazione del matrimonio in Italia" (1906); *Opet*, "Zum Brautkauf nach altalamannischem Recht", in "Festgabe für Hänel" (1907), 177–213. The argument of a work by Ficker on betrothal and espousal in the 1100s and 1200s, worked out by him in 1886–87, but never published, has been made known by *v. Voltelini* in *Jung*, "Julius Ficker (1826–1902), ein Beitrag zur deutschen Gelehrtengeschichte" (1907), 514–619; *Köstler*, "Muntgewalt und Ehebewilligung in ihrem Verhältnis zu einander nach fränkischem und nach langobardischem Recht" in Z². R. G., XXIX (1908), 75–135; *Roeder*, "Zur Deutung der angelsächsischen Glossierungen von 'paranympha' ('pronuba'), ein Beitrag zur Kenntnis des angelsächsischen Hochzeitsrituells", in K. Gesel. Wiss., Göttingen, "Nachrichten" (1909), 14–21; *Leicht*, "Troctingi e paraninfi nel matrimonio langobardo", in Atti del Reale Istituto Veneto, 1909–1910, 69 *et seq.*, 851–865; *Opet*, "Brauttradition und Konsensgespräch in mittelalterlichen Trauungsritualen, ein Beitrag zur Geschichte des deutschen Eheschliessungsrechts" (1910), *cf.* *Köstler* in Z². R. G., XXXI (1910), 617–620; *Lenz*, "Ein Beitrag zum frühkirchlichen Eheschliessungsrecht" in Deut. Z. Kirchenr., XX, (1910), 272–296; *Rodeck*, "Beiträge zur Geschichte des Eherechts deutscher Fürsten bis zur Durchführung des Tridentinums", in *Meister's* Münsterische Beiträge (new series, XXVI, 1910); *Koebner*, "Die Eheauffassung im späteren Mittelalter", in Arch. Kult. G., IX (1911), 136–198, 279–318; *Opet*, "Die Anordnung der Eheschliessungspublizität im Capitulare Vernense", in "Festschrift für O. Gierke", (1911), 245–254; *Schmitt-Falkenberg*, "Eine Studie über das Verlöbnis in England mit einer Einführung über die englische Rechtsentwicklung im allgemeinen" (1911).

into special systems for different religious confessions or Territorial churches. It is only in the modern period that the State has again assumed control of the regulation of the marriage contract.

(I) **The old Germanic law of Marriage Contract.** — (1) *Wife-abduction and wife-purchase.*—(A) WIFE-ABDUCTION ("Frauenraub", wife-" rape "). There can be no doubt that, just as among the people of India, Greeks, Romans, Slavs, and many other non-Indo-Germanic races, so also among the primitive Germans the abduction of women had at one time the effect of creating the marriage relation. Indubitable evidences exist of this fact. Like the Indian and Grecian epics, the sagas and poems of the primitive Germans ascribe to their most celebrated heroes the abduction of women by violence; and that this poetry rested upon a basis of reality, — although indeed one which had for the most part already disappeared, — is shown by historical examples, among which none is more celebrated than that of Arminius, who by abduction won in marriage Thusnelda, the intended wife of another.[1] These reports are confirmed by the legal sources: in some of the Germanic folk-laws there still occur provisions according to which the 'raptor' retained as wife a woman he had abducted against the will of her kindred from whom he captured her; or at least retained her when she herself acquiesced in the abduction or thereafter chose to remain with him.[2] It can be proved that the abduction marriage was still known among the North Germans in the age of the Vikings, and in the peculiar statutory wife-abduction of northern legal sources it continued even much later. Reminders of this one-time institution of bride-abduction have been preserved also in many marriage customs among Germanic and Slavic races, widespread even to-day, which considerably increase the weight of other evidences. Thus, among rural populations the wooing of the bride frequently still has an apparently warlike character. Something like a simulated investment of the bride's house is undertaken by the friends of the bridegroom; often, the bride conceals herself after the marriage ceremony and must be captured, in which connection feigned battles take place among the boys and girls; throughout Germany, moreover, there is known as a marriage game a custom in accord with which the bride is abducted by the

[1] *Brunner*, "Geschichte", I (2d ed.), 95.
[2] *Brunner*, *op. cit.* *Cf.* *Fehr*, "Hammurapi und das salische Recht, eine Rechtsvergleichung" (1910), 77.

youth of the village.[1] It is consistent with all this that the marriage ceremony ("Trauung", "Hochzeit") was known in the East and West Germanic laws as "bride-flight" ("Brautlauf", "Brautlauft", from "laufen", "currere", to run); these names reflect the fact that it was the bringing home of the bride that constituted the most essential element in the marriage contract.

There is a theory, — wholly without basis, notwithstanding that it is championed by some Germanists (Dargun, Heusler), — that this rape-marriage was "the normal marriage of primitive law"; [2] that the rape of women was originally the only valid form in which marriage could be consummated among the primitive Germans, and that only in time was there developed from it a peaceful, contractual mode in which marriage could be established. Schröder justly remarks [3] that "marriage contracted between the children of neighbors with the knowledge and consent of their families must have been the starting point in the case of every race not wholly bestial." In the case of the primitive Germans the further fact is especially important that among them, as among many other primitive peoples, so-called endogamous marriages seem to have been the rule; that is, marriages between members of the same sib. The sib, however, was a frith-union (*supra*, p. 114), and excluded as between its members blood-feuds, hostilities, and acts of violence. In the case of such marriages, therefore, there must always have been a peaceful form of contract. Just as in the old law of India marriage by violent abduction of women was ordinarily permitted only to the members of the military nobility, so among the primitive Germans rape-marriage was doubtless never the rule but always an exception, and could have been especially common only when the question was one of winning in marriage the daughters of another sib, of an alien line ("Stamm", family), or of a conquered race.

(B) Wife-purchase ("Frauenkauf"). — The original form of marriage contract among the primitive Germans was wife-purchase. We meet with it in the oldest legal sources as the prevailing, and the only legal, form in which marriage could be consummated. In this respect, also, the oldest Germanic law agrees exactly with conditions that are attested with equal clearness among most of the other Indo-Germanic races in their earliest

[1] *Dargun*, "Mutterrecht und Raubehe", 134.
[2] *Schröder*, "Lehrbuch" (5th ed.), 70.
[3] *Op. cit.*

antiquity, and which have been preserved among some of such races down to the present day; for example in India, where even today wife-purchase is widely prevalent in many regions as a form of marriage among the ordinary people,[1] and among the Russians, where marriage is still, in the mind of the rural folk and in reality, a matter of purchase, and is treated in the most matter-of-fact way as a question of goods and prices.[2] Again, among the early Germans the consummation of marriage was a juristic act, which was concluded between the bridegroom and his kindred on one side, and the father or guardian who held mundium over the bride and her kindred on the other side; and in which the bride herself participated solely as the object of the sale and not as a contracting party. Hence the Frankish folk-laws still spoke of "uxorem emere", "feminam vendere", "pretium emptionis", "pretium nuptiale", "puella empta"; and the Scandinavian law-books of "kaupa", "byggja konu" (to buy a wife, to bargain). In Germany the expression "kaufen" (to buy), for "to marry", long survived in many regions the custom itself, and has been preserved down to modern times, indeed even to the present day, as for example in Holland "where popular speech still designates the bride as 'purchased' ('verkocht', 'verkauft')."[3] It is true, as already mentioned (p. 592), that older legal phraseology employed the expressions "Kauf", "kaufen" (sale, to buy) in a far wider sense than that which is usual to-day, applying them to every bilateral contract; to every contract which in Amira's words can be called in any sense a "trade" ("Handelschaft"). Relying upon this circumstance, Maurer [4] and Amira [5] deny to the marriage of Germanic law the character of a purchase in the present sense of that word. But despite this pertinent definition of the term, it can scarcely be doubted that the primitive Germans, when they chose their wives by contract, saw in the transaction by which they so procured them nothing more than an actual purchase; that in their eyes there was no difference in the transaction, as such, whether they purchased a woman to be a wife or a servant. This conclusion is not inconsistent with the fact that the purchase of a wife was distinguished from all other purchases both by its object — a free woman, and by its pur-

[1] *Jolly*, "Recht und Sitte, Grundriss der indoarischen Philologie und Altertumskunde", Vol. 2, Heft 8 (1896), 52.
[2] *Schrader*, "Sprachvergleichung und Urgeschichte" (3d ed.), 323.
[3] *Brunner*, *op. cit.*, 97.
[4] "Vorlesungen", II, 506 *et seq.*
[5] "Recht", 111.

pose — the creation of a mundium that protected the entire freedom of the woman. Nor is it inconsistent with the fact that the will of the bride herself may also have come to be considered, at least in fact, at an early date. Although bride-purchase was therefore distinguished by the special agreements that accompanied it, and which were lacking in other contract forms for the purchases of women, there was nevertheless involved in it, as in every contract of sale, an exchange of goods and a purchase price. The purchase price was called dower ("Wittum", "Widum"; Old High G. "widemo", "widem"; A. Saxon "weotuma"; Burgundian "wittimon") or hire-money ("Mietgeld"; Lombard "metá"; "Miete", "Lohn",—hire, wage). In Latin it was known as "pretium nuptiale"; "pretium emptionis", "dos." To be sure, fixed statutory tariffs for the dower ("Wittum") were declared in the folk-laws, at least in the Frankish period, but these probably had no absolute, but only a relative, significance; possibly that of a minimum limit. On the contrary free agreement was probably the original and ordinary form. Indeed we are frequently told, for example in the Scandinavian sagas, of a bargaining concerning the sum. The creation of the marital community for life by a transaction of sale, — it nowhere appears in more repulsive form than in some of the Anglo Saxon laws,[1] — has to our feelings a cold-blooded and brutal character. But that can be no reason for doubting that the actual nature of this form of marriage was a sale; especially when one remarks how widespread this view has been and still is among races of the past and of the present day. Even now it cannot be regarded as extinct in many social strata of the German folk.

(2) *Formal requisites of a marriage consummated by contract.* — (A) The original simple act of the marriage contract. — Since Sohm's investigations it has been certain that marriages consummated contractually were always controlled by the general rules of contract law. Indeed the study of the forms in which marriage was consummated has served to make clear the general principles and development of the Germanic-German law of contract. Marriage by contract, like every other legal transaction, and particularly every sale, was originally consummated as a non-credit transaction. This spot transaction was composed, indeed, of two different elements; but it combined these, exactly as

[1] *Aethelberht* (601–604), cc. 77, 31; *Liebermann*, "Die Gesetze der Angelsachsen", I (1903), 7 *et seq.*, 5. *Von Amira*, "Recht", 112, detects in these rules principles that have been further developed in the later law.

did the oldest conveyances of land, into an act single in time and in law. When the offer of marriage, which ordinarily preceded the contract, had been accepted, and when an agreement had been reached concerning the conditions — particularly the price and the time — of the nuptials, then the legal ceremony, upon whose publicity great weight was laid, was consummated within the circle of blood "friends." For marriage was an affair of the sib; it was a marriage under the family-law.[1] This legal act was so executed that the performances of the two parties followed alternatively: the bridegroom counted out into the hand of him who held mundium over the bride, for her sib, the price agreed upon, and he who held the mundium gave ("tradieren", "trauen", to deliver) the bride to the bridegroom. Thereupon followed the leading of the bride home to the house of the bridegroom, — the bride-flight, — where cohabitation ("Beilager") was consummated in a public manner; and with this the marriage ceremony was concluded, and the existence of the marriage begun. The father, brother, or the next male relative of the sword-kin was empowered to betroth and to give the bride. If she were a widow it was the nearest male connection of her first husband in conjunction with her blood-friends; whose place was taken, in case of their refusal, by the kindred of the widow. The betrother ("Verlober") received for his participation a marriage gift from the bridegroom.

(B) Betrothal and nuptials.—This simple marriage act, which we must assume for the Germanic period, became divided in the Frankish period into two acts, the two elements theoretically involved in it being separated in time, — exactly as was the case with the Sala and the investiture in conveyances of land (*supra*, pp. 241 *et seq.*).

(a) *The betrothal* ("Verlobung"). — The first act essential to the consummation of the marriage, which corresponded to the "Sala", was the betrothal ("desponsatio"; A. Saxon "beweddung"; Old Norse "foestning"). This was the contract of alienation, which continued for a time to be concluded between the bridegroom and the bride's sib, represented by the holder of mundium over her. To be sure, under the influence of Christianity increasing respect was paid to the bride's will, but no importance was at first attributed to this legally. In accordance with the general rules of the law of contracts, this contract of alienation could originally be concluded only as a real-contract

[1] *Brunner*, Z². R. G., XVI (1895), 103.

(*supra*, pp. 503 *et seq.*). That is, the bridegroom was bound to perform first the act incumbent upon him, — the payment of the purchase price; he thereby obligated the other contracting party to the counter performance, which after the appearance of credit transactions was postponed to a later time. However, just as the payment of handsel, symbolic of the full purchase price and in place of complete pre-performance, came in time to be considered sufficient in a sale to obligate the other party to counter performance, so in the betrothal men were contented if the bridegroom delivered an earnest ("arrha"), a payment on the purchase price. Among the Franks this symbolic mundium-money ("Mundschatz") amounted to a solidus (= 10 denarii) and one denarius; in the betrothal of a widow, — in which connection it was known as a "Reipus" (ring-money),[1] — three solidi and one denarius. The payment of this slight sum was preserved for centuries in regions of the French law as a marriage custom. At the marriage of Louis XVI and Marie Antoinette there still figured thirteen denarii, — which, indeed, are reported to be still in use in some parts of France;[2] and it is reported of the marriage of the Count of Paris, celebrated in 1864, that the Count, to conclude the same, handed to his young wife a few gold and silver coins.[3]

Although the payment of the earnest might preserve to the betrothal the character of a real contract it nevertheless became possible to conclude it in the form of a wed-contract; that is, to consummate it as a formal, instead of a real, contract. In this case the bridegroom obligated himself to a later payment of the dower ("Wittum") by handing to the mundium-holder of the bride a "wadia"; whereupon, — since the staff did not have the effect of binding the other party, — a "wadia" was likewise handed over by the guardian, in order to assure the bride's future delivery. Moreover, there might easily occur here, as in all cases, a confusion of earnest-money ("arrha") and staff ("wadia"), of real and formal contract (*supra*, pp. 501, 506 *et seq.*).

The nature of the betrothal was altered in still another respect. It became usual to regard the mundium over the bride, rather than her own person, as the object of the sale which the bride-

[1] *Gierke* is of another opinion, "Schuld und Haftung", 359 *et seq.*, in particular 362, n. 103.

[2] *Viollet*, 419; *Brissaud*, 1015.

[3] In a letter of the chemist *A. W. v. Hofmann*, in "Berichte der deutschen chemischen Gesellschaft", XXXV (1902), 78.

groom must acquire with the purchase price. This explains the fact that among the Lombards the purchase price was also known as "mundius", among the Frisians as "muntsket" ("Muntschatz"), and among the North Germans as "mundr." At the same time, this change of view must have had rather theoretical than practical importance so long as the mundium continued to involve extensive powers of control.

On the other hand it was of the greatest practical importance that the purchase money came in time to inure to the bride herself instead of her sib. From the mundium-holder's custom of delivering to her the whole or a part of the "Wittum" there was developed a legal claim of the bride to that amount of property. By this change, however, the meaning and purpose of the performance incumbent upon the bridegroom was also altered: he no longer gave the sum agreed upon in order to purchase the bride from her sib, but in order to make her a gift ("Zuwendung") which was intended to serve her as a maintenance-portion ("Leibgedinge"), as support for her when a widow. The "pretium" became a "dos"; the "puella empta" became a "puella dotata." With this change the giving of the dower ("Wittum"), once essential under the Germanic law to the validity of the marriage (*infra*, § 94), completely lost its importance from the 1100 s onward.

To these changes was added the following. As already mentioned, the bride was originally simply the object of the betrothal contract, and it marked an advance when regard was also paid to her will (in the beginning at least actually, and later legally as well), and her consent required. But when the legal position of women began gradually to improve, this purely passive participation of the bride ceased, and the rôles of the parties were reversed. "Whereas the father (or guardian) of the bride had theretofore concluded the betrothal contract, though with the consent of the daughter, she now betrothed herself, a mere right of consent, that is a veto upon the contraction of the marriage, being conceded to her father (or guardian) as a remnant of his old right of betrothal."[1] The father or guardian thenceforth appeared as the betrother only in the case of a bride under mundium. The betrothal thus became a contract concluded between bridegroom and bride; they were the contract parties who made the mutual promises of marriage. But in this form also, of course, the betrothal continued subject to the existing rules of contract

[1] *Sohm*, "Eheschliessung", 52.

law. Afterward as before, it was concluded either as a weakened real contract by the delivery of earnest-money by the bridegroom, or as a formal (a wed-) contract by the mutual delivery of staffs; in which connection, however, as already mentioned, staff and handsel might easily be confused with one another. Following Roman-Italian usage, a ring was the customary handsel in Germany ("subarrhatio cum anulo"). It was entirely consistent with the nature of the "arrha" that only *one* ring was originally given, and this by the bridegroom to the bride; for the ring, the betrothal ring, was the last remnant of the old purchase-money; with it the bridegroom betrothed the bride, and the bride, by putting it on her finger, obligated herself to marital fidelity. When the custom of exchanging rings later developed, the mutual gift and acceptance of the rings replaced the mutual delivery of staffs, and represented the formal act of a wed-contract. However, as in the case of other contracts so in that of betrothal the weaker forms of oath or hand-clasp also sufficed for its consummation.

(b) *The nuptials* ("Trauung"). — The betrothal was followed, when the day agreed upon arrived, by the delivery of the bride from her mundium-holder to the bridegroom. This was the "traditio puellæ" (A. Saxon "gifta"), which, as already remarked, exactly corresponded in legal significance and outward form to the investiture in a conveyance of land. It was performed as a public and solemn act in the bride's home in the presence of the kindred of both parties. It was accompanied by the marriage feast. The legal formalities observed in this connection were long the same as those that once accompanied the original simple act by which marriage was consummated. They corresponded, in part, to the usages customary in adoption. Along with the bride there were delivered to the bridegroom certain symbols of espousal—preferably a spear, as the token of the mundium that passed therewith to him for the future; the hair of the bride, which she had until then worn loose, was done up, her head was veiled, a mantle was thrown about her, and so on; the bridegroom grasped her hand,[1] and probably stepped upon her foot, or set her upon his knee as if she were an adopted child; frequently, also, he delivered to her a present. The final act, afterward as before, was the festive leading of the bride home to the bridegroom's house, where, at least in the North, a common cup once more rejoiced the entire marriage company. Thereafter

[1] *Cf. v. Amira*, "Handgebärden" (*supra*, p. 11), 241 *et seq.*, 244.

came the occupancy of the nuptial-bed in the presence of witnesses, frequently by torch-light; a custom which remained usual throughout the Middle Ages, persisting longest in the case of princely marriages, but also among the laboring classes down into the 1600 s. The Law Books of the zenith of the Middle Ages emphasized more frequently and with greater stress than did the Frankish sources the importance of marital cohabitation as the act most decisive for the consummation of the marriage's legal consequences. The beginning of the marital community of goods, in particular, was very often made dependent upon it. This moment was expressed by phrases of the most varied character ("when the woman gets into the man's bed"; "when the cover is drawn over them"; "when the woman disrobes before the man's bed", etc.).[1]

The consequences of dividing the marriage ceremony into two acts, the betrothal and the nuptials, was that neither of these alone sufficed to establish the marriage relation. Of course the betrothal, like all other contracts, produced certain legal effects. It obligated the guardian to perform the marriage ceremony at the time agreed upon, and it obligated the bridegroom to take home the bride and to pay the purchase money whose payment was temporarily respited. Whoever failed to perform these obligations was punished for breach of the betrothal contract; the guardian was ordinarily obliged to give back the "Wittum" in case this had already been paid, and to pay an equal amount as damages; the bridegroom lost the "Wittum." In addition to this, the betrothal created a personal obligation of fidelity on the part of the woman; so long as she was a mere object of sale, this could have been created by giving her a present, and later it was created by the handsel that was given her. Under many legal systems an affianced woman who was guilty of sexual intercourse with another man might be punished as an adulteress. Her betrothed, as well as her mundium-holder, had an action against a third person who seduced her, with or without her consent. But the marriage relation was first created by the espousals, which, however, could be consummated only after betrothal.

That betrothal and nuptials were equally necessary preconditionals to the creation of a legally valid marriage, and continued to constitute one act legally, is shown by the generally prevalent

[1] *Cf. Fehr*, "Die Rechtsstellung der Frau und der Kinder in den Weistümern" (1912), 60 *et seq.*

custom of performing in connection with each the formalities that were usual in the other. So for example, the Lombard law, in the case of betrothal, when the "meta" had been paid or wagered (given as a wed), the bride was delivered by her mundium-holder symbolically ("per baculum"), but then immediately handed back by the bridegroom. It was more common to repeat the formalities of betrothal in the nuptials: the bridegroom once more paid the simulated purchase price (the earnest-money) and the parties once more declared their will to marry, just as they had already done in the betrothal. In particular, a ring was delivered or rings again exchanged in the nuptials: with this step the engagement ring became a marriage ring ("mahelfingerlin"). This is also the explanation of the fact that expressions were employed to designate the married couple that were derived from the betrothal, — "Ehegespons", "promessi sposi", "épouser", "to spouse", "to wed", "vermählen" (that is, to promise, to betroth; from "mahal" = speech, address, modern "Gemahl").

When, at the zenith of the Middle Ages, self-betrothal by the bride took the place of betrothal by her guardian, the nuptial "giving" in the sense of an investiture had outlived its usefulness. The "traditio puellæ" was transformed into a self-espousal ("Selbsttrauung") of the bride, into a mutual giving by the bridal couple. To be sure, the influence of the older viewpoint of the law continued to be shown in a peculiar manner. For that form of self-espousal which first became predominant was "a 'giving' through a third person who was freely chosen by the bride, or as the case might be by the bridal couple."[1] This third person thus became a Salmann or fiduciary ("Treuhänder") to whom the bride gave herself "in trust" ("auf Treue"); that is, "merely to the end that he should deliver her to her betrothed."[2] Who the third person might be was immaterial. He might be a near relative but that was not necessary; any trustworthy man, preferably one of advanced age but always a layman, was asked to assume this rôle. The essential thing was that he was not, like the guardian, chosen to coöperate because of any right of kinship, but merely by virtue of a commission; he was no "born" ("geborener") but a freely "chosen" ("gekorener") guardian. He consummated the nuptials by certain words with which he pronounced the marriage benediction; they were no longer completed by a marriage act but by a marriage formula. The transi-

[1] *Sohm*, "Eheschliessung", 67.

[2] *Sohm*, *op. cit.*, 68.

tion from the old to the new usage can be traced in certain remarkable records of legal and cultural history. In a Swabian nuptial-formula of the 1100 s it is still the true, the "born", guardian who as the nearest male relative gives ("antwortet") the bride to the bridegroom together with the symbols of marriage, — namely seven gloves (the "wadia" given by the bridegroom), a sword, a golden ring, a penny, mantle, and hat, pronouncing at the same time the words: "wa ich iu bevilhe mine muntadele (Mündel) ziweren triwun und ze iueren gnaden, und bit iuch durch die triwe als ich si iu bevilhe, dar ir ir rehte voget sit, und ir genadich voget sit, und daz ir nit palemunt (treuloser Vormund) ne werdent." ("Because I give over to you my ward to your faith and mercy and beg you by the faith by which I entrust her to you that you will be her right and kindly keeper and that you will not become faithless to your trust.") On the other hand, in a nuptial-formula of Cologne of the 1300 s there is talk merely of a certain "somebody" who consummates the marriage simply with the following words: "Ich bevelen uch zô houff up Frentzer Erden myt Goulde ind Gesteynen, Silver ind Gould, beyde nâ Francken Wyse ind Sassen ee, dat urre geyn den anderen layssen en sall umb Leyff noch umb Leyt, noch um geyn Dynck dat Gott an eme geschaffen hait odir geschaffen mach layssen werden." [1] ("I enjoin you, on Frankish soil with gold and precious stones, with silver and gold, both according to Frankish manner and Saxon law, that neither of you shall leave the other for love or woe nor for any other thing that God has created in you or may create in you.")

(C) RELIGIOUS BENEDICTION.—Inasmuch as marriage was everywhere in Europe regarded, in the first half of the Middle Ages, as a secular juristic act, — in accordance with the old view of the Germanic races, and in agreement also with the viewpoint of the Roman law, — there was no place in such act for participation by ecclesiastical agents. But at this most important moment in life the Germanic peoples, from the earliest times, felt the need of a religious consecration. In the heathen period the mind of the gods was sounded in advance by lot; in the North the betrothal was consecrated by Thor's hammer, or the young wife was led three times around the hearth upon which a fire had been lighted for the gods; —and so on. After the adoption of Christianity these heathen usages were displaced by the benediction of the young people pronounced by a priest after the

[1] *Sohm, op. cit.*, 67, 69, 320 f.

espousal. Frankish capitularies expressly prescribe this in accordance with the Church's precepts. Inasmuch as the nuptials, particularly the lay- (the Salmann) form above discussed, were preferably performed in the Middle Ages before the church door ("ante valvas ecclesiæ"), — before the "bridal-door" (the main door of the north side being, for this reason, frequently so known), — in order to assure to it the greatest publicity possible, the newly married couple could immediately thereafter enter the church with the marriage party to hear the marriage mass and receive, thereafter, the Church's blessing. Often, however, the benediction took place only on the day following the marriage, on the morning after cohabitation; for example, Günther went to the mass with Brünhild, Siegfried with Kriemhild, only after the bridal night. But these usages did not alter in the least the purely secular character of the marriage. Whether or not the priest was present, as was natural, before the church door during the marriage ceremony, at any rate his ecclesiastical function began only after the conclusion of the legal ceremony.

(II) **The Ecclesiastical Law of Marriage.** — (1) *The Canon law of marriage.* — From the 1100 s onward, the secular law was displaced, in Germany as elsewhere, by the marriage law of the Church. True, the formal side of the marriage law had from the earliest times been less important to the Church than its substantive aspect, — that is, the question of any impediment to marriage, above all one resulting from kinship. Relying upon the Bible, it assumed in this respect a far stricter attitude than did the Germanic law. For though the latter emphasized from the beginning the equality of status, — which, on the other hand, was immaterial from the Church's point of view, — it originally permitted marriages between kindred of all degrees, save parents and children, permitting in the Christian period, after marriages between brothers and sisters, which were once permitted, had ceased to be practiced, marriages with brothers- and sisters-in-law, and even marriage with one's step-mother. In the same way the Church began an obstinate struggle against the divorce law of the Germanic races (*infra*, § 92). It succeeded in establishing its contentions in both matters, for it found a way to withdraw from the lay courts all suits involving the personal rights of the marriage relation, and to establish for these, as ecclesiastical matters, an exclusive jurisdiction in the ecclesiastical courts. It followed as a matter of course that the rules of the ecclesiastical law thenceforth became controlling in answering the question whether a marriage formally valid had been created, since that question was decided in the ecclesiastical courts. Next, the Church demanded the participation of ecclesiastics in the marriage ceremony. A simple means existed by which to establish such coöperation. It was only necessary to convert the presence of the priest at the marriage, which was already customary, into a participation essential to the legality of the nuptials, by demanding that no layman should in future conduct the marriage ceremony as a "chosen" guardian, but that this should be done by the priest who afterwards pronounced the Church's blessing. In other words the Church forbade marriage by laymen and commanded marriage by ecclesiastics. In fact secular marriages thereafter disappeared from legal life. The priest took the place of the old guardian. But notwithstanding that the nuptials were now consummated by a priest, and had thereby been transformed into an act subject to the Canon law, the ceremony was not, — as was, for example, confirmation ("Firmung"), — a priestly act, resting upon the priestly power of consecration. Marriage, according to the dogma of the Catholic Church, was a sacrament; the dispenser of the sacrament, however, was not the priest but the marriage couple themselves. The nuptials still remained a secular ceremony; the ecclesiastical ceremony continued to lie merely in the pronunciation of the Church's blessing upon a marriage already concluded.

The displacement of the lay guardian by the priest in the giving ("Trauung") of the bride was not, however, the sole result of subjecting marriage to the rules of the Canon law. This had the further effect that the formal requisites of secular law, particularly the old division of the ceremony into betrothal and nuptials, were displaced by the totally different ecclesiastical law of marriage. This ecclesiastical marriage law, — which can here be only briefly referred to beyond a reference to the literature of the Canon law,[1] — adopted from the beginning the rule of the classic Roman law of marriage: "nudus consensus facit nuptias"; though, to be sure, there was added to this, as an entirely new conception, the doctrine of the sacramental nature of marriage. As a result of regarding the meeting of the parties' wills as the constitutive element in marriage, without declaring any form

[1] In addition to the discussion of this matter in *Sohm's* "Recht der Eheschliessung", compare among other works the elaborate exposition in *Scherer*, "Handbuch des Kirchenrechts", II (1891, 2d ed., 1898), §§ 109 *et seq.*, with abundant references.

whatever to be legally necessary thereto, — not even the ceremony prescribed by the Church, — the duality of betrothal and nuptials in Germanic law was so far paralleled that the distinction between "sponsalia de futuro" ("accipiam te uxorem", or "maritum"), corresponding to the betrothal, and "sponsalia de præsenti" ("accipio te"), — the former involving a declaration of will directed to the future, the latter one directed to the present, — was elevated by Pope Alexander III to universal law. However, just as the importance of the betrothal had already come to be greatly lessened in the Germanic law, so that it became usual to repeat its formalities in the nuptials, so under the classic Canon law only the "desponsatio de præsenti" sufficed, of itself, to create the marriage; although the "desponsatio de futuro" could be transformed into a marriage by the consummative act of "copula carnalis." The Church retained these views. Even the great dangers and evils that resulted from the possibility of clandestine marriages, — particularly the frequent occurrence of bigamous relations, — although they did induce her, probably following the French example, to introduce at the Lateran Council of 1215 the publication of bans, and repeatedly to insist more sharply upon the celebration of marriages "in facie ecclesiæ" (that is before priests and witnesses), — could not induce her to abandon the principle of the power of consensus to create the marriage. The Church continued to require no legal form for that contract which, above all others, is in need of definite forms. No wonder that the Canon law of marriage thereby became, as has been aptly said, "a maze of flighty fancies and misapplied logic." [1]

In order to minimize these evils, the Council of Trent undertook in its celebrated decree "Tametsi" a reformation of the Canon law of marriage which, in the main, ended its development. Thereafter as before it permitted marriage to originate in the declaration of will on the part of the bridal couple, but required for this declaration of will one absolute element; it *must* be made in the presence of a priest and two witnesses. Owing to this rule it became thenceforth impossible to transform informal "sponsalia de futuro" into marriages by "copula carnalis." But at the same time the Council thereby renounced performance of the marriage ceremony by ecclesiastics, and so the nuptials in toto. The priest became a mere witness whose presence was required (in an extreme case, indeed, only passively) in order to

[1] *Pollock* and *Maitland*, "History", II, 387.

solemnize by his mere presence the marriage actually concluded by the bridal couple through a formal " desponsatio de præsenti."[1] The rôle that had fallen to the priest as successor of the old lay guardian was thus again taken from him: his words no longer had consecrative effect; they no longer conveyed the bride, but merely evidenced the act of giving (" Traditionshandlung ") performed by the bridal pair themselves. In so far as the Tridentine law regarded the marriage as resulting, not from a ceremony in the church but from a secular juristic act of the bridal couple, its position was consistent, therefore, with the old national views of the Germanic races. On the other hand, in making essential only *one* act, namely the formal consensual declaration of marriage, it definitively abandoned those views, thus rounding out the development earlier begun. The Tridentine marriage law became effective only in parishes where the decrees of the Council were published, but the legal uncertainty that resulted from this in Germany has recently been removed by the papal bull " Provida " of January 18, 1906, which has subjected all Catholic marriages in Germany to the decree " Tametsi." Finally, the decree " Ne temere " of August 2, 1907, effected a transformation of the decree " Tametsi ", — one, moreover, which is consistent with the tendency of the most recent German civil law of marriage, — by providing (especially) that the priest must be voluntarily sought and must voluntarily officiate.

(2) *The Protestant law of marriage.* — The evangelical law of marriage maintained down into the 1700 s the viewpoint of the medieval marriage law of the church to the extent that it rejected the doctrine of the sacramental character of marriage; but, on the other hand, it also regarded marriage as originating in a declaration of will by the bridal couple. Unlike the Council of Trent, however, Luther and his followers attempted to do away with the evils resulting from distinctions between betrothals by treating only the conditional " sponsalia de futuro " as true betrothals (still permitting these, however, to become marriages by " copula carnalis "), while on the other hand declaring all public betrothals, — that is, unconditional betrothals consummated directly with the consent of parents or before witnesses, or with the coöperation of the church, — to be " sponsalia de præsenti ", in other words, marriages. For this reason, after the conclusion of such a public betrothal, an action was given to compel the wedding, with compulsory execution; and for the same reason

[1] *Sohm, op. cit.*, 193.

such "sponsalia de præsenti" could be dissolved only in the same manner as marriages, and their breach was treated as adultery. At the same time, here also, consummation of the marriage was first realized by actual cohabitation, which was effected by "copula carnalis." Though the older Protestant marriage law therefore differed in this respect from the Canon law, nevertheless, like that, it required that the betrothed couple should cause themselves to be given in marriage and that their union should be consecrated by a priest. The act of the priest, as a "chosen" marriage-guardian, was intended to create the marital community for life, and to make the legal relation of marriage a relationship of fact.[1] The betrothed parties, although they were already husband and wife, were nevertheless expected to begin their married life, and in particular to consummate the "copula carnalis", only after benediction was pronounced upon their relation by the Church. An act of the Church, and not the mere natural act that was sufficient in law, was intended to be the beginning of married life. If the betrothed couple were actually living together as husband and wife, they must espouse each other a second time. Thus the German medieval law remained vital in the marriage ceremony of the older Protestant marriage-law to the extent that in this also marriage was an act of delivery performed by a third person, the priest; which delivery, in connection with cohabitation, completed the marriage ceremony begun with the "desponsatio." To be sure, its importance, as compared with the desponsatio, was very much less than that of the medieval nuptials ("Trauung") as compared with the betrothal ("Verlobung").

This older form of the Protestant marriage law, derived partly from Canon and partly from original Germanic law, was done away with in the Evangelical church as a result of the reaction against the use of Canon law that was inaugurated by Just Henning Böhmer. Protestant legal theory of the 1700 s denied to the consensual declaration of the bridal pair efficacy to constitute the marriage, attributing such power solely to the wedding consummated by the priest. With this change the parties' agreement again acquired merely the significance of a first and preparatory act, a preliminary contract, which indeed gave rise to certain duties but could not be perfected as a marriage except through an ecclesiastical marriage; which was a certain approximation to the old Germanic law. At the same time, and for the first time in

[1] *Sohm, op. cit.*, 233.

the long evolution of the marriage law, marriage became a purely ecclesiastical ceremony. It was the declaration of the priest, — which he made as an ecclesiastical act and by virtue of his churchly office, — and no longer the will and declaration of the bridal pair, that created the marriage. The secular legislation of many German States also adopted the view of this later Protestant marriage law, prescribing, in accord with it, ecclesiastical nuptials for Protestant subjects.[1]

(III) **The Marriage Law of the Modern State.** — The Reformers, while rejecting the theory of the sacramental nature of marriage, clung without qualifications to the view that the law of marriage was a part of the Canon law and therefore must belong to the jurisdiction of the church courts; but the revival of religious life that was stimulated by the Reformation, the actual conditions produced by a division of religious faiths, and finally the intellectual tendencies that were attaining supremacy as embodied in the law of nature, led nevertheless to a fundamental break with the view of the medieval Church, and to secularization of the marriage law and the marriage ceremony. A fundamental transformation of marriage into a purely secular legal act, performed exclusively before public authorities, was first realized among the Puritans of England and Scotland, as a result of religious motives whose influence was there most effectively felt, and which proved able to enforce their demand that marriage should be a simple consensual declaration of the bridal pair before the assembled community. Such was the civil marriage introduced by Cromwell in 1653 into Great Britain; an institution that was abolished shortly after his death. Civil marriage was prescribed in these same years throughout the Netherlands as a result of considerations primarily practical and political, due to the various faiths of citizens of different States, — and after individual States had taken steps in this direction as early as the 1500 s for their own territories; absolutely in the case of dissenters and alternatively in the case of members of the reformed church. In the later development, however, especially in Germany, it was not so much the English and Dutch legislation that was influential as that of France, where civil marriage was introduced as an obligatory type of marriage, first by a statute of 1792 and then by the Code Civil, as a result of certain ideas of natural law concerning the relation of State and Church.

[1] For example, Prussian Allg. L. R., II, 1, § 136: "A perfect and valid marriage is consummated by the espousals before the priest." § 81: "It is not necessary that a formal betrothal shall precede every marriage."

To be sure, civil marriage was recognized in Germany, at first, only in a few States outside the regions of the French law; and when the German Fundamental Rights of 1848 demanded it, and the Prussian constitution, under their influence, prescribed it (Art. 19) for Prussia, men were content for the moment to introduce the "facultative" form of civil marriage in cases of necessity (*i.e.* for those persons who could not be married in the church, as for example dissenters and Jews). However, after certain States later adopted compulsory civil marriage (Frankfort 1850, Baden 1869, Prussia 1874), this was introduced for the entire Empire by the Imperial Act of Personal Status of February 6, 1875. With this step the Canon law of marriage, so far as it has been recognized by the State, was abrogated. It was conceded, henceforth, merely the character of a rule binding, at most, upon the conscience. This view has been adopted, and indeed even more decisively established, in the codification of the German law, since the present Civil Code not only prescribes for the marriage contract the outward form of an obligatory civil ceremony, excluding any participation by representatives of the Church, but also regulates exhaustively and exclusively the substantive preconditions and the legal effect of the relation. As respects the form of the marriage ceremony, it has so modified the imperial statutes of personal status as to free itself from the last traces of the Protestant ecclesiastical rules, returning to the Tridentine and the classical Canon marriage law to the extent of attributing to the civil official (whose declaration consummates the marriage, under the law of 1875, in the same way as that of an evangelical pastor) merely the functions of a recorder, such as was the "parochus proprius" of the Tridentine law. It is not the declaration of the public official that creates the marriage, but the unqualified and immediate declaration of will by the bridal couple; though this must be made personally and simultaneously in the presence of such official, who is authorized to receive it. With this change the marriage ceremony has again become an act of secular private law, as it was down to the 1100 s. The division of the marriage ceremony into two equally essential acts is not recognized in the present civil law of marriage; no more than it was in the Tridentine law. True, the Civil Code also regulates betrothal by some provisions that have given rise to important differences of opinion respecting the present legal nature of that institute; but betrothal is not, under the present law, an absolutely necessary requisite for the creation of a legal marriage.

§ 92. **The Dissolution of Marriage. — (I) Dissolution by Death.** — The purpose of marriage being limited to the life of the parties, the ordinary cause of its dissolution has always been the death of one of the spouses. The consequences that result therefrom, as regards the surviving spouse, with reference to rights of property and legal relations to the children will be discussed below (§§ 94 *et seq.*). As regards remarriage by the surviving spouse, this was of course always unrestricted in the case of the husband. On the other hand, the *remarriage of the widow* [1] seems to have been looked upon with disfavor, in the earliest times, among many of the Germanic racial branches. Tacitus remarks that among some peoples the widow ordinarily followed her husband into death.[2] And although doubts might be raised respecting the fact reported, and especially his explanation of it, nevertheless there do exist other traces of this custom, which as is well known was most prevalent in India. The Scandinavian Saga of Nanna "pictures the wife as dying of grief, and burned with her husband upon a funeral pyre"; "Brynhild orders that she be burned with Sigurd"; [3] among the Herulians, the widow hanged herself beside the body of her husband; among the inhabitants of Ditmarsch, the marriage of a widow was still regarded at the end of the Middle Ages as highly scandalous; and among the North Frisians no widow marries even at the present day, as Müllenhoff, himself a North Frisian, reports.[4] The most illuminating explanation of the voluntary death of a widow is possibly found in the custom of primitive times of burying with a dead man a part of his property (*infra*, § 111); the widow, along with slaves and maid servants, belonged to this "death- (dead man's) portion" ("Totenteil").[5] At the same time the aversion to a widow's marriage, the demand that the widow "should not move her widow's-chair", cannot have been generally prevalent. On the contrary, it is a certainty that marriage of the widow with a kinsman of her husband was a widespread custom among primitive Germans from the earliest times; and that according to the folk-laws of the Frankish period "the marriage of widows was not only freely permitted, but the law protected the widow's right of remarriage against impediments which selfishness might possibly

[1] *Martin Wolff*, "Zur Geschichte der Witwenehe im altdeutschen Recht", in Inst. öst. G. F., XVII (1896), 369–388.
[2] "Germania", c. 19.
[3] *Grimm*, "Rechtsaltertümer", I, 622.
[4] *Müllenhoff*, "Deutsche Altertumskunde", IV, 313.
[5] *Brunner*, "Geschichte", I (2d ed.), 109.

place in her way."[1] Since the widow was subject during life to the sex-guardianship of her dead husband's sib, and her husband's kindred could therefore control her right of remarriage, there was evident danger of their improperly profiting at her expense: the sib, in order to retain her property and her labor, might permit either no remarriage or only remarriage with another member of the sib. The folk-laws adopted different means to restrain this danger of exploitation. Some, as for example the Lombard and the Saxon law, gave to the widow's own blood-friends ("Magen") the control of her betrothal which was originally held by the blood-friends of the dead husband, in case of its abuse by the latter; others, like the Icelandic law, from the beginning, gave the power of betrothal to the widow's kindred; still others, finally, like the later Salic Law, granted the widow an unrestricted right of self-betrothal. Only a transitory authority was enjoyed by the provision of the "Lex Salica" that kindred not interested in the heritage of the husband, — that is his kindred on the spindle-side, — should exercise the right of betrothal, and should receive from the second husband the ring-money ("Reipus") as a betrothal fee; the idea being that they would act more impartially than the kindred of the first husband, who were interested in the inheritance. When the bride's right of self-betrothal became general, later in the Middle Ages, all these restrictions upon remarriages by widows, derived from the old betrothal-right of the sex-guardian, disappeared. And although the rule existed in Germanic law, and is still recognized in the law of the Civil Code (§ 1313), that a widow may contract a second marriage only on the expiration of a certain period since the dissolution of her former marriage, the reason for this is entirely different: it is designed to avoid uncertainty concerning the paternity of children borne by the widow after the dissolution of the first marriage.

(II) **Divorce** ("Ehescheidung"). — There was always recognized in Germanic law, as in the laws of kindred races, a possibility of dissolving marriage even during the life of the spouses, notwithstanding its theoretical continuance for life that distinguished it from other forms of sexual union. However, in Germany as elsewhere, the secular law of divorce was displaced, even earlier than the secular law of the marriage contract, by the Church's international law of divorce, which was dominated by quite different ideas. Only in modern times has the State again

[1] See *Brunner's* essay on the "Reipus", cited *supra*, p. 591, at 1292.

assumed the legal regulation of this matter, thereby restricting the Canon law of divorce to the field of conscience. Thus the law of divorce has passed through the same three stages as has the law of marriage contracts.

(1) *The Old German law of divorce*[1] recognized three forms of divorce.[2] (A) In the oldest Germanic law a STATUTORY DIVORCE resulted from the outlawry of one of the spouses. Inasmuch as an outlaw was expelled from all legal communion with his fellows this necessarily broke his (or her) marital bonds. His wife was regarded as a widow; he could no longer have by her legitimate children. Thus, in the medieval formulas of judicial outlawry ("Verbannung") and prescription by vehmic right ("Verfehmung"), the judge pronounces the wife of the outlaw "a notorious widow" and his children "notorious orphans"; and similarly, medieval legal systems treated as illegitimate a child begotten on his wife by a man while in prison.

(B) But marriage could also be dissolved by the will of the spouses. Like the oldest law, the law of the Frankish period still recognized "an absolute freedom of DIVORCE BY MUTUAL AGREEMENT."[3] The separation agreement was concluded between the husband and the sib of the wife. This was the normal form of divorce.

(C) Finally, there existed a form of DIVORCE AT THE WILL OF ONE PARTY. But the right to exercise this existed, originally, in favor of the husband only. It implied an originally unlimited power in the husband to free himself from his wife by repudiating her. In those times, however, of which the earliest sources preserved to us afford us exact information, such repudiation of a wife was permitted by the law only in certain cases. The most important ground for repudiation was commission of adultery by the wife, or other equally serious breach of marital fidelity, as for example a secret attempt upon her husband's life. But certainly there was also included among the legal grounds for divorce among the primitive Germans sterility of the wife, as a defect which prevented the begetting of children, which was the chief purpose of the marriage. Charles the Great, for example, repudiated his Lombard wife for this reason after a short-lived marriage. "After the marriage law ceased to recognize sterility as a ground for divorce of marriage, the same end was attained by permitting a

[1] *Geffcken*, "Zur Geschichte der Ehescheidung vor Gratian" (1894).
[2] *Brunner*, Z². R. G., XVI (1895), 105 *et seq.*
[3] *Heusler*, "Institutionen", II, 291.

consummation of a marriage only after the woman's fecundity was put beyond doubt by facts that were manifest before marriage." [1] Customs designed to secure the same end are, as is well known, still met with among the rural population of Germany. Of course, if the husband repudiated his wife without legal cause this violation of the law involved consequences prejudicial to him, — in particular, he became liable to pay a bót to his wife's kindred, who might make feud upon him; but even an unlawful separation resulted, nevertheless, in a dissolution of the marriage.

It was only in the Frankish period and under the influence of the Roman law that the wife was empowered, in a few cases, to declare herself free of her husband by her own act; for example, in case of extreme mistreatment. The custom developed in the Frankish systems of law in accord with which "the widow laid keys and a purse upon the corpse or upon the coffin of her dead husband, thereby renouncing in his favor her rights to the marital property" [2] (*infra*, § 95), was a unilateral form of separation which was consummated by the wife after the death of her husband.

(2) *The ecclesiastical law of divorce.* (A) THE DIVORCE LAW OF THE CATHOLIC CHURCH. — Already in the Frankish period the secular law of divorce was hard pressed, and from the 1900 s was entirely displaced, by that of the Church. From this time on the Church enjoyed an exclusive jurisdiction of divorce actions, and since it also proved capable of substituting judicial divorce for the private divorce of the old Germanic and Frankish law it was in a position to enforce in such actions its own substantive law of divorce which rested upon ideas totally different from those of the secular law. The Canon law of divorce rested upon the principle that a marriage consummated by "copula carnalis", and thereby made a sacrament, was indissoluble. "It must excite astonishment and wonder that the Church was able to elevate to the rank of a legal rule, in the midst of a world of barbarism, an ideal so high as that of the indissolubility of marriage." [3] To be sure, it by no means succeeded in absolutely enforcing this rule. The indissolubility of the marriage bond was in large part a fiction in the Middle Ages, especially among the highest social classes.[4] As a concession to the actual facts of life, separation without dissolu-

[1] *Brunner*, *op. cit.*, 107.
[2] *Brunner*, "Geschichte" (2d ed.), 39.
[3] *Marianne Weber*, *op. cit.* (*supra*, p. 61), 262.
[4] *Finke*, in the Inter. W. Sch. (*cf. supra*, p. 61), IV (1910), 1292.

tion of the marriage bond was finally introduced (definitively by the Tridentine law). This was the so-called "separatio quoad thorum et mensam"; but even this did not permit remarriage by the spouses so separated. The Canon law, by recognizing clandestine contracts of marriage (*supra*, p. 606), created widespread uncertainty respecting the legality of marriages consummated in a manner formally correct. Thus, the Church, by exaggerating its idea of the indissolubility of marriages, renounced the higher ideal of purity in the marriage relation. Under the dominance of the Canon law of divorce, which received its final form in the decrees of the Council of Trent, nothing was left to the secular law beyond the right to regulate the effect of the separation which the Canon law thus permitted upon marital property and the legal relations of parents and children.

(B) THE PROTESTANT LAW OF DIVORCE assumed from the beginning a position sharply contrasted with that of the Canon law in that it recognized the possibility of a dissolution of the marriage bond. This was a step in advance, but it was offset by the fact that it rejected the action for divorce developed in the Canon law, and reintroduced the old right of self-divorce. However, self-divorce was later forbidden and an official decree of divorce required. Adultery was recognized, without exceptions, as ground for divorce; whereas the agreement of the spouses was in no case recognized as such. As to other matters there was vacillation for a long time, especially as respected desertion, until finally the more liberal view prevailed that divorce should be permitted for moral delinquencies. But along with this there was recognized a separation from bed and board for a definite or indefinite period.

(3) *The divorce law of the modern State.* — Modern State legislation contented itself, at first, with recognizing the ecclesiastical law of divorce. As regards Catholic subjects this position was adhered to in the modern codes. They recognized the indissolubility of marriage as respects the bond (and so the Austrian law, even to-day), but for the most part increased the number of reasons which justified a separation from bed and board. An intermediate position was adopted by the Prussian "Landrecht" in providing that when a right of separation was recognized in the ecclesiastical court this should have the effect of a divorce under the private law. On the other hand, the codes abrogated the ecclesiastical right of divorce theretofore conceded to evangelical subjects, and replaced this by a State law of divorce that facili-

tated divorces in the utmost possible degree, in accord with principles of natural law and utilitarian considerations. The Prussian "Landrecht" went furthest in this direction. It permitted divorce in case of insurmountable aversion, as in cases of childless marriages, — granted, to be sure, always by a court, — in case "it appears from the nature of the evidence that such repugnance is so strong and so deeply seated that absolutely no hope remains of reconciliation and a realization of the ends of the marriage" (II, 1, § 718 a).

In the 1800 s the ecclesiastical law of divorce was finally replaced by that of the State, which thereby became legally binding upon Catholic subjects also. As a result of this there existed at first an extreme diversity in the law, since the state statutes differed greatly in their definition of legal grounds for divorce. Later, however, this subject was also regulated uniformly for all Germany, upon the principle of an absolute secularization of divorce, by the imperial statute of personal status of February 6, 1875. The divorce law of the Civil Code has now in turn displaced that. The Code has retained, in theory, the viewpoint of the Personal Status Act, for unlike the Catholic law it recognizes divorce. It has followed the latter only so far as to give a choice between divorce and that separation from bed and board ("abrogation of the marital community") which prevents remarriage and which was rejected in toto by the Personal Status Act; but it provides that when one spouse has brought an action for separation, divorce must be granted upon demand of the other party, and that when a separation has been granted either spouse may demand divorce upon the basis of that judgment (§§ 1575–1576). However, though the demands for a complete abrogation of the ecclesiastical divorce law and for an exclusive competence of secular courts in divorce cases were thus unqualifiedly realized, nevertheless, as respects the substantive law of divorce, there was a decided departure from the doctrine of the law of nature. In the 1840 s the attempt had already been made in Prussia, during the ministry of Savigny, to replace by some stricter regulation the right of free divorce under the State law, and the present Civil Code has realized this aim by adopting the rule that divorce or separation can only be pronounced, aside from cases of incurable insanity, when there has been misconduct ("Verschulden") on the part of one or of both spouses. The Code has laid down a few absolute grounds for dissolution of marriage, — that is, those that give a right to divorce (adultery, bigamy, unnatural practices, attempt upon the plaintiff's life, wilful desertion); and in addition permits the judge to dissolve a marriage ("relative" causes for divorce) when either party "by serious violation of marital duty or dishonorable or immoral conduct" has effected "such a fundamental derangement of conjugal relations" that the innocent spouse "cannot be expected to continue the marriage" (§ 1568). The same principles have been adopted by the Swiss Civil Code (§§ 137–158), which likewise recognizes separation in addition to divorce, adds relative to absolute causes of divorce, and aside from cases of insanity (and also, of course, in case of relative grounds for divorce) requires misconduct ("Verschulden") on the part of one of the parties.

§ 93. **Personal Legal Relations of the Spouses.** (I) **The Older Law.** — The husband, in the patriarchal family of the prehistoric Indo-Germanic period, enjoyed in the marriage a position so superior to that of woman that language had no word for the conceptions "marriage", "spouses", or "parents." Similarly, the mundium of the old Germanic law still involved a subjection of the bride to the unlimited power of the man to whom she was given in marriage. And though the moral standards of society ("Sitte") might accord to the "legitimate" wife a position of respect that distinguished her from concubines and servants, and might attribute to her a higher value as the most important worker in her husband's household, she was nevertheless legally at the mercy of his caprice. Even in the Middle Ages the "brutal formula" was still occasionally used that she was "his chattel."[1] Legally, she occupied the same position in relation to him as a child subjected to his mundium; and in token of this, forms of adoption were common in the marriage ceremony (*supra*, p. 600). The husband had the right to kill his wife. This power, certainly originally unlimited, was later subjected to certain preconditions, at first by social moral standards and then also by law. The principal cause which long continued to justify a husband for killing his wife was adultery on her part. As for the third person, adultery was originally regarded not as a true crime but as an unlawful interference with the husband's rights, and moreover the legal consciousness of the primitive Germans was dominated by a deeply rooted conviction

[1] *Brunner*, "Geschichte", I (2d ed.), 101, referring to low Frankish legal systems. He cites from the Flemish coûtume of Ardenburg the rule that a husband may cut open his wife and warm his feet in her blood, provided only that he sew her up again and she remain alive.

that the wife could be guilty of the crime as against her husband, but not, conversely, the husband as against his wife. This "inequality of sexual morality" not only prevailed, of course, so long as the acquisition of several wives and unlimited sexual intercourse with "secondary" ("Neben-") wives and concubines was permitted to the husband, but continued under the supremacy of monogamy. The Church always energetically championed in this matter the equality of the sexes, but struggled along in vain before it was able to enforce its view, which was morally far the higher. Adultery by the wife also entitled the husband to drive her with curses from his house, and thus dissolve their marriage (*supra*, p. 613). In other cases his disciplinary power over his wife gave him the right to lock her up and deprive her of food. Indeed, he could sell her; and this not only as a punishment but also in order to free himself, with the money so realized, from pressing pecuniary difficulties.[1] The most brutal application of this commercial conception of marriage was doubtless illustrated when two Icelanders exchanged their entire possessions in lands and chattels, including their respective wives; the wife of one, to be sure, hanged herself as a result, but the other peacefully submitted.[2] Everywhere, moreover, the husband possessed the right to chastise his wife as he would a servant. As late as in the Nibelungenlied, Kriemhild tells us how Siegfried has beaten her body blue because of her useless chatter. In the skevin-book of Brünner (of about 1315) it is recommended to the husband to exercise moderately his right of chastisement, but the right itself is clearly recognized; and in 1431 a Breslau husband promised to chastise his wife, in future, with switches only, as was fitting and consistent with the fidelity and honor of a worthy man.

Although in the course of the Middle Ages it became increasingly rare to resort to the legal powers that were the extreme consequences of the husband's power of mundium, the power nevertheless was maintained in theory. Even the Church strove, in this matter, to strengthen the husband's position. Starting with the idea that woman was a being of inferior worth and that marriage was created, essentially, solely in order to avoid the sins of the flesh, it taught, upon the strength of the Apostle's words, that the wife should be subject to the husband. And the result of

[1] According to a report in the "Allgemeine Zeitung" of 1844, no. 8, cited by *Wackernagel* in *op. cit.*, p. 585 *supra*, a case occurred in England as late as 1844 in which a man sold his wife in public market.

[2] *Maurer*, "Vorlesungen", II, 638.

this was that when sex-guardianship over unmarried adult daughters became less prominent (*supra*, pp. 65 *et seq.*), the husband was recognized as the mundium-holder ("Muntherr") of his wife; or as the medieval legal sources were accustomed to express it her "guardian", "steward", or "master", the "principal" in the marriage relation.[1] Whereas in the older law the mundium passed from the bride's mundium-holder ("Gewalthaber") to the bridegroom only as the result of a betrothal and nuptials in accordance with law, remaining with the guardian in case her marriage was consummated without his consent, in the later Middle Ages the husband's guardianship sprang directly from every legally valid marriage as a rule of objective law, without further formalities.

In the face of all this it means little that the wife is characterized in the Law-Books as the "companion" of her husband.[2] For this relation of fellowship, which began with cohabitation, was confined to the fact that the wife shared the name and the status of her husband, and that his domicile was determinant of her own. In other respects it did not restrict in the least the husband's guardianship.

However, as already remarked, there gradually resulted a weakening of the powers and an increase in the protective duties implicit in the right of mundium (*supra*, p. 585). This transformation, naturally, also affected the husband's guardianship, which thenceforth came to signify, primarily, his duty to represent his wife in court, even where she herself was a litigant. At the same time, the Saxon town-law already permitted the wife to appear independently in court. The wife found support in her family against abuses of her husband's guardianship; the protection once accorded her in a right of divorce disappeared with the displacement of the secular by the Canon law of divorce.

(II) **The Modern Law.** — Even in later centuries the personal legal relations of the spouses remained subject, in essentials, to the principles of the medieval marital-stewardship ("Ehevogtei"). True, it was retained under this express name in only a few legal systems; but even where the name was abandoned nothing was actually altered, generally speaking, in the legal relations of the parties. Even the great intellectual currents of modern times

[1] Ssp., III, 45, § 3; Swsp., 10, 2 (G); Ostfries. Landrecht, II, 109 (1515).

[2] Note the continuation of Ssp., III, 45, § 3. *Cf. Fehr*, *op. cit.* (p. 61 *supra*), 37.

brought about no fundamental change. The reception of the Roman law, which in its final form no longer recognized a "manus mariti", was unable to overcome in this matter the native legal customs; for it was possible to appeal from it to the authority of the Canon theory that the husband was the "principal" of the marriage relation. The Evangelical doctrine also maintained this view without qualification; though it is true that by familiarizing the people through the translation of the Bible with the high regard for marriage expressed in the Old Testament, it contributed much toward a spiritual deepening of the significance of the marital relation. Even the law of nature, though it made marriage under its contract-theory a partnership of two originally equal individuals, nevertheless assumed a complete subordination of the wife to her husband; it merely derived this subjection, theoretically, from a voluntary agreement of the parties. This view also prevailed in the great modern codes. The Prussian "Allgemeines Landrecht", for example, emphasized on the one hand the mutual moral duty of the spouses, regulating by this principle their personal relations even in the most intimate matters; but on the other hand it none the less declared the husband to be the principal of the marital partnership, whose will should be decisive in their common affairs (II. 1, § 184). It conceded that assaults by the husband need not under all circumstances be ground for complaint on the part of the wife, but did not mention his earlier power of moderate chastisement, — which was still recognized by the Bavarian Territorial Law and by many other of the regional systems. Again, it still assigned to the husband the representation of his wife in court, in accord with the general legal conditions of that time, denying her as a rule all independent rights of litigation, and attributing to him a presumptive power of attorney. As respects this last point, a fundamental change took place in the course of the 1800 s, full litigant capacity being conceded to all women, equally whether married or unmarried, — first in the case of women engaged in commerce, then as to those engaged in industry, and finally, under the imperial Code of Civil Procedure, as to all women. On the other hand the present Civil Code retains the principle that the decision of all matters affecting their common life during marriage belongs to the husband; the wife, however, need not obey if he abuses this right of decision (§ 1354). Moreover, the Civil Code has adopted the traditional rules, borrowed from the Prussian "Landrecht" and other modern codes, that make the wife share the domicile, name, status, and nationality of the husband, ascribe to her the right and duty of caring for the home, and require her to labor in the household and business of her husband as circumstances require. As an offset to these duties and as compensation for her renunciation of the right of independent choice, the Code, in common with earlier legal systems, accords her, in addition to her so-called key-right ("Schlüsselgewalt", *infra*, § 95), a claim against her husband for support suited to her rank; although she must in turn support him in case of necessity (§ 1360). The rule of the Swiss Civil Code is in general the same. True, the husband is still expressly designated in it as the "principal of the community" (§ 160); but on the other hand the view is more strongly emphasized that "marriage is a community" whose advancement the spouses are bound "to forward by harmonious coöperation", and whose representation, though primarily incumbent upon the husband, rests also upon the wife.

§ 94. **The Law of Marital Property:**[1] (1) **of the Folk-laws.**

(I) **The Point of Departure in the Historical Development.** — The law of the marital community of goods is that part of Ger-

[1] The leading work is *Schröder's* "Geschichte des ehelichen Güterrechts in Deutschland", Vol. 1 (1863) covering the age of the folk-laws, Vol. 2 (in three parts, 1866, 1871, 1874) covering the age of the Law-Books. *Cf.* therewith *Schröder*, "Das eheliche Güterrecht und die Wanderungen der deutschen Stämme" in Hist. Z., XXXI (1874), 289–311. Furthermore, *Hasse*, "Beitrag zur Revision der bisherigen Theorie von der ehelichen Gütergemeinschaft" (1808); *Runde*, "Deutsches eheliches Güterrecht" (1841); *Gerber*, "Betrachtungen über das Güterrecht der Ehegatten nach deutschem Recht", in *Ihering's* J. B., I (1857), 239 *et seq.* and also in the "Leipziger Dekanatsprogramm" of 1869, both articles reprinted in the author's "Gesammelte Juristische Abhandlungen" (1872), 311–371; *Roth*, "Über Gütereinheit und Güterverbindung", in J. B. gem. R., III (1859), 313 *et seq.*; *Hänel*, "Die eheliche Gütergemeinschaft in Ostfalen", in Z[1]. R. G., I. (1861), 273 *et seq.*; *Sandhaas*, "Fränkisches eheliches Güterrecht" (1866); *v. Martitz*, "Das eheliche Güterrecht des Sachsenspiegels und der verwandten Rechtsquellen" (1867); *Agricola*, "Die Gewere zu rechter Vormundschaft" (1869); *Roth*, "Das deutsche eheliche Güterrecht", in Z. vergl. R. W., I (1878), 39 *et seq.*; *Huber*, "Die historische Grundlage des ehelichen Güterrechts der Berner Handveste" (1884); *Adler*, "Eheliches Güterrecht und Abschichtungsrecht nach den ältesten bairischen Rechtsquellen" (1893); *Brunner*, "Zu Lex Salica", tit. 44: 'De Reipus'" (p. 591 *supra*), "Die fränkisch-romanische Dos", in K. Preuss. Akad. Wiss. Sitz., Ber. 1894, 545–574, "Die Geburt eines lebenden Kindes und das eheliche Vermögensrecht" in Z[2]. R. G., XVI (1895), 63–108; *Stern*, "Der Ursprung der sächsischen Leibzucht" (1896); *v. Wyss*, "Die ehelichen Güterrechte der Schweiz in ihrer rechtsgeschichtlichen Entwicklung" (1896); *Schröder*, "Das eheliche Güterrecht nach dem BGB in seinen Grundzügen" (3d ed., 1900); *Behre*, "Die Eigentumsverhältnisse im ehelichen Güterrecht des Sachsenspiegels und Magdeburger Rechts" (1904); *Bartsch*, "Eheliches Güterrecht im Erzherzogtum Österreich im 16. Jahrhundert" (1905); *Caillemer*, "L'origine du douaire des enfants" in "Studi di diritto . . . pubblicati in onore di V. Scialoja", II (1905), 249–278; *Arnold*, "Das eheliche

manic private law which presents by far the greatest complexity and disunity. In the course of its development it has assumed very diverse forms, which in part followed one another chronologically and in part existed simultaneously throughout greater or smaller jurisdictions. Down to the present day the legal map of Germany has not presented as regards any other matter a picture even approximately as motley. But this development of the marital community of goods, notwithstanding it was marked in such extreme degree by particularistic characteristics and led to such a variety of legal forms that it is difficult to survey them, has nevertheless always been dominated by a few leading ideas. Although the evidence of the oldest legal sources already reveals various forms of community in the legal systems of the different racial branches, this development is doubtless to be traced to beginnings common to all branches of the Germanic race. In view of the general character of the Germanic marriage, the origin can have been no other than the house-lord's unlimited power over all property of the household, the sole ownership of the husband in all marital property. Whatever property the bride brought with her into the marriage passed, like her person, under the power of her husband; at the most, those objects remained her own that were intended for her exclusive use. The husband's

Güterrecht von Mühlhausen i. E. am Ausgang des Mittelalters", in *Beyerle's* "Beiträge", I (1906); *Kiesel*, "Die Bedeutung der Gewere des Mannes am Frauengute für das Ehegüterrecht des Sachsenspiegels", no. 85 (1906) of *Gierke's* "Untersuchungen"; *E. Heymann*, "Zum Ehegüterrecht der heiligen Elisabeth", in Z. Ver. Türin. G., XXVII (new ser. X, 1908), 1–22; *Hradil*, "Untersuchungen zur spätmittelalterlichen Ehegüterrechtsbildung nach bayerisch-österreichischen Rechtsquellen, I: Das Heiratsgut" (1908), and *cf. A. B. Schmidt* in Z². R. G., XXXI (1910), 636–638; *Hradil*, "Beiträge zur Geschichte des süddeutschen Ehegüterrechts" in Z². R. G., XXX (1909), 304–310; *Franco*, "Vicende storiche della dote romana nella pratica medievale dell' Italia superiore", in "Archivio giuridico F. Serafini", LXXX (1908), 393–490; *Kapras*, "Eheliches Güterrecht im altböhmischen Landrechte", in Z. vergl. R. W., XXIII (1909), 106–208; *Hradil*, "Zur Theorie der Gerade", in Z². R. G., XXXI (1910), 67–130; *Steiner*, "Das eheliche Güterrecht des Kantons Schwyz mit vergleichenden Hinweisen auf das eheliche Güterrecht des schweizerischen Zivilgesetzbuchs", in *Egger's* Zür. Beiträge zur R. W., XXVII (1910), and *Stutz* in Z². R. G. XXXI (1910), 657, 658; *Schupfer*, "La comunione di beni tra coniugi, a propositio di recenti studi", in "Rivista italiana per le scienze giuridiche", XLVIII (1911), 57–72, 241–263; *Reich*, "Das Ehegüterrecht in den deutschen Teilen von Steiermark, Kärnten und Krain", in "Festschrift zur Jahrhundertfeier des oesterreichischen allgemeinen bürgerlichen Gesetzbuchs" (1911), II, 361 *et seq.*; *Bartsch*, "Das eheliche Güterrecht in der Summa Raymunds von Wiener Neustadt", in Wien. K. Akad. Wiss., Sitz. Ber., CLXVIII (1912), 7th essay; *E. His*, "Das eheliche Güterrecht in den Tessiner Rechtsquellen, seine Grundlage im langobardischen und vulgär-römischen Recht", in Z. schweiz. R., LII (new ser. XXX, 1911), 85–143.

exclusive rights under the property law corresponded to his absolute power in personal relations. His ownership was limited, to be sure, by the fact that it was controlled by the family-law: the marital property constituted a household estate that necessarily remained dedicated to the purposes of the marriage, and which therefore, above all, could not be alienated from the children (*supra*, p. 304; *infra*, § 98); but the wife had no share in this community of rights in household property which existed between the father and the sons. This idea of an undivided property in the husband was relaxed, however, in favor of the wife as early as in the age of the folk-laws. Their provisions, admittedly debatable in many respects, by no means show (if we accept the prevailing opinion — though this is contested by Huber and Heusler, who champion a sole property of the husband in the household estate even under the folk-laws),[1] such a subjection of the wife's entire property to her husband's ownership as was peculiar to the original law. On the contrary they already recognize her ownership of certain portions of the marital property. This important advance was a consequence of the gradually increasing legal and economic independence of women, especially of their capacity to inherit, although this extended at first solely to chattels, and only later to land (*infra*, § 107). "The increasing improvement in woman's position was the real leaven in the entire later development of the law of marital property."[2]

So soon as daughters became capable of holding and inheriting property within their own families, they were in a position to bring with them in marriage property of considerable value to their husbands; for their kindred were thenceforth bound to indemnify them for their renunciation, upon marriage, of herital rights in their father's estate. Again, when the wife came to be regarded as the subject of independent property rights, her husband's gift to her, especially the "Wittum" that was developed from her purchase-price, might become her property. With this step the original undivided marital estate necessarily disappeared. It was now possible, for the first time, to speak of an actual marital community of goods in the sense of a regulation of the spouses' legal rights, created by their marriage, in the property constitut-

[1] Here again quite a different view is adopted by *Ficker*, who, in harmony with his assumption of an original equality of women with men under the inheritance law, argues for a total separation of the property of the two spouses as the original form of the Germanic law of marital property. See his "Untersuchungen zur Erbenfolge", IV, 291 *et seq.*

[2] *Huber*, "Schw. Privatrecht", IV, 386.

ing the marital estate; for it was only now that property existed in which not merely the husband but also the wife had rights; it was only thenceforth that there existed, during marriage, a wife's, in addition to the husband's, estate.

(II) **Constitution of the Wife's Estate.** — The property of the wife in the age of the folk-laws might consist of the following elements recognized by law:

(1) *The dowry, or marriage portion* ("maritagium"; "Aussteuer"; "Heimsteuer", really "Heisteuer", "hiustüre"; "Heiratssteuer", — marriage "contribution"). The "maritagium", that is the "property that was given with the wife incidentally to her marriage, either by the house of her parents or by the household community to which she belonged",[1] consisted originally (so long, namely, as women were incapable of holding property) simply of the "wife's supply of clothing and adornments."[2] Jewels, festive dresses, ornaments such as mirrors, combs, etc., — the "ornamenta muliebria", "matronalia", "matrimonialia", — made up its content. An old native expression for it was "Gerade"; though first used in the Saxon legal sources of the age of the Law-Books, this is already suggested in the Frankish period in the Thuringian "rhedo" and the Burgundian "malahereda." The "Gerade" was a gift, customary but nevertheless essentially voluntary. As just mentioned, even in the Frankish period it no longer passed into the husband's ownership. With the recognition of the herital capacity of women their marriage portion became more extensive than the objects belonging to the paraphernalia ("Gerade") proper. It was extended first to the chattels that were given with the wife, and by which she was indemnified for her renunciation of claims in her father's property; and later to lands. The marriage portion already shows this character in the 600 s among the Lombards, whose "faderfio" even then included money and immovables and was regarded as a herital composition. In the other racial branches the change took place only later. During the existence of the marriage other acquisitions of property might be added to the dowry; particularly, in case it was not a herital composition, the portion of her parents' heritage later accruing in her favor, and further, among most Germanic racial branches, presents.

(2) *The dower* ("Wittum"). This was a gift by husband to

[1] *Brunner*, "Grundzüge" (5th ed.), 226.
[2] *Schröder*, "Lehrbuch" (5th ed.), 318.

wife which was developed from her purchase price, and which was long regarded among the Franks, the Visigoths, and the North Germans (and doubtless originally among all Germanic races) as a necessary and, indeed, the principal, token of a legal marriage.[1] In the Latin sources this payment by the husband to the wife bears the name "dos". As Tacitus (Germ. 18) already tells us, among the Germans the "dos" was not brought by the wife to the husband, but by the husband to the wife; a statement which, however, certainly rests upon a misunderstanding to the extent that this gift was not yet given, at that time, to the bride herself but to her kindred (*supra*, p. 598). The peculiar change in the meaning of the word "dos" was mainly due to the influence in the oldest Frankish law of the "donatio ante nuptias", which was probably adopted by the Roman law from the legal systems of the provinces, and which in the later Roman period ordinarily preceded the delivery of the "dos" and was returned as the "dos" by the wife to the husband. It was therefore known as a "donatio ante nuptias in dotem redacta"; and this may eventually have led to the use of the word "dos" to designate the husband's gift. In the earlier period the "Wittum", which was intended to serve the wife for maintenance in widowhood after her husband's death, consisted among the wealthier classes of chattels (money, cattle, serfs). Among the propertied classes of the Franks the chattel "dos" was replaced, at the latest in the 600 s, by a "dos" of immovables which was ordinarily delivered by a "traditio cartae" (*supra*, pp. 244 *et seq.*). This was the "dos conscripta." As already stated, dower was a gift legally necessary to the creation of a fully valid marriage. In case it was not fixed by agreement, the wife was given a claim for dower to an amount statutorily determined, — the "dos legitima." In the older Salic Law a third of the husband's movable and immovable property (the Salic "tertia" and the "douaire" of the French medieval law) belonged to the wife as dower.

(3) *The morgive* ("Morgengabe", morning-gift). — The custom in accord with which the husband made a present to his young wife on the morning after the bridal night goes back to the earliest times; it may be that it was developed without any reference to marriage, and persisted as a remnant of pre-marital

[1] *Ficker*, "Untersuchungen", III, 350, cites as authority for this the "Landrecht" of the county of Saarbrück (1321?), in which the husband is required to give his wife dower in order that she may not be repudiated after his death by the children and heirs or be taken for a servant-maid, or for a light woman who had been living with him in dishonor.

conditions.[1] This morgive ("donum matutinum") long preserved its original character of a "pretium virginitatis"; for which reason the rule still prevailed in places in the Middle Ages that no morgive was due to a widow who remarried, but on the contrary must be paid by her in case she married an innocent youth. So long as the wife did not receive the dower herself, and even afterwards when no dower was delivered to her but only a morgive, — that is in cases of unlawful and unequal marriages (which for this very reason were known as "morganatic" — *supra*, p. 99), — the morgive satisfied at the same time that purpose of securing the wife's position under the property law which was satisfied in other cases by dower. When existing concurrently with dower it possessed merely the ethical significance indicated. Perhaps, however, it served a legal purpose even then, namely as a public notification of the consummation of the marriage by cohabitation.[2] For this reason some legal systems, for example the Alamanian folk-law and the Sachsenspiegel, provided in special rules how the wife must prove the receipt of the morgive, in case of dispute; namely by independent oath ("Eineid") given on breast and plait of hair, which among the Alamanians was known as "nasthait" (perhaps from the lace, "Nestel", that held the dress together at the breast). The morgive was often delivered in large amount even in addition to the dower, but among many racial branches it became merged, in time, with the dower in a single gift. This was the case, notably, among the Lombards, where this gift ordinarily consisted of a fourth part of the husband's property (the Lombard "quarta").

(III) **Legal Relations during the Existence of Marriage.** (1) *The ordinary form* of the marital community of property in the folk-laws was that the ownership of the wife's estate, constituted of the portions above indicated, was not in the husband, but in the wife. The husband, however, by virtue of his mundium, held possession of all the wife's property: as a result of the marriage the property of the bride was delivered to him, and he likewise held in his own hand his gifts to the bride. In this manner, the distinct ownership of the property being preserved, but the entire marital estate united in the possession of the husband, the result was that as early as in the folk-laws the original

[1] *Ficker, op. cit.*, III, 396.
[2] This suggestion is made by *Fockema-Andreae*, "Hexoud nederlandsch burgerlijk recht", II, 167: "man erkende door de morgengave, dat de bijslap had plaats gehad."

undivided property had been replaced, in the main, by a system of community property. This has been variously known as that of a "Güterverbindung" (Bluntschli, Heusler), "Gütereinheit" (Gerber, Beseler, von Martitz, Gengler), or "Güterscheidung" (Brunner), — "combined", "unsevered", or "several" estates.[1] But it is usually designated by the name, certainly illogical, of "administrative community" ("Verwaltungsgemeinschaft"), that is an administration by the husband of the entire community (Schröder), — the essential nature of which is found in a mere physical union of the two portions of the marital property, which does not result in any legal community of the spouses with reference thereto. The husband, thus receiving the seisin of the wife's estate, received with it, on the one hand the right to take the profits, and on the other hand the duty of administration. His own property he held in usufruct and administered as owner; that of his wife as her mundium-holder or guardian ("Vormund"). Thanks to this seisin "in mundium" ("zu rechter Vormundschaft", "of guardianship"), as it was customary to say in the later Middle Ages, he could control his wife's entire estate. He could even alienate her chattels independently; but he required her coöperation for the alienation of her lands. His control of his own property was restricted to the extent that he may have given his wife rights therein; as was the case, for example, with the "dos conscripta", the Frankish "tertia", and the Lombard "quarta." On the other hand, the wife could not dispose of anything inter vivos, with the exception of the paraphernalia, without the consent of her husband. The wife's estate was not liable for her husband's obligations.

(2) Some of the legal systems of the Frankish period had already departed from this principle of distinct estates to the extent of recognizing a true legal community as respects so-called *acquests* ("Errungenschaften"), — that is, such property as was acquired by the spouses during marriage, by labor or by juristic act, for value; an idea also reflected in the dower, which consisted of a fraction of the husband's property. Whereas the majority of legal systems treated the acquests as falling under the ownership of the husband, the Salic and Ripuarian systems, by statutory recognition of a practice of customary law, conceded to the wife, in addition to the "dos" of movables (but not in addition to the "dos conscripta") and the morgive, an independent right in a third of the acquests.[2] Further, among the Westphalians the

[1] Z². R. G., XVI, 66.

[2] "Lex Ribuaria", 37, 1.

wife received half of the acquests, whereas among the Ostphalians and the Angrivarians she was obliged to content herself with the "dos";[1] in which connection it is disputed whether the Westphalian acquest-community existed only when a child was born to the marriage and destroyed ("killed") the "dos", — in this case a dower ("Wittum") consisting of a life-portion ("Leibzucht"), — by its birth (Schröder), or whether it also existed in childless marriages, that is in addition to the claim to the "dos" (Brunner, Heusler).

(IV) **Legal Relations after Dissolution of Marriage.** — If the marriage was dissolved, particularly if one of the spouses died, the marital property which until then was physically united in the seisin of the husband became separated into its legal portions. The consequences of this varied according as the husband or the wife died first, and according as the marriage was "inherited" or "unherited"; that is, according as it was or was not survived by at least one child born in wedlock. Under many legal systems the important question was whether the marriage had been fruitful, — that is, whether a living child had been brought into the world as a result of it; for certain legal consequences were dependent upon this fact, even though the child later died before its parents. We must doubtless, with Brunner, explain this peculiar institute by the fact that the birth of a child deprived the husband of the possibility of dissolving the marriage for sterility of his wife. After this, it was a natural step to recognize a closer community between the spouses.

(1) *After the husband's death* the dower fell to his widow in accord with its appointed end of serving as her maintenance, and similarly the morgive. In many cases, however, it was received merely as inalienable property ("Eigentum") for life, inasmuch as these gifts, in case of an "unherited" marriage, reverted after the death of the widow to the kindred of the husband, as the giver (reversionary right = "Rückfallsrecht", known in the later French law as "droit de retour"); whereas in case of an "inherited" marriage they were sequestered for the children. Whatever else belonged to the wife, — her marriage portion, and other property acquired by inheritance or gift, — was thenceforth subjected to her independent ownership. Among the Westphalians, in case of a sterile marriage the "dos" was given to the widow for life and reverted after her death to the giver or his heirs; in case of a fruitful marriage, she received as compensation

[1] "Lex Saxonum", 47, 48.

for the destruction of the "dos" worked by the birth of a child some indemnity, as for example the right for life to live on and enjoy the usufruct of the lands of her dead husband. Among the Ostphalians and Angrivarians the same rule existed, in case of a sterile marriage, as for the Westphalian widow. But among them the widow also received a "dos" in case of a fruitful marriage, with the difference that a reversion was here not recognized, the "dos" falling either to her children, or, if none survived her, to her nearest kindred. Everywhere, so long as she remained single, the widow was ordinarily given a right to live on the lands of her dead husband which had been devised to the children.

(2) *After the wife's death* the morgive always, and the dower in case of an "unherited" marriage, reverted to the widower, as the giver; on the other hand, in case of an "inherited" marriage the dower fell to the children. In case of a sterile marriage the widower was bound to return the dowry to the donor thereof or to his heirs; on the other hand, under the law of the Alamanians and Bavarians, he retained for life the property of the wife, including the dowry, when a living child had been born. A different rule prevailed among the Lombards, where the husband, as the holder of the mundium, was the sole heir of his wife.

§ 95. **The Law of Marital Property: (2) The Medieval Systems. (I) General Development and Common Principles of the Medieval Systems.** (1) *The administrative community and the community of goods.* — In the post-Frankish period the development of the marital community of goods followed various lines. Some legal systems clung to the rule of the folk-laws; that is, to the purely physical union of the entire marriage property in the hand of the husband, which involved no legal community between the spouses. Others, on the other hand, went further in the direction of extending the wife's property rights, abandoning the distinction of her special estate, uniting this with that of the husband into a collective ("Gesamt") estate, and conceding to the wife the same property rights in this collective estate as to the husband. With this step, those legal systems of which the last was true became distinct, as systems of community of goods ("Gütergemeinschaft", "Güterverbindung", "Güterscheidung") from those that maintained a mere administrative community ("Verwaltungsgemeinschaft"). A community of goods signified, therefore, an intimate union into an indivisible whole of the individual pieces of property that were derived from husband and from wife, the whole being subject to their mutual rights of collective ownership. The wife was given, here, the same rights in the husband's property included in the collective estate as he possessed in her property. If this community extended to all property of the spouses men spoke of a "*general*" *community* of goods. But the community might also be limited to certain pieces of property, special estates of each spouse being distinguished alongside the common property of the two, — which was a "*limited*" *community* of goods. In the case of the *acquest-community*, merely the acquests, — that is (above, p. 627) property acquired during marriage by labor or by juristic act for value, — fell into the collective estate; in the case of a *chattel community*, merely the chattels brought into the marriage and the acquests thereafter acquired.

Economic relations, and ethical factors associated with these were determinant of the preservation of the administrative community or the adoption of the community of goods. As Heusler has convincingly shown,[1] the old idea of family-property ("Familienvermögen") remained vital among large masses of the rural population, especially in Northern Germany; and this even after daughters had become entitled to inheritance in lands. Chattel property long continued to play only an unimportant rôle in these regions; the economic and social position of families was dependent upon family-lands ("Familiengut"), which were protected against alienation and disintegration by the heirs' rights in expectancy and rights of co-alienation (*supra*, pp. 304 *et seq.*), and which were inherited by generation after generation. We can therefore understand that even as regards those lands, portions of the family possessions, which the daughters took with them as marriage portions, there was no definitive renunciation; they continued to be regarded as part of the family lands. They could not be united, therefore, with the husband's property into a legal entity; they never fell to him, but were either inherited by the children, or in case of his wife's death without children reverted to her family. This treatment of the property brought by the wife into marriage was, however, not limited to her landed property. For, as Huber remarks,[2] in the maintenance of this division between the wife's and the husband's property there was reflected at the same time a certain mode of thought, a proneness to the preservation of traditional matters, whose influence might also be felt in cases where the wife brought no lands into

[1] "Institutionen", II, 303 *et seq.*
[2] "Schw. Privatrecht", IV, 393.

the marriage. It was because of this conservative attitude of mind that no necessity was felt, under the legal systems now in question, of giving the wife rights in her husband's property.

On the other hand, in those regions and among those classes of the population where the chief part of the marital property did not consist of landed possessions inherited through generations, but of acquests, a tendency prevailed to develop an intimate fusion of the property of the two parties into a more or less comprehensive community of goods. Already in the Frankish period the acquests had caused the abandonment, in some legal systems, of the system of separate estates. That they played such a part can be readily understood. For "where the property is constituted, changed, and enlarged, by the activity and labor of the parties, the fusion of the wife's property with the estate of her husband is materially facilitated."[1] The influence of this tendency was felt, above all, in the cities. In marriages of burghers, artisans, and merchants "contracted between the different elements, old and newly immigrated, of the city population", the idea of a family-estate naturally became less prominent, since they ordinarily founded an entirely new house, with an independent economic basis. Much the same was true of marriages among the servile ("hörigen") classes.

The movement, however, by no means proceeded in such manner that the circumstances determining it could have created the three systems just named in forms everywhere identical. The administrative community, the limited, and the general community of goods, are not types of the medieval law of marital property in the sense that, — to use Heusler's words,[2] — "all legal systems of marital estates are to be forced into these three classes, and that all brought into one class have exactly the same content, precisely as all personal servitudes may be grouped under 'ususfructus', 'usus', 'habitatio', and 'operæ', thereby receiving for all time a fixed and definite content." The administrative community and the limited and the general community of goods are, rather, mere generalizations for the grouping of those legal systems in which there appear more or less clear tendencies, respectively, toward the separation or the union of the two estates. There existed in the Middle Ages, not precisely three but an infinite number, of legal systems of marital property. There did exist, however, only two "Motive", two principles which made it possible in theory to assign these infinite variations to one or the

[1] *Heusler*, "Institutionen", II, 304. [2] *Op. cit.*, II, 365.

other of those systems. Which of these principles predominated in a given legal system depended, as already remarked, primarily upon general economic conditions; and the great diversity of these naturally resulted in a great variety of systems of marital estates. When these appear to us (as they often do) to be an arbitrary combination of different legal rules, this may frequently be due, therefore, merely to the fact that the actual foundations are no longer discernible. Moreover, there was another circumstance that greatly furthered diversity of development; namely the fact that systems of marital property were very often carried from place to place. The colonists who removed to Eastern Germany, especially, took with them into their new home their native laws, and the cities that were there founded were endowed with the marital property law of the mother-cities. In such cases there might result a very different development upon the old and common basis.

(2) *The "mundium" of the husband.* — But however divergently the development proceeded, the old mundium of the husband was preserved in all medieval systems of marital property as the basis, also, of the spouses' relations under the property law. Whether ownership by the wife was recognized as respected her property, or a collective ownership of collective property was conceded to her with her husband, the rule always prevailed that the husband was "steward" and "master" of his wife (*supra*, p. 619) in the law of marital property. This marital stewardship ("Ehevogtei") of the husband had the effect, in all systems, of subjecting the wife to his will. Everywhere, she was incapable of independent action, and independent control of her own property, without his consent; everywhere, the administration of the collective marital property belonged to him. We may therefore, with Heusler,[1] perceive in the statement of the Sachsenspiegel, "man unde wif ne hebbet nein getveiet gut to irme live" (I, 31, § 1), — by which was meant that the property of the wife passed to the hand of the husband, — the fundamental principle that controlled the entire medieval German law of marital property. Nor was this by any means one peculiar to the administrative community; the Sachsenspiegel, whose system is based upon the community of goods, repeats it in almost the same words: "man unde wip mugen niht gehaben dehein guot gezweihet" (W, 33; L, 34). Everywhere, accordingly, the husband held the seisin of his wife's property. And in this seisin "in mundium", as it is

[1] *Op. cit.*, II, 380.

called by the Sachsenspiegel,[1] there is expressed an idea common to all legal systems of marital property, which loses authority only where reservations in favor of the wife have been made by express contractual provision. Nowhere did German legal systems accept the principle of the Roman law of dotal property, which not only kept the property of husband and wife legally distinct, but also conceded to the latter the management of her own property. On the contrary the German wife was unable to affect by independent action the marital property. If she contracted debts unbeknown to her husband, or concluded other contracts without his consent, this bound neither the property of the husband nor that of his wife of which he held the seisin; if she alienated without his consent and coöperation things belonging to the marital estate, the husband could demand them back, without more ado, from the acquirer. An independent dispositive power was conceded her only as respected transactions of everyday life, necessary for the conduct of the household. Thanks to this "key-power" ("Schlüsselgewalt") she could contract debts of small amount, limited by statute; and, similarly, she bound her husband by transactions concerning articles intended for her personal use (veils, cloth, and flax; dresses, jewels, and distaffs). In case of the sickness or absence of the husband, as well as in other cases of necessity, her dispositive powers were increased; also, the administration of the property might be withdrawn from the husband by a court because of his poor management, and in this case his power passed to his wife, at least wherever sex-guardianship no longer existed. Women engaged in commerce and trade, — who carried on an industry with the consent of their husbands, — were everywhere freer.

(3) Finally, reference must be made to a fact which is universally characteristic of the medieval German law of marital property; namely, that the statutory law could be supplemented or altered in a great extent by *marriage contracts*, which were themselves in large part an embodiment of customary law that had long been in a state of change. These marriage contracts ("Eheverträge", "Eheabreden", "Ehestiftungen", "Gedinge", "Eheteidinge", "Brautlaufsbriefe", and the like; marriage contracts, agreements, settlements, etc.) sometimes referred to the gifts which should be made by the wife or by the husband for the purposes of the marriage. In these cases they conformed to the prevailing law of marital property, which treated them as a

[1] Ssp., I, 31, § 2. *Cf. Heusler, op. cit.*, 381.

supplement, partly necessary and partly customary, to its own rules. At the same time it might easily happen that what was originally required to be established by contract, — as for example the reservation of ownership in the wife's marriage portion, — became in time statutory or customary law. After this change the necessity of special arrangements came to be less felt. They became dispensable in ordinary cases in the absence of extraordinary agreements to the contrary, and were preserved only among the rich and prominent classes, where it was necessary to regulate particularly complicated relations. Another kind were marriage contracts entered into for the purpose of amending the existing law. In so far as this was not absolute in its nature — and this was usually the case — there existed here also complete freedom of contract. The general rule prevailed, "contract breaks the law of the land" ("Gedinge bricht Landrecht"). Gratuitous gifts, however, also continued to exist. In particular, the view (already referred to) became controlling in this connection that the birth of a child changed the nature of the marital estate, and by creating a closer legal community under the property law between parents and children prevented any arbitrary disposition of property. This was expressed in the legal maxim, "begetting children breaks a marriage settlement" ("Kinderzeugen bricht Ehestiftung"). Marriage contracts were made before a court or before witnesses and under the modern legal systems exclusively in writing, usually before marriage, and preferably with the coöperation of kindred, particularly those of the bride; but they were also permitted during marriage.

(II) **Systems of Administrative Community.** (1) *The Ostphalian law.* (A) HUSBAND'S ESTATE AND WIFE'S ESTATE. — The Ostphalian-Saxon law, whose national (Territorial) form found its classical expression in the Sachsenspiegel, and whose urban form was embodied par excellence in the Magdeburg town-law, retained with slight exceptions the old administrative community of the folk-laws, thereby preserving this down into recent times. The words above quoted (p. 632) from the Mirror give a striking expression of the principle that the wife, together with her property, became subject to her husband's mundium; that the husband, in return for conducting the business and carrying the burdens of the marriage, received seisin "in mundium" in his wife's property; and that consequently the marital property constituted, to that extent, an "undivided estate." But this was only a physical union; as respects the ownership, the different parts of the property remained distinct.[1] This was unqualifiedly true of land, which was the chief form of property under the agricultural conditions of Ostphalia, and as respects which the idea of family-estates, above mentioned, was of decisive influence. Just as the husband remained the sole owner of his land, so the wife remained the sole owner of the lands brought with her in marriage; and whatever immovable property she acquired during the marriage by inheritance, gift, or exchange, likewise passed into her exclusive ownership. And it was the same with chattels. True, the statements of the sources referring to these present great difficulties, for which reason differences of opinion exist in respect to this matter that have not yet been overcome. The Saxon law distinguished in a peculiar way a certain part of the marital movable property by designating it with the old traditional name of "Gerade" (paraphernalia), using the word in a technical sense. The paraphernalia of Saxon legal sources consisted "of objects intended for the wife's personal use and of objects used by her in her management of the household."[2] The sources give exhaustive lists of these.[3] Now it was these paraphernalia, and not the chattel property actually brought by the wife into the marriage, that passed, with few exceptions, to her kindred upon dissolution of the same; whereas all objects that did not belong to the paraphernalia, — so-called "Ungerade" (non-paraphernalia), — passed to the husband or his heirs. The peculiar thing here was that the economic use of the individual things, and not their origin, was decisive of their legal fortune at the moment marriage was dissolved. During the continuance of the marriage it was therefore impossible to say what chattels would finally be recognized as property of the wife. For this reason Heusler[4] sees in the treatment of the Saxon paraphernalia an element of community.

(B) LEGAL RELATIONS DURING THE CONTINUANCE OF THE MARRIAGE. — Thanks to his seisin "in mundium", the entire marital property was, as already mentioned, subject to the husband's administration and usufruct. Of course he was not restrained by the assent of his wife in the disposition of his own property. He possessed equally unlimited powers of disposing of all chattels, inclusive of those owned by his wife, — he could alienate her chattels with-

[1] Ssp., I, 31, § 2.
[2] *Brunner*, "Grundzüge" (5th ed.), 227 *et seq.*
[3] For example Ssp., I, 24, § 3.
[4] *Op. cit.*, II, 390 *et seq.*

out being compelled to make compensation therefor; even when he bought lands with his wife's money they became his property and not hers. On the other hand, in dispositions of his wife's lands he was bound by her consent and that of her next heirs; only in cases of actual necessity could the consent of the wife, when lacking, be made good judicially. The wife was denied all independent dispositive powers over her property.[1] As respects the treatment of debts, since the husband could freely dispose of the movable property of the wife, this was also liable, at least under the Magdeburg town-law, to his creditors; on the other hand, of course the wife's immovable property was not so liable. As respects debts of the wife contracted before marriage, her property continued liable for these during the marriage. As already mentioned, she could not be made liable by dispositions of the marital property undertaken by her independently while married; though doubtless, after dissolution of the marriage, she could be held liable through her property, — since this was thereafter again in her seisin, — for debts that had nevertheless been so contracted.

(C) Legal relations after dissolution of marriage. — With such dissolution there resulted a division of the marital property, in which connection it was immaterial under the Ostphalian law whether the marriage was fruitful or sterile, "inherited" or "unherited." The surviving spouse, therefore, took his own immovable property, and that of the dead spouse went to the latter's heirs. As respects chattels the same rule prevailed; only, as already remarked, the wife received as her own upon the death of her husband, not the marriage portion ("Heiratsgut") that she had brought into the marriage, but the paraphernalia as this existed at the moment the marriage was dissolved, and which, it follows from what has been said, might also include articles received or acquired from her husband. On the other hand she was bound to deliver to her husband's heirs whatever other things might still exist of those included in her dowry; and all acquests also were included in the exclusive property of the husband, — of course these last were unimportant under rural conditions. In addition to the paraphernalia the widow received, for the purpose of enabling her to continue the management of the household, a half of the provisions present on the estate at her husband's death, — the so-called "Musteil" ("cibaria domestica"); and she also had the right to remain in the house of her dead husband until the end of the thirtieth day and to live

[1] Ssp., I, 45, § 2.

at the expense of the estate, without the heir's having a right to expel her by virtue of the seisin that passed to him upon the husband's death.[1] "Until the thirtieth day and on that day services were held for the dead in the church; during this time the quiet of the house where he died might not be disturbed, and the widow, freed of cares for shelter and subsistence, should enjoy a quiet stay in her accustomed home. Only with the thirtieth day did the clearing of the house and the removal of her things begin", and the division of the inheritance take place; and this led, under manorial conditions, to the rule that similarly "by the thirtieth day every thing must be settled as to what she claims from the dead and the heritage, in order that the removal of the same might begin immediately upon the expiration of the thirtieth day."[2] If the wife died, the husband was bound to deliver the paraphernalia to the daughter or to another nearest female relative of the wife, — the so-called "niece's paraphernalia" ("Niftelgerade"); and this even when the existing paraphernalia had been received or acquired from him. In default of female kindred the niece's paraphernalia fell to the court. The husband could retain for himself only a few indispensable household articles: bed, table, bench, and stool, — the so-called "Heerpfühl."[3]

(D) CONTRACTUAL LAW OF MARITAL PROPERTY. — The statutory law of marital property, as it is presented in the Sachsenspiegel, sufficed for the simple economic conditions of Ostphalia, and therefore supplementary contractual agreements were necessary only to a slight extent. Here also, however, some such agreements were customary. Some of them referred to marriage gifts from the husband to the wife delivered under marriage contract. The husband was accustomed to deliver to his wife a "maintenance" portion ("Leibzucht") in which was perpetuated the old "dos" of the "Lex Saxonum" (*supra*, p. 627); it was originally composed of land, and later also of money. Though the ownership of such objects remained in the husband, he was restricted in his power of disposing of them by the end to which they were dedicated, and similarly his heirs were obliged to leave them to the widow for usufruct during her life. Besides the "Leibzucht" there was also preserved the old custom of the *morgive*. According

[1] Ssp., I, 22, §§ 1, 3. *Homeyer*, "Der Dreissigste", in Akad. Wiss., Berl., "Abhandlungen" (1865); *Siegel*, "Der Dreissigste, insbesondere nach Hofrecht", in the Krit. Vj., VII (1865), 275 *et seq.*

[2] *Heusler*, "Institutionen", II, 567 *et seq.*

[3] Ssp., III, 38, § 5.

to the Sachsenspiegel this was a voluntary gift ("Zuwendung") made to the wife under contract; but definite limits were set to it.[1] It was only later that a statutory morgive was developed among the nobles. According to the Saxon town-law the contractual ("gelobte") morgive of money was ordinarily promised on the betrothal day in the family circle, the bridegroom binding himself at the same time, however, to renew ("volfuren") his promise in the sacred ("gehegtes") folk-court.

The legal separation of the property of the two parties was ill adapted, in itself, to secure the rights of the wife; for the husband, by virtue of his large dispositive powers over the marital property, could completely destroy the rights of his wife by sale or other alienation, particularly as economic conditions became increasingly those of a money economy. Consequently, *contracts for the security of the wife's property* steadily became more numerous. The Sachsenspiegel names, as such a means, the "Ursale",[2] — that is, a "judicial conveyance of the husband's lands into the hands of a curator of the wife, in ownership or in pledge."[3] The same purpose was served by contracts, developed in systems of town-law, that gave to the wife a reserved-estate ("Vorbehaltsgut") that did not become subject to the administration of the husband, but was subject to her own administration and disposition. It also was conveyed to a trustee ("Treuhänder") or curator. These contracts served the purpose, especially in the cities, of disintegrating the Territorial legal systems of paraphernalia. For such law, in its old form, was actually justified only so long as the wife brought practically only paraphernalia (aside from land) into the marriage as her dowry.

(2) *Other systems of administrative community.* — (A) A pure administrative community, or system of distinct marital estates, prevailed in a number of Swiss legal systems,—notably in those of Zürich and Thurgau and in the original cantons; and in even a clearer form than in the Ostphalian law, because the institute of paraphernalia was unknown to them, and therefore the chattel estate could also be exactly divided according to the origin of the chattels. There prevailed here, absolutely, the rule: "wife's property shall neither wax nor wane"; that is, the wife or her heirs, when the marriage was dissolved, should receive exactly that which she took unto the marriage, or its value. The chattels which she brought into the marriage her husband was bound to

[1] Ssp., I, 20, §§ 1, 8. [2] *Ibid.*, 44.
[3] *Schröder*, "Lehrbuch" (5th ed.), 762.

secure by his lands, — "Zu Erb und Eigen legen" ("to lay upon heir and property"); that is "he pledged his lands, or charged them with a rent equivalent to the value of the property so contributed, for that purpose." [1]

(B) Finally, under some legal systems the administrative community was not recognized generally but only in cases of "unherited" marriages. This was the case in THE FRISIAN AND THE WESTPHALIAN LAW. The Westphalian administrative community was originally identical with the Ostphalian law of the Sachsenspiegel; but the paraphernalia were done away with in it at an early day, a complete statutory division of marital estates being thereby realized in the case also of chattels. Quite unlike the Ostphalian law, however, the Westphalian took the view that the wife was the heiress of her husband. After the death of her husband the widow received, as heiress, in addition to her own property that reverted to her, a half of the remaining property, constituted of the portion brought to the marriage by the husband and the acquests; and, conversely, in case of the predecease of the wife the husband was required to return only half of her property to her heirs, — notwithstanding that he was not ordinarily designated as an heir. This rule was observed, notably, in Soest and in Münster, and in the legal systems dependent upon those cities; and above all in the Lübeck law, which was based upon that of Soest.

(III) **Systems of Marital Community.** — Unlike the legal systems that maintained a division of the marital property, a unification of the property of husband and wife was established in most parts of Western and Southern Germany; that is, in the greatest portion of the regions of the Frankish, Westphalian, Thuringian, Swabian, and Bavarian laws. The effects of this were particularly evident in case of dissolution of the marriage, but in some respects even during its continuance. Moreover, the community existed, — in so far as no special estate was reserved by marriage contract, — by force of law; sometimes as respected all portions of the marital property, sometimes as respected definite portions thereof, and sometimes in all and sometimes only in "inherited" or fertile marriages.

(1) *Limited community of goods.* — The Frankish and the Westphalian law had recognized the wife's rights in marital acquests already in the period of the folk-laws; and even in the post-Frankish period of the Middle Ages the Frankish law retained an

[1] *Heusler*, "Institutionen", II, 331.

acquest-community as the system of marital property that took effect, by force of statute, in all marriages. This Frankish acquest-community also became the dominant rule in Thuringia, in the cities of the Saxon Harz, and in the greatest part of Swabia, Bavaria, and Austria. The Frisian law recognized it as applying to "inherited" marriages, and in part to marriages that remained without issue after the expiration of a year ("überjährige Ehen"). Many legal systems also extended the community to the chattels brought into the marriage (*community of chattels*).

(A) Legal relations during marriage. — In all these legal systems the marital estate, constituted either of the acquests alone or of the entire movable property plus lands later acquired as acquests, was a solidary mass, a collective ownership of which inhered in the two spouses "in undivided shares, which were inseparable during the continuance of the community."[1] The spouses constituted in relation to this collective property a community of collective hand. Inasmuch, however, as the husband, as the head of the marital community, enjoyed a marital stewardship even in these legal systems, he controlled in them also the administration, usufruct, and alienation of the collective property. On the other hand, precisely as in the systems of administrative community, he could dispose of the lands standing in the separate ownership of the two spouses, — even of his own lands, — only with the coöperation of his wife, — that is, only with collective hand; from which it follows that alienation with collective hand was not in itself necessarily indicative of an existing collective ownership. As respects the special estates of the two spouses existing along with the collective estate, — in other words, primarily, as respects the lands brought into the marriage, — the same principles prevailed as in the administrative community; the husband held the seisin of the wife's special estate, but the profits of the acquests accrued in this case solely to the collective estate. As respects liability for obligations, some, as obligations of the collective estate, bound both the community property and the husband's special estate; others bound only the special estate of the wife. The obligations of the collective estate included not only obligations assumed by the husband in furtherance of marital interests and by virtue of his dispositive powers ("community obligations") but also all special obligations incurred by him personally (for example, even his obligations for torts); also the wife's obligations, alike those incurred before

[1] *Gierke* in *Holtzendorff*, I, 538.

marriage and those which she assumed during marriage within the authority of her "key-power" or with the consent of her husband. The husband was liable for all obligations of the collective estate not only with the collective property but also, as just stated, with his own special property; this was the converse of the dispositive power that was accorded to him. Under the Frankish legal systems a widow could free herself from this liability imposed upon the collective property, — for which, upon the death of her husband, she became ipso facto liable, — "by laying upon the death-bed or the corpse, or upon the coffin or the grave of her husband, her keys or her girdle (from which the keys hung)."[1] It is Brunner's view that this key-right of the widow goes back to the idea of a separation under the property law after the death of the husband (*supra*, p. 614).

(B) LEGAL RELATIONS AFTER DISSOLUTION OF MARRIAGE. — In case of an "*unherited*" *marriage*, the special estates of the spouses passed to the sides from which they were respectively derived; whereas the collective estate was divided between the survivor and the heirs of the dead consort. The division was effected in accordance with the old Frankish rule, two-thirds falling to the husband's kindred as "sword" or "spear" portion and one-third to the wife's kindred as a "spindle" or "distaff" portion; or else there was an equal division. However, the surviving spouse was ordinarily given a maintenance-portion for life ("Leibzucht") in the special estates and the acquest-share, and a right of inheritance in the chattel-share of the deceased consort; and some legal systems even accorded him (or her) the ownership of the dead spouse's share of the acquests, so that in this way all the acquests and chattels, — in other words the entire collective estate, — passed into the exclusive ownership of the survivor. These principles, which prevailed in the Frankish law as respects "unherited" marriages, became established in the Frisian law, though with certain variations, in the case of "inherited" marriages, since the Frisian law, as already mentioned, recognized a community of chattels only in the case of "inherited" marriages, and an administrative community in the case of "unherited" marriages.

Moreover, in the case of "*inherited marriages*", there prevailed in most systems of acquest and chattel community the so-called law of "Verfangenschaft" ("sequestration", devolution).[2] Ac-

[1] *Brunner*, "Grundzüge" (5th ed.) 228, "Geschichte", I (2d ed.), 39.

[2] *Mayer-Homberg*, "Zur Entstehung des fränkischen Verfangenschaftsrechtes" in Westd. Z. G. K., XXXI (1912), 1–133; also separately under

cording to this, all the property included in the marital estate was divided into two masses, one consisting of "free" and the other of the "sequestered" ("verfangene") property. To the "free" property belonged all the chattels. They passed to the surviving spouse, whose collective ownership theretofore existing was accordingly transformed by the death of the other spouse who had held with the survivor in collective hand ("Gesamthänder", his "collective-hander") into an absolutely free sole-ownership, as a result of the benefit of survivorship characteristic of rights in collective hand (*supra*, p. 235) so that he could dispose of them thenceforth absolutely. To the "sequestered" property belonged all lands which the spouses had possessed down to the dissolution of the marriage; including those that had been, during the continuance of the marriage, in the sole ownership of the survivor. Of these lands, thus sequestered for the children, the survivor might continue to enjoy usufruct and administration, but except in case of actual necessity he (or she) could thereafter alienate them only with the children's consent. Thus the children's right of sequestration (concerning whose legal nature very different opinions are held) effected a consolidation of the lands, inasmuch as these (even those that were before in the ownership of the deceased), as well as the chattels, passed after the death of one spouse into the sole ownership of the survivor, — although, to be sure, an ownership limited in time, namely for life, beyond which lay the irrevocable claim of the children. If the surviving parent remarried he took with him into the new marriage the sequestered property, but the children of the first marriage alone, and not the children of the second, had herital rights therein. On the other hand the children of the first marriage were fully secured by this right, and had no claim to other property of the second marriage. In order to avoid this unlike treatment of children of the first and second marriages, which was felt to be unequal, partitions were often made between the parent who remarried and the children by the first marriage ("Vorkinder"); and, in connection with this practice, there was developed, beginning in the second half of the 1200 s, a statutory right of partition ("Teilrecht") which was "a wholesome reform of the right of sequestration."[1] It compelled the parent who remarried to come to an agreement with the children of the first

the title "Studien zur Geschichte des Verfangenschaftsrechtes, I. Band: Zur Entstehung des fränkischen Verfangenschaftsrechtes" (1913).

[1] *Schröder*, "Lehrbuch" (5th ed.), 759.

marriage and to deliver them immediately a portion of the "free" and of the "sequestered" property. Under this rule the partition was made either simply by halves, or upon the basis of sword and distaff kindred, or per capita. In this way the "first" children were definitively satisfied, and the parent who remarried took into the new marriage, as free property, the portion still remaining to him.

(2) *The general community of goods.* — As already remarked, many medieval systems of marital property established not simply a limited but a general community of goods. Some of them accomplished this by extending the acquest and chattel community to the entire marital property. This was first done in the Frankish and Westphalian laws, where the requirement that dispositions of land be made by collective hand even under a limited community of goods (*supra*, p. 640) had the result of developing a collective ownership of the spouses in those portions, also, of the marital property. In many places, particularly in the cities of Frankish and Bavarian-Austrian territory, statutory recognition of this form of marital estate originated in a custom by which spouses mutually devised their entire property, to one another. The general community of goods was first developed in the lowlands of the upper and lower Rhine as far as Holland and Flanders, as well as in Westphalia and Thuringia; from these regions it spread into the lowlands of the Weser, toward Hamburg and Lübeck, Mark Meissen and Mark Brandenburg, Lausitz, Silesia, Prussia, Bohemia, and Moravia. It was also widely prevalent in the regions of the Swabian, Bavarian, and Austrian laws, and was introduced into many cities of Magdeburg law in place of the Saxon paraphernalia. A few legal systems regarded it as arising only when a child was born from the marriage, and as determining upon the death of all children, — so, for example, the Westphalian-Lübeck law that spread from Soest. This consideration, however, was generally disregarded, following the example of the Frankish law.

(A) LEGAL RELATIONS DURING MARRIAGE. — The general community of goods, in its legal essence, was "a community in collective hand that fused the entire property of both spouses into one entity, their shares therein being undivided and uncollectible during the continuance of the community."[1] It was distinguished from the limited community of goods by the fact that the community attached by force of law to all property brought into the

[1] *Gierke* in *Holtzendorff-Kohler*, I, 538.

marriage or later acquired, intimately uniting it in a collective estate belonging equally to both spouses. There existed, therefore, no statutory separate estates; but, on the other hand, there was nothing to prevent the spouses from reserving particular pieces of property, by marriage contract, as separate property. Yet even under this system, which emphasized most decidedly the equality of husband and wife in property rights, the husband was the holder of the mundium and the head of the marital community, and therefore alone entitled to administer and represent it. To be sure, his dispositive power was variously limited in different legal systems. Although he could everywhere dispose independently of the chattels, he was bound in most systems, as regards the lands, to secure the coöperation of his wife; only a few allowed him to act with entire independence as to them also. As for the treatment of obligations, the same principles prevailed as in the case of the limited community of goods. The spouses constituted with respect to the collective property a community of obligations ("Schuldengemeinschaft"). Obligations binding the collective estate included all obligations assumed by the husband, and such obligations of the wife as were incurred either before her marriage or in transactions within her marital competence. The husband was liable for these obligations of the collective estate with his special estate, also, if such existed; whereas under most legal systems the wife was liable only with the collective property under all circumstances, and could free herself even from this liability, as in the case of a chattel community, by a renunciation made in legal form (above, p. 640).

(B) Legal relations after dissolution of marriage. — Generally speaking, it was usual to distinguish between "unherited" and "inherited" marriages; although many legal systems, notably those of the Lower Franks and Westphalians, maintained a rule equally applicable in all cases. In the case of the "*unherited*" *marriage*, some legal systems permitted a partition of the property immediately upon or after the thirtieth day, following the death of either spouse, the survivor taking from the collective estate a certain part as his (or her) sole property for the future. In the older legal systems this share of the survivor was usually a major portion. Especially common was partition into thirds, two of these falling to the survivor; but this was frequently true only of the widower's sword-portion, whereas the widow was obliged to content herself with the distaff-portion of a third. On the other hand, a division into halves was usually a result only of a later legal development. Still other legal systems admitted no partition whatever, but provided that the surviving spouse should receive the entire collective property. This was a rule which corresponded exactly to the principle of collective hand, being an accrescence of the portion of one commoner, freed by death, for the benefit of the survivor ("längst Leib, längst Gut": "so long property as life in the body"); but later it was ordinarily regarded as a right of inheritance of the surviving spouse in the share of the dead consort.

If the marriage was "*inherited*", then according to many legal systems, notably the Frankish, all the property fell to the surviving spouse in sole ownership; but it was then bound, as in the case of the limited community of goods, by the children's right of sequestration which attached to the lands. Another widespread rule was that the children should take the place of their dead parent, and continue the community of goods with the survivor for common profit and loss (*infra*, § 98). In this connection, in turn, very different provisions prevailed concerning the time and the basis of the partition thus temporarily postponed but later to be realized. For the most part, the children could demand such when they reached majority, or when the daughters wished to marry, or when the parent proved a poor manager, and particularly when he contracted a second marriage. On the other hand, where a usufruct for life in the children's share existed in favor of the surviving parent the community continued under the second marriage and the partition could be made only upon his death.

(3) *Regulation by contract.* — The extraordinary complexity of the law of the marital community was considerably increased in consequence of the fact above adverted to (pp. 632 *et seq.*) that in addition to the systems provided by statute special contractual rules were introduced and acquired wide prevalence, partly before the establishment of the former and partly in association with them; and also because in many regions the various statutory systems of marital community were ordinarily supplemented by contractual rules of traditional origin, particularly by voluntary gifts ("Zuwendungen") between the spouses. Thus, for example, among the noble classes of West and South Germany a so-called "dower" marriage long enjoyed great favor along with the statutory forms of marital estates. In this the wife received from her husband a gift which originated in a union of the old dower ("Wittum") with the morgive. For the rest, it was

regulated substantially like the administrative community. It was customary in many regions to adjust such gift to the value of the marriage portion brought with her by the wife; to the end that, as the husband retained the dowry ("Heimsteuer") of the wife upon her death, so the wife upon his death should receive an equal benefit in the form of this "Widerlage" ("Gegengeld", — counter-money; "contrados", "augmentum dotis").

§ 96. **The Law of Marital Property: (3) The Modern Law. — (I) General Development Since the Reception.** — If the result of the medieval legal development was an extraordinary diversity in the law of marital property, this diversity was still further increased in the modern period, by the Reception and by a statutory activity of various governments which frequently took the form of pure arbitrariness, disregarding as useless even a knowledge of the existing legal systems. Thus, in many places "the continuity of legal development was broken, alien systems were introduced, and it was often left to accident which principle should be established in modern legislation."[1] Although individual systems had spread in the Middle Ages without regard to the territorial bounds of different racial branches, there could no longer be any talk of larger regions in which a definite system exclusively prevailed; at the most it might be said that a preference existed in North Germany for the administrative and the general community of goods, and in West Germany for the chattel community. The condition of the law was most of a medley in Middle and South Germany, where the boundaries of various systems of marital property often ran through one village. Not rarely, also, several systems of marital property were recognized in one and the same district; and what is more, not only were "inherited" and "unherited", and first and second marriages, treated in the traditional manner of the older law, but marriages between parties of different status by birth or occupation, and of different religious faiths, were treated according to different principles. So, for example, in Würzburg the dotal system prevailed as to marriages of imperial knights, but otherwise the rules of the general or acquest community; in the older Hessian portions of Hesse-Cassel the dotal system prevailed for the higher classes and the acquest community for the lower; in Augsburg the acquest community for industrials, and the dotal system in other cases; in Hechingen, the community of goods for Christians and separate estates for Jews; in Mecklenburg, Germanic law (for

[1] *Stobbe*, IV (3d ed.), 149.

the most part Lübeck law and the law of the Old March) in most of the cities, but in some of them a Germanic law modified by, and in still others a pure, Roman law, — Roman law, also, for all privileged persons, and with few exceptions for the entire open ("platte") country.

In view of this devotion to particularism, even some of the great modern codes renounced any attempt to introduce a uniform law of marital property for the entire territory of the State. The Prussian Allgemeines Landrecht adopted the so-called "local" ("Regional-") principle. That is, while it regulated the law of marital property, primarily and in principle, according to an independent system which represented a modification of the Saxon administrative community, and which prevailed in the absence of other agreement, it also left in authority along with this, within their respective territories, those provincial statutes and regulations ("Statuten") which established a general or an acquest-community, — although adopting even as to these systems numerous rules designed to give to such regional systems of marital community a certain uniformity of basis, and particularly for guidance in doubtful questions. This general system was intended to govern, therefore, only in so far as no other rule was provided in the regional systems. Nevertheless the system of the general community of goods thus established by State law attained cardinal importance. In the first place, it prevailed whenever a community of goods was agreed upon by contract outside the regions where such community existed by force of law; it was later introduced as a statutory system into the province of Posen and in some districts of Pomerania; finally, a codification of the law of marital estates in the general sense of a general community of goods closely related to that of the Landrecht was effected for the province of Westphalia and for those parts of the Rhine Province in which the "Landrecht" prevailed by a law of April 16, 1860. The Code Civil followed another course. Rejecting the "regional" principle, it recognized several systems of marital property: preferentially, the chattel community, which it recognized as the statutory system whenever a marriage contract contained only a bare declaration that the marriage was contracted under the law of community of goods, or when no contract was made. Beside this, it permitted other contractual agreements, and laid down, as a basis for these, provisions concerning the acquest-community, the general community of goods, the system of separate estates, and the dotal system.

(II) **Specific Systems of Marital Property.** — In addition to the systems of the administrative, general, and limited community of goods to which the medieval development had led, the Roman dotal system was adopted, as already mentioned, as an additional system of marital property in consequence of the Reception. Indeed the authority of common law was ascribed to this by the jurists. However, the native statutes and practices offered such resistance as to exclude the Roman law from entry into practical legal life save to a very slight extent. But though the Roman law actually displaced the native only in a few regions, it nevertheless attained a very considerable influence; so much so that the Roman concepts were thenceforth preferably treated as norms in applying the rules of the Germanic law, and in legislation. And in the scientific statements that were now first attempted of these various systems they necessarily furnished the guiding principles.

While a certain force, albeit weak, tending toward uniformity was involved in the scientific method thus generally observed, a stronger check upon particularistic legal development was found in the fact that certain general principles everywhere remained controlling even in modern times, — alike in the native Germanic systems, notwithstanding their divergent development in details, and in the dotal system of the common law. In consequence of this the inconsistencies in the two systems had a more superficial effect than must otherwise have been the case.

These common principles included, in the first place, the old rule that the husband, as the principal in the marriage relation, should bear the burdens of the marriage, and was therefore entitled, so far as a special estate was not expressly created for the wife, to take possession of and to administer the wife's entire property. Under all the Germanic systems the wife continued, therefore, to be restricted in her dispositive powers; without the consent of her husband she might neither alienate her property nor charge it with liabilities. In accordance with the older Germanic law, it was only within the scope of her "key-power", and further in case of the husband's incapacity or in case of an independent business carried on by the wife with her husband's assent, that an unrestricted capacity of action was attributed to her. The regions of the common law of dower right ("Dotalrecht") were the only ones where these principles had no authority; since there, in accordance with the Roman rules, a wife had the same capacity for action as an unmarried woman.

Moreover, unlike the Roman law, which gave the spouses only a limited power of contractual disposition over their rights in the marital property, the principle of free contract was quite generally preserved. Only the modern regional systems required the observance of certain forms (writing, judicial or notarial authentication) and also, frequently, publication. The present Civil Code has followed the example of Bremen and Oldenburg in introducing, to satisfy the last two requirements, an entry in the register of marital property; the commercial register having theretofore been used, to some extent, in place of this. With the exception of the Code Civil most of the modern systems permitted the conclusion of marriage contracts not only before but also during the existence of the marriage.

For the rest, the individual systems at the end of their development, — *i.e.* at the end of the 1800s, — were related to each other, as regards their territorial prevalence and general principles, approximately as follows:

(1) *The administrative community.* (A) JURISDICTION.—In the form defined by the Prussian "Landrecht", this prevailed as a statutory system in almost all of Silesia, in certain circles of the provinces of Pomerania and Brandenburg, in the province of Saxony, and in East Friesland. It also prevailed in the greater part of the province of Brandenburg, including the city of Berlin, by virtue of the Constitutio Joachimica of 1527; in the Kingdom of Saxony, by virtue of the Saxon Code; and further, in the Saxon-Thuringian principalities and in Anhalt, in parts of Schleswig-Holstein and Hannover, in Oldenburg, in Lübeck, and in most of the cities of Mecklenburg law (for example Rostock, Wismar, Schwerin, etc.). At the end of the 1800 s some twenty-one million persons lived under this system.

(B) LEGAL RELATIONS DURING MARRIAGE.—On the whole, the old legal rules prevailed in this type of marital estate, save that the powers of the husband, which were once the result of his seisin " in mundium ", were now construed as a marital usufruct (" usufructus maritalis "), notwithstanding that there was here no usufruct in the sense of the Roman law, — his power to alienate specific portions of the wife's property, in particular, being irreconcilable with the Roman usufruct. To the estate of the wife belonged property brought with her in marriage or acquired for value during its continuance; it became immediately subject to the administration and usufruct of the husband, and in the case of money and fungible things passed to his ownership.

The profits of her property and also, in particular, whatever she acquired by her labor became the property of her husband. However, she could be given a reserved-estate by contract, and in this the husband had no rights. As for her lands, the husband could not dispose of these without her consent, since an entry in the Land Book was necessary. The husband was liable to his wife for an efficient administration of the property. To insure this the statutory pledge right which the Roman law gave her to secure her " dos " was extended to cover all the property brought with her in marriage; there was later developed from this a statutory hypothecary title. Under most legal systems only the property of the husband, — together with the profits of the wife's property brought with her in the marriage, — was liable for his obligations; on the other hand, the husband's property was also liable for the obligations of his wife in case he had given his consent to the contract she concluded.

(C) In case of dissolution of marriage by death there ordinarily resulted immediately a division of the marital property, the surviving spouse receiving in addition to his or her own property a part of that of the deceased, by virtue of a right of inheritance recognized in his or her favor. This was the " statutory portion." Often, however (under some legal systems only in case of "unherited" marriages), no partition was made, the property being left intact and either given to the surviving spouse as a whole or assigned in shares to such spouse and the heirs of the dead. This was called a " community of goods mortis causa." In the case of " inherited " marriages a choice was often given to a surviving spouse, either to the widow only or also to the widower, whether he or she would divide all the marital property theretofore physically united ("Grund-" or "Totteilung": landed-partition, partition mortis causa), or first take out his own property and then divide the remainder with the children or other heirs of the deceased. In regions of the Saxon law the rules of chattel succession established in the Sachsenspiegel and the Constitution of Electoral Hesse prevailed as to widowers, whereas a widow had a choice between the re-delivery of her marriage portion and her right to the statutory portion. In place of this principle a variant rule, more closely resembling that of the Prussian "Landrecht", was introduced for the Kingdom of Saxony by a statute of December 29, 1829. This statute abandoned the community mortis causa (which, however, remained in authority in Berlin and Mark Brandenburg, by virtue of the Joachimica, in cases where the survivor did not withdraw his property from the collective mass), and gave to the surviving spouse in addition to his own property, which reverted to him, a statutory portion that was variously measured according to the nearness in kinship of the other heirs of the deceased. That is: if there were descendants one-fourth, or if more than three lines of descendants were represented a child's portions; if there were ascendants, or brothers or sisters, or nephews or nieces, a third; otherwise the survivor inherited the half or the entire heritage. In default of descendants the surviving spouse also inherited the ordinary bed and table linen, as well as furniture and household utensils (a reminiscence of the old paraphernalia). Further, the voluntary gifts of the old law, the morgive, maintenance portion ("Leibzucht", and "Widerlage"), dower ("Wittum"), paraphernalia, and compulsory portion ("Musteil") were preserved in many regions, especially among the noble classes, and in their case partly as statutory claims.

(2) *The general community of goods.* (A) JURISDICTION.—This system of marital estate was very widely prevalent in Germany, more especially in the North. In Prussia it prevailed in East Prussia (save as to nobles), in West Prussia, and in Posen, in the lowlands of Pomerania, in Westphalia, and in those portions of the Rhine province that were subject to the "Landrecht," — in all of which it was uniformly regulated by the statute of 1860 just mentioned; in the Hohenzollern principalities, in parts of Schleswig-Holstein, Hannover, and Hesse-Nassau. Further, in many districts of Bavaria, in some portions of Hesse-Darmstadt, in some cities of Mecklenburg, in Thuringian districts, in Lippe-Detmold, in Bremen, and in Hamburg. A population of some eleven million lived under the law of the general marital community in 1900.

(B) PRINCIPLES APPLICABLE DURING THE CONTINUANCE OF MARRIAGE. — In general the old rules remained in authority. Difficulties arose from the juristic theory above referred to, for here was a relation that could not be forced within the Roman categories of sole ownership and co-ownership by ideal shares, however much many jurists strove to construct such a Romanistic co-ownership, endeavoring for this purpose to discover in the marital community a "societas" or a "communio." However, the hopelessness of this attempt, in particular the impossibility of basing the participation of the spouses upon the principle of quotal rights ("Quoten"), made it necessary to undertake the solution of a question from the Germanic viewpoint. Of the jurists who followed this course, some it is true, advanced a theory certainly indefensible, alleging that the spouses constituted by their union a new and independent subject of rights, — either a juristic person or an unclearly conceived association, — to which the marital property belonged. This theory of a juristic person was championed especially by Hasse,[1] who contended that the spouses lost their previously existing rights, in toto, to this "mystic person" of which they were members, without retaining therein the slightest share as individual subjects of rights. This view, however, although it for a time dominated legal literature (Eichhorn and Albrecht accepted it) was entirely too artificial to be capable of maintenance. The consequences, also, to which it led were in part in open conflict with the actually existing law. The outcome was that a theory eventually triumphed which, — adopting ideas (*supra*, p. 239) first expressed by Justus Veracius, but modifying the Germanic "condominium plurium in solidum" that was assumed by him and his followers, — regarded the marital community of goods as an application of Germanic ownership in collective hand, in the sense which has been explained (*supra*, pp. 235 *et seq.*).

(C) Relations after dissolution of marriage. — The provisions in modern legal systems concerning the consequences of a dissolution of marriage varied greatly in details, but on the whole they always adopted one of the three rules already recognized in the Middle Ages. Either, — as was especially common in cases of "unherited" marriages, — the collective property was divided between the surviving spouse and the next heirs of the deceased in a certain ratio (usually by halves, but also, still, according to sword and distaff shares and the like); or, — as was especially frequent in cases of "inherited" marriages, — a continued marital community was established between the survivor and the children; or the entire marital property passed to the survivor. When a partition was made, many legal systems, in accord with traditional principles, granted the survivor, besides his share of the collective estate, a so-called "Beisitz" ("by-sitting"), — which was a usufructuary right for life or for some other period in the portions of the children or other heirs of the deceased consort. In many other legal systems, however, the surviving parent enjoyed more than this "Beisitz", which involved ad-

[1] "Beytrag zur Revision der bisherigen Lehre von der Gütergemeinschaft" (1808).

ministration and usufruct of the portions of the children. Instead of giving the children their separate shares, there was established, namely, by force of law, between him and them a "continued" community of goods ("fortgesetzte"). In this, as in the marital community of goods during marriage there existed a community of collective hand in the unapportioned shares of the estate, and a common management for common profit and loss; and in this relation of collective hand the children and their issue took per stirpes the place of the dead spouse. To the collective estate there belonged the whole property as it existed at the dissolution of the marriage and the later acquests of the surviving parent; on the other hand, later acquests of the children were not included, but constituted their own separate estate. The administration of the collective estate fell to the surviving parent under the same rules as to the husband in the marital community; consultation of the children was necessary to the same extent as was, in that, the consent of the wife. Under all circumstances, remarriage by the surviving spouse worked a dissolution of the continued community. Under many legal systems the surviving spouse's exclusive right of inheritance was recognized in the case not only of "unherited" but also of "inherited" marriages; nevertheless, in the latter case the ownership thus acquired was not limited, as in the continued community, by rights of collective hand, but by the children's rights in expectancy.

(3) *The limited community of goods.* (A) THE ACQUEST-COMMUNITY prevailed in 1900 among a population of about ten millions; particularly in the regions of the Franconian law, in parts of Hesse-Darmstadt and Electoral Hesse, in Nassau, Wetzlar, and Frankfort (by virtue of the Franconian Ordinance of Territorial Courts of 1618, the Territorial law of Solm of 1571, the Territorial law of Mainz of 1755, and the Frankfort Reformation of 1611); further, in parts of the Rhine province of Prussia (district of the "Judicial Senate" of Ehrenbreitstein), in Schleswig-Holstein (in Ditmarsch, Fehmarn, Nordstrand), in Hannover, Thuringia, in great areas of Old Bavaria (by virtue of the Bavarian Territorial Law), and finally in Württemberg (by virtue of the Württemberg Territorial Law of 1610).

(B) THE CHATTEL COMMUNITY prevailed, as the statutory system of the Code Civil (which in its codification followed especially the Custom of Paris) in the lands of the French law; that is, in the Rhine province of Prussia to the West of the Rhine as well as in the greatest part to the East; also in Rhenish Hesse, in the

Oldenburg principality of Birkenfeld, in the Bavarian Palatinate, and in Alsace-Lorraine. Also in Baden, by virtue of the Baden Territorial Law, and finally in Schleswig-Holstein by virtue of the Jutland Law. Some nine million people lived under this system.

As respects the system of the *limited community* of goods, reference may be made to the remarks already made upon the medieval law (*supra*, pp. 639 *et seq.*), since the legal principles governing it were preserved intact, notwithstanding the great diversity that of course existed in details; and since, moreover, the rules of the general community of goods and those of the administrative community continued to be applied, respectively, to the collective estate and to the special estates ("Einhandsgüter") of the spouses. Special rules prevailed in the French law respecting liability for obligations.

(4) Finally, the *dotal system of the common law* became established in Electoral Hesse, in scattered portions of Westphalia, Pomerania, and Hannover; in Lauenburg, in many districts of Bavaria and Hesse-Darmstadt, in the rural regions of Mecklenburg, in Brunswick, etc. It was the rule for about three million persons. The Austrian Civil Code also based its law of marital property, substantially, upon the principles of the Roman dotal system.

The Roman law, in its pure form, was very sharply contrasted even with that Germanic system which most resembled it, namely, the administrative community. For it rested upon the principles that marriage involved no change whatever in the position of the married person under the property law; that the property of the married couple remained separate, equally as regarded ownership, administration, and disposition; that the husband had no other rights in the property of the wife (her so-called "parapherna") than she might see fit to grant him, — for which reason, also, her acquests increased her "parapherna" only; and that marital obligations bound the husband exclusively, the wife sharing the liability only in case a "dos" was given for her. This "dos" passed into the husband's ownership, but was required to be restored to her after dissolution of the marriage. Further, whereas under Germanic law the husband might alienate the wife's land with her consent, the "fundus dotalis" was absolutely inalienable according to Roman law. Moreover, the Roman law recognized a herital right of a surviving spouse only in default of kindred of the dead consort, and in addition the herital right of a poor widow.

This Roman law of dotal property, however, was adopted in its pure form only in the rarest cases. In the regions of the common law, as well as in the statutes that recognized that, it suffered many modifications in the sense of the Germanic law, for which reason the system was ordinarily known as "the modified dower system." In particular, here again the entire administration and usufruct of the wife's estate, notwithstanding this was kept separate from his own property, was ordinarily given to the husband in recognition of his traditional mundium, — the distinction between the dotal property and the paraphema thus losing, of course, its practical importance, for with this change the dower system came closer to the administrative community. In the same way alienations of the "fundus dotalis" were permitted with the consent of the wife and approval of the court. At times, also, there was recognized an acquest irreconcilable with the Roman law. And finally, the Roman rules of succession "bonorum possessio unde vir et uxor" and the herital right of poor widows were replaced by the statutory herital-portion of Germanic law.

(III) **Establishment of Legal Uniformity.** — The Civil Code made an end of this condition of the German law of marital property, — a condition which was intolerable, and impossible of continuance in a unified country. True, historical antecedents and prevailing conditions did not permit the introduction of such a single exclusive system as was realized in the Austrian and the Saxon Codes. Even the principle of contractual freedom, which the Code recognized in agreement with the earlier law, would not have sufficed to reconcile the variety of legal customs prevailing in different parts of Germany. Hence the Civil Code, rejecting the principle of local option ("Regionalprinzip"), has adopted the course followed by the Code Civil in providing several systems of marital property. Two of these systems, — the administrative and usufructuary system (*i.e.* the administrative community) and that of separate estates, — it has laid down as "legal" systems. The former is assumed as the normal system when nothing else is agreed upon at the time of marriage; the latter, on the other hand, when a woman of limited capacity for juristic acts marries without the consent of her statutory representative, or when any other system of marital property in which spouses have theretofore been living is ended during the continuance of marriage, or when spouses whose marital community has been abolished reëstablish such community. It also regulates the general, the acquest, and the chattel communities when established contractually as the marital property system; so that the spouses can make these systems the basis of their contract by a simple reference to the respective sections of the Code. They can also adopt voluntarily the statutory system of distinct estates or any other whatever as they may please, provided they be not immoral or opposed to the purposes of marriage. Nor may they refer in their contract to a statute which is no longer in force, nor to a foreign statute. Although the present Civil Code has conformed in general to the principles of the legal systems that prevailed before 1900, its provisions nevertheless include many modifications in the case of all four systems. Here again the primary consideration of the legislator has been to give greater security to the wife's legal position; one of the most significant novelties being that under the statutory rules for the administration and usufruct of the wife's reserved-estate, — as to which no powers of administration or usufruct exist in favor of the husband, — all those things belong thereto which the wife acquires by her labor or by independent prosecution of an industry (§ 1367). Whether the best means have everywhere been adopted for the attainment of that end and whether it has already been attained so far as might reasonably be desired, is a question that cannot here be discussed; and a detailed consideration of the law as at present existing must also be dispensed with.

The Swiss Civil Code has solved in the same manner as the German the legislative task of establishing uniformity in the law of marital property, — the forms of which, in Switzerland also, were formerly very diverse. Like the German Code it makes the normal statutory system that of a joint estate ("Güterverbindung"), though this is differently regulated in details; and besides this, as an extraordinary form, it recognizes that of distinct estates; placing at the disposition of the parties, moreover, the systems of general, limited, and continued marital community of goods, all of which it regulates, and any of which the parties may adopt by contract. It has also introduced the register of marital property.

CHAPTER XII

CHILDHOOD

§ 97. **Legitimate Children:**[1] (1) **Personal Legal Relations between Parents and Children.** (I) **Paternal Authority.** — (1) *Nature and extent of paternal authority.* — In accord with the patriarchal organization of the family in Indo-Germanic and Germanic races, the house-lord, by virtue of his mundium, was the absolute master of his wife and children. Clear traces have been preserved down into the Middle Ages of the fact that this paternal authority, precisely like that of the husband, was legally unlimited, and therefore included extraordinarily extensive powers, notably an absolute power of discipline and punishment. The father could dispose absolutely at will of the life and death of his children. He had the right to expose them after birth, to repudiate, to enslave, to sell, to kill them. Here also, in agreement with the general development of the concept of mundium (*supra*, pp. 584 *et seq.*), the ameliorations that at first were demanded only by social standards ("Sitte") gradually became legal restrictions. In the age of the folk-laws this state of affairs was realized: the father enjoyed such powers only in case of the existence of certain circumstances defined by law, and he was frequently required,

[1] *Cf. Fehr*, "Die Rechtsstellung der Frau und der Kinder in den Weistümern" (1912), 87 *et seq.*

even in undertaking merely severe chastisement, to have the coöperation of the family or the sib. That this power over freedom and life might be exercised, however, in the cases so recognized, the law expressly contemplated. For example, as respects the power of sale it was expressly provided as late as in the "Edictum Pistense" of the Emperor Charles II, of 864, that a father might sell his children into slavery in case of his own actual necessity. A similar rule was adopted so late as in the Schwabenspiegel; though whether it actually reflected the legal conditions of that time appears doubtful,[1] for with increasing culture and under the influence of Christianity these hard and cruel expressions of paternal power naturally came to conflict with the popular consciousness of right. On the contrary, the duties of the father became more prominent, — to protect his child and to represent it in court. The absolute power which he originally could exercise to compel the marriage of his daughters became weakened into mere rights of betrothal and assent to marriage (*supra*, 599).[2] Notwithstanding this change, however, of the three forms in which the mundium appeared in the family law (marriage-stewardship, paternal power, guardianship), it was "the paternal power which preserved most markedly throughout the Middle Ages the original characteristics of house-lordship." [3] The view continued to prevail that the father's mundium, in contradistinction to that of the guardian, was intended to serve the individual interest of the holder. The father disposed of the child "not merely in order to train it, to determine the course of its life, to marry it, but also in order to utilize its labor in his own service." [4] Consequently, this emphasis of the father's interest appeared especially in relations of the property law (*infra*, § 98).

After the Reception, the father's duty to care for his children was treated in the law of persons as decidedly the chief element in his household power. It was required that he should exercise for the best interest of the child the right of training him, of determining his religious faith, of appointing his guardians. For this

[1] Swsp., 357 (L); *cf. Schröder*, "Lehrbuch" (5th ed.), 765, who denies convincing force to the corresponding passage in the sermons of *Geiler von Kaisersberg*, because they were derived from this uncritical note of the Schwabenspiegel.

[2] *Köstler*, "Die väterliche Ehebewilligung, eine kirchenrechtliche Untersuchung auf rechtsvergleichender Grundlage", No. 51 (1908) of *Stutz's* "Untersuchungen", and "Muntgewalt und Ehebewilligung in ihrem Verhältnis zueinander nach langobardischem und fränkischem Recht", in Z². R. G., XXIX (1908), 79–135.

[3] *Heusler*, "Institutionen", II. 442.

[4] *v. Amira*, "Recht" (2d ed.), 114.

reason the principles of the law of guardianship were more and more applied in the modern codes to the legal relations existing between father and children, the father, like the guardian, being subjected, although less strictly, to a governmental supervision in the nature of guardianship — in certain cases the supervisory Guardians' Court ("Obervormundschaftsgericht") was empowered or required to interfere. The Civil Code has likewise conformed in this matter to the earlier law, providing for official interference by the Guardians' Court in certain cases. This is required, for example, when the father has grossly violated his duties, or when he desires to conclude in the name of the child certain particularly important juristic acts. The Swiss Civil Code has applied these ideas still more logically. True, it sharply distinguishes, on the one hand, the parental power from the guardian's power; but on the other hand it protects the children by prescribing more explicitly and in greater detail than in other codes the parents' duties, by requiring (like the German Code) in certain cases a guardian's assent to parental acts, and, finally, by conceding to the public authorities extensive rights of interference, — for example, the removal of the child from an environment that seriously threatens danger from tubercular infection.[1]

(2) *The origin of paternal authority.* — (A) LEGITIMATE BIRTH. — According to the oldest law the father's power was not based upon the fact that he had begotten the child but upon his mundium over the mother. The father acquired paternal power over those children only who were born to him by a wife who was subject to his mundium as husband; that is, by his legal wife. If the wife was under the mundium, not of her husband but of another person (*e.g.* of her father), her children became subject to the latter's mundium; and on the other hand all children by a legal wife, even though they were not the children of the husband, became subject to the husband's mundium. But as has already been mentioned (*supra*, p. 43), the fact of birth by a legitimate wife was originally not sufficient, in itself, to give the child a right to enter the family and house-lordship of the father. For it depended upon his will whether he would adopt it or make use, instead, of his power of exposure. This stage of the law was succeeded in the early Middle Ages by another. The Church's influence forced the abandonment of the power of exposure, and thereafter the sole fact of birth constituted the basis of paternal power, — only legitimate birth, however, birth in lawful wedlock.

[1] See *Tuor*, "Das neue Recht" (p. lv *supra*), 193 *et seq.*

To this was added in medieval theory a requirement that the child should also have been begotten during marriage; children conceived before and born during marriage were not regarded as legitimate, and subsequent marriage had no legitimizing effect upon their status ("Stellung").[1] However, a father must have possessed the power expressly to recognize such a child as his own; and there thus developed, as early as the later Middle Ages, an opposite view according to which the only fact of importance was birth during marriage, the husband possessing a right to deny his paternity only in case of unseasonable birth, and to refute the presumption of the child's legitimacy. No fixed rules existed in the older law for the decision of the question whether a child should be regarded as born too early, or (after dissolution of marriage) too late. Unlike the Sachsenspiegel, the Schwabenspiegel and various other medieval legal sources fixed a certain number of weeks for the duration of pregnancy; and after the Reception authority was acquired by the rule of the common law, namely, that birth might take place at the earliest on the 182d day, and at the latest ten months after conception. The modern codes have also conformed in principle to this rule, although the period has somewhat varied. The present Civil Code has declared for the 181st and 302d days, both inclusive (§ 1592); the Swiss Civil Code (§§ 254, 252) has adopted the 180th and the 300th days. The earlier modern codes likewise contained detailed provisions respecting the evidence by which the presumption of the child's legitimacy, arising from birth within the period adopted, could be rebutted by the father, — but only provided he had made no express or tacit admission of legitimacy. In place of the specific evidence which they required to show the *impossibility* of paternity (which must be based upon impotence, separation, lack of cohabitation, earlier pregnancy of the wife, and the like), — any allegation of sexual intercourse by the wife with other men being disregarded, — the present Civil Code has laid down the general rule that the child is not legitimate when it is manifestly impossible, under the circumstances, that the wife could have conceived it by her husband (§ 1591). The provisions of the Swiss Civil Code (§ 254) are similar.

(B) Adoption of children.[2] — The adoption of children was certainly known in the primitive Germanic and even in the Frank-

[1] Ssp., I, 36, § 1.

[2] *Pappenheim,* "Über künstliche Verwandtschaft im germanischen Recht", in Z². R. G., XXIX (1908), 304–333; "Die Pflegekindschaft in

ish period, at least among some Germanic racial branches; the expression "Affatomie" ("affatomire", Frankish "fathumjan" = to receive into the narrowest circle of the kindred, the "fathum") being employed to designate it among the Franks. In other words, there was an artificial creation of the filial relation; along with and modeled upon which there existed among the North Germans an artificial relationship of brothers and sisters ("blood"-brotherhood), and among the West Germans a brotherhood "of oath" ("angelobte Brüderschaft", "affratatio", "agermanament"). The adoption of a son, which was permitted only to childless parents, or to others with the consent of all the issue of their body ("leibliche Kinder"), was effected by "handing over the child to the adoptive father, whereupon the latter performed some action that showed his recognition of the paternal relation":[1] he handed him weapons and thereby declared him able-bodied ("wehrhaft"), he clipped his hair ("capillaturiæ"), set him upon his knee or his lap, wrapped him in his own mantle, embraced him. The child was thereby adopted into the household of the adoptive father, and consequently was subjected to his household mundium. This Germanic adoption had no effects, however, within the law of inheritance. This ancient institute everywhere became less prominent in the later course of legal development, and in some legal systems (as for example in the English) adoption remained absolutely unknown. But wherever still practiced in the Middle Ages it was no longer the basis of paternal authority, for legitimate birth alone had been become decisive of the latter. With the Reception, the Roman institute of adoption was introduced into Germany. It also attained no great practical importance, however; the greater nobility did not recognize it at all. At the same time, the rules of the Roman law were modified both in the common law and in the modern codes; in particular, a single institute, which resembled most nearly the "adoptio minus plena", was substituted for the three Roman forms ("arrogatio", "adoptio plena", "adoptio minus plena"). By the adoption of a child under modern law a relation is established which is copied after that existing between actual ("leiblich") parents and children, without, however, producing all the legal consequences of natural

der Graugans", in "Festgabe für Brunner" (1910), 1–15; *Rietschel*, art. "Adoption" in *Hoop's* "Reallexikon", I (1911), 38 *et seq.*, and art. "Blutsbrüderschaft" in *ibid.*, 297.

[1] *Brunner*, "Geschichte", I (2d ed.), 103.

childhood, or breaking all relation of the adoptive child with its natural family. The Civil Code has conformed in most respects to the preëxisting law. But whereas this did not give to the adoptive father the rights of a natural father in the property of the adoptive child, — the administration and profit of the property of a minor adoptive child being given, on the contrary, to its natural father or guardian, and of an adult adoptive child to himself, — the present Civil Code has given to the adoptive parent both complete paternal power over, and usufruct of the property of, an adoptive child under age (§ 1757). On the other hand it has withdrawn from the adoptive parents all rights of inheritance in the property of the adoptive child (§§ 1759, 1764), while leaving to such child, in accord with the earlier law, its rights of inheriting both from its blood kindred and from its adoptive parents (but not from the latter's kindred). The Swiss Civil Code has taken the same attitude (§§ 264–269).

(3) *Determination of paternal power.* — It has already been remarked under the law of persons (*supra*, pp. 55 *et seq.*) that, from the earliest times, the primitive Germanic and later German law treated the father's house-power over his children as ending, not with their attainment of a certain age, nor with the declaration of their majority by the grant of arms (" Wehrhaftmachung "), but with their departure from the paternal household.

In the case of sons this departure ordinarily occurred when they established their own households, which was customarily associated with their marriage, although it was not impossible, particularly in rural regions, that they brought their wives to their father's estate (" Hof "), and so remained in the paternal household even after marriage. In early times an economic separation was involved, also, in their joining the retinue (conutatus) of a lord, and this ended the paternal power. In order to terminate the father's power without division of the household resort was had in the Frankish period to a simulated adoption, the child being adopted by a third person who then returned it to its father's house. It may be assumed that a son who had reached majority could demand emancipation from the paternal household, and either an accounting for his property or a suitable outfit. According to later legal sources, a division of the household, when it was not the consequence of marriage, required " a formal legal act, by which the father, in court, ' cut his son off from bread ', at the same time assigning to him a certain income; an action which was known as ' exseparare ', ' emancipare ', ' foris familiare ', 'mettre hors de pain et pot', 'to cut off bread and duty.'"[1] The mundium of the father was no longer reconcilable with the child's economic independence, with the "possession of his own hearth and pot"; for so long as the son dwelt in the father's house, so long as he "brought home honest ('keusches') bread", or "ate jam and bread of his parents", use could be made of the most important of paternal powers, the usufruct of the child's property. A partition of property was therefore the decisive fact. In some legal systems this had the effect of terminating the paternal power even when the son continued to live in his father's house after the partition, — that is, as the master of his own estate, distinct from that of his father; or when he returned to his father's house after an absence of some duration (defined by statute). In this case, the formality of a judicial decree of partition was always necessary.

The daughters were always freed of paternal power by marriage, so long as sex-guardianship existed only by marriage, since they, by force of law, were subject to the mundium of their husbands.

Even after the Reception both these grounds of the old Germanic law for the determination of paternal power everywhere retained their force. Although later legal theory designated them "emancipatio Saxonica" (sometimes, "tacita"), this was not because they embodied particularistic Saxon law, for the old rules in part retained authority especially long in South Germany, — in Switzerland down into the 1800 s, and in places even until 1881; "but because it was a custom in North Germany, from the 1500 s onward, to designate as 'Saxon' any rule of native law that had maintained itself against the Roman."[2] Against this deeply rooted legal idea that Justinian institute of emancipation, which could only result from an express release ("Entlassung") from the father's power, made little headway in practice, notwithstanding its recognition by the common law and its adoption in most of the modern codes. The difficulty of proving in any particular case an actual economic separation and independence of households resulted more and more in modern times (earliest of all in the Austrian and the Moravian law) in a treatment of paternal power as terminating upon the child's attainment of majority, or upon the declaration of his majority.

[1] *Brunner*, "Grundzüge" (5th ed.), 229.
[2] *Heusler*, "Institutionen", II, 441.

This rule has been adopted also by the Civil Code (§ 1626), following the example of the Austrian Code, the Code Civil, the Zürich Code, and other statutes. Even as respects minor daughters the paternal power, therefore, no longer terminates with their marriage; only the parent's duty of personal care then ceases. That the Swiss Civil Code (§ 14), on the other hand, has again adopted the old rule "marriage give mundium", has already been remarked (*supra*, p. 59). The parents retain, however, a claim to household services against a child, even though adult, that remains in the paternal household. And just as the older law recognized destruction of the father's power, aside from the ordinary reasons for its termination, in certain extraordinary cases, — by forfeiture, by enfranchisement, by adoption, — so in the present law there exist similar provisions.

(II) **The Legal Relation of the Mother to her Children. Parental Power.** — According to the view of the Germanic and German law, the powers that inured to the father over his children were, as already mentioned, consequences of the mundium that belonged solely to him as house-lord. Inasmuch as the wife, exactly like the children, was subjected to this mundium, instead of sharing control over them with the husband, it followed that there existed in the older Germanic law only a paternal, but no maternal and consequently no parental, power over children. True, the mother was not "as respects the power of the father a child among children, but enjoyed a motherly authority over her own children that the law could not ignore":[1] she was bound to coöperate in the physical and spiritual care and education of the child, and the chief responsibility in this connection doubtless rested, ordinarily, upon her. Doubtless there also existed on the child's part a duty of obedience to both parents. For these reasons the French legal sources and law-books spoke of the "garde ou mainburnie" exercised over the children by "père et mère."[2] That this personal authority of the mother did not affect the paternal power, however, follows from the fact that the last word was everywhere conceded to the father. This is also seen, for example, in the Roman law, which did not regard the "patria potestas" as in any way lessened by the power of training and caring for the child that was conferred, under some circumstances, upon the mother, to the exclusion of the father.[3] It is

[1] *Huber*, "Schw. Privatrecht", IV, 486.

[2] *v. Salis*, "Beitrag zur Geschichte der väterlichen Gewalt nach altfranzösischem Recht", in Z². R. G., VII (1887), 137–204.

[3] *Ibid.*, 153.

possible that the Germanic law, had it continued to develop without interference, might have evolved from the powers enjoyed by the mother (the right of training, the right of consenting to marriage, of naming a guardian, and particularly, the right of guardianship accorded by some statutes to a widow) a parental power inuring more or less equally to both the parents; just as this happened (notably as regards the marital community of goods) in the customary law in France, where it received statutory recognition in the Code Civil. In Germany, however, such a development was temporarily prevented by the reception of the Roman law, which had no place for a parental power. The demand made by the law of nature for a transformation of paternal into parental power was acceded to in but few statutes, and even in these only as respects particular rules. The Civil Code introduced for the first time a fundamental improvement in this matter upon the earlier law: it has created a unitary institute of parental power. This parental power, whose substantive content is of traditional extent, although subject as already remarked to governmental oversight and coöperation, inheres primarily in the father; the final word, also, always rests with him. But the mother is empowered as well as he to fulfill independently the duty of personal care; above all, in case of incapacity on the father's part or when his parental power is suspended the full parental powers pass to the mother (save that in these cases, and also when the father is placed under guardianship as a dipsomaniac, the right of usufruct in the child's estate remains in the father); and finally, a widow completely takes the father's place, so that the appointment of a guardian is unnecessary. The wife, however, may be given an adviser ("Beistand"); and a widow, in case of remarriage, loses her powers, except those of personal care for the child. With these rules of the German law the Swiss Civil Code substantially agrees.

§ 98. **Legitimate Children: (2) Relations under the Property Law. (I) During the Continuance of Paternal or Parental Power.** (1) *The older law.* — In the view of Germanic law children were always regarded as capable of holding property, and although all the earnings from the labor of a child living in its father's household may possibly have inured, originally and generally, to the father, nevertheless children could acquire separate property by inheritance, particularly from the side of their mother, or by gift. Naturally, however, the relations of children under the property law were shaped by the father's right of mundium, just as they were adjusted on the other hand to the conception of the household estate. The property of the children, like that of the wife, constituted a portion of the household property, and therefore the father received in it also, by virtue of his household mundium, a seisin "in mundium"; that is, a right of usufruct and a duty of administration. But it remained the property of the child. The father was bound to deliver it to the child unlessened in value upon the termination of his paternal authority; and consequently with indemnity for any diminution of value resulting through his fault. The rule prevailed, "children's property shall neither increase nor diminish", "children's property is 'iron' property."[1] Inasmuch as the father held a seisin "in mundium" he disposed freely of the child's chattels, just as a husband disposed of the chattels brought with his wife in marriage under the system of administrative community. On the other hand, in alienations of and charges upon the child's lands he was subject to the owner's assent in the same way as in the law of marital estates; save that the child could give such assent only after attaining majority, so that the effectiveness of such dispositive acts remained, until then, doubtful. The child itself was unable to make legally binding dispositions of its property. On the contrary, any juristic acts it concluded were ineffective as against the father, exactly as were those of his wife. Moreover, the child itself was not bound by juristic acts concluded during its minority; it could revoke them within a year after attaining majority, and only when this was not done did they acquire definitive efficacy. The father, therefore, held the property of his child absolutely in his hand; all the profits therefrom went to him; so long as his paternal power existed he need deliver nothing from the child's estate.[2] In contrast to and as the reverse side of this far-reaching right, in which the nature of the paternal mundium, as a power existing in the father's interest, was most evidently expressed, the old law recognized the rule that the father was liable with his own property for torts committed by the child (*supra*, pp. 530, 580), and could not free himself from such liability, under principles generally recognized, except by abandonment of the child, — that is, by driving him from the household community. It was only in the course of the Middle Ages that the majority of legal systems restricted this paternal liability to the child's property then in the father's hands. With these strong rights of the father in his children's property there was united (a point particularly important in the

[1] Ssp., I. 11. [2] *Heusler*, "Institutionen", II, 448.

early medieval law) a right of the children in the property of their father; a right which, as already remarked, continued to be influenced by the old collective right of the household, — constituted of father and children, — in the family-property. The children, in whom was "honored the future continuation of the house",[1] were conceded rights in expectancy and of co-alienation (*supra*, pp. 304 *et seq.*) that limited in their interest the ownership of the father, and assured to them rights of coöperation in dispositions of the household lands. Later, it is true, this strong right in expectancy became less prominent, being limited to a claim for maintenance in the paternal house and, in default of independent property, a proper outfit ("Ausstattung") on departure therefrom.

(2) *The modern law.* — After the Reception the Roman theory of the "peculium" was united with the native traditional institutes, and that property whose usufruct and administration continued to be accorded to the father in the old manner was regarded as a "peculium adventicium regulare", *i.e.* as property subject to restrictions ("unfree" property); whereas the property that was recognized as the child's own ("free") was treated in accordance with the rules of the "peculium castrense" or "quasi castrense." In this process, however, the concept of the "free" property was generally considerably enlarged, — for example by the Prussian "Landrecht" and the Code Civil, — so as to include in it all acquests which a child living under mundium owed to occupancy of a public office, or to scientific or artistic dignities or activities, to its skill, to its industry, or to other services for other people. This concept the present Civil Code has also adopted (§ 1651), adding to its content things intended exclusively for the child's personal use (§ 1650), so that now its "free" property corresponds to the wife's reserved-estate under that system of marital property in which the husband enjoys the profits and administration. In this "free" property, — which modern legal systems, including the Civil Code, have treated as including the Roman "peculium adventicium irregulare" (property that is given to the child upon condition that the father shall hold powers of administration only), — the father enjoys no usufruct; although he does hold a tutelary administrative power, exercisable solely in the child's interest, so long as it is a minor. The father administers and collects the profits from all its other property, — that is, from the "unfree" property, — under the same rules as the hus-

[1] *Huber*, "Schw. Privatrecht", IV, 488.

band collects them from property brought with the wife in marriage, although with greater freedom. Nevertheless, under the present Civil Code he requires for the performance of certain juristic acts an authorization from the Guardians' Court. Under modern legal systems, including the Civil Code, only the child's own property is liable for its debts. The Swiss Civil Code gives even greater freedom to the parents, and defines in somewhat different manner the amount of the child's-property that is excepted from the parent's usufruct (§ 290 *et seq.*).

(II) **After Termination of Paternal or Parental Authority.** — When the father's authority was terminated by the son's departure from the paternal household or by the daughter's marriage, there resulted, of course, a complete severance of the property relations theretofore existing between father and child. If, on the other hand, death terminated the father's paternal power or the parental power of the mother, it was not always necessary that a partition of the property should be made between the surviving parent and the children. On the contrary it was a widely prevalent custom to continue the old community household, such parent and the children remaining in possession "in undivided seisin" ("ungeteilte Were").

The legal nature of this relation depended upon the particular system of marital property that had prevailed during the marriage; it has therefore already been discussed in the sections relative to that subject (pp. 628 *et seq.*, 649 *et seq.*, 641 *et seq.*).

Beyond a reference to that discussion we will here only repeat that wherever an administrative community prevailed it was commonly continued after the father's death in the form of the widow's "Beisitz", either until the children's departure from the parental household or so long as the widow lived or remained unmarried. This rule was especially common in the Ostphalian law. Later, there was frequently recognized (for example in the revision of 1856 of the Lübeck law) a so-called "community of goods mortis causa", by virtue of which the property that had been physically united in the hands of the husband was left, after the death of either parent, in the hands of the survivor as a legally unitary mass. The majority of modern statutes, however, — as for example the Prussian "Allgemeines Landrecht," — abandoned the community mortis causa, and treated the marital property as always dissolved under these circumstances; the children inherited the property of the dead parent, while a surviving husband received a statutory portion. The Civil Code treats every right of the father in the maternal heritage (" Muttererbe ") and every right of the mother in the paternal heritage (" Vatererbe) as extinguished by the child's majority; nevertheless the usufruct in such heritable portion of the children may be given to the surviving spouse by a disposition mortis causa.

Wherever there existed a community of goods, the older law, as has been already mentioned, adopted various measures in order to postpone a partition of the property between the surviving spouse and the children after the death of one consort. Either such survivor was given a possession involving rights of administration and usufruct in the children's shares, — the collective property being apportioned in ideal shares between such survivor and the children (this rule prevailed, for example, in East and West Prussia and in Posen); or, where the entire marital estate passed into the sole ownership of the surviving spouse, the children were given an interest in property " sequestered " (" verfangen ") for them, at least to the extent of an irrevocable right in expectancy to the whole future heritage of their surviving parent (so, for example in Hamburg and Bremen); or, finally, in place of a continued marital community proper (" communio bonorum prorogata "), which could only exist following a general community of goods, the relationship of collective hand that existed between the parents was regarded as still existing between the surviving parent and the children. This last rule had earlier existed (for example) in Westphalia, and also in Hamburg and Bremen in favor of the widow, and has been adopted by the Civil Code. It recognizes the continued marital community as arising by rule of law after a general community of goods in default of other agreement, and in place of a chattel community as a result of special agreement.

All community relations between a surviving parent and children terminated, save with rare exceptions, in case of remarriage by the surviving spouse. Nevertheless, it was necessary under some circumstances to prolong the community through such a second marriage, particularly on account of the difficulties associated with partition, and the prejudices that might result therefrom. Herein lay the reason for the appearance of the institute of " single proles " (" Einkindschaft ", " unio prolium ") [1] which was developed most especially in the territory of the Franconian law between the 1200 s and the end of the 1600 s.

According to the older Franconian law, agreements creating a

[1] *Herbert Meyer*, "Die Einkindschaft" (1900).

"single proles" (single family), which usually were made before or immediately after the contraction of a second marriage, were contracts between the children of the first marriage on the one hand, and the spouses in the new marriage on the other hand, by which the children of the first marriage (the "Vorkinder", "first children") were made the legal equals, in herital rights, of the expectant children of the second marriage (the "Nachkinder", "second children"). The first children renounced their rights in the property of the first marriage in favor of the spouses of the second marriage, and in exchange were substituted by the latter in the position of actual children of the second marriage. They thus acquired precisely the same rights, as respected property and inheritance, as the second children. The children of the two marriages being thus treated as issue of one marriage for these purposes, there naturally soon came to attach to the contract consequences purely of family-law. It was only later that this institute of "Einkindschaft" came to be regarded as strictly a contract of inheritance, and therefore again restricted to effects within the law of inheritance; an irrevocable contractual right of inheritance being conceded, however, to the children. Inasmuch, however, as injustice might be involved in the equalization under the inheritance law of children of different marriages, and the contract might be a risky one either for the first or (possibly) for the second children, it frequently happened that in case the first children brought property into the second marriage, — and probably also as regards the second children, — that a corresponding advance was agreed upon, which was paid to them by way of preference in the future division of the inheritance. The Prussian Landrecht made such an advance to the first children obligatory. This institute of "Einkindschaft" ended with the death of all the children, with their departure from the parental household, with the death or divorce of the spouses, and doubtless also when the second marriage proved childless, or when one of the spouses died and the other remarried. Its termination could also be demanded by the children and ordered by the court. "Einkindschaft" continued to exist after the Reception, particularly in the regions of Franconian law, but also for example in Hamburg, Bremen, Lübeck, and Riga, and was regulated by many modern statutes (for example in the Prussian "Landrecht"), but in recent times it has more and more tended to disappear from legal life. Many legal systems were unfriendly to it, some, as for example the Austrian Code, denying it legal validity; and others, as for example the Baden Territorial Law, abolishing it. The Civil Code, like the Code Civil, has abrogated it by failure to adopt it; since 1900 agreements creating "Einkindschaften" are invalid. The Swiss Civil Code has taken the same attitude.

§ 99. **Illegitimate Children.**[1] (I) *The older Germanic Law.* — Inasmuch as the ancient Germanic law recognized, in addition to marriage, other forms of sexual union, illegitimate birth was by no means a ground at that time for lessened legal capacity or for a lower social status. Children begotten outside wedlock by a free man upon a free woman during notorious cohabitation, that is in concubinage (so-called "Kebs-", "Friedelehe"; Spanish "barraganía"), were known, — because they were not born of a marriage publicly contracted by betrothal and espousal, and as contrasted with "full-born" (Lombard "fulboran") children, — by names such as Old High G. "hornung", Old Norse "hornungr" (= begotten in a corner, "Winkelkind"), Mid. High G. "banchart" ("Bankert", begotten on a bench); among which the Germanic-Romanistic (or Celtic?) word "bastard" seems to belong. Inasmuch as the father held no mundium over a free concubine for lack of betrothal, the children that were begotten upon her were not subject to his mundium but to that of her guardian. Nevertheless, if they had been recognized by their father they belonged to his household and his family, along with his legitimate children. Illegitimate sons of this class, therefore, because of their belonging to the household, had herital rights in their father's property along with his legitimate sons; at least limited rights. In consequence of this principle the illegitimate offspring of rulers, both among the North and East Germans and also among the Franks, shared with the legitimate succession to the throne, and inherited the royal treasure and the royal lands. So late as under the Merovingians royal bastards were the exact equals, under the inheritance law, of the king's legitimate sons. But among the Carolingians their position became less favorable: as against legitimate sons they no longer had any right of succession to the throne, being entitled to succeed only in default of legitimate issue. It was by virtue of this right that Arnulf ascended the

[1] *Wilda*, "Von den unecht geborenen Kindern", in Z. deut. R., XV (1855), 237 *et seq.*; *Maurer*, "Die unächte Geburt nach altnordischem Rechte", in K. Bayer. Akad. Wiss., Sitz. Ber., 1883, 3–86; *Brunner*, "Die uneheliche Vaterschaft in den ältesten germanischen Rechten", in Z². R. G., XVII (1896), 1–32; *W. Sickel*, "Das Thronfolgerecht der unehelichen Karolinger", in Z². R. G., XXIV (1903), 110–147; *Rietschel*, art. "Bastard" and "Beischläferin", in *Hoop's* "Reallexikon", I (1912), 174–177, 214–216. *Cf. Fehr*, *op. cit.* (p. 657 *supra*), 261 *et seq.*

German throne. The best known proof of the fact that it also existed among the West Frankish Normans is the case of William the Conqueror; the nickname "Bastard" always clung to him. However, as already mentioned, it was always a precondition to the inclusion of recognized bastards in the household of their father, and to their claims of inheritance, that they should have been born of a free woman. Under most legal systems the children of an unfree woman were likewise unfree, in accord with the principle that "the child follows the worser hand", and a right of inheritance was totally unknown among unfree persons. Among the West Germanic racial branches the position of concubinal children was most favorable among the Lombards. They there enjoyed, equally with legitimate children, statutory rights of inheritance and rights in expectancy, a share in the betrothal gift paid upon the marriage of their legitimate and illegitimate sisters, and likewise in the wergeld payable for a brother who was killed; and they were counted among the oath-helpers of the family. According to the Lombard law, indeed, a son begotten in concubinage upon a man's own slave seems to have been regarded as personally free if his father recognized him, without its being necessary that he be first formally emancipated.[1]

The position of illegitimate children became worse under the influence of the Church. This was a necessary consequence of its battle against every form of sexual intercourse outside of marriage. "The ill-will of the Church toward illegitimate children went hand in hand with its condemnation of sexual unions between men and women outside of marriage. Just as the Church's 'horror sanguinis' led eventually to the base status of the executioner, so its 'horror adulterii' had the effect of lessening the legal capacity of illegitimate children."[2] True, there were long preserved many traces of their one-time membership in the family; as for example the right enjoyed by bastards among the old imperial nobility, down into the 1700 s, to bear the name and arms of their father. But the legal status in which unfree illegitimate children had earlier found themselves was now attributed to all persons of illegitimate birth. "As respects the capacity of bastards to inherit, or at least of bastards who died without descendants born in wedlock, French, Dutch, and German legal systems of Frankish origin start from the principle, 'neque genus neque gentem habent bas-

[1] *Brunner*, art. just cited, 15.
[2] *Brunner* in Z². R. G., XXIII (1902), 199 *et seq.*

tardi', 'bâtards n'ont point de ligne.'"[1] With few exceptions, all illegitimate children, including those born free, lost their right to inherit from their father, retaining merely a right of inheritance from their unmarried mothers, — this, however, always. At a time when a passive herital capacity was accorded to all unfree persons, or when unfreedom itself had become a waning institution, this rule was justified by the argument that although illegitimacy of birth might be recognized as against the father no child could be a concubinal child in relation to its mother: "nul n'est bâtard de sa mère", "ten oensien van de moeders syn onechte kinderen soo veel als echten." By far the most unfavorable position of illegitimate children was that assigned them in the Saxon law. Under this they lost even the right of inheriting from their mother and her kindred; moreover, they could transmit property to their children only, who were likewise regarded as illegitimate under all circumstances.[2] Only a few systems of town-law treated illegitimate children better. A few other legal systems (for example the Frisian) made it possible for the father to make gifts to his illegitimate child without the necessity of the heir's consent, — so-called "bastard gifts" ("Hornungsgaben"). With the right of inheritance there also disappeared the right of succession to the throne. The Sachsenspiegel lays down the rule that a German king must have been born free and in wedlock.[3] The consequences of blemished civic honor, to which all persons of illegitimate birth were subject, have already been discussed under the law of persons (*supra*, pp. 106 *et seq.*). At the same time, medieval legal theory required of the father that he should show regard for and contribute to the support of his illegitimate children, notwithstanding that they neither belonged to his household nor were subject to his paternal authority.

(II) **The Modern Development.** — That the status of illegitimates improved only very slowly in modern times has already been remarked in the Section (§ 14) dealing with civic honor. The stigma of illegitimate birth was strongly emphasized down into the 1700 s; it is only since then that the institute of "baseness" ("Anrüchigkeit") has disappeared. On the other hand there has persisted down into the present law the rule that an illegitimate child is not legally related to its father; a rule to which an exception has been made by the Civil Code (§ 1310, 3)

[1] *Brunner* in same, XVII, 26 *et seq.*
[2] Lüneburg Reformation of 1577, V, 2.
[3] Ssp., III, 54, § 3.

solely in the case of kinship as an impediment to marriage. In further development of the view of the Germanic law already mentioned, and in agreement with the rules of the Canon law, there has been given to the child, as against its father, a claim for maintenance; but no more. Most legal systems conceded this right not only when the father had voluntarily admitted his paternity but also when he had been adjudged the father in an action for the establishment of paternity. This action was available equally to the child and to the mother. On the other hand the Code Civil prohibited any investigation of paternity ("la recherche de la paternité est interdite"), so that under it a compulsory contribution of the father for the maintenance of the child was impossible.[1] The Civil Code has adopted the first named (so-called "paternity") principle; it recognizes an action for the proof of paternity, but it gives this to the child alone (§ 1708). The illegitimate child, therefore, belonged and still belongs, as respects legal relations, to its mother only. It bears her name and occupies in relation to her family, under the present Civil Code (§ 1805), as formerly under the common law and the Saxon law, the position of a legitimate child; whereas other legal systems, as for example the Prussian "Landrecht", regarded such a child merely as related to its mother in some sort of kinship. The mother was generally conceded a right to care personally for the child. This right the Civil Code also accords her,—but not parental power. For this reason it was always necessary to name a guardian for an illegitimate child, the mother's father being given first preference for this position. The Civil Code, following the Prussian statute of guardianship, declares the maternal grandfather to be the statutory guardian of the child; but it also permits the appointment of the mother herself as guardian in preference to her father (§ 1778). The provisions of the Swiss Civil Code (§§ 302–327) vary in many respects from those of the German. Among other things, in order to protect the mother and child to the utmost possible extent as against one who begets children out of wedlock, it gives the mother an action to establish paternity (§ 307); further, it adopts the so-called "recognition with consequence of status" ("Zusprechung mit Standesfolge"), which gives to the illegitimate child, even as against the father, certain rights of kinship, namely those of "bastard kinship" (§ 325).

[1] The rule of the Code Civil has recently been abolished in France also by a statute of November 16, 1912.

(III) **Legitimation.**[1] — The favorable position of illegitimate children in the old law explains the fact that a legitimation of bastard children was unknown, speaking generally, to the West Germans. Among the Norwegians there was known an adoption of an illegitimate child into the family of its father in the form of "Schuhsteigung" ("stepping in the shoes"). It was only the aggravation of their situation that set in in the Middle Ages that made necessary the removal in individual cases of the stigma of their birth. For this reason, the Popes adopted in the 1100 s the "legitimatio per rescriptum principis" of the Roman law as "legitimatio per rescriptum papae", and this example was soon followed by the secular princes. Frederick I first adopted the institute in Germany; as a matter of fact he seems to have transplanted it to Germany from his Sicilian chancery. Later rulers exercised it in part personally; in part they conveyed the right of its exercise to others; in particular it was regarded as a right regularly included in the office of the Palatinate counts. After the Reception the institute attained the authority of common law (without the adoption of the restrictive provisions of the Justinian law), although no uniform regulation of the institute was attained.

Legitimation by subsequent marriage, which was taken over from the Roman into the canon law by Pope Alexander III, was first carried to Germany toward the end of the Middle Ages. Up to that time there was there recognized only the adoption of children born before marriage; which was realized by the parents' taking them under their mantle or girdle before the altar, — "mantle"-children. In the eyes of Germanic law, marriage without this formality effected no change in the legal position of children born before wedlock.[2] The Roman-canonic institute encountered at first in Germany an exceedingly hostile reception; which was only altered when it became, with the general Reception, a part of the common law. The grant to legitimized children of full powers under the law of family and inheritance decidedly contradicted the popular consciousness of law, particularly in North Germany.

Most of the modern codes regulated the institute of legitimation in both its forms; not, however, the Code Civil or the Baden Territorial Law. The present Civil Code recognizes both legiti-

[1] *Kogler*, "Die legitimatio per rescriptum von Justinian bis zum Tode Karls IV" (1904), and "Beiträge zur Geschichte der Rezeption und der Symbolik der legitimatio per subsequens matrimonium", in Z². R. G., XXV (1904), 94–171.

[2] Ssp., I. 36, § 1, *supra*, p. 660.

mation by subsequent marriage and that by declaration of legitimacy. But in the case of the latter, although it permits the child to acquire the rights of legitimate issue as against the father, it does not recognize any relations whatever of kinship between such legitimized child and the other children or kindred of the father. A child legitimized in this manner acquires a right of inheritance only from the father, as does the latter from the child. On the other hand, the status of a legitimate child is accorded without reservation and without qualification to one legitimized by a subsequent marriage. The Swiss Civil Code has abandoned this double treatment: children legitimized by judicial decree, together with their own legitimate descendants, are made by it the equals of legitimate issue in relation to both their father and mother (§ 263).

CHAPTER XIII

GUARDIANSHIP

§ 100. **General Development of the Law of Guardianship.**[1] (I) **The Older Law.**—The German law of guardianship had its historical and conceptual origin in the Germanic mundium. Guardianship was, in its essence, mundium over those free persons lacking in self-mundium ("Selbmündigkeit") who were subject neither to the husband's mundium as wives nor to the father's mundium as children. There were subjected to it, therefore, above all, fatherless minors, unmarried adult women, and lunatics. Like the mundium of the family law it was purely a household power. In the most primitive times it may have belonged to the head of the "greater" family, but in that period back to which we are led by the oldest form of the Germanic-German law of guardianship the subject of this tutelary power was the sib: the oldest form of the German law of guardianship was a collective guardianship of the sib. This is the form that still prevails in unmodified form in the Anglo-Saxon legal sources; and similarly in the monuments of North Germanic law, particularly the Norwegian and Danish, the participation of the sib in guardianship still clearly appears. The entire body of adult independent male members of the sib held over such dependent members

[1] *Kraut*, "Die Vormundschaft nach den Grundsätzen des deutschen Rechts" (3 vols., 1835, 1847, 1859); *Rive*, "Geschichte der deutschen Vormundschaft", Vol. I: "Die Vormundschaft im Rechte der Germanen" (1862), Vol. 2 (in 2 parts): "Die Vormundschaft im deutschen Recht des Mittelalters" (1866, 1875).

"their protecting, and if the interest of the family required their powerful, hand."[1] In this connection it was already the custom at an early date to entrust the administration of the guardianship to the nearest male blood-relative of the ward in the male line, that is to the nearest sword-kinsman ("Schwertmagen", sword-friend). From this custom there was developed in most legal systems of the Frankish Empire the rule that such sword-kinsman was the guardian ("Vormund"; Old High G. "foramundo", "gêrhabe"; Old G. "muntporo", "muntwalt"; Mid. G. "momber") of the ward by virtue of birth. Thus the sib's collective guardianship was displaced by the individual guardianship of the nearest sword-kinsman; in place of the guardian chosen ("gekoren") by the sib there appeared the "born" ("geborener") guardian, and the sib's collective guardianship shrank to a supervisory guardianship.[2] But even where this was the case traces of the old conditions were preserved, in some cases until far into the Middle Ages, notably in the legal systems derived from the Salic Law and in the Frisian law. Such were: a coöperation of the kindred in the marriage of wards; the power of the sib, under certain preconditions, — for example when the "born" guardian by birth proved incapable, — to choose another guardian; participation in the administration of the ward's property, for which purpose a committee was frequently created; etc. In the main, however, the question who was entitled in any particular case to assume the guardianship was henceforth decided according to the rules governing the right of inheritance. Like this, the right of guardianship was a family right resting upon blood relationship and determined by the degree thereof. After the death of the house-lord the nearest sword-kinsman exercised household-power over minor sons and unmarried daughters, or else he took such dependent kindred into his own household. It followed from the nature of guardianship that it implied precisely the same powers that were possessed by the house-lord over his wife and children; and that, like every other mundium, it originally emphasized the rights of the mundium-holder far more than his duties; that is, it did not so much burden him with duties as procure him benefits, at least when the ward possessed property. The guardian was, indeed, bound to maintain the ward, and in case of necessity care for his or her education; and in the case of daughters to provide them also with dowry ("Ausstattung") upon

[1] *v. Amira*, "Recht" (2d ed.), 107.
[2] *Brunner*, "Geschichte", I (2d ed.), 125.

their marriage. But just as the father had a seisin "in mundium" of the property of his child, so the guardian had such in the property of his ward, and it secured him the entire economic returns thereof. Indeed, the dominant idea in the institute of guardianship, also, may originally have been not the interest of the ward, but that of the guardian; a point that has been emphasized in particular by Heusler.[1] In fact, such dependent members of the sib, if they had been left to themselves, would have endangered the interests of the sib or of their own next kinsman. The sib, and afterward the nearest male kinsman, took them under mundium in order that the sib property might not be squandered by them, in order that their defective litigant capacity might not prejudice them in a way that must also cause damage to the kindred, in order that the claims arising from rights to bots might not remain unsatisfied; and so on.

It was decisive of the development of guardianship, however, that its old character as mundium was abandoned, and that the care of the ward was made its essential element. With this change its legal character was fundamentally altered. The beginnings of this transformation went back to early times. The sib's oversight over the administration of the guardian it appointed, — an oversight which as already mentioned continued in many places, as to certain powers of the kindred, even after the disappearance of collective guardianship proper,—restricted the guardian, and protected the ward against his arbitrary will. The idea involved in this first received effective application when the State itself assumed that position of a superior guardian which was once occupied by the sib. This task it earliest assumed among the Lombards, where the judge was appealed to for official intervention in lawsuits, in alienations of property, and in partitions of the heritage of minor wards. In the Frankish Empire the king proclaimed the care of widows and orphans to be, at least theoretically, a duty of the State. In the Frankish capitularies it was repeatedly impressed upon the judges to dispose first of all lawsuits involving such weak persons; the king, as their protector, claimed the right to assume the mundium over them himself, in default of kindred. For a time, however, things went no further in Germany than "these theoretical rudiments."[2] It was only in the Middle Ages that such oversight by the state was developed;

[1] *Heusler*, "Institutionen", II, 480 *et seq.*
[2] *Brunner*, "Grundzüge" (5th ed.), 231; "Geschichte", I (2d ed.), 331 *et seq.*

first of all in the cities, where the magistrates were in many places regarded as the guardians of orphans, — as the "protecteurs et suprêmes tuteurs des orphelins", as they were called for example in Bruges. Consequently, the first modern ordinances of guardianship were issued in the cities. Under these, special official boards were created at an early period for the control of guardians; for example, in Nuremberg as early as 1399 two salaried city officials, who entered all matters relating to guardians in a special book, and who were to apply in difficult questions to the town council, — but in other cases to keep silence! In the 1500 s improvements were introduced upon the basis of a report by a deputation that had been sent to Venice to study the practices there observed. Similar boards and deputations subordinate to the town council were created in Basel, Leipzig, Vienna, Görlitz, and elsewhere.

This encroachment of public authority upon an institution that was originally purely one of the family law could not have been possible if the idea that the exercise of guardianship was a family right, resting upon blood relationship and therefore ordinarily irrevocable, had not lost vitality, owing to the increasing loosening and dissolution, particularly in the cities, of the old and formerly firmly solidary family groups. Precisely as inheritance based upon the will of the testator was introduced to supplement the statutory herital rights of kinsmen, in consequence of the recognition of dispositive freedom mortis causa (*infra*, §§ 110 *et seq.*), so from the 1200 s onward it became possible and usual for the father, instead of entrusting his children to the mundium of the sword-kinsman next thereto entitled, the "born" guardian, to name in his last testament a guardian of his free choice. And when the possibility of a "chosen" guardian had once been recognized, the choice and appointment of a guardian could also, in case of necessity, be left to the court. Thus, in addition to the guardian appointed by virtue of his kinship, — which the Sachsenspiegel still recognizes as everywhere the ordinary rule,[1] — and the guardian chosen by the father, there appeared the guardian appointed by public authority; and soon judicial confirmation was also required for the guardian nominated by the father.

That, of course, altered the legal position of the guardian. He was no longer the holder of the mundium, who was entitled to enjoy without an accounting the profits of the ward's estate of which he held the seisin. He became a representative of the ward under the oversight of public authorities, responsible to public officials

[1] Ssp., I. 23, § 1.

for proper administration. A usufruct in the ward's estate no longer existed in his favor, — and naturally he was therefore no longer under the duty of maintaining the ward from his own property. The assumption of the guardianship was no longer a right, but a duty; no citizen could decline it, he could only claim in return for the burden of his stewardship a reward ("Vogtslohn").

(II) **The Modern Development.** — Although these new views concerning guardianship took root only with difficulty in many regions, especially where the old solidarity of the family was longest preserved, they nevertheless everywhere became established in the second half of the Middle Ages, thus giving to the institute of guardianship in Germany a form essentially uniform. This suffered no principal change as a result of the reception of the Roman law. The rules of the latter, although partly divergent, exercised only a slight influence. Although its distinction between the tutelage of "impuberes" ("Unmündige") and the curatorship of "minores" ("Minderjährige") was in some places adopted in connection with the two periods of infancy of the Saxon law (*supra*, p. 57), there was here involved nothing more than a superficial adaptation, which was later again done away with; in the main, guardianship of all minors ("Minderjährige") was treated as a uniform institute.

Further, guardianship preserved down into recent times the characteristics of public office which it acquired during the second half of the Middle Ages; but with this difference, that this official character was enforced with increasing strictness, — alike as respects the mode in which the guardianship was established, the obligation to assume it, its far-reaching control by public authorities, and their coöperation in all important transactions as well as in the definition of the guardian's rights and duties. The institute of guardianship was one of the few matters of private law with which the legislation of the old Empire concerned itself; but because of the hesitancy felt in interfering with the private law, its regulation was left to the imperial police ordinances, and was established by these only in broad outline ("Reichspolizeiordnungen" of 1548 and 1577), — so that in this field, also, of the law the most important changes were effected by State legislation. It was precisely through this that the authority of government was ever more extended. Whereas under the older codes the guardian so bound actually to conduct the administration, and required the assent of the Supervisory Guardians' Board ("Obervormundschaftsbehörde"), — or of the town council in cities, and in modern States generally that of a court,—only in more important matters, the administration of the office eventually passed, under many legal systems, to the public authorities themselves, the guardian becoming a mere agent of the Guardians' Board, and so bound simply to execute what the latter ordered. The Guardians' Board acquired most nearly unlimited power in Prussia and Austria, reflecting the omnipotence of an absolute police-state. The Prussian "Landrecht" therefore characterized the ward, logically enough, as "committed to the care of the State", and the guardian as the "procurator of the State", who was appointed to exercise in its behalf the "oversight and care" incumbent upon it.

But in the course of the 1800 s, a reaction took place against this exaggeration of public ("Ober-") guardianship. The guardian has again been entrusted, as formerly, with the independent conduct of his office, though under the oversight and direction of the Guardians' Board, whose assent he requires in certain important matters. This was the theory, notably, of the Prussian Ordinance of Wardship of July 5, 1875, the most important of modern statutes regulating guardianship, whose principles have passed with slight changes into the present Civil Code.

The idea of oversight over the guardian was embodied in the French law in a peculiar institute distinct from the German institute of public guardianship. In it, the old powers of the sib as a guardian were continued in the institute of the family-council. The Code Civil, following the older law, introduced this as an obligatory legal institute, assigning to it those duties which fell in Germany to the Court of Wards ("Vormundschaftsgericht"). Consisting of a mediator ("peace-judge") and six of the ward's blood or marriage relatives, it was empowered to name the guardian in default of provision by the parents, control the administration of the estate, and give or refuse assent to important acts. The Prussian Ordinance of Wardship adopted the family-council of the French law, but it permitted the organization of this only when the father or the mother of the ward so ordered, or when the kindred or the guardian so requested. Under that ordinance it consisted of a judge ("guardianship-judge") and at most five other male persons; it possessed all the rights and duties of the Court of Wards. The Prussian statute prescribed in addition that in important matters, either at the instance of the parties or of his own motion, the judge should hear the opinions of three near kinsmen of the ward. These provisions of the Prussian law have been adopted with slight changes in the present Civil Code. The Swiss Civil Code also permits the transfer to a family-council of the authority and duties, and the responsibility, of a Guardians' Board.

(III) **Cases in which Guardianship Existed.** — From the earliest times guardianship over infants, *i.e.* guardianship on account of age, has been the most important part of the law of guardianship. The principles of this were mainly developed within that institute. The further discussion of this section may be restricted to it. Though guardianship of adult unmarried women, — sex-guardianship, — played an important rôle in earlier times and in part down almost to the present day, and has disappeared from the law only in its latest form, this has already been discussed under the law of persons (*supra*, pp. 61 *et seq.*).

Other forms of guardianship over adults had and have less importance. It has also already been mentioned that under earlier legal systems persons physically infirm could be placed under guardianship (*supra*, p. 71); and the Civil Code (§ 1910) has permitted the institution of a curatorship for them, equally with the deaf, the blind, and the dumb, who are incapable of attending to their own affairs. In the same way (as has also been remarked *supra*, p. 71) persons of unsound mind were subjected to guardianship under the older Germanic law; never, however, under modern law unless a formal interdiction has been decreed. Guardianship of persons of unsound mind has likewise been regulated by the Civil Code in essential agreement with the pre-existing law. In general this is controlled by the principles of age-guardianship; a few deviations, — for example, the rule that it can be terminated only as the result of an official abrogation of the interdiction, — are evidently necessary.

Further (as already mentioned above, pp. 72 *et seq.*), after the Reception and as a development of the Roman "cura absentis", the care of the property of a missing person was brought within the concept of guardianship, being designated a "cura anomala." This existed from the 1500 s to the 1700 s as an institute of the common law, but was thereafter abandoned in consequence of a closer adherence to the Roman law. The Civil Code has abolished it, introducing in its place a curatorship of missing persons.

Finally, as respects the guardianship of prodigals reference may likewise be made to earlier remarks (pp. 72 *et seq.*). The Civil Code has added to this a guardianship of dipsomaniacs. The Swiss Civil Code, going still further, has provided that a wicked course of life may be a ground for guardianship; and also that every adult person shall be under guardianship who has been condemned for one year or longer to imprisonment.

(IV) **Curatorship.** — A so-called "curatorship" ("Pflegschaft") was introduced for certain cases in the modern law, to some extent in imitation of the Roman law. This was distinguished from guardianship ("Vormundschaft") by the fact that the curator did not, like the guardian, take the place of a father or mother, but was appointed alongside of the subject of paternal or parental authority or of a guardian in order to care for particular affairs of a child or of a ward. Such curatorships, however, were also recognized for unborn persons ("curator ventris"); for possible future issue not yet even conceived, as *e.g.* possible future heirs of fideicommissa; for unspecified heirs ("curator heraditatis iacentis"); for missing persons; for infirm persons; etc. The present Civil Code, following the example of the Prussian law, has retained the curatorship as an independent institute along with guardianship. Under it a curator is nominated for any person subject to parental power or to guardianship whenever the parents or the guardians are actually prevented from or legally incapable of attending to any duties of their office; also, for a person who is physically or mentally infirm, and consequently unable to attend to his own affairs; for a missing person (the Prussian law treated the care of deaf-mutes and missing persons as guardianship, and not curatorship); for a child conceived but not yet born; for an uncertain and unknown person in interest; and for property collected by public subscription for a temporary purpose (§§ 1909–1910). Curatorship is regulated, in general, by the rules of guardianship. The curatorship of the German law corresponds substantially to the assessorship ("Beistandschaft", "curatelle") of the Swiss Civil Code.

§ 101. **Guardianship of Minors.**[1] (I) **Preconditions.** — Incapacity for self-mundium ("Unmündigkeit") and default of paternal authority necessitate the establishment of a guardianship on account of age.

The most important facts respecting the limits of infancy, — of "impuberes" ("Unmündige") and "minores" ("Minderjährige"), which coincided in the view of the old Germanic law, — have already been stated (*supra*, pp. 54 *et seq.*). Default of paternal authority was and is, of course, ordinarily due to the father's death; but even in his lifetime a guardianship may become neces-

[1] See *Fehr, op. cit.* (657 *supra*), 167 *et seq.*

sary. This was the case under medieval law when the father was actually incapable of caring for the child, — for example, because he entered a cloister and thereby became dead to the world (*supra*, pp. 48 *et seq.*); and also, according to some legal systems, when the mother had died, although sometimes only when the widower contracted a second marriage. In the modern law all such rules have been done away with. A case requiring guardianship ordinarily arises during the lifetime of the father only when paternal authority is in abeyance for legal reasons, or has been abolished, or when the child has been released from parental authority without having attained the rights of majority. On the other hand, in the earliest legal systems, wherever an exceptional parental power was accorded to the mother the father's death did not necessitate a guardianship. Inasmuch as the Civil Code, as already mentioned (*supra*, pp. 664 *et seq.*), has recognized in theory a parental power in the mother, a case requiring the appointment of a guardian exists only when both parents have died or when they have lost their parental power, which in the case of a surviving mother occurs as a consequence of her remarriage. Cases are rare in which guardianship is established during the continuance of parental power because the parent does not have a right to represent the child in personal and property relations.

(II) **Appointment and Personal Qualifications of the Guardian.** (1) *The appointment.* — As already mentioned, after collective guardianship by the sib had become less prominent in the older law, the guardianship passed without legal formalities to the nearest sword-kinsman, as the "born" guardian of the ward. If he was ineligible ("untauglich") to assume it, the next kinsman became eligible. Although other kindred, particularly the maternal sib, were later made eligible, and although many legal systems (as for example the West Gothic, Burgundian, and Bavarian) even conceded the administration of wardship to the mother or to other female kindred of the ward, this striking fact is perhaps explainable, where no Roman influences can be assumed, as an after-effect of the old collective guardianship: the sib, to whom the power was even elsewhere reserved of naming the guardian, chose such women because it expected of them the most careful attention to the interests of the ward.[1] But for the most

[1] *Ernst Mayer* relies upon this and other phenomena to develop the theory that the Germanic law of guardianship was based upon a system of relationship that rested on conditions of mother-right: "Der germanische Uradel", in Z². R. G., XXXII (1911), 41–228, particularly 174 *et seq.*

part the sword-kinsman of the ward remained the usual guardian,[1] and though later legal systems left to the widow the personal care of the children this was no more guardianship than it was a form of parental authority.

From the 1200 s onward, however, despite much resistance, and owing somewhat to the influence of the Roman law, the above-mentioned practice spread of appointing the guardian by testamentary disposition or contract subject to judicial confirmation. This naturally led to appointment by the public authorities, usually by a judge, as another usual manner in which the relation was legally established. Such public authorities were expected to interfere, above all, in cases where kinsmen were lacking and an appointment by the father failed, in order that no one might be without a guardian. The judge, so soon as he learned of such a case of necessity, was bound to appoint a guardian of his own motion. In some legal systems a further step was taken as early as in the Middle Ages; namely that even a guardian named by the father and a statutory guardian were required, before entering upon their duties, to apply to the public authorities in order that these might instate them in their office. With this change the statutory right was transformed into a mere claim to special consideration by the judge in making an appointment. The imperial Police Ordinances of 1548 and 1577 provided in quite general terms that every guardian should receive his administrative powers by virtue of a governmental decree, and should take oath at the same time to perform his duties faithfully and conscientiously. The complement to this right of the court to nominate was its power to remove an unfaithful guardian (a " balemund "). This rule has also been retained in all modern statutes regulating guardianship. In every case of guardianship that arose an official appointment of the guardian was held necessary. The judge, — whom kinsmen, registrars of personal status, priests, and communal officials were bound to aid in this function, — was required to inquire whether a fit guardian had been appointed by due and lawful act of the parents, or whether in default of such disposition there was available a proper kinsman lawfully entitled to the guardianship. In case there was, the judge was legally obligated to appoint such person as guardian (" confirmatio iuris Germanici "); otherwise he was bound to find a suitable person of his own motion, and to entrust the guardianship to such person. These three situations, which were already defined in the medieval

[1] *Brunner*, "Geschichte", I (2d ed.), 124 *et seq.*

law, corresponded superficially to the three ways in which guardians were appointed under the Roman law; and they were therefore designated in the common law as "tutelae testamentariae", "legitimae" and "dativae"; inexactly, to be sure, inasmuch as a judicial appointment was required in all cases, so that all guardians were in this sense "tutores dativi." The statutory qualifications for appointment based upon kinship came in time to be of very little consequence.

Under the Civil Code the guardianship must be offered (aside from persons appointed by the parents) to the paternal and maternal grandfathers of the ward; an unwedded mother, though she may be named the guardian of her child, has no legal claim to such appointment. In other respects the judge is free in his choice; he should, however, hear the Orphans' Court of the commune, consult in the first place the blood and marriage relations of the ward, and show regard for its religious faith. Every guardian is appointed by the Court of Wards subject to an obligation of faithful and conscientious conduct of his office. This obligation is imposed by a hand-clasp, instead of by oath.

Totally different is its regulation in the Swiss Civil Code. While this recognizes no legal claims at all to the guardianship, it does provide in quite general terms that unless there are weighty reasons to the contrary the Guardians' Board shall, in choosing, give preference to a proper near kinsman or to the husband of the ward; and also shall respect a designation made by the ward, or by his father or mother (§§ 380–381). If there is available for guardian neither a suitable kinsman nor a trustworthy designated guardian by such persons, then an official guardianship must be created.

(2) *Several guardians. Supervisory guardianship.* — As contrasted with the ordinary case in which one guardian is appointed, many earlier legal systems (for example, the law of Lübeck, Bremen, Hamburg, Frankfort, Vienna, and also the Frisian law) sought to realize greater security by the appointment of several guardians; in which case, in addition to the paternal kindred, either the maternal kindred were given recognition or guardians were appointed by public authority along with the guardian entitled under statute. This practice was retained in many modern legal systems also, particularly in the wardship ordinances of the Hansa cities. On the other hand, under the Saxon Code and the Prussian Wardship Ordinance the court ordinarily appointed only one guardian, whether for a single ward or for several brothers

and sisters. The present Civil Code has adopted the same rule, although permitting the appointment of several guardians in certain cases.

Special guardianships existed in the Middle Ages to care for special legal relationships; notably, "guardianships" of lands located abroad and of fiefs. These are found also in the modern period, and even to-day, particularly in the dynastic statutes of the greater nobility where they are usual when a minor member of a family has possessions in different (and to-day, consequently, foreign) States.

Inasmuch as the institute of public ("Ober-") guardianship was less developed in the French than in the German law, the Code Civil, — following the example of the Roman law in recognizing a division of the guardian's obligations between a "tutor gerens" and a supervisory "tutor honorarius", — provided for the appointment, in addition to the ordinary guardian, of a supervisory guardian ("tuteur subrogé", "Gegenvormund") to oversee the former, coöperate in certain actions, and, particularly, intervene whenever the interests of the ward conflicted with those of the principal guardian. The Prussian Wardship Ordinance and the present Civil Code (but not the Swiss Civil Code) have taken over from the French law this institute of supervisory guardianship. Under them, however, the appointment of a supervisory guardian is obligatory only when the guardianship involves the administration of an estate of some size, and provided the guardianship is not entrusted to several guardians. In other cases the appointment of a supervisory guardian rests in the court's discretion. The parents may forbid such appointment in connection with a guardian named by them.

(3) *Personal qualifications of guardians.* — Although it was originally left to the free judgment of the sib, and later to the discretion of a judge, to decide whether a person entitled by virtue of blood relationship to the office of guardian possessed the other requisite qualities, nevertheless certain general principles always prevailed, and are found expressly stated in the sources. No women, no aliens, no priests, no outlaws, no persons of weak mind, and no enemies of the ward's father, might be appointed guardian. Further, equality of birth and of course self-mundium were required of a guardian. After the Reception the incapacity of women was generally retained. A sole exception, which existed in many medieval legal systems, was made in favor of the mother and grandmother. The capacity of women as guardians was

first unqualifiedly recognized in the present Civil Code, but even now a married woman can be appointed guardian only with the consent of her husband. Further, there have been retained or newly introduced the incapacity of persons incapable of juristic acts and persons themselves under the mundium of others, of bankrupts during bankruptcy, of persons who have been deprived of rights of civic honor (save in cases involving the guardianship of descendants), and finally of persons barred from appointment by the testamentary disposition of the ward's father or mother. The ineligibility of priests and civil officials, which depends upon the rules of the Canon law and the administrative law of the particular States, still exists to the extent that they can be appointed only after the grant of a permission, if such be prescribed by the State law. The incapacity of aliens is no longer important as respects Germans since the establishment of a general German citizenship by Article 2 of the Imperial Constitution. Difference of religious faith is no longer ground of incapacity; but, as already mentioned (*supra*, p. 687), according to the express injunction of the Civil Code regard should be shown to the religious faith of the ward.

(4) *Grounds for refusal of a guardianship.* — When guardianship had ceased to be exclusively a right of blood relatives and its official character had become predominant, its acceptance came to be regarded as a general duty of citizens; and only very definite reasons have since then been held justification for a declination of the office. In the medieval sources, however, any uniform rule is still lacking. After the Reception many legal systems adopted the excuses recognized by the Roman law, — so, for example the Prussian Territorial Law and the Prussian Wardship Ordinance. Others, on the other hand, left the decision of any particular case to the judge's free discretion. Generally speaking, advanced age (formerly, until seventy years; in modern legal systems and under the Civil Code sixty years), a large number of minor children, occupancy of public office, and military service were recognized as sufficient reasons for a declination. A right of declination was also given to one of whom security was required. The same right is enjoyed under the Civil Code by a person who is already charged with two guardianships or curatorships, and by one to whom the proper discharge of the office would either be impossible or an especial burden because of sickness, infirmity, or distance from his residence; also by anyone who is offered the office of a co- (" Mit- ") guardian, and by every woman (§ 1786). The provisions of the Swiss Civil Code (§ 383) are similar.

(III) **Legal Position of the Guardian.** (1) *The older law.* — By virtue of the mundium he possessed under the family law, the "born" guardian of the older law had power over the ward's person, and a seisin "in mundium" of the ward's property. His legal relation to the ward corresponded exactly to that of a father to his son. In personal relations he had the powers that resulted from house-lordship; and therefore, originally, a power of punishment, although this became restricted so early as the Frankish period to a brother acting as guardian. In relations under the property law the guardian was not, as might be supposed, a mere administrator of the ward's estate, but took "the ward's property into his power by virtue of his legal claim to the seisin thereof that resulted from his appointment to the guardianship."[1] For this reason he brought an action in his own name, and not in the name of the ward, against any third person who refused to deliver objects belonging to the estate.[2] Of course his seisin of the estate also gave the guardian its profits; but he could not dispose of the substance, for here again the rule prevailed that the property of a person subjected to the mundium of another who assumed control thereover, must remain unimpaired: "the ward's estate shall neither grow nor lessen."[3] Upon the termination of his administration the guardian, when he delivered the property to the ward upon the latter's attainment of majority, was bound to inform him of its condition; but so long as he acted as guardian he was neither bound to make an accounting nor to give security. The ward's chattels he could freely dispose of; but his dispositions of lands were subject to a right of revocation by the ward on attainment of majority. Choses in action of the ward were enforced by the guardian in his own name; but if he made debts the guardian was not bound to recognize them, no more than a father was bound to recognize those of his child or a husband those of his wife. The guardian was liable for damages that resulted from the ward's torts — originally with his own property, later in the first instance with the estate of the ward[4] — no matter in what form the action might be brought against him. Conversely, in case of wrongs ("Missetaten") against the ward the guardian was regarded as the person injured, and he was entitled to collect the bôt; although this was restricted already in the Frankish period to injuries that affected his rights as guardian. Thus, there resulted from these rules as early as the first half of the

[1] *Heusler*, "Institutionen", II, 495.
[2] "Lex Burgundionum", 85, 2.
[3] Ssp., I, 11.
[4] Ssp., II, 65, § 1.

Middle Ages a judicial representation of the ward by his guardian in criminal cases. Under the private law, however, the guardian could not appear as the ward's representative so long as litigant representation was unknown therein. The guardian could not obligate and bind the ward in any manner; he could conclude legal transactions and contract debts in his own name only. If he paid such debts with the property of the ward during the continuance of the wardship he was liable to his ward for their amount; if he alienated lands the ward could, upon attaining majority and within a year and a day, demand them back from any holder. Conversely, the ward, because of his imperfect capacity of action, could not conclude juristic acts that were of final binding effect upon himself; like a child under its father's mundium ("Hauskind") he had the right of revocation upon attaining majority. Consequently, all transactions which he entered into remained provisional, as did alienations of lands made by the guardian.

(2) *The modern law.* — Whereas the old usufructuary form of guardianship still prevailed in the Sachsenspiegel and the Saxon town law, — in addition to which it also persisted in localities under the medieval Franconian law and in the Frisian-Holland law, — there appeared from the 1300 s onward (in other words before the Reception), first in South Germany and then in North Germany, in the place of these principles derived from the mundium of the family-law, and in necessary connection with the transformation of that mundium into an obligation to care for the ward under public oversight, a new regulation of the legal relation between guardian and ward whose essence may be characterized as "a bare administration of an estate, subject to an obligation of accounting."[1] The recognition of powers of attorney in the private law made it possible to make the guardian a representative of the ward capable of declarations legally binding upon the latter. This advance was doubtless rendered necessary by the disadvantages of the provisional character of transactions relative to the ward's estate, just referred to. Henceforth, either the guardian was permitted to act in the ward's name or the ward was permitted to act personally with the consent of his guardian.[2] The latter power was first utilized in alienations of his lands, but later also in contracting liabilities required by his necessities. In the old law there could be no question such

[1] *Schröder*, "Lehrbuch" (5th ed.), 768.
[2] "Rechtsbuch nach Distinktionen", I, 44, 4.

as this, "because the guardian was obliged to maintain the children at his own expense so long as it served his purposes to retain them under his mundium";[1] the profits of the ward's property furnishing him the necessary means. With the disappearance of this usufructuary right the necessity arose of making it possible for the guardian to assume obligations in the interest of the children. But when the guardian could conclude juristic acts that could obligate the child, albeit only with the latter's consent, the ward's property was "delivered much more unreservedly to the guardian than formerly, and was much more exposed to danger from his dishonest or unconsidered actions";[2] since the rule had formerly prevailed, without qualification, that "the ward's estate shall neither grow nor lessen." For this reason the usufruct of the ward's property was taken from the guardian, first from the "chosen" guardian and then from the one appointed by court, and later from the "born" guardian; and his administration was subjected to an oversight by public officials which constantly became more stringent. In alienations of the ward's lands he was bound to reinvest the proceeds in other lands, to safeguard the ward's moneys in ways precisely defined, to render a yearly account of his administration, and also, frequently, to give security and deliver an inventory.

The theory that was thus attained in the later Middle Ages, and which was sanctioned by the Imperial Police Ordinances of the 1500 s, was preserved and in details elaborated in modern times. In this process, however, the influence of the Roman law remained merely superficial. Under the modern law of guardianship the guardian is a representative of the ward and acts in the latter's place, although his coöperation is necessary in certain cases. It is only exceptionally, — for example in the case of purely beneficial acts, — that the ward can make, quite independently, a legally effective declaration of will. The present Civil Code also gives the guardian powers of representation which entitle and obligate him to care for the person and the property of the ward. In a considerable number of cases he requires the assent of the Court of Wards, but here again it is the guardian who acts and not the official body. By virtue of his personal duty to care for the ward's spiritual and physical welfare the guardian is bound to attend to its education and support. His representative duty still appears in criminal cases only in so far as he is bound to defend

[1] *Heusler*, "Institutionen", II, 505.
[2] *Heusler*, *op. cit.*, 506.

the ward, and to bring actions for offenses ("Antragsdelikten") committed against him. In civil cases he is bound to conduct the suit in the ward's place and to take oath for the ward when the latter is incapable of taking such. The care of the ward's estate involves the obligation of making an inventory. As respects his administration of the property, the statutes and the Civil Code lay down a great number of rules that must be strictly observed; in many cases official ratification is required. He is forbidden to make use of the property in any case for his own benefit. He must render an account, annually or at shorter intervals of time; and though the father can release from this obligation a guardian by him appointed, he must nevertheless, under the present Civil Code, hand in at definite intervals of time a report upon the condition of the estate. Upon the termination of the guardianship the property must be redelivered, and a final accounting made which must be audited by the state.

(IV) **Termination.** — The guardianship is ordinarily ended by the ward's attainment of majority, but also of course by the latter's death; likewise by a declaration of death, by adoption, and by a resubjection to parental authority. In earlier legal systems the acceptance of public office, admission to the bar, and also marriage, involved the termination of guardianship; but these effects have not been recognized by the existing law, save that in the case of female minors the guardianship is restricted after their marriage (provided this takes place with the consent of the guardian) to representation in their personal affairs, administration of the wife's reserved estate, and the giving of consent to such of the husband's administrative acts as require the wife's assent. In Switzerland marriage frees every person from the mundium of others (*supra*, p. 59).

As in the medieval law, so also in the more modern law and in that of the present day a judge may remove an unfaithful guardian. Such a removal may be made at the instance of the ward or of the court's own motion; the guardian may be deprived, in the same way, of particular rights. The position of a guardian, as such, is of course also forfeited by one who himself becomes incapable of legal action, or who loses the other qualifications necessary for the conduct of his office. The guardian may also resign his office when conditions intervene that would originally have entitled him to decline the assumption of the office.

BOOK V. THE LAW OF INHERITANCE

Chapter XIV

GENERAL PRINCIPLES

§ 102. **Origin and Nature of the Germanic Rules of Succession.**[1] (I) **The Historical Point of Departure.** — However obscure and controverted may be the beginnings and the oldest rules of the Germanic law of inheritance, it seems nevertheless permissible to assume that the historical source of the Germanic, and therefore also of the German, law of inheritance was the original collective ownership of the kindred; a source of which the later law never lost consciousness. For the Germanic law of inheritance, in its essence, has always remained primarily a law of blood inheritance, a family-law. This family-law, however, developed only gradually into a law of inheritance. The origin and development of this branch of the law were closely and necessarily associated with the origin and development of private property. Therefore rights of inheritance in chattels became possible earlier than rights of inheritance in lands. So long as all property, aside from the few objects of personal use such as weapons and clothes that were buried with their owner (*infra*, §§ 107, 110), remained in the collective ownership of the sib group, the individual members of this—that is the heads of its households ("Hausväter")—receiving a mere right of usufruct in the lands and chattels (the cattle and agricultural implements) of the sib, the latter's collective ownership was unaffected by the death of any individual member. It was merely the persons of the members entitled to

[1] *Siegel*, "Das deutsche Erbrecht nach den Rechtsquellen des Mittelalters" (1853).

such usufructuary rights that changed. Later, the chattels passed from the sib's collective ownership into the ownership of its individual members; not, however, at first, nor for a long time, into their unqualified individual ("Sonder-") ownership. On the contrary, they became the collective property of the families. The house-lord and the heirs united within his household and under his household authority, — that is, his sons, — constituted as respects the household estate a property community, in which the father as the representative of this community was indeed accorded a primary right, above all the usufruct of the household property, but the sons were also recognized as co-holders of rights with him, and were conceded an irrevocable right of succession. If the father died they took his place, thus making actual a right already existing in his lifetime. "The restraint upon the alienation of the sequestered estate ('Gebundenheit der Verfangenschaft') was now transformed into a rule of succession;"[1] they could thenceforth partition the family estate among themselves, or remain upon it in undivided community as owners in collective hand (*supra*, pp. 139 *et seq.*). Within the family, therefore, there were in fact originally involved no rights of inheritance whatever, but merely a "community succession" in the collective property; or as the case might be, if one of the sons died during the lifetime of the father or after his death but during a continued community, a question of benefit of survivorship ("Anwachsung").[2] The principles of ownership in collective hand, and not any special principles of inheritance law, determined the legal nature of the family-property and its partition among the members of the family. If no members of the household community in collective hand who were capable of ownership were living, the household property reverted to the sib. But so soon as this had ceased to be a holder of collective rights, either as to all property or at least as to movables, there became necessary some definite rule of partition; that is, a necessity arose for a law of inheritance in the strict sense. A similar development later took place in the case of lands in so far as these also passed into the ownership of the sib families, becoming a part, and indeed the most important portion, of the household property. With the disintegration of the house communities the rules that had been developed in the inheritance law to define the gradation and interrelation of the more remote kindred became controlling also within the limits of the household;

[1] *Huber*, "Schw. Privatrecht", IV, 541.
[2] *Heusler*, "Institutionen", II, 528.

but the original distinction between the household, constituted of the parents and the children, and the sib, which was entitled to inherit only after the household, led to a differentiation and variant treatment of a "narrower" and a "wider" circle of heirs that long remained of great importance in the definition of the legal order of succession (*infra*, § 107).

(II) **Customary, and Contractual and Testamentary Succession** ("gesetzliches und gewillkürtes Erbrecht"). — It is clear from the above that the right of inheritance was not substantially different either in origin or (at first) in nature from other family rights; precisely like them, it was based upon blood relationship. The blood relatives had the right and the duty to exercise guardianship over the dependent members of the sib; as the "sib of the dead hand", they received the wergeld paid for a fellow sibman who was killed and divided it among themselves, and were liable as "the sib of the living hand" for the raising of a wergeld payable by one of their fellows; they were bound to support an impoverished blood friend in need of help; similarly they were entitled by virtue of blood relationship to the estate set free by the death of one of their fellows. It is noteworthy that in the legal theory of the later Middle Ages the duty of support and the right of inheritance were still regarded as mutually necessary complements, — if the estate fell to the commune or to the State for default of kindred entitled to inherit, this was justified by the fact that the duty of support, the burden of caring for the poor,[1] was borne, in the last analysis, by these public groups. True, this connection later became less evident. The right of support retained in the modern law, — in the Civil Code only as between kindred in direct line, but in the Swiss Civil Code also as between brothers and sisters, — has been set apart from the rules of the inheritance law as an independent institute restricted within a narrow range of application. Who was heir depended, therefore, in the view of the Germanic and the early German law solely upon blood. The inheritance law was withdrawn, in principle, from arbitrary regulation by man: "solus deus heredem facere potest, non homo." "Whatever the dying man lets fall must fall into the hand of the heir appointed by nature."[2] There existed in the beginning no voluntary succession of inheritance, but a customary ("gesetzliche") succession only. The deceased was unable to alter by his juristic act the rights of his kindred, or to

[1] *Rietschel*, art. "Armenrecht" in *Hoop's* "Reallexikon", I (1911), 1234.
[2] *Heusler*, "Institutionen", II, 531.

create in the place of that fixed by nature another order of succession; for the right enjoyed by the legal heirs was in principle irrevocable. This fundamental characteristic of the old Germanic law of inheritance, which was observed and described by Tacitus with entire correctness, seemed to him to stand in striking contrast to the Roman law,[1] which based the order of inheritance primarily upon a testator's will, and only secondarily upon rights of intestate succession enjoyed by the kindred. But the strict Germanic order of succession was in entire agreement with the general conditions and views of a primitive and unindividualistic society. Moreover, it was identical with the original institutions of other Indo-Germanic races. Thus, for example, among the Greeks the testament was first introduced by Solon; and even among the Romans the testamentary freedom that is recognized in the Twelve Tables, — which moreover was very much restricted, as regarded form, by the coöperation of the "comitiae", — seems to have applied (as has recently been shown) only to non-mancipable chattels, that is to say to "pecunia" ("Kleinvieh": calves, sheep, goats, and pigs); and not yet to the "res mancipi" (slaves and "Grossvieh": cattle proper) that made up the most important part of the estate.[2] In time the German law, developing rudiments that were already present within it at an early day, came to recognize a voluntary testamentary order of succession (*infra*, §§ 110–13), which was determined either by contract or by unilateral testamentary disposition of the deceased. Nevertheless it may safely be said that despite the equal effect that was conceded in Germany (unlike France) to the testate order of succession, intestate succession resting upon blood relationship remained the rule, testamentary succession being regarded only as a variant system created for a special case; which was expressed in the proverb "wer will wohl und seelig sterben, der lasse sein Gut den rechten Erben" ("he who would die well and blessed should leave his property to the legal heir"). The statutory order of inheritance failed to take effect only when the deceased had concluded a contract or had made a testament otherwise defining the order of succession. The same is true also in the law of the present day. "Our statutory order of succession is no 'order of intestate succession,' and cannot be based upon the presumptive will of the deceased."[3] This view is given clear

[1] "Germania", 20.

[2] *Mitteis*, "Römisches Privatrecht bis auf die Zeit Diokletians", I (1908), 82.

[3] *Gierke* in *Holtzendorff-Kohler*, I, 546.

expression in the arrangement of the Civil Code, which begins its provisions respecting the inheritance law with the statutory order of succession, following this with a regulation of testaments. The Swiss Civil Code proceeds in the same manner.

(III) **Unitary and Segregate Succession.**[1] — As already mentioned, the German law of inheritance was developed independently as respects chattels and lands, and has always preserved certain differences in the order of succession to lands and to chattels although the effect of this distinction was much profounder in the English law, in which it has remained to the present time. This fact shows that the theory of the Roman law in its final form, according to which the heir continued the legal personality of the deceased in the entirety of his legal relations, was originally wholly foreign to Germanic law. While lands and chattels were subjected to a different order of inheritance there could of course be no talk of the idea that "the subjective unity which characterized the property in the hands of the deceased"[2] survived in the person of the heir. In this sense, therefore, the concept of universal succession was foreign to Germanic law, but, as Heusler has shown,[3] in another sense it also recognized a "universal succession." For it is characteristic of and essential to every system of succession "that a complex of property rights and relations passes by virtue of a single title." The heir is substituted in the legal relations that pass to him by the single legal act through which he acquires the heritage, and not by virtue of various acts, each for the transfer of a particular right, which would otherwise be necessary. However, it was not necessary that the entire property should pass to the heirs or to one heir, as was theoretically the case in the Roman law (general succession). Again, when only certain classes of legal relations fall to the heir, as for example only the assets included in the estate and not the obligations, their transfer is effected under the single title of a unitary succession. Again, in the German medieval law the heir had an action against any person who himself claimed to have a right in the heritage or who contested the right of such complainant thereto: namely an action "von erves wegene" ("on account of the heir"), which compelled a defendant who lost the suit to deliver the objects whose possession he had

[1] *Frhr. v. Freytagh-Loringhoven*, "Der Sukzessionsmodus des deutschen Erbrechts" (1908); with which compare *J. Gierke* in Z². R. G., XXX (1909), 426–429.

[2] *Gierke, op. cit.*, 546.

[3] "Institutionen", II, 532 *et seq.*

withheld. This Germanic action for the heritage, like the Roman "hereditatis petitio", can only be explained as a universal succession in the special sense indicated.[1] It may therefore be said that the property falling to the heir passed to him as an objective unity, without regard to the question whether it constituted the entire property of the deceased or only a certain part of that. Consequently, inasmuch as this concept of unitary succession that underlay the Germanic rule of succession by no means required a unitary treatment of the heritage, it was possible to divide this into special ("Sonder-") estates, and to transmit these in different manner to the heirs. This idea received a very elaborate development in medieval law. Not only was the variant treatment of land and chattels under the inheritance law retained, but there were also formed within the one and the other category special masses or complexes of property ("Vermögensinbegriffe") subject to peculiar principles of inheritance. Of real estate, the fief, manorial lands, entailed lands ("Stammgüter"), restricted herital lands ("Erbgüter"), and family fideicommissa were thus subjected to a different rule of succession than the fee ("Eigen") of the Territorial law; and heritable ("Erb-") and purchased ("Kauf-") estates were distinguished (*supra*, p. 167). Among chattels the paraphernalia ("Gerade") and the warrior's accoutrements ("Heergewäte"), particularly, were the objects of special rules of inheritance. The paraphernalia (*supra*, pp. 629, 637), after dissolution of the marriage by death of the wife, passed into the "niece" ("Niftel-") seisin of her nearest female kinswoman. The "Heergewäte" or "Heergeräte" consisted of the military equipment, weapons and charger, which were once buried with the dead warrior in his grave or burned with his body (*infra*, § 110), and were reserved after the dying out of this custom to the son or the nearest sword-kinsman.[2] In the law of Upper Germany, Flanders, Brabant, and Friesland, and especially in the Anglo-Norman and French laws, there was also developed from the reversionary rights ("Wiederkehrrecht", *supra*, p. 628) common in the older law, — by virtue of which gifts, especially those to one's issue, reverted to the donor upon the donee's death, — an individual right of inheritance by parents in such gifts made by them to their issue ("droit de retour"). This was adopted

[1] "Institutionen" II, 539.

[2] "Lex Angl. et Werin", 31; Ssp., I, 27, § 2; *Klatt*, "Das Heergewäte", in *Beyerle's* "Beiträge", II, 2 (1908). See also *Keutgen* in Vj. Soz. W. G., VIII (1910), 178 *et seq.*; *Brunner*, "Zur Geschichte der ältesten deutschen Erbschaftssteuer" (see *infra*, p. 743), 25 *et seq.*

by the Code Civil.[1] That property which was not set apart under a special rule of succession was designated by the sources as the "heritage" ("Erbe") in the proper sense of the word, — so that the Sachsenspiegel, for example, declares that everything not belonging to the morgive and the paraphernalia of the wife is her heritage.[2] But these special cases of succession were also universal successions in the sense above indicated; namely, successions to masses of property ("Vermögensinbegriffe"), and not merely to specific things. First of all in the cities, and then after the Reception everywhere, the theoretical unity of the entire heritage was established, and the application of the Roman concept of a "universal" succession was thereby made possible in the sense of a "general" succession. At the same time the effects of the older view continued to be felt. For example it was nowhere possible to establish the Roman principle that inheritance must be based either solely upon testamentary succession or solely upon intestate succession. Again, liability for obligations continued to be differently regulated than in the Roman law, for the reason that the idea of a perpetuation in one person of the entire personality of the deceased found no footing. And above all, special rules of succession in particular forms of property were preserved in the regional systems (*infra*, §§ 114–16), and have been in part further developed by statute in very recent times.

§ 103. **Devolution of the Heritage.**[3] (I) **The Older Law.** — Since the heir was freed by the death of the deceased, according to the view of the Germanic law, merely from a limitation upon his powers (inasmuch as he then entered into the *administration* of an estate whose constituent elements had already *belonged* to him in the lifetime of the deceased[4]), and since it was clearly defined by statute *who* was heir by virtue of blood relationship, the heritage was logically regarded as passing to the heir immediately upon the death of the deceased. His acquisition of the estate was not dependent upon an act of will and an expression of will on his part. It was not the heir who must perform a juristic act; the deceased himself, by his death, effected the substitution of the heir in his place. As Brunner has shown,[5] it must be as-

[1] *Brunner*, "Über den germanischen Ursprung des droit de retour", in his "Forschungen" (1894), 676–765.

[2] Ssp., I, 24, § 3.

[3] *Cosack*, "Der Besitz des Erben" (1877); *Behrend*, "Anevang und Erbengewere", in the "Breslauer Festschrift für Beseler" (1885).

[4] *v. Amira*, "Recht", (2d ed.), 108.

[5] In the essay (cited *infra*, p. 740) on the continued life of the dead, 31 *et seq.*, in which it is shown that the primitive Germans, doubtless like

sumed that the deceased was conceived of in Germanic antiquity in a purely materialistic manner as himself active, as himself placing the heir in possession of the heritage by a juristic act that corresponded roughly to the legal formality of "exire" in the conveyance of land (*supra*, p. 242). This view is the explanation of the legal proverb already mentioned *supra* (p. 190), — which though attested only from the 1400 s onward perfectly expressed the primitive ideas here in question, — "der Tote erbt den Lebenden": that is, the dead person makes the living his heir ("erben" used transitively, as in the compound "vererben"). Therefore upon the death of the deceased the seisin of lands included in the estate also passed directly to the heir; a rule which likewise found expression in the French maxim "le mort saisit le vif", the dead seises the living. This was true even when the heir was absent or unknown, and when a third person not entitled thereto was in possession of the heritage. In these cases the lawful heir acquired, if not the physical, at least the ideal seisin of the heritage. There could never be a break in the seisin; "the hand of the deceased, cold and weak in death, let fall the ear of corn, the symbol of his land; but it fell, not to the floor, but into the hand of the heir; it had no time to become lordless."[1] Therefore, when the heir, particularly if he was not seised at the death of the deceased (that is, if he was not "sitting" upon the heritage at the death of the deceased), performed a legal and formal act of taking possession, and when in so doing he caused to be issued a judicial decree instating him in the possession (as was quite a common practice), this did not serve, as might be supposed, to create the seisin, but merely for its visible establishment and the defense of his right as against third parties. If he was prevented from taking possession by an abator who did not contest his right of inheritance but relied upon some special legal title, — as *e.g.* that of a vendee, — then the heir, in case he could not allege a violent dispossession, was obliged to bring an action against him as owner for delivery of possession. On the other hand, if such third person refused delivery because he claimed to be himself the heir, or because he contested the claimant's qualifications as heir, then the latter, relying upon his ideal seisin, brought an action for the inheritance ("von erves wegene"),

many other races in an early stage of civilization, regarded dead persons as subjects of rights and duties. The principles laid down on p. 46 *supra* that physical death was always regarded as the end of capacity for rights must be limited accordingly as respects the oldest period.

[1] *Heusler*, "Institutionen", II, 531.

which secured to him in litigation the preferential status of one enjoying seisin. In some medieval legal systems, particularly in those of the Netherlands, resort was had at the instance of the claimant to the heritage (whose claim must be made within a year and day after the death of the deceased) to a peculiar procedure called the right of "Erbhaus" or "Sterbehaus" (patrimonial-house, death-house). This was preserved in the Netherlands down into the 1800 s. If, namely, the abator refused to deliver the land to the person claiming to be heir, alleging himself to be the heir, then "the bench was erected", that is a session of the court was held, in the very house where the deceased died. Thereupon the claimant to the inheritance, proceeding as in the action of "anefang", that is grasping the door-post in a formal manner prescribed by law, demanded that his seisin be recognized. The court examined summarily the evidence submitted by the parties as heirs, and granted the seisin to that party who was able to produce the better proofs, thereby assuring to him the rôle of defendant in the action for the heritage, and meanwhile the authority to act as heir. If the occupant of the lands opposed no allegation of an independent right as heir to the claimant's demand for instatement in possession, yet wished to deliver them only after due proof of the legitimate heirship of the claimant and upon judicial authority, or if the judge had taken the heritage into his custody (*e.g.* because the heirs were unknown) an instatement of the heir by the court was common, in Germany as elsewhere. This was likewise required to be demanded within a year and a day, since "the death-house remained open" for that period only. Here again the one claiming as heir performed a formal act of taking possession "boven an dem dorstele und neden an der swellen" ("above on the door, and below on the threshold"); [1] at the same time he was required to give security "for the unconditional delivery of the heritage to whatever person might later present himself with better title." Thereupon the court instated him in possession. As the formula customary in Basel ran, it set him "in the power and seisin of all the heritage and property which the deceased had left at Basel and in the Holy Roman Empire." [2] Such judicial instatement ("Einsetzung") in possession was originally usual only in special cases that required the seisin to be established in a legally formal manner; but toward the end of the Middle Ages, doubtless under the influence of the Roman law, it became customary in

[1] *Cf. Heusler*, "Institutionen", II, 564. [2] *Ibid.*, 538.

many regions, particularly in South Germany, to entrust the control of the inheritance to the public authorities in all cases, and to prohibit the heir from himself reducing the heritage to possession. The "reformations" of town-law prescribed in general terms a judicial investiture, thereby sacrificing to be sure the Germanic legal principle of the immediate devolution of the inheritance. The heir was forbidden to take possession immediately upon the death of the deceased; he was required to observe, first, the "rest" of the heritage ("Nachlassruhe"). To this regard shown for the decedent and his widow was due the origin of the institute, already mentioned, of the "thirty days." (*supra*, p. 636); which however also inured to the benefit of the heir himself, since he need not until after the expiration of such term make answer to creditors of the deceased, claimants to the estate, or coheirs. On the other hand, the rules already mentioned concerning judicial investiture show that the retaking of possession must happen within a year and a day. After the expiration of such period, — in the case of lands after expiration of thirty-one years and a day, — the heir lost his right under the rule of preclusive prescription, unless he was in a situation of actual necessity. In this case the judge confiscated the property as heirless.[1]

(II) **The Modern Law.** — After the Reception the Roman rules regulating the devolution of the inheritance attained the authority of common law. Under them, a direct acquisition of the title, similar to that of the Germanic law, took place only in the case of children ("sui heredes"), an acceptance of the inheritance by the heir, either express ("hereditatis aditio") or tacit ("pro herede gestio"), being required in other cases. The Romanists were able to secure the rejection of the old Germanic principle by the common law notwithstanding that such rejection directly contradicted the popular sense of right, and some of the older and modern regional systems also abandoned it (for example, the "reformations" of Nuremberg and Frankfort, the Landrecht of Mainz, of Württemberg and of Bavaria, and the Austrian and the Saxon Codes), but many other regional systems retained it, at least to the extent of still regarding the title as passing to the heir directly upon the death of the deceased. These systems were followed by the Prussian "Landrecht" and by a Lübeck statute of 1862, — and this both as to statutory and testamentary succession; whereas the Code Civil retained the Germanic rule

[1] Ssp., I, 28.

only in the case of statutory heirs (the "héritiers légitimes" and the "légataire universel"). On the other hand, most of these same legal systems succumbed to the theory of the Roman law (which attained the authority of common law) that the possession of the heritage could be acquired only directly and not derivatively, inasmuch as they abandoned the direct transfer of possession to the heir and required a special act of taking possession on his part (*supra*, pp. 211 *et seq.*). The Civil Code has followed, in general, the Prussian law, and has thus again given general validity to the old Germanic law: so soon as the owner is dead, the heritage passes by force of law to the heir (§ 1942), and the possession also passes to him without further formalities, and without regard to the question whether or not the heir possess any actual control over the things included in the heritage (§ 857). Therefore, as in the old Germanic law there can now be no estate in abeyance ("ruhende"), and all disputes concerning the interpretation of this one-time institute of the common law have ended. The heir may, however, renounce the heritage that falls to him, provided that he declare within a certain time whether he will refuse or accept it, — that is, whether he will or will not make use of his right to renounce it; acceptance therefore signifies in the present law renunciation of the right to refuse the inheritance. The Swiss Civil Code has established for all Switzerland, for the future, the rule of the Germanic law governing the acquisition of the heritage. This had already existed in most of the German cantons.

Many "reformations" of town-law, and later numerous statutes, required that either in all or at least in certain cases the probate court must intervene in the settlement of the estate by publication of the testament, by delivery of the heritage to the heirs it appointed, and so on; and the modern codes also retained the view that the State is bound to see to the proper transfer of the property. The nature and the extent of such coöperation by the State was, however, variously defined. As contrasted with the Austrian Code, according to which no one might take possession of an estate by his own act but must litigate his right of inheritance in court, the Prussian "Landrecht," the Code Civil, the Saxon and the Zürich Codes were content, generally speaking, to prescribe a judicial "sealing" or division of the heritage only when the heirs were unknown, or missing, or minors, or when a petition was made to that effect; the Code Civil, moreover, provides the same in every case of testamentary succession. The Civil

Code, like the earlier codes, provides for the coöperation of the probate court. Under it (§ 1960) the latter is bound to care for the security of the heritage in case of necessity, — namely when the heir is unknown or when the heritage has not yet been unquestionably accepted; for which purpose it may order the attachment of seals, the deposit of money, commercial paper, and valuables, the preparation of an inventory of the property, the appointment of an administrator, and so on. In other cases it is left to state legislation to regulate in more detail the security of the heritage; save that there is a provision of the imperial law forbidding the testator to prohibit the sealing of the estates (as was permitted, for example, under the Prussian law). The Civil Code has taken over from the Prussian law, also, the voucher or "receipt" of inheritance ("Erbschein"), — unknown to the common, to the Saxon, and to the French law, — which is given to the heir by the probate court in witness of his right to inherit, and which enjoys public faith.

§ 104. **Liability for Obligations of the Deceased.**[1] — (I) **The Older Law.** — Inasmuch as purely personal legal relations are always necessarily non-heritable, and since the idea was unknown to the Germanic law that the legal personality of the deceased was continued in the heir, it necessarily followed that by no means all the legal relations to which the deceased had been a party were continued beyond his death. In particular, there was nothing in the Germanic law to prevent certain obligations from determining upon the death of the deceased. On the other hand, the heir was doubtless liable to some extent, even in the oldest Germanic law, for obligations of the deceased. To what extent this was the case is debatable, and "is a question that can hardly be answered with entire certainty from the sources as respects the earliest period."[2] The provisions of the folk-laws differ from one another. In some of them, — as for example in the Visigothic, Burgundian, and Lombard, — Roman influences are perceptible; most of them refer to liability for wergeld. But, as Heusler has shown,[3]

[1] *Stobbe*, "Über das Eintreten des Erben in die obligatorischen Verhältnisse des Erblassers", in J. B. gem. R., V (1862), 293–349; *Lewis*, "Die Succession des Erben in die Obligation des Erblassers nach deutschen Recht" (1864); *Frhr. v. Freytagh-Loringhoven*, "Die Schuldenhaftung des Erben nach den livländischen Rechtsbüchern", in Z². R. G., XXVII (1906), 92–118; "Beispruchsrecht und Erbenhaftung", in Z². R. G., XXVIII (1907), 69–102; *Rauch*, "Gewährschaftsverhältnis und Erbgang nach älterem deutschen Recht" (*supra*, p. 407), 550 *et seq.*; *Gierke*, "Schuld und Haftung", 90 *et seq.*

[2] *Heusler*, "Institutionen", II, 541.

[3] *Ibid.*, 541 *et seq.*

conclusions concerning other obligation cannot be drawn directly from the treatment of liability for wergeld, because the wergeld was from the beginning a liability of the entire sib or of the next heirs, "inasmuch as such composition was given to avoid the blood-feud, which similarly threatened the entire sib and not alone the killer." As respects the medieval law, the Sachsenspiegel, in a passage which, to be sure, is likewise much debated, gives us the information that certain obligations were regarded as not belonging to the heritage, and therefore as lapsing upon the death of the deceased; and that the heir's liability was limited to the value of the chattels inherited.[1] Purely personal obligations, such as those arising from larceny and robbery, and similarly all delictual obligations, were extinguished by the death of the deceased unless they had already been established and measured by a judgment or by composition. Among contractual obligations only those were heritable for which the deceased had received and left in the heritage a "wederstadinge", to use the expression of the Sachsenspiegel: that is, a value in exchange. By this there may be meant, as Heusler explains,[2] obligations that "have enabled the deceased to leave the heritage and the heirs to receive it in its existing form." In this case the word "wederstadinge" would not have had "the meaning of an actual and demonstrable increase of the inheritance", but that of "an act of performance ('Leistung') which, although no longer present 'in natura', nevertheless has helped to bring the heritage to the heirs in its present form." According to this principle, promises of gifts, promises of alienations, and also gaming debts, were non-heritable; but debts due for loans were heritable. The sources that follow the Sachsenspiegel, — equally those of the group of Magdeburg town-law and the Schwabenspiegel, and the town-laws of South Germany, — no longer recognized the requisite of a "wederstadinge." On the contrary they treated all contractual obligations of the deceased as constituting a portion of the heritage, merely recognizing certain special exceptions to this rule; as for example that of debts that violated the prohibition of usury by containing a promise of interest. That obligations of suretyship were likewise non-heritable under the older law has already been remarked (*supra*, p. 484); their heritable character was recognized only from the second half of the 1200 s onward, and in isolated cases. Now in so far as the heir was held liable for obligations of the deceased, this liability could be enforced under the older law,

[1] Ssp., I, 6, § 2.

[2] *Op. cit.*, 549.

— as this still found expression in the statement of the Sachsenspiegel, — only against the chattels he inherited. This principle was a consequence of the fact that the decedent had been free to dispose of his chattels only, while bound as regarded the lands by the heirs' rights in expectancy and of co-alienation. In fact "the freedom of lands from liability for debts was a necessary principle in the herital system of the old law", and Heusler[1] justly asks what meaning ownership in collective hand by the father and sons could have had "if the father had been able to contract debts that might compel the sons to abandon the estate in order to make them good." With the recedence, however, of the idea of estates limited by the heir's indestructible herital rights ("Erbgut") this rule also disappeared. It still properly found a place in the Sachsenspiegel, which held fast to the above idea and preserved intact the heirs' rights in expectancy and of co-alienation, but it is no longer to be found in the Magdeburg law, in the Deutschenspiegel or the Schwabenspiegel, nor in any of the later sources. In the second half of the Middle Ages, at least in Germany (in France and Belgium the old restriction was longer maintained), the rule held that the heir was liable for the obligations of the deceased with the entire estate, including the land. It was an after-effect of the old idea of the herital estate ("Erbgut") when, in the Lübeck law, the equality of "Kaufeigen" (*supra*, p. 167) was expressly attributed to "Erbgüter", in order that they might be devoted by the heir to the satisfaction of debts already contracted in reliance upon them (*supra*, p. 167). The heir, however, was always liable in theory with the heritage only, and not with his other property; it was only when he incautiously confused the two, or otherwise violated the rights of creditors, that he lost this privilege. On account of this "real" ("sachlich") character of the heir's liability he could free himself from every liability by an abandonment of the heritage to the creditors.

(II) **The Modern Law.** — With the Reception the Roman principle, which was opposed to the Germanic, became established both in the common law and in the regional systems; namely, that the heir became a personal obligor in the place of the deceased, and was therefore liable with his own property beyond the value of the heritage; and from this liability he could only free himself by executing an inventory of the heritage. Only the Saxon Code, which strangely enough clung in this point to the native

[1] *Op. cit.*, 552.

law, and similarly the Lübeck law, provided that the heir should be liable only to the value of the inheritance. The Prussian "Landrecht" also started with the principle of limited liability, but it later abandoned this, recognizing instead an unlimited liability when an heir, after taking possession without "reservation of an inventory", allowed a certain statutory period to elapse without preparing such and depositing it in court. To this extent the preparation of an inventory was here, exactly as in the common and the French law, actually an advantage, since it avoided the increased liability that was otherwise incurred. In the common law it was, further, a debated question whether the heir of a feudal estate ("Benefizialerbe") was liable as in the Justinian law to the amount of the estate, — so that the sum for which execution could be had by the creditors of the deceased against the heir's individual property was limited to the value of the inheritance, — or whether, as was assumed in the prevailing practice, his liability was limited to the specific things inherited, so that the creditors could enforce claims against his private property only so far as the value of such things had passed by the inheritance into his private estate. Some of the regional systems adopted the Roman viewpoint; others, as the Prussian "Landrecht" and the Saxon Code, adopted the milder view of the common-law practice, which was in accord with the Germanic law. The present Civil Code has conformed on the whole to the rule of the Prussian "Landrecht"; in particular, it does not impose upon the heir a liability beyond the value of the heritage; that is, it does not impose an unlimited liability to the extent of his entire separate property. Its complicated provisions have the effect of creating provisionally a loosely defined condition of unlimited but limitable liability, which may be definitively discharged in two ways. In case of the bankruptcy of the decedent's estate and an official administration thereof, and equally in case of a so-called plea of "insolvency" ("Erschöpfung", poverty, or "Unzulänglichkeit", insufficient assets), the heir is liable only to a limited extent. On the other hand, if an inventory period is allowed to the heir and he permits it to pass without presenting an inventory, or if he therein states the condition of the heritage falsely and to the damage of the creditor, he becomes liable without limitation.

§ 105. **Plurality of Heirs.**[1] — (I) **The Older Law.** — Succession by one heir among several of the same degree was unknown to the Germanic law, and equally under the German law the heritage

[1] See *Ernst Mayer*, work cited on pp. 585, 104 *et seq.*

passed to the co-heirs ("Ganerben") collectively; they were regarded as the successors of the decedent by collective right, to the same extent as a single heir. The apportionable rights and obligations included in the heritage also passed to the co-heirs without division. Thus there resulted a community of collective hand between the co-heirs. Indeed, as has already been explained (pp. 139 *et seq.*, 150 *et seq.*, 234 *et seq.*), these co-heir communities constituted one of the most important and most common applications of the principle of collective hand. In accord with that principle, each co-heir had for his part a share in the collective estate, notwithstanding that he could not have disposed thereof alone; on the other hand, he could demand at any moment a severance of the same, since impartibility of the collective estate, indissolubility of the community, was, as already seen, by no means essential to that principle. But just as this freedom of partition led, as is well known, to the greatest political evils in the field of public law, so also it involved great dangers within the private law. For, as is justly said in Freidank's "Bescheidenheit": "Breitiu eigen werdent smal, So man si teilet mit der zal" ("large estates become small if always divided by the number of children"). There existed a partial check upon this tendency, though certainly only a weak one, in that a co-heir's claim for partition could be excluded by contract; more effective was popular custom, which at least among the peasantry clung long and generally to undivided management.

If a partition of the heritage was made, then an old rule, observed particularly in the Saxon law, provided that the older should divide and the younger should choose;[1] because, as Jacob Grimm remarks, "to divide implies the maturer understanding, to choose implies the innocence of youth."[2] If more than two parts were involved resort was usually had to lot. Impartible things, and also lands, were frequently not alienated, but instead abandoned to one of the heirs, who was then bound to compensate the others either by payment of a certain sum of money or by a rent charged upon the land (so-called "Erbegelder", heir-money). To determine the value resort was had to the process of "Setzen zu Gelde"; that is, one of the co-heirs set a price at which he would take over the land or leave it to the other heirs as they might prefer. The one fixing the price was frequently chosen by lot, for example in Hamburg and Lübeck; frequently, however, particular heirs had a preferential right to

[1] Ssp., III, 29, § 2. [2] "Rechtsaltertümer", I, 660.

take lands included in the estate in return for indemnity given to the other co-heirs,—for example, in the case of peasant holdings the sons before the daughters, in the case of the paternal house the youngest, and otherwise the eldest son (*infra*, §§ 115–116). If nobody desired to take over the land it was sold, and the proceeds were divided among the heirs.

In the partition of the heritage, — the actual carrying out of which was ordinarily left to the heirs, although the public authorities came to intervene at an early date, especially when there were minor heirs,—the children were required, from the earliest times, to throw into a hotchpot gifts received by them from the deceased during his lifetime, such property being reckoned against them in the distribution in order to accomplish an equalization. To be sure not all gifts (" Gaben "), — for example, not presents (" Geschenke ") made by the father to a child under his mundium for necessities, such as clothing, weapons, horses;[1] nor the expenses of a daughter's marriage. On the other hand, the " outfit " (" Ausstattung ") that was given to a child when it left the paternal household was the chief among the gifts that must be thrown into the common estate for partition.[2] Of course if a child's rights had been entirely satisfied by such gifts there could be no question of a duty of contribution, since such a child did not share in the partition of the heritage.

(II) **The Modern Law.** — The joint ownership in collective hand which existed between co-heirs under the Germanic law, was displaced in the common law by the Roman co-ownership. Each heir received a fractional part of the specific things included in the estate; contractual claims and debts (" Forderungen und Schulden ") passed without formal division in proportion to the number sharing the heritage. In the same way the French and Saxon law provided that all apportionable rights should be distributed among the co-heirs immediately upon the vesting of the estate; in the impartible portions of the same, on the other hand, they acquired a co-ownership in undivided shares (" nach Bruchteilen "), so that each co-heir could immediately dispose of his share of the individual things included therein. On the other hand the Prussian "Landrecht", as already mentioned (p. 150), regulated the herital community as a community in collective hand, after the manner of the Germanic law. This has been followed by the Civil Code, though to be sure not without recognizing in various respects the principles of community in undivided

[1] Ssp., I, 10.

[2] *Ibid.*, I, 13, § 1.

shares. Thus, in particular, individual objects included in the estate can be disposed of, in accord with the principle of collective hand, only by all of the co-heirs together; whereas alienations of the entire estate can be made independently by each co-heir, in accord with the "quotal" principle, to the extent of his share; only, in the latter case his co-heirs' rights of pre-emption (*supra*, p. 400) restrict his dispositive freedom. As regards creditors and debtors of the decedent's estate, the co-heirs are liable and entitled collectively; on the other hand, as respects their legal relations among themselves during the continuance of the community, the rules of community in undivided shares are applied; so that every co-heir can demand at any time a dissolution of the community. Dissolution may, indeed, under the present law, be prohibited by testamentary disposition of the decedent; but only for a definite period of time defined by statute, and not absolutely, inasmuch as such a disposition becomes ineffective, theoretically, when thirty years have passed since the vesting of the inheritance. In general, actual dissolution is left under the present law to the co-heirs themselves; but the probate court may intervene at their instance, and the deceased also may regulate the dissolution by testamentary disposition. As respects the duty of hotchpot the rules of the Roman institute of "collatio" prevailed in the common law. Here again the Civil Code has followed for the most part the earlier Prussian law, which in substantial agreement with other modern codes and with many special statutes subjected to hotchpot whatever the child had received either as dowry ("Aussteuer") upon marriage, or to set it up in an independent household, trade, or other means of livelihood. But whereas the Prussian law extended the duty of hotchpot to ordinary presents from the decedent when these were lands or invested capital, the Civil Code restricts the duty of hotchpot to such gifts as are made as dowry or "outfit" ("Ausstattung"), and also, provided they exceed an ordinary amount, to gifts that are intended for professional training or for enjoyment as current income. Moreover, the testator can specially provide for the extension or restriction of these rules. Under the Civil Code, as under the earlier law, the duty of hotchpot always affects descendants only; but it applies under the Civil Code, — unlike the Saxon Code, but in agreement with the common and the Prussian law, — not only to statutory but also to testamentary succession, whenever the statutory rules of succession are declared by the testator to be the basis of his dispositions.

Chapter XV

INTESTATE SUCCESSION[1]

§ 106. **System and Degrees of Blood Relationship.** (I) **Stable and Unstable Sibs. Narrower and wider Circles of Kindred.**—In the earliest times the kindred coincided with the solidary agnatic union of the sib (*supra*, pp. 114 *et seq.*). The members of the sib,

[1] *Danz*, "Versuch einer historischen Entwicklung der gemeinrechtlichen Erbfolgeart in Lehen" (1793); *J. Chr. Majer*, "Germaniens Urverfassung" (1798), 82–105, and "Teutsche Erbfolge sowohl überhaupt als insbes. in Lehen und Stammgüter", I (1805; a continuation of the former book), 1–139; *v. Sydow*, "Darstellung des Erbrechts nach dem Sachsenspiegel" (1828); *Siegel*, "Die germanische Verwandschaftsberechnung mit besonderer Beziehung auf die Erbenfolge" (1853); *Wasserschleben*, "Das Prinzip der Successionsordnung nach deutschem, insbesondere sächsischem Recht" (1860); *Homeyer*, "Die Stellung des Sachsenspiegels zur Parentelenordnung" (1860); *Rive*, "Zur Frage nach dem Prinzip der Successionsordnung im germanischen Recht", in J. B. gem. R., VI (1863), 197 *et seq.*; *Wasserschleben*, "Die germanische Verwandt-

that is all persons who were descended from a common male ancestor or " truncal father " (" Stammvater "), were " blood-friends " (" Blutsfreunde ") in consequence of such descent. No other kinship, through wives and mothers, existed. In earliest times marriages may have been customary among the primitive Germans, as among other races, only between members of the same sib (endogamous marriages). But when marriages with women of other sibs had also become common (exogamous marriages) the wives thereby became absolutely isolated from their own

schaftsberechnung, Eine Replik" (1864); *Stobbe*, "Die Erbfolgeordnung nach den Magdeburger Schöffensprüchen", in his "Beiträge", 37–58; *Lewis*, "Zur Lehre von der Successionsordnung des deutschen Rechts", in Krit. Vj. IX (1867), 23 *et seq.*, XIV (1872) *et seq.*, XXII (1875), 400 *et seq.; Brunner*, "Das anglonormannische Erbfolgesystem, Ein Beitrag zur Geschichte der Parentelenordnung" (1869); *Kayser*, "Das Erbrecht nach den Edicten der langobardischen Könige", in Z[1]. R. G., VIII (1869), 466 *et seq.; Wasserschleben*, "Das Prinzip der Erbenfolge nach den älteren deutschen und verwandten Rechten" (1870); *Huber*, "Die schweizerischen Erbrechte in ihrer Entwicklung seit der Ablösung des alten Bundes vom deutschen Reich" (1872); *v. Amira*, "Erbenfolge und Verwandtschaftsgliederung nach den altniederdeutschen Rechten" (1874); *Rosin*, "Commentatio ad titulum legis Salicae LIX, 'de alodis'" (1875); *Gierke*, "Erbrecht und Vicinenrecht im Edict Chilperichs", in Z[1]. R. G., XII (1876), 430 *et seq.; Rosin*, "Der Begriff der Schwertmagen" (1877); *Miller*, "Das langobardische Erbrecht", in Z[1]. R. G., XIII (1878), 68–104; *Brunner*, "Sippe und Wergeld", in Z[2]. R. G., III (1882), 1–87; *Kohler*, "Zur Lehre von der Parentelenordnung" in his "Gesammelte Abhandlungen" (1883), 341–367; "Zwei Studien über das sogenannte Repräsentationsrecht", in same, 367–421; *Pappenheim*, "Zur Erbfolgeordnung des langobardischen Rechts", in Forsch. D. G., XXIII (1883), 616 *et seq.; Schanz*, "Das Erbfolgeprinzip des Sachsenspiegels und des Magdeburger Rechts" (1883); *Schröder*, "Über die Bezeichnung der Spindelmagen in der älteren deutschen Rechtssprache", in Z[2]. R. G., IV (1883), 1–15; *Opet*, "Die erbrechtliche Stellung der Weiber in der Zeit der Volksrechte", no. 25 (1888) of *Gierke's* "Untersuchungen"; *Frommhold*, "Beiträge zur Geschichte der Einzelerbfolge", no. 33 (1889) of *Gierke's* "Untersuchungen"; *Selig*, "Die Erbfolgeordnung des Schwabenspiegels" (1890); *Stutz*, "Das Verwandtschaftsbild des Sachsenspiegels und seine Bedeutung für die sächsische Erbfolgeordnung", no. 34 (1890) of *Gierke's* "Untersuchungen"; *Ficker*, "Untersuchungen zur Erbenfolge der ostgermanischen Rechte" (4 vols. and 2 half-vols., 1891–1904, incomplete); *Heymann*, "Die Grundzüge des gesetzlichen Verwandtenerbrechts nach dem BGB" (1896); *Vinogradoff*, "Geschlecht und Verwandtschaft im altnorwegischen Recht", in Z. Soz. W. G., III (1898), 1–43; *v. Dultzig*, "Das deutsche Grunderbrecht", no. 58 (1899) of *Gierke's* "Untersuchungen"; *Brunner*, "Kritische Bemerkungen zur Geschichte des germanischen Weibererbrechts", in Z[2]. R. G., XXI (1900), 1–19; *Rosen*, "Beiträge zur Lehre von der Parentelenordnung und Verwandtschaftsberechnung nach deutschem und österreichischem, jüdischem und kanonischem Recht", in *Grünhut's* Z. Priv. öff. R. Gegenw., XXVIII (1901), 341–404; *Caillemer*, "Études sur la confiscation et l'administration des successions par les pouvoirs publics au moyen âge" (1901); *Pappenheim* on *Kjer*, "Dansk og langobardisk Arveret" (1901), in Z[2]. R. G., XXII (1901), 356–399; *Gál*, "Der Ausschluss der Aszendenten von der Erbenfolge und das Fallrecht", no. 72 (1904) of *Gierke's* "Untersuchungen"; *Gross*, "Medieval Law of Intestacy", in "Select Essays A. A. L. H.", III, 723 *et seq.; Ernst Mayer, op. cit.* p. 585 *supra*, 104 *et seq.*

kindred (*supra*, p. 589). Therefore the issue of such marriages also remained members of the paternal sib alone. So long as these solidary or stable ("feste") sibs were the rule, the system of blood relationship was simple; it could be determined only by the greater or less distance from the common male ancestor; all blood relations could be arranged in groups of descendants more or less removed from him, and their relation to one another and to such truncal ancestor was easily determined. The matter became more complicated so soon as the maternal kindred also found legal recognition, which was the case from the beginning of historical times onward. Thenceforth children were no longer born merely into the paternal, but also into the maternal kindred; hence they became members of all those sibs into which the paternal and maternal kindred were divided. The sib of the wife became for the next generation the sib of the mother. Thus a division resulted within the solidary agnatic marriage relation.[1] Descent from a common male ancestor was then no longer alone decisive, but instead descent from a particular pair of parents. Each individual no longer belonged merely to that group of fellows who had with him a common ancestor through a male line of ascendants, but had also his own body of paternal and maternal blood relatives to which belonged at the most, along with himself, his brothers and sisters of the full blood. In this sense, to use Ficker's striking expression, the sib "changed" for each individual, or at least for each group of full brothers and sisters. With this step, the concept of blood relationship in the broader sense ("Blutsverwandtschaft"), inclusive both of agnates and cognates, replaced the older and narrower concept which had so designated the agnatic relative only; the unstable ("wechselnde") sib replaced the solidary or stable ("feste") sib.

The blood relatives were known as "friends" ("Freunde", "Holde", "Gesippen", "Gatten", "Gattlinge"); among the West Germans they were also known as "magen" (Old High G. "mâg"). No division within the kindred seems to have existed in the earliest period. Kinship was assumed so far as common blood could be established; a view which long retained vitality, and found expression for example in the legal maxim "the blood of friends boils even though it be but a drop" ("Freundesblut wallt und wenn es auch nur ein Tropfen ist"). On the other hand, most Germanic legal systems introduced divisions within the blood kinship at an early day, from practical considera-

[1] *Vinogradoff*, essay just cited, 42.

tions; although, to be sure, these were everywhere very loosely drawn.

The totality of the blood relatives, — which may be designated the "Magschaft" or blood-friends in the broad sense, as distinguished from the solidary agnatic group of the sib,[1] — was divided into paternal and maternal "Magen"; the former including kindred related through the father and the latter those related through the mother. The expressions "spear" ("Ger-", "Speer-") or "sword" friends, and "spindle" ("Spindel-", "Spill-") or "distaff" ("Kunkel-") friends had another significance. Sword-friends were the male kindred descended in a male line ("agnati masculi"); spindle-friends, on the other hand, were all the female kindred and *also* the male descendants of such. In the case of the "spindle-" friends, therefore, there was a peculiar extension of a name taken from the occupation of women, — and therefore intrinsically intelligible only as applied to them, — to men; a form of speech which has persisted down to the present day in such phrases as "female descendants" ("weibliche Nachkommenschaft")—for example in the Prussian "Landrecht"—as synonymous with "female line" ("weibliche Linie"). Moreover, the old legal terminology frequently applied the expressions "sword", "spear" ("lancea") and "spindle" ("Spindel", "Spinne", "fusus") to designate alike a male or female individual and the entire body of sword or spindle friends.[2]

Within the blood-friends ("Magschaft") in the broader sense, those persons who belonged to the same house-community constituted a narrower and especially close circle, the "Busen" ("fathum"; *supra*, p. 661). This included son and daughter, father and mother, brother and sister, — the "six hands of the sib" as they were called in the Frisian sources. This closer union and differentiation of the "family" in the narrowest sense, as distinguished from the wider circle of kindred, was a consequence of the disintegration of the "greater" or truncal family of primitive times into a group of agnatic sibs, within which in turn the "lesser-" ("Sonder-") families, — that is those narrowest groups which were united under the mundium of a "family-father", — became independent, solidary units, which increased

[1] With *Brunner*, "Geschichte", I (2d ed.), 113.

[2] "Lex Angl. et Werin.", 34: "Tunc demum hereditas ad fusum a lancea transeat." Compare the French legal maxim, "Le royaume de France ne tombe pas en quenouille (*Spindel*)."

in independence the looser the sib became and the more it was confused with the general concept of blood relationship or kindred. In the terminology of the old law, the members of this narrower circle of kindred were not counted at all among the blood-friends ("Magen") in the proper sense; the blood-friends, according to it, included only those kindred who stood outside of the house-community,—the "nephews" and "nieces" in the broadest sense. Thus, for example, the Sachsenspiegel still distinguished among the members of the sib — the "Sippegenossen", the "Sippezahlen", the blood relatives generally — those members thereof "who were reckoned among the blood-friends (Magen)", namely those who stood outside the narrowest circle of the house-community.[1] This distinction between the narrower circle of nearest related members, and the wider circle of blood-friends (of the "Magschaft" in the narrower sense) was of particularly fundamental importance in the oldest inheritance law.

(II) **System and Degrees of Kinship.** — Germanic law recognized various systems by which the wider circle of blood relatives, — the "Magschaft" or blood-friends in the broader sense, — were organized, and according to which their degree of kinship was measured.

(1) *Relationship by generations (the parentelic system).* — The natural lamination of the agnatic group of the sib in successive layers of descendants, or generations, was also retained in the systematic organization of the kindred composed alike of paternal and maternal blood-friends. Within the broad circle of the "Magschaft" distinct groups were formed, under this system, of all those persons who were related through their nearest common male ancestor or their nearest ancestral pair. It is the custom in modern legal science to designate these groups as "parentela" (also as "Stämme", "trunks"; "Linien", "lines"; "Glieder", "branches"). The old legal sources written in Latin, however, employ the expression "parentela" ("parentilla") in another sense; they designate by it the kindred generally, the "Magschaft" in the broader sense. According to the above system, therefore, the kindred of any individual member of the sib (the "propositus") were organized in distinct groups of his own descendants, the descendants of his parents, of his grandparents, of his great-grandparents, and so on. His own descendants, — children, grandchildren, great-grandchildren, etc., — constituted in relation

[1] Ssp., I, 3, § 3.

to himself, the first parentelic group, since he was the male ancestor of all of them. The *other* descendants of his parents, — in other words, his brothers and sisters and their descendants, his nephews and nieces, grandnephews and grandnieces, — constituted the second parentelic group. His grandparents and their descendants in so far as they did *not* belong to the first and second parentelic groups, — in other words, his uncles and aunts, his male and female cousins, and their children, grandchildren, and so on, — were included in the third parentelic group, inasmuch as all of them were related to him through their grandfathers or through their grandparents. And thus the enumeration continued. The calculation of kinship upon the basis of this system was very simple and natural. In the first place the rule held that the members of a nearer parentelic group were more nearly related to the "propositus" than those of a more distant parentelic group, inasmuch as they shared with him a nearer truncal-father. His nephews were more nearly related to him than were his uncles; for they and he had a common ancestor in his father, but his uncle and he had such only in his grandfather. Within any particular parentelic group, however, the degree of kinship was measured by the lesser or greater distance from the truncal-head or truncal-pair of that group. The uncle was therefore more nearly related to the "propositus" than was the cousin; for the uncle was the son and the cousin the grandson of the common male ancestor, the grandfather of the "propositus." Unlike the Roman, the Germanic law did not illustrate degrees of kinship under the symbol of an ancestral tree with its branches, but by the human body and its limbs and joints; and therefore they designated the generations derived from the truncal male ancestor as "knees" ("genu", "geniculum"). Eike von Repgow has described in a celebrated and much debated passage of his work how the Saxons applied the figure of the human body to the calculation of kinship, and especially to the determination of herital rights.[1] If two persons alleged kinship with a third, the "propositus" (who was ordinarily the intestate), they were bound in the first place to name a truncal-father who was common to them and the "propositus." If they named the same truncal-father, or at least truncal-fathers of the same generation, — in other words if both belonged, in relation to the "propositus", to the same parentelic group, — then in order to determine which of them was the nearer to such common male ancestor, a process of "Abstuppen", described by Eike,

[1] Ssp., I, 3, § 3.

was resorted to; that is, an enumeration of generations from the truncal-father to the claimants. Each of them took the outline of the human body (the "Gliederbild"), placed the common male ancestor at the head, and then with the right hand counted downward on its left side the generations intervening between himself and such truncal-father. In so doing the children of the truncal-father were placed, as the "first sib-group" ("Sippezahl"), at the neck; the grandchildren, as the "second sib-group", at the shoulder; and the following generations successively at the elbows, the wrists, the first, second, and third joint of the middle finger; the last generation that was considered under the law of inheritance, — the eighth sib-group (or the seventh group when reckoning only the "Magen"), — was placed at the finger nail, whence the name "nail-friends" ("Nagelmagen"). Whichever of such claimants occupied a higher joint was more nearly related to the truncal-father, and therefore also with the "propositus", than he who belonged in a lower group; persons belonging at the same joint were related in equal degree. If the claimants named truncal-fathers of different joints ascending from the "propositus"; that is, if they did not belong to the same parentelic group, then it follows from what is said above that "the downward reckoning of the groups was not necessary; if it was nevertheless made, it had no other value than when evidence whose immateriality becomes evident in the course of its presentation is nevertheless given in full."[1] In this calculation of kinship, therefore, the nearer parentelic group or "line" ("Linie") was first determined, and then, *within* such parentelic group, the lesser descent or interval from the parentelic head, — the higher "knee" or the nearer joint to the head indicating the nearer "degree"; and consequently this method of determining kinship could also be designated as a "lineal-gradual" scheme. It is clear that this mode of calculating kinship was adapted to an organization of kinship by generations or descendants, such as was usual from the earliest times. If it was desired to indicate numerically, according to this mode of reckoning, the interval of kinship between two persons, and if they were members of the same generation below the common ancestor, the matter could be simplified, for it was then sufficient to indicate the interval once (so-called "reckoning by double-joints"). For example, it was said that the children of brothers and sisters, who were members of the second generation from their common truncal-

[1] *Stutz, op. cit.*, just above, 57.

father (their grandfather), were related in the second degree to one another; whereas in counting downward by "joints" from the truncal-father both the lines of descendants from him to the cousins must have been reckoned, and it must have been said of *each* cousin that he stood in the second generation from the grandfather. The matter was not so simple when the two persons belonged to different generations, that is were unequally removed from the common male ancestor; for example, the one as a grandchild of the truncal-father in the group (joint) of first cousins, the other as a great-grandchild in that of second cousins. As nothing else was here possible, the interval upon both sides was indicated: "unus in quarta, alius in tertia progenie sibi pertinet", says the Capitulare Compendiense of 757 (c. 3), — that is, they are related to one another in the fourth and the third generation from the truncal-male ancestor.[1] This mode of calculating kinship, by counting the generations descended from the truncal-father, passed from the Germanic into the Canon law; though there the example of the Old Testament may possibly also have been influential, since the reckoning of kinship by generations was also the old national system of the Jewish people. At all events it is found from the 700 s onward in Anglo-Saxon and Frankish, and indeed in all Germanic, legal sources of the Church, and was also adopted by the Pseudo-Isidorian Decretals. This Germanic-Canonic mode of reckoning differed in an important respect from the Roman. For the latter counted the generations lying *between* two persons and measured by this the degree of kinship; so that brothers and sisters were related according to the Roman system in the second, and not as in the Germanic in the first, degree; and the children of brothers and sisters were related in the fourth, and not in the second degree. The fundamental distinction between the Roman and the Germanic mode of reckoning has been justly placed in the fact that the Roman law regarded a human being as an isolated individual, as a "persona", and in reckoning kinship considered individual persons only as links; the Germanic law, on the other hand, regarded the persons concerned as members of units constituted of "generationes", — in other words it took the generation, from the beginning, as the link, and counted only *its* removal from the ancestor.[2] Wherever the old distinction was preserved between a narrower and a wider circle of kindred there resulted in the case of the latter, — as the passage above quoted from the Sachsenspiegel shows, — a "retarded enumeration":

[1] *Heusler*, "Institutionen", II, 590. [2] *Ibid.*

the first generation of children, who occupied the neck, were not blood-friends ("Magen"); on the contrary, the first sib-generation ("Sippezahl") that was reckoned among the blood-friends was the second generation of descendants, that is the grandchildren, who occupied the shoulder; the second group of blood friends ("Magschaft") was the third generation of sib-fellows ("Gesippen"), that is the grandchildren, occupying the elbow; and so forth. And consequently the "nail-friends" ("Nagelmagen"), included in the eighth "Gesippe", were the seventh "Magschaft." This retarded count was likewise adopted in the Canon law. In time, however, it ceased to be practised therein, and in the later German sources it was also abandoned; for example, already in the Schwabenspiegel. Enumeration by generations in any form was abandoned in many parts of Germany at an early day in favor of the Roman enumeration by degrees, which eventually everywhere acquired authority. In the law of inheritance, however, the former remained very important.

(2) *Relationship by stocks.* — Another organization of the kindred, namely in so-called stocks ("Stämme") and quarters ("Teile"), was associated with the appearance of the unstable sib and the inclusion of the cognates within the circle of the blood-friends. Just as the "Magen" were ordinarily divided into paternal and maternal blood-friends according as they belonged to the paternal or the maternal sib (*supra*, p. 714), so many legal systems arranged in special groups those persons related through each one of the four grandparents, and those related through each one of the eight great-grandparents. This arrangement, which was also common among the North Germans, was maintained among the Frisians and the Low Franks (in the law of Holland, Zealand, and Flanders) down into the Middle Ages. The four "Stämme" of the grandparents, — that is, the descendants of the four pairs of great-grandparents, — were known among the Franks as "Vierendeele", and among the Frisians as "Klüfte"; the eight "Stämme" of the great-grandparents, — that is, the descendants of the eight pairs of great-great-grandparents, — were known among the Franks as "Achtendeele" or "half-Vierendeele", and among the Frisians as "Fechten" or "Fänge." The entire group of kindred was therefore also known as the "Achtzahl" (Old High G. "ahta"; Old Norse "oett"). This arrangement of kindred is seen with especial clearness in the derivative systems of the Salic law in connection with the action for homicide and in the homicide wergeld, in which connection four

members of the group of second cousins ("Achtersusterkinder" = "Andergeschwisterkinder") frequently appeared as representative of the four "quarters" of the sib. It was important in the law of guardianship, inasmuch as the sib's supervisory guardianship was exercised by the four "Vierendeelen" of the "Magschaft." Finally, it played a leading rôle in the law of inheritance, for in default of the first and second parentelic groups the inheritance passed by virtue of the so-called "Schependomsrecht" (that is, the inheritance law of South Holland and Zealand, derived from Frankish origin), half and half to the blood-friends of the paternal and the maternal side, and in default of these to the four "Vierendeele", and finally to the eight "Achtendeele."[1]

(3) *Relationship by cousin-groups.* — An arrangement of the kindred which though descended from great antiquity has left its plain traces in the terminology of kinship that is usual even today in Romanic languages, is the reckoning by cousin-groups, proof of which was first given by Ficker.[2] In the Spanish language, which served Ficker as the basis of his investigation, the uncle is designated as "tio", the nephew as "sobrino"; but the cousin as "primo hermano", "primo carnal", or simply as "primo", — that is to say, as the "first", the "first brother." In addition to the "primo", however, there are recognized in Spanish a "secundo", "tercero" and "quarto hermano"; the "secundo" is a second cousin; and so on. The "primos", that is the cousins, are grandchildren of the same grandfather; the "secundos" are great-grandchildren of the same great-grandfather. To the Spanish "primo hermano" there corresponds the French "cousin" ("consanguineus"; in Italian, "cugino"), "cousin germain", also known simply as "germain", — the Flemish "rechtzweer"; to the Spanish "secundo", the French "cousin en autre" or "second", and the Flemish "anderzweer"; to the Spanish "tercero", the French "cousin en tierce", the Flemish "derdezweer"; and so on. These first, second, third, etc. cousins are always equally removed from their common male ancestor; they are in the same generation, or, if they be thought of as united by a direct horizontal line instead of as united by a broken line passing through the common ancestor, they stand upon the same horizontal line. When the first cousins, and not the brothers and sisters, are thus designated as "first brothers", we have here an-

[1] *Brunner* in Z^2. R. G., III, 51.
[2] "Untersuchungen zur Erbenfolge", I, 303–86.

other application of the "retarded" count above referred to (p. 720); which here also resulted from the fact that the brothers belonging to the same household were not reckoned among the blood-friends in the narrower sense. This mode of reckoning by cousin-groups offered great advantages in all cases where it was important to group together all kindred included in the same generation with the "propositus"; as for example all the able-bodied men of the sib who were of approximately the same age, and upon whom lay the obligation of the blood-feud. Although this enumeration by cousin-groups is certainly, as already remarked, very old, the further contentions of Ficker that the parentelic organization was derived from it as an earlier type, and that it can be explained only by the Canonic system of retarded count, are not supported by convincing proofs.

§ 107. **Succession of Kindred to the Inheritance.** (I) **The Older Law.** — (1) *The oldest sources.* — The scanty and in large part enigmatic testimony of the sources of the Germanic and Frankish periods certainly justifies a confident assumption (as already mentioned, — *supra*, pp. 694 *et seq.*) that the oldest rule of herital succession rested upon a distinction between a narrower and a wider circle of heirs, in accord with the general historical development of the family, and that this distinction continued to be maintained after the requirement of a common house-community had been abandoned as regarded the next heirs. On the other hand it is only with difficulty that evidence can be drawn from those sources for an answer to the question according to what rule the more remote kindred were called to the inheritance, and whether an identical rule was everywhere observed in this connection. The treatment under the inheritance law of those included within the narrower kinship-group also remains obscure at many points. The oldest explicit evidence is the statement of Tacitus, in which the children of the deceased, the brothers, the father's brothers, and the mother's brothers are named as the next heirs.[1] From this order of succession it may at least be concluded that the inheritance by children from the father, the omission of sisters and sons of sisters, and the inclusion of the "patruus", are inconsistent with the assumption of a system of mother-law;[2] whereas the mention of the mother's brother is sufficiently justified by the new rôle played by the cognates

[1] "Germania", 20.

[2] *Brunner*, "Geschichte", I (2d ed.), 106. Ernst Mayer has again advanced, very recently, another opinion.

(*supra*, p. 590). Great difficulties are presented, further, — to mention particularly only one passage, — by the celebrated title "De alodis" of the "Lex Salica."[1] According to the reading of the four oldest of the oldest group of manuscripts, this provides that in the case of the intestate's death without children the mother shall be heir; in her absence, brothers and sisters shall follow; and in default of these, also the sisters of the mother. Again, according to it he shall take the estate who is the nearest among the maternal blood-friends ("de illis generationibus"); at the end it provides that in the case of lands no share in the estate shall inure to women, but that the entire estate should fall to those who were brothers on the paternal side. Among the many explanations of this that have been attempted down to the present time that of Brunner[2] appears the simplest and the most illuminating. According to him Title 59 is by no means an exhaustive statement of the Salic law of inheritance; on the contrary it is merely an individual statute regulating the succession of the maternal friends in the inheritance. Consequently this Title cannot be used, as has often been attempted, as evidence of the existence of mother-law; which, for that matter, is contradicted by the fact that no mention is made of the mother's brother. Inasmuch as the only question involved is the herital succession of the maternal blood-friends, the paternal blood-friends are not even mentioned; and likewise the part of the chattels of the heritage to which the maternal blood-friends are entitled to succeed is assumed, as something already known, — probably an equal division of the chattels took place, even at that early day, between the groups of paternal and maternal blood-friends, just as in the later legal system of the Low Franks. That the latter were completely excluded by the male line from inheritance of lands is expressly mentioned at the end (§ 5). As respects the maternal blood-friends, however, this Title indicates a complete rule of succession: the mother, the brothers and sisters (who to be sure may also be paternal blood-friends, or even exclusively such because having a common father, but are here involved, along with maternal half-brothers and sisters, merely as persons having a common mother, — in other words as maternal blood-friends), the sisters of the mother, and the remaining maternal blood-friends in the order of their degree of kinship. As for the Salic order of inheritance among paternal blood-friends, we may assume, — in

[1] "Lex Salica", 59, 1.
[2] In his "Kritische Bemerkungen" (*supra*, p. 713), 12 *et seq.*

analogy to this rule laid down for the maternal blood-friends, and in view of the succession-tables of the Ripuarian folk-law,[1] — a system according to which first the father, then brothers and sisters with a common father, and then the sisters of the father succeeded a childless intestate. The kindred expressly named in these succession-tables all belonged to the house-community of such childless intestate's father. Since the deceased left no children, — and ordinarily he was doubtless young and unmarried, — there followed father and mother, brother and sisters; and unmarried sisters of the father and (a peculiarity of the Frankish law) the mother if living as dependent members in the households of a brother or a married sister (parents of the deceased). As respects the order of succession of more remote paternal and maternal kindred, the Frankish folk-laws, like many other sources, content themselves with the laconic remark that in such case the "proximior" or "proximus" shall be entitled. The order of succession was therefore assumed as something known.

Nevertheless, despite this silence it can hardly be doubted that the parentelic system in the sense above explained was employed very widely indeed, even in the oldest law, as the guide in determining the order of inheritance. The records of the folk-laws not only offer no evidence inconsistent with the parentelic system but may be understood, with least straining of interpretation, in a sense favorable to it.[2] In the Middle Ages it was doubtless the most widely prevalent system, so that the theory which assumes it to have been the oldest and most prevalent system of kinship and herital succession in the Germanic and German law appears to be perfectly supported by the sources, though it is true that a long-continued dispute has been conducted over this hypothesis. As early as the 1700 s the students of the feudal law, in which the "lineal-gradual" system prevailed without question, endeavored to establish the existence of the system in the older Germanic legal sources. "A complete victory was won for these Germanic views by Danz's really important work."[3] In later times, however, this was displaced by the writings of Majer, which appeared shortly thereafter; he was of the opinion that the parentelic system could already be read between the lines of the order of succession indicated by Tacitus. During the 1800 s the Ger-

[1] "Lex Ribuaria", 56. 1.

[2] *Heusler*, "Institutionen", II, 597 *et seq.*

[3] *Rosin* in the essay in *Grünhut's* Z. Priv. öff. R., XXVIII, 371, cited *supra*, p. 713.

manists were divided into camps of parentelic and anti-parentelic champions. Although in earlier times the former theory was predominant, its position was apparently seriously weakened by the attacks of Siegel and Wasserschleben; scholars like Amira and Ficker declared against it, others like Lewis, Stobbe, and Maurer, declared the question not yet ripe for answer. In quite recent years, however, conditions have changed to the advantage of the parentelic system, since very recent investigations, in part due to these controversies, have considerably strengthened the historical evidences of an early and widespread prevalence of parentelic groups.

(2) *The parentelic system.* — (A) IN GENERAL. — In the later Middle Ages the parentelic system prevailed, as is demonstrable, throughout a great part of Switzerland and many parts of the Rhine country, Austria and the Tyrol; it was assumed and explained as existing law by the authors of the Schwabenspiegel and the legal systems therefrom derived, and most probably also by Eike von Repgow.[1] Further, as has been recently proved, it prevailed in the Netherlands, in the greatest part of the regions of the French customary law, as well as in the Anglo-Norman law, whose principles were maintained unchanged in England, as regarded succession to immovable property, for more than 500 years and were codified for the first time in 1833.[2] As the rule of succession under the feudal law it was applied throughout Germany. In the parentelic system the first heirs were the children of the deceased, — "the breast-heirs" (the "Busen", "bosom-kindred" in the narrower sense), — and their descendants. These were followed by the parents of the decedent, — the so-called "Schoss" ("lap"); and only thereafter by the brothers and sisters. This "lap-succession" ("das Kind fällt in der Mutter Schoss": "the child falls in its mother's lap"), which is attested by most of the folk-laws and also by the Sachsenspiegel,[3] reflected the old view that the children were related to their parents by a closer blood bond than to their brothers and sisters; and moreover was required by the strict parentelic system, since the parents stood at the head of the second parentelic group. After the brothers and sisters there followed their issue, in other words the entire parentelic group of the parents; and after them, in the third place, the parentelic group of the grandparents; in the fourth place, that

[1] Compare the passage from the Ssp., I. 3, § 3 cited on p. 716.
[2] *Heymann* in *Holtzendorff-Kohler*, I, 834.
[3] Ssp., I. 17, § 1.

of the great-grandparents; and so on, — always, in the first place, the truncal-pair of parents as the heads of the "lines", and then their issue in the order of removal from them. The limitation of kinship that was introduced already in Germanic times as respects rights of inheritance had the effect of cutting off the right to succeed to the heritage at a definite point, — though, to be sure, a point that was variously fixed. Some certain generation, counting downwards and upwards from the decedent, was the last one entitled to inherit. According to the Sachsenspiegel this was the sixth sib-generation ("Sippezahl") that was included in the blood-friends ("Magschaft"), namely the group occupying the third link of the finger; the "nail-friends" being no longer heirs. Of the issue of the deceased, therefore, the last ones entitled to inherit were the great-grandchildren of a great-great-grandchild (that is the seventh generation, or the sixth body of blood-friends, following him). Of the collateral kindred, it was the seventh generation descended from the great-grandfather of his great-great-grandfather. Certainly an exceedingly wide range of relationship!

(B) Representation. The three-line system. — The parentelic system may be applied with greater or with less strictness. In particular there is the question whether effect shall be given to the right of representation (so-called "Eintrittsrecht", "right of entry"); that is, whether the grandchildren of the deceased shall enter in the places of their dead fathers, the sons of the deceased, — whether they shall "represent" the latter in the division of the estate. It is debatable whether in the oldest Germanic law of inheritance there existed at all, in addition to a son's right of inheritance, a similar right in remoter issue; or whether, when the decedent left only grandchildren, in other words children of dead sons, these grandchildren were excluded by surviving brothers of the deceased, their great-uncles. (For the parents of the deceased would, as matter of fact, hardly be considered in such cases.) If one assumes that there originally prevailed such a preference of brothers over grandchildren, then one is bound to derive this, with Heusler,[1] from the fact that as an after-effect of the primitive sacredness of the bond between brothers and sisters a grandfather felt less near to his grandchildren than to his brothers. At all events the exclusion of the grandchildren by the brothers must have been evidence that the idea of the house-community, of the narrower circle of heirs, was still stronger than that of succession

[1] "Institutionen", II, 579 *et seq.*

by generations. In the time of the folk-laws, however, a right of the remoter issue to inherit seems to have been for the most part already recognized; so that not only the children but all the descendants of the deceased were entitled to succeed as of the first line, and only after them the brothers as members of the second parentelic group. Wherever remoter descendants enjoyed herital rights the question might also arise whether the grandchildren should also be granted the right to represent their fathers. An occasion for such succession (per stirpes) was offered when the deceased was survived by a son and the son of another dead son, — in other words a grandson. Should the grandson be excluded by the son, his uncle, or should he succeed in place of his father, and so divide the heritage with the other son, his uncle? The idea of such a representation ("Eintritt"), however natural it might be to a system of inheritance based upon a truncal-organization ("Stammgliederung"), was originally unknown to Germanic law. The rule prevailed: "the nearer to the blood, the nearer to the estate" ("Je näher dem Blut, je näher dem Gut"); that is, within the parentelic group of the decedent's descendants inheritance was determined by the degree of kinship. The danger of a prejudicial parcellation of property, particularly of the landed possessions of the family, that was involved in such equality of sons and grandsons under the inheritance law, weighed heavily against such a right of representation. Sporadic attempts to introduce it by way of legislation, such as the statute issued in 595 by King Childebert II for the Austrasian Franks,[1] could not overcome the strong resistance of the common people. Especially characteristic was the course of events in the case of the Saxons. This question of the right of representation was there decided by judgment of God in a judicial combat that took place at Stela in 942, and inasmuch as the champion of the grandsons conquered, in their favor, — but only to the extent of the case there submitted for decision, namely in favor of sons' children as against other sons.[2] Even in later times this restriction was strictly maintained; the Sachsenspiegel recognizes rights of representation to no greater extent.[3] It was only in the course of the Middle Ages that the right of grandsons in the estate became firmly established, doubtless in consequence of the frequent preferment of grandsons by their grandparents, by which they were put in the

[1] Childebert, II decretio, c. 1 (M. G., Cap. 1. 15).
[2] "Widukindi, res gestae Saxon.", II, 10.
[3] Ssp., I. 5, § 1.

"shoes" of their deceased parents.[1] However, the right of representation did not pass in Germany beyond these mere beginnings, generally speaking, until acquaintance was made with the Roman law. Still less was the German law inclined to recognize rights of representation in cases where only remote descendants were present, of the same degree but the issue of different sons of the deceased; for example, three sons of a dead elder son and two of a dead younger son. In this case the estate was not, as might be supposed, divided into two parts, one being given to the first three grandchildren, one-sixth therefore to each, and the other half to the other two grandsons, one-fourth to each. On the contrary, as the rule of the Sachsenspiegel already cited shows, it was divided per capita, one-fifth being therefore given to each grandson in the case supposed. For the rule prevailed "Soviel Mund, soviel Pfund" ("so many mouths, so many pounds").

While this preferment of descendants to all collateral relatives, which was being painfully established with the right of representation, marked a victory for the parentelic system, the reverse was true when some legal systems made the ascendants a special group of heirs, thereby making a threefold division of these into descendants, ascendants, and collaterals, — the so-called "*three line system.*" Moreover, in some legal systems all ascendants were preferred to collaterals, possibly because of the special relation of piety in which the deceased stood in relation to them. More often, however, the opposite was the case: the herital right of ancestors, which was generally recognized in the Frankish period, was limited or even wholly abolished in favor of the collaterals, their descendants, — at least as regards certain portions of the heritage (usually restricted herital estates, "Erbgüter"). It was not desired that the property should again come to the hands of ancestors, who for the most part enjoyed a secure economic position, but that they should remain in younger hands. The heritage should pass downwards, and not upwards: "the property runs as the blood" ("Das Gut rinnt wie das Blut"; "les propres ne remontent pas"; "geen good klimt gaarne"). This principle assumed various forms in Germany in the regions of the Frankish law, and also in the Netherlands and Flanders; it prevailed in the French and in the Anglo-Norman law. Rights of parental reversion (so-called "Fallrecht") were usually associated with the exclusion of the ascendants.

[1] *Schröder*, "Lehrbuch" (5th ed.), 770.

(C) SEX DISCRIMINATIONS. — The order of succession was influenced to an extraordinary extent by the different treatment of the sexes in the inheritance law. Even if one starts with the prevailing theory that Germanic law, in accord with the original military character of Germanic civilization and the patriarchal organization of its family, denied to women capacity to hold property and therefore capacity to inherit (*supra*, pp. 64, 628), this rule had already been weakened, by the beginning of historical times, to a mere preferment of males and "male kindred" in the inheritance law. This, however, was characteristic of its entire medieval development. The right of parental reversion ("Fallrecht", "ius recadentiae") developed in many medieval systems, — particularly in the Frankish, Swiss and Frisian, — was an echo of the fact that rights of kindred related through the mother were recognized in the inheritance law only at a late day as compared with those of members of the old and purely agnatic union of the sib. According to this right the lands of a person who died without descendants, or of one who died without ascendants or descendants, reverted to that side from which they originally came; although frequently, as already mentioned, with exclusion of direct ascendants, — "restricted herital estates retrace the way whence they came" ("Erbgut geht wieder den Weg, daher es gekommen"; "het goet moet gaen, van dar het gekomen is", "the goods shall go whence they came"; "paterna paternis, materna maternis.") It was another expression of the same idea, — found equally in the old Frankish legal systems and in the medieval systems of Flanders, Holland, Saxony, Alamania, and Friesland, — when a quotal partition was made (usually an equal division into halves) between the paternal and the maternal blood-friends of each parentela, instead of an apportionment to the sides whence the property originally came; so that the paternal and maternal kindred, though indeed treated equally, were nevertheless treated as special natural groups. This system prevailed, notably, in the French coûtumes (so-called "fente" or "refente").

The unlike treatment of the sexes that had earlier prevailed resulted, however, not only in a separation of the kindred related through women from the paternal blood-friends, but above all in a postponement of women to men of the same degree of blood. The folk-laws, it is true, all give to women a herital right in place of the claim to maintenance that was alone originally conceded them; but all of them with the exception of the Visigothic postponed daughters to sons within the narrower circle of heirs, either in all cases or at least in the case of lands (as in the Lex Salica) [1] or of family-estates (as in the Lex Ribuaria); [2] and also frequently restricted succession by remoter heirs to the sword-friends, that is to the men of the male line. On the other hand, a woman of nearer degree later came to be preferred to a remoter male, in accord with the parentelic theory, as the Sachsenspiegel, for example, shows.[3] In the wider circle of heirs sex completely lost its one-time influence. Whereas in rural regions the postponement of daughters to sons as respects inheritance of lands was maintained not only throughout the Middle Ages but, in the inheritance of particular kinds of estates, down into modern times (*infra*, §§ 114–16), in the cities the equality of sons and daughters under the inheritance law was established already in the Middle Ages.

(D) Postponement of brothers and sisters of the half-blood. — Many medieval legal systems postponed brothers and sisters of the half-blood in various ways to those of the full blood, in accord with the unlike treatment of paternal and maternal blood-friends. For example, according to the Sachsenspiegel persons of the half-blood were postponed an entire degree,[4] and according to other legal systems a half degree, to the full blood. Some legal systems gave to brothers and sisters of the half-blood only half the share of the heritage that fell to those of the full blood; they permitted them to inherit, not like the latter "with both hands", but only "with one hand."

(3) *Other systems.* — The peculiarities above mentioned were mere "variations of the parentelic system",[5] which, while indeed creating a great complexity in the legal systems recognizing them, nevertheless did not affect their substantial basis. But there existed in the Middle Ages a few legal systems in which there was observed a system of succession irreconcilable with the parentelic order. There are here in question certain town laws of Lower Germany, — among others those of Dortmund, Goslar, Hamburg and Eisenach; also certain Swiss dooms and Frisian statutes and Scandinavian legal systems; and, above all, the judicial practice of the Magdeburg skevins. There was here no

[1] "Lex Salica", 59, 5. *Cf.* p. 723 *supra.* Chilperich was the first to give rights of succession to daughters, brothers, and sisters of the deceased in lands, in default of sons; so that an escheat to the commune took place only in the absence of all these heirs, — Edictum Chilperici (561–584), c. 3 (M. G., Cap. 1, 8).

[2] "L. Rib.", 56. *Cf.* p. 724 *supra.*

[3] Ssp., I, 17, § 1. *Cf.* p. 725 *supra.*

[4] Ssp., II, 20, § 1.

[5] *Gierke* in *Holtzendorff-Kohler*, I, 549.

principle of successive rights of parentelic groups. Many of these legal systems preferred collaterals, particularly brothers and sisters, — *i.e.* members of the second parentelic group, — to more remote descendants, particularly grandsons, — *i.e.* members of the first parentelic group; and all treated as equals the collateral kindred of different parentelic groups, for example cousins (third parentelic group) and grandsons of brothers and sisters (second parentelic group), or children of cousins (third parentelic group) and children of great-uncles (fourth parentelic group). There may be here involved in part an after-effect of the old distinction between the narrower and the wider circle of heirs, or in part an influence of the Roman law that was already felt; which last was doubtless furthered by the "arbor consanguinitatis" adopted in the Canon law and known in Germany from the 1300 s onward. But however one may explain these peculiar facts, at all events this system of succession, — which in the last analysis "appears as a pure 'gradual' system, modified by the peculiar position of the parents, the brothers, and the children of the decedent in the 'neck' of the Saxon skeleton of kinship",[1] — was unimportant as compared with the parentelic system, if for no other reason than the limited area of its authority.

(II) **The Modern Development.** (1) *Transformations in the common law of the Roman law adopted at the Reception.* — The Justinian system of intestate succession gave the first right to inherit to descendants; the second to ascendants, brothers and sisters of the full-blood and children of the latter; the third to brothers and sisters of the half-blood and their children; and the fourth to all other cognates in the order of their degree of kinship. Despite some fundamental differences, it possessed many similarities to the prevailing parentelic system; for example, the unqualified preference of descendants, the postponement of collaterals of the half-blood, the equal division of the estate among paternal and maternal ascendants of the same degree ("divisio in lineas") that took place in case of pure ascendant succession, and the composition of the second class of heirs, which was at least remotely similar to and reminds one of the "three-line-system."[2] These similarities were influential in procuring the acceptance of the Roman law of intestate inheritance, although not without strong opposition. Its triumph was attributable fully as much, however, to the circumstance that it possessed, in addition to the above, certain qualities that satisfied the special

[1] *Heymann*, "Grundzüge" (*supra*, p. 713), 16. [2] *Ibid.*, 27.

needs of the time and gave full effect to ideas theretofore present in the Germanic law only in rudimentary form. Among these, in particular, was the right of "representation", which took account of the fact that not only the heir but his entire line were economically enriched by his inheritance, and which was now generally applied. Hence it was that even the legislation of the Empire interfered — a rare case — to secure in this matter the adoption of the alien law. Rights of representation, after having been provisionally adopted, at least as respects grandchildren, at the Diet of Freiburg in 1498, — although still repudiated on the authority of the Sachsenspiegel as respected first cousins, — were introduced at the Diet of Augsburg in 1500 for descendants generally, and at the Diet of Worms in 1521 for the children of brothers and sisters (first cousins) along with these latter. True, these resolutions of the Diet, notwithstanding their observance was impressed upon the estates of the Empire by the edict of the "Reichsregiment" of 1521, by no means acquired authority everywhere in the Empire; in Saxony, particularly, their enforcement was resisted, and the Diet of Speier, in 1529, was obliged to recognize the partition "per capita" of the German law in the case of succession by first cousins. Accordingly, partition per stirpes ("Stammteilung") was permitted only when persons of unequal kinship (for example brothers and sisters and the children of deceased brothers and sisters) inherited together; and this involved, in fact, the triumph of a principle of Germanic law, although of course contemporaries were not conscious of this. They justified these as well as other notable deviations from Roman law with the theory (which originated in Italy and was now acquiring supremacy also in Germany) that the right of representation was a succession "ex alieno iure"; that the representative succeeded only as the heir of the person he represented, or at least by virtue of the latter's right, — a baseless fiction. Inasmuch as some of its consequences qualified the rules of the Roman law, its effect was to fortify the native against the alien system. In still other respects there were continued in Germany, in the theory and practice of the common law, the endeavors to assimilate the Justinian law to the principles of the parentelic system which had been earlier initiated in Italy. In particular, an attempt was made to transform the second Roman class of heirs into the second parentelic group of the Germanic law; namely, on one hand by including in it not only the children but also the more remote descendants of brothers and sisters, and on the other hand by excluding from it the more remote ascendants, including the grandparents; notwithstanding that this procedure, as respects the last point, directly contradicted the clear words of the 118th Novel. In the same way an attempt was made to extend the equal division of the heritage between paternal and maternal kindred of the same degree, prescribed by Justinian in the case of succession by ascendants, so that this division should be made not merely once, but should be repeated, as in the case of the French "refente", with respect to more remote ascendants. In case of pure ascendant succession, however, the Romanistic practice frequently retained, in addition, a division of the estate among the "sides" whence the property originally came, in accord with the Germanic law. The irreconcilability of these Germanic hybrids with the pure Roman law was first perceived by the Historical School of the 1800 s. At the same time, even in the face of the proofs it presented, two of these "unhistorical" and therefore "erroneous" variations proved capable of survival in practice; namely, partition per capita among first cousins and the complete equality of first cousins with ascendants; that is, even when no brothers and sisters of the decedent were living.

(2) *The regional systems.* — The circumstance that Territorial legislation, with few exceptions, — such, for example, as the Brandenburg "Constitutio Joachimica" (which adopted the Justinian law in its pure form), — was considerably influenced in most points by Germanic ideas, was of still greater importance in preserving the vitality of the Germanic rules than was the modification of the Roman law undertaken in the common law. These particularistic systems, as well as the judicial practice of the common law, attempted above all to adapt the second Justinian class of heirs to the Germanic law. Two groups of legal systems are distinguishable: the one adopted the three-line-system, the other the parentelic system.[1]

(A) To the FIRST GROUP, which may be designated the Saxon, there belonged a large number of Saxon legal systems. They followed the judicial practice of the common Saxon law, according to which, unlike the Sachsenspiegel and the judicial practice of Magdeburg, all ascendants, and later all collaterals, were entitled to inherit simply according to their degree of kinship. Similarly, most of the modern Saxon statutes adopted a system (which was also introduced in the 1600 s into the duchy of Magdeburg) according to which four classes were successively entitled

[1] *Heymann*, "Grundzüge" (*supra*, p. 713), 16.

to the succession, — first the descendants, then the ascendants, thereafter the brothers and sisters and their children of the whole and the half-blood, and finally all other collateral kindred.

(B) The SECOND GROUP of regional systems adopted the second course, namely the transformation of the second class of the Justinian system. They excluded from this the more remote ascendants, and added to the children of brothers and sisters the remoter descendants of the latter; the result was the second parentelic group. This arrangement, which preceded recognition of the pure parentelic system, is already to be found in some of the older town codifications (as in the Hamburg statutes of 1603, the Breslau statutes of 1577, and the Lübeck codification of 1586); but, above all, it was adopted in the great codifications of the modern period.

It received particularly clear expression in the Prussian Landrecht, whose provisions were framed by its drafters with conscious reference to the Germanic law. Under it the kindred inherited in five classes. The first was constituted of descendants, with strict application of the principle of representation; the second, of the parents; the third, of the brothers and sisters of the full blood; the fourth, of brothers and sisters of the half-blood and their descendants in conjunction with the ascendants of higher degrees, in such manner that one-half of the estate passed to the brothers and sisters of the half-blood and their descendants, the other to the higher ascendants according to the degree of their kinship; the fifth, of the more remote collateral kindred, strictly according to the degree of their relationship. Here, consequently, the first and the second parentelic groups were regulated in strict agreement with the Germanic law save that the brothers and sisters of the half-blood were not included in them, although they were preferred to all other collateral kindred. In other respects the system of the "Landrecht" was Roman. "The 'Landrecht' was the first German regional legal system that repudiated the erroneous conception of succession per stirpes as a right of succession 'alieno iure', applying the pure Roman principle of the unity of the stock ('Stammeinheit') to the entire body of the decedent's descendants and his brothers and sisters. Further, the distinction between the paternal and the maternal lines exercised no influence; not only was the 'ius recadentiae' expressly repudiated, but even the Justinian 'divisio in lineas' was done away with among descendants, so that ancestors of equal degree share per capita." [1]

[1] *Heymann*, "Grundzüge" (*supra*, p. 713), 38.

The Code Civil adopted a system akin in its principles to the Prussian Law. Its classes are: 1st, descendants; 2d, parents, and brothers and sisters with all their issue; 3d, ascendants; 4th, collaterals. But (among other things) it retained in large measure the distinction of the Germanic law between the paternal and the maternal kindred, as in the old French "fente."

Whereas these codes applied the principles of the parentelic order to the nearer kindred only, and therefore continued in theory to represent Romanistic systems more or less considerably modified in the sense of Germanic law, the Austrian legislation (if we disregard a few earlier particularistic statutes, — the inheritance statute of Joseph II, of 1786, and the Civil Code, which agrees with that) has led the way in establishing the parentelic system for the more remote kindred as well, partly under the influence of the law of nature, and partly following the example of the feudal law; so that, under it, it is only after the complete exhaustion of one parentelic group that the members of the following group have their turn.

The inheritance law of the kingdom of Saxony was regulated in agreement with the Austrian Code, first by an edict of 1829 and later by the Civil Code. But here the preferment given in the older common Saxon law to all ascendants was retained. The Saxon order of succession was adopted in some other Saxon states (Weimar, Altenburg, Gotha, Reuss). A similar system prevailed in Frankfort, Bremen, and in parts of Schleswig-Holstein.

(III) **The Existing Law.** — The present Civil Code has given the parentelic system the authority of common German law, although not with the same consistency as was observed in the Austrian Civil Code; for it restricts the right of representation, which the Austrian Civil Code extended to all parentelic groups, to the first three orders (descendants, parents and their descendants, grandparents and their descendants). Succession takes place in all of these according to stocks ("Stämmen"), and in the second and third according also to lines ("Linien"). In the fourth (great-grandparents and their descendants) and the following orders, however, which include all the more remote ancestors of the deceased and their descendants, succession is according to the nearness of the degree of kinship; there is no limit to the right of inheritance. The Swiss Civil Code, on the other hand, has once more applied the right of representation with entire consistency, and to all stocks ("Stämmlinien") whatever. But on the other hand it has introduced a limitation upon the statutory right of inheritance: the fourth parentelic group, the stock of the great-grandparents, no longer enjoys any statutory right of inheritance; the commonwealth takes its place. In Germany also there exists at present an intention to introduce in favor of the state a limitation upon statutory rights of inheritance.

§ 108. **Succession by Spouses.** — The fact that many Germanic legal systems gave to a surviving spouse a right of inheritance, at times extensive, in the property of the dead consort has already been mentioned in the account of the law of the marital property (*supra*, pp. 650 *et seq.*, 668), and therefore requires here only brief mention. The provisions of the Roman law, which accorded herital rights to spouses only to an extent exceedingly limited, were adopted in only a few regions. For even where the Roman dotal law was recognized in other respects, the local statutes ordinarily gave the surviving spouse a right of inheritance along with the other kindred of the deceased, — frequently, to be sure, only after them. It was a rare exception when the law of Mark Brandenburg wholly denied such a right of inheritance, giving to the spouse instead of this a mere right to convert into a general community of goods mortis causa an administrative community that existed during the continuance of the marriage, in which case the surviving spouse received half of the entire property derived from both sides. Most of the regional legal systems clung to the old view "that the surviving spouse ought to receive more than his or her heirs would have received had such surviving spouse died first."[1] The right in the estate given to such survivor, — which, since it was not supported by the common law but by regional statutes, was called, as already mentioned, a "statutory portion" ("successio coniugum statuaria"), — varied greatly in extent. Sometimes it referred to a certain quota of the estate, sometimes to things of a particular kind, especially chattels. Often it consisted of a right of usufruct in all the property of the dead spouse or in a fraction thereof; indeed, even the quota of the community property that was set apart for the surviving spouse under the rules of marital property was sometimes, although incorrectly, conceived of as an interest of inheritance. Many statutes went so far as to declare the survivor sole heir of the decedent (Lüneburg, Hildesheim, Fulda, Nördlingen). Most legal systems gave to the spouse a right of inheritance graduated according to the presence of other heirs; the proportions introduced by the Prussian "Landrecht" have already been referred

[1] *Gierke* in *Holtzendorff-Kohler*, I, 550.

to (*supra*, p. 651). Whereas the Saxon code adopted a similar although a simpler rule, the Code Civil permitted a spouse to take the inheritance only when the deceased left no kindred entitled thereto. Many legal systems declared the statutory portion to be an irrevocable herital right, — in other words a right to a compulsory portion; others ascribed such compulsory character to a quota of the intestate property only; still others, like the Austrian Civil Code, recognized no compulsory portion whatever, but merely an absolute ("fester") right to a suitable maintenance. The Civil Code has conceived of the surviving spouse's statutory right of inheritance, which is independent of the law of marital property, as a collective right of succession. The surviving spouse receives when there is issue a fourth, and in conjunction with kindred of the second order, or in conjunction with grandparents, a half of the estate; excluding other kinsmen, however, as sole heir. The half of the estate is an irrevocable compulsory portion, or is revocable only for reasons which would justify divorce. The Swiss Civil Code treats the surviving spouse far more favorably still. If there are no descendants he or she receives the entire inheritance, one part thereof in ownership and another part for usufruct; the relative amount of these two portions being determined by the stock ("Stammlinie") that is entitled to the inheritance in conjunction with the survivor. If adult issue are present the survivor receives, as he may choose, either a fourth of the estate in ownership or a half in usufruct.

§ 109. **Rights of Escheat.**[1] — In the absence of an heir statutorily entitled there were recognized in the medieval law certain rights of escheat. These represented, in part, consequences of the original collective ownership of blood or local groups; in part they rested, like seignorial rights of escheat, upon relations of real or personal dependence; and still others appeared as statutory herital rights of corporate associations ("Körperschaften") in the property of their members. The most important rôle was played by the general right of escheat of the crown or state.

(I) **Herital rights of neighbors** ("vicini"), that is of the commune, in lands owned by mark associations ("Markenverbände"), which are evidenced by the oldest Frankish sources, were a consequence of the original collective ownership of the sib after this became a local group. As already mentioned (*supra*, p. 730), this

[1] *Tomascheck*, "Das Heimfallsrecht, mit einem Rechtsgutachten über das Heimfallsrecht der Städte Wien und Prag" (1882); *Bär*, "Das Kadukrecht der Stadt Danzig", in Z. Westpreus. G. Ver., LI (1909), 21–52.

right took effect, according to the "Lex Salica", when the deceased left no sons. The edict of Chilperich, in turn, gave precedence to the daughters and brothers and sisters, at least, over the commune. But it was only in the course of the 600 s, after the right of grandsons to succeed per stirpes had already been introduced for Austrasia in the course of the 500 s, that all rights of the commune restrictive of the kindred's rights of inheritance were done away with. The old collective rights of the commune were so weakened as to become mere rights of preëmption (apportionment of the mark by lot: "Marklosung", "Nachbarlosung"; *supra*, p. 400).

(II) **Feudal rights of escheat** existed in early times in favor of persons freeing others in the property of such freedmen; as respects the highest classes, therefore, in favor of the king. There was here involved, originally, an actual right of inheritance on the part of the lord, which in the case of the Franks and the Anglo-Saxons excluded even children, but in the case of other legal systems was postponed to them. In the case of serfs this right of inheritance was weakened in the Middle Ages into a right of escheat that took effect only when no heirs were present who were members of the same community (vill); and which was also postponed, in isolated cases, to the right of escheat enjoyed by the royal treasury. A great rôle was played, further, by the rights of escheat of land-lords ("Leiheherr") in lands they leased. These were recognized equally in the case of inferior tenures, in the absence of nearer heirs, and in the feudal law, according to which the fief escheated to the lord (*supra*, p. 341) if a vassal died without heirs of his body and there existed neither subtenure ("Afterleihe") nor contract ("Gedinge") to the contrary.

(III) **Statutory succession rights of corporate associations and foundations** were also recognized as early as in the Middle Ages, although only infrequently. Thus it was sometimes provided that the tools of a dead craftsman should pass to the craft-gild; the University of Vienna received a right of escheat in the estates of its professors, doctors, masters, bachelors, students, beadles, and servants in default of heirs; a right of escheat existed in favor of religious establishments and hospitals in the estates of persons who died within their walls; etc. The statutory herital rights of charitable institutions, orphans' homes, and hospitals have been retained in modern legal systems, though they have been quite differently developed in details. Sometimes a limited right of inheritance was recognized in favor of prisons in the property of dead prisoners. The Introductory Statute of the present Civil Code has maintained intact (§ 139) those provisions of State law which give a herital right to the state treasury, or to other juristic persons, in the estates of persons supported by or under the care of the State or of such other juristic person.

(IV) **The right of escheat of the public treasury** in heirless estates was recognized already in the Frankish period. When it was applicable depended of course upon the question how far the kindred's right of inheritance extended. In the Middle Ages this right of the Empire passed in almost every Territory to the Territorial ruler; although in a few imperial cities, as for example in Frankfort, the crown's right remained intact down into the 1500 s. In the terminology of the medieval sources, this right was exercised by the "judge" ("Richter"), — that is, by the princes who were enfeoffed by the crown with rights of jurisdiction, and in the cities by the city authorities, — for his own profit. That is, when no heirs presented themselves, and particularly if none had presented themselves by the thirtieth day, the judge took possession of the estate, retained it under his control, and waited for a year and a day to see whether any one would claim it. The chattels he might devote to his own profit at the expiration of this time; the rights of the heir in lands were barred by prescription only after thirty-one years and a day. In the cities the estate was frequently divided; for example, a third might be delivered to the city, a third to the Church or the poor, and a third to the lord. In modern times the right of escheat was generally attributed to the State as an incident of sovereignty; in exceptional cases it was attributed to manorial lords as an incident of their power of judicature, and in rare cases to particular urban communes and corporations. The latter right has been preserved by the Introductory Statute to the Civil Code; the former (the right of manorial lords) has been abrogated. It was a controverted question in the common law whether the State treasury possessed a mere right of occupancy in heirless estates or became the heir, but modern codes have generally treated it as a statutory heir. Thus, according to the Civil Code the State or, as the case may be, the imperial treasury, is a statutory heir; only it cannot, like a true heir, refuse the inheritance (§ 1936). The Swiss Civil Code (§ 466) likewise provides that when the decedent leaves no heirs entitled to the heritage it shall fall to the canton or the commune, subject to rights of usufruct in favor of great-grandparents and the brothers and sisters of grandparents.

Chapter XVI

TESTAMENTARY SUCCESSION

§ 110. **Gifts "mortis causa" in the Old Law.**[1] (I) **Adoption in the Frankish Law and the Lombard Herital Contract.**—The very nature of the Germanic law of inheritance, as a law of kinship based exclusively upon blood relationship, necessarily wholly excluded, originally, testamentary dispositions of the estate. "Whoever, upon his death, left members of his household or sib who were entitled to inherit by rule of law, could appoint no other heir."[2] Only he who had no heir could create one. The oldest Germanic

[1] *Pappenheim*, "Launegild und Garethinx", no. 14 (1882) of *Gierke's* "Untersuchungen"; *Hübner*, "Die donationes post obitum und die Schenkungen mit Vorbehalt des Niessbrauchs im älteren deutschen Recht", no. 26 (1888) of *Gierke's* "Untersuchungen"; *Richard Schmidt*, "Die Affatomie der Lex Salica" (1891); *Schupfer*, "Thinx e Affatomia" (1892); *Gmür*, "Die Entwicklung der letzwilligen Verfügungen nach den Rechtsquellen des Kantons St. Gallen" (Dissertation, 1894); *Brunner*, "Der Totenteil in germanischen Rechten", in Z². R. G., XIX (1898), 107–139, "Das rechtliche Fortleben des Toten bei den Germanen", in Deut. Monatssch. ges. Leben, VI (1907), 18–32; *Bartsch*, "Seelgerätstiftungen im 14. Jahrhundert, Ein Beitrag zur Geschichte des Testaments in Österreich", in "Festgabe für Amira" (1908), 1–58; *Gál*, "Totenteil und Seelteil nach süddeutschen Rechten", in Z². R. G., XXIX (1908), 225–238; *Kogler*, "Seelenrecht und Pönfall in Salzburg und Tirol", in "Festgabe für Brunner" (1910), 175–186; *Robert Müller*, "Die Vergabungen von Todeswegen im Gebiet des Magdeburger Stadtrechts", in Thüringisch-sächsische Z. G. K., I (1911), 71–98, 187–226; *Ehrenzweig*, "Die Schenkung auf den Todesfall" in the "Festschrift zur Jahrhundertfeier des (österreichischen) allgemeinen bürgerlichen Gesetzbuchs" (1911), II, 625 *et seq.*; *Falco*, "Le disposizioni 'pro anima,' Fondamenti dottrinali, forme giuridiche" (1911); *Rietschel*, "Der 'Totenteil' in germanischen Rechten", in Z². R. G., XXXII (1911), 297–312; *Bigelow*, "The Rise of the English Will", in "Select Essays A. A. L. H.", III, 770 *et seq.*; *Bruck*, "Die Schenkung auf den Todesfall im griechischen und römischen Recht, zugleich ein Beitrag zur Geschichte des Testaments, I. Teil: Das griechische Recht bis zum Beginn der hellenistischen Epoche" (1909).

[2] *Heusler*, "Institutionen", II, 621.

law recognized a peculiar institute which served this purpose, a herital contract ("Erbschaftsgedinge"), which is most clearly revealed to us in the Frankish "affatomie" already mentioned in connection with adoption (*supra*, p. 661), and in the Lombard herital contract the "thinx" or "gairethinx." It seems permissible to assume that it was originally the folk that appointed an heir to an heirless man; and that though the appointment of the heir was later left to the deceased, there was still required a coöperation of the popular assembly, or of the king who took its place. This is explained by the fact that the right of escheat of the commune or of the king was rendered valueless by such creation of an artificial heir; which therefore required the assent of whoever enjoyed such right of escheat. The origin of this juristic act explains its peculiar form, which was similar to that usual in the grant of arms ("Wehrhaftmachung"), emancipation, and adoption. Among the Lombards, this contract of inheritance was concluded in public meeting of the folk-court ("thinx"), the deceased delivering a spear ("ger") to the contractual heir by the hand of a third person, the "spear-pledge" ("Speerbürge"), whence the name "gairethinx" or "thingatio."[1] In the Lombard "gairethinx" the character of the institute as one belonging to the family-law, — namely as one for the creation of an heir, an "heredem appellare", "in hereditatem adoptare", — is still plainly visible, notwithstanding that the transaction is already permitted in the case of mere default of children and parents. The Salic "affatomie", however, notwithstanding it is also very ancient in form, already shows the beginning of a weakening of the institute into a mere transfer of property. Originally performed as one act, the transaction was divided in the Salic Law into three acts, publicly performed and distinct in time. The first was the manual tradition of a "festuca", in place of a spear, to the trustee ("Salmann", "Treuhänder"); this act was performed in the minor folk-court ("gebotenes Ding") and indicated at once the person of the intended heir and the amount of the gift contemplated in his favor. The second act consisted in the Salmann's moving into the house of the deceased and there performing the "sessio triduana", by which he made evident in traditional and visible manner the vesting of the seisin (*supra*, p. 191). As the third act, which was required to be performed within a year, there followed, finally, the delivery of the "festuca" to the contractual heir in the presence of the royal court or in

[1] "Roth", 172.

the major folk-court ("echtes Ding"). There was therefore no longer any question, here, of the adoption of the intended heir into the narrowest circle of heirs, the "Busen"; the most essential part of the transaction, which alone required performance before the royal court or the major folk-court, was the final act of transfer by the Salmann. In the courts of the Frankish period the "affatomie" became transformed into a mere gift to take effect on death. Out of the "spear-pledge" of the "Lex Salica" there was developed, by changes which began even under that statute, a "Salmann of unlimited powers conferred by a real contract, who upon the death of the deceased was bound to make the conveyance to the intended heir."[1] The addition of a middle-man, however, remained a dispensable element; the Lex Ribuaria already permitted the gift ("adfatimus") by the delivery of a document. The old forms were thus preserved in a weakened form, but made to serve a new purpose.

(II) **Gifts "mortis causa."** — Inasmuch as "affatomie" and "gairethinx" created an artificial heir to take the place of a natural heir who was lacking, they did not contradict the principle that a dead person's estate might pass only to his heirs. The right in expectancy of the next heirs, which was based upon the idea of the household property, made impossible both gifts inter vivos and gifts mortis causa by which parts of the heritage could have been alienated from those entitled in expectancy. It was only gradually that the development of the "free-portion" secured to the decedent the power freely to dispose of a certain portion of his property. This free-portion, according to Brunner's illuminating suggestion, was developed from the "dead man's portion" ("Totenteil") that was recognized in the oldest Germanic law; that is, from that part of the movable estate that was laid with the dead man in his grave or burned with him, in order that it might aid him to reach the kingdom of the dead comfortably and free from danger and enable him to continue there his accustomed mode of life.[2] This death-portion was regarded as the dead man's own share in his estate, given to him for his own use in his life beyond the grave. In the case of rulers it consisted of rich treasures, — think, for example, of the riches that were buried with Alaric in the Busento! In the case of warriors it always included charger and weapons. That the cremation of widows was possibly connected with the same idea has already

[1] *Schröder*, "Lehrbuch" (5th ed.), 348.
[2] *Rietschel*, *op. cit.*, 740 *supra*, takes exceptions to *Brunner's* views.

been suggested (*supra*, p. 611). It was a widespread custom to set apart a third of the movable estate as the death-portion, from the part belonging to the heirs. This remained longest influential in the English law; in the older English legal sources (Glanville, Bracton) this three-fold division of the movable estate into the wife's part, the bairn's part, and the dead's part was treated as a common "consuetudo terræ." Under the influence of Christian ideas the death-portion, which had its roots in heathen mythological ideas, lost its importance. It was no longer buried with the dead man in order that it might serve his personal use in another world, but was given to the Church or to the poor, in order that it might serve the good of the dead man's soul. The old death-portion thus became in Christian times a soul-portion ("Seelteil", "-gerät", "-schatz", "-ding").[1] This historical process, and the tenacious perdurance of the primitive views, is most tangibly evidenced in a Bavarian ordinance of 1806, which contains provisions regulating dispositions of property "wherein the poor soul of the deceased is made his universal heir." As respects that portion of his property which was to be devoted after his death to the good of his soul, it was of course natural to permit the deceased himself to make provisions for that purpose. Thus the free-portion was first used to make gifts to the church. In the folk-laws it was expressly recognized that the father, either after the departure of the children from the paternal household or, as was generally permitted even in the Carolingian period, without such departure, might freely dispose for the good of his soul of his share in the household-property, his free-portion.

According to the results of Brunner's researches[2] there must also be derived from the dead's-portion the institute of the "best-animal" ("Besthaupt") and other succession-tributes ("Sterbefall", heriot); those widely prevalent gifts of the medieval law that were due from dependent persons to their lord out of the movable estate, and which consisted of certain hereditaments, — often the best piece or head of cattle, the best garment, or not infrequently whatever the lord might choose (whence the name "Kurmede"), — or else a fixed sum of money. The heriot was originally conceived of as a debt of the dead person, not as one of the heir; and the right of the lord as a creditor's right, not as a right of inheritance. The heriot consisted, there-

[1] *Brunner*, in Z[2]. R. G., XIX, 120.
[2] *Brunner*, "Zur Geschichte der ältesten deutschen Erbschaftssteuer", in the "Festschrift für Martitz" (1911), 1–31.

fore, of that portion of the heritage which belonged to the dead person. "The vassal ('Schutzhörige') was bound to leave behind him as a final rent, as a last compensation for the protection by his lord which he had enjoyed in his lifetime, some part of that which he would have taken with him as a free man into the beyond." [1]

These gifts mortis causa, customary in the Frankish period, were not testamentary dispositions in the technical sense of those words; that is, they were not juristic acts revocable until the death of the testator. They were rather "juristic acts inter vivos to take effect upon death." [2] They belonged, not to the law of inheritance but to the law of things; they were not unilateral, but bilateral, juristic acts, in other words contracts. They were consummated either as "donationes post obitum" or as gratuitous gifts with reservation of usufruct, — legal institutes which though indistinguishable in their economic effects were perfectly distinguishable as respects their legal nature. The "donatio post obitum" was a conveyance of property that was made subject to a condition precedent. The condition was the death of the donor and the survival of the donee; however, in the ordinary case of gifts to churches, inasmuch as the happening of this condition was certain, the time specified in the gift was the time at which such gift was to take effect. Although the juristic act became potentially valid with the making of the gift its efficacy was perfected only at the instant of the donor's death. In the meantime no outward change took place; in law, however, the donee became the owner at the instant the gift was made. He received by it a seisin in expectancy, which took effect immediately upon the death of the donor, and though not at once perceptible, it restricted in the meanwhile the seisin remaining in the donor for life, so that the latter could no longer dispose of the substance of the thing so given. A gift subject to the reservation of usufruct was an absolute juristic act; it became effective immediately and without qualification; the proprietary seisin passed at once to the donee, as was frequently made evident by the performance of the "sessio triduana", and there remained in the donor merely a usufructuary seisin in the land. Between the donor and the donee there was created a relationship of tenure; the donor receiving the usufruct either of the identical land that

[1] *Brunner*, "Zur Geschichte der ältesten deutschen Erbschaftssteuer" in the "Festschrift für Martitz "(1911), 30.

[2] *Gierke* in *Holtzendorff-Kohler*, I, 551.

was the object of the gift ("precaria oblata") or of other lands belonging to the church ("precaria remuneratoria"), in return for which he ordinarily paid the church a rent. Both these transactions were ordinarily consummated by "traditio cartæ", in which connection resort was often had to the Salmann of the old Frankish adoption ("affatomie"), who was bound to perform the act of donation when the donor was for any reason, as for example sickness, unable to do so. Frequently, these transactions were performed in such a way as to indicate that the "donatio post obitum" should become effective, not upon the death of the donor but only after the death of a third person; or that the usufruct should be reserved not only to the donor but also to a third person, or only to such third person. In this way the heirs' rights in expectancy could be protected in case the free portion was exceeded. But inasmuch as gifts to ecclesiastical institutions enormously increased in number and amount in the 600 s and 700 s, forcing into the background the idea of the free portion, and inasmuch, further, as the requirement that the donor must dispose of his free portion exclusively for pious purposes was not strictly enforced, the right of donation was constantly extended at the expense of rights in expectancy.

Contractual gifts mortis causa under the law of things remained in use throughout the Middle Ages. They were employed not only in the old way in endowments for the good of the donor's soul, but were also resorted to between kindred, and for the gift of entire estates or shares in estates. Spouses assigned to each other in this way their respective properties; grandparents used them to divert their property to their grandchildren, in order to secure them rights of representation in place of their dead parents; they were even permitted for the purpose of making gifts of specific chattels or sums of money, — although only under certain preconditions, since chattels could not in theory be donated from the deathbed, and moreover the rule "donner et retenir ne vaut" stood in the way of such gifts (*supra*, p. 426). As respects the form in which such gifts mortis causa were consummated, execution in court took the place, generally speaking, of the "traditio cartæ" customary in the Frankish period; it was absolutely required in North Germany.[1] The requirement that such transactions be executed in a sacred ("hedged") folk-court was justified primarily on the ground that possible heirs could make effective in this way only their right to object to alienations ("Wider-

[1] Ssp., II, 30.

spruchsrecht"), and also that their interests could be protected by the judge. The peace-ban of the court had the effects of citation (*supra*, p. 202) seisin.[1] In South Germany, on the other hand, gifts outside of court under letter and seal were early recognized along with the judicial form.

These gifts under the early medieval law of things, which are called in the documents themselves "donationes irrevocabiles inter vivos" (in German, "Gemächte", "Geschäfte", "Gelübde"), changed their nature at an early day. As a result of their increasing adoption of elements of the inheritance law, there were gradually developed from them other juristic acts which, instead of creating present claims under the law of things, created future rights of inheritance, — namely, contracts of inheritance and wills.

§ 111. **Contracts of Inheritance.**[2] (I) **In general.** — If we understand by a "contract of inheritance" ("Erbvertrag") a contract that creates or that destroys the qualifications of an heir, then the "Gemächte" and "Geschäfte" of the Middle Ages were not yet contracts of inheritance in the technical sense. For although the person appointed to take the inheritance ("Bedachte", "intended heir") was frequently designated in them as the "heir", he was no actual heir but merely received through the transaction an immediate right involving more or less decisive consequences. The effect of the contract was not the instatement of an heir but an acquisition of ownership inter vivos. How little it was regarded as conferring the qualifications of an heir, is shown by the fact that the deceased frequently gave the intended "heir", meanwhile, a co-enjoyment of the property; in other words, entered with him into a community of collective hand, — the consequence of which was that upon the death of one commoner, the decedent, the share he left accrued to the other commoner, the intended heir. But just as the "Gemächte" led along one line of development to the testament, so it was possible to pass from it along another line to the contract of inheritance. Its character as a bilateral contract inter vivos was maintained, but there was united with this the appointment of the heir. Such contracts of inheritance earliest appeared as juristic acts between spouses, who thus assured to each other mutual and irrevocable rights of succession in their respective estates. Renunciations of herital rights were also concluded in this manner, by contract, in the late

[1] Swsp., 22 (G.).

[2] *Beseler*, "Die Lehre von den Erbverträgen" (3 vols., 1835, 1837, 1840).

Middle Ages. Nevertheless, the development of the contract of inheritance as an independent and universally recognized institute of the inheritance law was realized only after the Reception, and thanks to the work of the jurists; for though they at first repudiated such contracts as inconsistent with the view of the Roman law, they later recognized them, systematically developed them, and secured their adoption in judicial practice. For this reason Beseler found in the inheritance contracts of the modern common law a leading example of what he called "jurist-law" (*supra*, p. 31). Contracts of inheritance were also recognized in most of the modern codes. They were recognized in general terms by the Bavarian "Landrecht," the Prussian "Landrecht," the Saxon Code, and likewise by the Zürich Code, which has been followed by the Swiss Civil Code. The Austrian Code, however, has recognized them only between spouses, — indeed, it is only as contracts between spouses that contracts of inheritance have anywhere attained actual importance, — and the Code Civil solely in connection with marriage contracts between betrothed couples for the benefit of themselves and their expected children. The present Civil Code has likewise recognized the contract of inheritance as a contractual disposition mortis causa. As distinguished from a will it is not a testamentary ("letztwillig") disposition, but merely a binding contract; and as distinguished from the old gift mortis causa its effects are felt, not under the law of things but in the law of inheritance. As respects their content, inheritance contracts are either for the appointment of an heir, or contracts of legacy, or renunciations of inheritance.

(II) **Contracts for the instatement of heirs,** among which must be reckoned also the herital-brotherhoods of houses of the greater nobility, appear in various forms. Such a contract, when simply for the appointment of an heir, creates a unilateral right of inheritance on the part of one party to the contract; when a bilateral contract, it creates a mutual right of inheritance in both parties, in such manner that in case of invalidity of the one appointment the other also becomes invalid. When a "restitutive" contract, it passes the inheritance to a third person, the heir obligating himself to deliver the estate to such person; when a "dispositive" contract, it is concluded in favor of one who is not a party to the contract but who is to acquire the estate immediately upon the death of the decedent. The contract for the appointment of the heir either creates an entirely new right of inheritance ("pactum successorium acquisitivum") or guarantees a right of inheritance already existing ("pactum successorium conservativum"). It creates either a right of inheritance free of every other co-existent right, or a right that is conditional, limited in time, or otherwise restricted. It may refer either to the whole heritage or to a quota thereof. If it refers only to specific objects it is a contract of legacy. This has been generally recognized, — though its admissibility has been combated by many jurists (for example, Beseler), — in modern codes, and has been maintained intact in the present Civil Code as well as in the Swiss Civil Code. The legacy-contract creates merely a contract claim to a legacy. Whereas it was doubtful under the common law whether a contract for the appointment of an heir must be in a particular form, the prevailing opinion favoring its informality, modern statutes have required writing or execution in court, and the Prussian "Landrecht" and the Saxon Code even testamentary form. The latter rule has been followed by the present Civil Code, which prescribes the form of a judicial or a notarial testament. The Swiss Civil Code also requires the form of a public testamentary disposition. Such a contract gives the donee a right of inheritance which the donor cannot alone revoke, charge, or qualify. In other respects, however, he remains free to dispose of his property by juristic acts inter vivos; for example, he may alienate it. The older law, however, permitted the contractual heir to avoid a fraudulent ("dolose") alienation or at any rate a voluntary gift; and under the Prussian law he could also demand the appointment of a guardian for the deceased when the latter was squandering his property. The present Civil Code gives to the contractual heir the right to demand the return from a donee of voluntary gifts which the deceased has made to the prejudice of the contractual heir; this upon the theory of unjust enrichment. A contract for the appointment of an heir can be rescinded by the concurrent wills of the parties expressed in a contract of the same form; and also, exceptionally, by unilateral withdrawal, namely when such right has been reserved or when there exists a statutory justification therefor.

(III) **Renunciation of herital rights** is a contract by which one person renounces in favor of another a right of inheritance which he enjoys in preference to the latter. In this way every right of inheritance may be renounced, whether statutory, testamentary, or contractual, — the last by the third person for whose benefit the contract was made. Renunciations of inheritance, moreover, were informal in the common law, whereas in the present law they require a judicial or notarial form. As a result of the renunciation the party renouncing is eliminated from the line of heirs, so that in the absence of any other disposition mortis causa the next statutory heir is substituted in his place. Under the common law the party renouncing could not thereby bind his descendants; in the regional systems, however, — which have been followed by the present Civil Code and likewise by the Swiss Civil Code, — this was not only permitted in renunciations of statutory rights of inheritance, but was assumed as the intention of the parties in the absence of specific provision. Renunciations of herital rights by daughters of noble houses, for the regulation of which special rules of law were developed among the greater nobility and the imperial knightage, were particularly important. Their purpose was to prevent the equality of sons and daughters that would otherwise have existed under the inheritance law. The daughters upon their marriage were compelled to renounce by document, for themselves and their descendants, their rights of inheritance; though usually only in favor of the male stock (" bis auf den ledigen Anfall "). If the male line became extinct, so that the "female descendants", — that is (*supra*, p. 715), the kindred related through women, the spindle-friends, — became entitled, there arose "the much debated question, which has given rise not only to many law-suits but also to bloody wars",[1] whether the estate should pass to the renouncing daughters and their line, the "regressive" heirs ("Regredienterben"), or the daughters or other next relatives of the last possessor (the "Erbtochter") of the male line be called to the inheritance. Whereas the Imperial Chamber of Justice (of the old Empire) regularly decided in favor of the regressive female heirs, prevailing opinion has recently aligned itself, generally speaking, upon the side of the females of the male line ("Erbtochter").

§ 112. **The Testament.**[2] (I) **The Older Law.** — When the old gifts mortis causa became true contracts of inheritance, this signi-

[1] *Gierke* in *Holtzendorff-Kohler*, I, 553.

[2] *Fr. v. Wyss*, "Die letzwilligen Verfügungen nach den schweizerischen Rechten der früheren Zeit", in Z. schweiz. R., XIV (1875), 68 *et seq.*; *Demuth*, "Die wechselseitigen Verfügungen von Todes wegen nach alamanisch-Züricherischem Recht in ihrer geschichtlichen Entwicklung bis zur Gegenwart", no. 65 (1901) of *Gierke's* "Untersuchungen"; *Friese*, art. "Testament" and "Seelgeräte" in the glossary to his and *Liesegang's* ed. of the "Magdeburger-Schöffensprüche", I (1901), 833 *et seq.*; *O. Löning*, "Das Testament im Gebiete des Magdeburger Stadtrechts", no. 82 (1906) of *Gierke's* "Untersuchungen"; *Pappenheim*, "Eigenhändiges

fied a change in their content but not in their form. A transaction under the law of things was transformed into one of the inheritance law, — the intended heir ("Bedachte") no longer received a present right, but a claim mortis causa; the transaction, however, remained a bilateral contract. On the other hand, when such gifts became testaments, in the medieval sense, there was therein involved primarily a change of form; bilateral transactions became unilateral dispositions mortis causa, and inasmuch as they acquired the quality of revocability they became unilateral testamentary dispositions. That such unilateral testamentary dispositions were inconsistent with the most important principles of the Germanic law of inheritance has already been remarked; we can understand, therefore, why they were able only very gradually to gain recognition and prevalence. And wherever the idea retained vitality of a right in expectancy in the heritage and the household-property, or a general conservatism prevailed, as in Saxony, men struggled with a special obstinacy against such unilateral transactions, and clung tenaciously to the requirement of execution in court, — as in the judicial practice of the Magdeburg skevins of the 1200 s and 1300 s.

The first of such unilateral testamentary dispositions to become established were those for the good of the donor's soul. Along with these, however, the contractual form of the law of things remained common throughout the Middle Ages. That the recognition of the efficacy of the unilateral testament was most readily conceded in these particular instruments can be readily understood if one recalls their origin in the free-portion and the dead's-portion. They were gifts which by old and deeply rooted view were regarded as necessary even when blood relatives were present. This view, as already mentioned, was supported by the Church with its exceedingly effective weapons; he who made no testamentary gift for pious purposes was denied confession and absolution, and to be obliged to die "intestatus" and "inconfessus" was regarded, naturally, as a great misfortune. At the same time, it was zealously endeavored from the side of the secular law to restrict such gifts for the donor's soul within narrow limits. Although the requirement of physical health (*supra*, p. 425) was in time abandoned, and dispositions were recognized that were

Testament und Testierfreiheit im früheren Recht Schleswigs" in the "Festgabe des 28. deutschen Juristentages" (1906); *J. Merkel*, "Die justinianischen Enterbungsgründe, eine rezeptionsgeschichtliche Studie", no. 94 (1908) of *Gierke's* "Untersuchungen"; with which compare *A. B. Schmidt* in Z². R. G., XXIX (1908), 387–391.

made by the donor upon his death-bed for the good of his soul, nevertheless it was frequently provided that in such cases a certain modest portion might not be exceeded.

However, by the second half of the Middle Ages the institute of the unilateral testamentary gift had already gained for itself a greatly widened area of authority. In this extension of gifts for the donor's soul to testamentary dispositions of varied nature the influence of the Church, which assumed jurisdiction in cases of wills and championed in theory the freedom of dispositions mortis causa, was of decisive importance. So also was the example of the testaments that had always been common among the clergy. The Church had very early devised means to moderate the formal requirements of the Roman law of wills. The testaments of ecclesiastics were reduced to the form of a protocol either before a priest and two witnesses or before an official of the ecclesiastical court or before a notary, and were recorded by such registrar, or written down by the testator himself in a private document, or orally declared by him upon his death-bed to those about him.[1] The laity now followed this example with increasing frequency. How rapidly and in what particular form unilateral testamentary dispositions of laymen might spread, depended upon many special circumstances and therefore varied in different regions. Execution as a mere private document was at first frequently forbidden; submission of the testament to a court or the city council, or its sealing by the council, or its drafting before two councilors or two skevins, or other like requirements being, on the contrary, prescribed. Although the requirement of a certain publicity was thus preserved, the decisive thing, nevertheless, was the fact that the presence of the intended heir in court and his acceptance of the gift were abandoned, alike in testaments of laymen and of ecclesiastics. In exceptional cases, — as for example in case of severe sickness, — the testator's appearance before the official board was also dispensed with; a deputation of the city council was sent to his home, and he declared his last will in their presence. After this it was only a short step to declare sufficient the delivery of the document to the public authorities. In many regions the Canonic form of drafting in the presence of a priest and two witnesses also became usual, but this was prohibited by the secular authorities from the 1400 s onward. These secular testaments were also restricted as regards their content, — namely to dispositions of specific hereditaments; for which reason they

[1] *Heusler*, "Institutionen", II, 647.

resembled more the Roman "legatum" than the Roman testament. In particular, the nomination in them of the heir was not, as in the Roman law, an absolutely indispensable requisite. Statutory succession could therefore be combined with testamentary succession; in so far as there was no testamentary disposition, the kindred succeeded under the statutory rule. Inasmuch as the testament involved a great danger to the family it was endeavored to protect the interest of kinsmen by legislation; a difficult task, which resulted at first in "an oscillation between the owner's complete freedom to dispose of his own by last will, and the family's claims upon the property of its member."[1] It was only under the guidance of the Roman law that sound principles were finally established in this matter.

(II) **The Modern Law.** — After the Reception many rules of the Roman law of wills became established in Germany, but in many other points the native rules were maintained.

(1) As respects *the form of the testament*, the legislation of the Reception period adopted the Roman private testament of seven witnesses, but it did not require, to adopt the words of the Nuremberg Reformation, the observance of the "elaborate niceties of the common written law." They acquired no authority, moreover, in legal practice. On the contrary the traditional forms continued to be extremely widely prevalent, — the "judicial" testament, made either by a personal declaration in court of the testator's last will or by a personal delivery of a sealed or unsealed writing, and along with this the notarial testament, of the same possible varieties. These also passed into the modern codes, and were adopted by the present Civil Code as equally valid forms. The French and Austrian law recognized in addition the holographic testament, and this has likewise been recognized by the Civil Code as the common law form. Along with ordinary forms of testament there were, and still are, recognized extraordinary forms subject to less strict conditions. The principles of the Swiss Civil Code agree in all respects, in this matter, with the German.

(2) As respects *the content of the testament*, in the common law the Roman rule became dominant; namely, that it must contain a nomination of the heir. The majority of the regional statutes, and among the Codes the Bavarian and Prussian "Landrecht" and the Austrian Code, clung to the same rule. Testamentary dispositions without nomination of an heir were, however, recognized

[1] *Stobbe*, V, 214.

as codicils. On the other hand, many codes remained true to the old view and declared the nomination of an heir not a necessary part of a testament. This was true of the Code Civil, the Saxon Code, and the Lübeck Statute of 1862. These have been followed by the present Civil Code and the Swiss Civil Code. The Roman rule "nemo pro parte testatus pro parte intestatus decedere potest" therefore attained only a very limited authority, and disappeared from the modern law. The German law not having reached independently (as already mentioned) a satisfactory compromise between the principle of the testator's freedom and the interests of his family, the Roman substantive law of the compulsory portion was adopted, though to be sure with important changes, especially the abrogation of the formal requisites of the Roman succession by necessity. Thenceforth all kinsmen were obliged to submit to a restriction of their statutory right of inheritance; but descendants and ascendants, to some extent brothers and sisters, and also a surviving spouse, received in exchange an absolute right to a certain share of their statutory portions. The present Civil Code has done away with the right of brothers and sisters to a compulsory portion; in other respects it has followed in essentials those modern codes which adopted the Roman law as their basis, like the Prussian "Landrecht." Consequently, as under this and the common law, so under the Civil Code the heir of necessity who is passed over in the will or insufficiently remembered, has no right as heir to the compulsory portion so withheld from him, but merely a claim as a creditor of the testamentary heirs for the value of whatever fraction of the estate should have been left to him as a compulsory portion. In contrast to this rule, the French and the Swiss law restricted within much narrower limits the testator's power to disinherit his heirs or to reduce their share, conceding him dispositive powers over that portion only which was not reserved for his next heirs; so that these became co-heirs as respects the compulsory portion to which they were entitled. In the Swiss Civil Code it was found impossible to establish a uniform regulation of the law of compulsory portions, save as a system subsidiarily applicable.

(3) *Joint testaments.* — Joint ("gemeinschaftliche", *i.e.* "community") testaments, later particularly common in the case of spouses, were developed in the legal practice of Germany from the 1300 s onward. Though not inconsistent with the principles of the Roman law these had found in that no detailed regulation, and consequently German judicial practice and legal theory

oscillated, in their treatment, between the principles of the Roman testament and those of the Germanic contract of inheritance. In form, the joint testament was an ordinary simple testament. Aside from "common" testaments ("testamenta simultanea"), which were those by which several persons willed their property by one and the same instrument, there were distinguished as sub-varieties of the joint testament, mutual wills ("testamenta reciproca") and mutually conditional ("korrespektive") wills. In the former, two persons appointed each other mutually as heirs, or otherwise remembered one another. In the latter the two dispositions were so dependent upon one another that the one testament stood or fell with the other. The present Civil Code, following the example of the Prussian "Landrecht" and the Austrian Code, has recognized such joint testaments between spouses. In the common and in the Saxon law they were recognized without qualification; in the French law, on the other hand, they were prohibited in all cases. The Swiss Civil Code does not recognize them.

§ 113. **The Executor.**[1] (I) **The Older Law.** — The institute of the trustee ("Treuhänder") or Salmann, which we meet with in its most ancient form in the Frankish adoption ("affatomie") and in the Lombard "gairethinx" (*supra*, pp. 741 *et seq.*) was placed at the testator's service in the most liberal manner by the medieval law. In the older period, in which testaments were unknown, — *i.e.* until about the 1100 s, — it was gifts made mortis causa for the good of the donor's soul, "donationes pro anima", that were frequently consummated with the inclusion of a Salmann. Inasmuch as the "traditio cartæ" that was the effective element in these transactions usually took place in the church as a "traditio super altare", there arose in the case of the donor's incapacity, — and of course men frequently resolved to

[1] *Beseler*, "Von den Testamentsvollziehern", in Z. deut. R., IX (1845), 144–222; *Alfred Schultze*, "Die langobardische Treuhand und ihre Umbildung zur Testamentsvollstreckung", no. 49 (1895) of *Gierke's* "Untersuchungen"; *Beyerle*, "Grundeigentumsverhältnisse und Bürgerrecht im mittelalterlichen Konstanz, I, 1: Das Salmannenrecht" (1900); *Caillemer*, "Origines et développement de l'exécution testamentaire, époque franque et moyen âge" (1901); *Maitland*, "Trust und Corporation" in *Grünhut's* Z. Priv. öff. R., XXXII (1904), 1–76; *Heymann*, "Geschäftsanwälte und Treuhandgesellschaften als Vermögensverwalter nach englischem und deutschem Recht, eine rechtsvergleichende und rechtspolitische Betrachtung", in "Festgabe für K. Güterbock" (1910), 561–596, "Trustee und Trustee Company im deutschen Rechtsverkehr", in "Festgabe für Brunner" (1910), 473–537; *Holmes*, "Executors in earlier English Law", in "Select Essays in A. A. L. H.", III, 737 *et seq.*; *Caillemer*, "The Executor in England and on the Continent", in *ibid.*, 746 *et seq.*

make such gifts "pro anima" in the very face of death, — the necessity of entrusting a third person with the performance of the act of tradition. Moreover it was a favorite practice, which echoed the old theory of the death-portion, to have the tradition take place on the day of the burial as a "donatio pro sepultura", in which case, since the donor was no longer among the living, a trustee ("Treuhänder"), an "eleemosinarius", was again necessary. And the employment of such a trustee might also recommend itself because the donor, in case he had concluded the contract with the trustee only, and not directly with the ecclesiastical foundation, could more easily rescind the contract. The position of the "Treuhänder" became still more important in the 1100 s and 1200 s when unilateral "letzwillige" ("of last will") dispositions, — *i.e.* testaments, — appeared side by side with, and later in place of, the bilateral contractual gift mortis causa, so that the Salmann became an actual executor. True, the carrying out of a "donatio pro anima" was still a regular part of his obligations, since these new testaments usually contained such gifts; indeed, as already mentioned, they were at first exclusively unilateral testamentary endowments for sacred vessels and vestments. But the duties of the Salmann increased in pace with the broadening scope of the testament. They were entrusted with the liquidation of the decedent's estate; they were bound to perform his last will, to undertake the distribution of the estate, and incidentally thereto to compromise the hostile interests of the heirs; they were appointed to protect the will, against legatees and especially against the heirs, but also against third persons; frequently they were charged at the same time with the guardianship of the widow and children; and the duty of attending to the burial was also laid upon them. In this way these executors — Salmanns, "Seelgeräter", "testamentarii", "eleemosinarii", "wadiarii", "fideiussores", "spondarii", "fideicommissarii", or however else they might be known — played a very important part during the Middle Ages in all parts of the Occident. This was very especially true in England, where there was developed from them the institute of the trust, peculiar to the English law, though it merely applies in a special manner legal ideas universal in Germanic law. The executor, in accord with the principles of the Germanic law of things, and like the Salmann who was employed in gifts mortis causa and in conveyances inter vivos, received the seisin, namely an exclusive seisin, in the chattels of the estate, — a legal power under the law of things that had the appearance of ownership qualified by the end to which the property was appointed, and which differed from complete ownership merely in that he was entitled to exercise his rights solely for the purpose of performing the last will of the testator. Even long after the appearance of the testament, therefore, either an immediate seisin or one subject to the condition precedent of the donor's death was conveyed to the executor, as to the old Salmann in gifts mortis causa, by a tradition in the form of a symbolic investiture. Though the executor was thus endowed with extensive powers and his position made very strong even as against the heirs, certain securities existed against the misuses of this absolute power, on the one hand in the liability of the executor to the heirs, — though this is not exactly common in the sources, — and still more in the fact that his position was regarded as a public office. He was therefore not only required to deliver an inventory and to publish the testament, — and under the Canon law, also to take oath and give security, — but was otherwise subjected to a strict oversight of the public authorities which the ecclesiastical and secular courts vied in enforcing.

(II) **The Modern Law.** — This institute of the executor, which was quite unknown to the Roman law, was generally retained in Germany after the Reception, as in other countries. It also passed into all the modern codes, including the present Civil Code. The Code Civil alone, which was here influenced by the Roman law, still contains only the barest trace of this institute, once widespread in the old French as in other Germanic legal systems. But inasmuch as the Roman concepts did not suffice to explain it and the Germanic ideas that underlay it long remained undiscovered, many controversies resulted concerning its legal nature. The executor's powers were explained, now as a mandate of the testator that continued effective after his death, — notwithstanding that this was irreconcilable with a unilateral testamentary nomination of an heir, which was particularly common, — and now as a statutory right of representation in the nature of a guardian's, or again as a special office with which he was entrusted. Other scholars explained the executor as a mandatary of the heirs, notwithstanding that it was precisely his independence in relation to them that was the essence of his office; or as a representative of the decedent's estate, as such. It follows from the history of the institute that the executor has always been a trustee ("Treuhänder") in the sense of the Germanic law, and is such to-day; that is, he is not a representative of another's right, but a trustee

("Vertrauensmann") of the testator endowed with independent rights, who exercises such rights in his own name although in the interest of the heirs. For this independent right is limited in the old way by the requirement that it must be exercised in accord with the will of the testator. In fact there is still visible in the modern executor a plain trace of the primitive idea of a representation of the dead.[1] Whether an executor shall or shall not be named depends upon the testator's will; and his powers are also determined in the same manner. Statutory rules take effect, in essential matters, only in default of and as a supplement to the testator's directions. The executor is responsible to the heirs and legatees for the performance of his obligations; but he is also subject to the continual oversight of the probate court.

[1] *Brunner*, "Geschichte," I (2d ed.), 40.

CHAPTER XVII

SPECIAL RULES OF SUCCESSION IN THE INHERITANCE OF LANDS

§ 114. **The Inheritance of Fiefs. Feudal Succession.**[1] (I) **The Older German law.** — As has already been remarked (*supra*, pp. 373 *et seq.*) in the general description of feudal tenure, a fief was conveyed only for such time as both parties to the feoffment might live, since it presupposed a personal relation of fidelity between lord and vassal. When the heritable character of the fief later became established there was developed in consequence of its military character a special law of feudal inheritance, which differed in important respects from the general principles of the inheritance law and which led to a sharp distinction between feudal succession in the fief and succession in the fee. Moreover, the circle of those who were entitled to succeed as feudal heirs was originally very narrowly limited within the body of kinsmen capable of feudal services (pp. 337 *et seq.*). In the beginning, as already mentioned, only the son of the vassal seems to have been capable of succession to the estate;[2] it was only later that a right of inheritance was extended to all descendants, such as was expressly recognized, for example, in an imperial decision delivered by King Albrecht in 1299. Herital rights of collateral kindred were unknown to the German feudal law. It was only by feudal contracts ("Lehnsverträge") that herital rights could be given to more remote kindred. Since partition of the fief

[1] See *Ernst Mayer*, "Der germanische Uradel" (*supra*, p. 585), 106 *et seq.*

[2] "Sächs. Lehnr.", 21, § 3.

would have lessened its capacity to satisfy feudal services, the general principle of the inheritance law that the heritage must be divided among the heirs of equal degree could not be applied in feudal succession. Unless a feoffment was made in collective hand (*supra*, p. 340) the lord might enfeoff only one of the feudal heirs. If no such feoffment was made, then ordinarily the oldest son came, in time, to receive the investiture; a rule which was established in the main by contract but was also recognized to some extent by statute.

(II) **The Lombard and the Modern Law.** — Unlike the German feudal law, that of the Lombards extended feudal succession not merely to descendants but also to collaterals. This was already the rule of the feudal Constitution of the Emperor Konrad II, of 1037,[1] and it was "the starting point in the succession system of the 'Libri Feudorum', and generally of the later feudal law, according to which every right of inheritance was limited and controlled by the concept of the 'feudum paterum', 'ervelen.'"[2] In consequence of this principle, ascendants of a feudal tenant were excluded in all cases from succession to the fief, because the feoffment of the deceased did not affect them. Therefore, also, only those collateral kindred had a right of succession who were themselves descendants of an earlier feudal tenant. Collaterals who were not the issue of a former tenant, and to whom the fief was therefore a "feudum novum", were not included among kinsmen entitled to inherit. An extension of herital rights in favor of other collaterals could be effected by contract only. This rule was also received into Germany, and in Mecklenburg led, as already mentioned (*supra*, p. 346), to the institute of "Reversal"- cousins. Equally in the Lombard feudal law and in the later feudal common-law of Germany many doubts resulted from this admission, — albeit in theory only qualified, — of collateral kindred. According to the Lombard law the descendants of the last tenant succeeded first to the inheritance, in accordance with the principle of representation. Later, since ascendants were excluded, the collaterals succeeded (the brothers in the first place) on the ground that the fief was as to them a "feudum paternum"; here again the sons of dead brothers succeeded in their place. Finally, the more remote collaterals succeeded in such manner that those kindred were preferred who had the near-

[1] "Edictum de beneficiis regni italici" (Lib. Feud., 5. 1, c. 4; M. G., Constitutiones, I, 90).

[2] *Heusler*, "Institutionen", II, 614.

est common male ancestor with the deceased, and again, as among these, those of nearer in preference to those of more remote degree. But it was precisely this preferment of the "Linie" within the collateral kindred in the larger sense, — in other words the recognition of the parentelic or "lineal-gradual" system, — that was combated, it being alleged that the Libri Feudorum embodied a different system. In the one view, which was formerly followed by the imperial courts, the preferment of the line was entirely disregarded and the degree of kinship between the decedent and the more remote collaterals was made decisive (pure "gradual" succession of the Roman law). In the other view, which prevailed in some princely houses, advantages in degree of kinship were disregarded, and the next line called to the inheritance without regard to the degree of kinship and with absolute enforcement of the right of representation (pure "lineal" succession). There can be no doubt, however, that the "lineal-gradual" system of succession, that is the parentelic system, alone satisfied the requirements of the "Libri Feudorum". In Germany, also, this found wide acceptance, and according to the better view was regarded as the common law; being observed as such, for example, in the judicial practice of Mecklenburg, Brunswick, Hamburg, and Württemberg. It was frequently united with the principle of primogeniture, so that as between several lines of equal degree preference was given to the line of the first-born, and within that again to the first-born. The authority of common law was also claimed, by many scholars, even for the other theories; and some statutes recognized pure "lineal" succession, — for example the Prussian "Landrecht" and the Bavarian Feudal Edict. Under the Lombard feudal law different principles prevailed according as a descendant or a collateral kinsman (an "agnate" in the sense of the feudal law) succeeded, the death of the feudal tenant giving him succession, also, in such tenant's allodial lands. Such an "agnate" might refuse the allodial estate and take the fief alone, in which case he became liable, not for the general, but only for the feudal obligations of the deceased. But the descendant had no such right to refuse the estate; on the contrary he was bound to accept the allodium with the fief, and therefore all the liabilities of the deceased as well. The power which was thus accorded to the "agnate" was justified by the fact that he did not acquire the fief from the last, but rather from the first, tenant; that is, from the common male ancestor of the "agnate" and the vassal last deceased, or as it was said "ex pacto et providentia maiorum." This distinction, although not everywhere accepted, passed over into the common law, notwithstanding that the succession of descendants was also conceived of later as a "successio ex pacto et providentia maiorum." Wherever the right of renunciation was also given to descendants it was therefore said, — in order to remain consistent with the "Libri Feudorum", — that there existed a "family" ("Stamm-") fief, a "feudum ex pacto et providentia maiorum." This was contrasted with a heritable fief, a "feuda hereditaria", in the case of which the right of renunciation was denied equally to collaterals and descendants. However, this distinction remained a much debated one.

When the fief was not willed to one alone of several feudal heirs in equal degree, each generally succeeded to a part under the Lombard feudal law, according to the principles of quotal co-ownership (*supra*, p. 343); but in German legal systems succession in collective hand was commonly preserved. However, it was often provided, also, that only one should receive the fief, and indemnify the others; in which case, in some systems, fixed principles in the nature of primogeniture or of entail applied. In Mecklenburg, in case one of several feudal heirs demands a dissolution of the herital community, the one who shall take the estate is determined by lot ("Kavelung"). The estate is then assigned him at a "reasonable and brotherly price", and the value thus determined serves as a basis in determining the indemnity due to the others.[1]

§ 115. **Succession to Entailed Family Estates and under Family Trust-Entails.** (I) That the **Entailed family estate** ("Stammgüter") of the greater noble houses, as estates limited ("gebundene") by an irrevocable right in expectancy in favor of kindred entitled to the inheritance, were subjected by autonomous enactment to special rules of succession, has already been remarked (*supra*, pp. 308 *et seq.*). Ordinarily a rule of individual succession was established, and in a majority of cases primogeniture. An indemnity was required for after-born sons and daughters which was ordinarily less than the compulsory portion required in other systems.

(II) **Succession under family trust-entails** (fideicommissa) was likewise subjected, as already mentioned (*supra*, p. 315), to a special rule adapted to the purpose of the institute, and based upon the feudal principle of "successio ex pacto et providentia maiorum." Ordinarily the donor appoints the order of succes-

[1] *Stobbe*, V, 347.

sion for the fideicommissum in the deed of donation. If this is not done, and if no alternative statutory order is provided, then the ordinary statutory rule of succession applies. Succession under fideicommissa is almost always individual succession with preferment of greater age (" *Majorat* " *in the wider sense*), as contrasted with the preferment of lesser age (" *Juniorat* "), which occurs only rarely in family fideicommissa. This " majorat ", in the broad sense, may assume various forms:

(*A*) "Seniorat" (seniority). In this system the oldest member of the entire family succeeds, without regard to the line or degree of kinship. Modern statutes, as for example, the Prussian "Landrecht", have abolished seniority or have excluded it by prescribing other systems.

(*B*) "Majorat" in the narrow sense. — In this the estate goes to the nearest kinsman of the last occupant capable of inheriting, according to the degree of kinship. As between several persons entitled in the same degree preferment is given to greater age. In the application of this principle in its pure form the right of representation plays no part, so that for example the younger son of the last possessor precedes a grandson of an older son already dead.

(*C*) Primogeniture, which is also the rule under family trust-entails. In this, in accord with the principles of the parentelic system, the nearer parentelic group precedes the more remote, and within each parentelic group the elder line precedes the younger; at the same time the right of primogeniture prevails, along with absolute enforcement of the right of representation. Therefore the son and grandson of an elder son precede a younger son of the last possessor. In case cognates possess a subsidiary herital right, then, in case of complete extinction of the male line, that cognate succeeds to the inheritance who is the nearest kinsman, capable of inheritance, of the last possessor; whence the preferment of " Erbtochter " and their descendants to " regressive " female heirs and their issue (*supra*, p. 749). Once the fideicommissum, however, has passed to the female line, the preferment of males again becomes immediately applicable.

Secundo-, tertiogeniture, etc. are family fideicommissa that are established for the second, third, etc. line of a family. Therefore, if one line of entail becomes extinct the fideicommissum passes to the second. If all become extinct it reverts to the main (" Haupt- ") line.

§ 116. **Succession in Peasant Estates.**[1] — Even in the case of peasant holdings the general principle prevailed, theoretically, in the Middle Ages, that heirs of equal degree divided the heritage. However, as already mentioned (*supra*, pp. 709 *et seq.*) attempts were made in various ways to minimize the danger to the free agricultural population that was involved in a parcellation of land. When land was inherited by common heirs it was customary in many regions to abandon it to one of them, the so-called " Anerbe " (" single ") heir; but the others, originally, might remain sitting on the land until their rights were redeemed. Again, the father frequently designated one of his sons as his principal (" Haupt- ") heir, either himself indemnifying the other sons at the same time, or imposing upon such principal heir the duty to indemnify them. The impartibility of the estate might also be established by contract. In regions subject to manorial law it was customary for the lords to promulgate for their manors independent rules of inheritance which, in the lord's interest, excluded partition. There was thus developed, — for the most part by the growth of customary law, but in places by virtue of statutory rules, — a herital system for peasant estates which was the counterpart for such holdings of the special order of succession in noble houses, and which was ordinarily known as " Anerbenrecht " (system of single heirship). In some rural districts this system was maintained in modern times, and down even to the present day. It was adopted and regulated in many Territorial ordinances of the 1600 s and 1700 s; for example in Schleswig-Holstein, Brunswick, Lippe, Schaumburg-Lippe, Altenburg, Waldeck, and in the ad-

[1] *v. Miaskowski*, "Das Erbrecht und die Grundeigentumsverteilung im deutschen Reiche", in S. Ver. Soz. Pol., XX (1882) and XXV (1884). *Frommhold*, "Die rechtliche Natur des Anerbenrechts" (1886); *v. Dultzig*, *op. cit.*, p. 713 *supra*; *Hermes*, art. "Anerbenrecht", in H. W. B. Staatsw., I (3d ed., 1909), 470–481; *Sering*, art. "Vererbung des ländlichen Grundbesitzes", in W. B. der Volksw., II (3d ed., 1911), 1137–1146, and "Erbrecht und Agrarverfassung in Schleswig-Holstein auf geschichtlicher Grundlage, mit Beiträgen von Lerch, Petersen und Büchner", Vol. VII (1908) of "Die Vererbung des ländlichen Grundbesitzes im Königreich Preussen"; with which compare *Pappenheim* in Z[2]. R. G., XXX (1909), 429–436; *Guggenheim*, "Das bäuerliche Erbrecht des schweizerischen Zivilgesetzbuchs verglichen mit dem kantonalen Recht und den deutschen Anerbenrechten, in "Züricher Beiträge zur Rechtswissenschaft", XXV (1909); *Clasen*, " Schleswig-Holsteinisches Anerbenrecht in seiner geschichtlichen und heutigen Gestaltung" (Rostock dissertation, 1912); *Rörig*, "Agrargeschichte und Agrarverfassung Schleswig-Holsteins, vornehmlich Ostholsteins", in Z. Ver. Lübeck. G. A. K., XIV (1912), 137–150; *Reineke*, "Die Entwicklung des bäuerlichen Erbrechts in der Provinz Westfalen von 1815 bis heute", in *E. Frhr. v. Kerckerinck zu Borg*, editor, "Beiträge zur Geschichte des westfälischen Bauernstandes" (1912), 107–163.

ministrative district of Cassel. This law of single-heirship, thus handed down from ancient times, was very commonly treated as a "juniorat", in Schleswig-Holstein mainly as a "majorat", and more rarely as a "minorat." In some localities, although by no means everywhere, it was a compulsory right, testamentary dispositions to the contrary and partition of the land being prohibited. The extent to which the single-heir was preferred varied. Frequently, his right took the form of a special right of inheritance in the estate, as compared with which the other brothers and sisters enjoyed either a mere ordinary right of inheritance in the remainder of the heritage, or at most a right to be indemnified out of the land ("Hof").

It is possible that the rule of ultimogeniture ("Jüngstenrecht") goes back, in origin, to the youngest son's right of choice indicated in the Sachsenspiegel (*supra*, p. 709).

The principle of the testator's dispositive freedom, which acquired supremacy with the reception of the Roman law, was necessarily hostile to the rights of the single-heir. In fact it had already restricted the territory within which this prevailed to one of relatively slight extent when the measures of agricultural reform that were adopted at the beginning of the 1800 s also deprived the system of its essential material basis; and modern theories of economics denied it any sound justification in principle. Consequently, in the greater number of German States it was done away with either simultaneously with the promulgation of the statutes for the emancipation of the peasants or soon thereafter. As a custom of the peasantry it continued to enjoy the miserable existence of an institute that was gradually losing all vitality and was apparently destined to complete disappearance. In the second half of the 1800 s, however, a different view became predominant; one which had its origin precisely in these old regions of single-heirships in Northwestern Germany. This view regarded the common law of inheritance as a great obstacle to the preservation of a strong peasantry. It was now endeavored, therefore, to fortify and further develop the principles of the system of single-heirship by special legislation. For this purpose, after Bavaria and Baden had led the way in the 1850 s without any great success, there was introduced, at first only in certain districts of Prussia and other States, an "indirect" or "mediate" intestate right of single-heirship so devised as to apply exclusively to such holdings as had been entered at the instance of their owners in a "roll" of the estate ("Höferolle", "Landgüterrolle"). The model for this system was found in a Hanoverian Ordinance of Rural Estates of 1874, which was followed by similar ordinances in Lauenburg, Westphalia, the administrative district of Cassel, Brandenburg, Schleswig-Holstein, and Silesia, as well as by "Höfegesetze" in Oldenburg and in Bremen. Inasmuch, however, as this system proved unsatisfactory, a "direct" right of single heirship was either introduced anew or newly regulated by more modern statutes. This was done in Prussia (1896) in the case of lands subject to rent charges ("Rentengüter") and colonial ("Ansiedelungs-") estates (*supra*, p. 289); in Westphalia and in five administrative circles of the Lower Rhine (1898); in Baden (1888, 1898) as regards impartible manorial estates in the Black Forest; in Brunswick and in Schaumburg-Lippe. In Mecklenburg single-heirship and impartibility had already been prescribed for heritable leaseholds by statutes of 1869 and 1872. Under these statutes certain classes of estates, which are specifically described, are subject by rule of law to rights of single-heirship that take immediate effect in the absence of specific testamentary disposition. Such lands are noted in the land-book, at the instance of the registry officials, as lands subject to single-heirship. Other lands subject to single-heirship may be registered at the instance of the parties interested. In this form, also, the right of single-heirship is "a special rule of succession in the land with all its appurtenances",[1] but it is not a right in expectancy that restricts the testator. He is entitled, in the first instance, to designate the single-heir; in default of such designation, the descendants and brothers and sisters of the decedent, together with their descendants, become entitled in order of age, with preferment of the male sex. In many places a right of single-heirship also exists in favor of a surviving spouse. Co-heirs have a claim to indemnity, for the calculation of which exact rules are prescribed. Under the law in its latest form an indemnification that remains unpaid may be registered against the land as a rent. The Swiss Civil Code has endeavored to attain the same end as the German Code by the provision (§ 620), that in case a cultivated farm is included in the estate, and one of the heirs declares his willingness to undertake its management and appears fitted to do so, it shall be assigned to him as a whole, in so far as it constitutes a natural unity for purposes of agriculture, subject to the indemnification of the others. If the necessary indemnities would charge the land to an amount exceeding

[1] *Gierke* in *Holtzendorff-Kohler*, I, 558.

three-fourths of its calculated value, the person assuming the management may demand a postponement of partition. In this case the co-heirs constitute a community of collective hand in the produce (§ 622).

INDEX

www.ingramcontent.com/pod-product-compliance
Lightning Source LLC
LaVergne TN
LVHW102102300926
849161LV00001B/1
* 9 7 8 1 5 8 4 7 7 0 6 5 7 *